Architectural Modeling in Revit®

The BIM House 2015 - Volume I
2nd Edition

Rob Danner

© 2015 Rob Danner

ALL RIGHTS RESERVED. No part of this book may be reproduced, transmitted, stored, or used in any form or or by any means including but not limited to photocopying, scanning, digitizing, Web distribution, information networks, or information storage and retrieval systems, without the prior written permission of the author.

Autodesk, AutoCAD, Revit®, Revit® Architecture are registered trademarks of Autodesk.

ISBN-13: 978-1535385367

ISBN-10: 1535385367

Note to the reader

Author / publisher do not warrant any of the products listed in this book, nor does the author make any claims that the methods shown in this book are suitable for a specific practice or project. Furthermore, construction methods implied herein are not to be taken as good practice, or as meeting local building codes. By following the instructions contained herein, the reader willingly accepts all risks associated with such instruction, and agrees to hold the author / publisher harmless of any claim arising out its use.

2nd Edition Updates

This edition of the text in no way changes the final outcome of the project. Changes in the text are limited to clarifications and typo corrections only.

Table of Contents

- Preface v
- About This Book vi
  - Who Should Use this Book? vi
  - What You Will Need vi
  - Conventions Used vii
- Chapter 1: Project Setup, Layout, and Basic Walls 1
- Chapter 2: Adding Roofs, Floors, and Wall Attachments 43
- Chapter 3: Interior Walls Refinement / Adding Doors & Windows 83
- Chapter 4: Adding Components 117
- Chapter 5: Section Views & Graphic Overrides 149
- Chapter 6: Ceilings 165
- Chapter 7: Foundation and Topography 197
- Chapter 8: Compound Elements & Model Refinement 229
- Chapter 9: Structural Elements 263
- Chapter 10: Porch Construction 295
- Chapter 11: Stairs & Railings 331

Dedication

The number of people who have influenced and supported me over the years, and have in some way either directly or indirectly contributed to the creation of this book, are far too great to list. However, I would like to name a special few who stand out.

First, I'd like to thank my loving wife Lisa, whose unconditional support and encouragement through my many endeavors over the years has never wavered. Thanks for believing in me.

Next, I'd like to thank all of my BIM students over the last five years who have used various published and unpublished versions of this book and put up with typos, updates, and various errors; particularly those who weren't shy about bringing those errors to my attention! I can't imagine a better editing process than one where the users are also the editors!

Finally, I'd like to thank my friend and colleague Professor Mike Murphy, who has been instrumental in helping me adapt to the world of teaching. Without his insistence on me teaching the BIM curriculum at South Puget Sound Community College, this book would never have been conceived.

Preface

Welcome to Architectural Modeling in Revit®. The exercises in this book were originally developed to accompany a Building Modeling curriculum, currently taught by the author at South Puget Sound Community College. It incorporates a workflow-based approach, where tools and concepts are introduced as needed based on the progression of a project.

This version of text has been significantly updated for 2015; not only for the 2015 version of Revit, but the instructions, workflow, and insights have been refined to address various areas of difficulty repeatedly identified by students.

This 1st volume of a two-volume set will take you through initial modeling of a residential project. You will focus primarily on developing your building modeling skills. If you decide to continue on with Volume II, you will learn how to extract information out of the model, as well as how to develop drawing sheets, create presentation views, work with linked Revit models, and explore other more advanced topics.

The workflow in this book is just one of many possible approaches to progressing through a project. As you become more proficient with the software, or go to work for someone who has established standards, your workflow and the way you approach a project will likely vary, depending on company standards, preferences, etc. The point is that there are many ways in which to achieve a desired end result with Revit®.

The exercises in this book are fairly well detailed, and walk you through the process with detailed step-by-step instructions. Nothing is arbitrary, and accuracy will affect the integrity of the model. Keep in mind that Revit® can be deceptively simple; it might appear that your model is coming together nicely on the surface, when in reality it could be a "house of cards" if good practices are not followed.

Regarding the State of the Industry

The AEC industry is constantly evolving. Job descriptions and individual roles are dramatically changing with the adoption of BIM. Many larger architectural firms no longer employ "draftsman." However, many larger contractors have adopted BIM, which opens up a whole new set of opportunities.

It's important to remember why anyone would use BIM. The accuracy of the information, and the ability to extract the information is key. As the industry is demonstrating, there seems to be an endless number of ways of leveraging the information out of a building model.

Bottom line: as you work through this course, remember you're not necessarily learning how to be a "modeler." Rather, your developing an understanding of how to use a set of tools. How you use these tools in this course may be very different from how you're asked to use these tools in a job. Therefore, the deeper your understanding of the many tools used in BIM and how they interact, the more marketable you will be.

About This Book

Who Should Use this Book?

In the Classroom

This book has been designed as a workbook to help reinforce concepts learned elsewhere, whether in a classroom, or through other means such as online training videos, etc. The book is most effective when used as part of an instructor-led curriculum; however, that's not to say it can't be used outside of the classroom with positive results.

For the Beginner

While it's possible to work through this book without any supplemental instruction, it's not recommended for the beginner. The step-by-step instructions clearly walk you through each exercise; however, the underlying "why" is usually not discussed in depth. Furthermore, troubleshooting problems is a skill that's acquired over time and usually comes with experience. As a beginner, it's always best to have some guidance when it comes to problem solving.

For the Intermediate User

If you have some experience using Revit, this book should help to reinforce concepts that you're already familiar with, as well as expose you to some new or alternative methods for completing various tasks in Revit. Once again, this book doesn't always cover the underlying "why" in depth, and is therefore best accompanied by some form of supplemental instruction.

What You Will Need

To complete the step-by-step instructions in this book you will need a PC running Revit 2015. Additionally, various chapters instruct you to use "instructor-provided" content, such as project templates, families, and project files.

If you are using this book in conjunction with a course, your instructor may have you use alternative content. If you are working through this book on your own, feel free to supplement your own content as you wish. If you'd like to use the content as instructed, you may download it at the following URL.

 http://www.allthingsrevit.com/bimhouse

Conventions Used

This book incorporates a unique approach to communicating tool actions, as well as related parameter settings. Most often, activation of a tool is communicated by a color-coded banner rather than a sentence. The idea is that as you get more used to seeing these banners, it will be quicker for you to get through that step because you can "see" the tool rather than read a wordy sentence instructing you to activate a tool.

As you progress through the chapters, certain tool banners may be omitted for certain operations that are repeated frequently, and with which you should already have been familiarized. In this case, the tool banner will be replaced with specific text formatting to help you identify the tool name.

In addition to the color coded banners, included in this section is also an explanation of the various icons and text formatting you will find throughout the book.

If you are new to the Revit® User Interface, you'll want to keep this section handy and refer to it while learning the interface. This will help you relate the interface to the conventions used.

Text Formatting & Special Characters

Throughout this book you will periodically see the following special characters:

- **[ ]** will be used to identify a key, or key sequence on the keyboard.
- **< >** will be used to encapsulate a generic placeholder, typically n a filename, where you will need to replace the entire string, including the < > with unique information.

Additionally, you will regularly see the following text formatting:

- *Italic-medium:* This is used as a reference to something named in a project, such as a parameter, view, or sheet. Additionally it may refer to a file or family name.
- **Bold**: This has two uses, but in both cases indicates an action.
    1. A keystroke, or keystroke combination, the name of a tool, or menu selection when used in a sentence instructing you to perform an operation.

       Example 1: **[Ctrl]+C** or **[Ctrl]C** both indicate simultaneously pressing the *Control* and the *C* key on the keyboard (the + key is never pressed with these key combinations).

       Example 2: "**Align/Lock** the wall to the reference plane..." may appear in a sentence instructing you to use the *Align* tool, and then *Lock* the alignment.
    2. Parameter value input. This can be either selecting a value from a predefined set, or keying a value into a field.
- Example: Both of the above formats used together:

  Length: **12' 6"** means enter the value *12' 6"* entered into the *Length* field.

Icons

Various icons are used to draw your attention to different details or information. Each one has a different purpose in the type of information it communicates.

This is a tip. It contains useful or additional information related to the current topic or tool. It's not mandatory reading, but can be helpful in that it may provide an alternate method or shortcut for achieving a result. Additionally, this will be used as a reminder of something previously learned that's relevant to the current topic.

This indicates additional information or further explanation on the current topic or tool.

This is a warning, or something of a critical nature. Failure to acknowledge this may result in a compromised model, undesired results, or just general hair-pulling frustration!

Tool Banners

All tool banners referring to the *primary* tools located on the ribbon will will be colored in blue, whereas tool banners referring to contextual tools will be colored in green to coincide with contextual ribbon tabs in the Revit® UI. The term *primary* is used to refer to the tools that are normally always available on the ribbon. *Contextual* tools are context-specific and only appear when an element selection is made or a primary tool is activated.

The following example illustrates a series of banners you may see prompting wall placement.

		Wall	WA
Tab	Panel	Split Button ▼	Tool Button
Architecture	Build	Wall	Wall: Architectural

	Modify | Place Wall		
	Draw		
	Line		
Height Level 2	Location Line: **Core Face: Exterior**	Chain: ☑	Offset: **0' 0"** Radius: ☐

Properties
Type: **Basic Wall: Generic - 6"**
Top Offset: 2' 0"

ABOUT THIS BOOK

The following descriptions and illustrations break down each of the banners shown in the previous example, and relate them back to the Revit® user interface components.

Primary Tool Banners

Primary ribbon tool banners typically contain three rows of information, but will periodically contain fourth row. The following example illustrates the content and purpose of each row for the Wall tool.

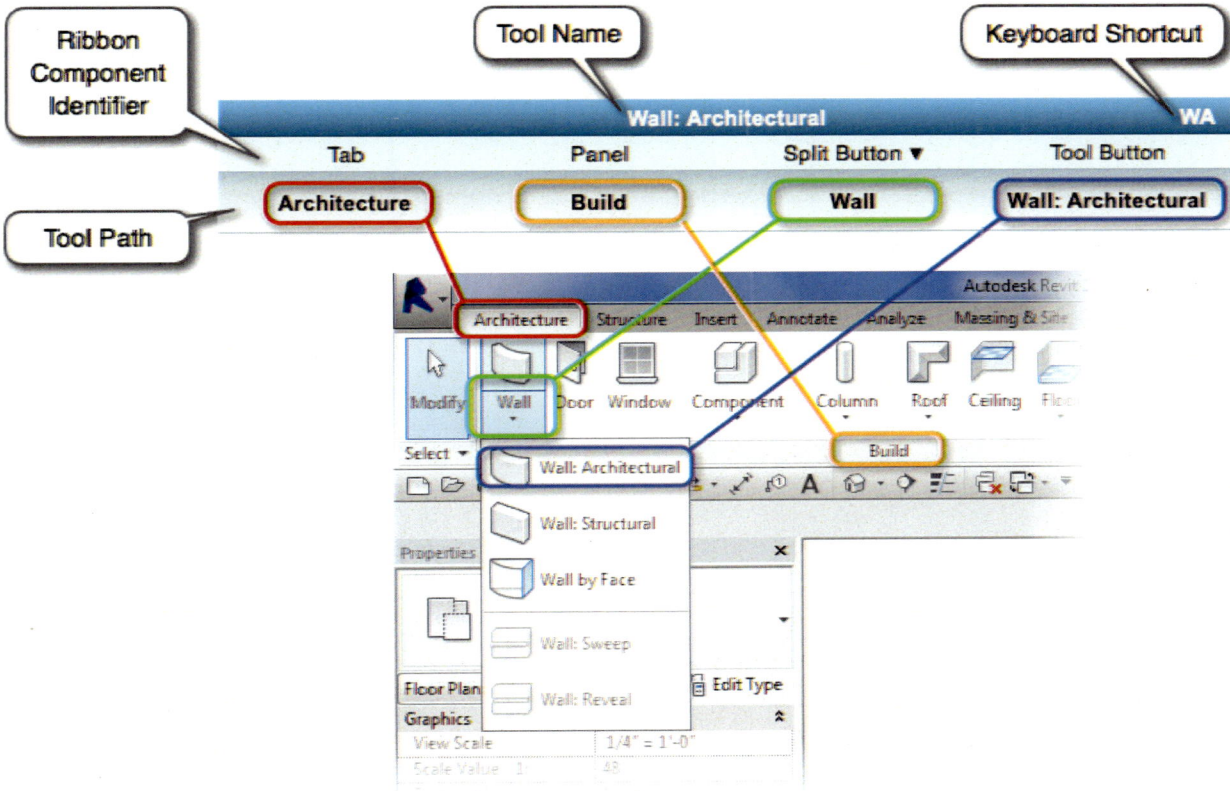

Tool Banner Example: Activating the Wall Tool

Contextual Ribbon Tab Banners

Contextual ribbon banners are constructed similar to the primary ribbon banners, but some rows serve a different purpose. Understanding of these differences is important to avoiding confusion early on in the exercises. The following example illustrates the content and purpose of each row for the Place Wall contextual ribbon tab.

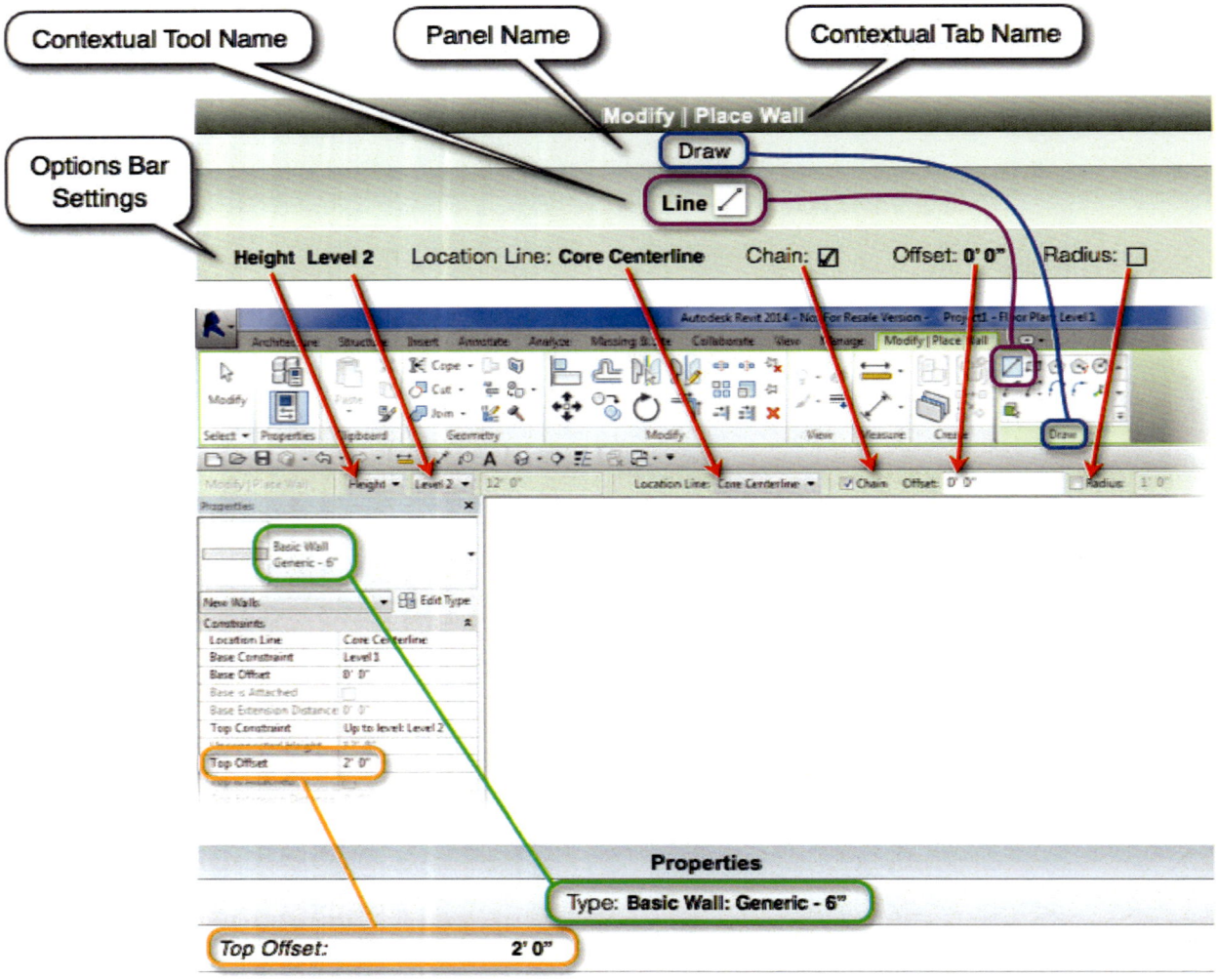

Contextual & Properties Banner Example: Activating the Wall Tool

Properties Banners

Lastly, sometimes additional property values need to be set within the properties pallet when using a tool. In this case the properties banner will be used as illustrated above. The example shown specifies the wall type to be used, as well as a change to the Top Offset property. Note that only those properties requiring change will be listed.

Variations on Tool Banners

You will regularly encounter variations on tool banners with respect to the illustrations previously shown. Each tool has a unique set of options and properties, and to show each combination would likely take an entire book in itself. However, the following illustrate some of the more general variations.

Operation Using the Application Menu

Example of a banner for an operation within the Application Menu. These banners are easily identified by the Revit® icon, which corresponds to the Application button in the Revit® user interface.

QAT 📂	Open Project	[Ctl]+O
Operation	Option	File Name
Open ▶	**Project**	**filename.rvt**

Tool Banner with Options Bar Settings

Example of a banner for a modify tool, which includes tool behavior settings in the Options bar. Note the Options bar is not green, as there is no contextual ribbon tab for this tool.

	Align	AL
Tab	Panel	Tool Button
Modify	**Modify**	**Align**
Multiple Alignment: ☑	Prefer: **Wall faces**	

Contextual Ribbon Tab With Type Selector

This is a simplified contextual ribbon tab for a tool that does not utilize any contextual tools; only options. It additionally includes the Type property setting.

	Modify	Elevation	
Attach to Grid: ☐	Scale: **1/4" = 1'-0"**	Reference other view: ☐
	Type: **Interior Elevation**	

Contextual Ribbon Tab Without Options Bar Settings

Modify	Place Ceiling
Ceiling
Automatic Ceiling

Chapter 1

Project Setup, Layout, and Basic Walls

Overview

This chapter is intended to get you started on your class project, which you will be working on throughout this course. You will define the building layout, as well as model the exterior shell of the building using generic walls. Make sure to start with the correct project template provided for this project.

Learning Objectives

In this chapter you will practice project set up, building layout, basic constraints, and importing CAD files. After completing this chapter you should have a basic understanding of:

- Starting a new project using a project template
- Saving your work
- Setting up project information, location, and default units
- Adding and editing levels
- Duplicating views
- Importing CAD files
- Using reference planes to aid the building layout process
- Adding walls and manipulating basic wall properties
- Creating simple wall types
- Using the *Align*, *Move*, and *Trim* modify tools
- Applying *Alignment* and *Pinned* constraints

Project Objectives

- Define basic project information
- Establish a project location
- Set up all required levels
- Create a building layout using reference planes
- Model generic exterior walls on both the first and second floors

CHAPTER 1: PROJECT SETUP, IMPORT CAD, BASIC WALLS

Chapter Contents

Exercise 1.1: Project Setup 3
    Initial Project Setup 4
    Existing Views Setup 7
    Add Levels & Plan Views 8
    Duplicate Views 10

Exercise 1.2: Importing CAD Files & Creating a Building Layout 15
    Import the CAD Files 15
    Building Layout 16

Exercise 1.3: Adding Exterior Walls 21
    1st Floor Exterior Walls 21
    2nd Floor Exterior Walls 25

Exercise 1.4: Project Extents & Constraints Validation 28
    Project Extents 28
    Verifying Design Intent 30
    Pin The building layout 38
    Prepare Project for Submission 40

Exercise 1.1: Project Setup

Using the project template provided, start a new project and save it as follows.

 Make sure that you use the *new project* command and then browse for the template file specified below. <u>DO NOT use *file open* to open the template file</u>. When opening a template file directly, it can only be saved as a template!

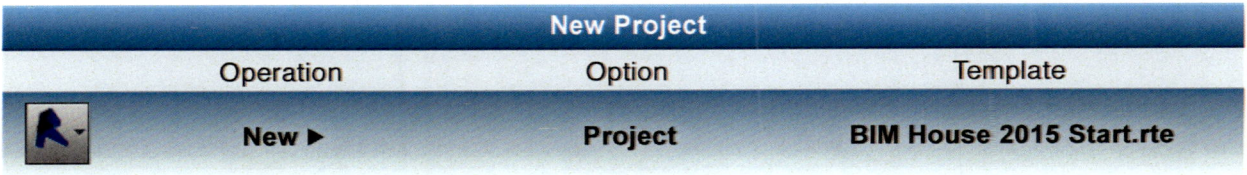

New Project		
Operation	Option	Template
New ▶	Project	BIM House 2015 Start.rte

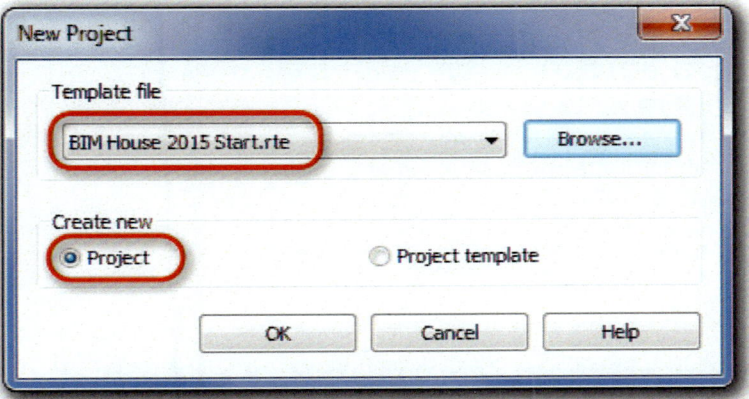

 Failure to start with the specified project template will result in missing parameters, and will require that you start over and redo any work completed using the correct template before moving forward with future exercises.

 When performing a *Save As*, you do not need to key in the extension as shown. This will be added automatically based on the file type specified. In the following step the file type specified is *project*, which results in an extension of *rvt*.

Save As (Project)		
Operation	Option	File Name
Save As ▶	Project	BIMHOUSE-EX01-1.rvt

CHAPTER 1: PROJECT SETUP, IMPORT CAD, BASIC WALLS

Initial Project Setup

Enter Basic Project Information

Project Information		
Tab	Panel	Tool Button
Manage	Settings	Project Information

1. In the Project Properties dialog box, enter the following information.

Instance Properties: Project Information

Parameter	Value	Comments
Project Issue Date		Enter today's date (*MM/DD/YYYY*)
Project Status	**PRELIMINARY**	
Client Name	**SPSCC**	
Project Address	**2011 MOTTMAN RD SW** **OLYMPIA, WA 98512**	Enter 2 lines as shown
Project Name	**BIM HOUSE 2015**	
Project Number	**BH-15**	
Student Name	*<name>*	*<first-initial>*. *<Last-name>* (all upper case); e.g., **J. DOE**

2. When done entering the information above, click **Edit...** next to the *Energy Settings* property to open the Energy Settings dialog box.

3. Set the *Building Type* property as illustrated below.

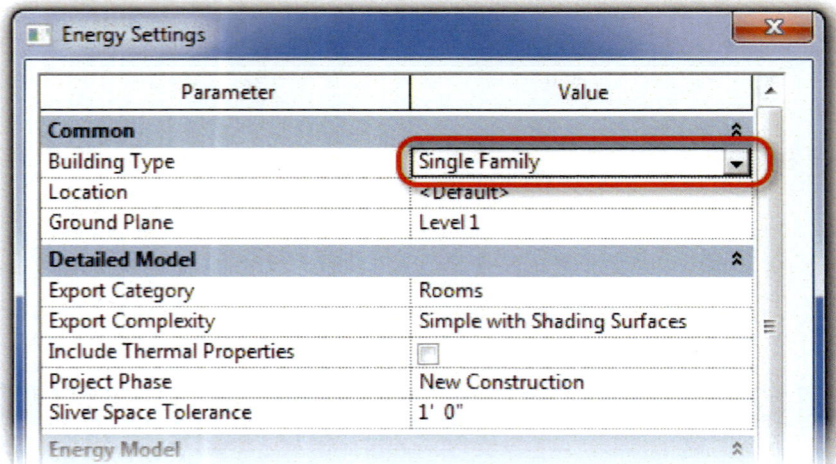

Energy Settings

4. When done, click **OK** twice to exit the Energy Settings and Project Information dialog boxes.

EXERCISE 1.1: PROJECT SETUP

Set Project location

Project Location		
Tab	Panel	Tool Button
Manage	Project Location	Location

5. In the Location Weather and Site dialog box, enter the following information.

Location Tab

Parameter	Value
Define Location by	**Default City List**
City	**Olympia, WA**
Use Daylight Savings Time	✓

6. Click **OK** when done.

 To quickly find a city from the drop-down list in the Location Weather and Site dialog box, click on the drop-down button to expand the list, then key the first letter of the city. This will take you to the first city in the list that starts with the keyed letter.

 An internet connection is required for the following steps, through "Set Default Project Units."

7. Reopen the Location Weather and Site dialog box...

Project Location		
Tab	Panel	Tool Button
Manage	Project Location	Location

8. Set the *Define Location by* drop-down selector to **Internet Mapping Service** as illustrated below.

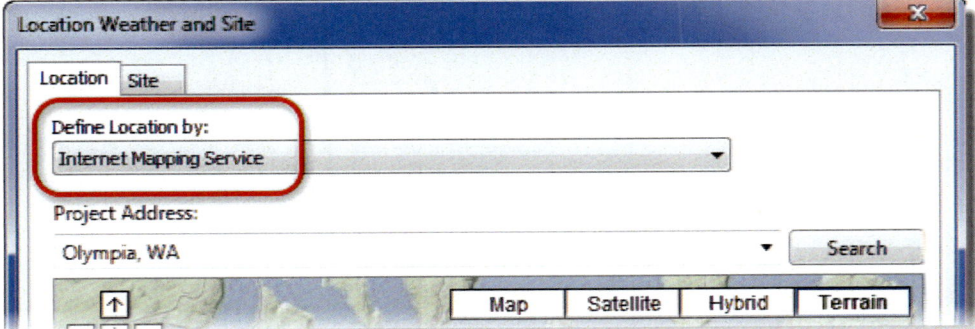

Internet Mapping Service

5

CHAPTER 1: PROJECT SETUP, IMPORT CAD, BASIC WALLS

9. Take notice of the *Project Address* field, then drag the location indicator (red pushpin with the house icon) to the approximate location of the SPSCC campus. Notice that the *Project Address* field now displays coordinates.

10. In the *Project Address* field overwrite the coordinates with the correct project address as you entered it into Project Information. You should only need to type the street number and name, then click **Search**. The location indicator will move to the exact location of the address according to the mapping service.

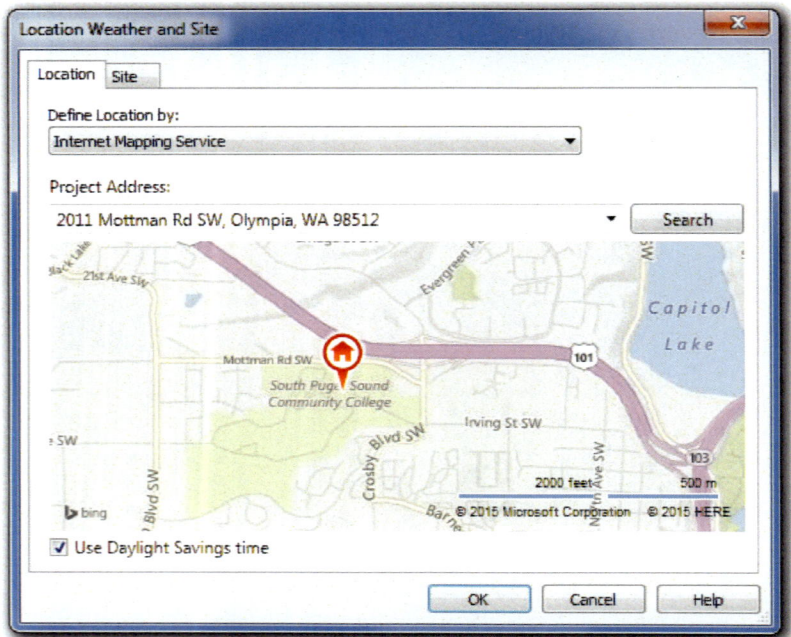

11. Click **OK** when done.

Set default project units

	Project Units	
Tab	Panel	Tool Button
Manage	Settings	Project Units

12. In the Project Units dialog box, click the format button for *Length*, and make the following changes.

Project Units: Length Format

Parameter	Value
Rounding	To the nearest 1/8"
Suppress 0 feet	✓ Checked
Suppress spaces	✓ Checked

13. Click **OK** twice to exit both dialog boxes.

Existing Views Setup

Edit View Scales

 Properties for multiple views can be edited simultaneously. In the Project Browser, click on all views you wish to edit while holding down the **[ctrl]** key to create a selection set.

1. Using the Project Browser, select each of the views listed in the table below. When the view, or group of views is selected, use the Properties Palette to change the *View Scale* property to **1/4" = 1'-0", then** click **Apply** or shift focus away from the Properties Palette to apply the new value.

 DO NOT use the *View Control Bar* when simultaneously editing values for multiple views.

2. When done, all views EXCEPT *Site* should have a view scale of **1/4" = 1'-0"**.

Views Requiring View Scale Change to 1/4" = 1'-0"

Floor Plans	Ceiling Plans	Elevations (Building Elevation)
Level 1	Level 1	East
Level 2	Level 2	North
		South
		West

Rename Levels

3. Open the *South* elevation view either by double-clicking on it in the project browser, or by double-clicking on the elevation marker arrowhead in plan view.

4. Rename the levels as indicated in the table below. Make sure to use the upper & lower case letters, and all punctuation as indicated. Answer **Yes** when prompted with the dialog box *"Would you like to rename corresponding views?"*

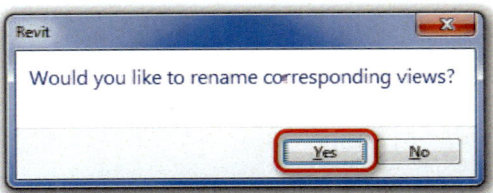

 Make sure to answer **Yes** when prompted to rename views.

 To edit a level name, first select the level, then click on the name field to activate it.

Level	Rename to
Level 1	F.F.L. 1st FLR
Level 2	F.F.L. 2nd FLR

Add Levels & Plan Views

1. If the *South* elevation view is not still open, open it now and create levels as follows.

Tab	Panel	Tool Button
	Level	LL
Architecture	Datum	Level

Modify	Place Level	
	Draw	
	Line	
Make Plan View: ☑	Plan View Types... **Floor Plan**	Offset: **0' 0"**

 The options banner above directs you to create only *Floor Plan* view types. You control this by clicking on **Plan View Types...** in the options bar, then selecting and/or deselecting the appropriate view types (default is all views selected). *Take note that this setting is remembered and saved in the Project file, not by session.*

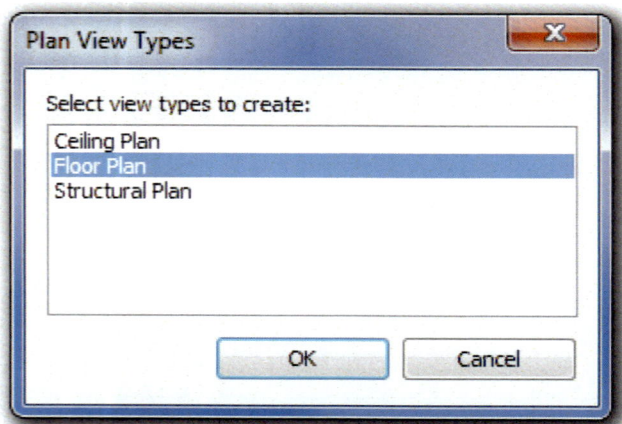

2. Sketching from left to right, while using *snap to remote* to align with the start and end points of existing levels, create three new levels *with corresponding plan views* as indicated in the table on the following page. Rename each level after creating it.

 Be sure to answer **Yes** when prompted to rename the corresponding view.

 You can rename each level immediately after sketching it without exiting the Level tool. After you complete the level, click the name field to activate it, then key in the new name and press **[enter]**. You can do the same for the elevation value if you want to change it.

New Levels with a Corresponding *Floor Plan* View

Level	Approximate Location in Elevation
T.O.W. STEM	Below F.F.L. 1st FLR
T.O.W. 1st FLR	Between F.F.L. 1st FLR & F.F.L. 2nd FLR
T.O.W. 2nd FLR	Above F.F.L. 2nd FLR

3. Change the Options Bar settings...

Modify	Place Level
Draw	
Line	
Make Plan View: ☐	Offset: **0' 0"**

4. Continue sketching the remaining levels indicated in the following table. Corresponding plan views will not be created.

New Levels without Corresponding Views

Level	Approximate Location in Elevation
FINISH GRADE	Below T.O. STEM WALL
T.O. FOOTING	Below FINISH GRADE
B.O. FOOTING	Below T.O. FOOTING

5. **Exit** the *Levels* tool when done.
6. Adjust the elevation values of the new levels as indicated in the following table.

Final Level Elevation Values

Level	Elevation
B.O. FOOTING	-3' 2"
T.O. FOOTING	-2' 6"
FINISH GRADE	-1' 8"
T.O.W. STEM	-1' 0"
T.O.W. 1st FLR	8' 1 1/8"
F.F.L. 2nd FLR	9' 1 1/8"
T.O.W. 2nd FLR	17' 2 1/4"

CHAPTER 1: PROJECT SETUP, IMPORT CAD, BASIC WALLS

7. Make the level names and elevations readable by selecting an appropriate level, clicking the *Add Elbow* symbol, and adjusting the grips as necessary. When complete, your levels should look similar to the illustration below.

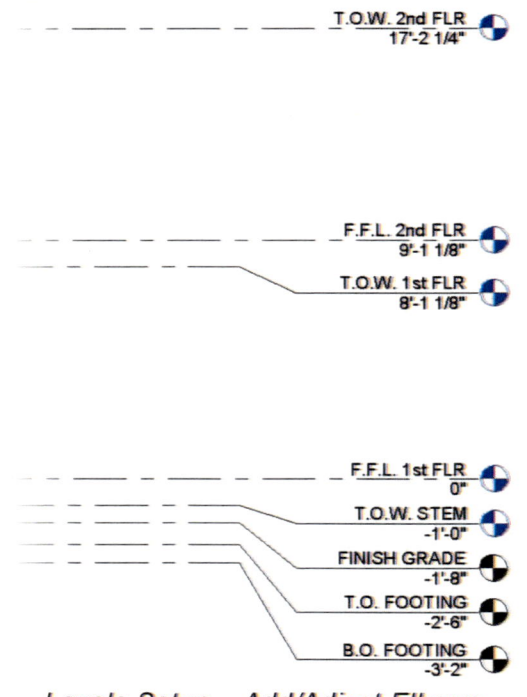

Levels Setup – Add/Adjust Elbows

 Levels with blue level heads have corresponding plan views (shown in the Project Browser), and levels with black level heads do not.

Duplicate Views

Duplicate an Elevation View

1. In the project browser, click once to select the *South* elevation view (it's not necessary to open it), then duplicate it as follows.

Duplicate View			
Tab	Panel	Drop-down Button ▼	Tool Button
View	**Create**	**Duplicate View**	**Duplicate View**

 The new elevation view should be created, and simultaneously opened. If not, use the Undo command and repeat the previous step.

2. Use the Properties Palette to rename the new elevation view (*South Copy 1*) to **W-South - Constraints**, then click **Apply**. Verify the renamed view in the Project Browser.

EXERCISE 1.1: PROJECT SETUP

 Revit often provides multiple methods for accomplishing the same thing. Many operations can be accessed in the contextual menu. Just right-click on an element, then select the desired operations from the menu. Right-clicking on a view in the project browser provides shortcut access to common view editing operations, such as *Duplicate* and *Rename*.

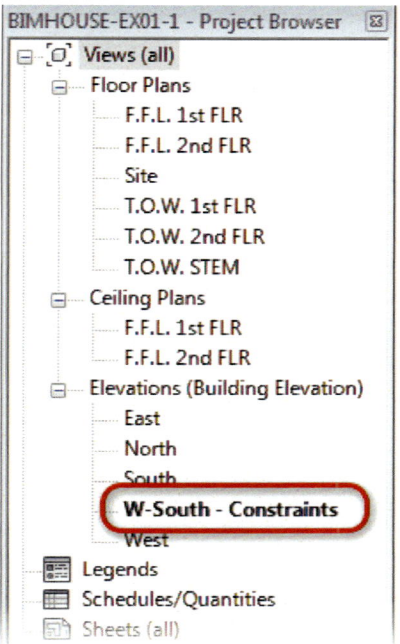

 This isn't the typical way of creating an elevation view. The more standard approach will be discussed in future lessons. What's important to realize is that every elevation view must have it's own elevation marker, and by duplicating a view we duplicate the marker.

Adjust the Location of the New Elevation Marker

When duplicating the *South* elevation view, the duplicated elevation marker in the plan view was placed directly on top of the existing marker. In the following steps you will separate the two markers

3. Open floor plan view *F.F.L. 1st FLR*.

4. Select the south elevation marker body by clicking on the box portion of the marker. Do not use a window or crossing selection.

5. Next, **click and drag** the marker off to the left as illustrated below.

Drag-Move Duplicated Elevation Marker

CHAPTER 1: PROJECT SETUP, IMPORT CAD, BASIC WALLS

Duplicate Floor Plan Views

The following steps outline the process for duplicating a view using the contextual menu (right-click). Use this process to duplicate the <u>floor</u> plan views listed in the table below. Be sure to create the correct number of copies for each view listed.

6. In the project browser, **right-click** on the view to be duplicated.
7. From the contextual-menu, select **Duplicate View ▶ Duplicate**.

 When creating multiple copies of a view, continue to duplicate the *same* view for subsequent copies. Do not make a duplicate of a copy, or the names will not correspond to view names referenced in future exercise steps.

Floor Plan Views to Duplicate

View to Duplicate	Number of Copies
F.F.L. 1st FLR	4
F.F.L. 2nd FLR	4
T.O.W. 2nd FLR	1
T.O.W. STEM	1

Rename Plan Views

8. Rename the duplicated plan views as indicated in the following table.

Rename Duplicated Floor Plan Views

Duplicated View Names	New Name
F.F.L. 1st FLR Copy 1	W-1st Floor - Constraints
F.F.L. 1st FLR Copy 2	W-1st Floor - Working Notes
F.F.L. 1st FLR Copy 3	W-1st Floor - CAD Import
F.F.L. 1st FLR Copy 4	1st Floor - Dimension
F.F.L. 2nd FLR Copy 1	W-2nd Floor - Constraints
F.F.L. 2nd FLR Copy 2	W-2nd Floor - Working Notes
F.F.L. 2nd FLR Copy 3	W-2nd Floor - CAD Import
F.F.L. 2nd FLR Copy 4	2nd Floor - Dimension
T.O.W. 2nd FLR Copy 1	Roof Plan
T.O.W. STEM Copy 1	Foundation Plan

9. Rename each of the ceiling plan views as indicated in the table on the following page. <u>Answer **NO** when prompted to rename corresponding levels and views.</u>

EXERCISE 1.1: PROJECT SETUP

Rename Ceiling Plan Views

Original Name	New Name
F.F.L. 1st FLR	RCP - 1st Floor
F.F.L. 2nd FLR	RCP - 2nd Floor

 Failure to answer NO when prompted to rename corresponding levels and views will result in both the corresponding F.F.L. floor plan views and levels to be renamed to match the ceiling plans, which is NOT the result we want! Beware that the default button in this dialog is Yes, so DON'T press [enter] as this will answer Yes!

10. Open an exterior elevation view and verify that the level names have not changed. If any of them contains "RCP - " use Undo to correct the problem, and then repeat the previous step.

11. Verify that your project browser contains all of the views illustrated below. If any extra views exist in your project, delete them now. (**Right-click** on view and select **Delete**).

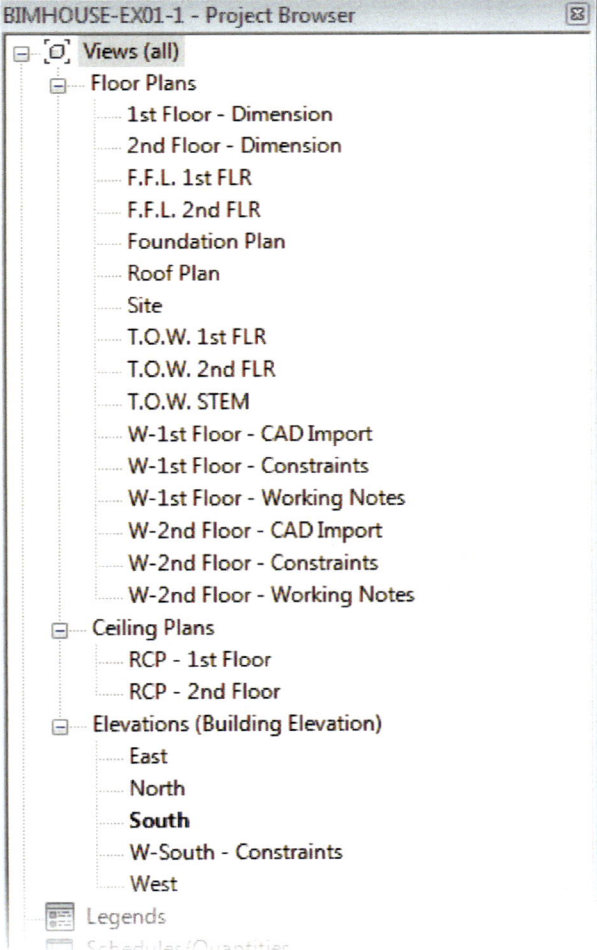

Project Browser: Completed View List

13

CHAPTER 1: PROJECT SETUP, IMPORT CAD, BASIC WALLS

⚠ If the view list in your project browser is not sorted in the same order as shown in the previous illustration, verify correct spelling, punctuation, and spaces in each name.

	Save (Project)	[Ctl]+S
Operation		
Save		

This concludes Exercise 1.1

Exercise 1.2: Importing CAD Files & Creating a Building Layout

Open Project		[Ctl]+O
Operation	Option	File Name
Open ▶	Project	BIMHOUSE-EX01-1.rvt

Save As (Project)		
Operation	Option	File Name
Save As ▶	Project	BIMHOUSE-EX01-2.rvt

Import the CAD Files

In the following steps you will be importing DWG files provided to you. Make sure you have these saved locally, and easily accessible prior to beginning.

1. Open the plan view *W-1st Floor - CAD Import*.

Import CAD		
Tab	Panel	Tool Button
Insert	**Import**	**Import CAD**

2. Navigate to the folder where you saved the provided DWG files, and import the file *BIMHouse-1st_Floor.dwg* using the settings shown below in the Import CAD Formats dialog box.

Import Dialog Settings: BIMHouse-1st_Floor.dwg

Parameter	Value
Current view only	✓
Colors	**Preserve**
Layers/Levels	**All**
Import units	**Auto–Detect**
Correct lines that are slightly off axis	✓
Positioning	**Auto - Origin to origin**

3. Click **Open** to finish the import operation.
4. Open the plan view *W-2nd Floor - CAD Import*

CHAPTER 1: PROJECT SETUP, IMPORT CAD, BASIC WALLS

Import CAD		
Tab	Panel	Tool Button
Insert	**Import**	**Import CAD**

5. Navigate to the folder where you saved the provided DWG files, and import the file *BIMHouse-2nd_Floor.dwg* using the same settings in the Import CAD Formats dialog box that you used for the previous import.

Building Layout

In the following steps you will outline the imported CAD geometry with reference planes. These reference planes will be visible in other views, and will serve as building layout guides, as well as datums to which building elements will be associated.

1. Open the view *W-1st Floor - CAD Import*.
2. Zoom in so that the building outline fills the current view window.

Reference Plane		RP
Tab	Panel	Tool Button
Architecture	**Work Plane**	**Ref Plane**

Modify	Place Reference Plane	
	Draw	
	Pick Lines	
Offset: **0' 0"**		Lock: ☐

⚠️ When using Pick Lines to create reference planes, take care not to pick any line more than once. Doing so will create multiple reference planes in the same location. This condition will not be apparent, and will cause major problems going forward. When clicking on an extent control of a reference plane, make sure it is pre-highlighted before clicking!!!

3. Place reference planes by picking the exterior faces of all exterior walls represented by the 1st floor imported CAD file.

   a) After each pick, extend both extents beyond the building footprint as illustrated on the following page.

EXERCISE 1.2: IMPORTING CAD FILES & BUILDING LAYOUT

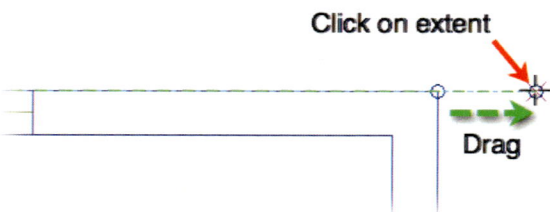

Extend Reference Plane Extents

b) Where more than one line segment defines a wall plane, pick only one of the lines, and then extend the reference plane using the extent control.

c) Include interior walls that separate livable space from the garage. Pick the side facing into the garage as illustrated below.

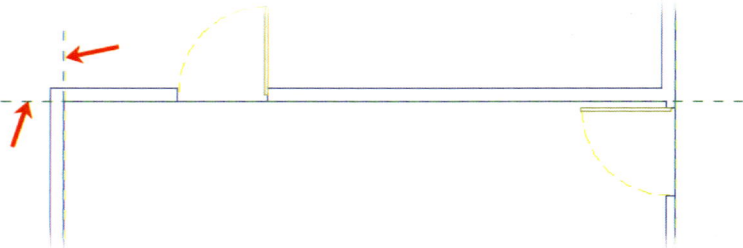

Interior Walls at Garage

4. Open the floor plan view *W-2nd Floor - CAD Import*.
5. Add the final reference plane by sketching it with the line tool...

Reference Plane		RP
Tab	Panel	Tool Button
Architecture	Work Plane	Ref Plane

Modify	Place Reference Plane
Draw
Line
Offset: 0' 0"

6. Sketch a single reference plane (sketching right to left) along the exterior face of the 2nd floor's south wall.
7. Extend the ends of any reference planes that still require adjustment beyond the wall boundaries as illustrated on the following page.

CHAPTER 1: PROJECT SETUP, IMPORT CAD, BASIC WALLS

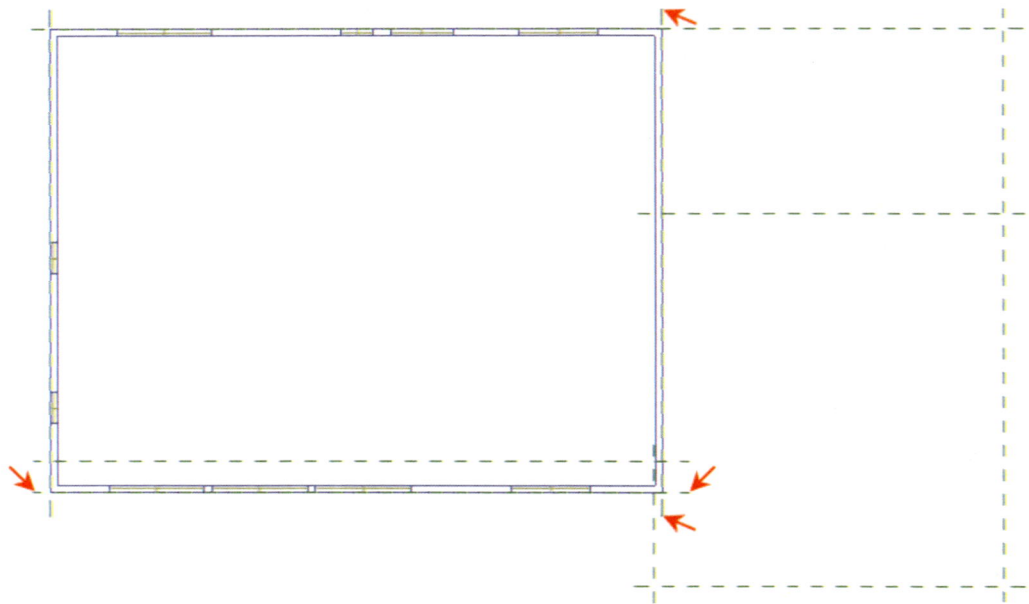

Reference Plane Adjustments in View W-2nd Floor - CAD Import

8. **Exit** the Reference Plane tool when done.

 As an alternative to adjusting the extent controls while the Reference Plane tool is active, you can first place all reference planes, then exit the tool. Then, individually pick each reference plane, and adjust its extent controls. This is less efficient, but it does lower the risk of multiple picks on a single line.

Verify Correct Number of Reference Planes

In the next steps you will ensure that no extra reference planes were created. If you discover an incorrect count, go back and find the extra reference plan and delete it.

9. With either one of the "... - *CAD Import*" views open, draw a crossing selection box over the entire floor plan, making sure to select all reference planes.

10. Examine the selection set using the Filter tool...

11. When the Filter dialog box opens, it should appear as illustrated on the following page. Note that the count column provides a total element count for each category in the selection set. You should have 9 reference planes at this time.

18

EXERCISE 1.2: IMPORTING CAD FILES & BUILDING LAYOUT

 If you have additional categories, such as Elevations and Views showing in the Filter dialog box, it's because you included elevation markers when you drew the crossing selection. Don't worry about this for now. The main purpose here is to verify the reference plane count.

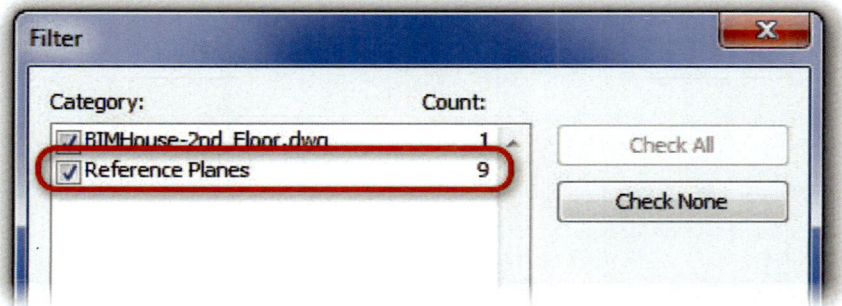

Selection Set in Filter Dialog Box

12. Click **OK** to exit the Filter dialog box.

13. Clear the selection by clicking the **Modify** button, or pressing **[Esc]** twice.

 Do not proceed with the following steps until you have verified that your project contains the correct number of reference planes!!!

Assign Names to Reference Planes

14. Select each reference plane one at a time and assign a name from the table on the following page. Refer to the illustration key below the table as a cross reference to the correct name in the table.

CHAPTER 1: PROJECT SETUP, IMPORT CAD, BASIC WALLS

 The numbers are used to key the reference planes in the illustration to a row in the table. DO NOT use these numbers as the actual name!

Named Reference Planes

Key Number in Illustration	Reference Plane Name
1	**Ext-West**
2	**Ext-North**
3	**Ext-East-1**
4	**Ext-East-2--Int-Garage-West**
5	**Ext-South-1**
6	**Ext-South-2**
7	**Ext-Garage-South**
8	**Ext-Garage-West**
9	**Int-Garage-North**

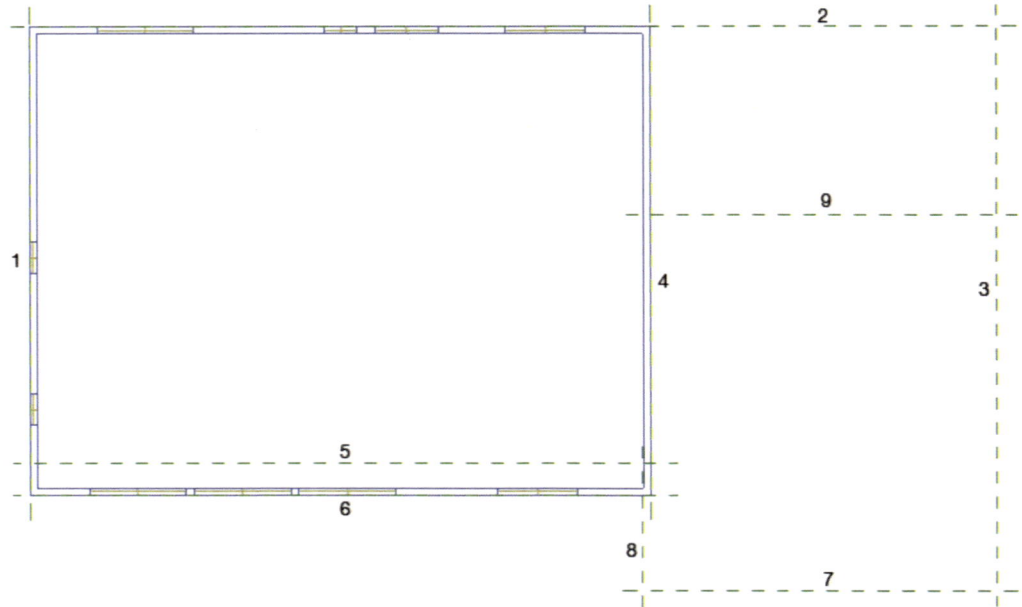

Reference Plane Name Key

QAT	Save (Project)	[Ctl]+S
	Operation	
	Save	

This concludes Exercise 1.2

Exercise 1.3: Adding Exterior Walls

QAT 📂	Open Project		[Ctl]+O
	Operation	Option	File Name
R	Open ▶	Project	BIMHOUSE-EX01-2.rvt

	Save As (Project)		
	Operation	Option	File Name
R	Save As ▶	Project	BIMHOUSE-EX01-3.rvt

1st Floor Exterior Walls

In the following steps you will add walls to the first floor. First you will place generic 6" walls to define the livable space. Then you will create a generic 4" wall type and use this to enclose the garage.

1. Open the floor plan view *F.F.L. 1st FLR*.
2. Activate the Wall tool, and set the properties as as follows.

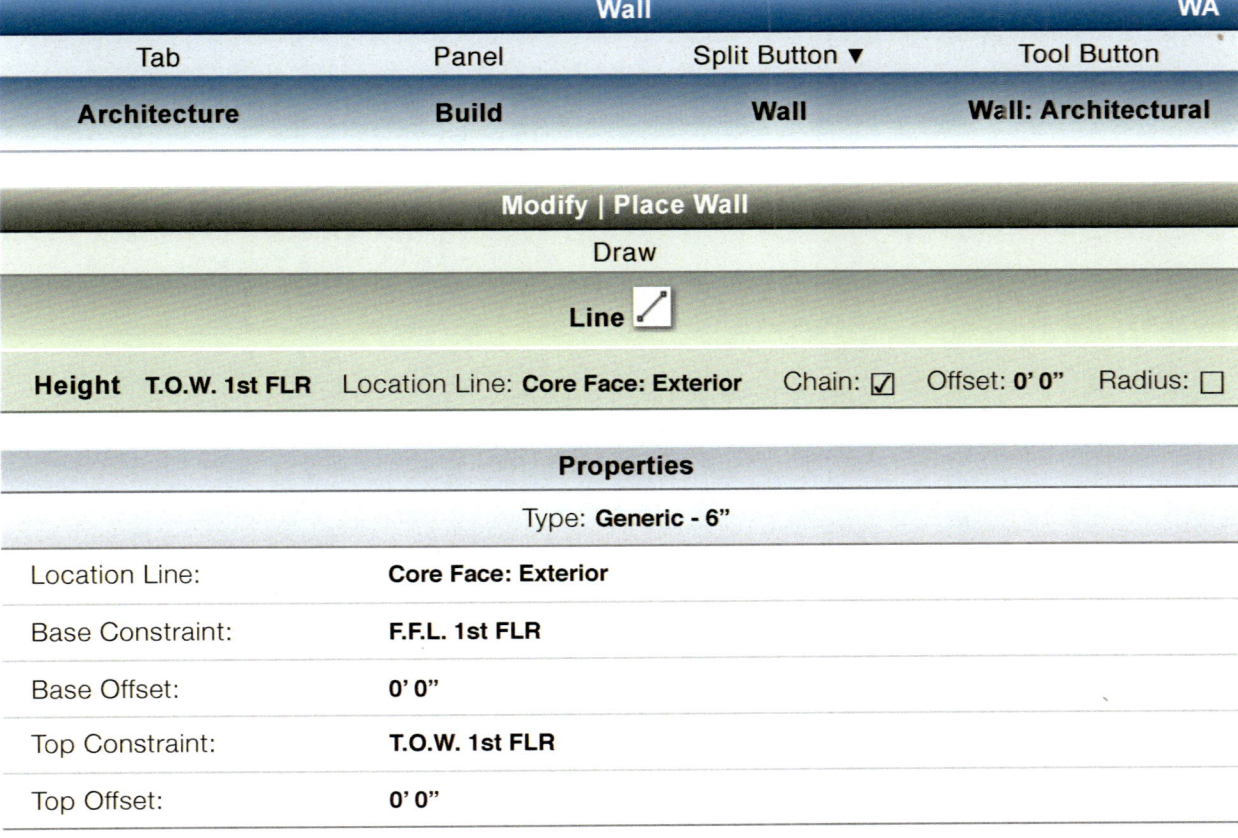

3. Sketch the Generic - 6" exterior walls of the livable area in a clockwise direction directly on the reference planes as illustrated below *(Snap wall ends to reference plane intersections)*.

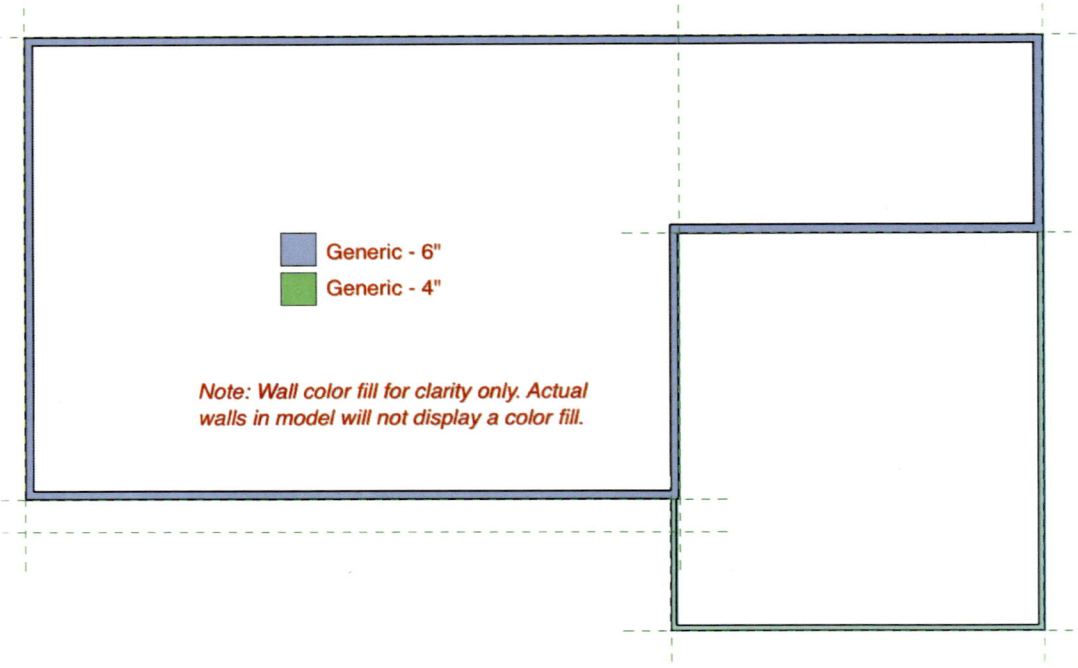

Create a New Wall Type

4. Verify the Wall tool is still active. If not, activate it now.

5. In the Properties Palette, click on **Edit Type**.

6. In the *Type Properties* dialog box, click on **Duplicate...**

7. Enter **Generic - 4"** for the name, then click **OK** to accept the new name.

8. Click on the **Edit...** button next to the *Structure* parameter in the Type Parameters pane to open the Edit Assembly dialog box.

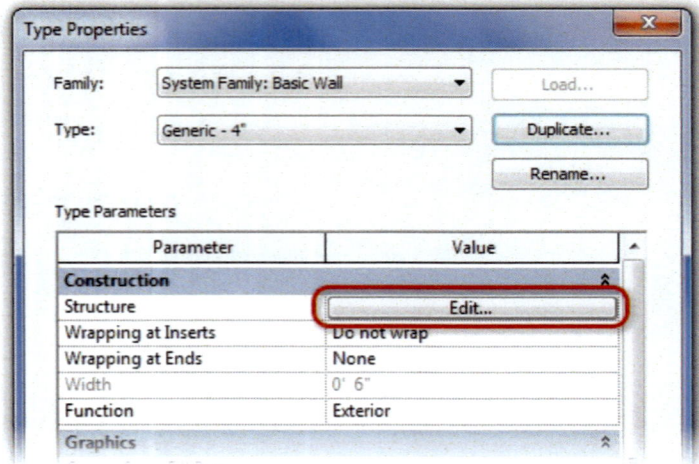

EXERCISE 1.3: ADDING EXTERIOR WALLS

9. In the Layers pane of the Edit Assembly dialog box, change the *Thickness* parameter for *Layer 2* to **0' 4"** as shown in the illustration below.

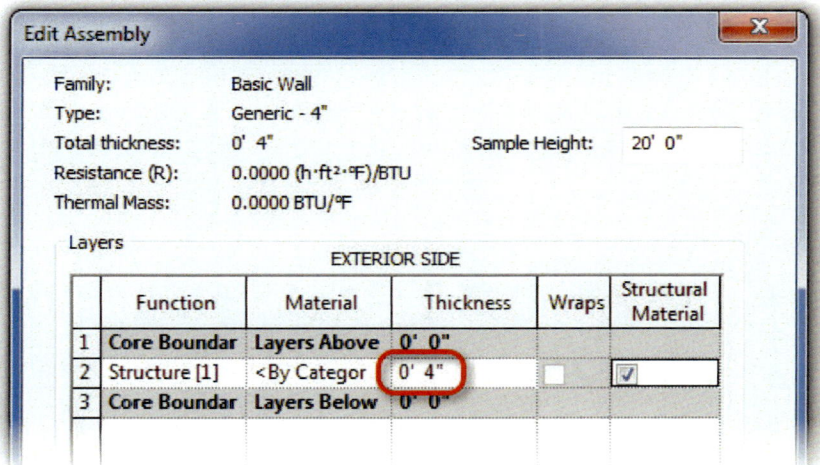

10. Click **OK** twice to exit all dialog boxes.

Add Garage Walls

11. Verify that the new wall type *Generic - 4"* is selected in the *Type Selector* located at the top of the Properties Palette, and continue sketching the garage walls starting at the northeast corner of the garage, and sketching in a clockwise direction to complete the garage as shown in the illustration on page 23.

12. **Exit** the Wall tool when done. Verify the join condition where the west garage wall meets the 6" walls appears as illustrated below.

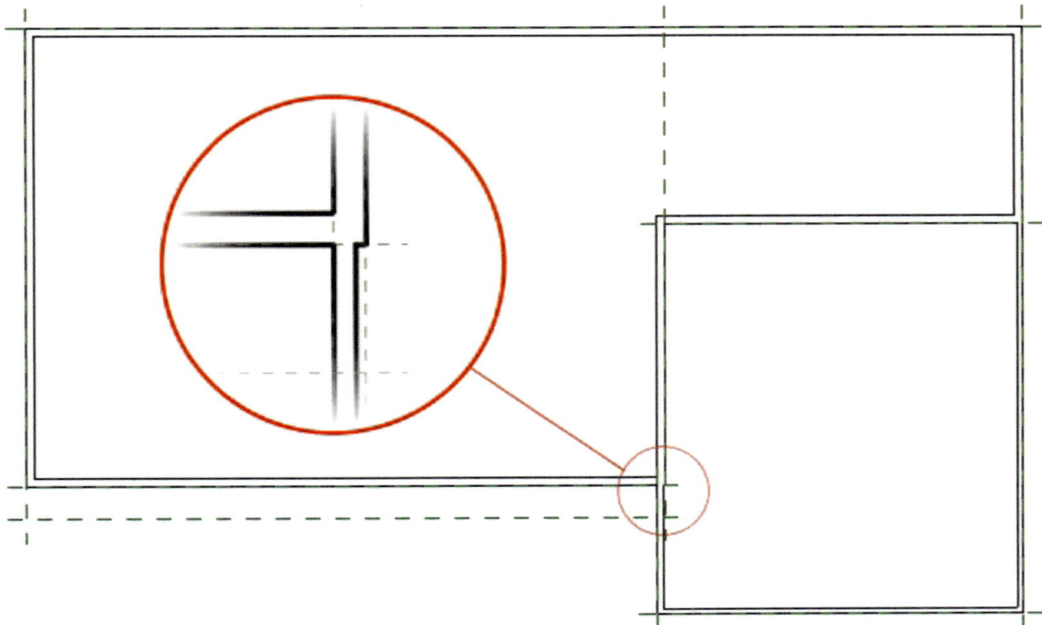

First Floor Exterior Shell Walls

CHAPTER 1: PROJECT SETUP, IMPORT CAD, BASIC WALLS

 Prior to moving on with the next steps, you should verify that all of the walls created are oriented correctly *(exterior side facing out)*, and that all of the wall location lines are set to **Core Face: Exterior**. Additionally, verify that all walls are located on the correct side of the reference planes as illustrated. It's an easy oversight for walls to be located and oriented incorrectly when first learning Revit. Therefore you should get in the habit of double-checking your work. Incorrect orientation and location line settings can have negative consequences later in the project resulting in rework, lost time, and major frustration!

Constrain 1st Floor Walls

In the following steps you will constrain the first floor walls to the reference planes. In upcoming steps this will be repeated on the second floor. Using this technique associates multiple elements to a common plane, which helps to maintain design intent.

13. Activate the **Align** tool and set its properties as shown in the following tool banner.

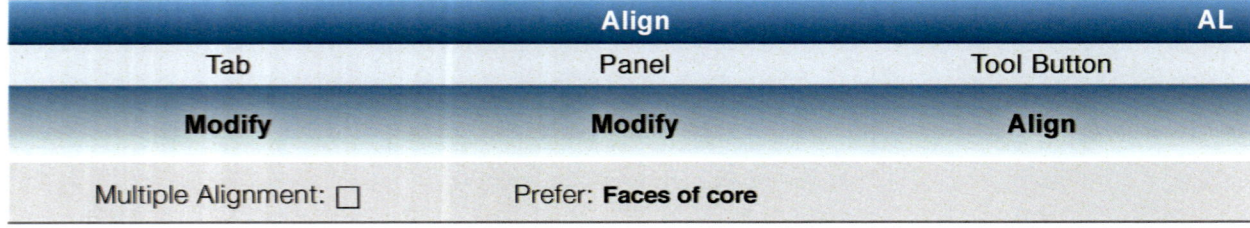

 Make sure you have not changed the *Detail Level* for the view in which you are working. It MUST be set to **Coarse**. Additionally, make sure to set the *Prefer* setting in the options bar to **Faces of Core** as shown in the tool banner above. *These steps are critical!*

14. **Align** and **Lock** the exterior *core face* of each wall to its associated reference plane. Immediately after each alignment operation, close the padlock icon to create the alignment constraint between the wall and reference plane.

15. **Exit** the Align tool when done.

EXERCISE 1.3: ADDING EXTERIOR WALLS

 Did I lock all of my walls? If you're not sure whether you locked all walls to a corresponding reference plane, there's a quick way to check it. First select all walls and reference planes visible in the view (a crossing selection works well for this), then click the **Activate Dimensions** button located in the Options Bar... *Voila*, all locks appear at once!

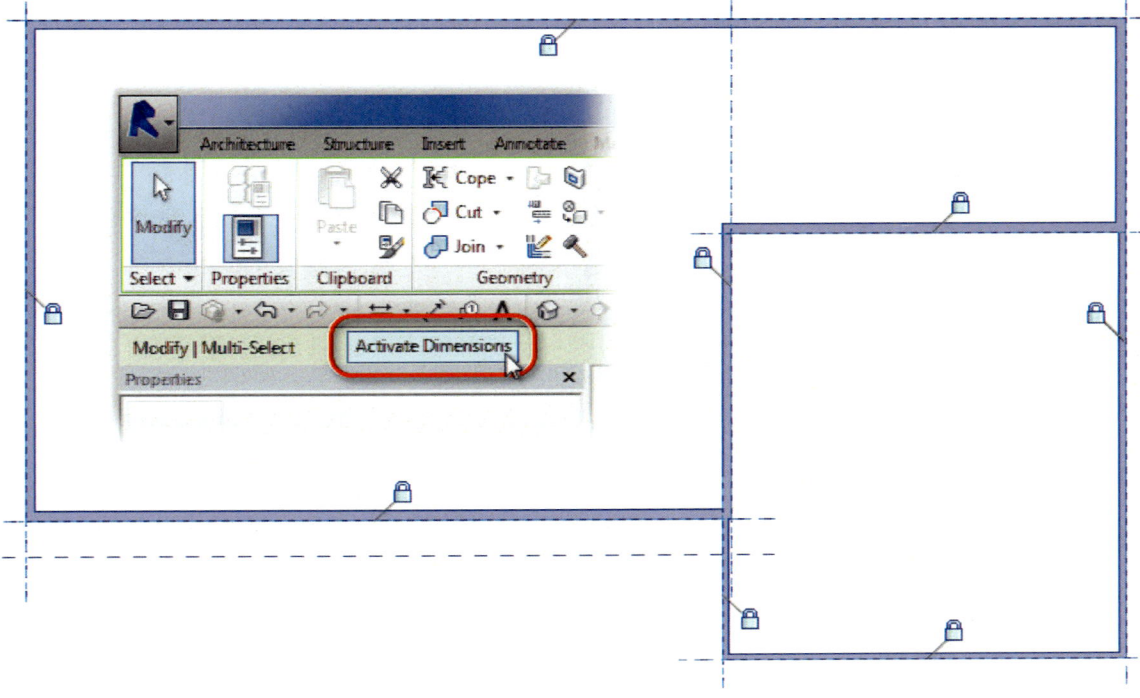

2nd Floor Exterior Walls

Next you will place the 2nd floor walls by using the Pick Lines tool.

1. Open the floor plan view: *F.F.L. 2nd FLR*.

   Notice that a half-tone image of the first floor walls is visible in the view. This is due to the *Underlay* setting in the View Properties.

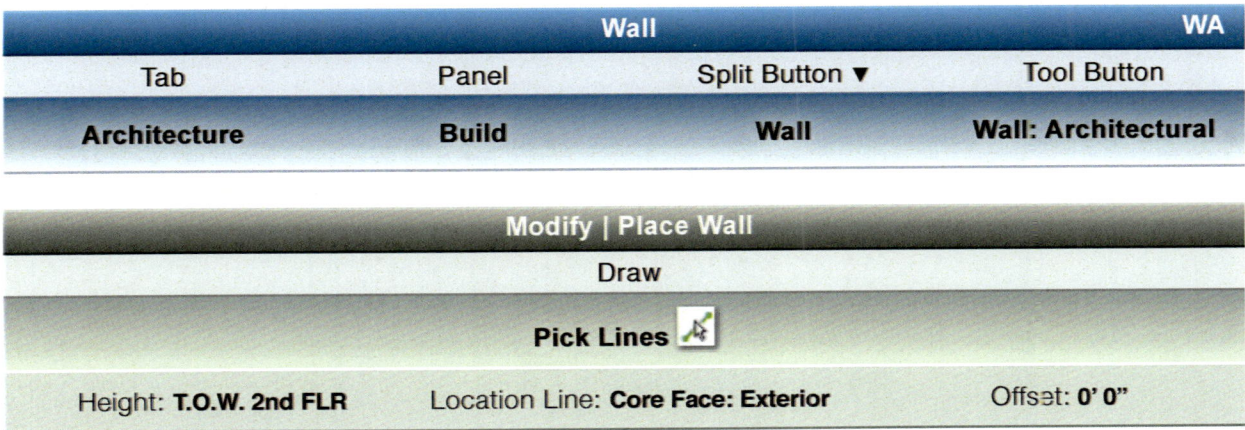

Tab	Panel	Split Button ▼	Wall	Tool Button	WA
Architecture	Build	Wall		Wall: Architectural	

Modify | Place Wall
Draw
Pick Lines
Height: **T.O.W. 2nd FLR**   Location Line: **Core Face: Exterior**   Offset: **0' 0"**

25

CHAPTER 1: PROJECT SETUP, IMPORT CAD, BASIC WALLS

Properties	
Type: **Generic - 6"**	
Location Line:	**Core Face: Exterior**
Base Constraint:	**F.F.L. 2nd FLR**
Base Offset:	**0' 0"**
Top Constraint:	**T.O.W. 2nd FLR**
Top Offset:	**0' 0"**

2. Place the 2nd floor exterior walls by picking the appropriate reference plane (*refer to the illustration below*). Verify exterior/interior faces of walls orient correctly. Notice that the walls all extend past the corners of the building to the full length of the reference plane. This is normal behavior when using the Pick Lines draw tool.

3. **Exit** the Wall tool when done.

Trim the Wall Ends to Clean the Corners

Trim/Extend to Corner		TR
Tab	Panel	Tool Button
Modify	**Modify**	**Trim/Extend to Corners**

4. Trim all wall corners where they cross as indicated in the illustration below.

 When using any of the the Trim/Extend tools, be sure to pick the portion of the element you wish to keep!

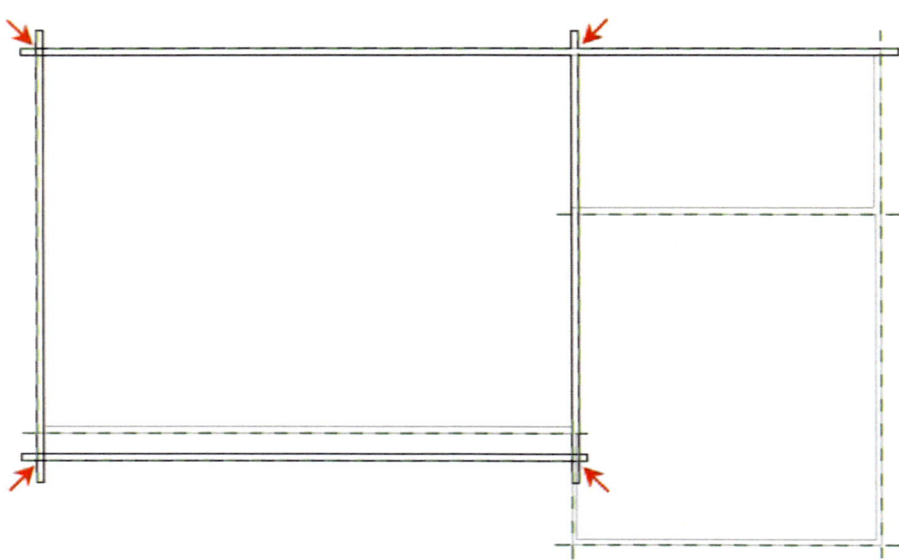

Trim Locations of 2nd Floor Walls

5. **Exit** the Trim/Extend tool when done. Your trimmed walls should appear as illustrated below.

2nd Floor Walls Trimmed

 As with the 1st floor walls, prior to moving on with the next steps you should verify that all of the walls created are oriented correctly *(exterior side facing out)*, and that all of the wall location lines are set to **Core Face: Exterior**. Additionally, verify that all walls are located to the inward facing side of the reference planes.

6. **Align** and **Lock** each wall to its associated reference plane.
7. **Exit** the align tool when done.

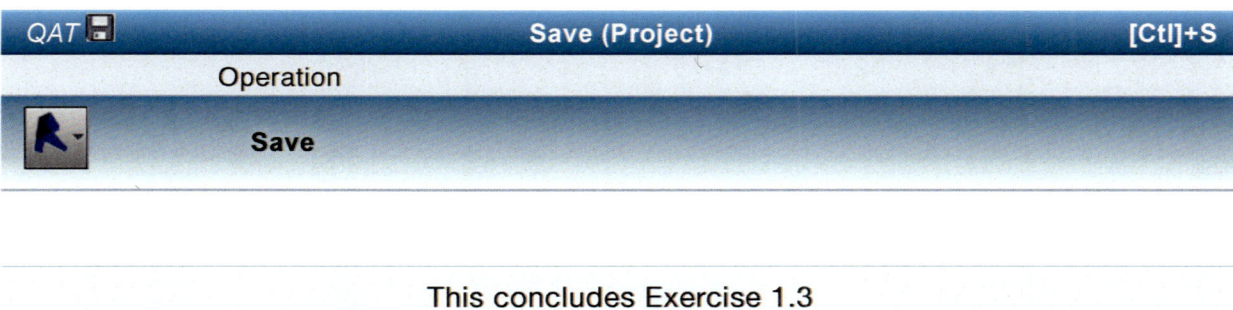

This concludes Exercise 1.3

Exercise 1.4: Project Extents & Constraints Validation

In the following steps you will adjust level extents, as well as elevation view marker locations. This will reduce the overall project extents, making the *Zoom to Fit* tool more effective. This has no affect on the physical properties of your model.

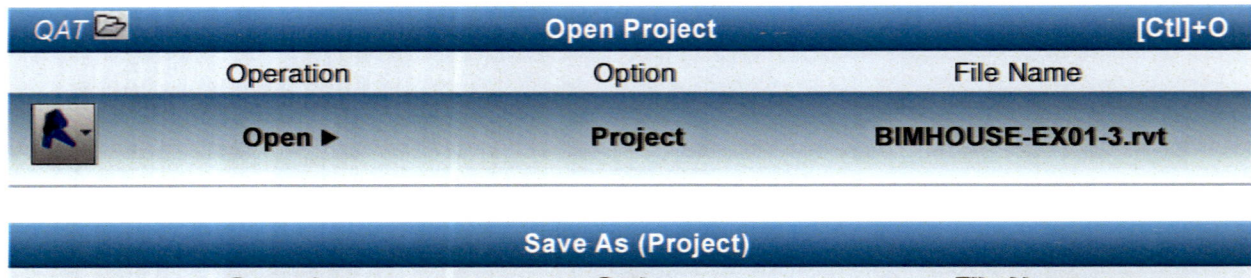

Project Extents

1. Open the floor plan view *F.F.L. 1st FLR*.

2. Zoom the view to fit using the Navigation Bar zoom tools **Zoom to Fit (ZF)**, or type **[ZF]**

3. Using either the crossing or a window selection method, select and move each of the elevation markers one at a time to the approximate location shown in the illustration below. Make sure both the body *and* the arrow are selected before performing the move.

 You can select and move both of the south elevation markers at the same time.

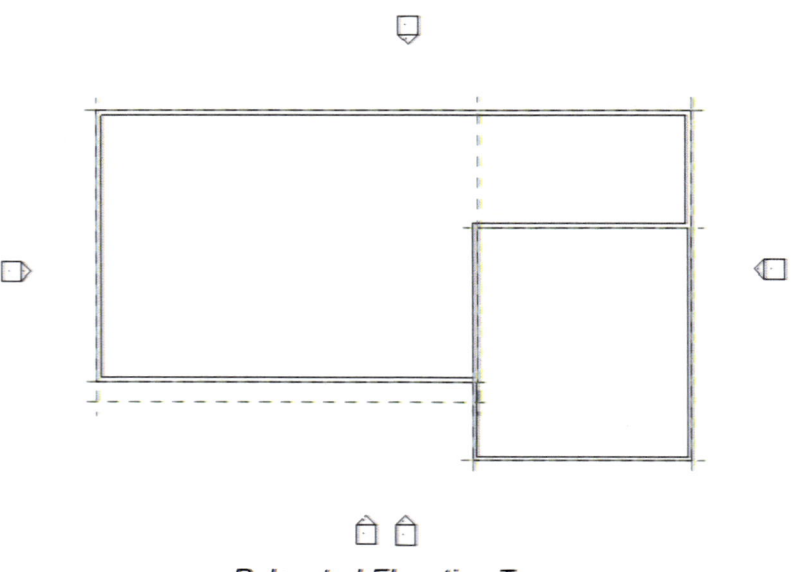

Relocated Elevation Tags

EXERCISE 1.4: PROJECT EXTENTS & CONSTRAINTS VALIDATION

4. Zoom the view to fit once again. The view should enlarge to fill the drawing area.
5. Open the *South* elevation view.
6. Select one of the levels, then click and drag the left 3D extents control to the right, and the right 3D extents control to the left so the view appears similar to the illustration below.

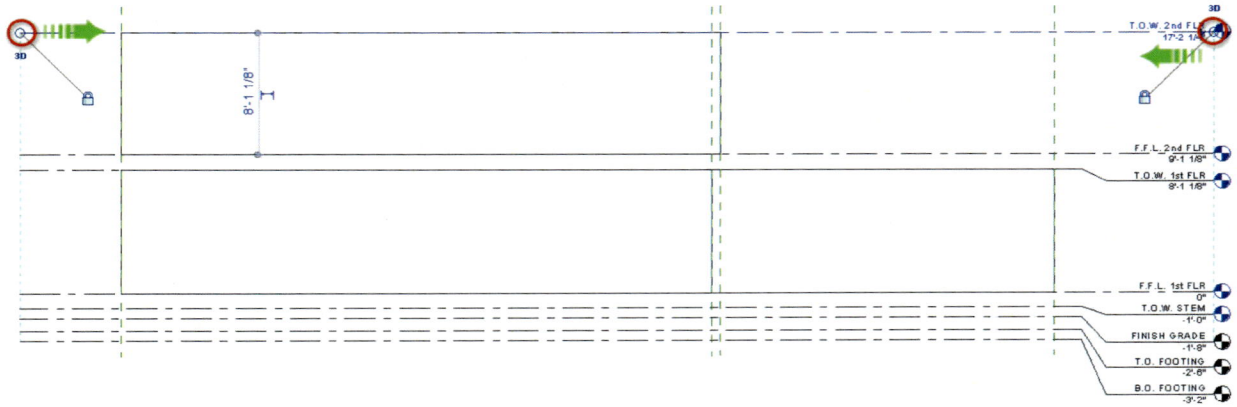

Adjust Level Extents – South Elevation View

7. Open the *West* elevation view.
8. Select one of the levels, then repeat the process so the view appears similar to the illustration below.

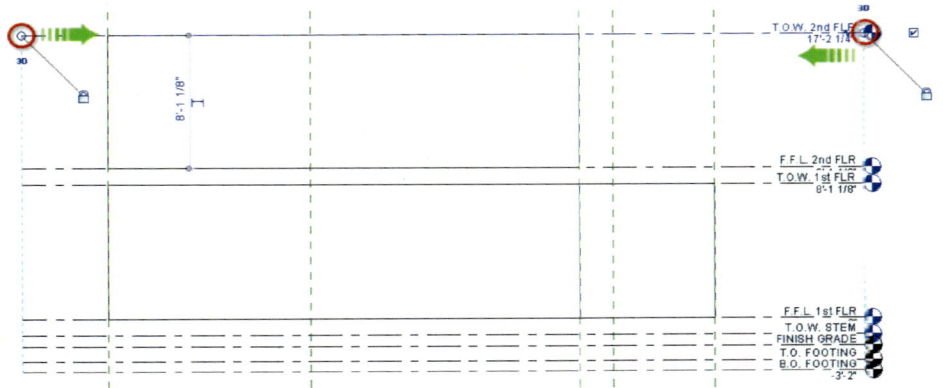

Adjust Level Extents – West Elevation View

 Did all level extents move together at each end? If not, it's possible that the ends were not aligned vertically using remote snapping while sketching the levels. Revit automatically groups (locks) all level extents that are aligned vertically, allowing them to be adjusted as a group. If any of your extents were left behind during adjustment, adjust that level separately until it snaps vertically to the rest of the level extents. It will then become part of that group, and will move together during future adjustments. If you *do* want to adjust an extent independently, select the level, click the padlock icon to unlock it, and then drag the level extent. Note that if you deselect the level before dragging the extent, it will automatically re-lock

29

Verifying Design Intent

Throughout the exercises in this workbook you should regularly make an effort to verify the integrity of your model and ensure design intent is maintained. In the following steps you will set up a couple of views to facilitate this process, as well as begin to learn how to check that design intent is being maintained.

Optimize View Graphics for Verifying Design Intent

In this section you will be introduced to Visibility/Graphics Overrides, which allow you to override the appearance of a single view without affecting other views. This topic will be covered in more detail in future chapters. Additionally, you'll be introduced to using the text tool, which will also be covered in more depth in future chapters. For now, just follow the steps carefully to achieve the proper results.

1. Open the floor plan view **W-1st Floor - CAD Import**. Notice that the imported CAD file is mostly covered by the added wall geometry.
2. Open the Visibility/Graphics Overrides dialog box...

Visibility/Graphics Overrides		VV / VG
Tab	Panel	Tool Button
View	**Graphics**	**Visibility/Graphics**

 You can also access the Visibility/Graphics Overrides dialog box from the Properties Palette.

The following table represents the target Visibility/Graphics Overrides settings for this view. The steps that follow will walk you through editing these settings.

Visibility Settings: CAD Import Views

Category Tab / Category / Subcategory	Visibility
Model / All Categories (master checkbox)	OFF
Annotation / Reference Planes	ON
Annotation / Text Notes	ON
Annotation / (All Remaining Categories)	OFF

3. Select the *Model Categories* tab, then **Uncheck** *Show model categories in this view*.

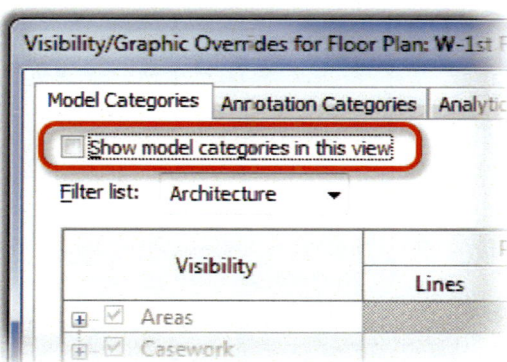

4. Select the *Annotation Categories* tab and do the following:

   a) Click the **All** button. This will highlight/select all categories.

   b) **Uncheck** any one checkbox in the categories pane. This will clear all checkboxes.

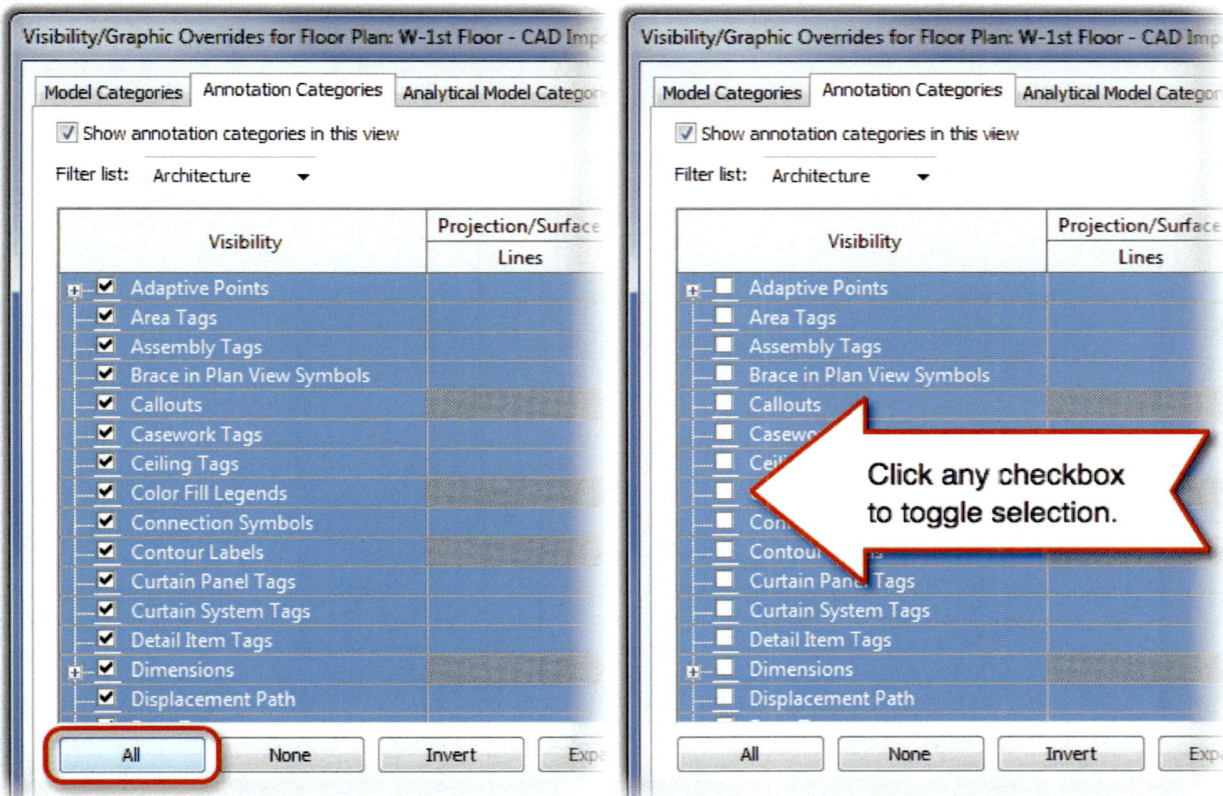

Select All Categories *Clear All Checkboxes*

c) Click the **None** button. This will deselect all categories.

d) Scroll down to locate the *Reference Planes* and *Text Notes* categories, and place a checkmark next to each one. This will keep reference planes and text notes visible.

 Rather than scrolling through the entire list of categories you can type the first letter of the category for which you are searching. This will scroll the list to the first category name beginning with that letter.

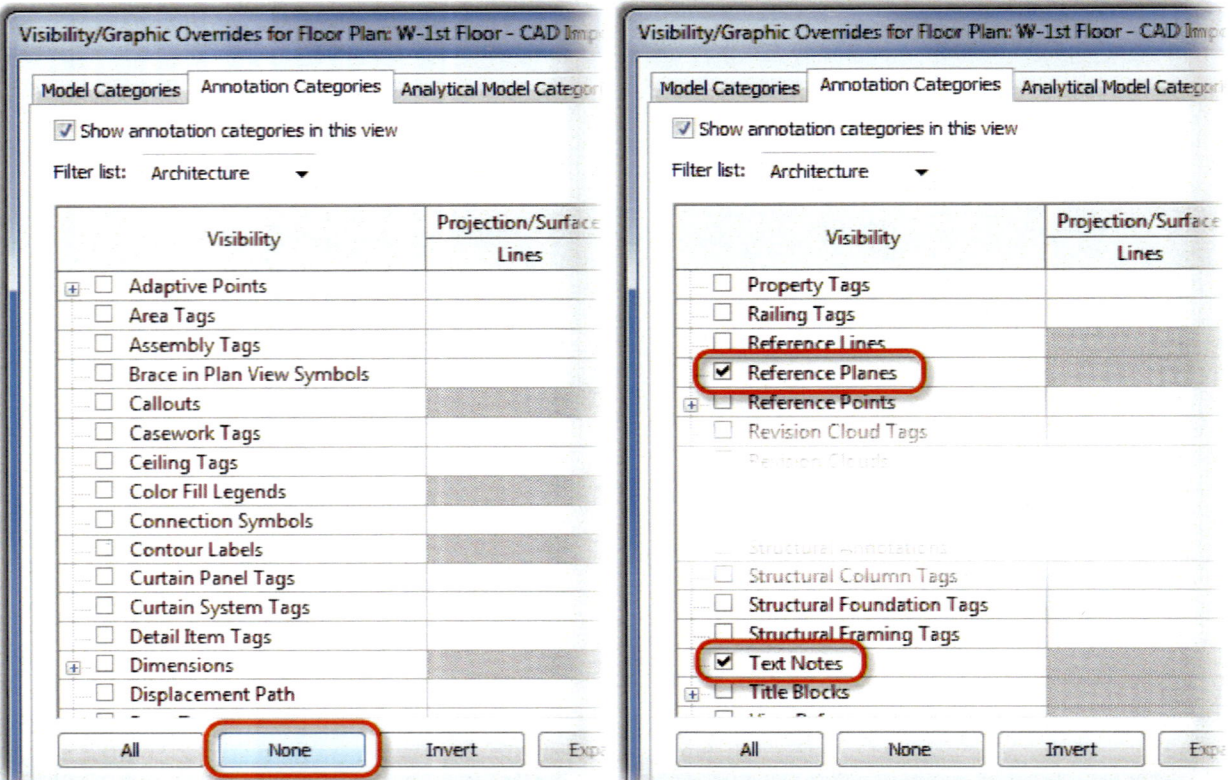

Deselect All Categories   *Select Reference Planes & Text Notes*

5. Click **OK** to close the dialog box and accept the changes. Your plan view should appear as illustrated on the following page.

EXERCISE 1.4: PROJECT EXTENTS & CONSTRAINTS VALIDATION

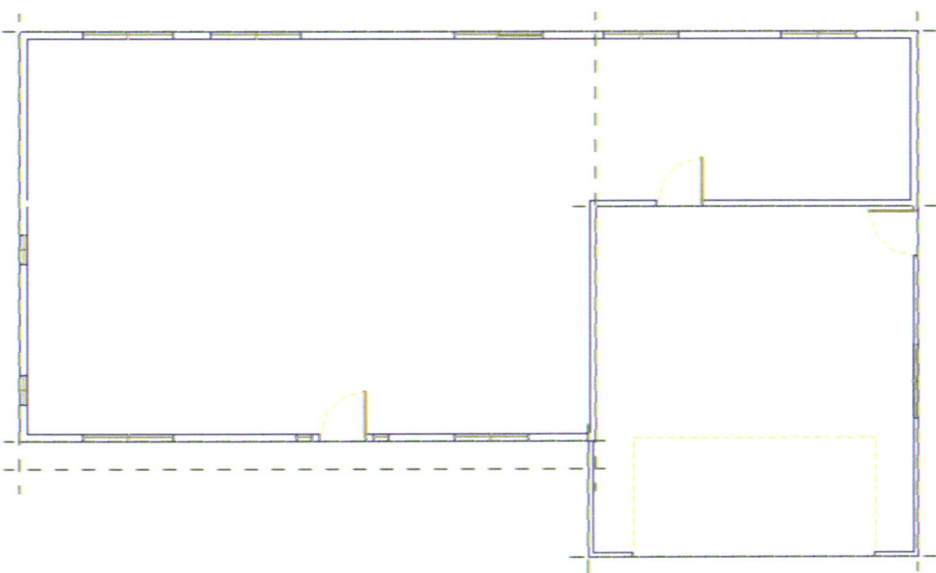

W-1st Floor - CAD Import with Visibility Overrides

<u>Set up View Graphics: W-2nd Floor - CAD Import</u>

6. Open the floor plan view **W-2nd Floor - CAD Import**.

Visibility/Graphics Overrides		VV / VG
Tab	Panel	Tool Button
View	**Graphics**	**Visibility/Graphics**

7. Repeat the previous steps (2 - 5) to achieve the required visibility settings for this view. When done, your plan view should appear as illustrated below.

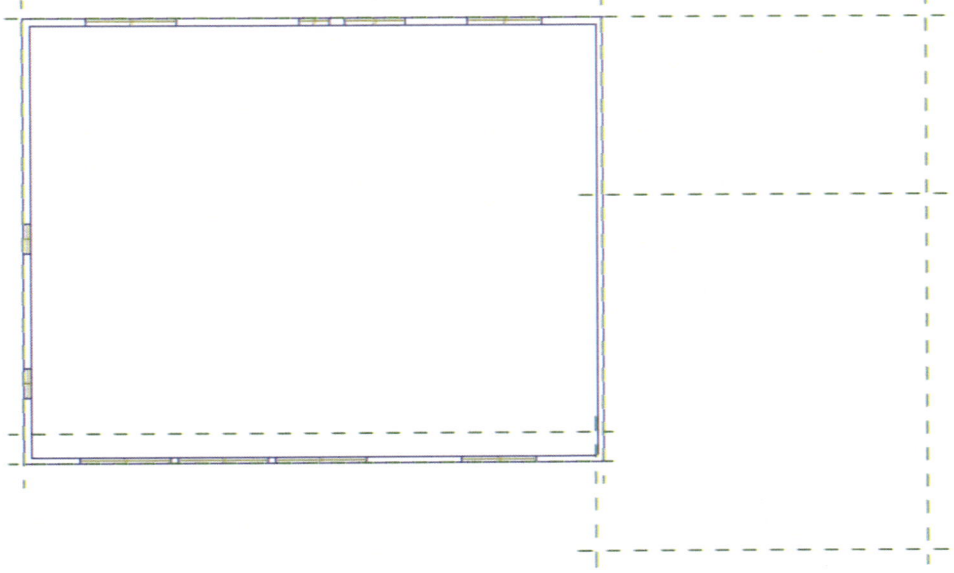

W-2nd Floor - CAD Import with Visibility Overrides

33

Add Text Notes

In the previous steps you adjusted the view graphics for the CAD import views to hide all but the reference planes, text notes, and reference geometry (CAD import). This serves two purposes:

a) First, it allows quick visual feedback on whether or not our building footprint matches the layout reference geometry.

b) Second, it allows us to reset the building footprint back to the reference geometry by aligning reference planes to the corresponding reference line of the CAD import.

 You've probably already noticed that whenever performing an align operation you are immediately presented with an open padlock, and so far you've mostly been instructed to lock it. This open padlock taunts new Revit users; the initial reaction is to lock it whenever you see it. A good rule of thumb is "*if you don't know why you're locking something, don't lock it.*"

When we realign a reference plane to the reference geometry we <u>never</u> want to lock it. We'll use a different type of constraint to hold reference planes in place. For now, we'll add a note to each of the CAD import views reminding us not to lock anything when working in those views.

8. Open the floor plan view *W-1st Floor - CAD Import*.

QAT A	Text	TX
Tab	Panel	Tool Button
Annotate	**Text**	**Text**

Properties
Type: **1/4" Arial**

9. Using the default settings (no leader), click in the graphics area at the location you wish to start the text.

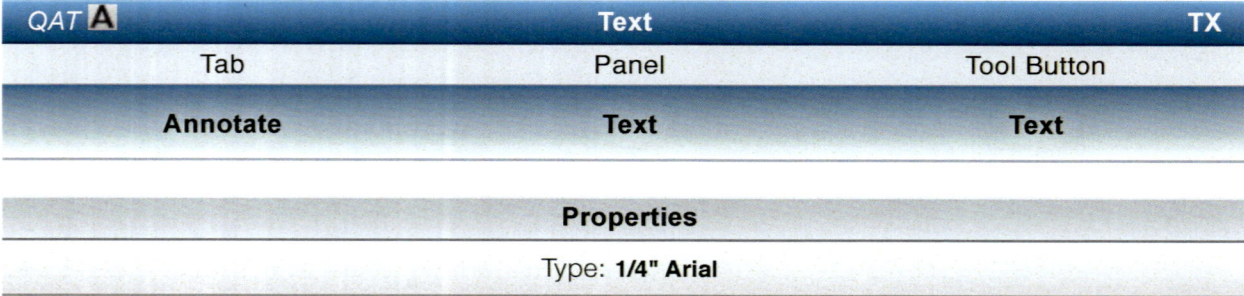

10. Enter the following text (*all upper case, all one line - don't use the [enter] key*):
DO NOT LOCK ANYTHING IN THIS VIEW. PIN REFERENCE PLANES AFTER ALIGNING TO IMPORTED REFERENCE GEOMETRY. NEVER UNPIN IMPORTED CAD FILE.

11. Click outside of the text box to complete the note, then click **Modify** or press **[esc]** twice to terminate the text tool.

12. Select the text note, then click on the right drag handle and drag it to the left. This will force the text to wrap. Continue dragging until you have two lines of text roughly the same length as illustrated.

13. With the text still selected, click and drag on the move icon in the upper left corner of the text box to move the note to the desired position.

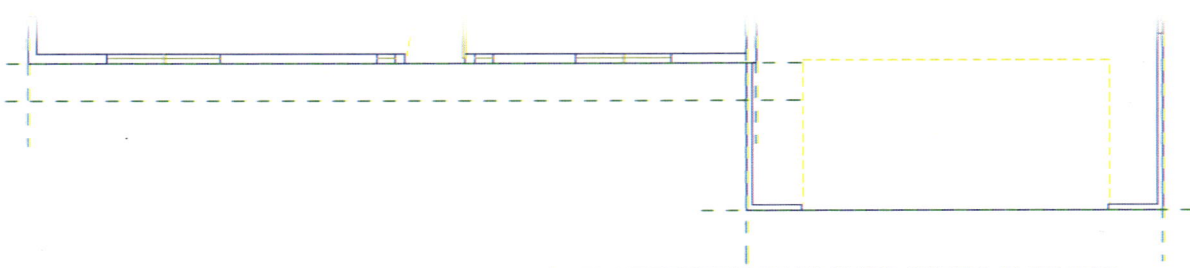

DO NOT LOCK ANYTHING IN THIS VIEW. PIN REFERENCE PLANES AFTER ALIGNING TO IMPORTED REFERENCE GEOMETRY. NEVER UNPIN IMPORTED CAD FILE.

14. Select the text note, the copy it to the clipboard...

Copy to Clipboard		[Ctrl]C
Tab	Panel	Tool Button
Modify	Clipboard	Copy to Clipboard

15. Open the floor plan view *W-2nd Floor - CAD Import* and copy the note into the current view...

Paste: Aligned to Current View			
Tab	Panel	Split Button ▼	Tool Button
Modify	Clipboard	Paste	Aligned to Current View

16. The text note should appear in the same location that you placed it in the original view.

CHAPTER 1: PROJECT SETUP, IMPORT CAD, BASIC WALLS

Flex the Model

In the following steps you will move reference planes, which should in turn move the associated wall geometry. This is also known as "flexing the model." Doing this will identify any missing or incorrect constraints.

17. Open/create a default 3D view, then close all hidden windows...

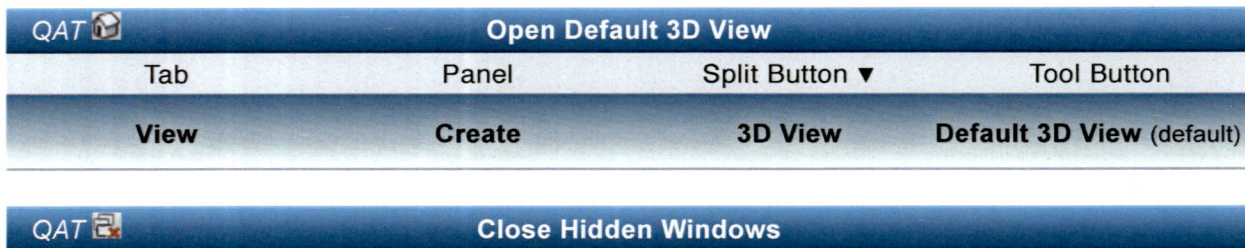

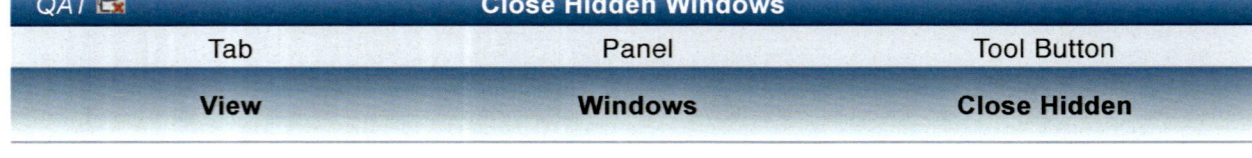

18. Using the View Control Bar (VCB), set the *Visual Style* to **Consistent Colors**. Your 3D view should appear as illustrated below.

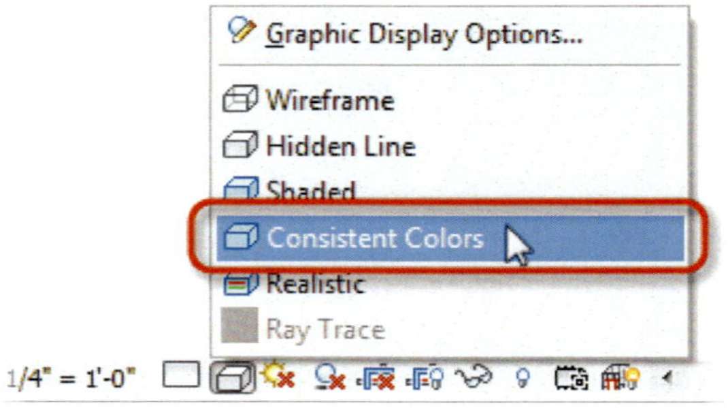

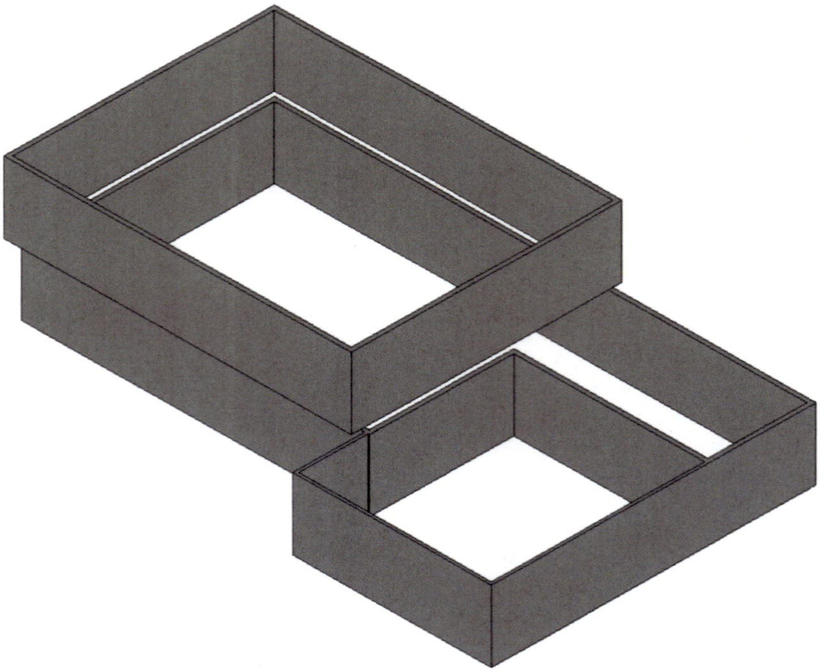

Default 3D View - Visual Style Set to Consistent Colors

19. Open the *South* elevation view.
20. Open the floor plan view *W-1st Floor - CAD Import*.
21. Open the floor plan view *W-2nd Floor - CAD Import*.
22. Tile the open windows...

Tile Windows		WT
Tab	Panel	Tool Button
View	Windows	Tile

23. Using the Navigation bar zoom tools, select **Zoom All to Fit (ZA)**, or type **[ZA]**. Your tiled views should appear as illustrated below.

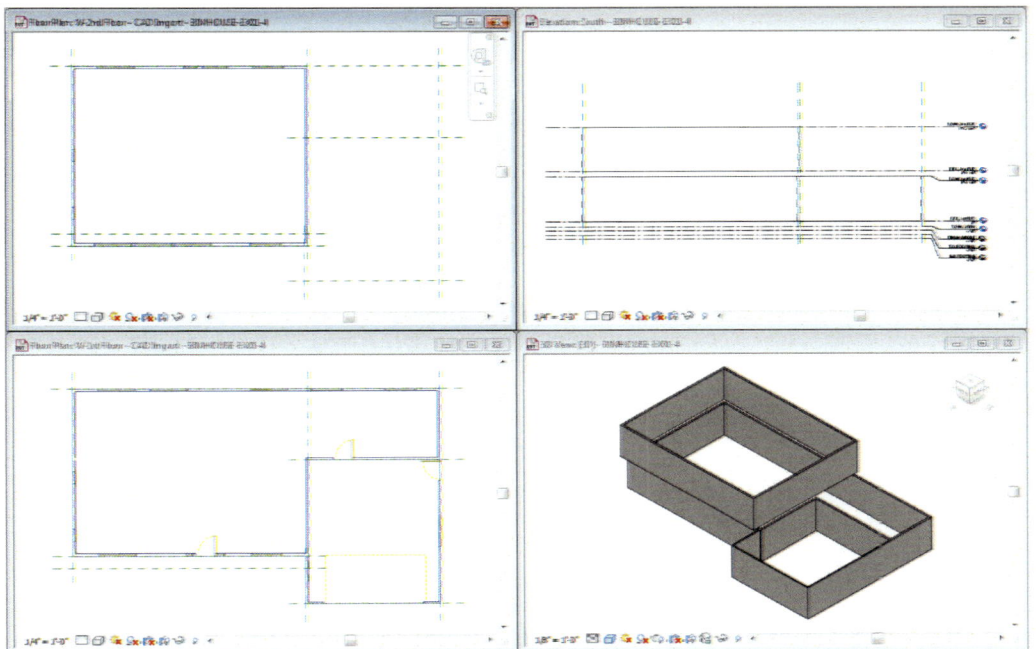

Four Windows Tiled

 In the next steps you will be moving datums to verify the associated model elements (walls) move with them. The undo history keeps track of your modeling steps, allowing you to go back to a previous point in time. To return any datum back to its original location after moving it, drop down the undo history and select the range of steps you'd like to undo. Whenever undoing more than one or two steps, it's always best to use the history list to be be 100% certain about what you're undoing.

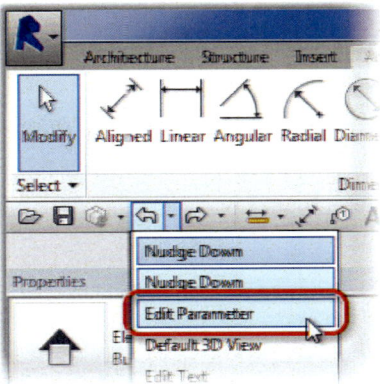

24. In the *South* elevation view, adjust the elevations of *T.O.W 2nd Floor* level up and down by entering alternate values into the elevation field. In the 3D view, verify that the top of the second-floor walls are tracking up and down with the level change. Reset each level's elevation back to its original value when finished.

25. Repeat the process for any of the other levels associated with the tops or bottoms of walls. Try using the Up/Down arrow keys to "nudge" the levels up and down. Additionally, try "nudging" at different zoom levels and notice the effect of length snapping.

26. From either of the floor plan views, move each reference plane one at a time. Verify walls that should be associated with the moved reference plane also move (*see information note below*). If any of the reference planes move independently of their associated wall(s), the wall was not properly aligned/locked to the reference plane. Go back and repeat the align/lock operation for the offending walls.

 There is a conflicting constraint condition with this model as it was created. Note that moving one of the two reference planes associated with the two west walls of the garage will also move the other wall and reference plane. This is a chain of constraints, and was created automatically by Revit. This will be discussed and corrected in the next chapter.

27. Maximize the floor plan view *W-1st Floor - CAD Import*, and zoom to fit [**ZF**].

28. Reset the reference planes to their original location by using the **Align** tool to realign each reference plane to its corresponding wall in the imported CAD geometry. (**DO NOT LOCK!**)

29. Open the floor plan view *W-2nd Floor - CAD Import*, and zoom to fit [**ZF**].

30. Reset the last reference planes on the 2nd floor to its original location by using the Align tool as you did in the previous steps. (**DO NOT LOCK!**)

Pin The building layout

1. The floor plan view *W-2nd Floor - CAD Import* should still be open. If not, open it now.

2. Using a window or a crossing selection, select all elements in the view, then filter the selection as follows.

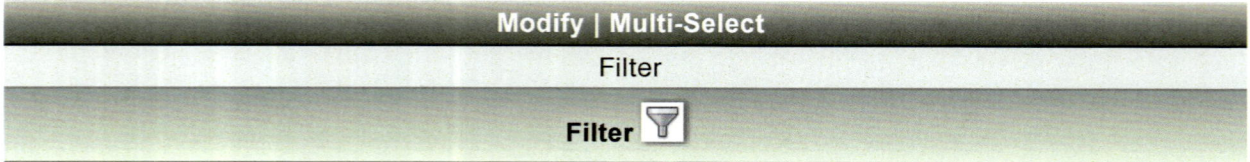

3. In the Filter dialog box, uncheck all categories *except* for *Reference Planes*. Alternatively, you can click **Check None**, then check *Reference Planes*.

 This is a good time to verify that the Reference Planes count column = 9.

EXERCISE 1.4: PROJECT EXTENTS & CONSTRAINTS VALIDATION

4. Click **OK**. This leaves only reference planes in the selection set.
5. Pin the reference planes as follows.

	Pin	PN
Tab	Panel	Tool Button
Modify	**Modify**	**Pin**

6. There should now be a push pin icon visible on each reference plane as illustrated below.

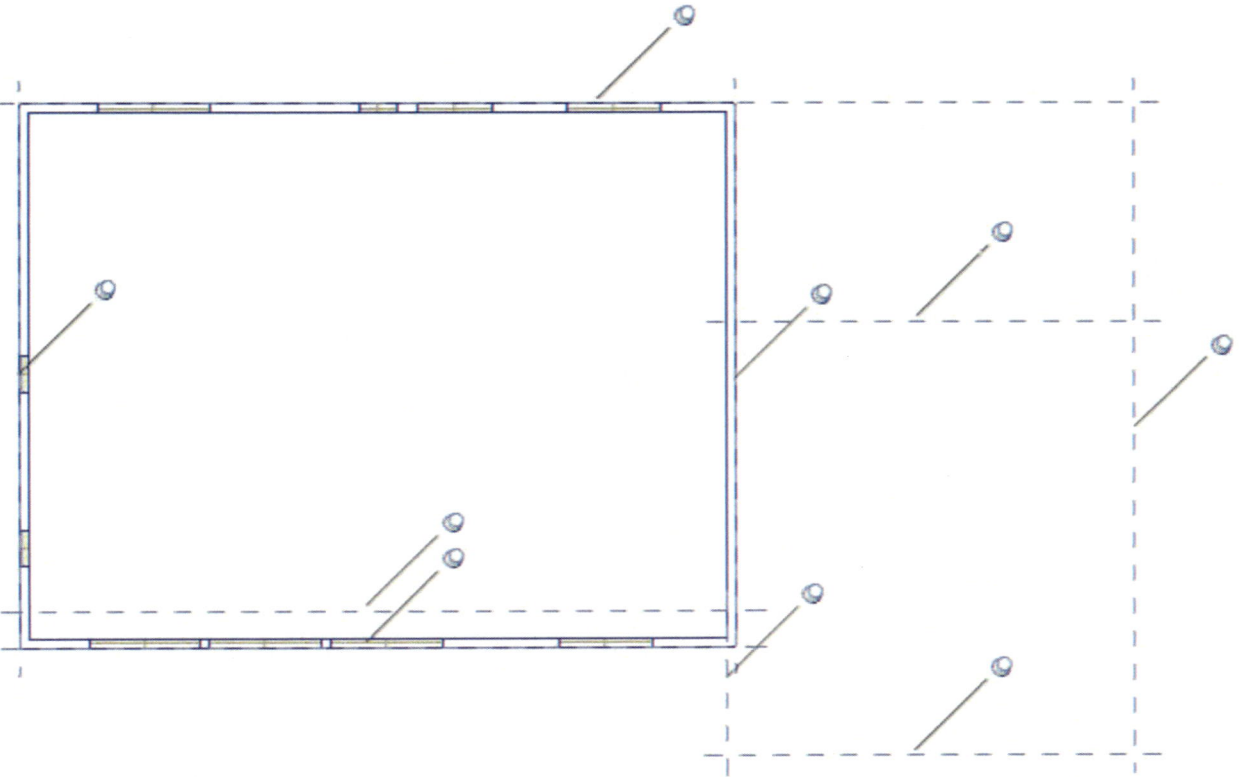

Reference Planes Pinned

7. Click **Modify** or press **[Esc]** to clear the selection.

 Using the filter tool to select only reference planes was and optional step since the only other element visible in the view is the imported CAD file, which MUST REMAIN PINNED AT ALL TIMES.

CHAPTER 1: PROJECT SETUP, IMPORT CAD, BASIC WALLS

Prepare Project for Submission

If you're using this workbook as part of a class curriculum, check with your instructor on whether or not the following steps are necessary. If you're working independently, you can skip these steps, then save your work and move onto the next chapter.

8. Close all views except for the default *{3D}* view.
9. Open the *South* elevation view.
10. Open the floor plan view *W-2nd Floor - CAD Import*.
11. Open the floor plan view *W-1st Floor - CAD Import* and tile windows...

Tile Windows		WT
Tab	Panel	Tool Button
View	Windows	Tile

12. Using the Navigation bar zoom tools, select **Zoom All to Fit (ZA)**, or type **[ZA]**. Your tiled windows should appear as illustrated below.

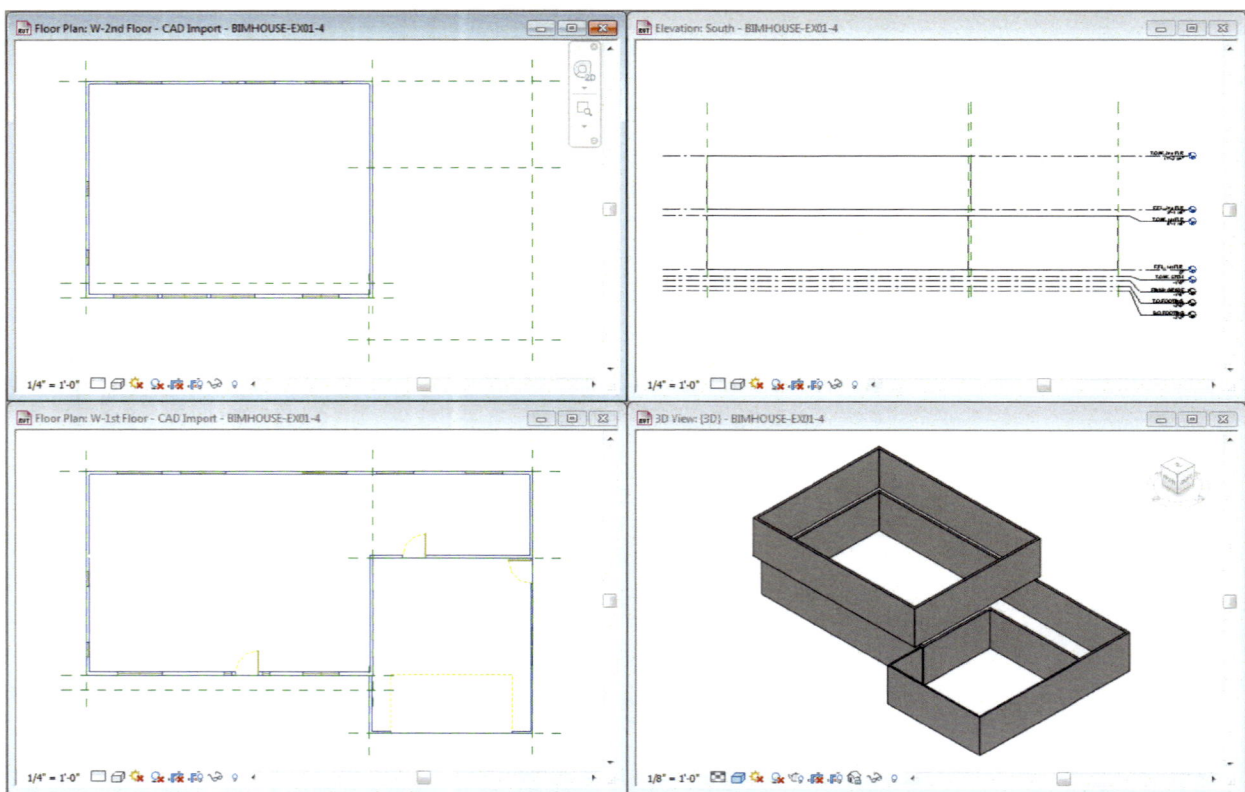

Four Windows Tiled - Final View Configuration for Chapter 1

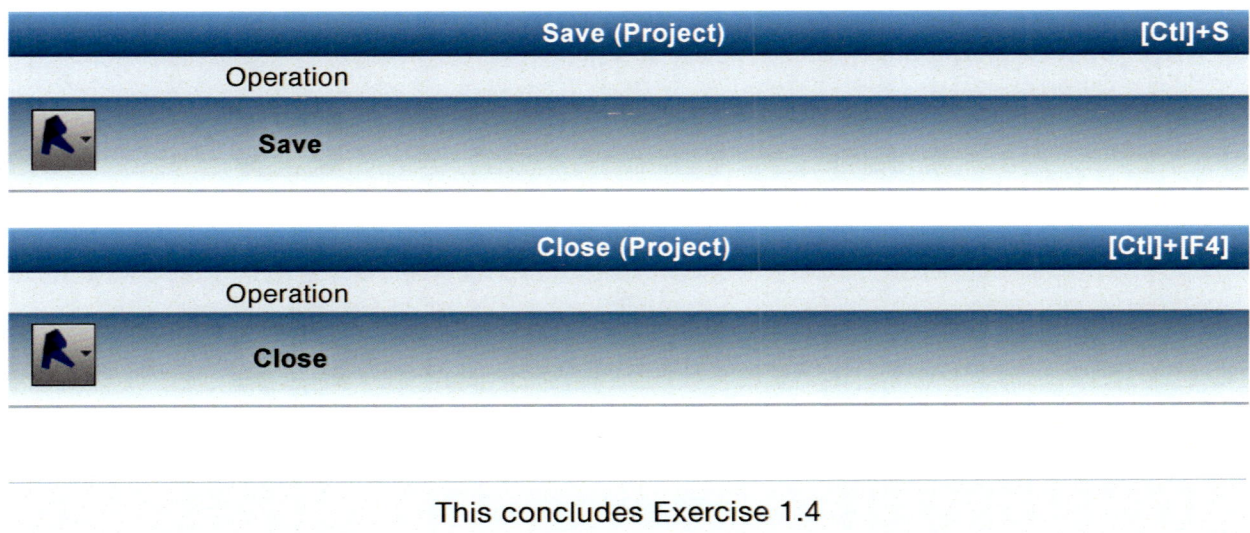

This concludes Exercise 1.4

Chapter Summary

In this lesson you were introduced to a variety of fundamental concepts, such as importing CAD files, using reference panes, and constraints. Additionally, you were introduced to the wall tool and basic wall properties. Throughout the course you will reinforce the concepts learned in this chapter, as many of them are key to creating a flexible model, while maintaining the integrity of the geometry and underlying information.

Chapter 2
Adding Roofs & Floors

Overview

This chapter is intended to introduce you to modeling elements created by using sketch mode, as well the attach tool to create relationships between vertical and horizontal elements. Additionally, you will practice several techniques learned in the previous exercise.

Learning Objectives

Throughout this chapter you will practice sketching various boundary-driven elements, as well as creating parametric relationships between elements. After completing this chapter you should have a good understanding of the following:

- Pitfalls associated automatic wall joins/relationships
- Manual wall joins
- Modeling floors & constraining boundaries
- Basic floor properties
- Modeling simple roofs by footprint & constraining boundaries
- Basic roof properties
- Various methods of accessing type properties dialog
- Using the Attach tool on walls

Project Objectives

- Correct a constraint conflict using manual wall joins
- Add generic floor elements
- Add generic roof elements
- Add generic gable end walls
- Add generic interior walls to the first and second floors

CHAPTER 2: ADDING ROOFS, FLOORS, AND WALL ATTACHMENTS

Chapter Contents

Exercise 2.1:	Resolving the Constraint Conflict	45
	Converting a Wall Join to Manual	45
	Cleaning Up Wall Joins	48
Exercise 2.2:	Modeling Floors	50
	1st Floor	50
	2nd Floor	52
	View the Model and Verify Associations	52
Exercise 2.3:	Modeling Roofs	54
	2nd Floor Roof	54
	1st Floor Roof	57
Exercise 2.4:	Add Gable Walls	65
	Create a New wall Type	65
	1st Floor Gable Walls	66
	2nd Floor Gable Walls	71
	Attach the Gable End Walls to the Roofs	72
Exercise 2.5:	Add Interior Walls	74
	1st Floor Interior Walls	74
	2nd Floor Interior Walls	79

Exercise 2.1: Resolving the Constraint Conflict

 There is likely an over-constrained condition with this model as it was created. Attempting to move either of the reference planes at the west side of the garage may generate the error illustrated. Failure to complete the steps in this section may result in ongoing problems throughout this project.

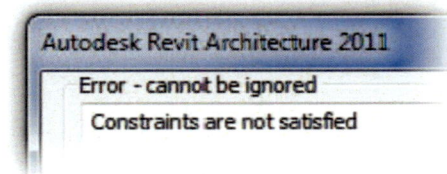

As you likely witnessed in the previous exercise, moving either of the two reference planes along the west wall of the garage resulted in both reference planes moving. Now, since all reference planes have been pinned, flexing the model will require temporarily unpinning the reference plane that you wish to move. Unpinning only one of the two reference planes related to the conflict, and attempting to move it will generate a *Constraints are not satisfied* error. The reason for this is twofold.

- First, we have two different walls, each locked to their own reference plane. This is intentional, and desired with respect to design intent.
- Second, the two walls were modeled co-planar along their west faces, and were automatically joined where they meet. This caused Revit to create an automatic relationship between these two walls. In other words, Revit sees that the two walls are aligned and joined at the time of creation, and then automatically locks this alignment.

These combined conditions result in the two reference planes being locked together *indirectly* through a chain of constraints. To correct this, we'll break the relationship and manage the join condition manually.

Converting a Wall Join to Manual

Open Project		[Ctl]+O
Operation	Option	File Name
Open ▶	Project	BIMHOUSE-EX01-4.rvt

Save As (Project)		
Operation	Option	File Name
Save As ▶	Project	BIMHOUSE-EX02-1.rvt

CHAPTER 2: ADDING ROOFS, FLOORS, AND WALL ATTACHMENTS

1. Open the floor plan view *F.F.L. 1st FLR*.

2. Zoom into the region along the west side of the garage where the three walls come together.

3. Select the west 4" garage wall as illustrated on the right. Notice that two padlock icons appear, one at each reference plane (or wall).

4. Click on the drag control (blue dot) where the selected wall meets the other two walls, and drag the wall and down and away from the other two walls.

5. Now, **right-click** on the same drag control, and from the contextual menu select **Disallow Join**.

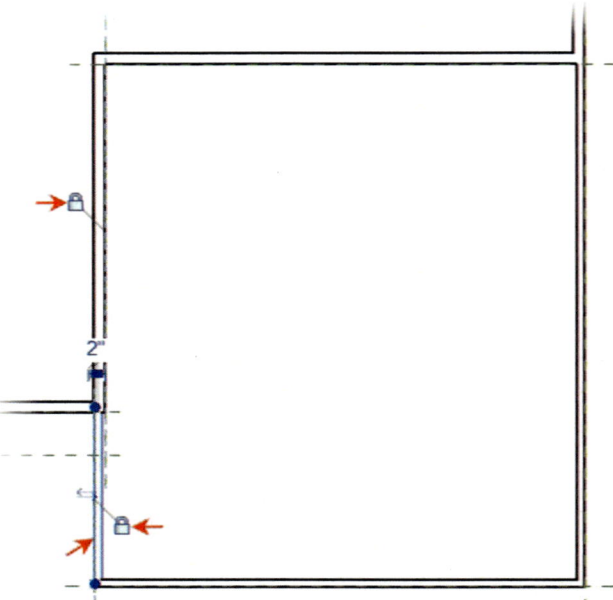

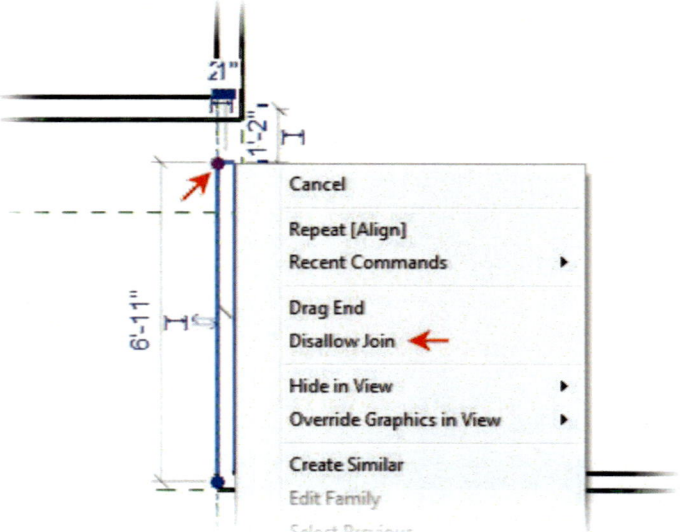

 By electing to disallow the wall join, the wall end will no longer automatically join to intersecting walls. This means automatic relationships will not be created and the wall will not track the intersecting walls if they are moved. Additionally, the graphics will not automatically cleanup between the intersecting walls.
In the steps that follow, we will re-create the relationship to the intersecting walls and clean up the graphic appearance manually.

46

EXERCISE 2.1: RESOLVING THE CONSTRAINT CONFLICT

	Align	AL
Tab	Panel	Tool Button
Modify	**Modify**	**Align**
Multiple Alignment: ☐	Prefer: **Faces of core**	

6. **Align** and **Lock** the free end of the west 4" garage wall (*previously set to Disallow Join*) to the reference plane *Ext-South-1* as illustrated below.

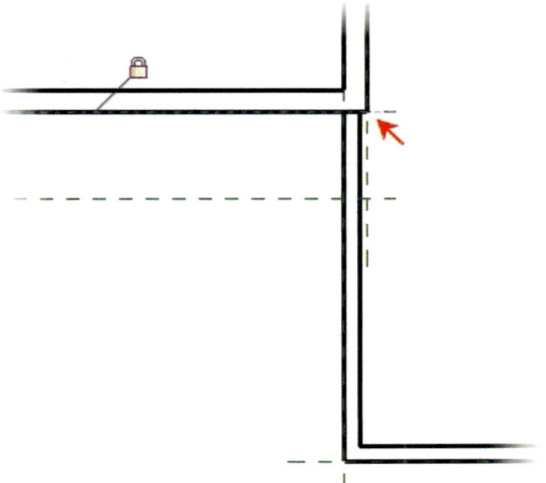

Wall End Aligned & Locked To Reference Plane

7. **Unpin** the reference plane *Ext-Garage-West* and move it left and/or right to verify that the model flexes correctly and without any errors as illustrated below.

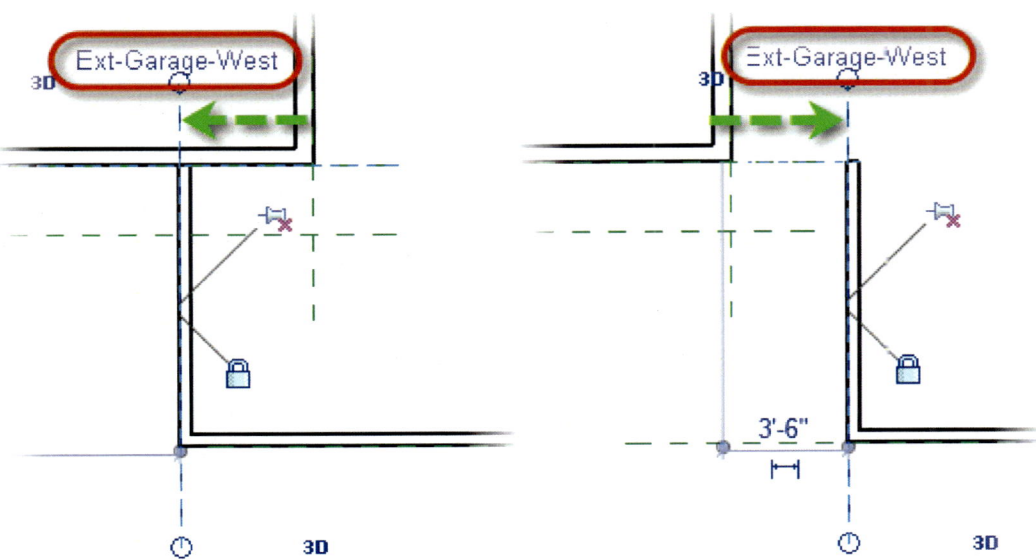

8. Return the reference plane *Ext-Garage-West* to its original location and re-pin it.

 As mentioned in the previous chapter, the undo history keeps track of your modeling steps, allowing you to go back to a previous point in time. To return the reference plane back to its original location and in its pinned state, drop down the undo history and select "Toggle Pin" or "Unpin," depending on the method you used to unpin it.

There's also a redo history, which allows you to go back the other way immediately after using undo.

9. **Unpin** and **move** reference plane *Ext-South-1* as illustrated. Verify the end of the 4" garage wall remains attached to the reference plane when moved.

10. When done, return the reference plane to its original location and **pin** it.

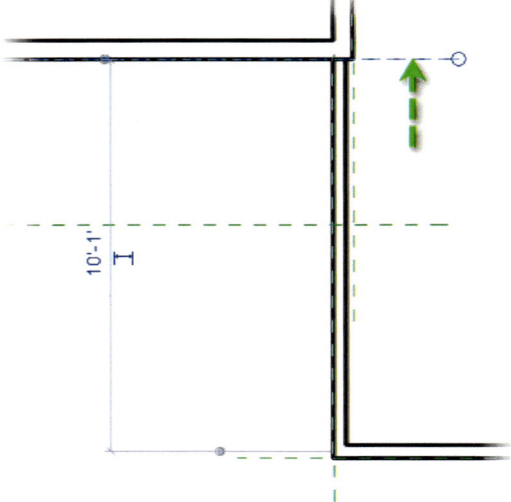

Cleaning Up Wall Joins

Since we've told Revit to disallow one of the walls to be joined, it no longer cleans up where it meets the other walls. In this case, or any other case where we wish to have geometry joined but Revit doesn't do it automatically, we need to use the *Join Geometry* tool.

Before we do this however, we want to make sure that the two 6" walls are joined in a manner that best represents design intent, and removes the possibility of related warnings.

Wall Joins		
Tab	Panel	Tool Button
Modify	Geometry	Wall Joins

1. Move the cursor over the wall intersection. When the box appears, click the intersection. This will reveal the current wall join configuration as shown in the following illustration.

2. In the options bar, click on **Next** to cycle through the available join options. When the wall join resembles the following illustration labeled *Best Configuration*, exit the *Wall Joins* tool.

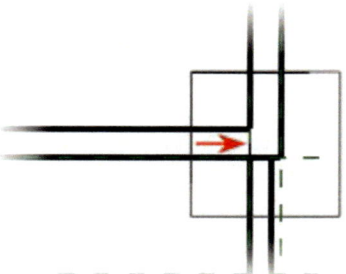
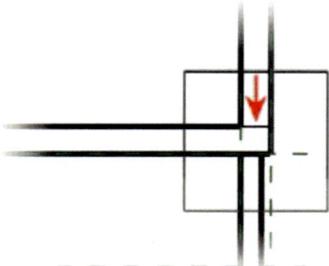

OK - May Cause WarningsBest Configuration

3. Pick the garage wall to be joined, then pick the wall to which it is to be joined. If you pick the incorrect wall, Revit will generate the warning shown to the right.

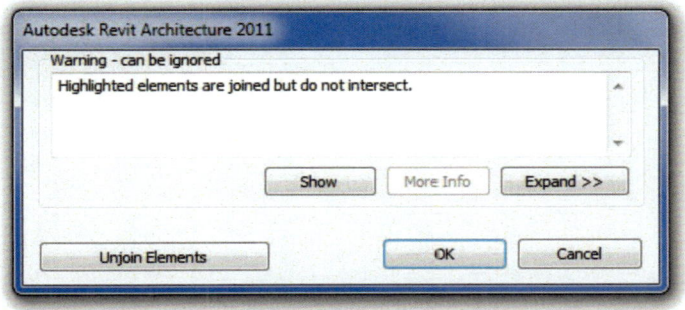

 You can join geometry that is not physically in contact. When you do this, Revit will generate a warning notifying you that "highlighted elements are joined but do not intersect." You can ignore this warning, or resolve it. If you know that the elements will never touch, then it is best to resolve the error by selecting **Unjoin Elements** in the warning dialog box. A large number of unresolved warnings in a project will add to the file size, and can affect performance. Therefore, it is best to resolve warnings whenever possible.

This concludes exercise 2.1

Exercise 2.2: Modeling Floors

In this exercise you will model floor elements for both the first and the second floor. The floor type used will be generic, which roughly represents the overall thickness of the floor structure. These floors will be replaced in future exercises with more accurate representations of floor composition and thickness.

 Parameter values, option bar settings, and sequence of steps throughout the following exercise steps were not randomly selected. Failure to set options and properties as instructed, and in the the sequence presented will result in unexpected behavior of your model going forward.

Open Project			[Ctl]+O
	Operation	Option	File Name
	Open ▶	Project	BIMHOUSE-EX02-1.rvt

Save As (Project)			
	Operation	Option	File Name
	Save As ▶	Project	BIMHOUSE-EX02-2.rvt

1st Floor

1. Open the floor plan view *F.F.L. 1st FLR* and add a floor...

Floor			
Tab	Panel	Split Button ▼	Tool Button
Architecture	**Build**	**Floor**	**Floor: Architectural**

Modify	Create Floor Boundary		
Draw	
Boundary Line	**Pick Walls**
Offset: **0' 0"**	Extend into wall (to core): ☑

EXERCISE 2.2: MODELING FLOORS

Properties	
Type: **Generic - 12"**	
Level:	F.F.L. 1st FLR
Height Offset From Level:	0' 0"
Room Bounding:	✓

2. Pick the six walls that define the livable area (only pick once on each wall) to create the floor boundary as illustrated below. Do not pick the exterior garage walls.

3. Verify that the boundary lines lie on the exterior side of the walls. If not, with one of the boundary lines selected, click on the flip arrow as indicated in the illustration below.

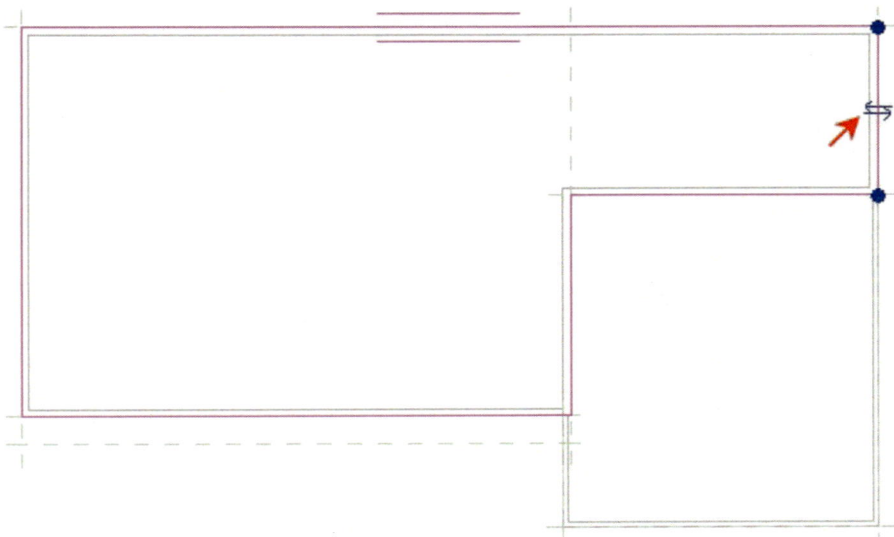

Floor Boundary Lines With Flip Arrow Visible

 At this point, don't worry about the span direction indicator lines. (The two short parallel lines on either side of one of the boundary lines)

4. When done, click the **Finish Edit Mode** button ✓ in the Mode panel of the contextual ribbon tab.

5. Clear the selection set (floor).

CHAPTER 2: ADDING ROOFS, FLOORS, AND WALL ATTACHMENTS

2nd Floor

1. Open the floor plan view *F.F.L. 2nd FLR*

2. In the Properties Palette, set *Underlay* to **None**. This will turn off the first-floor underlay, leaving only the second floor walls visible.

3. Create the second floor by repeating the steps used to create the first floor, but by picking the second floor walls. Use the same options bar settings and floor type, but verify the *Level* property is set to **F.F.L. 2nd FLR**. If it isn't, you likely have the wrong view opened.

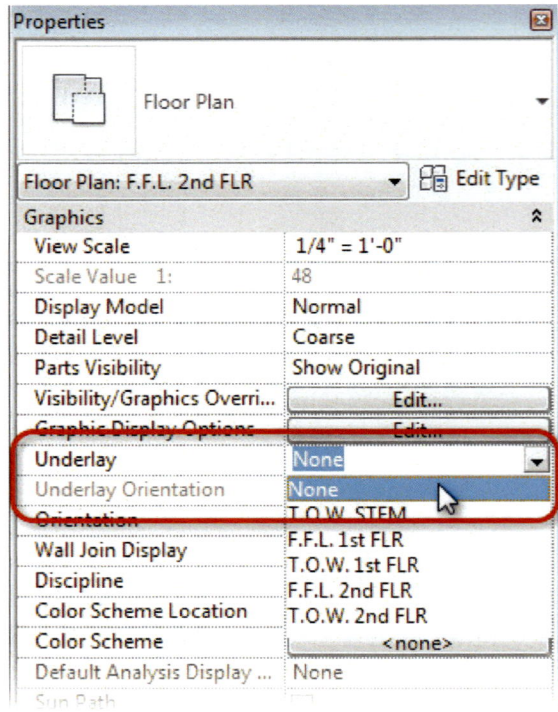

 When modeling elements, Revit will remember the family *Type* previously used for a specific tool. Using the previous example, the second time you activated the floor tool, the floor type defaulted to *Generic - 12"*. This holds true for other modeling tools such as walls and roofs.

View the Model and Verify Associations

1. Open the default *{3D}* view

2. Orbit the model around to view the added floors.

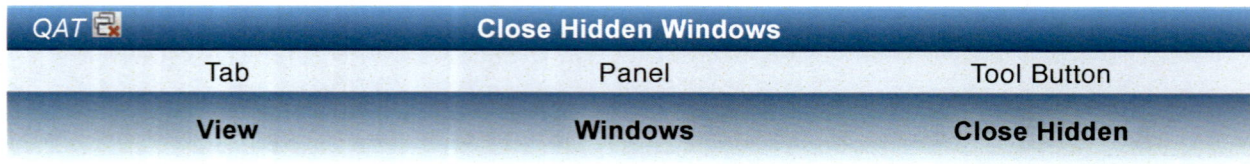

QAT	Close Hidden Windows	
Tab	Panel	Tool Button
View	Windows	Close Hidden

3. Open *W-1st Floor - CAD Import*.

	Tile Windows	WT
Tab	Panel	Tool Button
View	Windows	Tile

52

EXERCISE 2.2: MODELING FLOORS

4. Using the procedure used in chapter 1, flex the model by moving reference planes. In the 3D view, verify the correct walls and floor boundaries are moving with the reference plane. Additionally, <u>verify all floors extend to the exterior faces of the associated walls</u>.

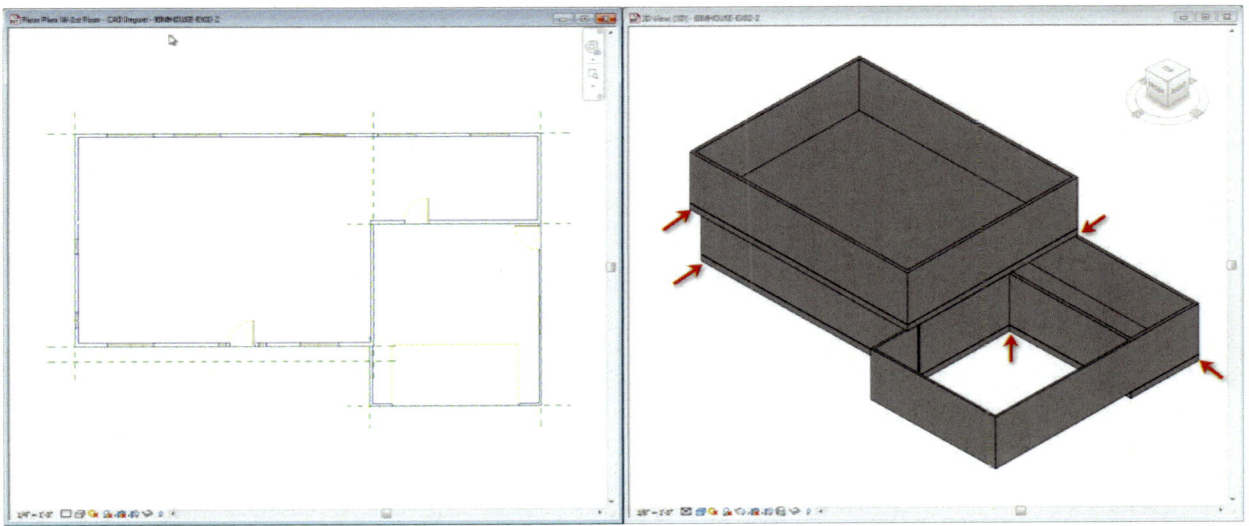

 Remember to return all reference planes to their correct positions and pin them!

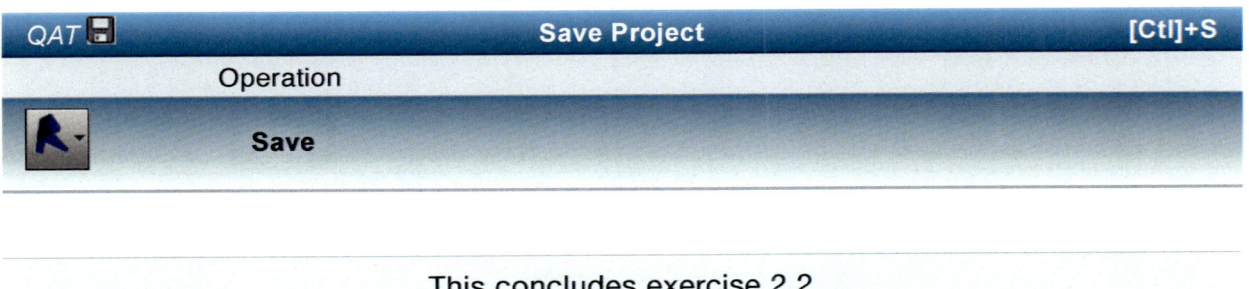

This concludes exercise 2.2

Exercise 2.3: Modeling Roofs

In the following steps you will create two roofs: one over the garage and adjacent living area, the other over the second-floor living areas. As with the floors, the roof will be generic, roughly representing the roof thickness.

⚠️ As with the previous exercise, failure to set options and properties as instructed, and in the the sequence presented will result in unexpected behavior of your model going forward.

Open Project			[Ctl]+O
	Operation	Option	File Name
	Open ▶	Project	BIMHOUSE-EX02-2.rvt

Save As (Project)			
	Operation	Option	File Name
	Save As ▶	Project	BIMHOUSE-EX02-3.rvt

2nd Floor Roof

1. Open the floor plan view *T.O.W. 2nd FLR*.
2. If the 2nd floor walls are not visible, set the *Underlay* view property to **F.F.L. 2nd FLR**.

Roof by Footprint			
Tab	Panel	Split Button ▼	Tool Button
Architecture	**Build**	**Roof**	**Roof by Footprint**

Create a New Roof Type

3. In the Properties Palette, click on **Edit Type**.
4. In the Type Properties dialog box, select **Generic - 9"** for *Type*.
5. Click **Duplicate...**
6. Enter **Generic - 5"** for the name, then click **OK** to close the Name dialog box.

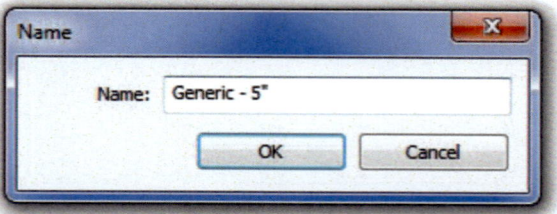

7. Click on the **Edit...** button next to the *Structure* parameter in the Type Parameters panel.

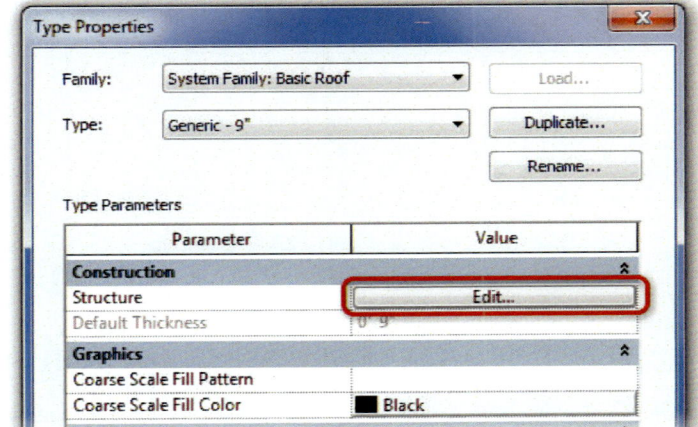

8. In the Layers panel of the Edit Assembly dialogue box, change the thickness parameter for Layer 2 to **0' 5"** as shown in the illustration below, then click **OK**.

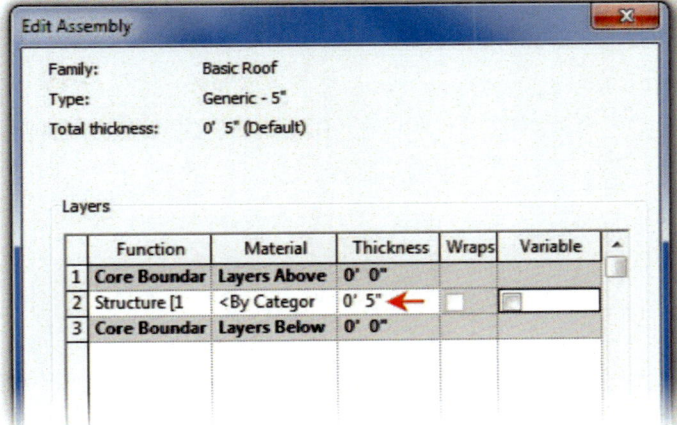

9. Verify the *Default Thickness* reads **0' 5"** as illustrated below, then click **OK**.

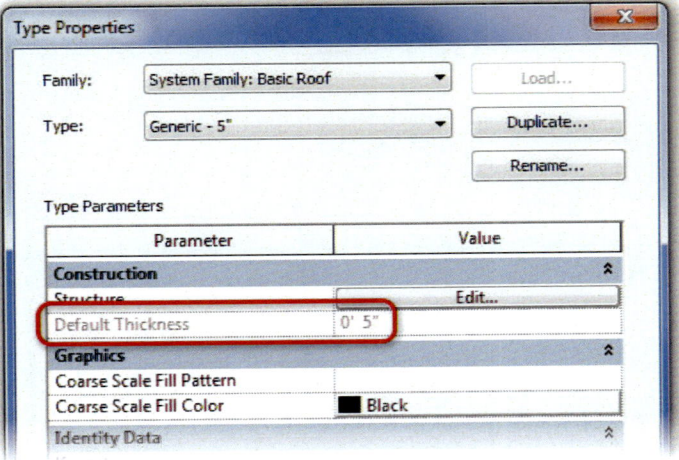

10. In the Properties Palette, verify the following Properties and Options Bar settings:

Properties	
Type: **Generic - 5"**	
Level:	T.O.W. 2nd FLR
Room Bounding:	✓
Base Offset from Level:	0' 0"
Cutoff Level:	None
Rafter Cut:	Plumb Cut

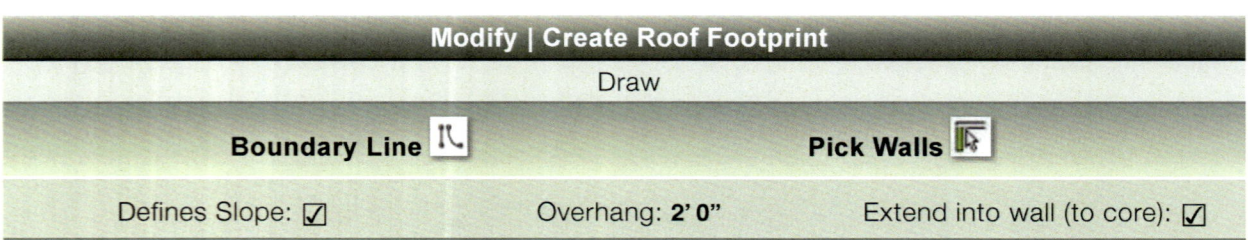

Modify | Create Roof Footprint		
Draw		
Boundary Line		**Pick Walls**
Defines Slope: ☑	Overhang: **2' 0"**	Extend into wall (to core): ☑

11. Hover over the north wall and move the cursor until the blue dashed reference line is located on the exterior side of the wall, then click on the wall to create the boundary.

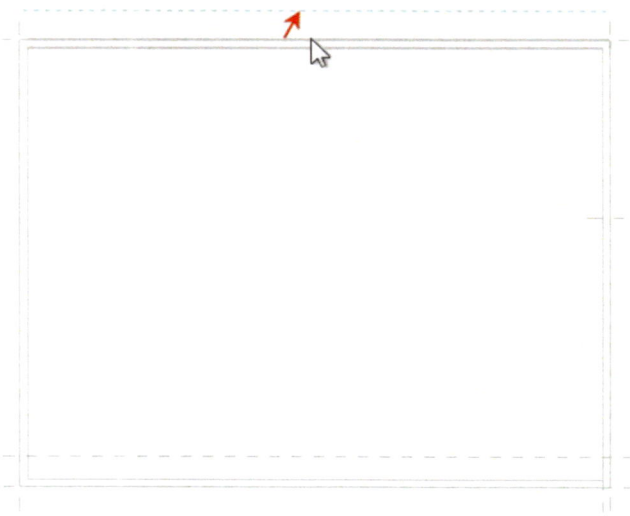

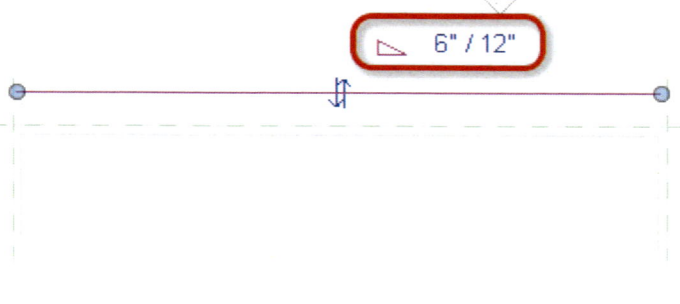

12. Immediately after creating the boundary line, click on the numeric slope value field and change it to **6"/12"** (you can just enter **6**, and Revit will know that it's 6"/12").

EXERCISE 2.3: MODELING ROOFS

13. Repeat the previous two steps to add a roof boundary line at the south wall, ensuring that the boundary line ends up on the exterior side of the wall.

14. Add the boundary lines that define the gable ends, but first change some of the options bar settings...

> Defines Slope: ☐   Overhang: **1' 0"**   Extend into wall (to core): ☑

15. Pick the east and west walls to add the boundary lines, ensuring that the boundary lines end up on the exterior side of the walls.

16. When done, click the **Finish Edit Mode** button ✔ in the Mode panel of the contextual ribbon tab. Your roof should appear as illustrated below. Don't worry that it appears cutoff at the moment. If you open the *{3D}* view you'll see that it's actually complete.

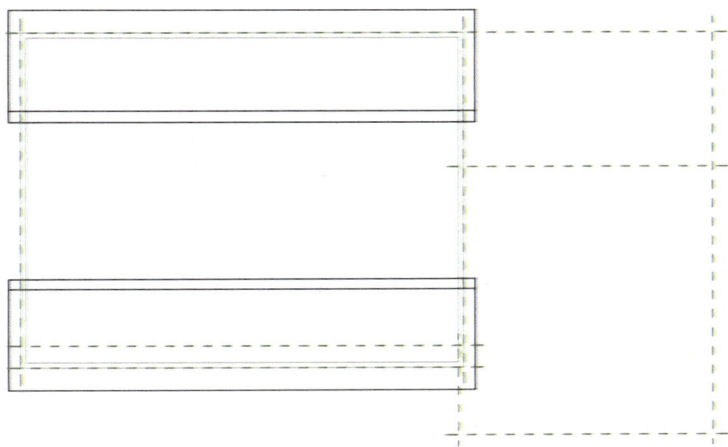

2nd Floor Roof Completed (T.O.W. 2nd FLR View)

1st Floor Roof

The first floor roof over the garage will require some careful association techniques to ensure the correct relationships are created, and the model meets design intent.

 Look ahead to see the finished result, as well as to study the related steps before beginning.

1. Open the floor plan view *T.O.W. 1st FLR*.
2. If the 1st floor walls are not visible, set the *Underlay* view property to **F.F.L. 1st FLR**.

Roof by Footprint			
Tab	Panel	Split Button ▼	Tool Button
Architecture	Build	Roof	Roof by Footprint

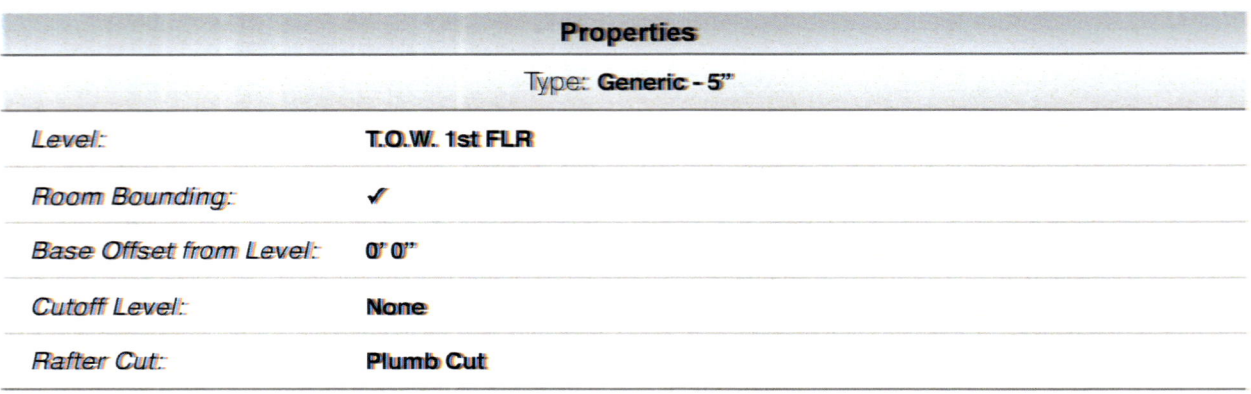

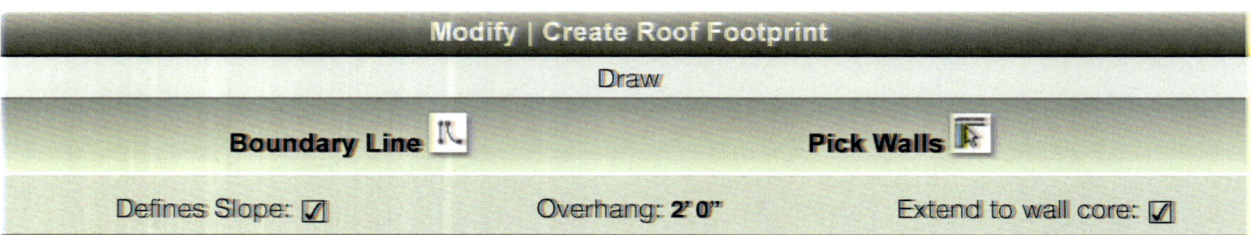

3. Set the default slope for all slope-defining lines:

   a) In the properties palette, select New <Sketch> from the drop-down list.

   b) Change the *Slope* property to **6"/12"**.

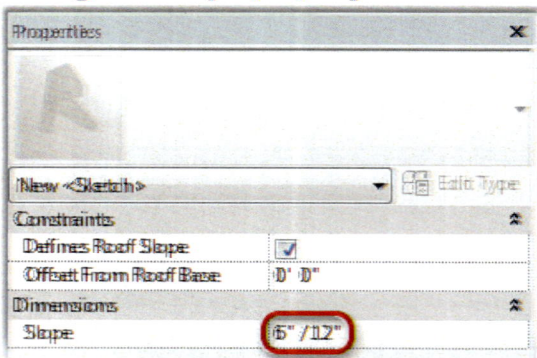
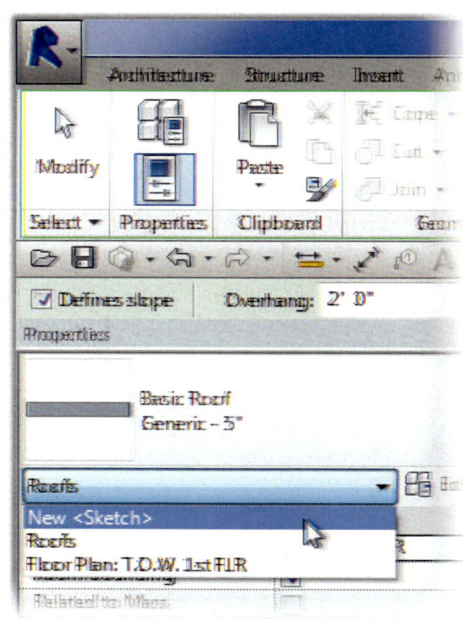

4. Pick the north and south walls at the *1st floor* (the underlay) to create the associated boundary lines. Don't worry that the north boundary line extends the full width of the building. You'll correct this shortly.

 Always be aware of the "Extend to wall core" setting. The default for roofs is deselected, and the default for floors is selected. Changes to properties or tool options, or interrupting the draw operation can cause this setting to revert back to its default state. Therefore, double-check before you click!

5. Add the boundary lines that define the gable ends, but first adjust options bar settings...

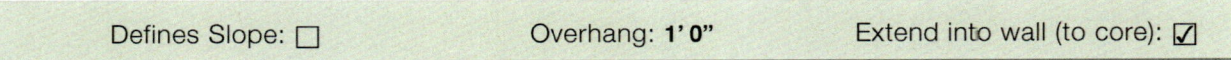

| Defines Slope: ☐ | Overhang: **1' 0"** | Extend into wall (to core): ☑ |

6. Pick the east and west garage walls to add the associated boundary lines as illustrated below.

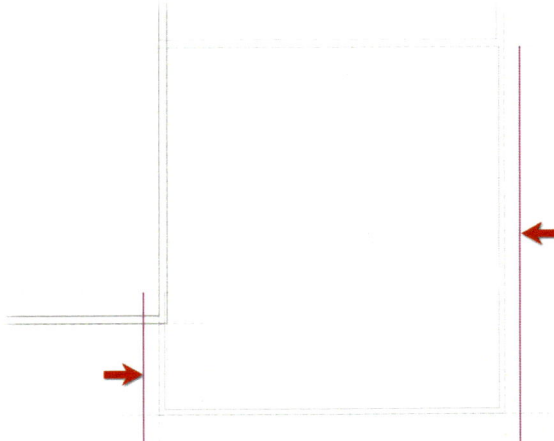

The remaining four boundary lines will be associated to reference planes. Three will be aligned and locked, and the other will be constrained at a fixed offset.

7. To add the boundary line where the roof wraps around the northeast corner of the second floor walls, pick the reference plane *Ext-East-2--Int-Garage-West*. Prior to clicking, make sure that the temporary blue reference is indicating that the line will be placed to the west of the reference plan as illustrated.

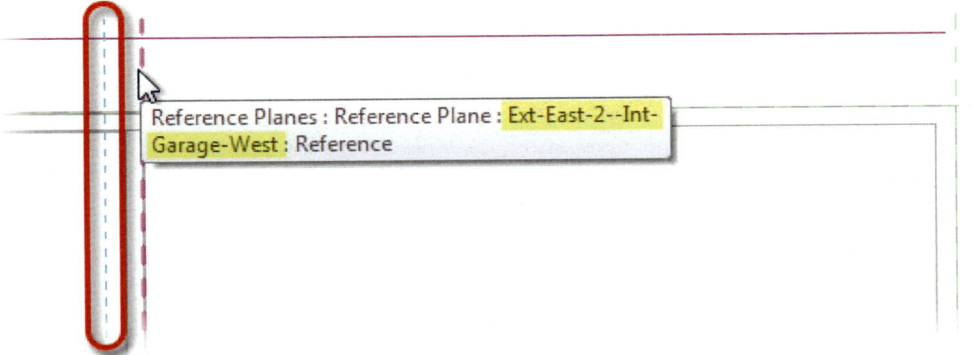

CHAPTER 2: ADDING ROOFS, FLOORS, AND WALL ATTACHMENTS

 When using the *Pick Lines* tool combined with a zero offset, the options bar provides a checkbox labeled "Lock." This is simply a shortcut that will create an alignment constraint automatically for each pick. You can still create the alignment constraint without selecting this option, but it requires you to click on the padlock after each pick.

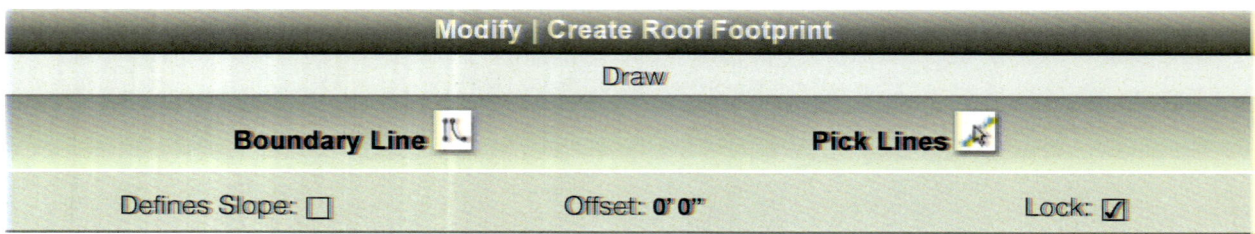

8. Pick the following *reference planes*:

    a) *Ext-North*

    b) *Ext-East-2--Int-Garage-West*

    c) *Ext-South-2*

 Be sure to verify – with either tool tips or status bar information – that you have a *reference plane* pre-highlighted *before* picking. If you pick a wall, this will cause problems in future exercises.

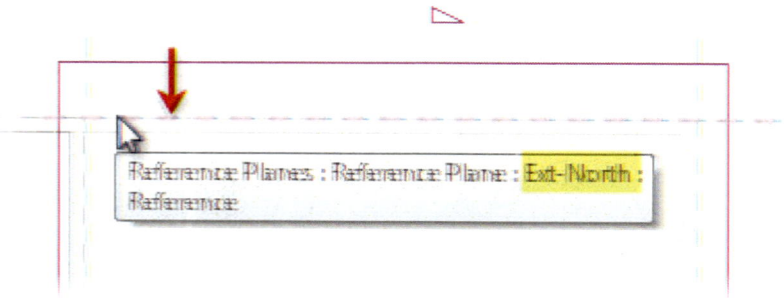

Pre-highlight / Pick Reference Plane 1

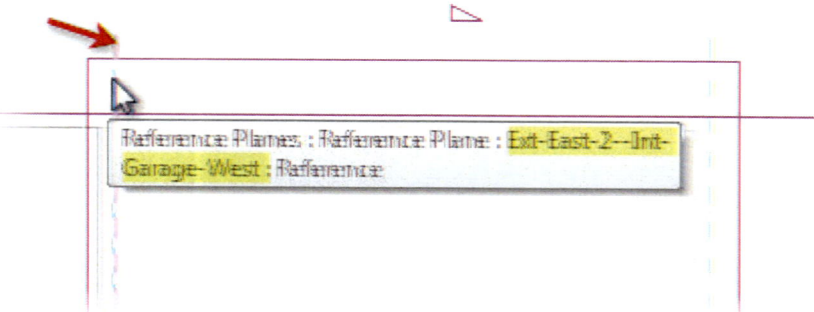

Pre-highlight / Pick Reference Plane 2

EXERCISE 2.3: MODELING ROOFS

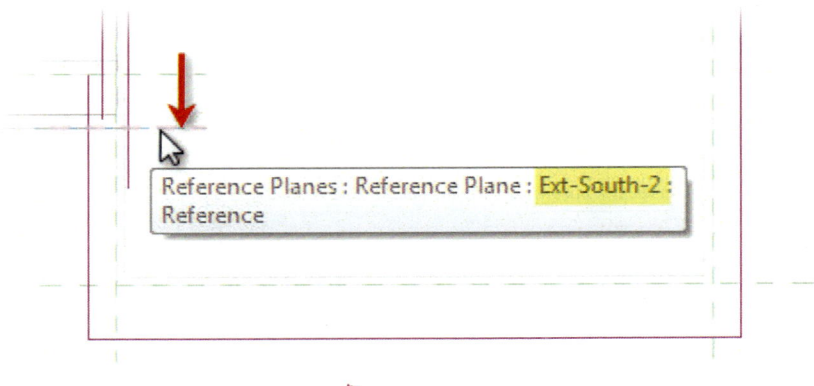

Pre-highlight / Pick Reference Plane 3

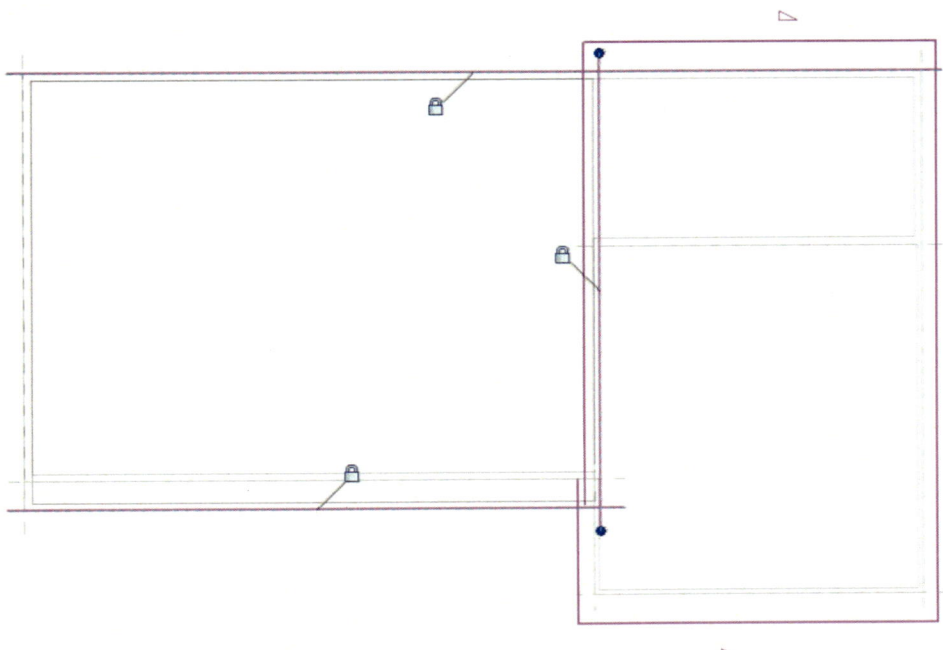

3 Reference Planes Picked / Boundaries Locked

Wall Pick with Negative Overhang Value

9. Click **Modify** to exit the Pick Lines operation.

10. Next you'll trim the boundary lines to create a closed loop sketch.

 Sketches for elements that require a boundary sketch must be a closed loop without any gaps or overlapping segments.

Chapter 2: Adding Roofs, Floors, and Wall Attachments

Trim/Extend to Corner		TR
Tab	Panel	Tool Button
Modify	**Modify**	**Trim/Extend to Corners**

11. Trim the boundary lines to achieve the closed-loop boundary as illustrated below.

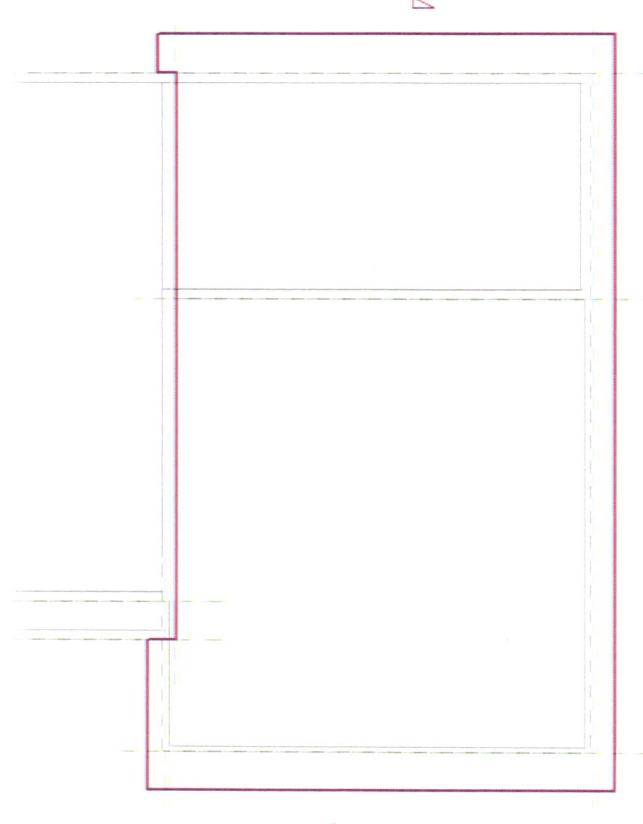

Completed Boundary Sketch

Add a Length Constraint

The boundary line defining the overhang where the roof wraps around the back of the house is not currently associated with any other geometry. Because of this, future design changes might cause the overhang to change unintentionally. To remedy this, we'll add a length constraint. A length constraint simply maintains a fixed distance between two elements. In this case, we want to fix the distance between the boundary line and the reference plane at 1"-0".

 Dimensions and length constraints will be covered in more detail in future chapters. For now, follow the directions on adding and locking the dimension carefully to ensure the proper outcome.

EXERCISE 2.3: MODELING ROOFS

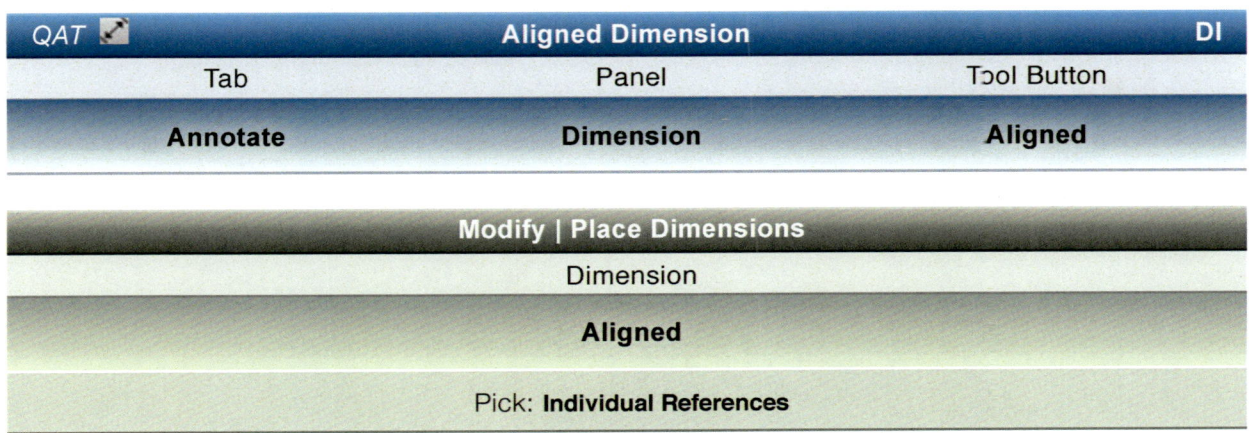

12. Click in the following order. Refer to the illustration below for specifics.

    a) Pick the roof boundary line.

    b) Pick the reference plane.

    c) Drag the cursor up and click where you want to place the dimension line to finish the dimension.

    d) Click on the padlock icon to lock the dimension.

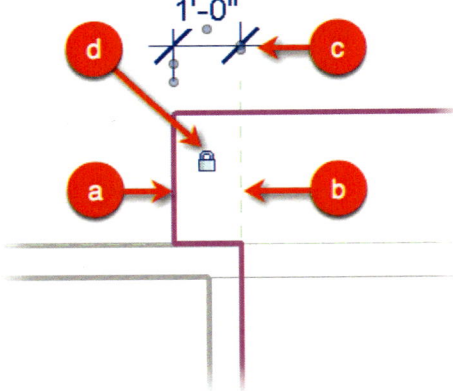

13. Click **Modify** or press **[esc]** twice to exit the dimension tool.

14. Click the **Finish Edit Mode** button ✔ to complete the roof.

QAT 📄	Open/Create Default 3D View		
Tab	Panel	Split Button ▼	Tool Button
View	Create	3D View	**Default 3D View** (default)

15. Examine the model using the *View Cube*. The newly created roofs should look like those in the illustration below.

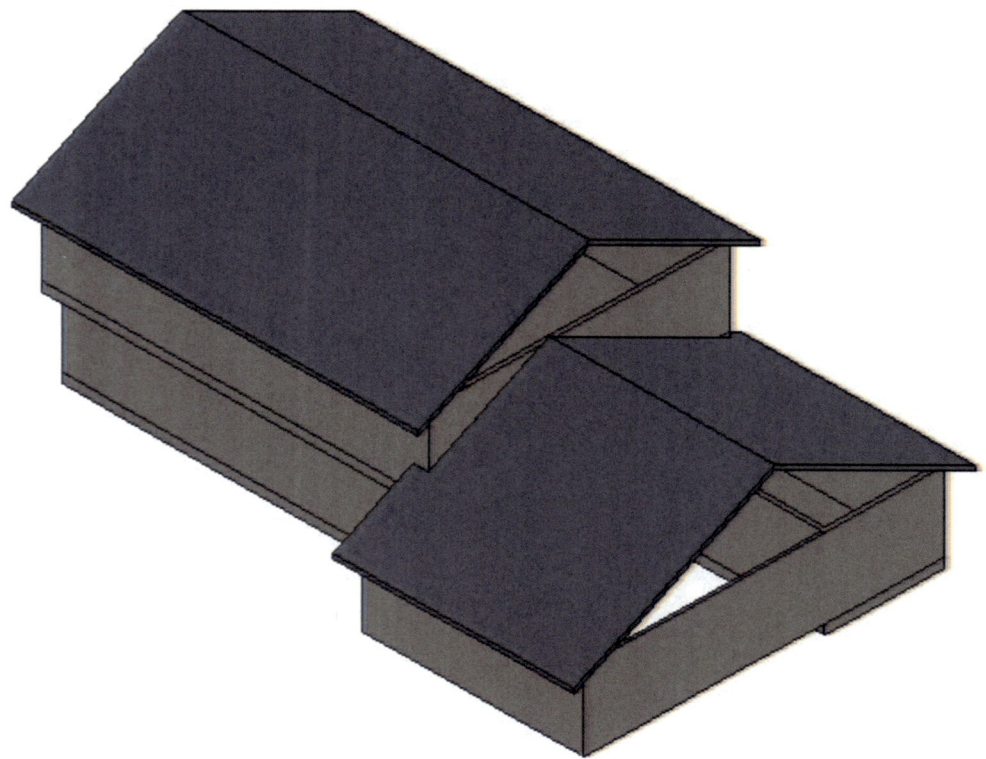

Generic Roofs Over 1st & 2nd Floors

 Consider testing the relationships between walls and roofs before continuing on. To do this, use the same process of unpinning and nudging reference planes as you did at the end of Chapter 1. Just remember to put reference planes back where they belong and re-pin them when you're done.

QAT 💾	Save Project		[Ctl]+S
	Operation		
	Save		

This concludes exercise 2.3

Exercise 2.4: Add Gable Walls

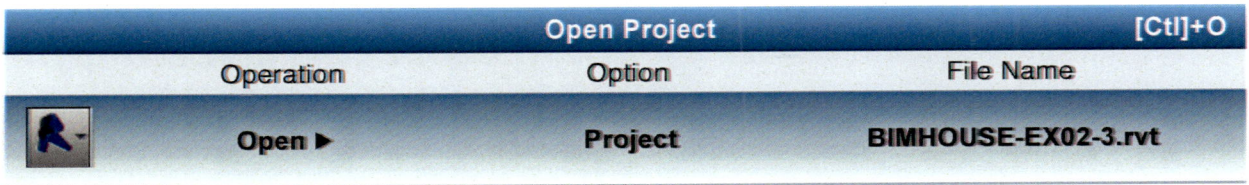

Open Project			[Ctl]+O
	Operation	Option	File Name
	Open ▶	Project	BIMHOUSE-EX02-3.rvt

Save As (Project)			
	Operation	Option	File Name
	Save As ▶	Project	BIMHOUSE-EX02-4.rvt

Create a New wall Type

In the following steps you will practice using the Project Browser to access families and their type properties.

1. In the Project Browser, expand the following tree: *Families* → *Walls* → *Basic Wall*

2. Under the Basic Wall branch, find *Generic - 4"* wall and open its Type Properties dialog box by doing one of the following:

    a) Right-click on it and select **Type Properties** from the contextual menu; or,

    b) **Double-click** on it.

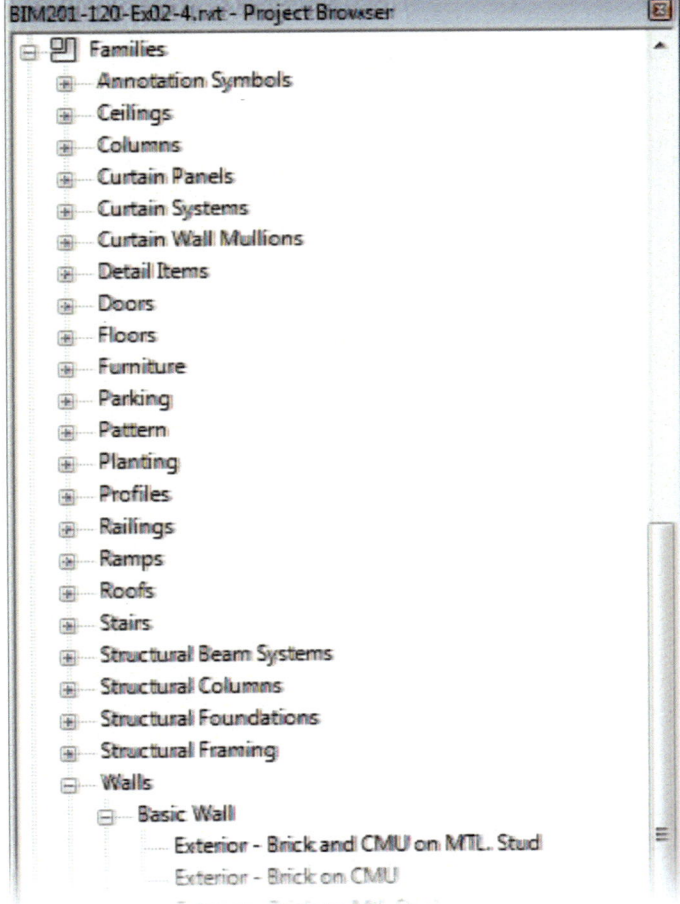

 From this point forward, the procedure for creating a new wall type is the same as creating a new wall type on-the-fly while the wall tool is active.

3. In the Type Properties dialog box, click **Duplicate…**
4. Enter **Generic - 2"** for the name, then click **OK**.
5. Click the **Edit…** button next to the *Structure* parameter in the Type Parameters pane.
6. In the Layers pane of the Edit Assembly dialog box, change the *Thickness* for Layer 2 to **0' 2"** as illustrated below.

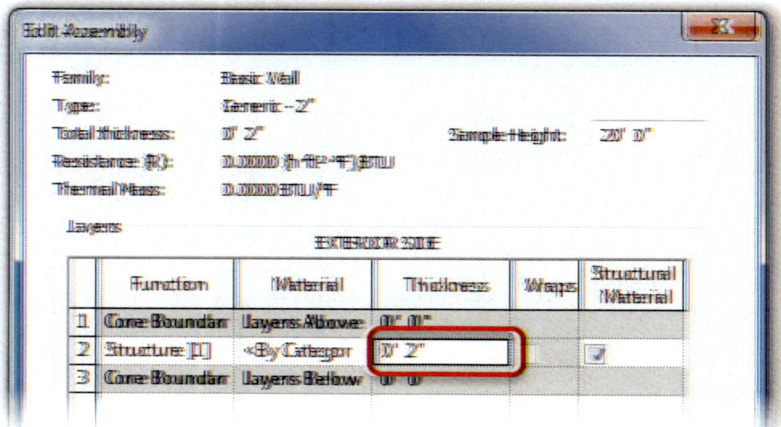

7. Click **OK** twice to exit all dialog boxes. The new wall type should now be visible in the Project Browser.

1st Floor Gable Walls

Add the Walls

1. Open the floor plan view *T.O.W. 1st FLR*, and add gable walls…

Tab	Panel	Wall Split Button ▼	WA Tool Button
Architecture	**Build**	**Wall**	**Wall: Architectural**

Properties			
	Type: **Generic - 2"**		
Base Constraint:	**T.O.W. 1st FLR**		
Base Offset:	**0' 0"**		

Modify	Place Wall			
	Draw		
	Pick Lines		
Height: **Unconnected** **3' 0"**		Location Line: **Core Face: Exterior**	Offset: **0' 0"**

EXERCISE 2.4: ADD GABLE END WALLS

2. Place two gable walls by picking the reference planes *Ext-Garage-West* and *Ext-East-1* as illustrated below. Make sure the wall orients correctly (exterior facing out).

 When pre-highlighting a reference plane prior to placing a wall, a dashed line will appear on the side of the reference plane where the wall will be located. When the Location Line is set to an exterior face, the dashed line will appear *opposite* the cursor location. This can be misleading and is somewhat counter-intuitive, so be careful!

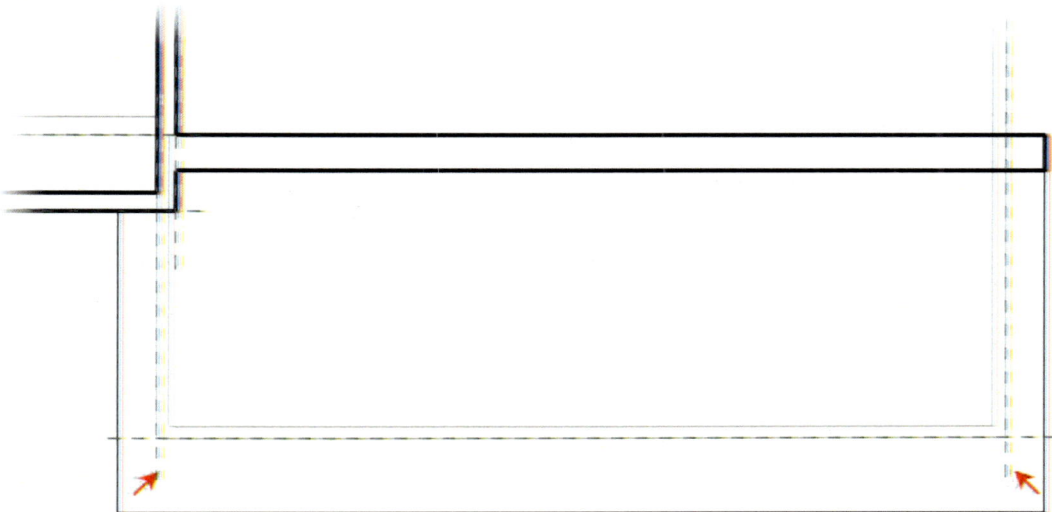

3. When picking on the reference plane on the west side of the garage, you'll receive a warning about overlapping walls. Don't worry about this, we'll fix it. Just close the warning dialog box.

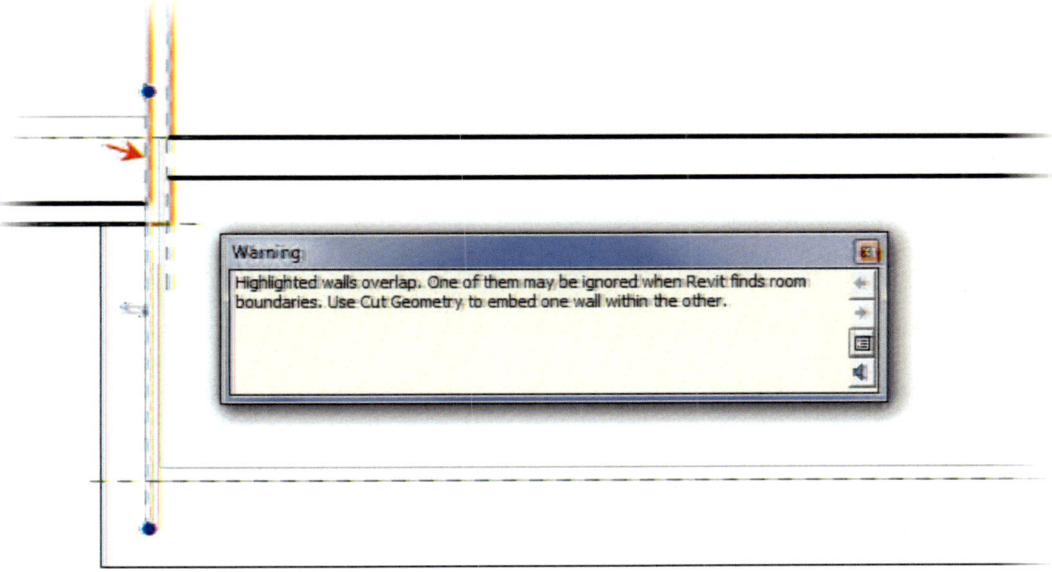

4. **Exit** the Wall tool when done.

Constrain the Gable Walls

Tab	Align	AL
	Panel	Tool Button
Modify	Modify	Align
Multiple Alignment: ☐	Prefer: **Faces of core**	

5. **Align** and **Lock** the south ends of both gable walls to reference plane *Ext-Garage-South*. Pick the reference plane first, and then the end of the wall. Remember to toggle the padlock to create the alignment constraint after each alignment operation.

 When using the Align tool, the first pick is always the target, or "move to" location, and the second pick is the element that will be moved. When edges are already coincident, the pick order doesn't matter.

Pick Order for Aligning Wall Ends

6. **Align** and **Lock** the north end of the east gable wall only to reference plane *Ext-North*.

 In the following steps, you'll be aligning and locking the core faces of generic walls to reference planes. Remember that for this type of alignment and constraint to operate properly, the *Detail Level* of the current view <u>MUST</u> be set to **Coarse**. Additionally, it's a good time to verify that the exterior wall faces are facing outward.

7. **Align** and **Lock** each gable wall to the reference plane you picked when creating the wall. To do this, first click on the reference plane, and then on the *exterior core face* of the wall. Remember to toggle the padlock to create the alignment constraint after each alignment operation.

Since you used pick lines to place the gable walls, they're already aligned with the reference planes. However, in order to create an alignment constraint (access the padlock), an alignment operation must be done regardless if the elements are already aligned.

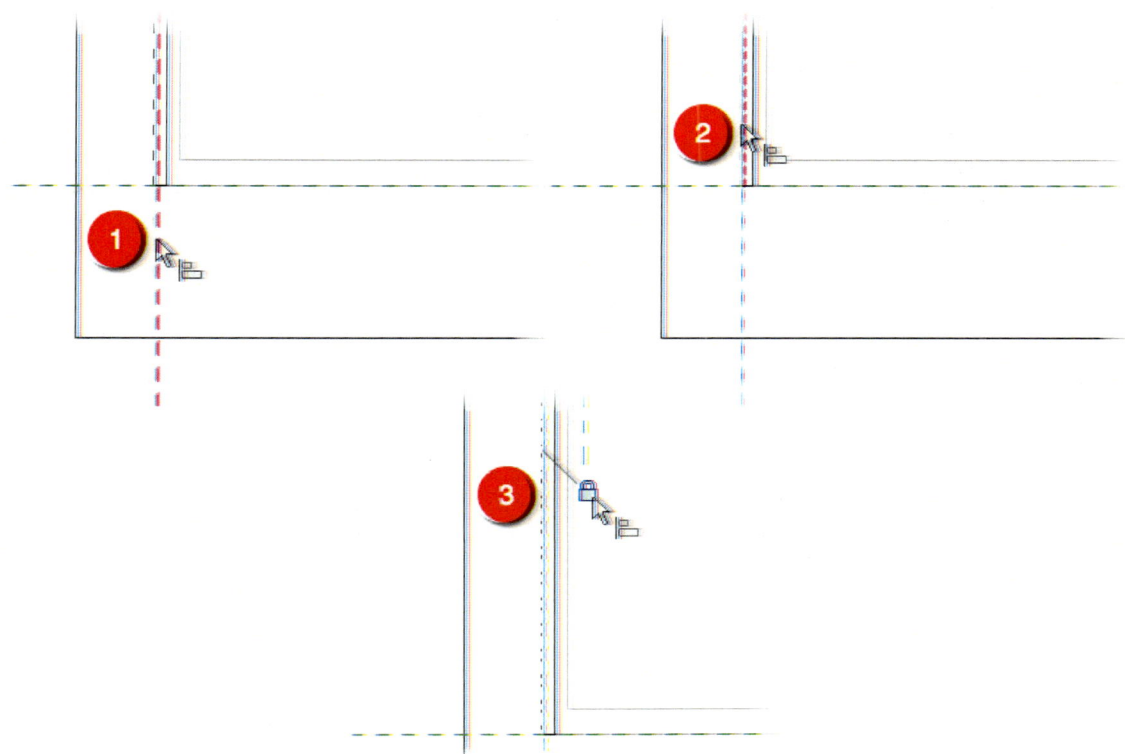

Pick Order for Aligning Wall Core Faces

8. **Exit** the Align tool when done.

CHAPTER 2: ADDING ROOFS, FLOORS, AND WALL ATTACHMENTS

Correct the Overlapping Wall Condition

9. **Click** on the gable wall on the west side of the garage to select it.

10. **Click** the drag control on the north edge of the wall, and drag the wall end down until it no longer contacts any walls, as shown in the illustration below. Make sure to drag it far enough so the end is not obscured by the roof surface.

11. **Right-click** on the same drag control, and select **Disallow Join** from the contextual menu.

 We are treating this gable wall join condition the same way that we treated the wall join beneath it at the very beginning of this exercise. Otherwise, the automatic constraint created between the gable wall and the coplanar 2nd floor wall will generate an error when attempting to flex the model geometry.

	Align		AL
Tab	Panel		Tool Button
Modify	Modify		Align
Multiple Alignment: ☐	Prefer: **Faces of core**		

12. **Align/Lock** the *end* of the wall to the reference plane *Ext-South-2* (*at the south wall of the 2nd floor*) as illustrated below.

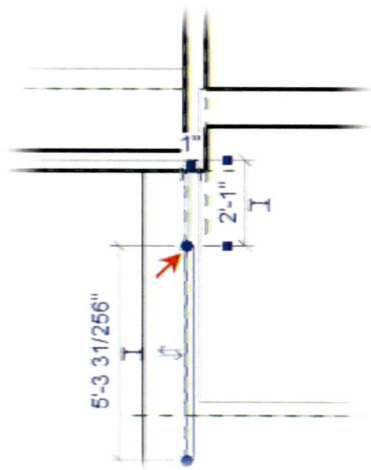   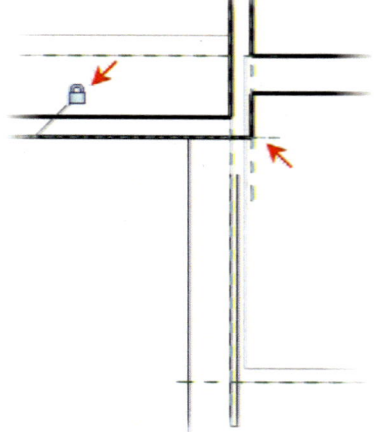

Drag Wall End & Disallow Join   Align & Lock Wall End To Reference Plane

 In the second illustration above, notice that you don't see where the gable end wall connects to the joining wall. This is because the wall is only 3' high, and the point where it disappears it is beneath the roof surface. Setting the *Visual Style* property for the current view to **Wireframe** would allow you to "see through" the roof if necessary.

13. **Exit** the Align tool when done.
14. Open the default *{3D}* view to observe the added gable end walls. Your model should appear as illustrated below.

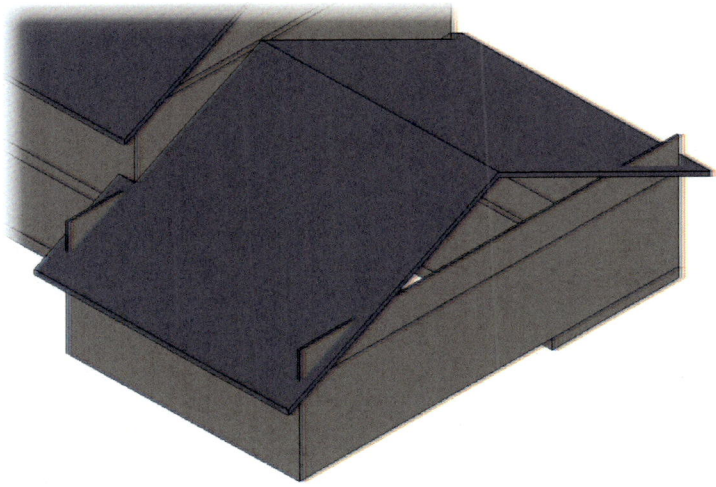

Gable End Walls at Garage After Placement and Alignment

2nd Floor Gable Walls

Add the Walls

Next you will place the gable end walls on the second floor. The procedure and end result is essentially the same as that for the first floor.

1. Open the floor plan view *T.O.W. 2nd FLR* and add the remaining gable walls...

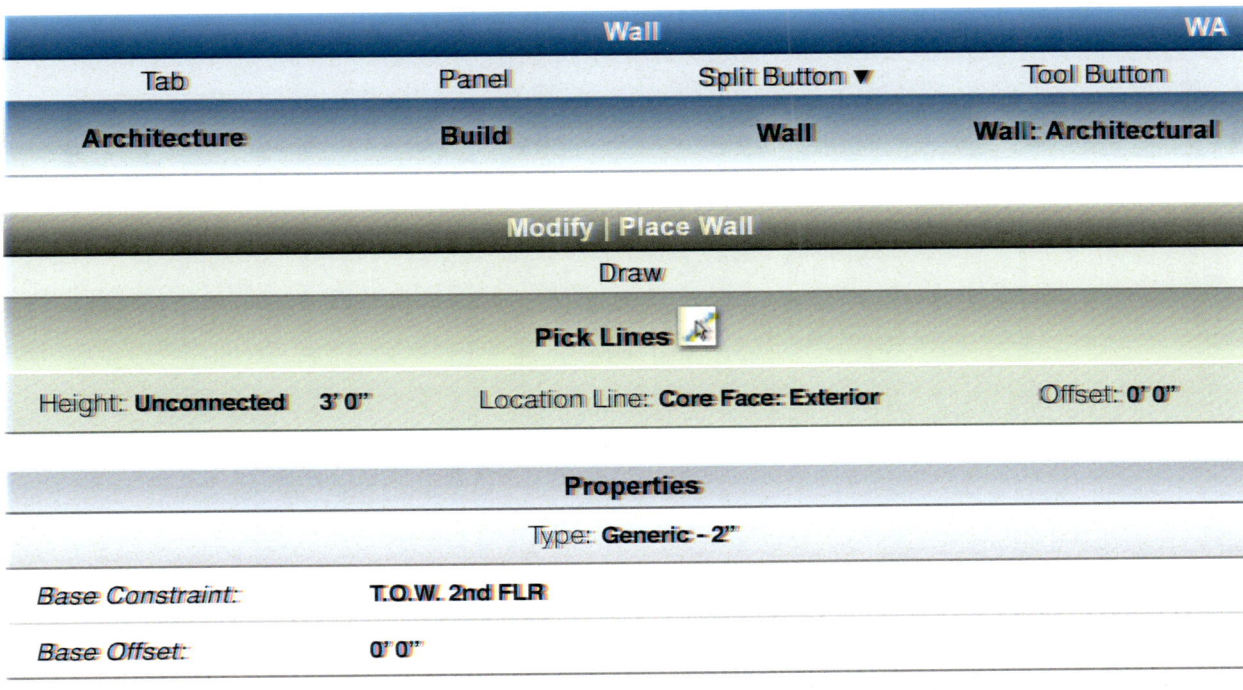

Wall			WA
Tab	Panel	Split Button ▼	Tool Button
Architecture	**Build**	**Wall**	**Wall: Architectural**

Modify | Place Wall
Draw
Pick Lines

Height: **Unconnected** 3' 0"	Location Line: **Core Face: Exterior**	Offset: **0' 0"**

Properties
Type: **Generic – 2"**

Base Constraint:	**T.O.W. 2nd FLR**
Base Offset:	**0' 0"**

2. **Pick** the reference planes *Ext-West* and *Ext-East-2--Int-Garage-West* (east and west ends of the 2nd floor) to add the gable walls. Again, make sure the wall orients to the correct side of the reference plane.

3. **Exit** the Wall tool after placing the two walls.

Constrain the Gable Walls

Align			AL
Tab	Panel		Tool Button
Modify	**Modify**		**Align**
Multiple Alignment: ☐	Prefer: **Faces of core**		

4. Using the same procedure as used for the first floor (refer to the previous steps as necessary), **Align** and **Lock** the *ends* of the new gable walls to the reference planes *Ext-North* and *Ext-South-2* (at the north and south faces of the 2nd floor). Remember to **lock** each wall end immediately after alignment.

5. Next, **Align** and **Lock** the exterior core face of each gable wall to the corresponding reference plane: *Ext-West* or *Ext-East-2--Int-Garage-West*.

Attach the Gable End Walls to the Roofs

QAT	Open Default 3D View		
Tab	Panel	Split Button ▼	Tool Button
View	**Create**	**3D View**	**Default 3D View** (default)

1. While holding down the **[Ctl]** key, select the two gable end walls at the 2nd floor, then activate the **Attach Top/Base** tool....

Modify | Wall
Modify Wall
Attach Top/Base
Attach Wall: **Top**

2. **Pick** the second floor roof. The tops of the two gable walls should assume the shape of the underside of the roof.

3. Repeat the process for the first floor gable walls and first floor roof. When done, your model should appear as illustrated below.

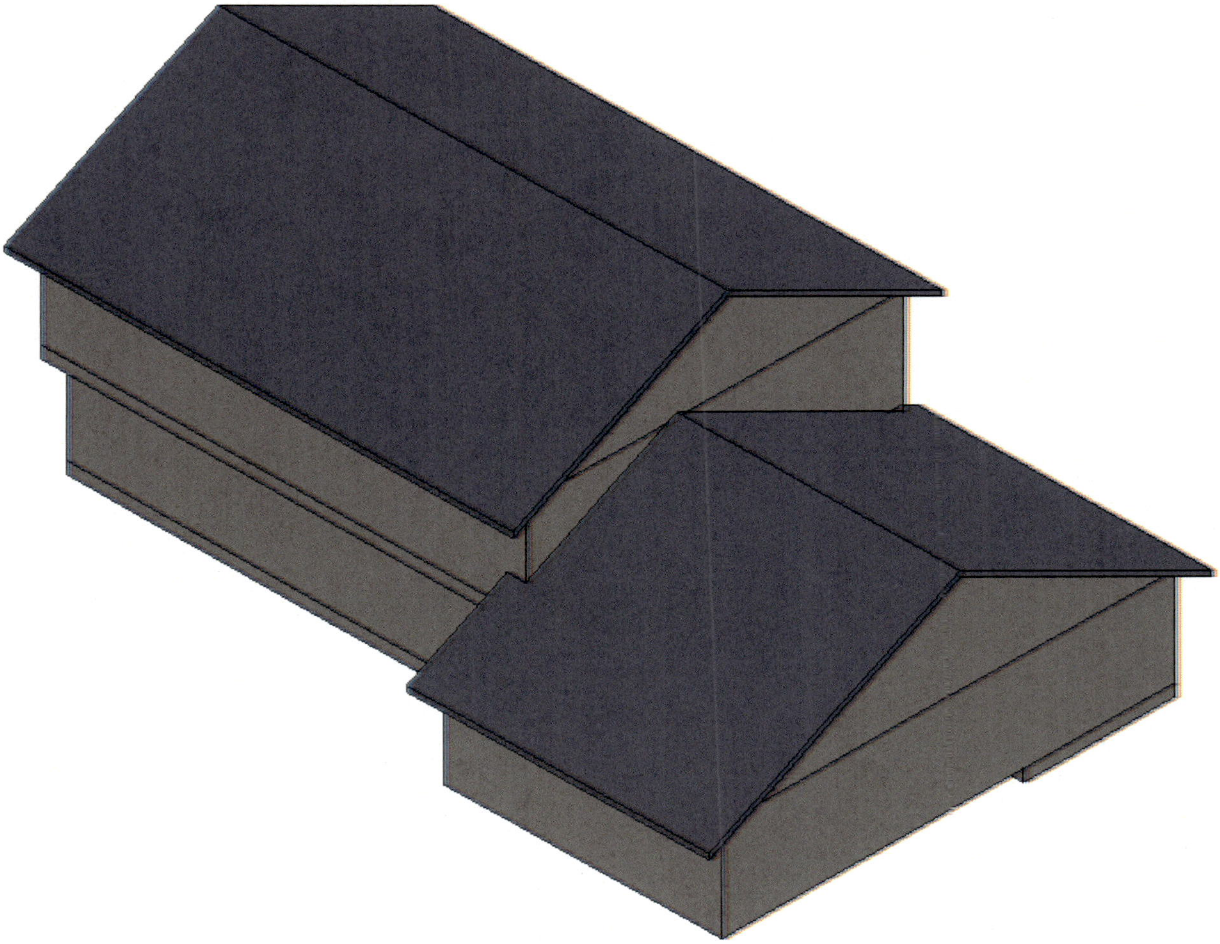

Completed Gable End Walls

 This is a good time to test the associations and flexibility of your model. Make sure to test *all* references at this point and correct any errors or elements that have become dissociated before moving on. You will continue to add more geometry to your model, making it more complex, which in turn makes it more difficult to troubleshoot.

QAT 💾	Save Project	[Ctl]+S
	Operation	
🅁	**Save**	

This concludes exercise 2.4

Exercise 2.5: Add Interior Walls

Open Project			[Ctl]+O
	Operation	Option	File Name
	Open ▶	Project	BIMHOUSE-EX02-4.rvt

Save As (Project)			
	Operation	Option	File Name
	Save As ▶	Project	BIMHOUSE-EX02-5.rvt

1st Floor Interior Walls

Add the East/West Bearing Wall at the 1st Floor

1. Open the floor plan view *F.F.L. 1st FLR*, and add the first of the 1st floor interior walls....

Wall			WA
Tab	Panel	Split Button ▼	Tool Button
Architecture	**Build**	**Wall**	**Wall: Architectural**

Properties	
Type: **Generic – 4"**	
Location Line:	**Finish Face: Interior**
Base Constraint:	**F.F.L. 1st FLR**
Base Offset:	**0' 0"**
Top Constraint:	**Up to level: T.O.W 1st FLR**
Top Offset:	**0' 0"**

Modify	Place Wall
Draw
Line ╱

Height: **T.O.W 1st FLR**   Location Line: **Finish Face: Interior**   Chain: ☐   Offset: **0' 0"**   Radius: ☐

2. Start sketching at the northwest corner of the garage wall as shown in the following illustration. Be sure to snap to the corner as shown.

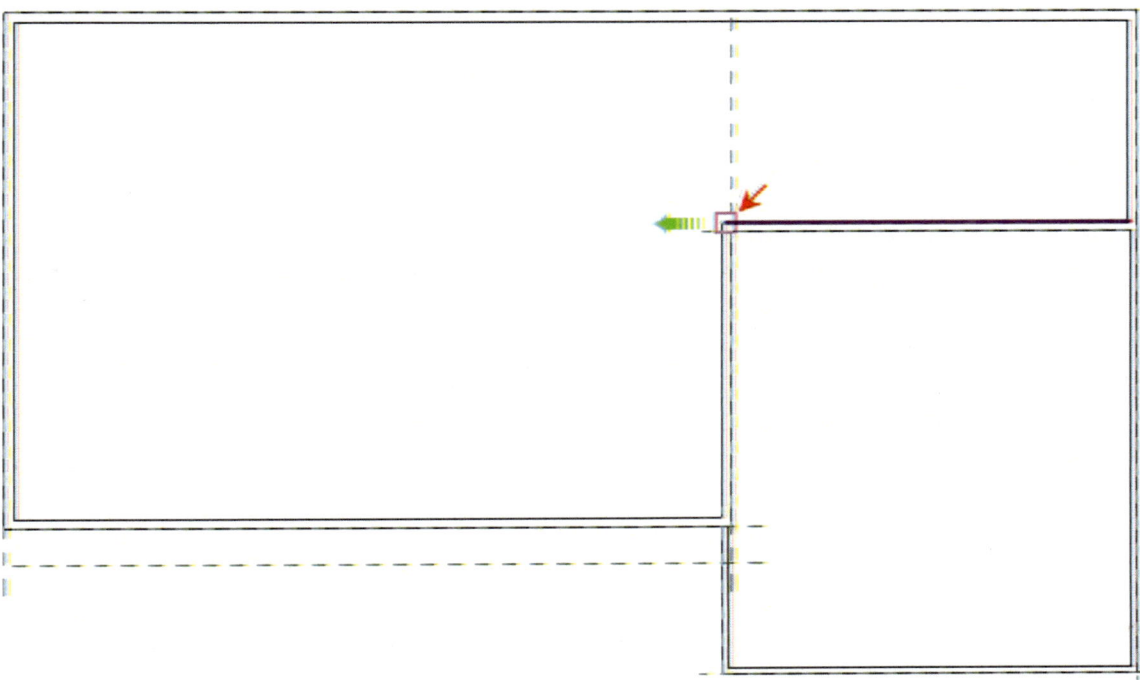

Start Interior Wall

3. **Sketch** to the left all the way to the west exterior wall to complete the wall as illustrated below.

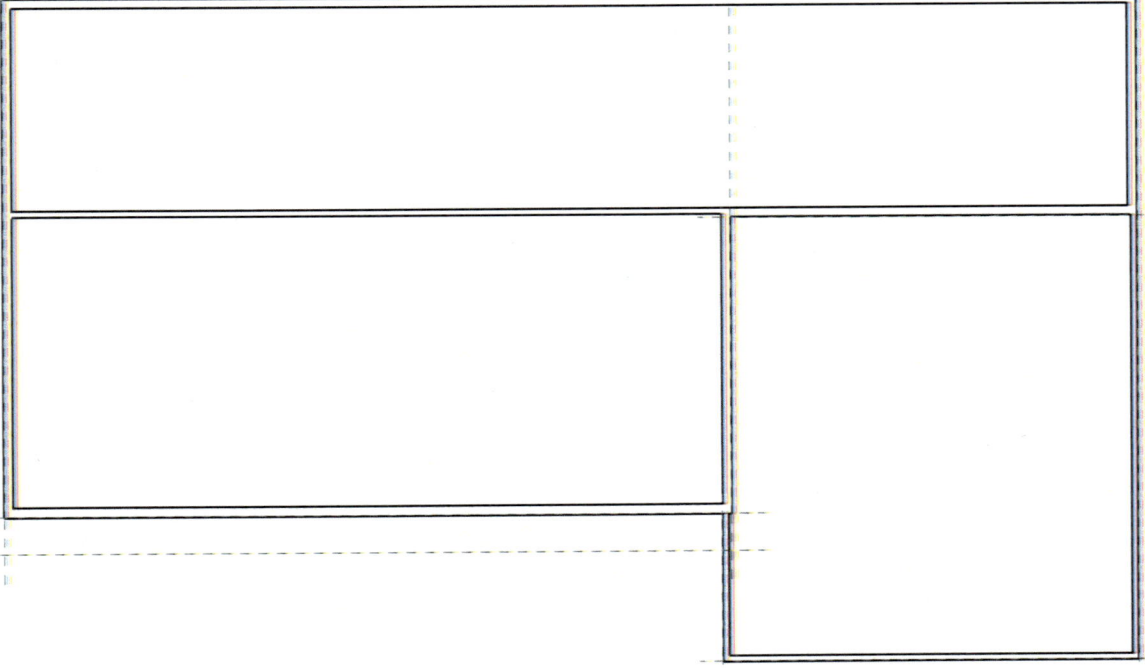

Completed Interior Wall

4. **Exit** the Wall tool.

5. Select the *Generic - 4"* wall you just sketched, verify the location of the flip arrow, and take note of the padlock on the reference plane.

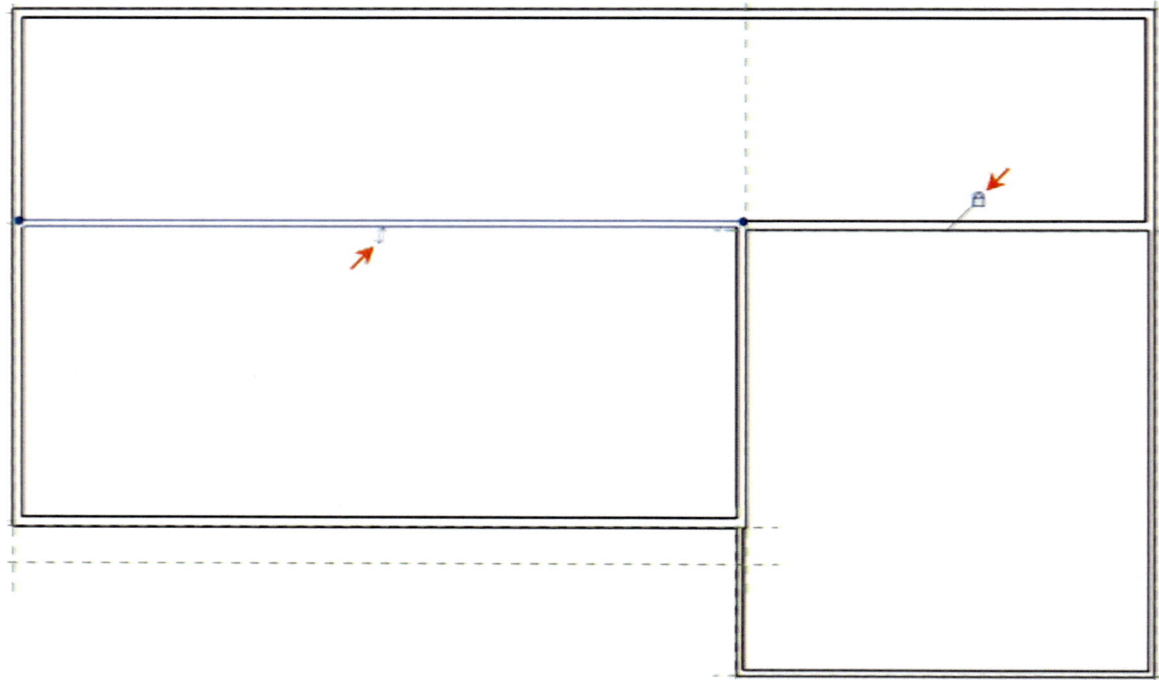

 You might recall from the beginning of this exercise that when walls are created and connected in a coplanar condition, Revit creates an alignment relationship between the coplanar surfaces. By sketching the previous wall as you did, the coplanar faces of the garage and interior walls are associated.

Verify Relationships

6. Select the *Generic - 4"* wall again, and try moving it up or down using the arrow keys on the keyboard. You should receive the error message illustrated below. Click **Cancel**.

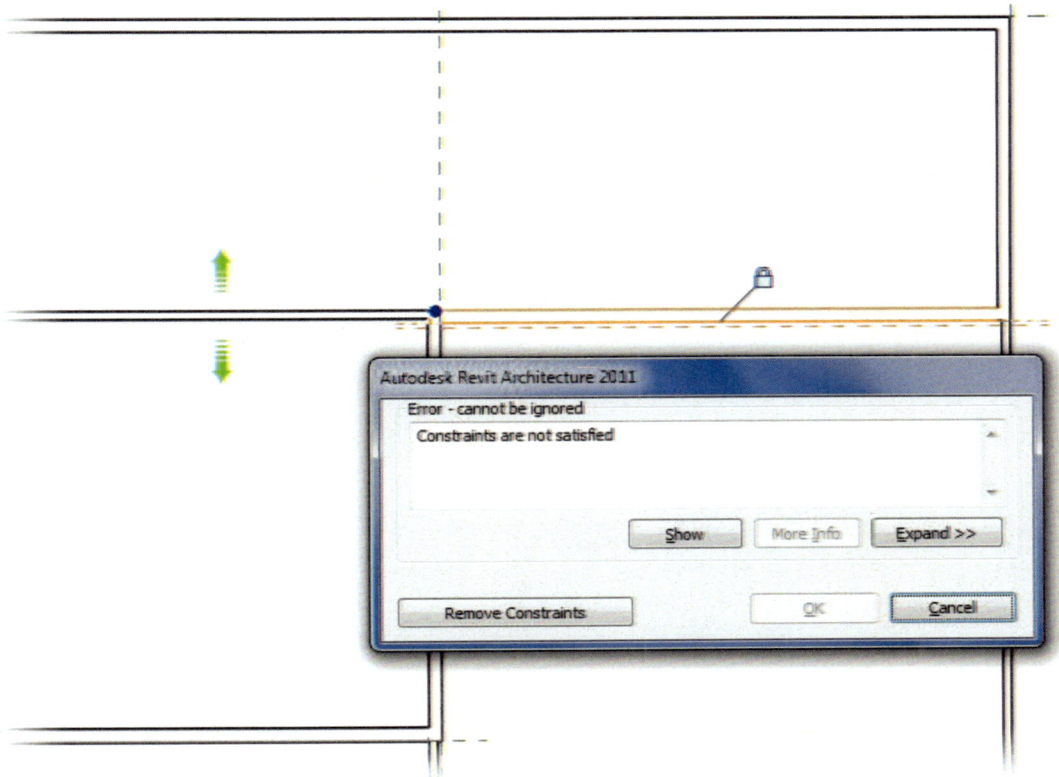

7. Select the reference plane *Int-Garage-North*, **Unpin** it, and move it up / down using the arrow keys on the keyboard. Both the garage wall and new interior wall should move together with the reference plane.

8. Return the reference plane to its original location and **Pin** it.

9. Select the *Generic - 4"* wall, and from the type selector in the Properties palette, change it to **Generic - 6"**. The wall should widen without errors, and the interior faces of the coplanar walls should remain coplanar. If you receive an error, it's likely that the new wall's location line is set incorrectly.

10. Return the wall type back to **Generic - 4"**.

 The alignment constraint created by Revit between the two walls can be broken through a series of steps involving separating the join, moving a wall, and then rejoining the walls. You will not be instructed at any time during any of the exercises to do this, so it shouldn't be a problem. However, be aware of this should you need to get creative with troubleshooting your model, or have some other reason to move one of the walls independent of the other. To recreate the constraint you will need to use the Align tool, and lock the faces of the walls together.

CHAPTER 2: ADDING ROOFS, FLOORS, AND WALL ATTACHMENTS

Add the Remaining 1st Floor Interior Walls

11. Open the floor plan view *F.F.L. 1st FLR*, and add the remaining 1st floor interior walls...

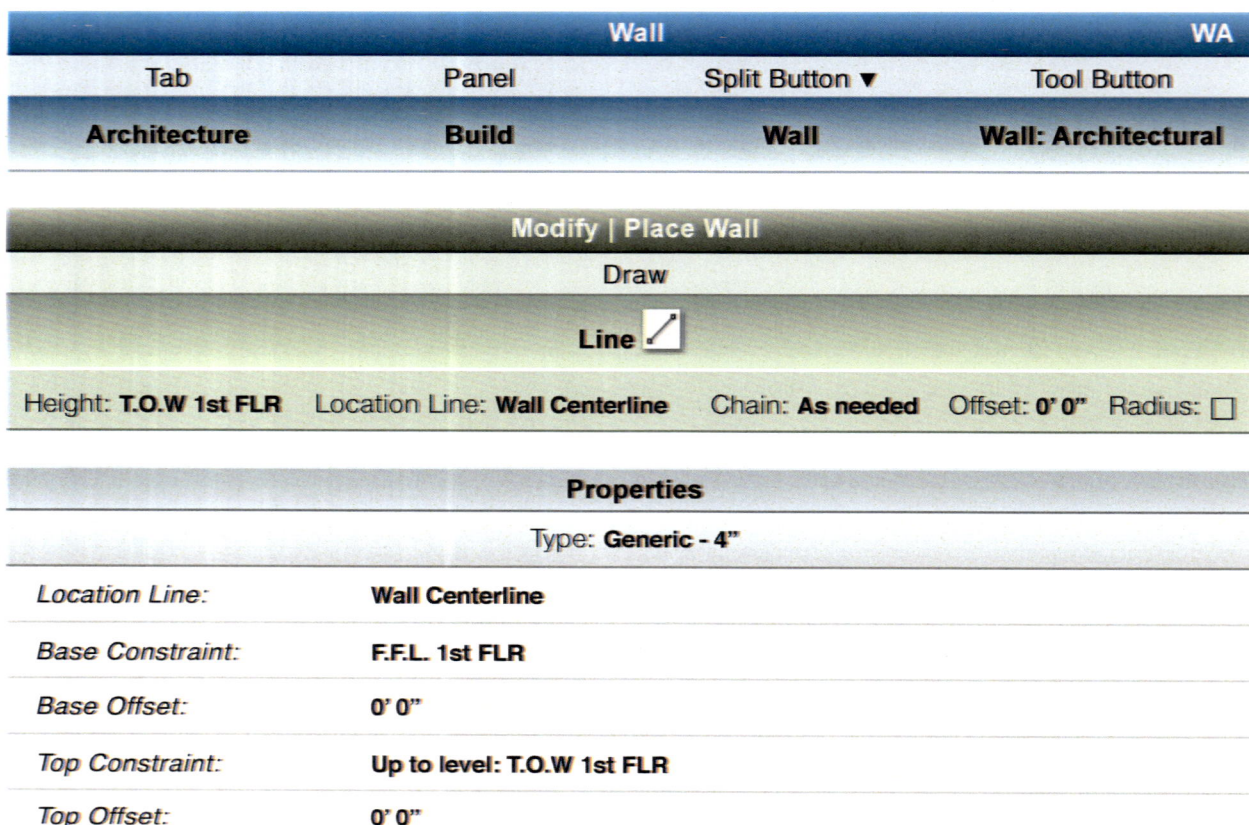

12. Sketch the remaining 1st floor interior walls roughly located as illustrated below. **Exit** the Wall tool when done.

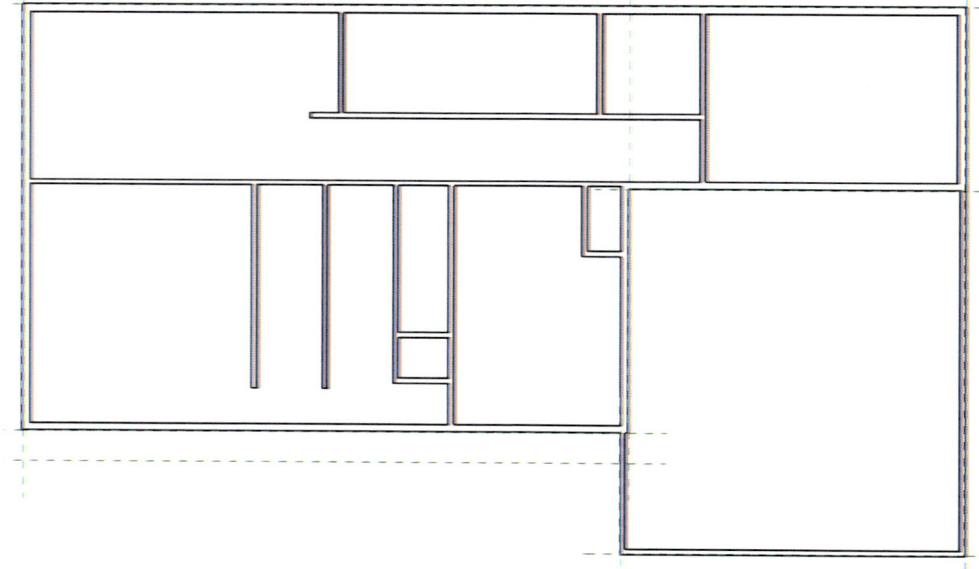

1st Floor Interior Walls – Approximate Locations

2nd Floor Interior Walls

1. Open the floor plan view *F.F.L. 2nd FLR*, and add the 2nd floor interior walls...

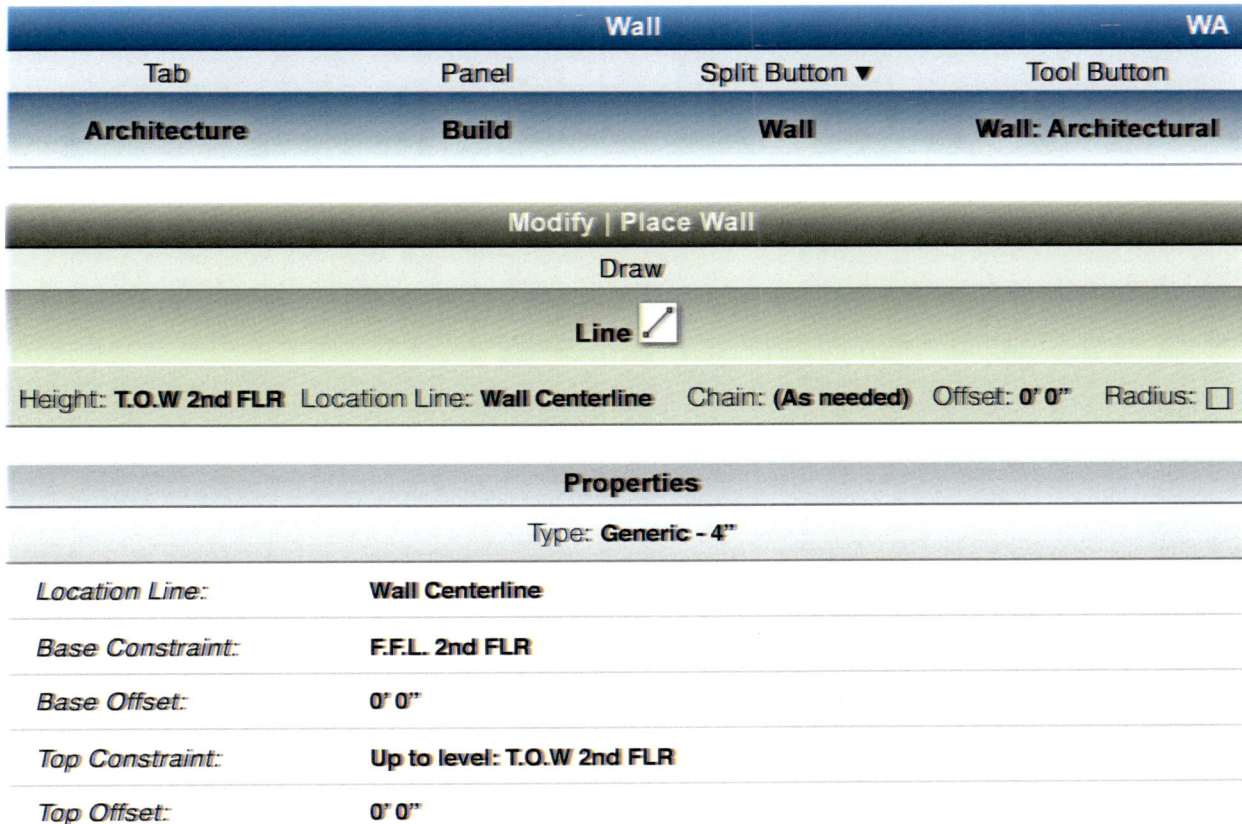

2. **Sketch** the 2nd floor interior walls roughly located as illustrated below, using as few wall segments as possible. In other words, don't create multiple wall segments along the same path. **Exit** the Wall tool when done.

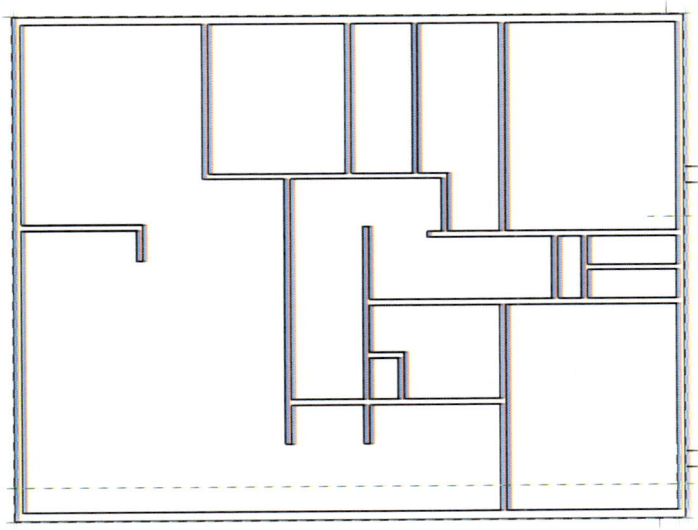

2nd Floor Interior Walls – Approximate Locations

You can verify the correct number of walls up to this point. To do so, open the {3D} view, select the entire model, then open the Filter dialog box. The wall count should read 49.

Although the wall *Location Line* property for most of the interior walls was specified as **Wall Centerline**, this may not be the best selection for all walls. You should typically try to consider how elements relate to each other, and if they were to change dimensionally, what part of that relationship is critical when attempting to maintain design intent. For right now, you haven't been given enough information to make that decision. However, you will be modifying wall properties as the design progresses and more information is available.

This concludes exercise 2.5

Chapter Summary

In this lesson you were introduced to the basics of creating floors and roofs, as well as how to manually override automatic wall joins. As you are probably beginning to see, creating a parametric building model requires considerably more thought about how elements relate, than simply drafting a 2D representation.

So far, elements have been kept generic, and we'll continue to do so up to the point where we have a fairly complete, yet basic representation of a house. We'll then go back and begin the refinement process by adding more complexity and specifics to the building elements.

Chapter 3

Adding Doors, Windows, and Wall Openings

Overview

This chapter will introduce you to using the Door, Window, and Component tools. Additionally, you will be introduced to view range and plan regions, and practice using temporary dimensions to refine your model.

Throughout this chapter you will need to refer to the floor plans provided in the file *BIM_House-Reference-15.pdf*.

Learning Objectives

After completing this chapter you should have a good understanding of the following:

- Temporary dimensions: settings and using
- Select All Instances tool
- Split Element tool
- Searching and downloading content from Autodesk Seek
- Loadable families
- Creating new door & window types
- Placing and orienting doors and windows
- Plan regions
- Opening families vs. wall opening tool

Project Objectives

- Refine the locations of interior walls
- Add relevant constraints between walls
- Populate the model with doors and windows
- Add plan regions to reveal elements above the cut plane
- Insert cased openings at interior walls

CHAPTER 3: INTERIOR WALLS REFINEMENT / ADDING DOORS & WINDOWS

Chapter Contents

Exercise 3.1: Wall Refinement 85
    Update the 4" Generic Walls 85
    Update the 6" Generic Walls 87
    Temporary Dimension Settings 88
    Refine Wall Locations and Properties - 1st Floor 88
    Refine Wall Locations and Properties - 2nd Floor 94

Exercise 3.2: Windows 98
    Load Window Families 98
    Create New Window Types 100
    Place Windows on 1st Floor 101
    Place Windows on 2nd Floor 103
    Adjust Window Header Heights 104
    Reset Visibility for Invisible Window 105

Exercise 3.3: Doors   **109**
    Load Door Families 109
    Place Doors on 1st Floor 110
    Download a Door Family from the Web Library 111
    Load and Place the Downloaded Family 112
    Place Doors on 2nd Floor 112

Exercise 3.4: Cased Openings 113
    Load Opening Family 113
    Place All Openings 114

Exercise 3.1: Wall Refinement

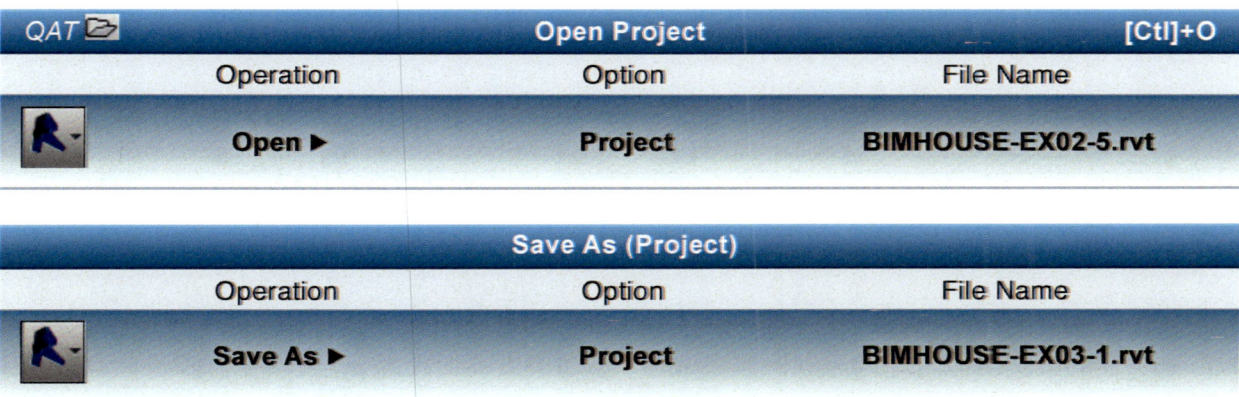

Update the 4" Generic Walls

The dimensions in the plans provided are based on actual framing member sizes. Therefore, before positioning the walls we'll change them to a type that accurately reflects framing member width (wall core thickness).

Change 1st Floor Interior Walls

1. Open the floor plan view *F.F.L. 1st FLR*.
2. **Right-click** on one of the interior walls, then from the contextual menu click **Select All Instances ▶ Visible in View** as illustrated below.

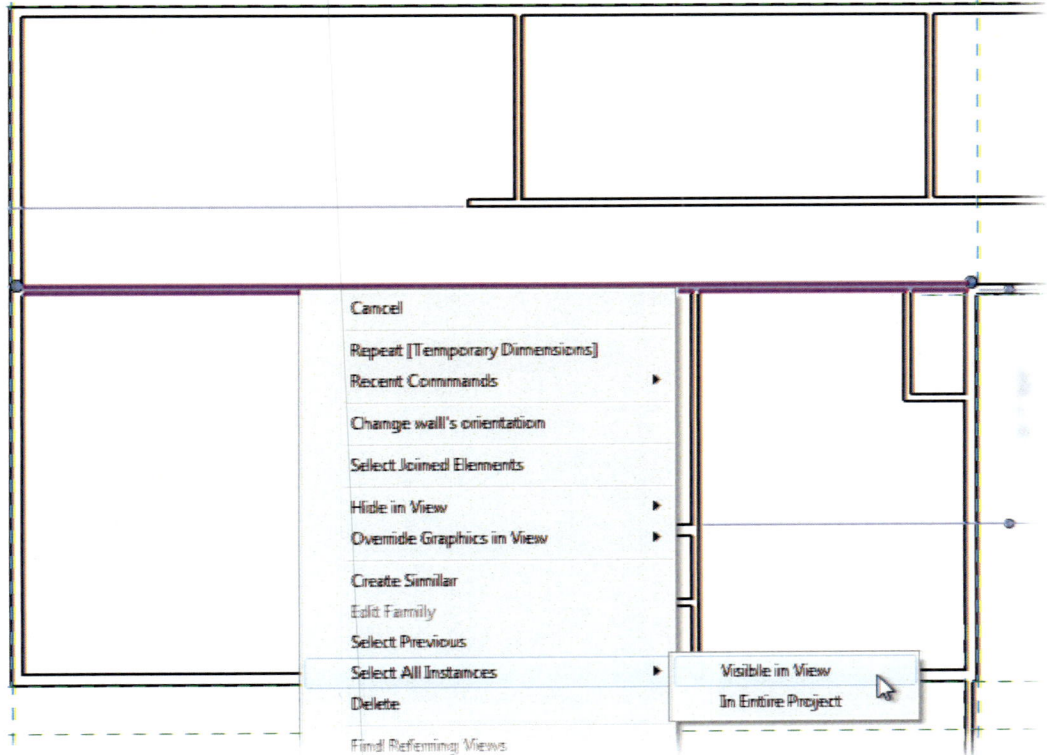

Note that all *Generic 4"* walls have been selected, including the three garage walls as illustrated below.

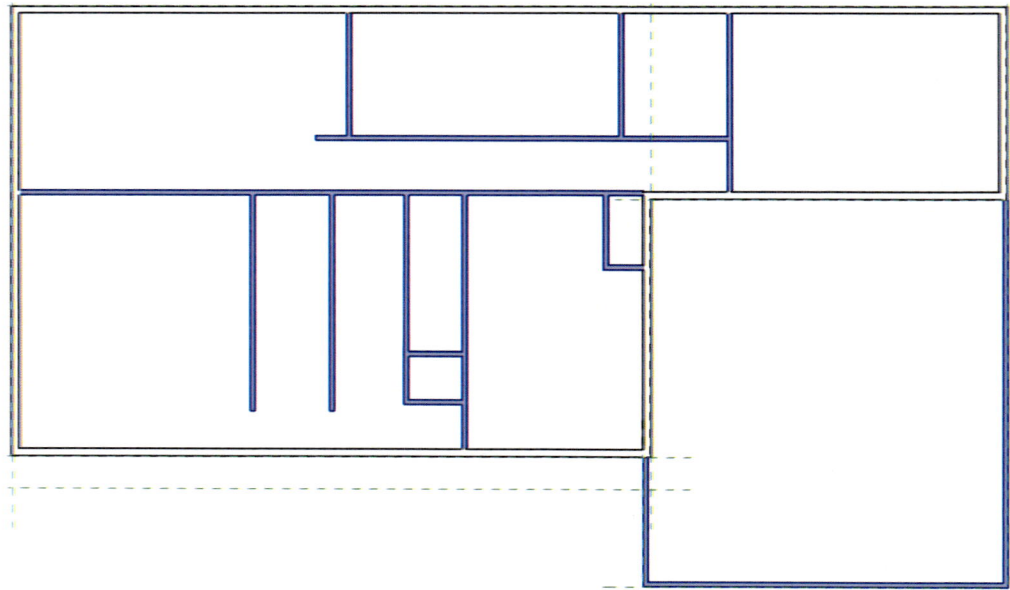

Generic - 4" Wall Selection Set

 You can see the number of elements you have selected on the right side of the Status Bar.

3. Click **Edit Type** in the properties palette to open the type properties dialog box for the *Generic - 4"* wall type.

4. Click **Duplicate...** and enter **Generic - 3 1/2"** for the name.

5. Click **Edit...** next to the *Structure* parameter to open the Edit Assembly dialog box.

6. Change Layer 2 *Thickness* to **3 1/2"**.

7. Click **OK** twice to exit all dialog boxes. All of the selected walls should update to the new type.

8. Clear the selection.

Change 2nd Floor Interior Walls

9. Open the floor plan view *F.F.L. 2nd FLR*.

10. **Right-click** on one of the interior walls, then from the contextual menu click **Select All Instances ▶ Visible in View**.

11. Expand the type selector in the Properties palette, and select **Generic - 3 1/2"**. All of the selected walls should change to the new type.

12. Clear the selection.

EXERCISE 3.1: REFINING THE INTERIOR WALLS LOCATIONS

Update the 6" Generic Walls

Create the Wall Type

In the following steps you will create another new wall type, however, you will use the Project Browser to access the wall family for duplicating and editing.

1. In the Project Browser, expand the following tree: *Families* → *Walls* → *Basic Wall*
2. Under the Basic Wall branch, find the *Generic - 6"* wall, **right-click** on it and select **Duplicate** from the contextual menu. A duplicate should appear directly below the original named *Generic - 6" 2*.
3. **Right-click** on *Generic - 6" 2*, select Rename from the contextual menu, and enter **Generic - 5 1/2"** for the name (press **[Enter]** when done).
4. With the *Generic - 5 1/2"* wall still highlighted, click on it again to open its Type Properties dialog box.
5. Click **Edit...** next to the *Structure* parameter to open the Edit Assembly dialog box.
6. Change Layer 2 *Thickness* to **5 1/2"**.
7. Click **OK** twice to exit all dialog boxes.

Apply the Generic - 5 1/2" Wall Type

8. Open the default *{3D}* view.
9. **Right-click** on one of the exterior *Generic - 6"* walls, then from the contextual menu click **Select All Instances ▸ In Entire Project** (*or* ▸ **Visible in View**).

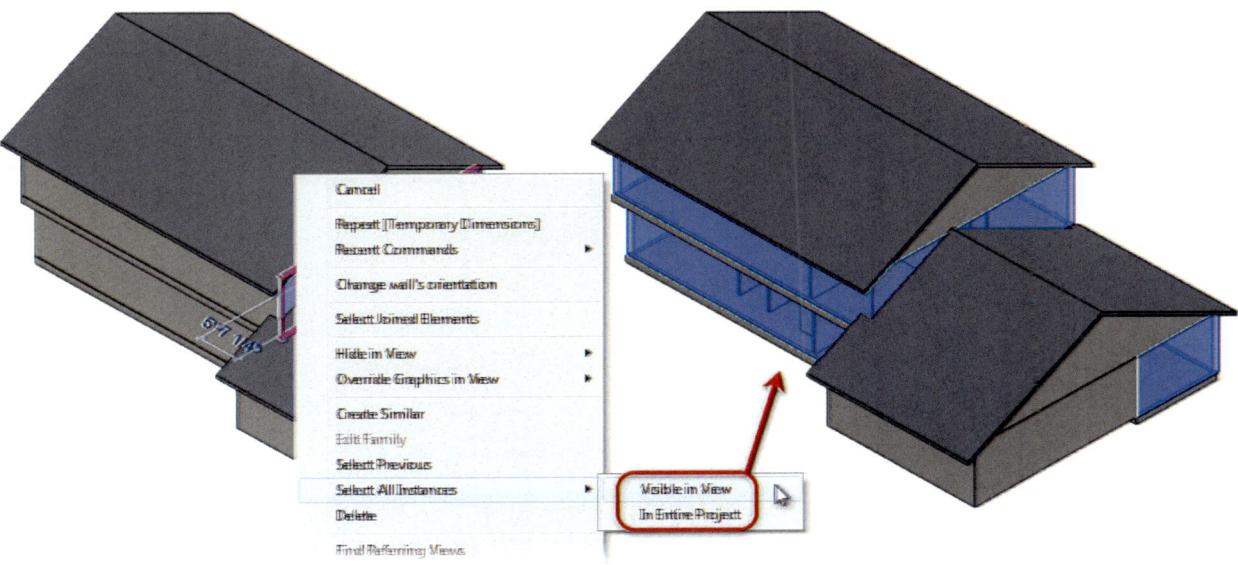

Select All Generic - 6" Walls in Model

10. Expand the type selector in the Properties palette, and select **Generic - 5 1/2"**. All of the selected walls should change to the new type.

Temporary Dimension Settings

In upcoming steps you'll be using temporary dimensions to refine the locations of interior walls to match the dimensions on the reference plan set. Since all dimensioning is referenced to the face of framing (Faces of Core), we'll want to make sure that our temporary dimensions are referenced the same way prior to adjusting the dimension. Whenever a wall is selected in Revit and temporary dimensions appear, the witness line can be toggled between the various references. They can also be dragged to a different reference, or a different element altogether. We can adjust the default behavior of temporary dimensions by specifying the initial placement of witness lines. Adjusting the settings to match the workflow can provide a minor productivity boost.

11. Open the Temporary Dimension Properties dialog box...

Temporary Dimensions			
Tab	Panel	Drop-down Button ▼	Tool Button
Manage	**Settings**	**Additional Settings**	**Temporary Dimensions**

12. Modify the settings per the following illustration, then click **OK** when done.

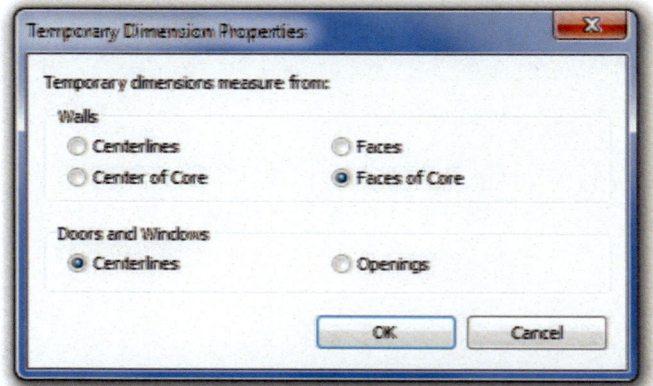

Refine Wall Locations and Properties - 1st Floor

1. Open the floor plan view *F.F.L. 1st FLR*.

Set Location Line for Stair Walls

2. Select the two walls that enclose the main stairway.

3. Using the Properties Palette, set the *Location Line* to **Core Face: Interior**.

4. Orient each wall so the exterior side faces away from the stairway area as shown in the following illustration.

 You will need to select each wall independently in order to access the flip arrow.

EXERCISE 3.1: REFINING THE INTERIOR WALLS LOCATIONS

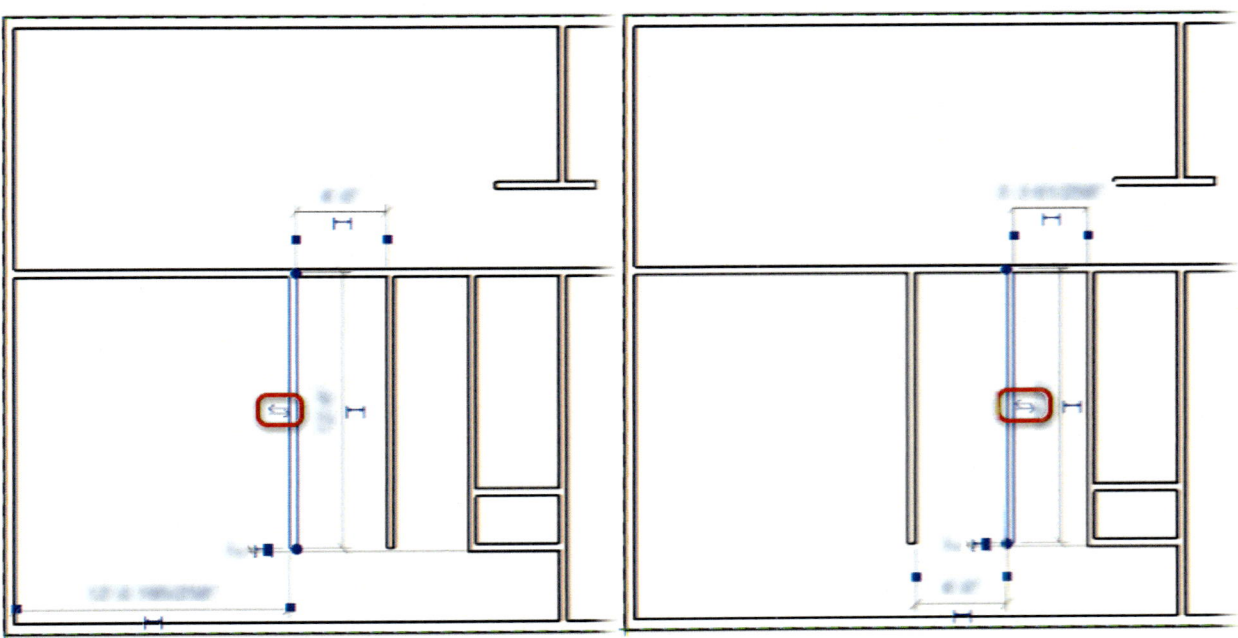

Stairway Walls - First Floor

5. Change the plumbing walls in the powder room and the laundry room to **Generic - 5 1/2"**.

 Refer to sheet **A201 - 1st Floor Note Plan** in the provided plan set for interior 2X6 wall locations.

Split & Adjust Walls

In the following steps you will use the Split Element tool to split a couple of walls into multiple segments.

6. Select the plumbing wall at the laundry room, use the flip arrow if necessary to orient the wall as illustrated, then set the wall's *Location Line* to **Core Face: Interior**.

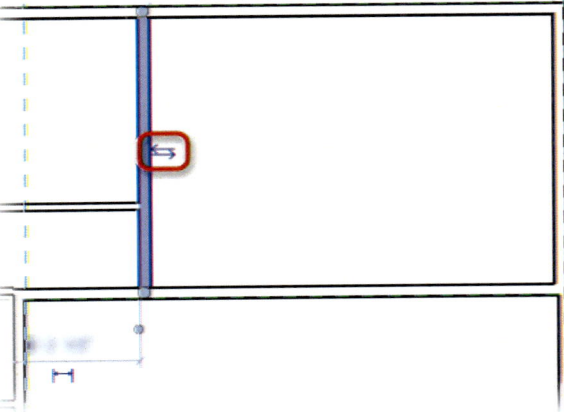

CHAPTER 3: INTERIOR WALLS REFINEMENT / ADDING DOORS & WINDOWS

	Split Element	SL
Tab	Panel	Tool Button
Modify	Modify	Split Element
Delete Inner Segment: ☐		

7. **Split** the wall at the location illustrated below, then **exit** the Split Element tool.

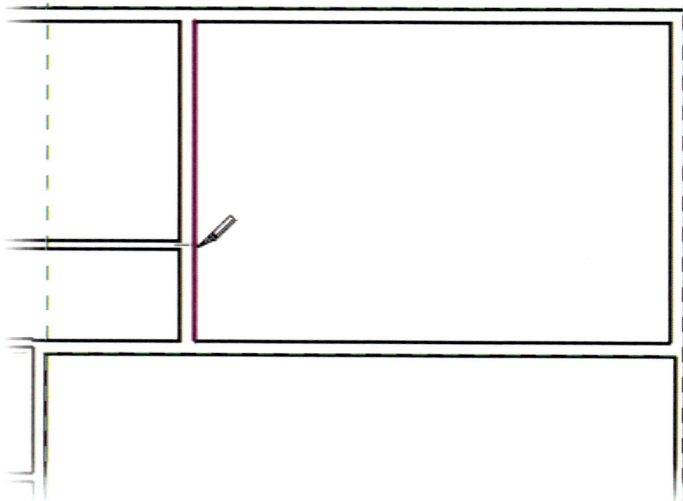

Split Plumbing Wall

8. **Align** and **Lock** the *exterior* side of the two walls illustrated below using **Wall faces** as the *Prefer* setting in the Options bar.

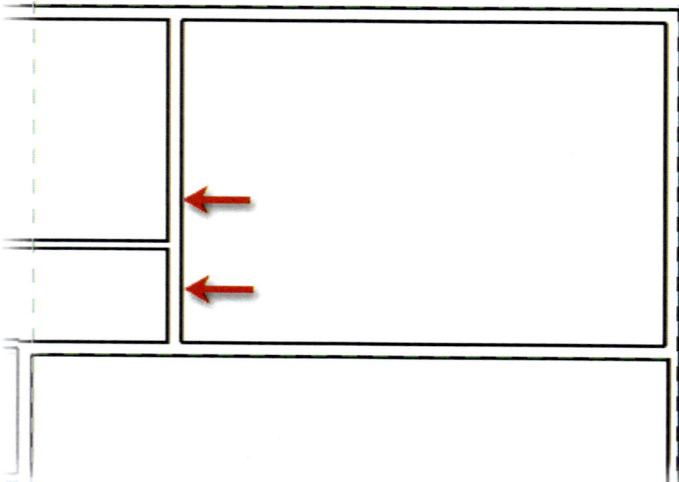

Align/Lock Wall Faces

9. Select the short wall at the end of the hallway as shown in the following illustration, change it to **Generic - 3 1/2"**, and set its location line to **Finish face: Exterior**.

EXERCISE 3.1: REFINING THE INTERIOR WALLS LOCATIONS

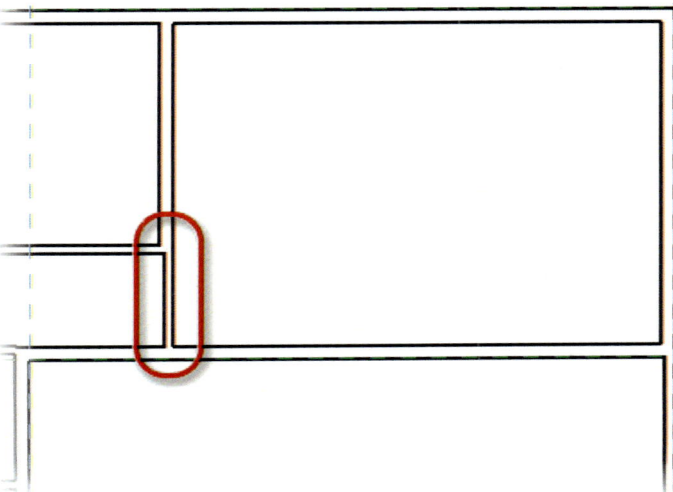

Change Wall Type to Generic - 3 1/2"

Split Element		SL
Tab	Panel	Tool Button
Modify	**Modify**	**Split Element**
Delete Inner Segment: ☑		

10. Split the long bearing wall at the end of the entry hallway at the two points illustrated below.

    The section of wall between the two split points should be removed automatically. If not, undo both splits and repeat this step after verifying the correct settings in the Options Bar. Alternatively, you can select the section of wall to be removed and delete it.

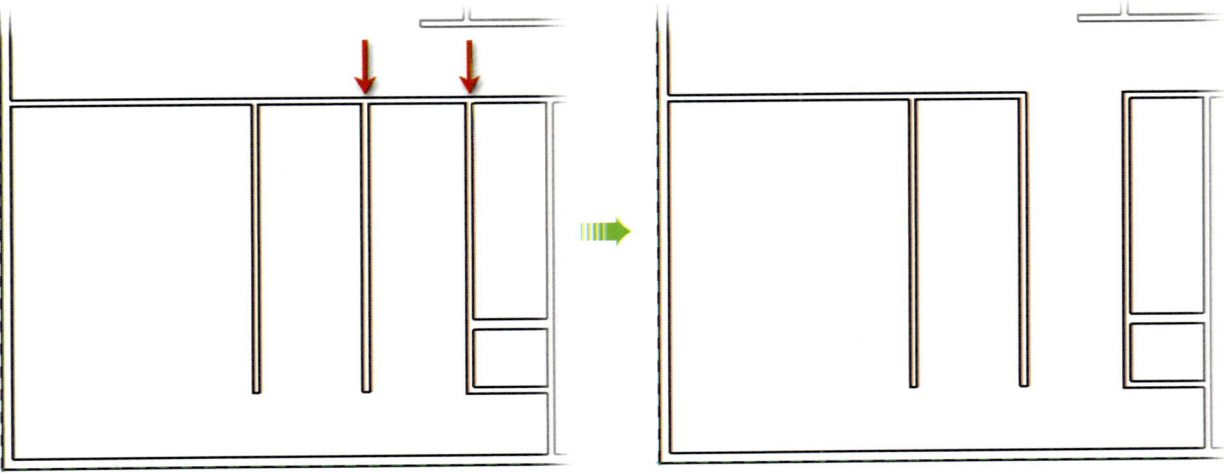

Split Locations   *After Split / Delete Inner Segment*

11. **Align** and **Lock** the interior side of the two wall segments illustrated below using **Wall faces** as the *Prefer* setting in the Options bar.

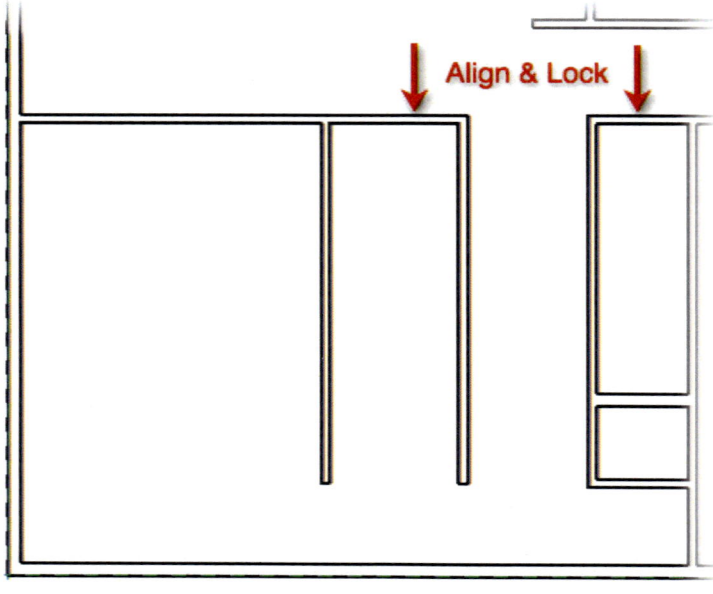

Align Wall Faces

12. Select the wall that will bound the west side of the main stairway, and drag its south end until it joins with the exterior wall as illustrated below.

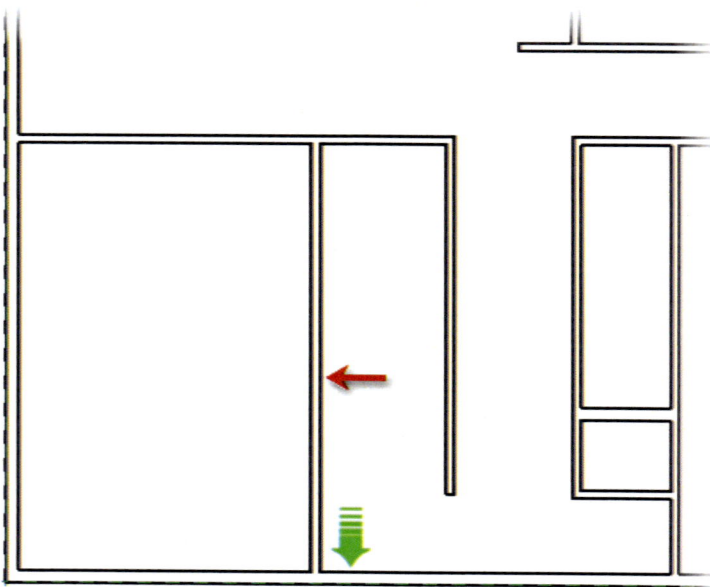

Extend Stairway Wall

Potential Broken Relationship

At this point you might have discovered a broken relationship between the interior wall and the corner of garage by the pantry. It can be identified by the 1/2" offset between walls as shown in the following illustration.

EXERCISE 3.1: REFINING THE INTERIOR WALLS LOCATIONS

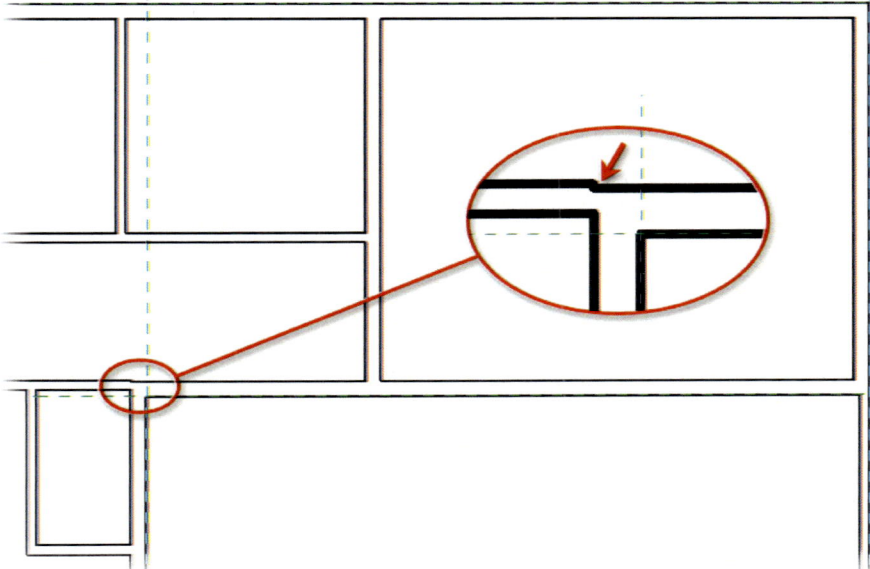

If this is the case in your model, **Align** and **Lock** the 3 1/2" wall *to* the 5 1/2" wall using **Wall faces** as the *Prefer* setting in the Options bar.

Position Interior Walls Using Temporary Dimensions

13. Following the procedure outlined below, refine the positions of the 1st floor interior walls per sheet *A101 - 1st Floor Dimension Plan* in the provided plan set. Dimensions shown in the plans are to *Faces of core* (face of framing).

    a. Select the wall you wish to move.

    b. Adjust the witness line locations of temporary dimensions as required.

    c. Select the appropriate temporary dimension value and enter the correct value.

    d. Repeat as required until all walls are in their proper location.

 Do not split any additional walls to form openings shown in the provided plans. Use the plans strictly for obtaining the correct positioning of the interior walls in your model. Openings will be added in a later exercise.

 You can toggle the location of a witness line for a temporary dimension by clicking on the associated drag handle. You can also click and drag a drag handle to move the witness line to another location, or to a completely different element. Revit remembers the adjusted witness line locations the next time you select an element in the view where the witness line was adjusted.

CHAPTER 3: INTERIOR WALLS REFINEMENT / ADDING DOORS & WINDOWS

Refine Wall Locations and Properties - 2nd Floor

Set Location Line for 2nd Floor Stair Walls

As with the 1st floor stair walls, the corresponding walls on the 2nd floor need to have their location lines and orientation set up correctly. Additionally, you will create a relationship between the 1st and 2nd floor stair walls using alignment constraints.

1. Open the floor plan view *F.F.L. 2nd FLR*.
2. In the Properties palette, set the *Underlay* view property to **F.F.L. 1st FLR**.

 Steps 3 - 5 below are to be carried out in the same manner as previously done on the 1st floor stair walls. Refer back to those instructions and illustrations as required.

3. Select the two walls that enclose the main stairway.
4. Using the Properties Palette, set the *Location Line* to **Core Face: Interior**.
5. Orient the exterior side of each wall so it faces out from the stairway area.
6. **Align** and **Lock** the interior side of each 2nd floor stairway wall *to* its respective wall on the first floor as shown in the illustration below. Be sure to set **Faces of core** as the *Prefer* setting in the Options bar.

 If the 1st and 2nd floor stair walls are overlapping prior to alignment, move the overlapping 2nd floor wall enough to fully expose the 1st floor wall. This will make wall selection during alignment easier.

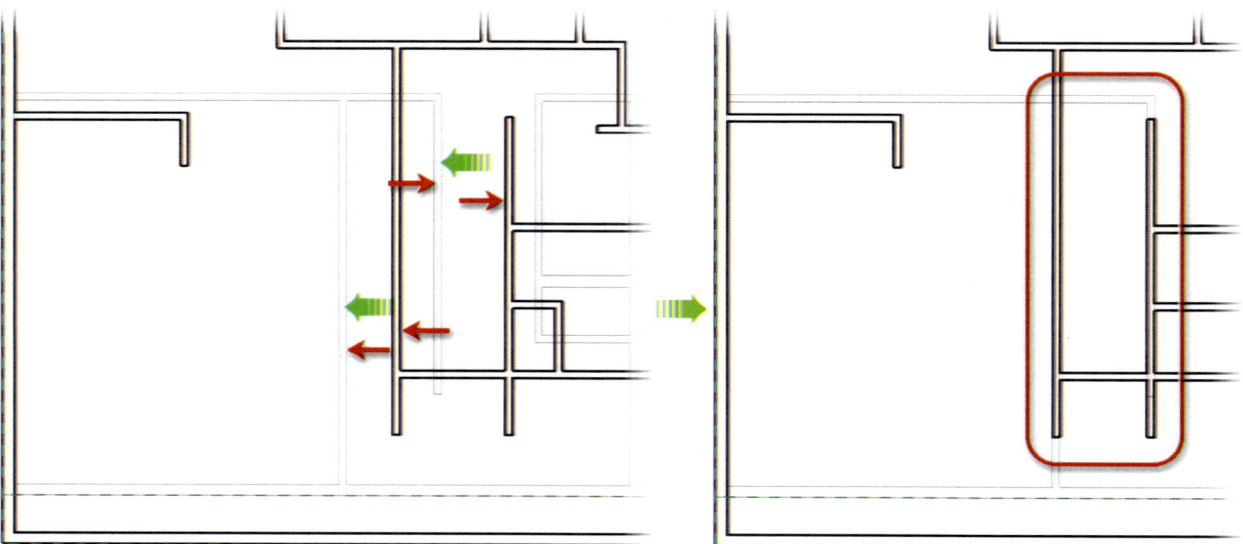

7. When done, the 1st floor stair walls should be directly below the 2nd floor stair walls.
8. Return the *Underlay* view property to **None**.

EXERCISE 3.1: REFINING THE INTERIOR WALLS LOCATIONS

Split & Adjust Plumbing Wall in Master Bathroom

In the following steps you will split a wall and then convert one of the segments to a 5 ½" wall, similar to what you did previously on the 1st floor laundry room wall.
Refer to sheet *A202 - 2nd Floor Note Plan* in the provided plan set for 2X6 wall locations.

9. Select the wall illustrated below, and change its orientation using the flip arrow if necessary.

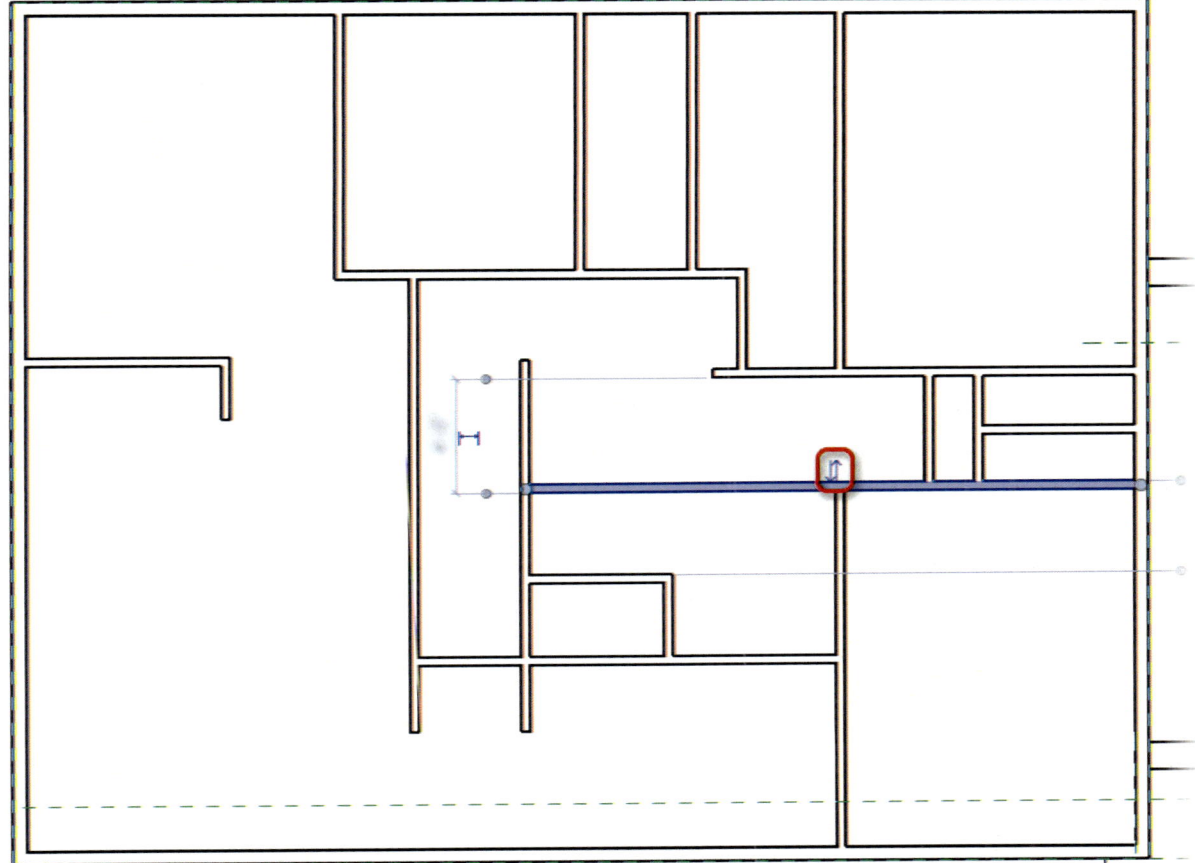

Wall Orientation

	Split Element	SL
Tab	Panel	Tool Button
Modify	**Modify**	**Split Element**
Delete Inner Segment: ☐		

95

10. Split the wall where indicated in the illustration below.

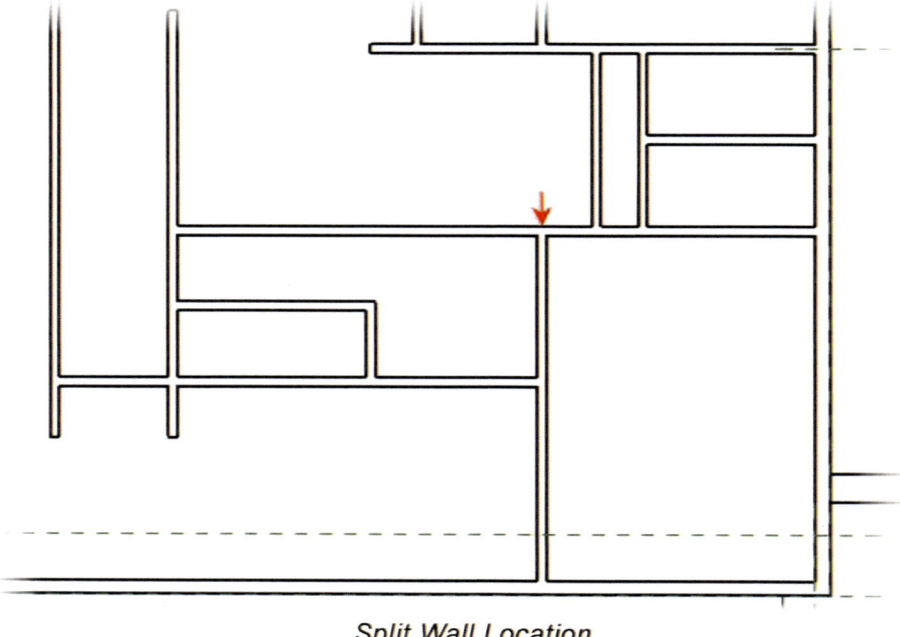

Split Wall Location

11. Select the plumbing wall at the master bathroom, and set its *Location Line* to **Core Face: Interior**.

12. Select the adjacent bedroom wall segment (resulting from the split operation), and set its *Location Line* to **Finish Face: Exterior**

13. **Align/Lock** the faces of the previously split wall segments using **Wall faces** as the *Prefer* setting in the Options bar.

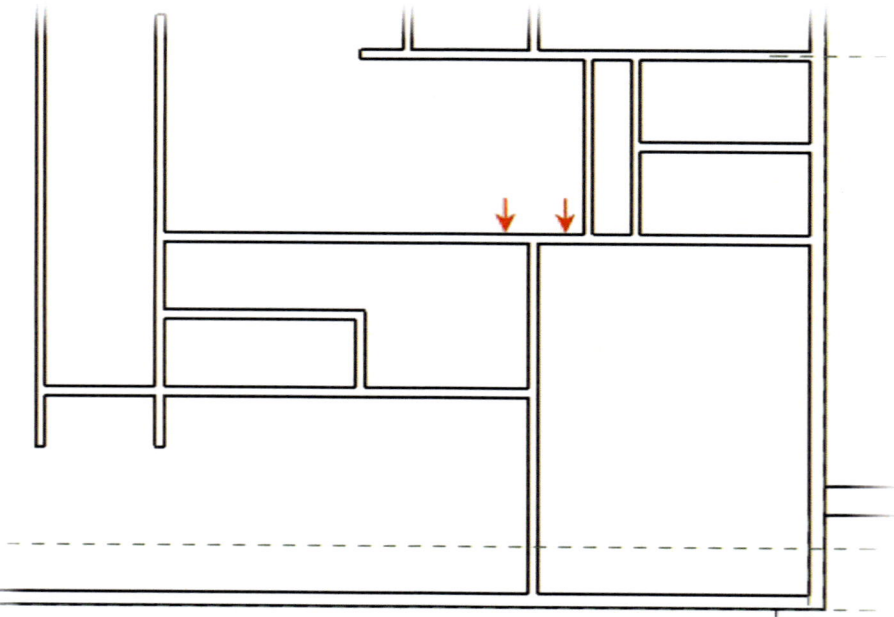

Align/Lock Bathroom/Bedroom Walls

14. Select the master bathroom plumbing wall and change it's type to **Generic - 5 1/2"**. The edge of the wall facing into the bathroom should remain fixed, and the wall should widen in and upward direction with the adjacent bedroom wall following it as illustrated below.

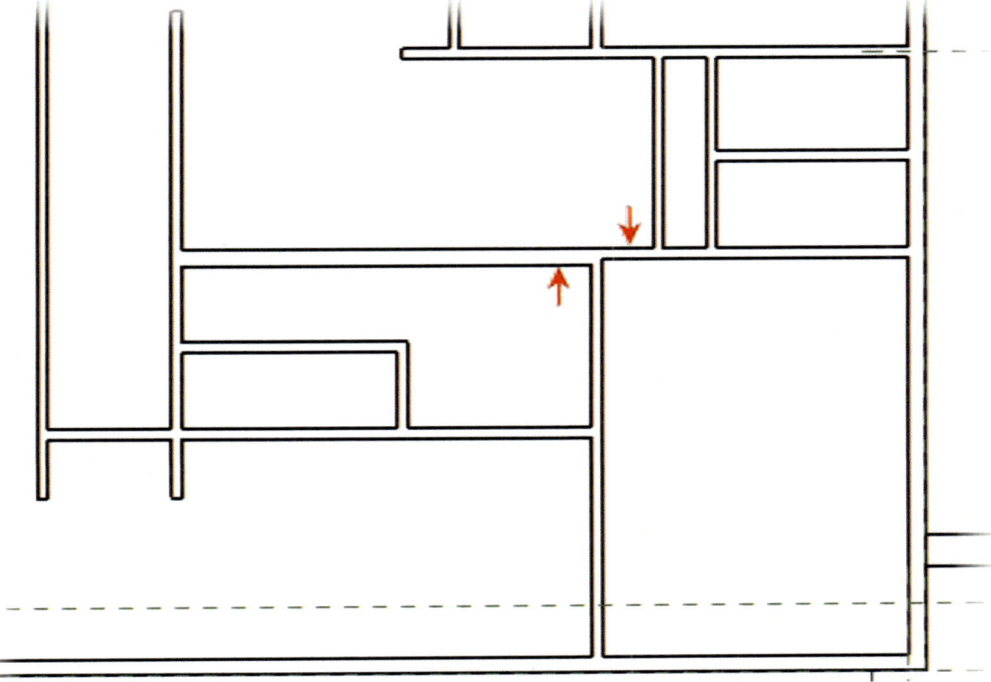

Bathroom Wall Updated to Generic - 5 1/2"

15. Using the same procedure as on the 1st floor, refine the positions of the 2nd floor interior walls per sheet *A102 - 2nd Floor Dimension Plan* in the provided plan set.

 As with the 1st floor, do not split any additional walls to form the openings shown in the provided plans. Use the plans strictly for obtaining the correct positioning of the interior walls in your model. Openings will be added in a later exercise.

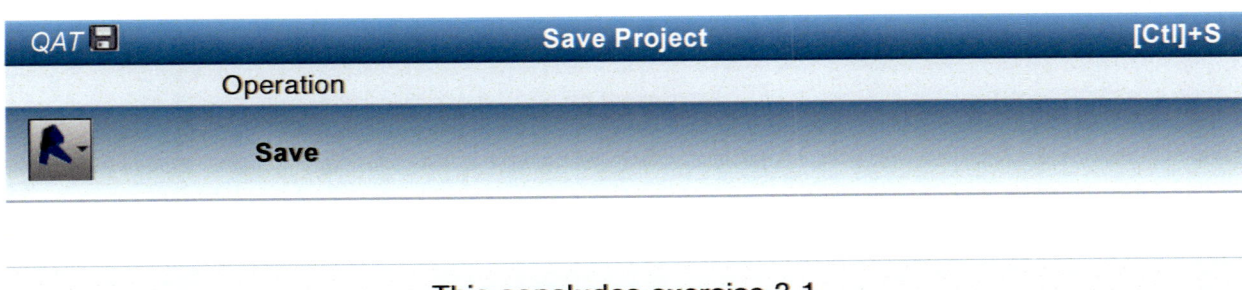

This concludes exercise 3.1

Exercise 3.2: Windows

There are are a number of ways to load families into a project. Depending on the current workflow, one may make be more productive than the other. We'll explore a couple of these methods throughout the remainder of this chapter.

There are numerous sources for loadable families (content), one of which is the stock library installed with Revit. Additionally, there are many online sources, some free, some fee-based. In these sections we'll be using Autodesk's online web library "Autodesk Seek" to download families that aren't available in the stock library.

QAT 📂	Open Project		[Ctl]+O
	Operation	Option	File Name
R	Open ▶	Project	BIMHOUSE-EX03-1.rvt

	Save As (Project)		
	Operation	Option	File Name
R	Save As ▶	Project	BIMHOUSE-EX03-2.rvt

Load Window Families

The default template used at the beginning of Chapter 1 doesn't contain any of the window families required for this project. Therefore, they'll need to be loaded into the project. Once loaded, you'll find that not all of the required sizes are included, which means you'll need to create a few extra types to satisfy the model requirements.

	Load Family		
Tab	Panel		Tool Button
Insert	Load from Library		Load Family

1. Load the window families listed in the table on the following page.

 After navigating to the ...*Imperial Library\Windows* folder, use **[ctrl]+click** to create a selection set and then click **Open** to load all three families at once (see illustration).

EXERCISE 3.2: WINDOWS

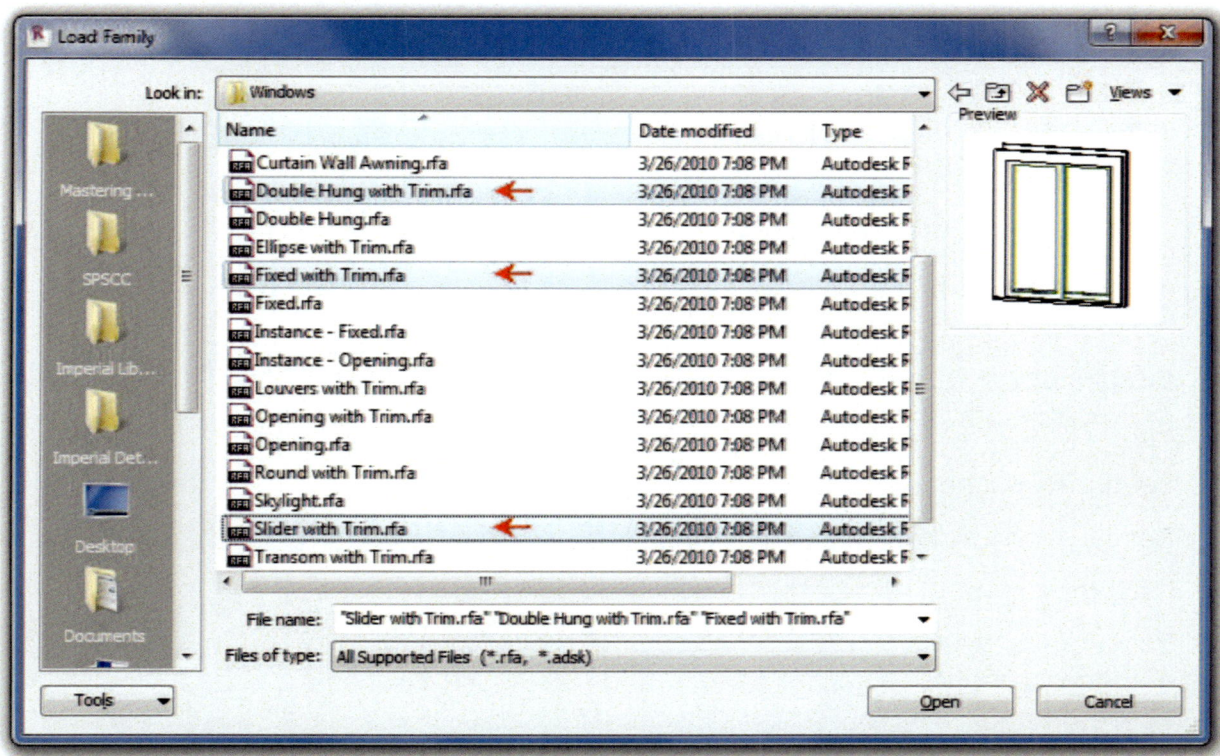

Window Families to Load

Family	File Location
Double Hung with Trim.rfa	...Imperial Library\Windows\
Fixed with Trim.rfa	...Imperial Library\Windows\
Slider with Trim.rfa	...Imperial Library\Windows\

2. Expand the *Families* tree in the Project Browser to reveal the newly loaded window families. By expanding a window family branch, we can see the available default sizes.

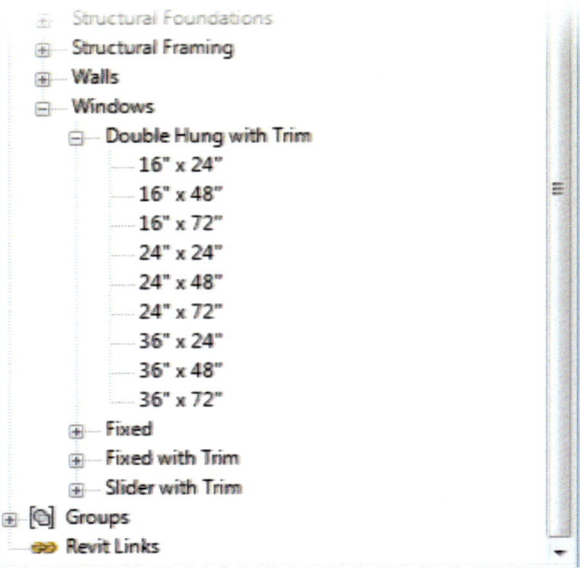

Create New Window Types

Since not all of the required window sizes (types) are available, we'll need to create them.

1. In the project browser, expand the window family branch named *Slider with Trim*.

2. Double-click on *36" x 24"* (or any other type within the family).

3. In the Type Properties dialog box, click **Duplicate…**

4. Enter **72" x 60"**, then click **OK**.

5. Set the *Height* parameter to **5' 0"**.

6. Set the *Width* parameter to **6' 0"**.

7. Click **Duplicate…**

8. Repeat the previous steps to create all of the types listed in the table below. Make sure to substitute the correct type names and parameters according to the type you are creating.

9. Click **OK** after creating the final window in each family.

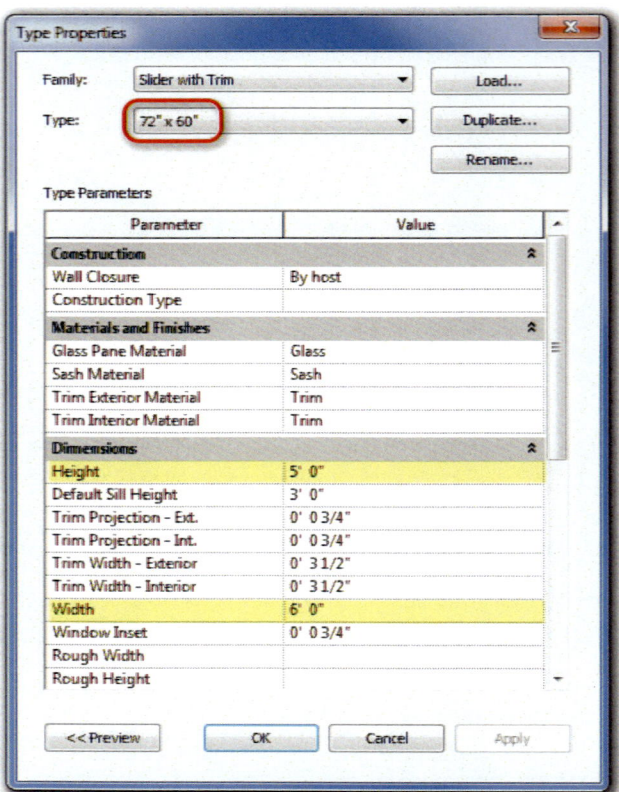

 Failure to click OK after creating the last type within the current family will result in the parameter edits being lost. The new window type will be retained, but the parameter values will be reset back to the values of the duplicated type.

 When creating a new family *Type*, it's often most efficient to duplicate a *Type* that shares the most similarities (parameter values) with the new type. This will minimize the number of parameter edits required in the new type.

New Window Types

Family	Type Name	Width	Height
Slider with Trim	72" x 60"	6' 0"	5' 0"
Slider with Trim	72" x 48"	6' 0"	4' 0"
Slider with Trim	54" x 48"	4' 6"	4' 0"
Slider with Trim	60" x 42"	5' 0"	3' 6"
Double Hung with Trim	24" x 60"	2' 0"	5' 0"
Fixed with Trim	18" x 60"	1' 6"	5' 0"

Place Windows on 1st Floor

1. Open the floor plan view *F.F.L. 1st FLR*.

Window		WN
Tab	Panel	Tool Button
Architecture	Build	Window

Modify	Place Window	
Mode	Tag
-	Tag on Placement (*Selected*)
(Varies)*	Leader: ☐

 The default setting for tagging on placement is *disabled*. Therefore, if you wish to have elements tagged as they are placed, you need to enable this setting prior to placement.

 If you place the window in the incorrect orientation, you can click on the flip arrow to reorient it immediately after placing it, without exiting the Window tool. However, you will need to manually relocate the tag(s) after exiting the Window tool.

2. * Set the tag orientation in the Options Bar to **Vertical** when placing east and west facing windows, and **Horizontal** for north and south facing windows.

3. Place all the windows as shown on sheet *A201 - 1st Floor Note Plan* of the provided plan set. Don't worry about exact location while placing the windows. Just focus on correct orientation.

4. **Exit** the Window tool when done.

 The Type number or "Type Mark" that shows in your window tags may differ from the provided plan set. Type mark values are assigned automatically by Revit. The order in which you created the new types will affect the numbering sequence, so if they don't match, don't worry about it. What's important is that each type has a unique number.

CHAPTER 3: INTERIOR WALLS REFINEMENT / ADDING DOORS & WINDOWS

5. Double check all of the window tags as follows:

   a) If the horizontal/vertical orientation is incorrect, select the tag and then in the Options Bar change the tag orientation control to either **Horizontal** of **Vertical** as required. Alternatively, you can press **[space]** with the tag selected to reorient it.

   b) If the tag is on the interior side of the building, it's possible that the window is installed with its exterior side facing inward. Select the window and, if the flip arrow is on the interior side of the building envelope, click on the **flip arrow** to reorient it. Either way, drag the window tag to the exterior side of the building so that it aligns to the other tags (use remote snapping to verify alignment).

Position the Windows

6. Position all of the windows using temporary dimensions as shown on sheet *A101 - 1st Floor Dimension Plan* of the provided plan set.

 Window families have multiple references built-in. Therefore, when selected you will see several temporary dimensions displayed, often stacked on top of each other. The trick is to toggle the witness lines of multiple temporary dimensions until they're overlaid on one another to look like a single dimension. Doing this prior to attempting to edit a dimension will make selecting the dimension easier, and ensure that you don't pick the wrong one.

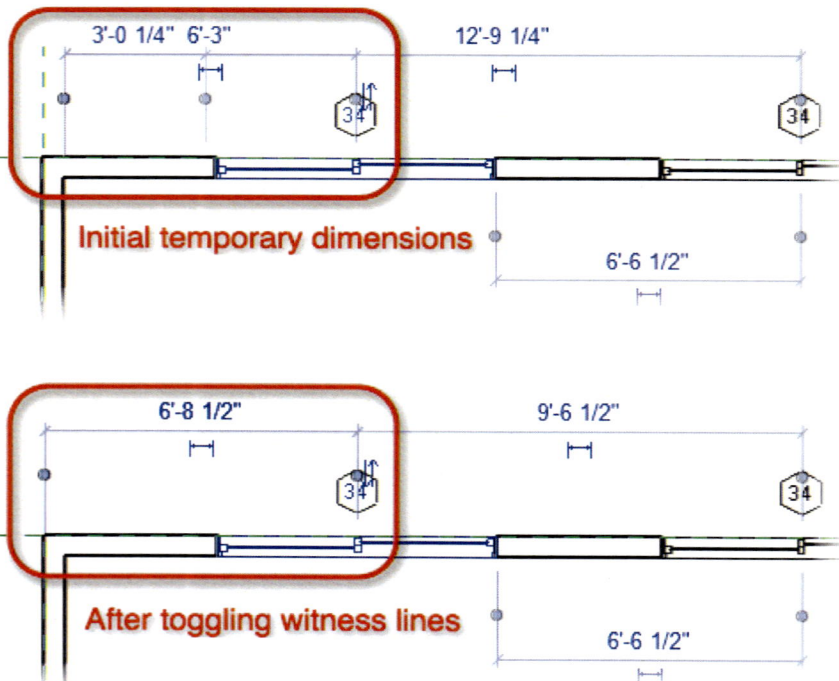

Place Windows on 2nd Floor

1. Open the floor plan view *F.F.L. 2nd FLR*.

2. Using the same procedure as on the 1st floor, place the 2nd floor windows shown on sheet *A202 - 2nd Floor Note Plan* of the provided plan set. Note that there is one required window type not yet created. We'll create this window "on the fly" while the Window tool is active.

   a) In the Properties Palette, click **Edit Type**

   b) From the *Family* drop-down list, select the family **Slider with Trim** as illustrated.

   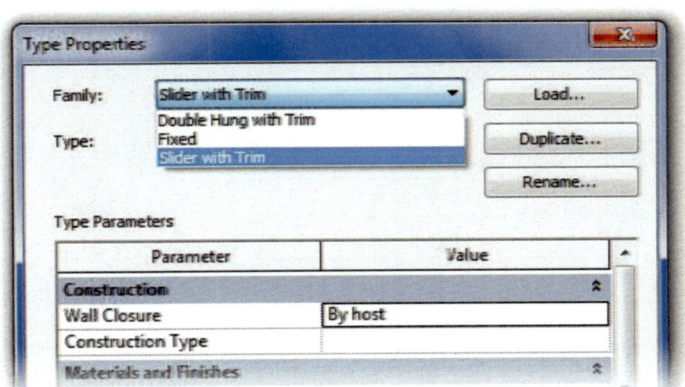

   c) From the *Type* drop-down list, select the type **48" x 24"**.

   d) Click **Duplicate...**

   e) Enter **48" x 12"** for the new name and click **OK**.

   f) Change the *Height* parameter to **1' 0"**, then click **OK**.

   g) Verify the new window *48" x 12"* is currently selected in the Properties Palette Type Selector, then place the window roughly per plan.

 The 48" x 12" window might not be visible after placing it. If this is the case in your model, the only indication that a window has been placed is the presence of the associated window tag. DO NOT continue to click expecting a window to appear!

Chapter 3: Interior Walls Refinement / Adding Doors & Windows

3. Place the remaining windows.
4. **Exit** the Window tool when done.
5. Verify window tag orientation and location as you did on the 1st floor.

Position the Windows

6. Position all of the windows using temporary dimensions as shown on sheet *A102 - 2nd Floor Dimension Plan* of the provided plan set.

 To select the hidden 48" x 12" window if it isn't visible, draw a window selection box around its location.

Adjust Window Header Heights

When placing windows in Revit, the window's elevation is based on the sill height property, which is unconventional and will therefore need to be corrected. Opening one of the exterior elevations, or the *{3D}* view will reveal windows of varied heights, but all with a consistent sill height. In the following steps we will correct this to consistent head heights.

1. Open the default *{3D}* view, then draw a selection box around the entire model.

2. In the Filter dialog box, do the following…
    a) Click **Check None**.
    b) Check the **Windows** checkbox in the *Category* pane.
    c) Click **OK**.

Your selection set should now include all windows in the model. Orbit the view to verify this, taking care not to click in empty space, which would clear your selection set.

3. In the Properties Palette, enter **7' 0"** for the *Head Height* property.
4. Click **Apply**, or shift focus to the drawing area. Your model should appear as illustrated below, with all windows sharing a common head height above their respective finish floor levels.

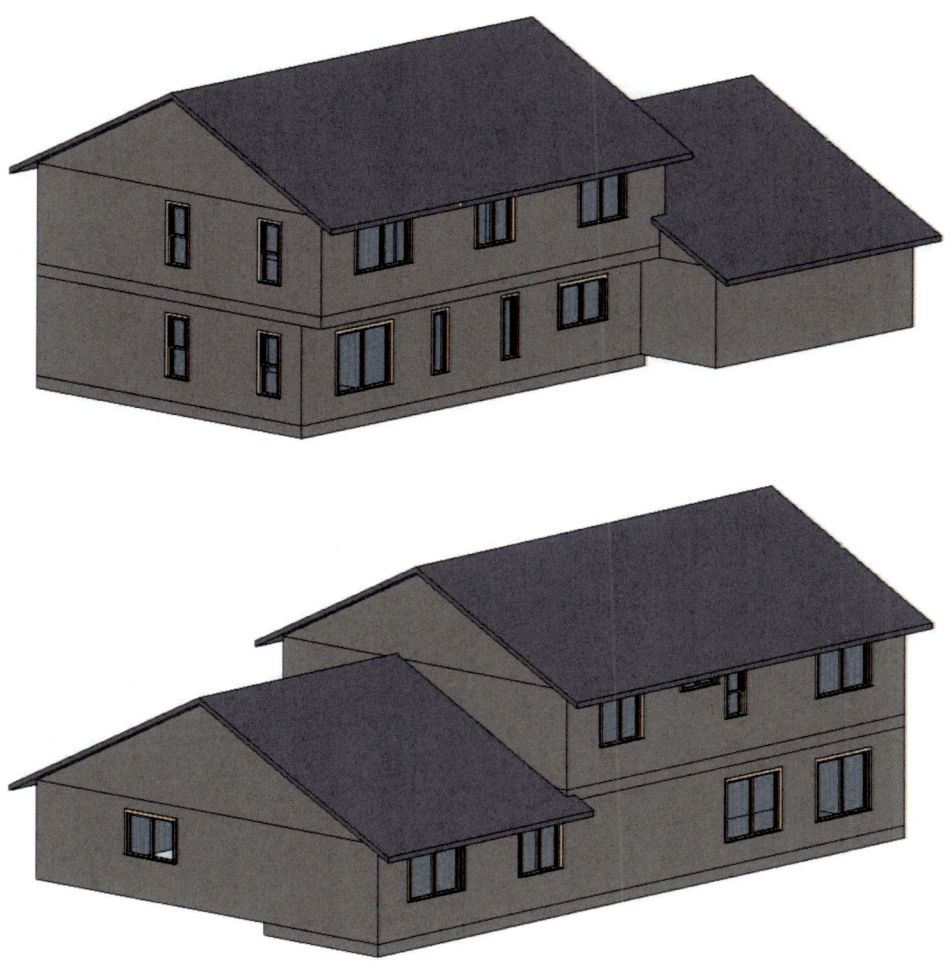

All Window Head Heights Consistent

 Since all windows in the project at this point share the same head height relative to their associated level, we were able to change them all at once. If the head height was different between floors, we would have had to do this one floor at a time from within each plan view.

Reset Visibility for Invisible Window

1. Open the floor plan view *F.F.L. 2nd FLR*.

 When the 48" x 12" window was originally placed, it may or may not have been visible depending on the sill height setting at the time it was placed. Regardless, setting its head height to 7' 0" caused this window to be hidden in plan view. This is due to the window geometry not intersecting the cut plane specified by the view range. This condition can be corrected with a Plan Region, which acts as an override to the default view range settings for the view in which it is placed.

2. Create a *Plan Region*...

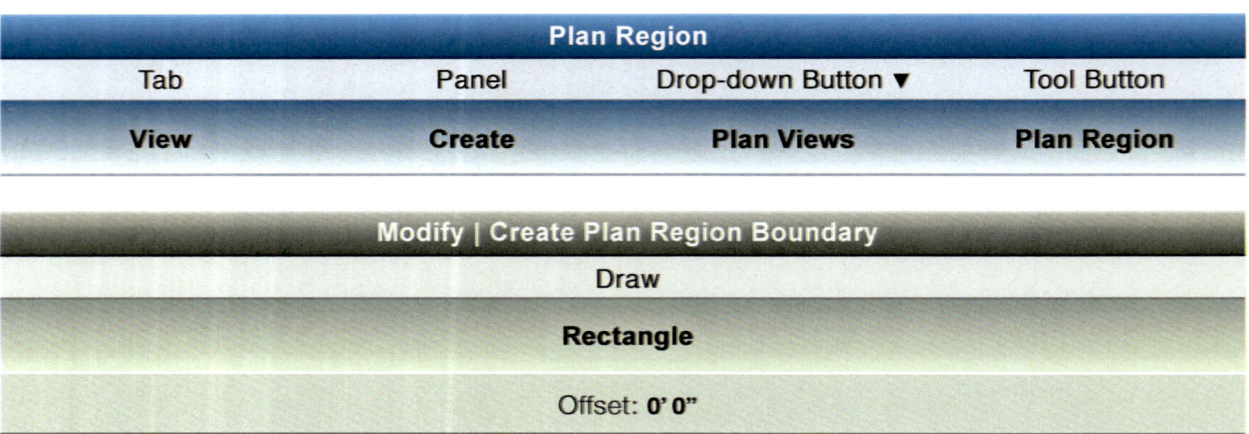

3. Draw a rectangle around the area of the hidden window as illustrated below. Don't worry about getting it exact. It can be adjusted later if necessary.

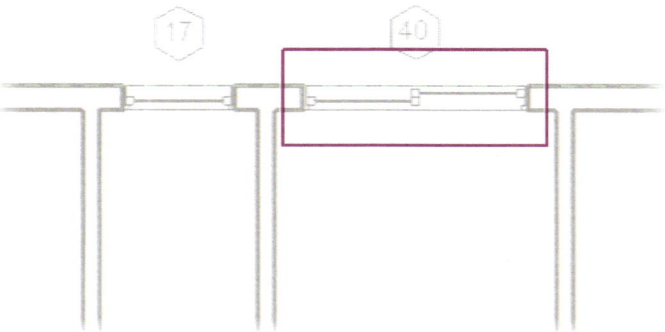

Plan Region – Sketched Boundary

4. Click **Edit...** next to *View Range* in the Properties Palette.

5. Set the *Cut plane* property to **6' 6"** as illustrated below.

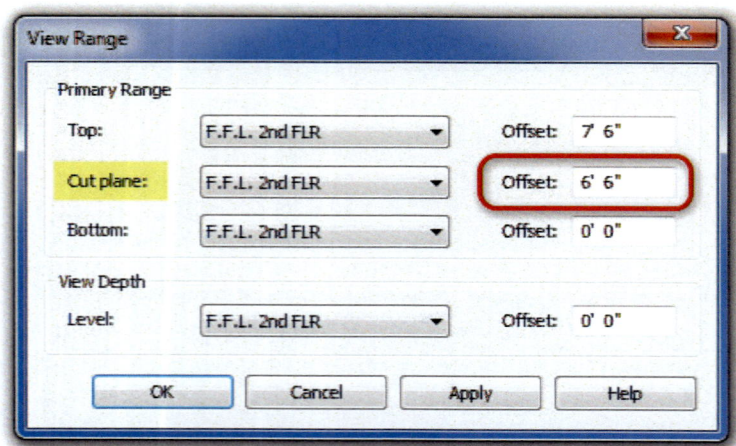

Plan Region Properties

6. Click **OK** to close the View Range dialog box.

7. Click the **Finish Edit Mode** button. ✓

   The area where the plan region was placed should appear as illustrated below.

   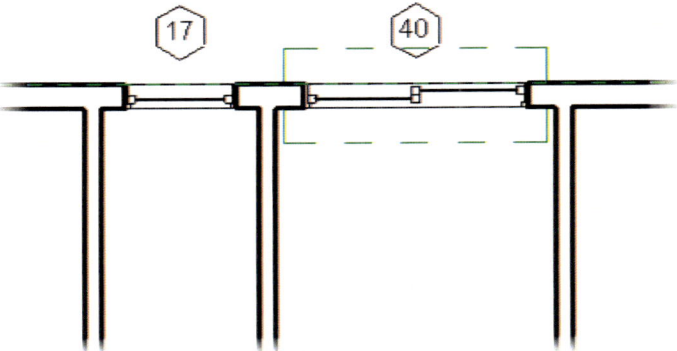

   Plan Region – Completed Boundary

 If the complete window is not visible, your plan region may not be large enough. To correct this, select the plan region, then resize it by clicking and dragging on the shape handles (arrowheads) as required.

 This is a good time to make sure the north exterior wall is correctly located to the imported CAD geometry. The plan region will not follow the wall if the wall needs to be moved.

Duplicate the Plan Region in Other 2nd Floor Views

8. Click on the plan region to select it. The Modify | Plan Region contextual ribbon tab should appear.

9. Copy the plan region to the clipboard...

			Modify | ***	[Ctrl]C
Tab		Panel		Tool Button
Modify		**Clipboard**		**Copy to Clipboard**

10. Next you will past the plan region to all of the appropriate 2nd floor plan views...

	Modify | ***		
Tab	Panel	Split Button ▼	Tool Button
Modify	**Clipboard**	**Paste**	**Aligned to Selected Views**

11. In the Select Views dialog box, select the following views. Hold down the **[Ctrl]** key when clicking to select multiple views.

    a) *Floor Plan: 2nd Floor - Dimension*
    b) *Floor Plan: 2nd Floor - Constraints*
    c) *Floor Plan: 2nd Floor - Working Notes*

12. Click **OK** to complete the paste operation.

13. Open each of the views selected in step 11 to verify the presence of the plan region.

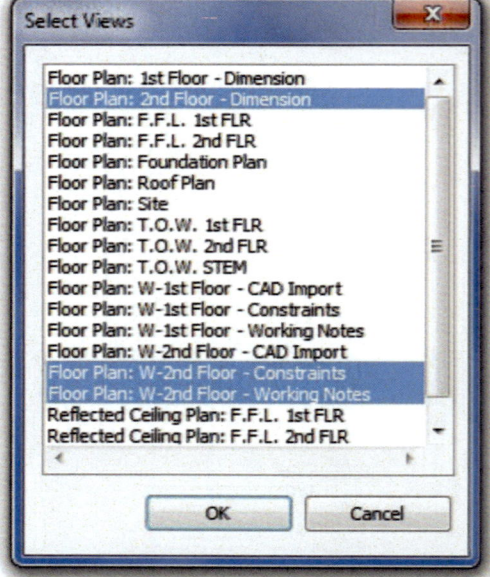

 Note that we omitted a few 2nd floor views from the paste operation. If you're curious, open each of these omitted views and see if you can determine why the plan region wasn't pasted into that view.

This concludes exercise 3.2

Exercise 3.3: Doors

QAT 📂	Open Project		[Ctl]+O
	Operation	Option	File Name
R	Open ▶	Project	BIMHOUSE-EX03-2.rvt

	Save As (Project)		
	Operation	Option	File Name
R	Save As ▶	Project	BIMHOUSE-EX03-3.rvt

The procedure for adding doors is very similar to that for adding windows. The major differences are:

- Doors are *typically* placed at 0'-0" relative to the associated level (view in which you are working). However, there can be exceptions to this.
- Door families *should* have a flip arrow that controls the door's hinge side, whereas this isn't necessary on some window configurations.

Load Door Families

The door family loaded with the default project template is a single-hinged flush door. We won't be using this door, so we'll need to load an alternative, as well as some additional door families that are required for the project.

Load Family		
Tab	Panel	Tool Button
Insert	Load from Library	Load Family

1. Load the door families listed in the table below.

Load Door Families

Family	File Location
Bifold-2 Panel.rfa	...Imperial Library\Doors\
Bifold-4 Panel.rfa	...Imperial Library\Doors\
Overhead-Sectional.rfa	...Imperial Library\Doors\
Single-Panel 2.rfa	...Imperial Library\Doors\
Sliding-2 panel.rfa	...Imperial Library\Doors\

CHAPTER 3: INTERIOR WALLS REFINEMENT / ADDING DOORS & WINDOWS

Place Doors on 1st Floor

In the following steps, you'll place doors for the families loaded so far.

1. Open the floor plan view *F.F.L. 1st FLR*.

Door		
Tab	Panel	Tool Button
Architecture	**Build**	**Door**

Modify	Place Door	
Mode	Tag
-	~~Tag on Placement~~ (*deselected*)

The Tag on Placement tool button in the Tag panel behaves as as it does when placing windows. In this case we *do not* want to tag doors on placement, as we will be placing a custom door tag in a future exercise.

2. Place all the doors as shown on sheet *A201 - 1st Floor Note Plan* of the provided plan set, *except for the pocket door in the powder room* (we don't have a pocket door family loaded yet). Again, don't worry about exact location while placing the doors; just focus on correct orientation.

    For door types (sizes) not available in the default family, duplicate an existing type, rename it, and adjust the dimensions in the Type Properties dialog box as required. This procedure is identical to that used for creating new window types in the previous exercise. Consider doing this on-the-fly on an as-needed basis.

Don't forget about using **[space]** to change the orientation of an instance before placing it, as well as the orientation arrows available immediately after placing it! Additionally, note how Revit will snap an element to be centered between two surrounding elements, such as two walls of a hallway, even if the resulting dimensions are finer than the current snap increment.

3. **Exit** the door tool when done.

Download a Door Family from the Web Library

Next we'll need to load a pocket door family that is not provided with the default installation of Revit. Therefore, we'll need to access Autodesk's web library and download a suitable family.

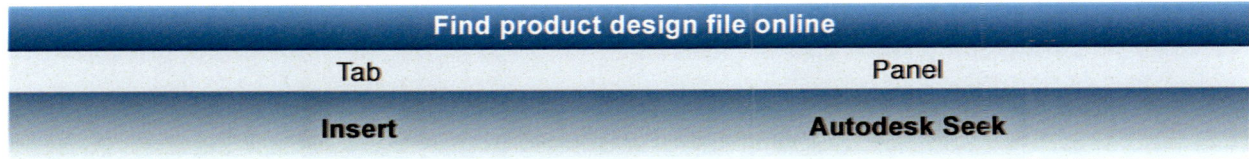

Find product design file online	
Tab	Panel
Insert	Autodesk Seek

1. In the *Search Autodesk Seek* field, type **pocket door**.

2. Click on the search (binocular) icon, or press **[Enter]**. This should open a web browser window to the Autodesk Seek website, with the targeted search results visible.

3. Click on **Single-Pocket** This should open a window revealing a couple of download options.

 You might need to filter the content to reduce the number of available options and make it easier to find the correct family. In this case, select **Revit Architecture (2)** under *Product Libraries*.

4. Check the box next to **Revit 2010 Imperial File**.

5. Set the download location drop-down list to **Save Selected to Local**, then click on **Download**.

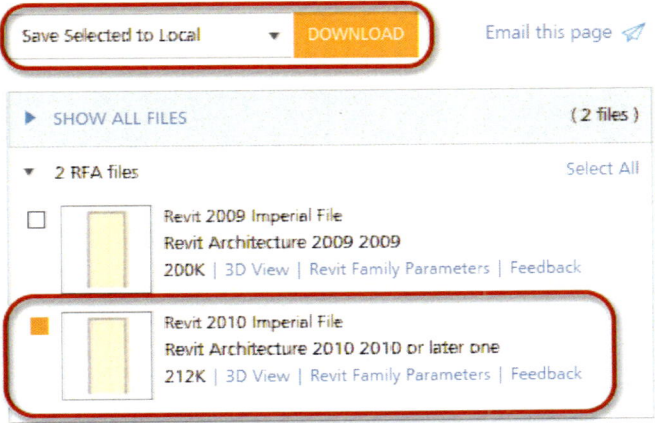

6. Sign into your Autodesk seek account, or create one. You might have to click on Download again after signing in.

7. Depending on the browser you're using, the language and/or controls for downloading the file may vary. If given any sort of option to *save as*, use this and save the file to a custom content folder on your hard drive. If you used save, and not save as, you'll want to move this file from the default download folder to your custom content folder.

> **DO NOT** save this family in the *Imperial Library* folder created as part of the default Revit installation. Additionally, do not change the name or open it.

8. Close the browser window when done.

Load and Place the Downloaded Family

	Load Family	
Tab	Panel	Tool Button
Insert	Load from Library	Load Family

1. Navigate to the folder where you downloaded the pocket door family, and load it into your project.

2. Next place an instance of the pocket door at the powder room per plan (you will need to create a new type).

	Door	
Tab	Panel	Tool Button
Architecture	Build	Door

Modify	Place Door	
Mode	Tag
-	Tag on Placement

3. **Exit** the Door tool when done.

4. Position all of the 1st floor doors using temporary dimensions as shown on sheet *A101 - 1st Floor Dimension Plan* of the provided plan set.

Place Doors on 2nd Floor

1. Open the floor plan view *F.F.L. 2nd FLR*

2. Using the same procedure as we used for placing doors on the 1st floor, place the doors on the 2nd floor per sheet *A201* and *A202* of the provided plan set. Create new types as required to satisfy size requirements.

3. **Exit** the Door tool when done.

4. Position all of the 2nd floor doors using temporary dimensions as shown on sheet *A102 - 2nd Floor Dimension Plan* of the provided plan set.

Exercise 3.4: Cased Openings

QAT 📂	Open Project		[Ctl]+O
	Operation	Option	File Name
R	Open ▶	Project	BIMHOUSE-EX03-3.rvt

	Save As (Project)		
	Operation	Option	File Name
R	Save As ▶	Project	BIMHOUSE-EX03-4.rvt

Load Opening Family

There are number of ways to create openings in walls. The easiest is adding a component that automatically cuts the wall with specified dimensions. You've already used examples of this by placing windows and doors. The cased openings will be added using the same approach. The biggest difference is that windows and doors each have their own category and dedicated tool, whereas opening families are assigned to the *Generic* category and are accessed for placement using the *Component* tool. The added benefits of creating openings using families are built-in view-based graphic representations such as overhead lines, additional geometry such as trim, and predefined sizes (family types).

Revit also provides a Wall Opening tool. This tool allows you to create free-form, one-off openings in walls. However, this tool doesn't come with any of the added benefits of using families, and is therefore best reserved for special circumstances.

Load Family		
Tab	Panel	Tool Button
Insert	Load from Library	Load Family

5. Navigate to the *Openings* folder in the Imperial Library.
6. Find, select, and load the file *Passage Opening-Cased.rfa*.
7. In the Project Browser, expand the *Generic Models* branch in the *Families* tree, then expand the *Passage Opening-Cased* family to view the available types.
8. Using any of the techniques used previously in this chapter, create any new types required for the project. Refer to the table on the following page for a list of required sizes.

CHAPTER 3: INTERIOR WALLS REFINEMENT / ADDING DOORS & WINDOWS

Required Opening Types

Family	Type Name	Width	Height
Passage Opening-Cased	36" x 80"	3' 0"	6' 8"
Passage Opening-Cased	72" x 80"	6' 0"	6' 8"
Passage Opening-Cased	114" x 80"	9' 6"	6' 8"

Place All Openings

1. Open the floor plan view *F.F.L. 1st FLR*.

	Place Component		CM
Tab	Panel	Split Button ▼	Tool Button
Architecture	**Build**	**Component**	**Place a Component**

2. Place the correct openings in the locations specified on sheet *A101* the provided plans.
3. Open the floor plan view *F.F.L. 2nd FLR*.
4. Place the remaining opening as specified on sheet *A202* of the provided plans
5. **Exit** the component tool.
6. Refer to sheets *A101 and A102* in the provided plan set, and position the cased openings using temporary dimensions.

QAT	Save Project	[Ctl]+S
	Operation	
	Save	

	Close (Project)	[Ctl]+[F4]
	Operation	
	Close	

This concludes exercise 3.4

Chapter Summary

In this lesson you were introduced to using temporary dimensions, loading and placing "loadable" families into a project, as well as other various tools and concepts. These tools and concepts will continue to be utilized as you move forward through developing this project.

 A good understanding of everything that has been covered so far is key to moving forward at the expected pace. If you struggled through these exercises, it is recommended that you repeat them until you feel comfortable with the concepts and the tools you are using. As we move forward, future exercises will gradually provide less explicit instructions on tools and concepts already covered.

Chapter 4

Adding Components

Overview

This chapter expands on using the Component tool introduced in the previous chapter. You will use this tool to place various types of casework, plumbing fixtures, and mechanical equipment. You will also learn about adding interior elevation views, and 3D section views to help you better visualize the model as it evolves. Furthermore, you will learn about model groups, as well as length and equality constraints as a means of controlling design intent. Throughout this chapter you will need to refer to the plans provided in the file *BIM_House-Reference-15.pdf*.

Learning Objectives

After completing this chapter you should have a basic understanding of the following tools and concepts.

- Interior elevation views and associated view markers
- Generic casework, mechanical, and specialty equipment families
- Various modify tools: Mirror, Rotate, Copy, Spacebar
- Create Similar tool
- Using Shape Handles to edit component instance properties
- Model groups

Project Objectives

When complete, you will have accomplished the following in your project:

- Create interior elevation and 3D section views
- Add cabinets and counter tops
- Place various appliances, plumbing, and mechanical fixtures
- Create model groups and apply constraints to maintain design intent

CHAPTER 4: ADDING COMPONENTS

Chapter Contents

Exercise 4.1:	**Interior Elevation Views**	119
	Add Interior Elevations: 1st Floor	119
	Add Interior Elevations: 2nd Floor	121
Exercise 4.2:	**Appliances & Casework**	123
	Add Appliances 1st Floor	123
	Create a 3D Section View	125
	Add Kitchen Cabinets & Countertops	126
	Add Vanity Cabinets & Countertops	129
Exercise 4.3:	**Plumbing & Mechanical Fixtures**	134
	Load Families	134
	Add Toilets & Tubs	135
	Add Sinks in the Kitchen and Bathrooms	136
	Constrain Sink Locations Within Counter Tops	137
	Add Laundry Sink	139
	Add Mechanical and Plumbing in the Garage	139
Exercise 4.4:	**Model Groups and Constraints**	141
	Create a Custom Dimension Type	141
	Apply Length Constraints	142
	Create Model Groups	143
	Apply Equality Constraints	145
	Associate Washer & Dryer with the Plumbing Wall	146

Exercise 4.1: Interior Elevation Views

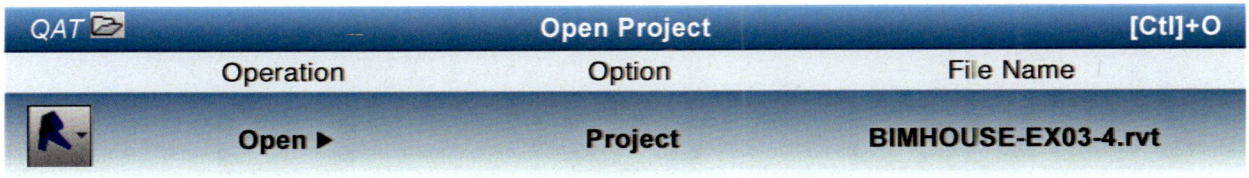

Add Interior Elevations: 1st Floor

1. Open the floor plan view *F.F.L. 1st FLR* and place an elevation view marker...

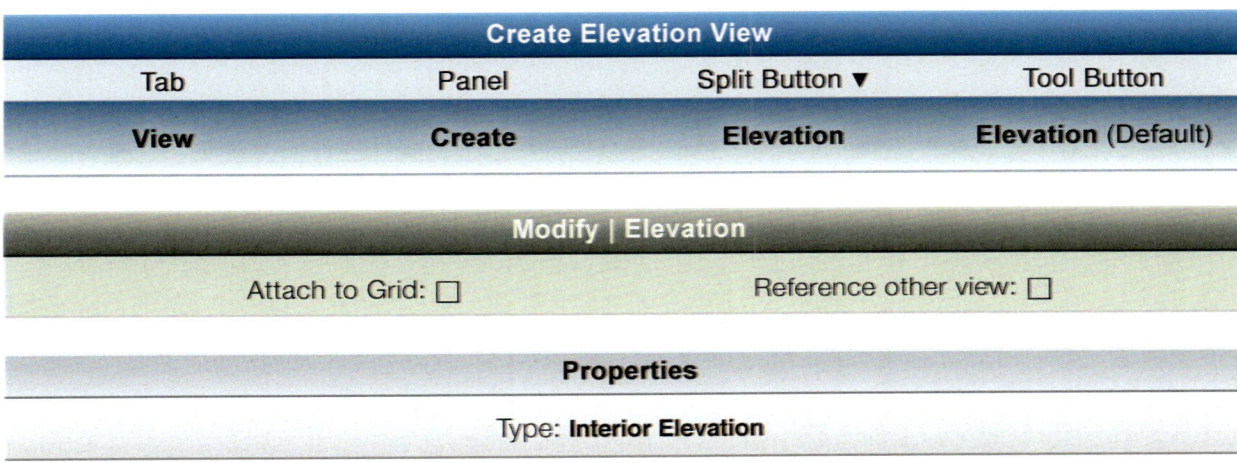

2. Place the elevation marker in the location and orientation shown in the illustration below.

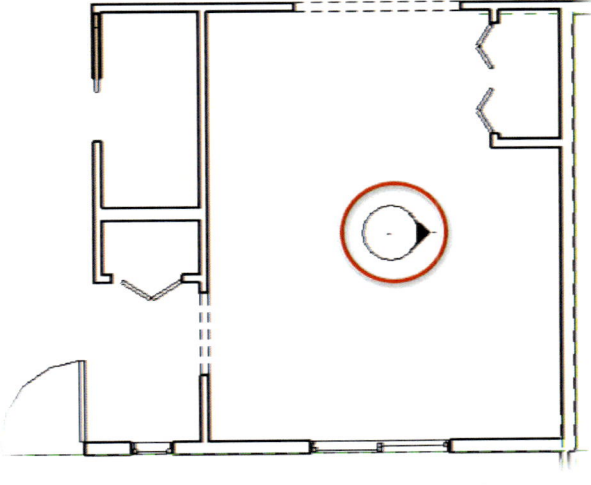

Interior Elevation Marker in Kitchen

3. **Exit** the Elevation tool after placing a single marker as shown.
4. Select the *circle* portion of the elevation marker you just placed.
5. **Click** the **checkboxes** as shown in the following illustration to create additional interior elevation views

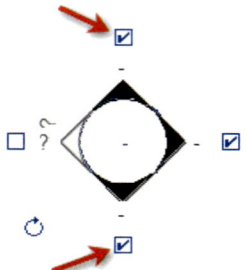

Enable Additional Elevation Views

6. Expand the project browser to see the new view category and added views.

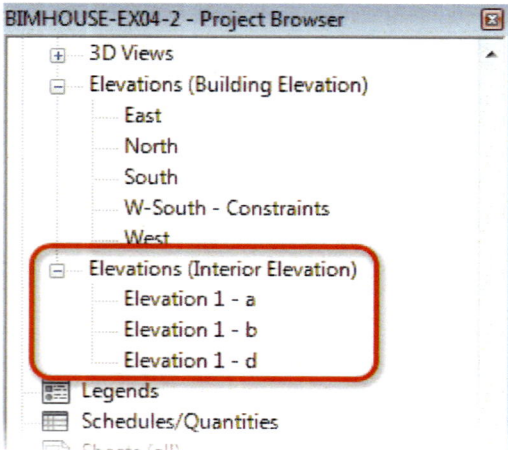

Interior Elevation View Category & Views

7. Select each elevation view independently, and rename it using the appropriate name from the following list.
   a) **Kitchen - North**
   b) **Kitchen - East**
   c) **Kitchen - South**

 To identify which default view name corresponds to which arrow on the view marker, briefly hover the cursor over one of the arrowheads and wait for the tool tip to appear, or look in the status bar. Either of these will reveal the view name associated with that arrowhead. Alternatively, you can select the arrow, which then opens the view properties in the Properties Palette. Here you can edit the view name as well.

8. Open the *Kitchen - North* interior elevation view by doing one of the following:

   ■ **Double-click** on the elevation marker *arrow* that corresponds with the view.

   ■ Navigate to the *Kitchen - North* view in the Project Browser, and **double-click** on it there.

9. Using the View Control Bar (VCB), set the *Detail Level* for the elevation view to **Medium**. Your view should appear as illustrated below.

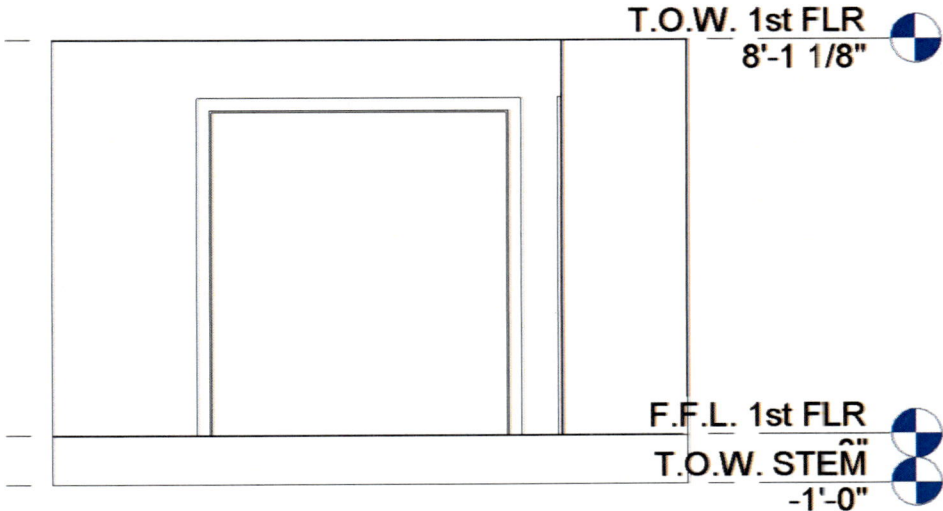

Kitchen - North Interior Elevation View

Add Interior Elevations: 2nd Floor

1. Open the floor plan view *F.F.L. 2nd FLR* and place an interior elevation view marker...

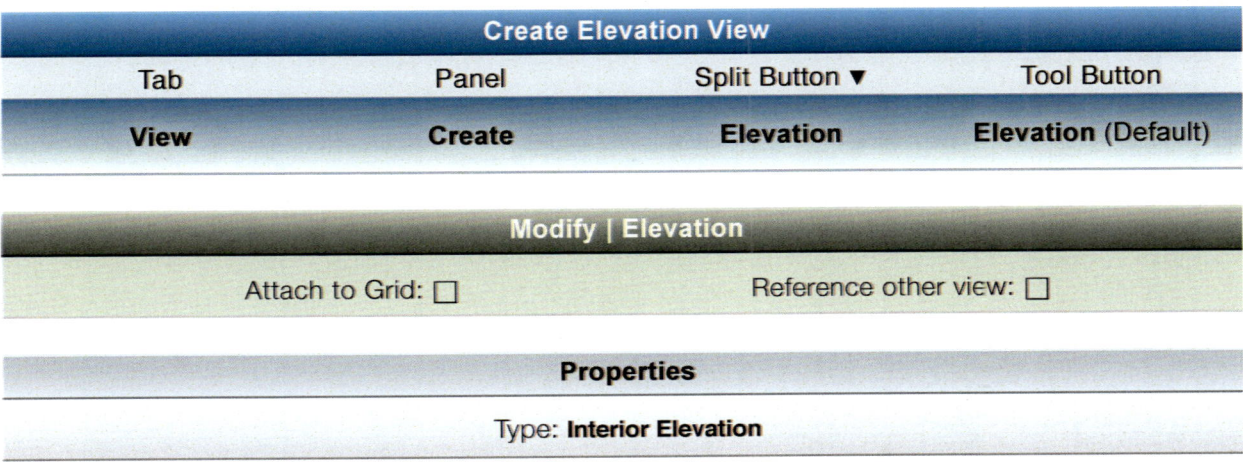

2. Place the elevation marker as located and oriented as illustrated below.

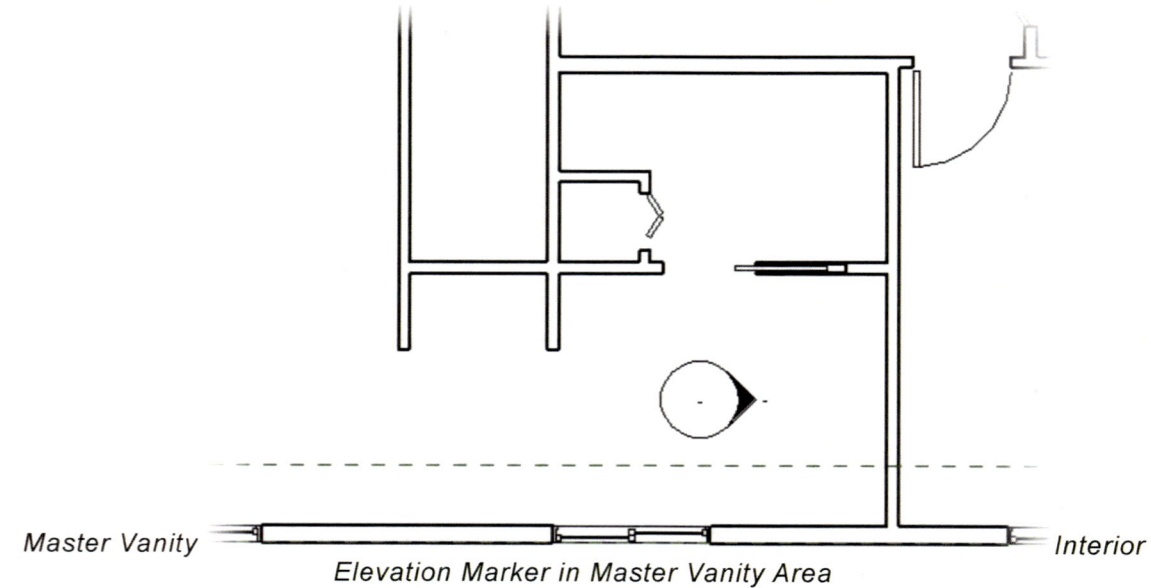

Elevation Marker in Master Vanity Area

 If the elevation arrowhead is not pointing in the desired direction, use the tab key to cycle through the available arrowhead selections prior to placing the elevation marker.

3. Rename the new elevation view to **Master Vanity**.

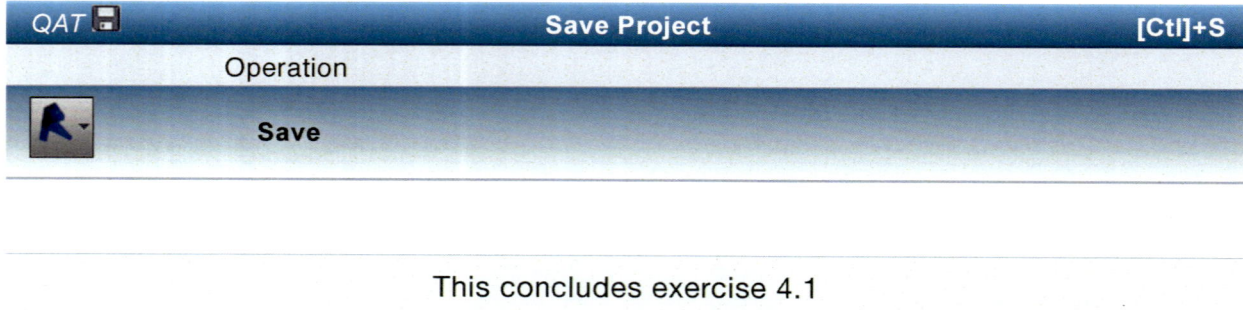

This concludes exercise 4.1

Exercise 4.2: Appliances & Casework

QAT 📂	Open Project		[Ctl]+O
	Operation	Option	File Name
🅁	Open ▶	Project	BIMHOUSE-EX04-1.rvt

	Save As (Project)		
	Operation	Option	File Name
🅁	Save As ▶	Project	BIMHOUSE-EX04-2.rvt

Add Appliances 1st Floor

1. Using the table below, load appliance families into your project.

Load Family		
Tab	Panel	Tool Button
Insert	**Load from Library**	**Load Family**

Custom family files downloaded from the web, or provided to you specifically for this project, should be saved in a custom content folder. DO NOT place custom content in any of the default Revit installation folders, including the libraries folders.

Specialty Equipment Families

Family	File Location	Use Type
Dishwasher.rfa	...Imperial Library\Specialty Equipment\Domestic\	24" x 24" x 34"
Dryer.rfa	...Imperial Library\Specialty Equipment\Domestic\	27" x 25" x 35"
Range.rfa	...Imperial Library\Specialty Equipment\Domestic\	30" x 26"
Refrigerator.rfa	...Imperial Library\Specialty Equipment\Domestic\	35" x 32" RH
Washer.rfa	...Imperial Library\Specialty Equipment\Domestic\	27" x 25" x 35"
Range Vent-Hood.rfa	*Provided Chapter 4 custom content*	30" Wide

2. Open the floor plan view *F.F.L. 1st FLR*.

CHAPTER 4: ADDING COMPONENTS

	Place Component		CM
Tab	Panel	Split Button ▼	Tool Button
Architecture	**Build**	**Component**	**Place a Component**

3. Place the family types specified in the previous table as illustrated below.

 The *Range Vent-Hood: 30" Wide* is placed directly over the *Range: 30" x 26"*.

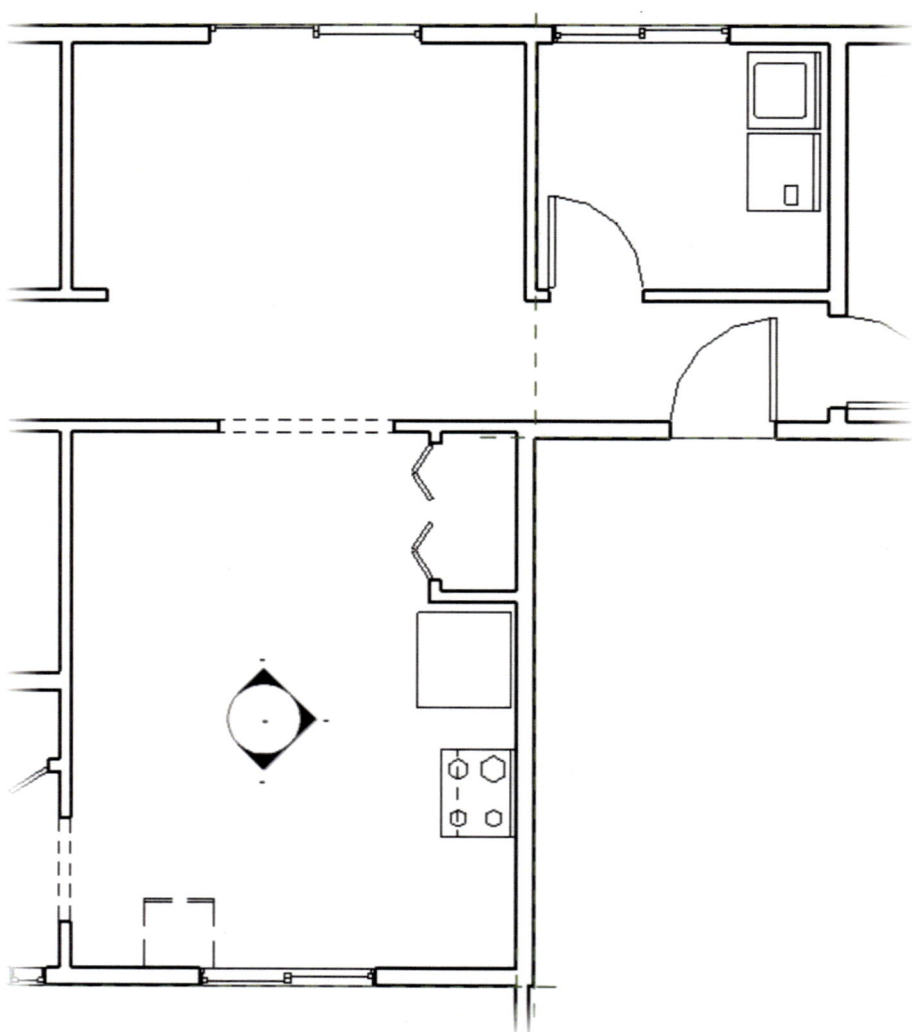

Approximate Appliance Locations

Create a 3D Section View

In the following sections you will be adding various elements to complete your kitchen. To help visualize the progress, create a 3D section view using following the steps below.

1. Duplicate the default *{3D}* view.

 If you need a refresher on how to duplicate a view, refer back to Chapter 1.

2. Rename the new view to **3D Section - Kitchen**.
3. In the Properties palette for the new 3D view, locate the *Section Box* property, and **check** the associated checkbox. You should see what appears to be a wireframe box around the model.
4. Click on the section box in the drawing area to select it. Once selected, 6 shape handles will appear.
5. Click and drag the shape handles to section the view to reveal the interior of the kitchen, similar to that illustrated below.

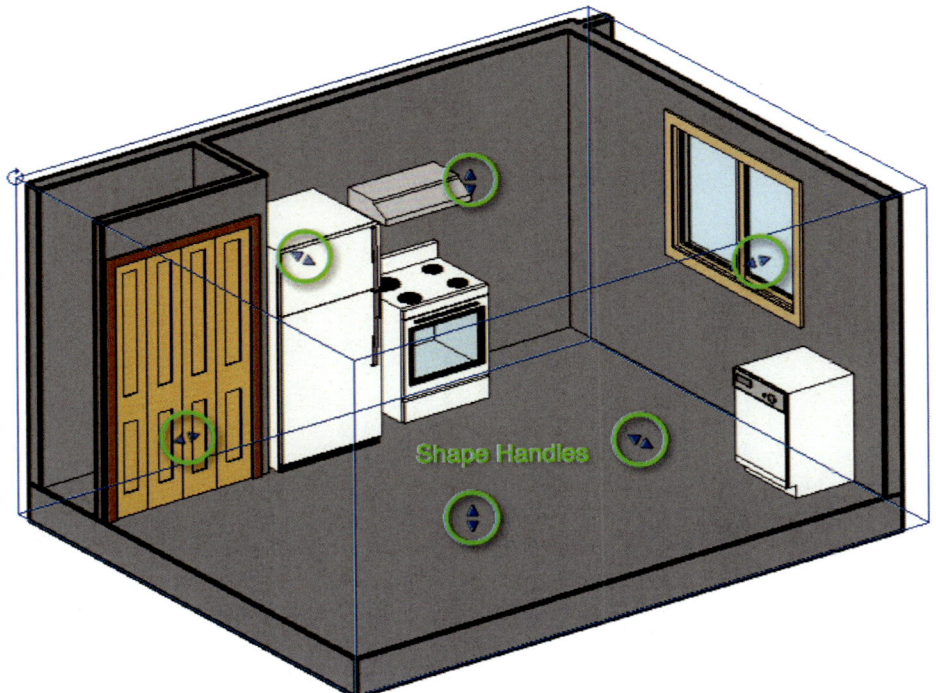

3D Section Box Around Kitchen

 Clearing the *Section Box* checkbox in the Properties Palette not only disables the section box, it also resets the section box boundaries. If you later decide to re-enable the section box, you will need to readjust the boundaries.

Add Kitchen Cabinets & Countertops

For this portion of the exercise you have some freedom to select and use a variety of content to personalize your kitchen layout.

 If you're working through this project as part of a formal course, you will be expected to create a complete kitchen layout with both base and wall cabinets complete with counter tops and fillers on at least 2 walls. It must look "finished" to receive full credit. If you're not sure where to begin, the illustrations on the following pages can be used as a guide, as well as an example of minimum content to be considered complete. Check with your instructor if you are unclear about these requirements.

General Guidelines

1. Countertops against walls should have a backsplash.

2. Use a countertop with a sink opening at the kitchen window. If you choose to use the corner unit illustrated, be sure to use the family provided for this project. Using a similar family from the Imperial Library or Autodesk Seek will create additional challenges when attempting to relocate the sink opening.

3. Use cabinet fillers as required to fill gaps between cabinets and walls, as well as gaps between cabinets where necessary.

4. Try to use a variety of cabinet families, including upper cabinets, to become familiar with the different types, as well as their unique behaviors.

5. If necessary, create additional types to suit your design. E.g., short upper cabinets to fit over refrigerator or range.

6. If you find that your kitchen design benefits from using appliances different those specified, you may replace any in the following list. However, if your model will be checked by your instructor using Model Review, be sure any replacement family contains the specified word within its name ("replacement Name Must Contain" column). Otherwise errors will be generated by the automated review process.

Appliance Families That May Be Replaced or Added

Family	Replacement Name Must Contain
Dishwasher.rfa	Dishwasher
Range.rfa	Range, Cooktop, Cook top, Oven *(any one)*
Refrigerator.rfa	Refrigerator
(Trash Compactor)	Trash

 Do not replace the *Range Vent-Hood* provided. You may create a new type if necessary. Additionally, do not apply any length or equality constraints anywhere at this time.

EXERCISE 4.2: APPLIANCES & CASEWORK

7. You can find most of the casework components illustrated in this workbook in the *...\Imperial Library\Casework* folder. Remember to check the provided content first.

8. If you decide to create a kitchen island that utilizes a low wall, create a new wall type named either **Generic - 3 1/2" Low** or **Generic - 5 1/2" Low** to use on the island.

9. Try working with a combination of floor plan, elevation, and 3D section views tiled. This will help visualize your design as it progresses.

 When measuring available space between walls to determine what size cabinets to use, consider that the generic walls will later be replaced with compound walls that include 1/2 thick gypsum wall board (GWB) layers. This will reduce the available space between any two existing walls by 1". Therefore make sure you have sufficient filler width to accommodate the shrinkage.

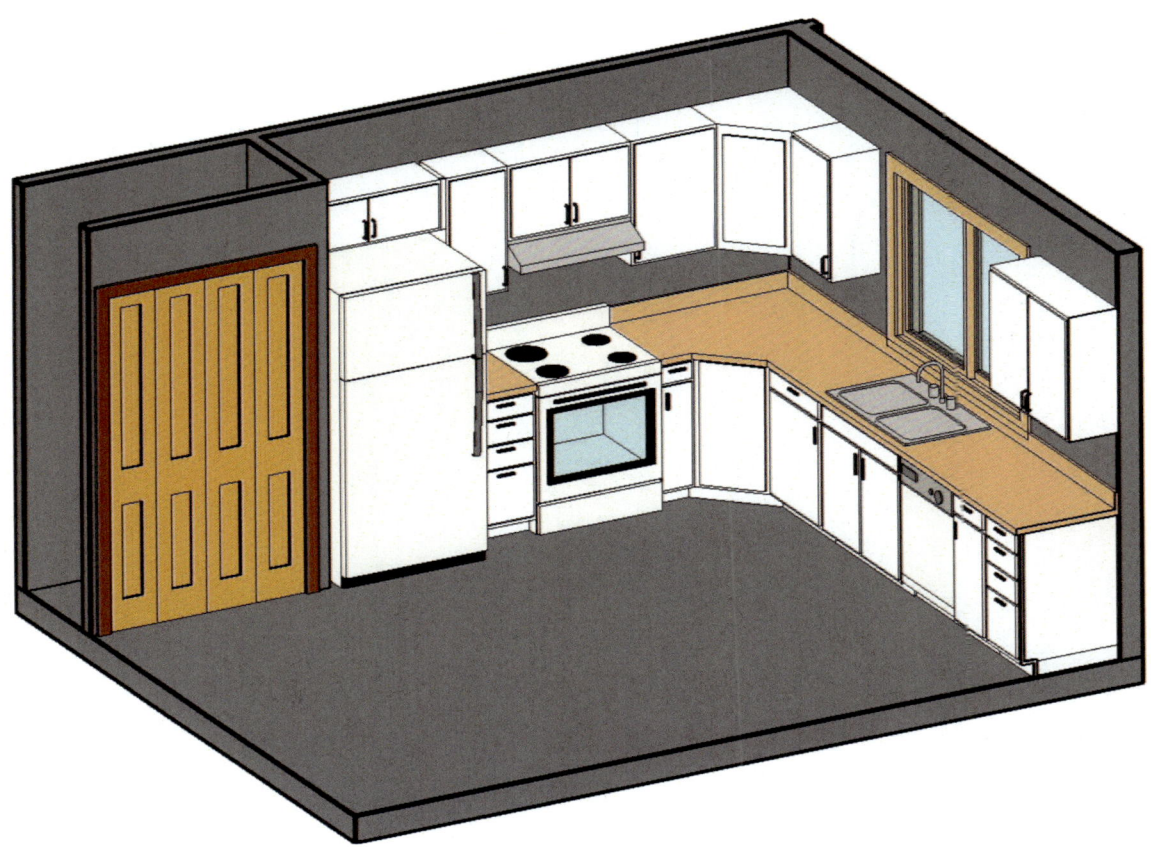

3D Section View

 The views illustrated above and on the following page include a kitchen sink. You are not required to place this component until the next exercise.

CHAPTER 4: ADDING COMPONENTS

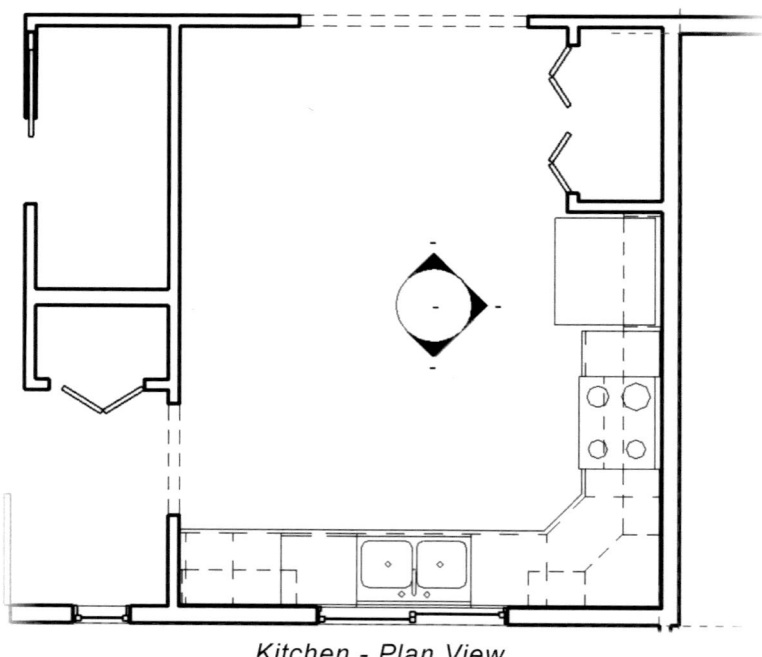
Kitchen - Plan View

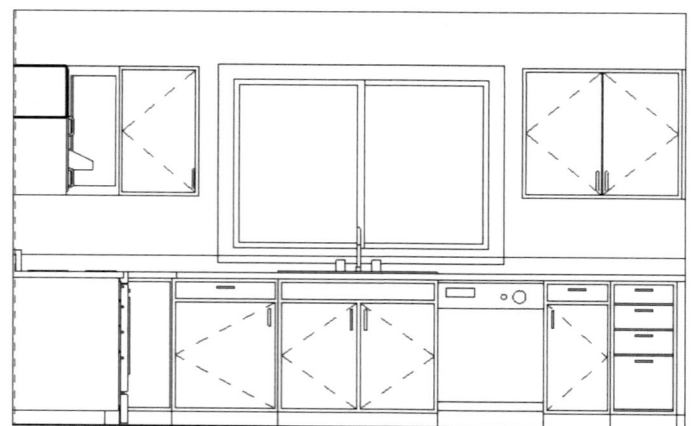
Kitchen - South Elevation View

Kitchen - East Elevation View

Add Vanity Cabinets & Countertops

Using the same procedures you used to place the kitchen cabinets and countertops, place the vanity cabinets and countertops as shown in the illustrations that follow.

Load Additional Cabinet and Countertop Families

Load Family		
Tab	Panel	Tool Button
Insert	Load from Library	Load Family

Using the following table, load the listed components into the project. Any folders listed are located in the Imperial Library folder.

 Do not substitute any of the custom families provided for this project!

Families to Load

Family	Located in Folder
Vanity Cabinet-Double Door Sink Unit.rfa	...\Casework\Base Cabinets\
Counter Top - Vanity - 1 Round Sink Hole.rfa	Provided Chapter 4 custom content
Vanity Cabinet-3 Drawers.rfa	Autodesk Seek
Counter Top - Vanity - 2 Round Sink Holes.rfa	Provided Chapter 4 custom content

1st Floor Powder Room

1. Open the floor plan view *F.F.L. 1st FLR*.
2. Refer to the illustration on the next page and place a base cabinet in the powder room...

Place Component			CM
Tab	Panel	Split Button ▼	Tool Button
Architecture	Build	Component	Place a Component

Properties
Type: **Vanity Cabinet-Double Door Sink Unit: 36"**

3. Place the cabinet centered against the south wall of the powder room.
4. Place the base cabinet fillers on either side of the cabinet...

 You need to create a new filler type named "Vanity" that matches the vanity counter height.

CHAPTER 4: ADDING COMPONENTS

Properties		
Type: **Base Cabinet-Filler: Vanity**		
Align		**AL**
Tab	Panel	Tool Button
Modify	**Modify**	**Align**
Multiple Alignment: ☐	Prefer: **Wall faces**	

5. **Align** and **Lock** the back of the base cabinet to the 2X6 wall.

6. **Align** and **Lock** each filler as follows:
   a) To the adjacent wall
   b) To the 2X6 wall
   c) To the adjacent face of the cabinet

7. Test the added constraints by nudging each of the three surrounding walls. Remember to return the walls back to their original location.

8. Next add the countertop…

Place Component			CM
Tab	Panel	Split Button ▼	Tool Button
Architecture	**Build**	**Component**	**Place a Component**
Properties			
Type: **Counter Top - Vanity - 1 Round Sink Hole: 31" Counter Height**			

9. Place the countertop with the splash against the south wall.

10. **Align** and **Lock** the countertop to the surrounding walls.

11. **Align** and **Lock** the sink hole center reference to the center reference of the base cabinet beneath it, as illustrated.

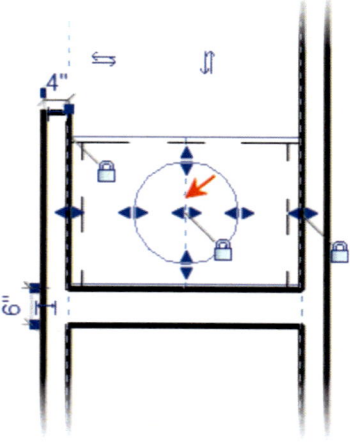

12. Test the added constraints by nudging each of the three surrounding walls, as well as the base cabinet (left/right). Remember to return everything back to its original location.

EXERCISE 4.2: APPLIANCES & CASEWORK

2nd Floor Master Vanity

The master vanity will have a counter top height of 36". The 3-drawer vanity cabinet downloaded from Autodesk Seek has the correct height to accommodate this. However, the double-door vanity sink base families do not. Therefore, in the following steps you will need to create a "Tall" version of an existing type.

13. Open the *F.F.L. 2nd FLR* floor plan view and maximize it.

14. **Close Hidden Windows**.

15. Open the *Master Vanity* interior elevation view.

16. **Tile Windows**.

17. Place the base cabinets...

Place Component			CM
Tab	Panel	Split Button ▼	Tool Button
Architecture	**Build**	**Component**	**Place a Component**

Properties
Type: **Vanity Cabinet-3 Drawers: 15"**

18. Place the cabinet roughly centered against the east wall of the master vanity area as shown in the illustration on the following page.

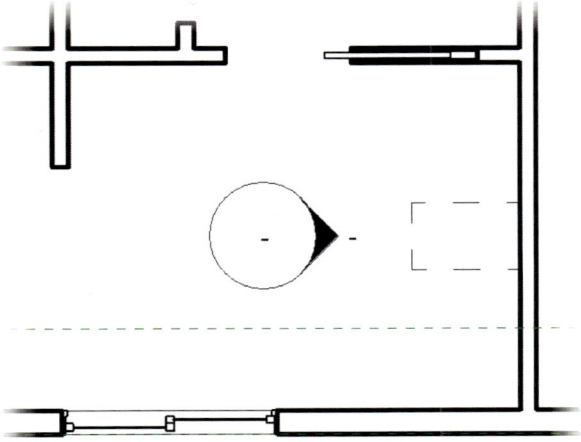

Master Vanity – Center 3-Drawer Cabinet

19. Place two double door sink base cabinets on either side of the drawer base...

CHAPTER 4: ADDING COMPONENTS

Properties
Type: **Vanity Cabinet-Double Door Sink Unit: Tall 30"**

 Create the new cabinet type by duplicating the existing type *30"*. Rename it to **Tall 30"**, and then change the *Height* parameter to **2' 10 1/2"**.

20. Place two instances of the new vanity base cabinet, one on either side of the 3-drawer unit as shown in the illustration to the right.

21. Add base cabinet fillers between each wall and the nearest cabinet.

22. **Align** and **lock** the fillers to the cabinets and the *faces* of all joining walls (*three locks per filler*).

23. Next place a countertop on the master vanity cabinets...

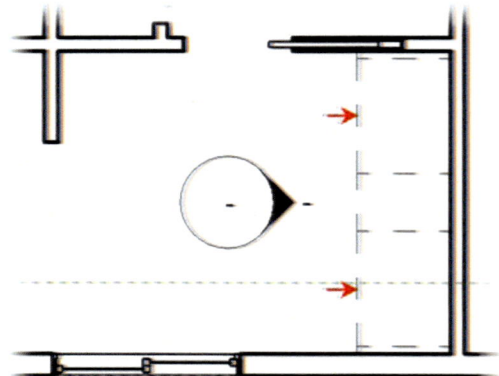

Place Component			CM
Tab	Panel	Split Button ▼	Tool Button
Architecture	**Build**	**Component**	**Place a Component**

Properties
Type: **Counter Top - Vanity - 2 Round Sink Holes: 36" Counter Height**

24. **Align** and **Lock** the countertop to the *faces* of all three surrounding walls.

25. **Align** and **Lock** each sink hole center reference to the center reference of the base cabinet beneath it as illustrated.

26. Verify the *Master Vanity* elevation view appears as illustrated below. If not, go back and make any necessary corrections before moving forward.

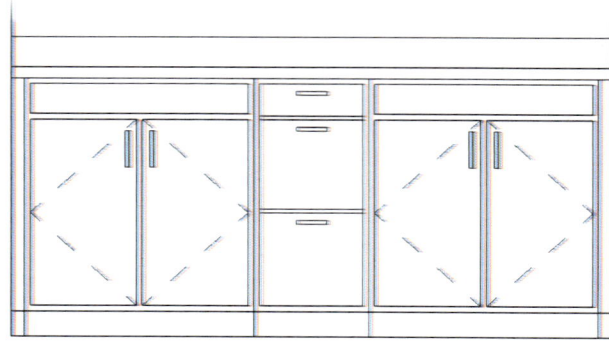

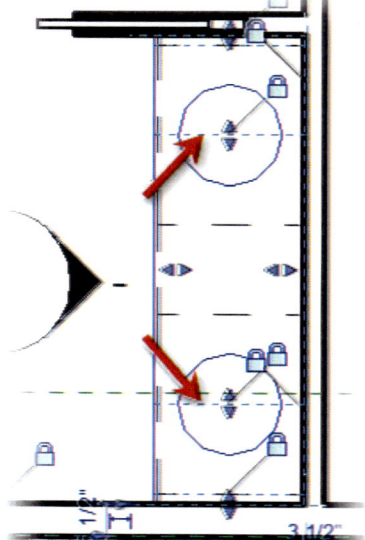

132

Place Component			CM
Tab	Panel	Split Button ▼	Tool Button
Architecture	Build	Component	Place a Component

27. Place a vanity base cabinet, fillers, and countertop in the secondary bath on the second floor following the same procedure used to place and constrain vanity components in the powder room. Refer back to those steps if necessary. Use the standard vanity height components (31" counter top height).

   Hint: you will need to use a narrower cabinet than that used in the powder room.

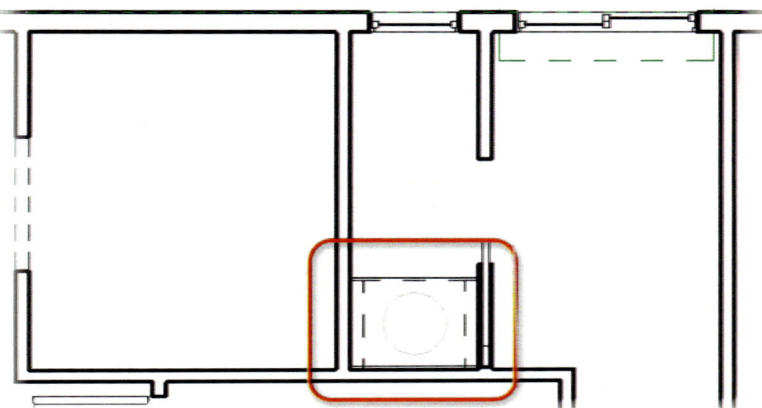

Secondary Bathroom Vanity at 2nd Floor

 Remember when measuring available space to determine what size cabinet to use, in future steps you will replace the generic walls with compound walls that include 1/2 thick GWB layers. This will reduce the available space between any two existing walls by 1".

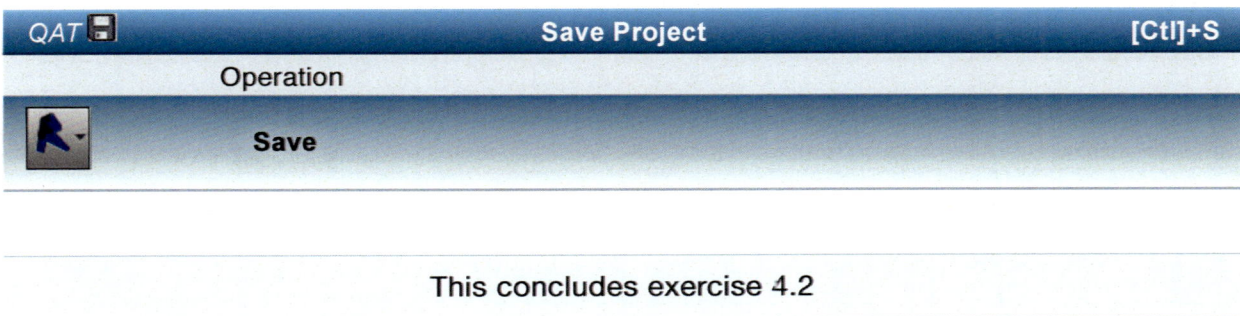

This concludes exercise 4.2

Exercise 4.3: Plumbing & Mechanical Fixtures

QAT 📂	Open Project		[Ctl]+O
	Operation	Option	File Name
🅡	Open ▶	Project	BIMHOUSE-EX04-2.rvt

	Save As (Project)		
	Operation	Option	File Name
🅡	Save As ▶	Project	BIMHOUSE-EX04-3.rvt

Load Families

Using the table below, load the listed components into the project...

Load Family		
Tab	Panel	Tool Button
Insert	Load from Library	Load Family

Families to Load

Family	File Location
Toilet-Domestic-3D.rfa	...Imperial Library\Plumbing\Architectural\Fixtures\Water Closets
Sink Vanity-Round.rfa	...Imperial Library\Plumbing\Architectural\\Fixtures\Sinks
Sink Kitchen-Double.rfa *	...Imperial Library\Plumbing\Architectural\\Fixtures\ Sinks
Tub-Rectangular-3D.rfa	...Imperial Library\Plumbing\Architectural\\Fixtures\Bathtubs
Water Heater.rfa	...Imperial Library\Plumbing\Architectural\Equipment\Water Heaters
Sink-Laundry.rfa	Autodesk Seek
Furnace.rfa	...Imperial Library\Mechanical\Architectural\Air-Side Components\Furnaces
Bollard 2.rfa	...Imperial Library\Site\Accessories\

 * The kitchen sink specified is optional. Your kitchen design may utilize a different sink.

In the steps that follow you will be working between the 1st and 2nd floor plan views *F.F.L. 1st FLR* and *F.F.L. 2nd FLR*. You will not be instructed when to switch views. Use the provided plan set to determine the location of the components that you're instructed to place.

If you open multiple views prior to activating a tool, you can switch between open windows using the **[Ctrl]**+**[Tab]** keys, and the tool will remain active. Double-clicking a view in the project browser to open it deactivates the tool. Alternatively, tiling multiple views allows you to click between open windows without deactivating the tool.

Periodically throughout the following steps you will receive a message indicating that there is no tag loaded for the type of family you're about to place, and whether or not you wish to load one. Answer **No** whenever you see this.

Add Toilets & Tubs

1. Place a total of 3 toilets according to the provided floor plans...

Place Component			
Tab	Panel	Split Button ▼	Tool Button
Architecture	Build	Component	Place a Component

Properties
Type: **Toilet-Domestic-3D**

2. **Align** and **Lock** the back of each toilet to the wall *face* behind it.

3. Don't worry about centering the toilets just yet. This will be addressed this in the following exercise.

4. Place 2 tubs...

Place Component			
Tab	Panel	Split Button ▼	Tool Button
Architecture	Build	Component	Place a Component

Properties
Type: **Tub-Rectangular-3D**

 The Tub-Rectangular-3D family is a "hosted" element, which requires it to be placed with its rear face against a wall. You must hover the cursor over a wall for the tub to appear.

5. Use **[Space]** to orient the tub prior to placing it, or the flip arrow after placing as required to properly orient it.

Add Sinks in the Kitchen and Bathrooms

1. Place a kitchen sink...

Place Component			CM
Tab	Panel	Split Button ▼	Tool Button
Architecture	**Build**	**Component**	**Place a Component**

Properties
Type: * **Sink Kitchen-Double: 42" x 21"**

 42" x 21" is the only type available in the Sink Kitchen-Double family. Feel free to create a type with alternate dimensions, or find an alternate sink family more suitable to your kitchen design. The illustrations of the kitchen in the previous section show a 36" x 21" sink. Remember to relocate and resize the sink hole in the counter top once you've established the final size and location of your sink.

2. Place 4 vanity sinks...

Place Component			CM
Tab	Panel	Split Button ▼	Tool Button
Architecture	**Build**	**Component**	**Place a Component**

Properties
Type: **Sink Vanity-Round: 19" x 19"**

3. Since the vanity in the master bath has a 36" counter height, and the standard vanity sink height is 31", you'll need to create a sink type to match...

    a) Duplicate *Sink Vanity-Round: 19" x 19"*.
    b) For the name enter **Tall 19" x 19"**
    c) Change the *Top Of Counter* parameter to **3' 0"**.
    d) Click **OK**.
    e) Place the sinks.

4. **Exit** the component tool.
5. **Open** the interior elevation view *Master Vanity*, and verify it appears as illustrated.

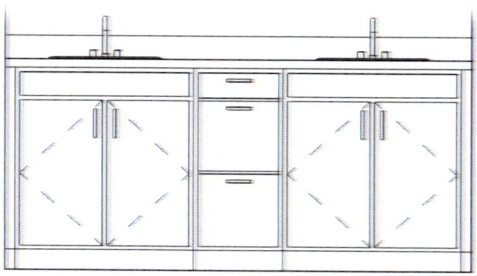

Constrain Sink Locations Within Counter Tops

In the following steps you will create relationships between the sinks and the openings in the counter tops. This will cause the sink and opening to stay together in the event of a design change. The steps outlined provide a general procedure for constraining sinks to counter top sink openings. Follow this procedure for every sink in the model.

Tab	Panel	Tool Button	
	Align		**AL**
Modify	**Modify**	**Align**	
Multiple Alignment: ☐	Prefer: **N/A**		

1. Pick the reference that defines the left/right centerline of the sink opening in the counter top. Use **[tab]** as required, while monitoring the tool tip and/or the status bar, until the correct reference is highlighted, then **click** to select it.

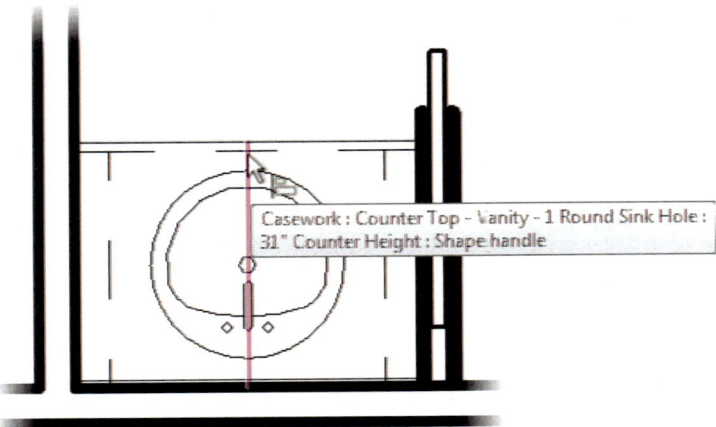

2. Pick the reference that defines the left/right centerline of the sink.

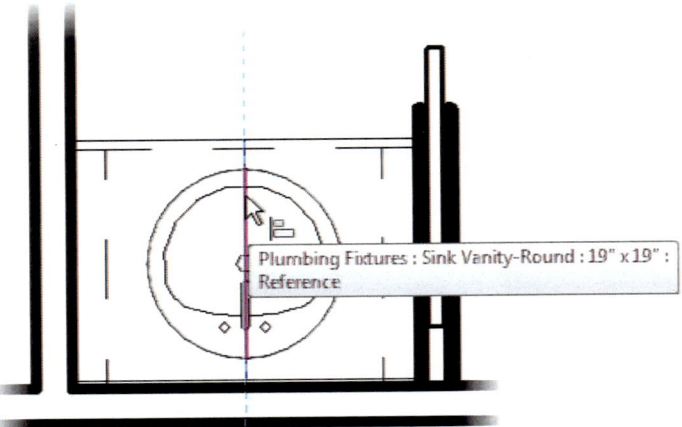

3. **Lock** the alignment immediately after the second pick.

4. Pick the reference that defines the front/back centerline of the sink opening.

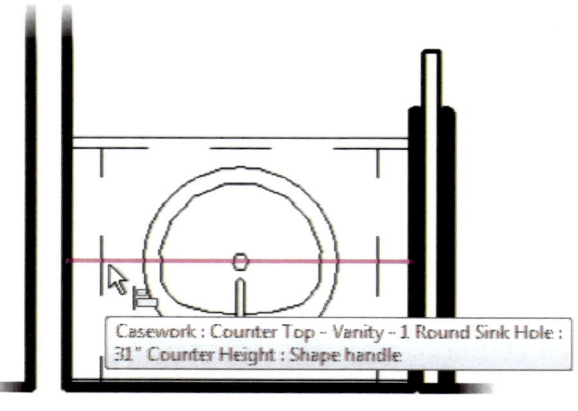

5. Pick the reference that defines the front/back centerline of the sink.

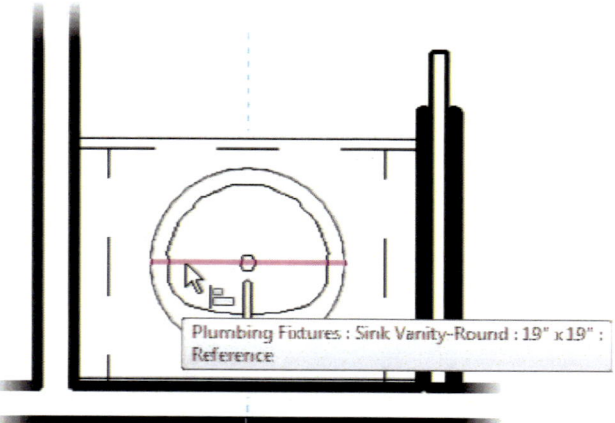

6. **Lock** the alignment immediately after the second pick.

 Make sure to test the constraints to ensure they were correctly applied.

7. Repeat the previous steps for the remaining sinks in the model.

Add Laundry Sink

1. Open the floor plan view *F.F.L. 1st FLR*.
2. Place a laundry sink in the laundry room as illustrated below...

Place Component			CM
Tab	Panel	Split Button ▼	Tool Button
Architecture	Build	Component	Place a Component

Properties
Type: **Sink-Laundry: 24" x 20"**

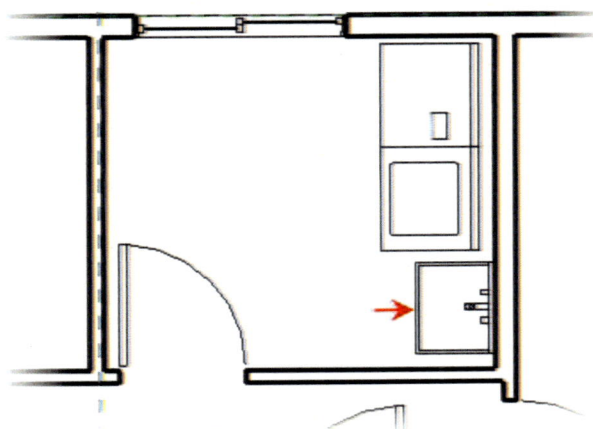

3. **Exit** the Component tool.
4. **Align** and **Lock** the back of the sink to the *wall face* of the 2X6 wall.

Add Mechanical and Plumbing in the Garage

In the following steps you will place three components in the garage: a furnace, water heater, and a bollard post. Refer to the provided floor plans for *approximate* locations.

Place Component			CM
Tab	Panel	Split Button ▼	Tool Button
Architecture	Build	Component	Place a Component

Properties
Type: **Furnace: 40" x 21" x 28"**

Level:	**F.F.L. 1st FLR**

Properties	
Type:	**Water Heater**
Level:	**F.F.L. 1st FLR**

Properties	
Type:	**Bollard 2: 9" Diameter**
Level:	**F.F.L. 1st FLR**

 At this point in our project, we've placed all of the windows, doors, components relative to *F.F.L. 1st FLR* or *F.F.L. 2nd FLR*. This works for everything in the livable portion of the house. However, the garage slab will be lower than *F.F.L. 1st FLR*, and therefore the components in the garage will need to be re-associated. This will be addressed in a future exercise, so don't worry about it for now.

QAT 💾	Save Project	[Ctl]+S
	Operation	
R	Save	

This concludes exercise 4.3

Exercise 4.4: Model Groups and Constraints

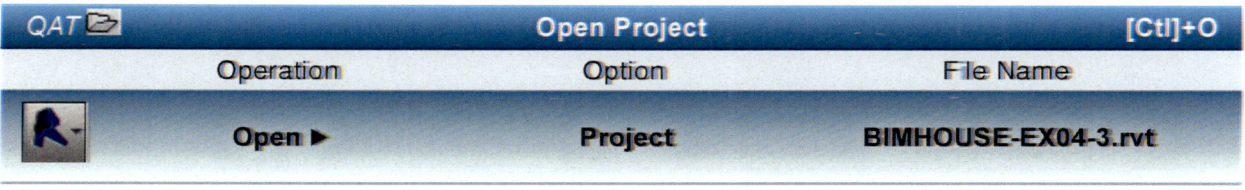

Create a Custom Dimension Type

In this section you'll be adding length and equality constraints, which are applied using a permanent dimension. To keep track of these constraints, we'll create and use a custom dimension type that displays in red. Additionally we'll place all of these related dimensions in the "constraints" views to help keep track of them.

Linear Dimension Types		
Tab	Expanded Panel ▼	Settings Button
Annotate	**Dimension**	**Linear Dimension Types**

1. In the Type Properties dialog box, Type should be set to *Linear - 3/32" Arial*. If not, select it now.
2. Click **Duplicate...** and enter **Linear - Constraints** for the name.
3. Click on the *Color* button in the Value column to launch the Color dialog box.
4. Pick the **Red** color swatch an click **OK**.
5. Click to select the **Bold** checkbox.
6. Click **OK** to accept the changes.

 The concept of creating and using a unique dimension type, as well as views dedicated to managing constraints is a preferred workflow of the author, and does not in any way represent Autodesk recommended practices.

Apply Length Constraints

1. Open the floor plan view *W-1st Floor - Constraints*.

QAT	Aligned Dimension	DI
Tab	Panel	Tool Button
Annotate	**Dimension**	**Aligned**

Modify	Place Dimensions	
	Dimension	
	Aligned	
Faces of Core		Pick: **Individual References**

Properties
Type: **Linear – Constraints**

> ⚠️ Be sure that you not only set the Options Bar setting to *Faces of core* when placing the following dimensions, but also make sure the detail level for the view is set to **Coarse**.

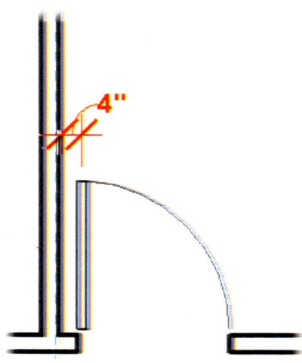

2. Place a dimension between the hinge-side of each interior door and the adjacent wall's *face of core*. Do this *only* for doors that are specified as being located 4" from the adjacent wall.

   If the dimension value equals 4" when placed, **lock** it while the dimension tool is active and continue on. Otherwise, you will need to adjust the door location as described in the next steps before locking.

3. **Exit** the dimension tool when done.

4. If any of the doors dimensioned are not located exactly 4" from the adjacent wall, adjust them as necessary now, then **lock** the corresponding dimension.

 Once a permanent dimension is placed, selecting a related element will activate it, just like a temporary dimension. Permanent dimensions can therefore be used like a temporary dimension to refine element position.

5. Open the floor plan view *W-2nd Floor - Constraints*.
6. Set the *Underlay* property to **none**.
7. Repeat the previous steps for the second floor doors.

Create Model Groups

In the kitchen and master vanity we could have tied all of the components together using alignment constraints. However, the more heavily a model is loaded with constraints, the more opportunity exists for errors. Therefore, it is a good practice to use constraints were they really matter, such as on the primary building components. Since we're mainly interested in keeping the cabinets and related appliances assembled together, we can place them into a model group. If a model group is moved, then all elements contained in that group are moved and maintain their position relative to one another.

 This is just one way of using model groups. Multiple instances of a model group can be placed in a model. When one instance of the group is edited, the rest update to match the changes.

1. Open the floor plan view *F.F.L. 2nd FLR*.

2. Create a selection set containing the following elements from the master vanity. These will be added into the new group.

   a) Base cabinets (3)
   b) Sinks (2)

 Do not select the fillers or the counter top. These elements are constrained and contain instance properties allowing them to flex when the surrounding geometry is moved. This is essentially dynamic updating of instance parameters. Parameter updates to elements inside of a group can only be performed in group edit mode. Otherwise attempting to flex an element inside of a group will result in an error.

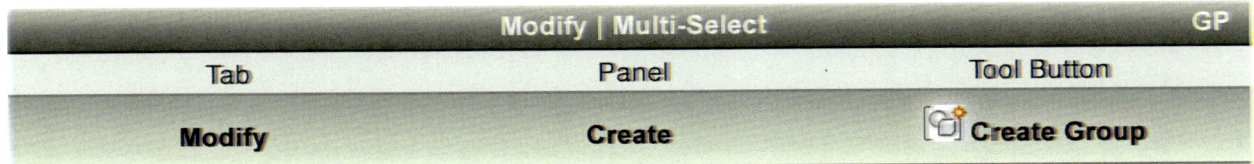

Tab	Panel	Tool Button
Modify	Create	Create Group

Modify | Multi-Select — GP

3. In the Create Model Group dialog box, enter **Master Vanity** for the name, and select the **Open in Group Editor** check box.

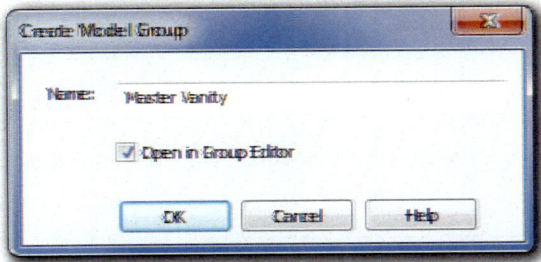

4. Click **OK**. The new group will open in the group edit mode. This mode is identified with the colored background, and the floating tool panel. Additionally, all items in the group are colored black and are selectable, and the remaining elements are shaded halftone and are not selectable.

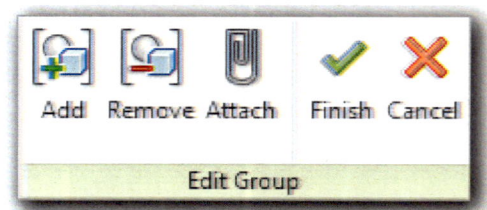
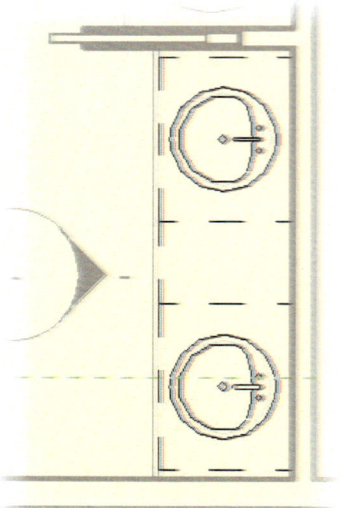

5. Click the **Finish** button (green checkmark) in the floating tool panel to complete the group.
1. Open the floor plan view *F.F.L. 1st FLR*.
2. Create a model group containing the following elements from kitchen. Remember not to include flexible elements in the group.

 Depending on your kitchen design, more than one model group might be required. Additionally, you may not want to include everything in the groups based on other constraints. If you modeled the kitchen as shown in the examples in this book, then only one model group will be necessary.

    a) Base cabinets
    b) Upper cabinets
    c) Sink
    d) Dishwasher
    e) Range
    f) Vent-hood

3. After completing the group(s) you will most likely need to constrain one ore two elements from each group to the adjacent walls with an alignment constraint. This is to ensure that the group(s) will move with the walls. To find out where constraints are needed, just move the adjacent walls (remember to use the reference planes to do this).

 Adding an alignment constraint to the group in the master vanity wasn't require because the sinks constrained to the counter top, which should be constrained to the back wall.

Apply Equality Constraints

1. Open the floor plan view *W-1st Floor - Constraints*.

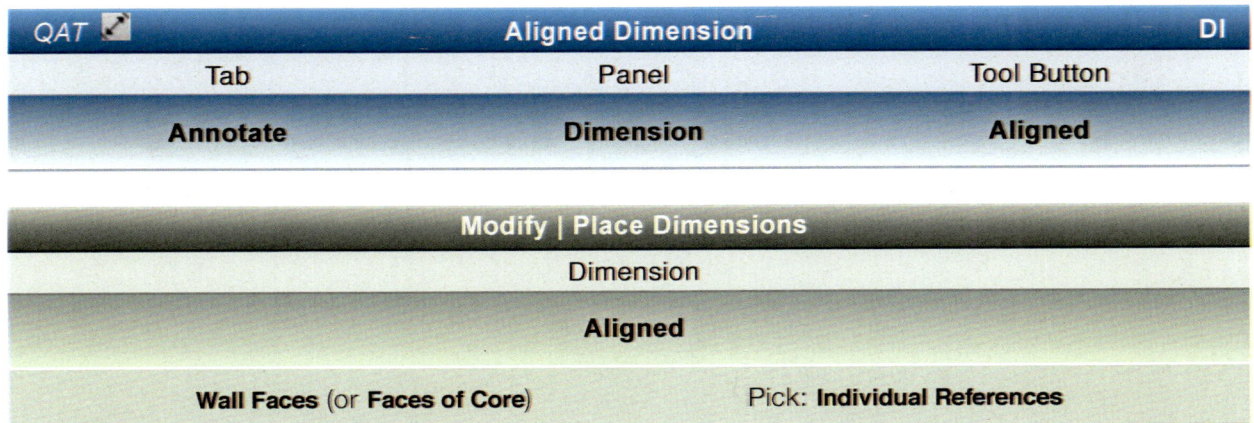

 Do not lock dimensions used to define equality constraints!

2. Place an aligned dimension between the centerline of the toilet, and the inner faces of the adjacent walls...

3. Immediately after the dimension is placed, click the **EQ** icon to create the equality constraint.

4. Repeat this step for the following elements:

   a) Vanity *base cabinet* in the powder room and the secondary bathroom on the 2nd floor

   b) Doors centered in hallways

   c) Closet doors

   d) Garage door

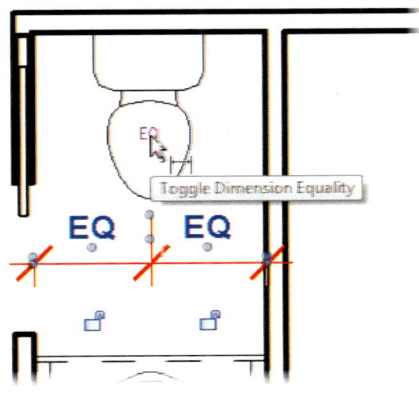

 An equality constraint applied to the master vanity group is unreliable and will likely fail. If not at first, then further into model development.

5. Open the floor plan view *W-2nd Floor - Constraints*.

6. Set the **Underlay** property for this view to **None**.

7. Continue to apply equality constraints to the following.

    a) Vanity *base cabinet* in the secondary bathroom

    b) Doors centered between walls

    c) Closet doors

    d) Master vanity group. If this constraint fails, try selecting the center reference of the 3-drawer cabinet prior to selecting the walls.

 Make sure to test all equality constraints for correct behavior.

Associate Washer & Dryer with the Plumbing Wall

The washer and dryer need some rear clearance to the plumbing wall. However, it would be nice to associate them with the wall. To accomplish this we could apply a length constraint as we did previously with the doors. However, in this instance we'll use the *Moves With Nearby Elements* option.

1. Select the washer and dryer in the laundry room, and in the Options Bar, check the *Moves With Nearby Elements* checkbox.

2. Clear the selection (click in empty space, or click **Modify**)

3. To test this relationship, move the interior plumbing wall behind the washer and dryer. The washer and dryer should track the movement of the wall.

 The *Moves With Nearby Elements* setting should be used with caution, as you don't have explicit control over which elements are considered "nearby." It is strongly recommended that you DO NOT use this option in conjunction with *any* other type of constraint, as the results can be unpredictable, and potentially plagued of with errors.

QAT	Save Project	[Ctl]+S
	Operation	
	Save	

	Close (Project)	[Ctl]+[F4]
	Operation	
	Close	

This concludes exercise 4.4

Chapter Summary

In this lesson you practiced placing various types of components, in addition to being exposed to some unique features of various families. Functionality and flexibility of families is primarily dependent upon how the family was created. This will vary greatly between families. Knowing whether or not a family was built properly, and will maintain desired constraints is largely a process of trial and error.

Chapter 5

Section Views & Graphic Overrides

Overview

This chapter is intended to introduce you to section views, as well as to the power of the graphics control within Revit. While various other applications use layers to control graphics, Revit uses categories, which is more simple and intuitive without giving up much – if any – control over the graphic representation of your views.

Learning Objectives

After completing this chapter you should have a basic understanding of the following tools and concepts.

- Creating section views
- Adjusting crop regions
- Modifying object styles settings
- Overriding visibility and graphics in views
- Creating and applying view filters
- Creating and applying view templates

Project Objectives

- Incorporate two primary section views
- Modify Object Styles for various categories to affect global graphics settings
- Visibility/graphics overrides on select views using filters
- Capture visibility/graphics overrides settings into view templates

Chapter 5: Section Views & Graphic Overrides

Chapter Contents

Exercise 5.1: Section Views 151
- Create Section Views 151
- Adjust Section Marker Graphics 152
- Open and Adjust Section Views 154

Exercise 5.2: Object Styles & Visibility Graphics Overrides 156
- Object Styles (Global Graphic Representation) 156
- Visibility/Graphics Overrides: By Category/Subcategory 157
- Visibility/Graphics Overrides: By Filter 158

Exercise 5.3: View Templates 161
- Create View Templates 161
- Apply View Templates 162

Exercise 5.1: Section Views

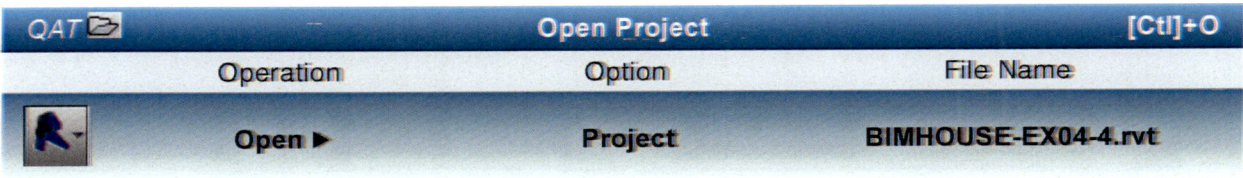

Create Section Views

1. Open the plan view *F.F.L. 1st FLR*.

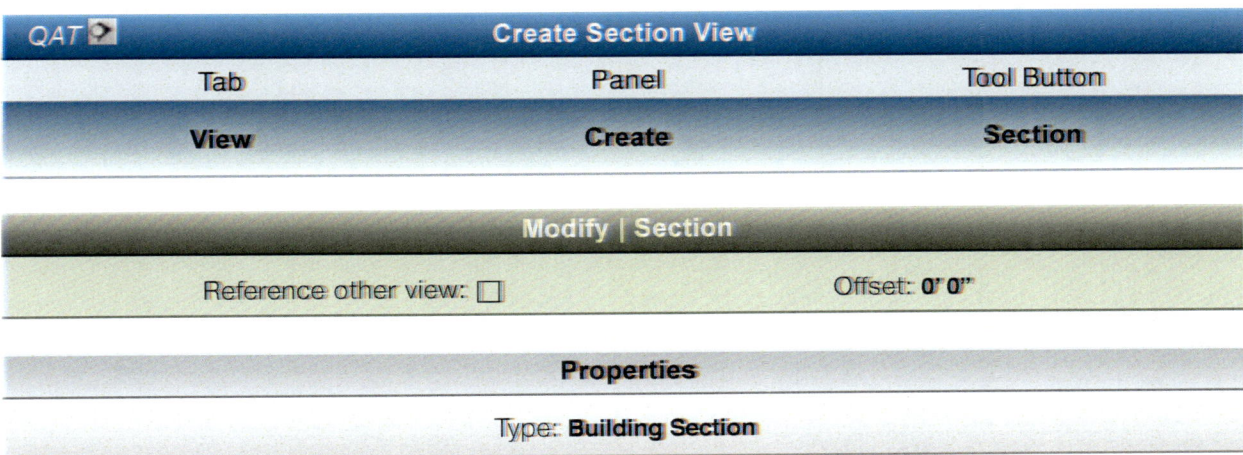

2. Sketch the first section marker from left to right. Refer to the marker labeled **[1]** in the illustration on the next page.

3. In the Project Browser, find the new branch titled *Sections (Building Section)* and expand it.

4. Rename the new section view to **Living-Kitchen-Garage (Cross)**.

5. Create another section view, this time sketching the marker from top to bottom. Refer to the marker labeled **[2]** in the illustration on the next page.

6. Rename the new section view to **Family-Stairs-Porch (Long)**.

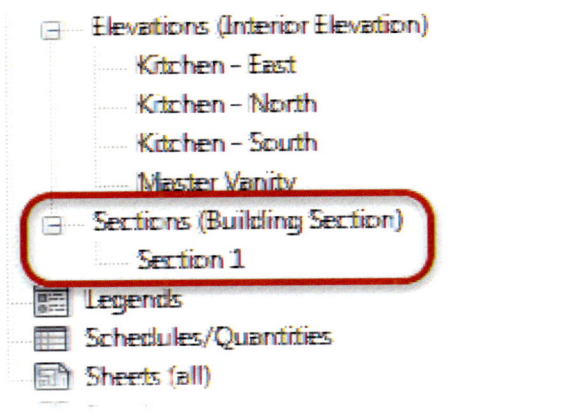

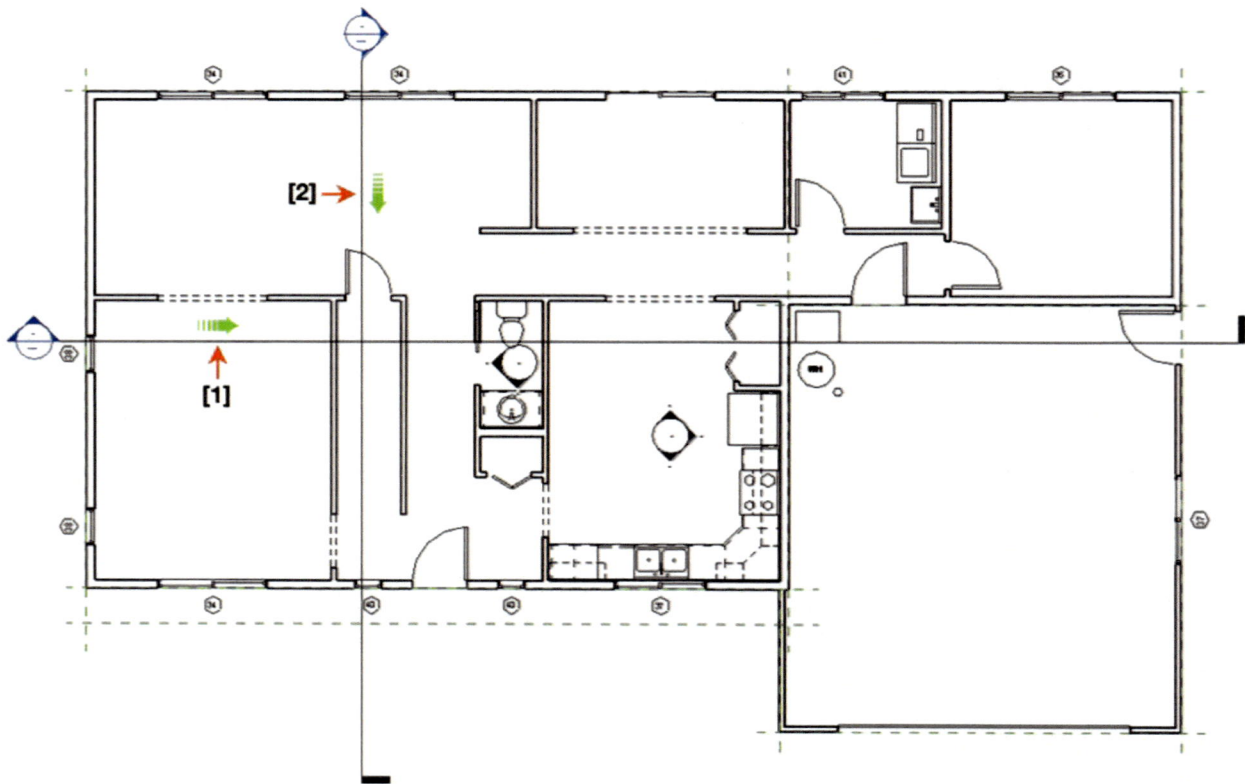

Place Section Markers

Adjust Section Marker Graphics

Convert the Section Tails to Section Heads

1. Select each section marker, one at a time, then at the tail end click the circular arrows icon to cycle through the options until it displays the section head symbol as illustrated below.

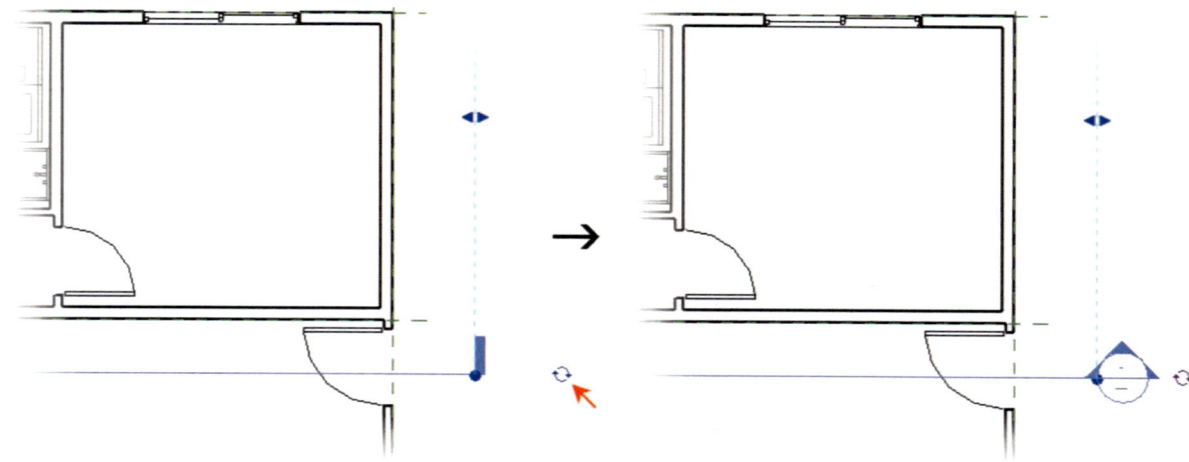

Convert Section Tail to Section Head

Place a Gap in the Section Lines

2. Select the longitudinal (North/South) section marker, then do the following:

   a) **Click** on the *Gap in Segments* icon (break symbol) on the section line.

   b) **Click/drag** the drag handles on the section line to achieve the results illustrated below.

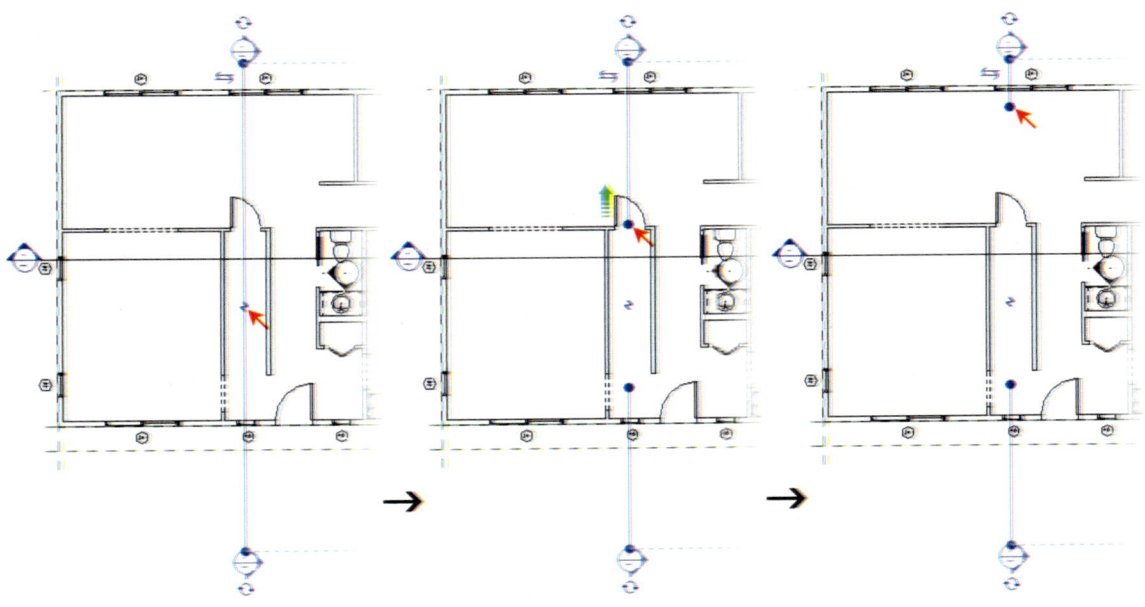

Place Gap in Section Line

3. Repeat the previous step on the cross section marker to achieve the results illustrated below.

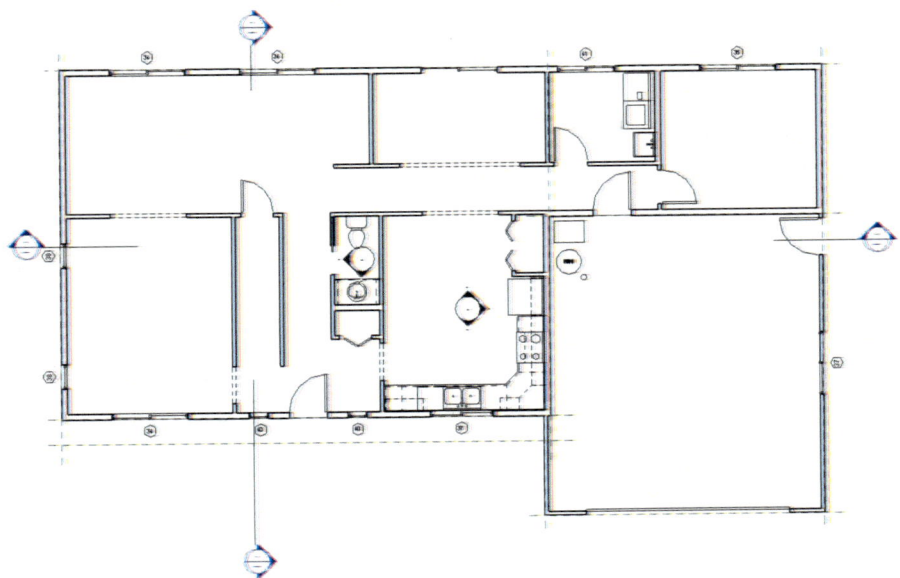

Section Marker Graphics Modified

4. Open the plan view *F.F.L. 2nd FLR* and verify the section marker gaps are present.

Open and Adjust Section Views

1. Open the section view *Living-Kitchen-Garage (Cross)*.
2. Using the VCB, set *Detail Level* to **Medium**, and **Hide Crop Region**. When done, your view should appear similar to the illustration below.

Section View Living-Kitchen-Garage (Cross)

3. Open the section view *Family-Stairs-Porch (Long)*.
4. Using the VCB, set *Detail Level* to **Medium**, and **Hide Crop Region**. When done, your view should appear similar to the illustration below.

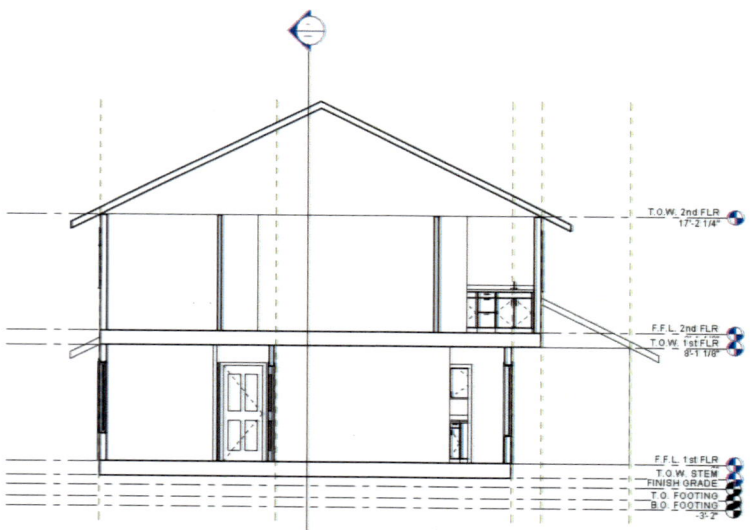

Section View Family-Stairs-Porch (Long)

 If any part of the model in either of the section views is not visible, adjust the crop boundary as required by first selecting it, then using the shape handle(s) to adjust its size as required.

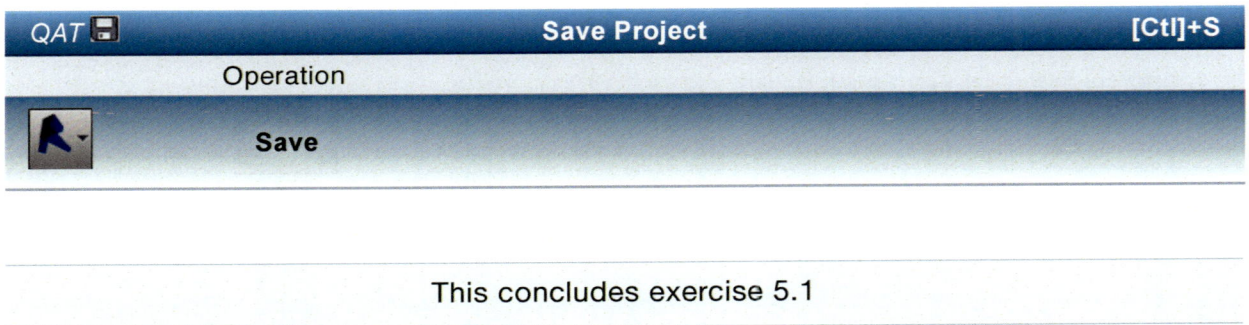

This concludes exercise 5.1

Exercise 5.2: Object Styles & Visibility Graphics Overrides

In the following section you will globally change the graphic representation for a number of categories and subcategories in your project. These changes will affect all views that have not been overridden. Additionally, you will apply overrides to specific views, which will change the visibility and/or graphic representation of various categories on a view-by-view basis only.

QAT 📂	Open Project		[Ctl]+O
	Operation	Option	File Name
🅡	Open ▶	Project	BIMHOUSE-EX05-1.rvt

	Save As (Project)		
	Operation	Option	File Name
🅡	Save As ▶	Project	BIMHOUSE-EX05-2.rvt

Object Styles (Global Graphic Representation)

1. Open the floor plan view *F.F.L. 1st FLR*.
2. Zoom into the kitchen area and take notice of the line weights for the counter tops and appliances.

	Object Styles	
Tab	Panel	Tool Button
Manage	**Settings**	**Object Styles**

3. In the Object Styles dialog box, make the changes listed in the following table.. You will need to expand a category in order to access any of its subcategories.

Object Styles Changes

Category / Subcategory	Line Weight	
	Projection	Cut
Casework / Cabinet	1	4
Casework / Counter Top	3	4
Specialty Equipment	2	

4. Click **OK** to accept the changes, and notice the change to the counter top and appliance line weights. Open any other plan view where these elements are visible, and they should be represented with the same line weights.

EXERCISE 5.2: OBJECT STYLES & VISIBILITY GRAPHICS OVERRIDES

Visibility/Graphics Overrides: By Category/Subcategory

The overrides applied in the next steps will affect all elements within an overridden category or subcategory. However, using overrides only affects the view in which the overrides are applied.

1. Open the floor plan view *F.F.L. 1st FLR*.

Visibility/Graphics Overrides		VV / VG
Tab	Panel	Tool Button
View	**Graphics**	**Visibility/Graphics**

 Notice that the name of the dialog box "Visibility/Graphics Overrides for..." includes the name of the view to which it applies.

2. Make the changes listed in the following table, then click **OK** to accept the changes. As with Object Styles, you will need to expand a category in order to access any of its subcategories.

F.F.L. 1st FLR

Category Tab / Category / Subcategory	Visibility
Model / Casework / Plan Rep - Below	OFF
Model / Casework / Sink Opening	OFF
Annotation / Grids	OFF
Annotation / Reference Planes	OFF

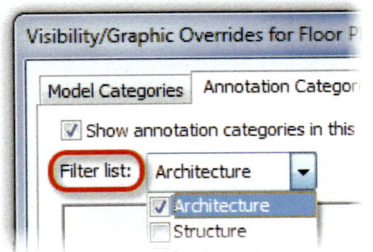 Depending on your user interface settings, you may be able to reduce the number of categories listed under each tab by manipulating the *Filter list:* setting.

1. Open the floor plan view *1st Floor - Dimension*.

Visibility/Graphics Overrides		VV / VG
Tab	Panel	Tool Button
View	**Graphics**	**Visibility/Graphics**

2. Make the changes listed in the following table, then click **OK** to accept the changes.

1St Floor - Dimension

Category Tab / Category / Subcategory	Visibility	Halftone
Model / Casework		✓
Model / Casework / Plan Rep - Above	OFF	
Model / Casework / Plan Rep - Below	OFF	
Model / Casework / Sink Opening	OFF	
Model / Mechanical Equipment		✓
Model / Plumbing Fixtures		✓
Model / Site		✓
Model / Specialty Equipment		✓
Model / Specialty Equipment / Dashed	OFF	
Annotation / Elevations	OFF	
Annotation / Grids	OFF	
Annotation / Reference Planes	OFF	
Annotation / Sections	OFF	

 Why set Grids visibility to *off*? In a future exercise we'll add grids to the project, and we won't want them visible in these views.

 Right-clicking on an element in an open view opens a contextual – or *shortcut* – menu, which gives you shortcut access to some of the Visibility/Graphics Overrides options.

Visibility/Graphics Overrides: By Filter

In the following steps you will define a selection set by with a filter. Filters are used to select a subset of elements within one or more categories. Once a filter is defined, it can be added to the Filters tab of the Visibility/Graphics Overrides dialog box. Any overrides applied to the filter will affect only elements that match the criteria defined by that filter.

Specifically, in the F.F.L... floor plan views, we don't want to see any "working" view markers, so we'll create a filter that selects only the view markers defined as working. Using V/G Overrides, we'll then set that filter selection set to be hidden. Presently, there is only a working building elevation marker in the plan views, and if you created them, some working interior elevation markers. In future exercises you will also add working section views, and those markers will be hidden by the filtered overrides as well.

EXERCISE 5.2: OBJECT STYLES & VISIBILITY GRAPHICS OVERRIDES

1. Open the floor plan view *F.F.L. 1st FLR*.

Visibility/Graphics Overrides		VV / VG
Tab	Panel	Tool Button
View	Graphics	Visibility/Graphics

2. Click on the **Filters** tab to open it.
3. Click **Add** to open the Add Filters dialog box.
4. Since the filter we need has not yet been created, we'll do this now. Click **Edit/New...** to open the Filters dialog box.
5. Referring to the illustration below, complete the following steps.

    a) At the bottom of the Filters pane, click the *New* icon

    b) Enter **View Markers - Working** for the name, then click **OK**.

    c) In the Categories pane, place a checkmark next to **Elevations** and **Sections**.

    d) To compress the list as shown in the illustration, optionally check the box for **Hide un-checked categories**.

    e) In the Filter Rules pane, set *Filter by* as follows:

    - **View Name** (*property by which to filter*)
    - **begins with** (*how the property will be tested, or the "operator"*)
    - **W-** (*value used by operator for comparison*)

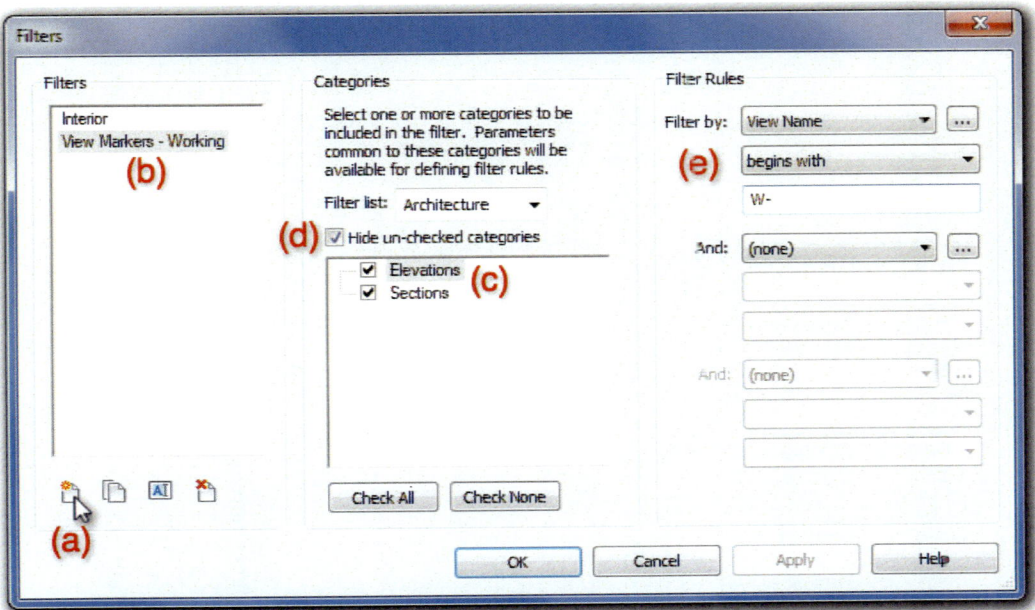

Filter Settings

6. Click **OK** to complete the filter.

159

7. In the Add Filters dialog box select **View Markers - Working**, then click **OK**. This should add it to the Filters tab of the Visibility/Graphics Overrides (V/G Overrides) dialog box.

    a) In the Filters tab of the V/G Overrides dialog box, clear the Visibility checkbox next to the filter name as illustrated below, then click **OK** to accept the changes.

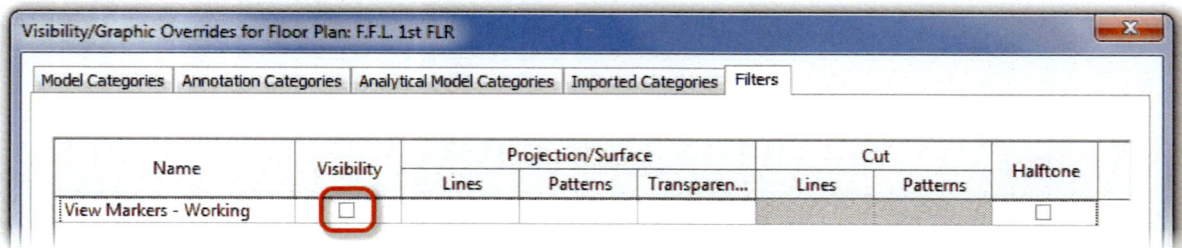

Filter Overrides

8. Your working elevation view markers should disappear from the view, provided they were named correctly, and the filter was set up properly.

 There's a peculiarity with hiding elevation markers with a filter. If only one view is associated with a marker and that view is hidden with a filter, the entire marker will be hidden, both body and arrow. However, if more than one view is enabled on a single marker, then only the arrows and view references will be hidden, not the body. This is regardless of whether or not all views are hidden by the filter. Therefore, if you created working interior elevation views with more than one view per marker, you will need to hide the body manually (by element).

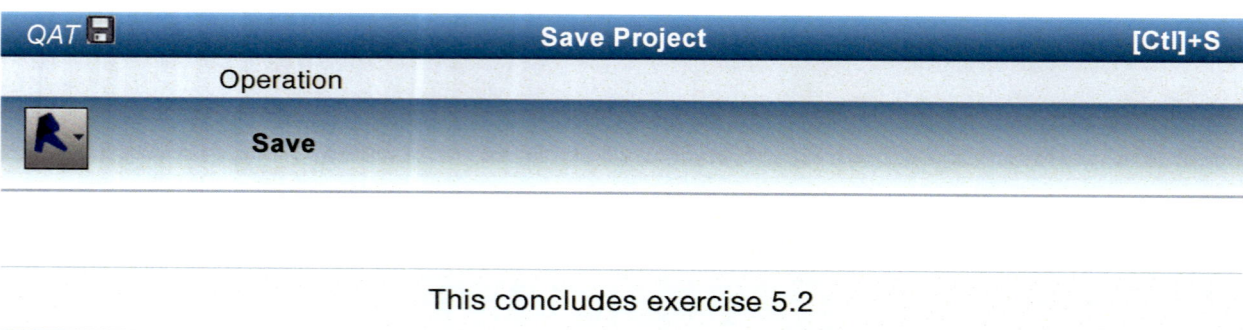

This concludes exercise 5.2

Exercise 5.3: View Templates

In this section you will create view templates to capture the graphic overrides you applied in the previous section. Having these override settings saved in templates will allow you to quickly apply the same overrides to other views as needed.

QAT 📂	Open Project		[Ctl]+O
	Operation	Option	File Name
R▾	Open ▶	Project	BIMHOUSE-EX05-2.rvt

	Save As (Project)		
	Operation	Option	File Name
R▾	Save As ▶	Project	BIMHOUSE-EX05-3.rvt

Create View Templates

Annotation Plan View Template

1. Open the floor plan view *F.F.L. 1st FLR*.

Create Template from Current View			
Tab	Panel	Split Button ▼	Tool Button
View	**Graphics**	**View Templates**	**Create Template from Current View**

2. In the New View Template dialog box, enter **Plan-Floor-Annotation** for the name, then click **OK**.
3. When the View Templates dialog box opens, click **OK** to accept all default settings.

Dimension Plan View Template

4. Open the floor plan view *1st Floor - Dimension*.

5. In the Project Browser, **right-click** on *1st Floor - Dimension* and select **Create Template From View...** from the contextual (shortcut) menu.

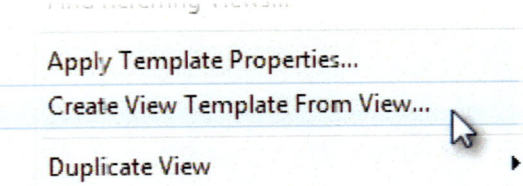

6. In the New View Template dialog box, enter **Plan-Floor-Dimension** for the name, then click **OK**.

7. When the View Templates dialog box opens, click **OK** to accept all default settings.

CHAPTER 5: SECTION VIEWS & GRAPHIC OVERRIDES

CAD Import Plan View Template

8. In the project browser, locate the floor plan view *W-1st Floor - CAD Import*, then **right-click** on it to open the contextual menu (no need to open the view), and select **Create View Template from View...**

9. In the New View Template dialog box, enter **Plan-Floor-CAD_Import** for the name, then click **OK**.

10. Once again, click **OK** in the View Templates dialog box to accept all default settings.

Apply View Templates

At this point, all we've done is capture the Visibility/Graphics Overrides into templates. Think of a template as a group of presets that can be applied when needed. In the following steps you will assign the new view templates to the appropriate views.

 There are two ways to update a view using a view template. The first is to simply *apply* the settings to the view. This updates the view, but allows further V/G overrides to be applied as needed. The second is to *assign* the view template in the view properties. This creates a link to the template, which makes the template the master control for the view. Further V/G overrides to any properties controlled by the template are not allowed. Any changes to the view template will be immediately reflected in views to which the template is *assigned*.

Annotation Plan View

1. In the Project browser, simultaneously select the two views *F.F.L. 1st FLR* and *F.F.L. 2nd FLR*.

2. In the Properties Palette, click on the button associated with the *View Template* property as illustrated.

3. Select *Plan-Floor-Annotation* from the Names pane in the Apply View Template dialog box, then click **OK**.

4. Open the floor plan view *F.F.L. 2nd FLR*, and verify that the graphic overrides match that of the *F.F.L. 1st FLR* plan view and that the *View Template* property is set to **Plan-Floor-Annotation**. If not, set it now.

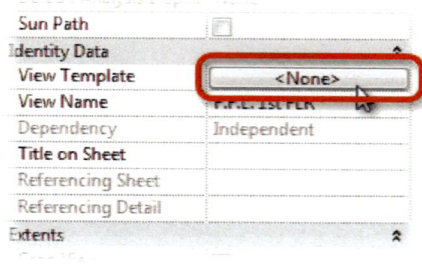

Dimension Plan View

5. In the Project browser, simultaneously select the two views *1st Floor - Dimension* and *2nd Floor - Dimension*.

6. Repeat the previous process and set the *View template* property to **Plan-Floor-Dimension**.

7. Open the floor plan view *2nd Floor - Dimension*, and verify that the graphic overrides match that of the *1st Floor - Dimension* plan view and that the *View Template* property is set to **Plan-Floor-Dimension**. If not, set it now.

8. Set the *Underlay* property to **None**.

 The *Underlay* property is not saved in a view template.

CAD Import Plan View

Although both of the CAD Import plan views should already have their graphic overrides applied, we still want to set the *View Template* property for both views to the correct template.

9. In the Project browser, simultaneously select the two views *W-1st Floor - CAD Import* and *W-2nd Floor - CAD Import*.
10. Repeat the previous process and set the *View template* property to **Plan-Floor-CAD_Import**.
11. Open each of the two views – *W-1st Floor - CAD Import* and *W-2nd Floor - CAD Import* – and verify correct view graphics and that the *View Template* property is set to **Plan-Floor-CAD_Import**. If not, set it now.

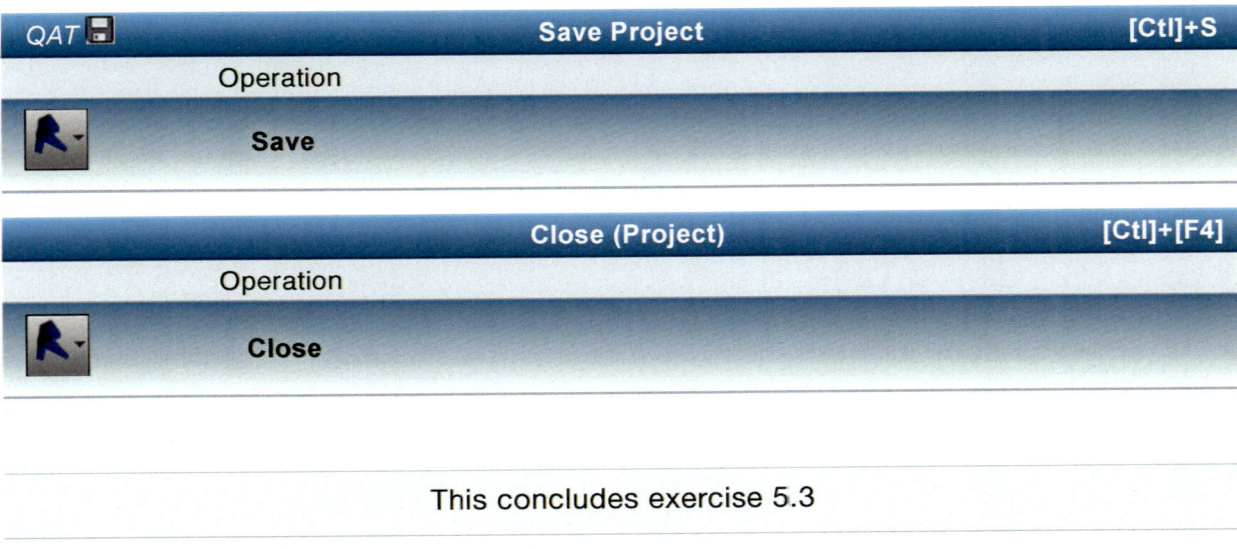

This concludes exercise 5.3

Chapter Summary

In this exercise you were exposed to the power of the graphics controls within Revit. Additionally, you have learned how to create view templates, which allow you to save a group of overrides and apply them to to any similar view at any time. What you have learned so far only scratches the surface, and you will gradually be exposed to more depth in future chapters.

Chapter 6
Ceilings

Overview

The typical, and default approach to creating ceilings in Revit isn't necessarily ideal for all applications. This chapter is intended to expose you to the various ways of modeling ceilings, and why one approach may be better than another. Additionally, you will be introduced to working in reflected ceiling plan views.

Learning Objectives

After completing this chapter you should have a basic understanding of the following tools and concepts.

- Modeling ceilings: "top down" and "bottom up"
- Creating compound ceiling types
- Creating a new material
- Controlling visibility, graphics, and view range in a reflected ceiling plan view
- Modeling walls and ceilings in a reflected ceiling plan view

Project Objectives

- Create new ceiling types
- Add ceilings on the 1st and 2nd floors
- Create a coffered ceiling
- Refine graphic representation in various plan views
- Create a working section view

Chapter Contents

Exercise 6.1: **Compound Ceilings** 167
- Set Up Views and Create Associated View Templates 167
- Create a Working Section View 173
- Create a New Ceiling Material 174
- Add a Ceiling Under the 1st Floor Roof 176
- Add a Ceiling Over the 2nd Floor 179

Exercise 6.2: **Ceiling Finish Layers** 182
- Coffered Ceiling in Living Room 182
- Create a Single-Layer 1/2" GWB Ceiling Type 188
- Set Up an Additional RCP View 189

Exercise 6.1: Compound Ceilings

The ceilings modeled in this exercise will serve two purposes: 1) to represent the roof truss bottom chord height; 2) to provide a drywall finish layer. The roof truss chord layer will be for representation purposes only, and will not contain any structural properties.

QAT 📂	Open Project		[Ctl]+O
	Operation	Option	File Name
R▼	Open ▶	Project	BIMHOUSE-EX5-3.rvt

	Save As (Project)		
	Operation	Option	File Name
R▼	Save As ▶	Project	BIMHOUSE-EX06-1.rvt

Set Up Views and Create Associated View Templates

T.O.W. View Graphics

1. Open floor plan view *T.O.W. 1st FLR*.
2. Adjust Visibility graphics overrides per the table below.

	Visibility/Graphics Overrides		VV / VG
Tab	Panel		Tool Button
View	Graphics		Visibility/Graphics

V/G Overrides: T.O.W. 1st FLR

Category Tab / Category / Subcategory	Visibility	Other
Model / Casework	OFF	
Model / Doors	OFF	
Model / Generic Models	OFF	
Model / Mechanical Equipment	OFF	
Model / Plumbing Fixtures	OFF	
Model / Roofs	OFF	
Model / Site	OFF	
Model / Specialty Equipment	OFF	
Annotation / Elevations	OFF	

3. Using the Properties palette, make the changes to the view properties indicated in the following table. When complete, your plan view should appear as illustrated below.

View Properties: T.O.W. 1st FLR

Parameter	Value	Alternate Access
Detail Level	**Medium**	VCB
Underlay	**F.F.L. 1st FLR**	
Underlay Orientation	**Plan**	
View Range...		
Top – Offset:	**0' 6"**	
Cut Plane – Offset:	**0' 6"**	
View Depth – Offset:	**-1' 0"**	

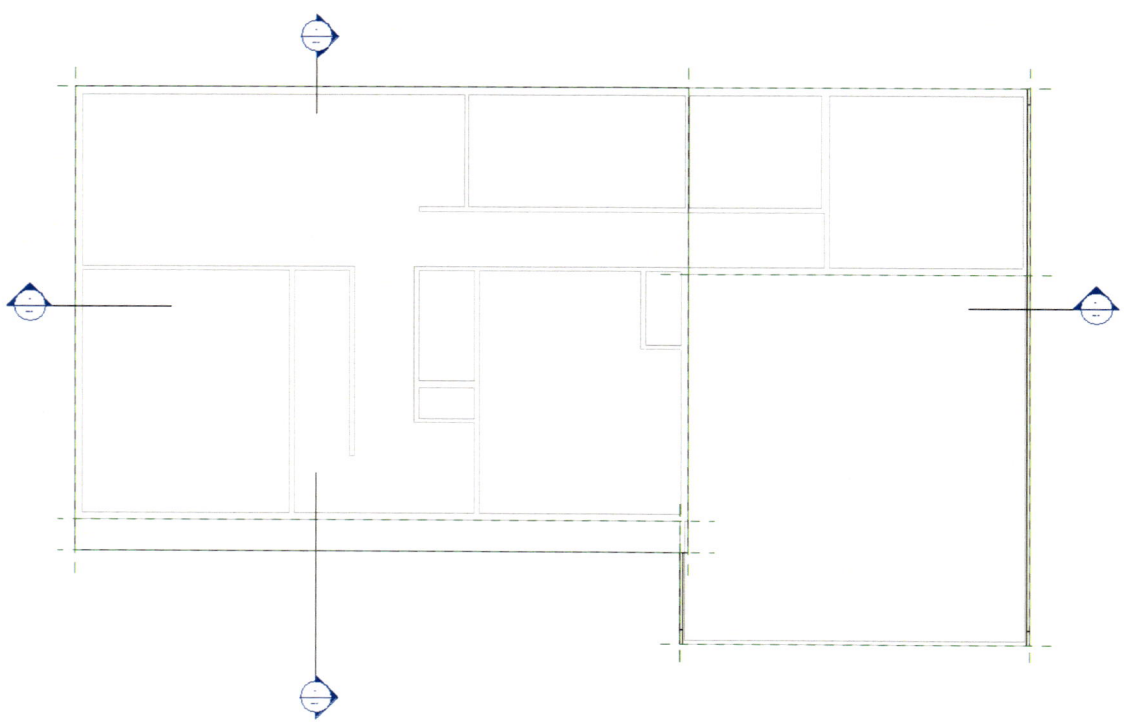

Create and Apply a View Template for T.O.W. Views

4. Using the techniques you learned in Chapter 5, do the following:

   a) **Create a view template** based on floor plan view *T.O.W. 1st FLR*, and name it **Plan-Floor-TOW**.

   b) Assign the new view template *Plan-Floor-TOW* to the *View Template* property of both *T.O.W. 1st FLR* and *T.O.W. 2nd FLR*.

EXERCISE 6.1: COMPOUND CEILINGS

Ceiling Plan View Graphics

In the following steps you will hide several categories using Visibility/Graphics Overrides. However, rather than using the Visibility/Graphics Overrides dialog box, you'll use the contextual menu instead, making the process much quicker.

5. Open the ceiling plan view *RCP - 1st Floor*.

6. Adjust the view range as indicated in the table below.

View Properties: RCP - 1st Floor

Parameter	Value	Alternate Access
View Range...		
Cut Plane – Offset:	7' 0"	

7. While holding down **[Ctrl]**, create a selection set by selecting at least one element from each category listed below. It doesn't matter which instance you pick, just pick at least one from each category. *Refer to the illustration on the next page for an example.*

   a) Elevation marker
      (either the body or the arrowhead)
   b) Section marker
   c) Roof
   d) Reference Plane
   e) Casework (upper cabinet)
   f) Door (garage door)
   g) Window

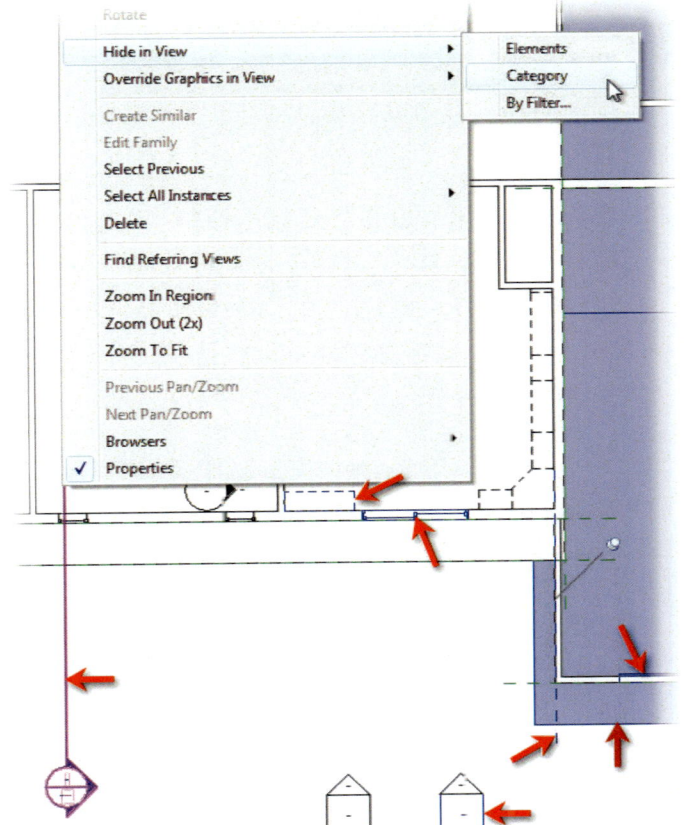

8. After you have the specified items selected, **right-click** anywhere in the drawing area and from the contextual menu select **Hide in View ▶ Category**.

   When done, the *RCP - 1st Floor* view should appear as illustrated on the following page.

CHAPTER 6: CEILINGS

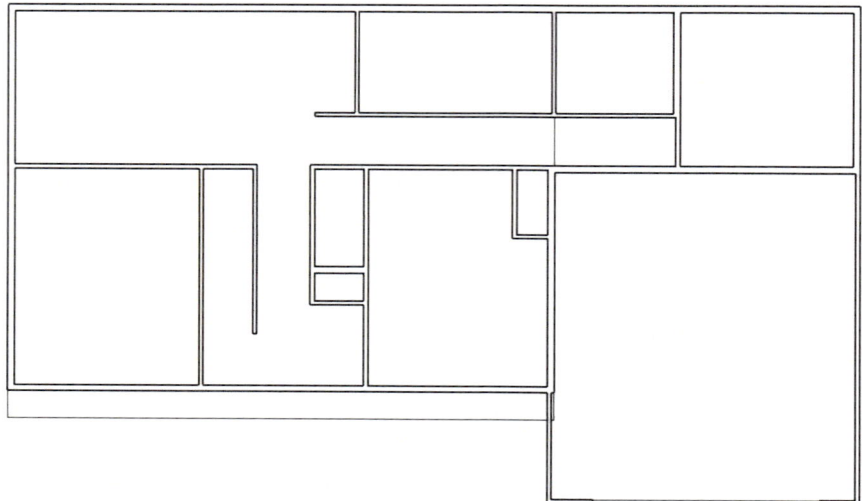

Modified View Graphics - RCP - 1st Floor

9. Open the Visibility/Graphics Overrides dialog box for the *RCP - 1st Floor* view, and make the additional changes shown in the table below.

V/G Overrides: RCP - 1st Floor

Category Tab / Category / Subcategory	Visibility
Annotation / Grids	OFF

10. Using the techniques you learned in Chapter 5, do the following:

    a) **Create a view template** based on ceiling plan view *RCP - 1st Floor*, name it **Plan-RCP**, and accept the default settings in the View Templates dialog box.

    b) Assign the new view template *Plan-RCP* to the *View Template* property of both *RCP - 1st Floor* and *RCP - 2nd Floor*.

Alternate RCP View Graphics & Template

The view settings applied so far may be appropriate for construction documents, but they also create some challenges when working in the view. In the following steps you will temporarily modify the graphic overrides to be more appropriate for working. You will then capture these additional overrides in a new view template, which can then be applied to other views, or temporarily applied whenever working in the current view.

11. Open the View Templates property manager...

Manage View Templates			
Tab	Panel	Split Button ▼	Tool Button
View	**Graphics**	**View Templates**	**Manage View Templates**

EXERCISE 6.1: COMPOUND CEILINGS

12. Select the view template *Plan-RCP* and **duplicate** it.
13. Name the new template **Plan-RCP-Working**.
14. Open the *V/G Overrides Model* by clicking on **Edit...**

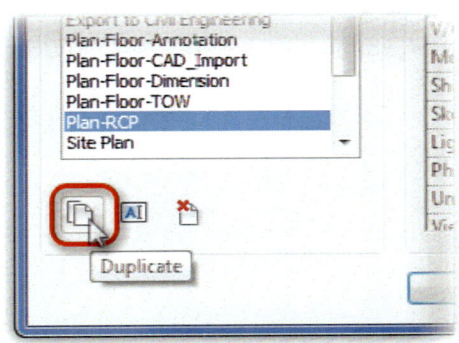

15. Make the following changes to the V/G Overrides (for the new view template *Plan-RCP-Working*).

V/G Override Changes: Plan-RCP-Working

Category Tab / Category	Visibility	Projection/Surface Patterns
Model / Ceilings		**Gypsum-Plaster** *(see illustration below)*
Annotation / Sections	ON	
Annotation / Reference Planes	ON	

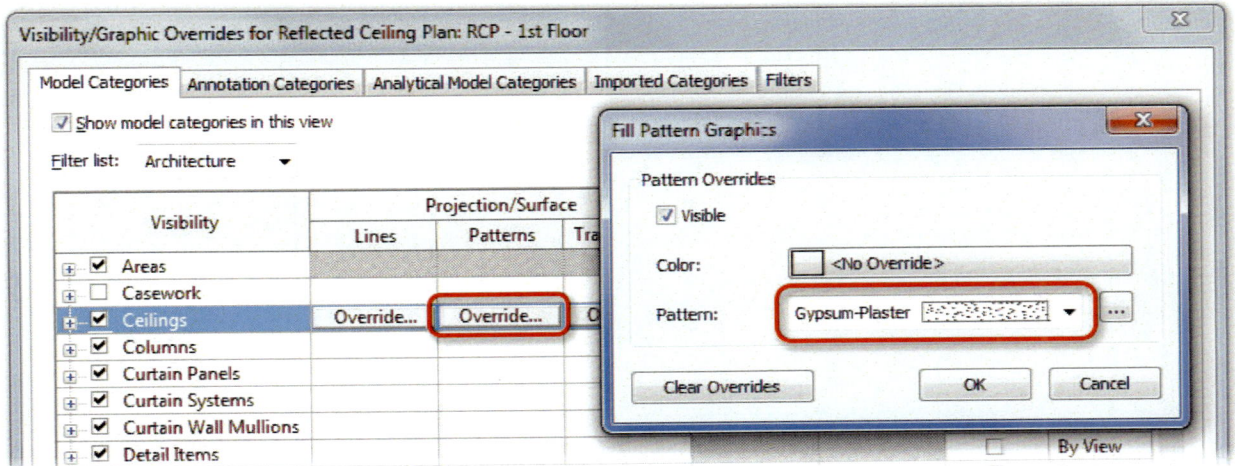

Surface Pattern Override: Ceilings Category

16. Click **OK** to close all dialog boxes and create the new view template.

171

CHAPTER 6: CEILINGS

 Having multiple view templates allows you to quickly change the appearance of a view to match workflow. Using the *Temporary View Properties*, you can temporarily apply a view template, and then restore the original settings when the temporary settings are no longer needed. After temporarily applying a view template the first time, that template will be added to a *Recent Templates* list in the *Temporary View Properties* menu, allowing quick access to it.

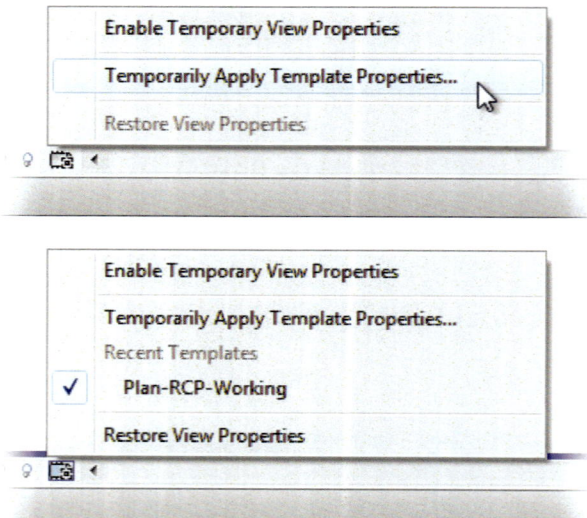

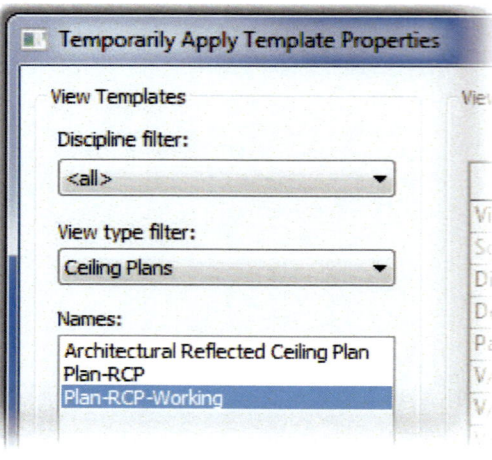

Create a Working Section View

1. Open floor plan view **F.F.L. 1st FLR**.

QAT ▸	Create Section View	
Tab	Panel	Tool Button
View	Create	Section

Modify | Section	
Reference other view: ☐	Offset: **0' 0"**

Properties
Type: **Building Section**

2. Draw the section marker as illustrated below.

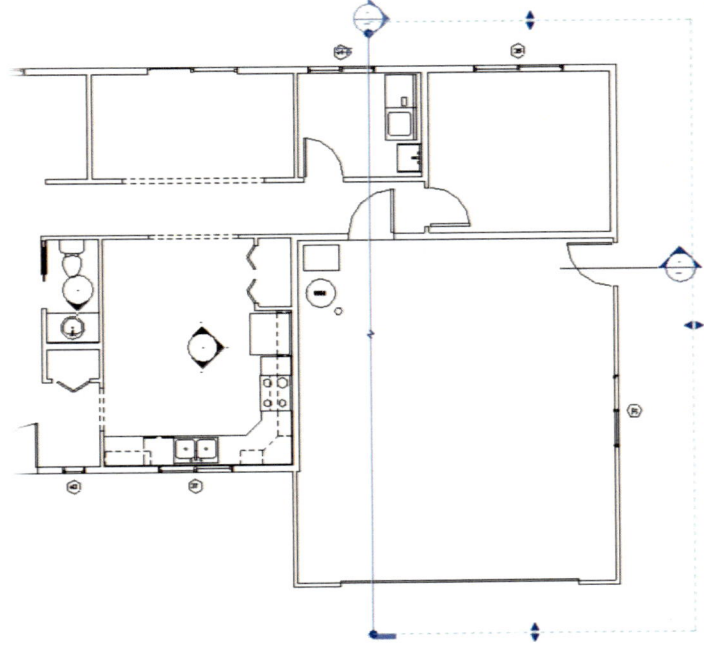

3. Rename the new section view to **W-Laundry-Garage (Long)**.

If F.F.L. 1st FLR was the active view when you renamed the section view, the section marker should have disappeared after you completed the renaming process. This is because we previously created and applied a filter in this view to hide all working section and elevation markers. The section marker will still be visible in other views where the filter or other related overrides have not been applied. *If the view marker did not disappear, double check the naming, as well as the filter criteria.*

Create a New Ceiling Material

In the following steps you will create a new material for use in a new ceiling type. This material will be used to in the bottom chord the truss layer. Refer to the illustration below for assistance on locating the various parts of the Material Browser.

1. In the search field at the top of the dialog box, type **wood** to filter the list.
2. Select the material *Structure, Wood Truss Joist/Rafter Layer* in the list of materials.
3. **Duplicate** the material.

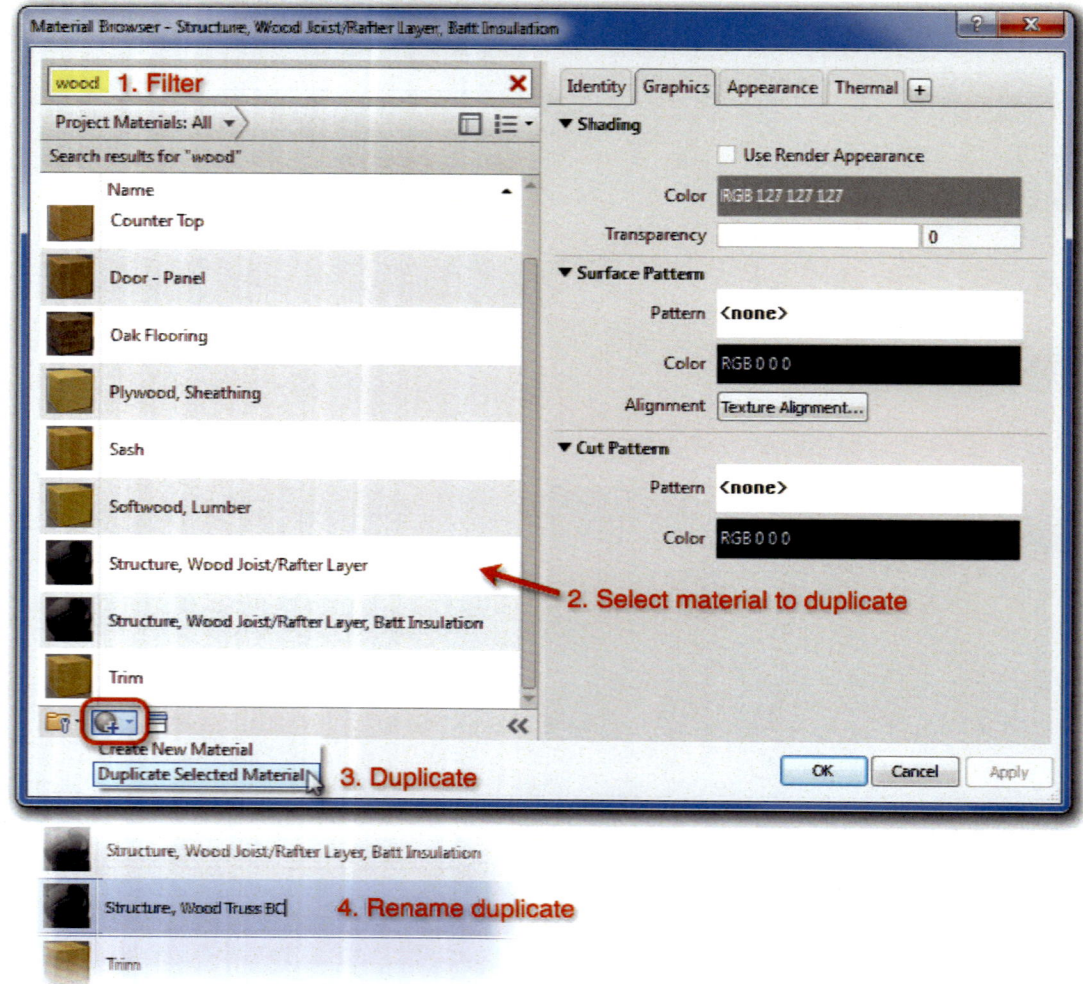

4. Enter **Structure, Wood Truss BC** for the new material name, then press **[enter]**
5. Click **OK** to exit the Material Browser dialog and create the new material.

EXERCISE 6.1: COMPOUND CEILINGS

Create a New Ceiling Type

1. In the Project Browser, navigate to the Families section and expand the following tree:

    Families → Ceilings → Compound Ceiling

2. **Double-click** on *GWB on Mtl. Stud* to open the Type Properties dialog box
3. Click **Duplicate...**
4. Enter **GWB on 4" Truss B.C.** for the name *(B.C. stands for "bottom chord")*, click **OK**.
5. Click **Edit...** *Structure* to open the Edit Assembly dialog box.
6. Modify the ceiling properties to match those shown in the table below. Refer to the illustrations that follow as a guide to assigning the material.

Ceiling Structure: Gwb On 4" Truss B.C

Layer	Function	Material	Thickness
1	**Core Boundary**	**Layers Above Wrap**	**0' 0"**
2	Structure [1]	Structure, Wood Truss BC	0' 3 1/2"
3	**Core Boundary**	**Layers Below Wrap**	**0' 0"**
2	Finish 2 [5]	Gypsum Wall Board	0' 0 1/2"

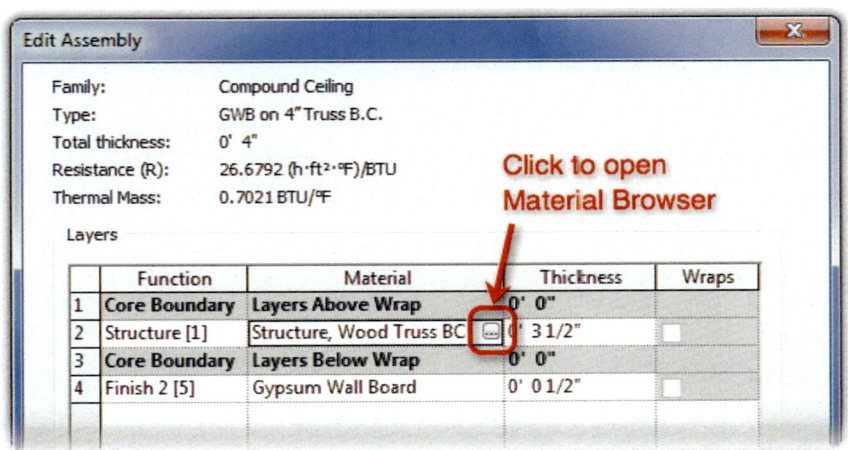

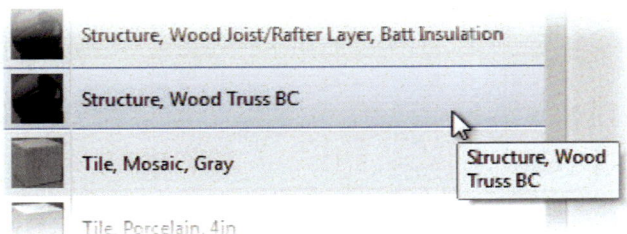

Select Material

7. Click **OK** to exit all dialogs and apply the changes.

175

Add a Ceiling Under the 1st Floor Roof

1. Open the floor plan view *T.O.W. 1st FLR*.

Ceiling		
Tab	Panel	Tool Button
Architecture	**Build**	**Ceiling**

2. On the contextual ribbon tab, click **Sketch Ceiling**.

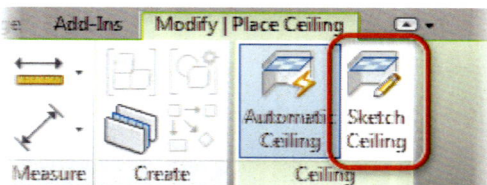

3. Set / verify the ceiling properties...

Properties	
Type:	**GWB on 4" Truss B.C.**
Level:	**T.O.W. 1st FLR**
Height Offset From Level:	**-0' 0 1/2"**
Room Bounding:	✓

 Offsetting the ceiling -1/2" is necessary to compensate for the thickness of the GWB. This allows the bottom of the truss layer to rest on the T.O.W. level.

Modify	Create Ceiling Boundary	
Draw	
Boundary Line	**Pick Walls**
Offset: **0' 0"**	Extend into wall (to core): ☑

4. Create a ceiling boundary by picking the walls shown in the illustration below.

 Where an arrow points to a gable wall, pick the *inside face* of the wall (2 places).

5. After picking all 6 walls, use the **Trim/Extend to Corner** tool to trim the boundary lines to create a closed loop, also shown in the illustration below.

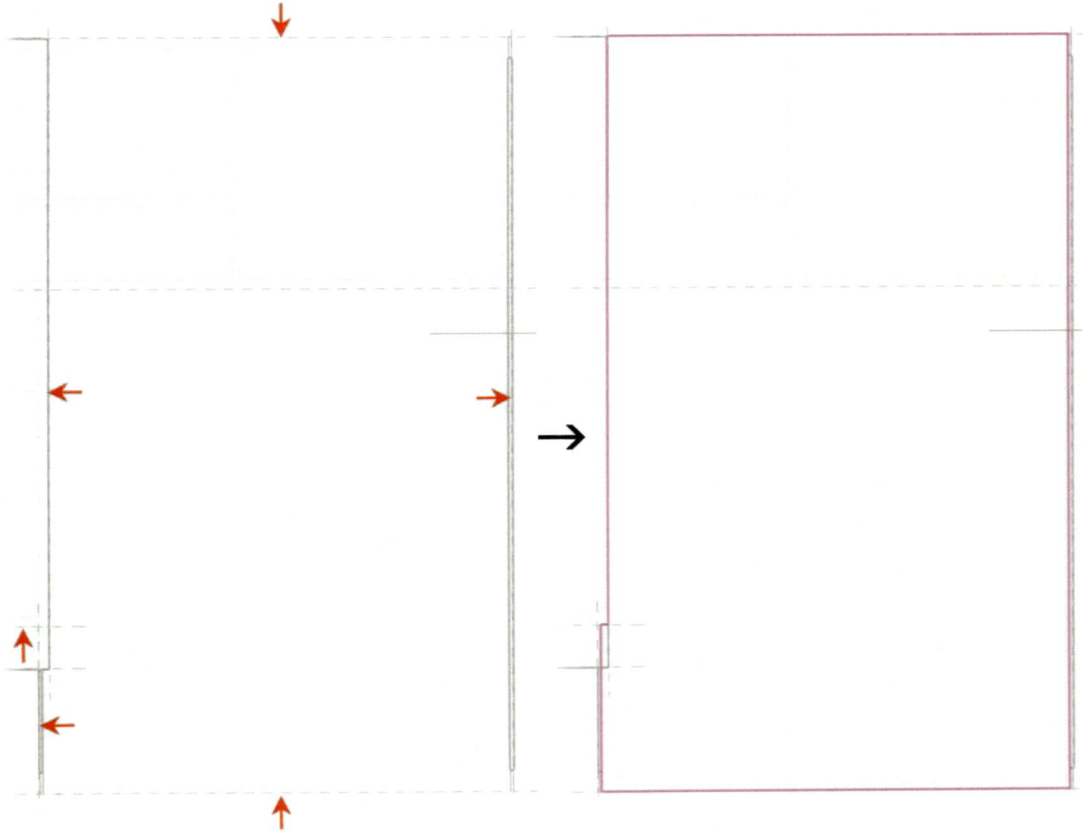

Pick Walls / Resulting Boundary - 1st Floor Ceiling

6. When done, click the **Finish Edit Mode** button ✓
7. Open the section view *W-Laundry-Garage (Long)*.
8. Set the *Detail Level* for the section view to **Medium**.

9. Zoom into the left side of the view (laundry area) to examine the overlapping conditions created by the new ceiling as shown in the illustration below:

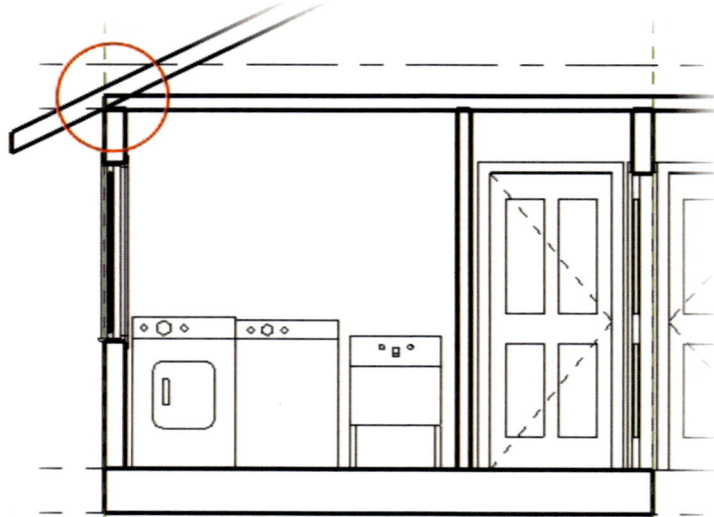

10. Use **Join Geometry** to clean up the overlapping conditions as illustrated below...

Join Geometry			
Tab	Panel	Split Button ▼	Tool Button
Modify	**Geometry**	**Join**	**Join Geometry**

11. Join elements in the following order:
   a) Join the four walls *to* the ceiling (pick wall first)
   b) Join the roof *to* the ceiling (pick roof first)

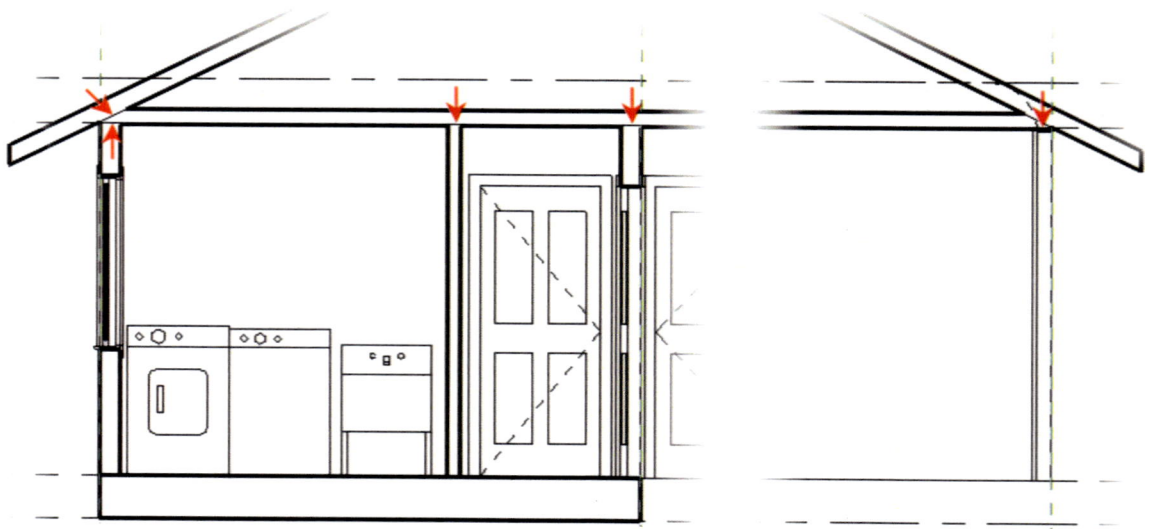

Join Geometry Locations

Add a Ceiling Over the 2nd Floor

1. Open floor plan view *T.O.W. 2nd FLR*
2. Adjust the crop region for the view so that it looks similar to the illustration below.

 To adjust the crop region, you will need to reveal it using the VCB.

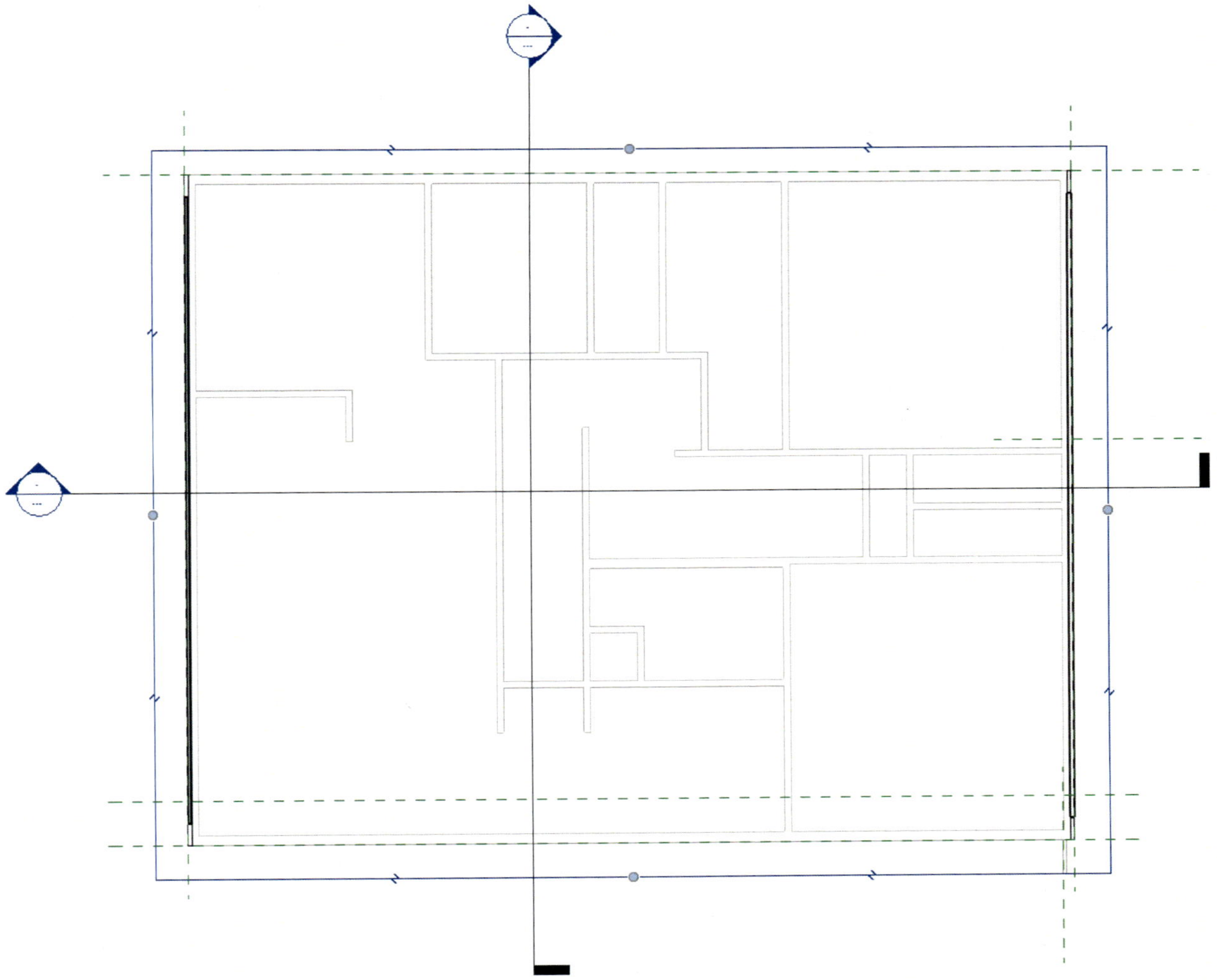

Adjust Crop Region

3. When done, **hide** the crop region.

CHAPTER 6: CEILINGS

Ceiling		
Tab	Panel	Tool Button
Architecture	Build	Ceiling

Modify	Create Ceiling Boundary
Ceiling
Sketch Ceiling

Properties
Type: **GWB on 4" Truss B.C.**

Height Offset From Level:	**-0' 0 1/2"**

Modify	Create Ceiling Boundary	
Draw	
Boundary Line	**Pick Walls**
Offset: **0' 0"**	Extend into wall (to core): ☑

4. Create a ceiling boundary by picking the walls as illustrated below.

 Where an arrow points to a gable wall, pick the *inside face* of the wall (2 places).

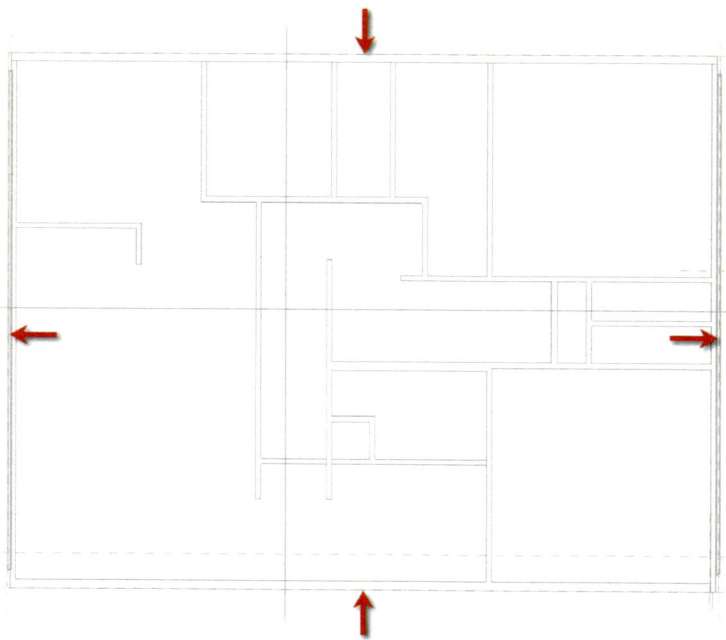

5. When done, click the **Finish Edit Mode** button ✓
6. Open the section view *Family-Stairs-Porch (Long)*
7. Use **Join Geometry** to join intersecting walls and roof to the 2nd floor ceiling, as you did in previous steps with the 1st floor ceiling. When done, your section should appear similar to the illustration below.

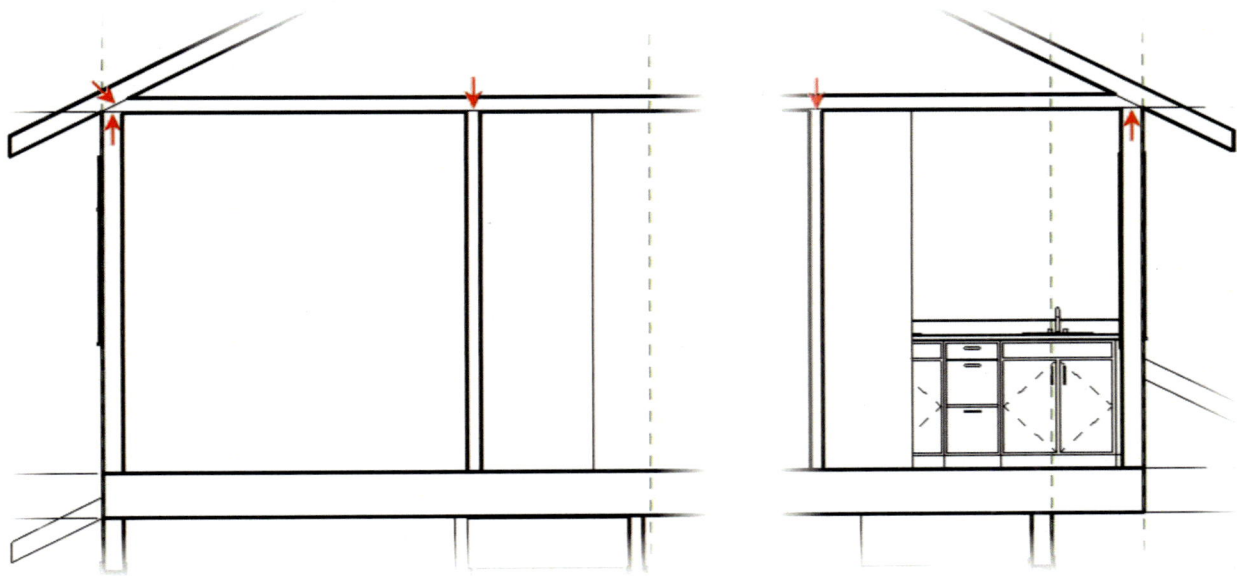

Joined Geometry at 2nd Floor

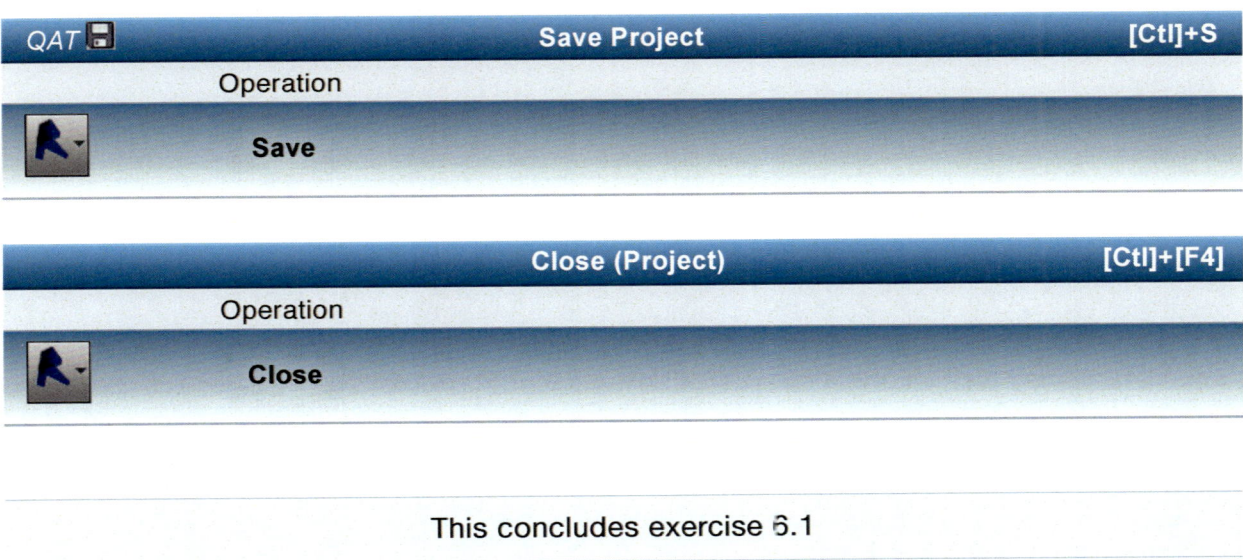

This concludes exercise 6.1

Exercise 6.2: Ceiling Finish Layers

The remainder of the ceilings in this chapter will represent finish and nonstructural framing elements only. When modeling these ceilings you will use the default Revit approach; that is, create them from within a reflected ceiling plan view.

The ceiling construction on the 1st floor will include a coffered ceiling in the living room. You will model soffit walls to create the vertical component of the coffer. These wall elements will be modeled first in order to provide a boundary between the two different ceiling elements in that room.

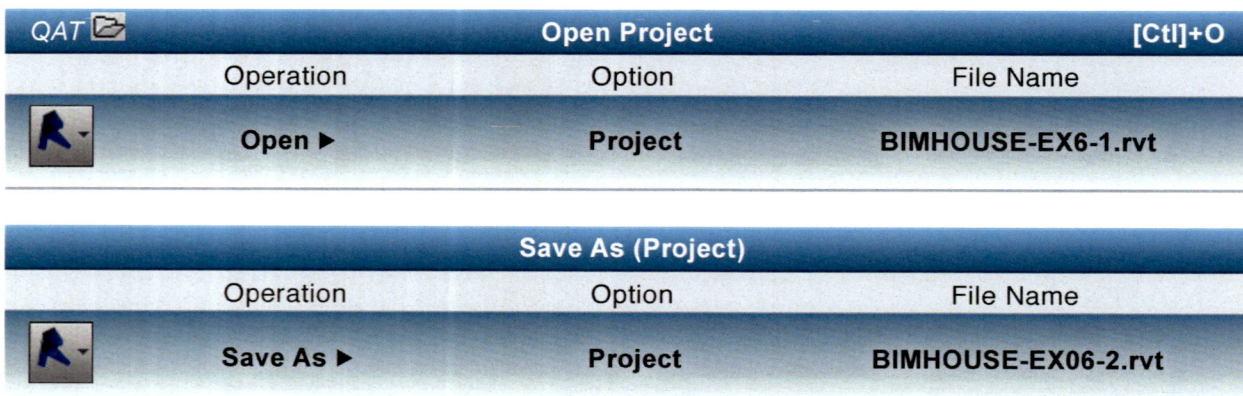

Coffered Ceiling in Living Room

Add Soffit Walls

In the following steps you will place a a series of soffit walls to create the vertical component of the coffer. Since this requires a unique wall type, you must first create it; you'll do this on-the-fly while the wall tool is active. Additionally, while working in this view you will temporarily apply the working view template created in the previous exercise.

1. Open the ceiling plan view *RCP -1st Floor*.

2. In the VCB, click the **Temporary View Properties** icon, and then select **Temporarily Apply Template Properties...**

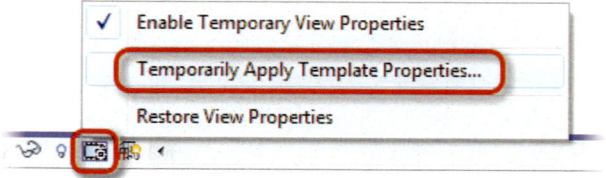

3. Select *Plan-RCP-Working* from the list and click **OK**. The view graphics should update to show section markers, reference planes, and a surface pattern on the existing ceiling. If not, go back to the previous exercise and check the view template properties.

 If you previously applied this view template using Temporary View Properties, the it should be available to select under the Recent Templates section in the pop-up menu.

EXERCISE 6.2: CEILING FINISH LAYERS

4. Add the soffit walls...

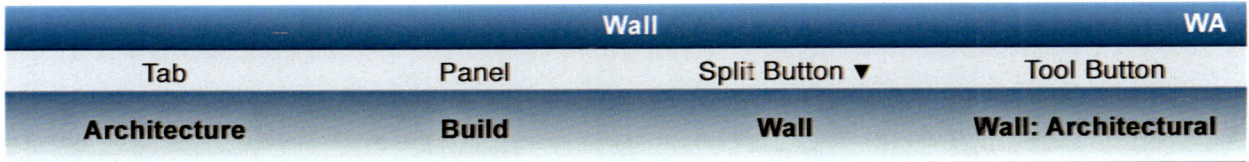

Wall			WA
Tab	Panel	Split Button ▼	Tool Button
Architecture	Build	Wall	Wall: Architectural

5. Select *Generic - 3 1/2"* for the type, then click **Edit Type**.
6. Click **Duplicate...** and change the name to **Generic - 3 1/2" Soffit**.
7. Set the *Function* property to **Soffit**.
8. Click **OK** to finish creating the wall.

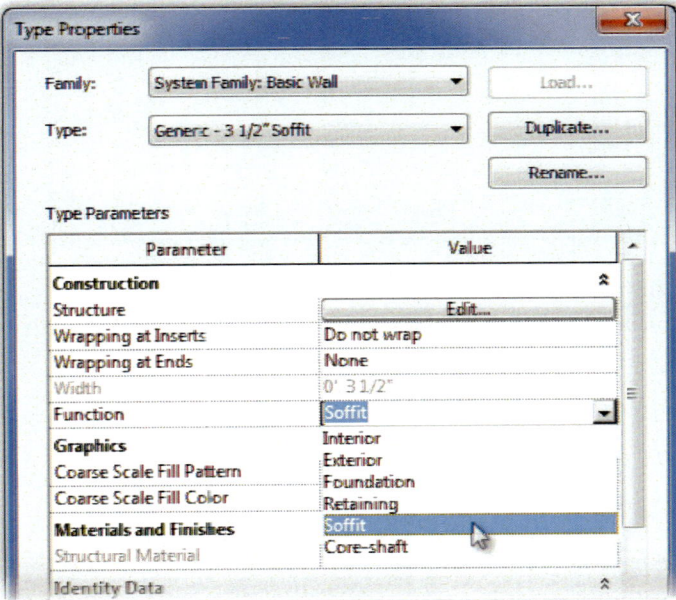

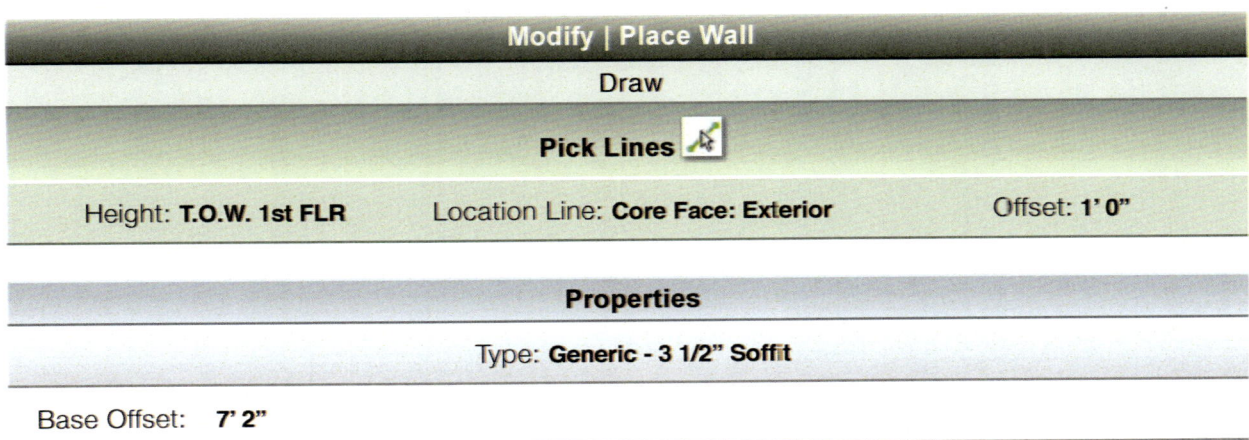

Modify	Place Wall		
Draw		
Pick Lines		
Height: **T.O.W. 1st FLR**	Location Line: **Core Face: Exterior**	Offset: **1' 0"**

Properties
Type: **Generic - 3 1/2" Soffit**

Base Offset: **7' 2"**

CHAPTER 6: CEILINGS

9. Place 4 soffit walls by picking the interior side of the walls that define the living room as illustrated. Make sure the the dashed blue location indicator line is showing on the interior side of the living room prior to each pick.

10. **Exit** the wall tool when done.

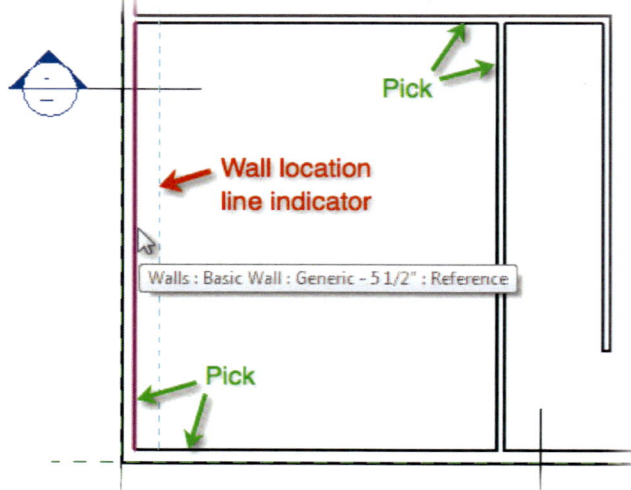

Trim/Extend to Corner		TR
Tab	Panel	Tool Button
Modify	Modify	Trim/Extend to Corners

11. **Trim** the four walls so they form a continuous rectangular chain as illustrated below.

12. **Exit** the Trim tool when done.

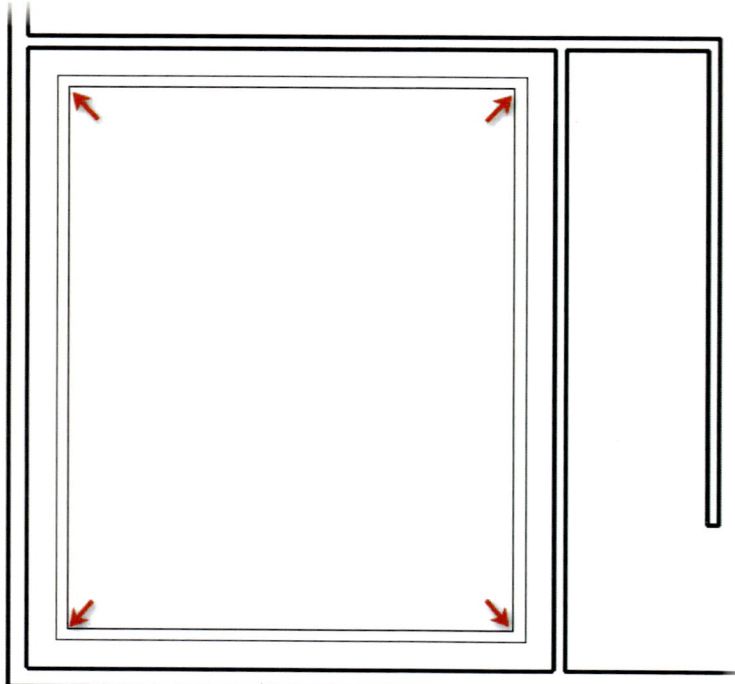

Create a New Ceiling Type

1. In the Project browser, locate the *GWB on 4" Truss B.C.* ceiling you created earlier, select it, and then open the Type Properties.

2. Click **Duplicate**... and enter **GWB on 4" Wood Furring** for the name.

3. Open the Edit Assembly dialog box, and change the *Structure [1]* layer material to **Structure, Wood Joist/Rafter Layer**.

4. Click **OK** twice to exit all dialog boxes and complete the ceiling type.

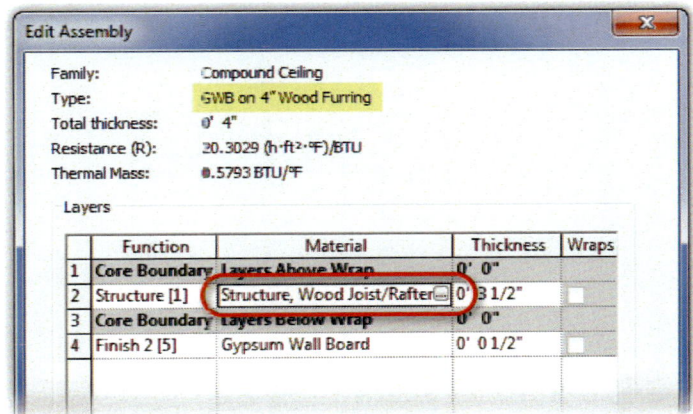

Place the Furred-down Ceiling

Ceiling		
Tab	Panel	Tool Button
Architecture	Build	Ceiling

Modify | Create Ceiling Boundary
Ceiling
Sketch Ceiling

Properties
Type: **GWB on 4" Wood Furring**

Level:	**F.F.L. 1st FLR**
Height Offset From Level:	**7' 2"**

Modify | Create Ceiling Boundary	
Draw	
Boundary Line	Pick Walls
Offset: **0' 0"**	Extend into wall (to core): ☑

5. Create the ceiling boundary with two closed loop sketches as illustrated below by picking the corresponding walls. Trim any excess lines as necessary.

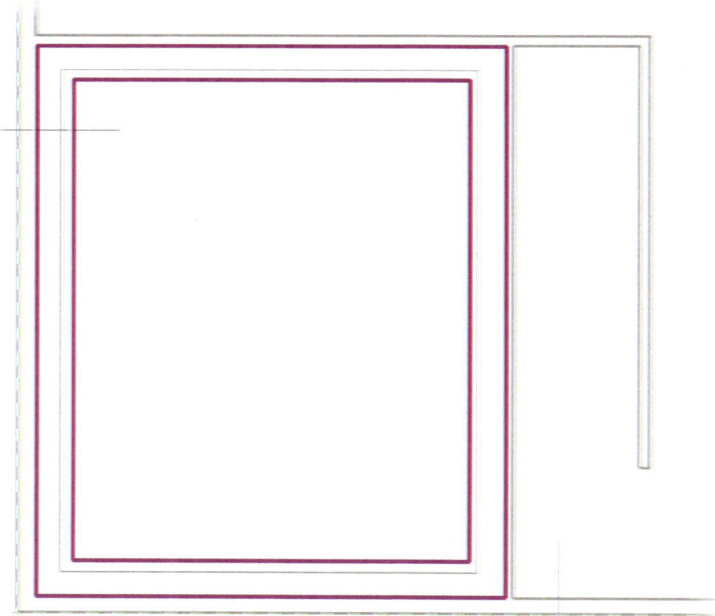

6. When done, click the **Finish Edit Mode** button ✓
7. Open the section view *Living-Kitchen-Garage (Cross)* and verify the ceiling is properly located in elevation, as illustrated below.

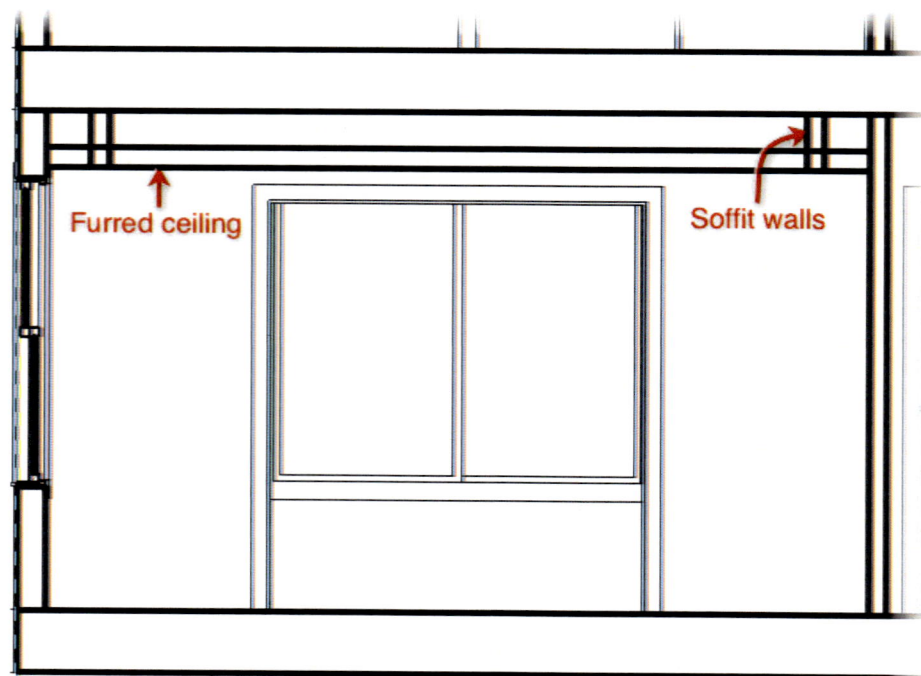

8. Open the ceiling plan view *RCP -1st Floor*.

9. Join the soffit walls to the ceiling using the *Multiple Join* option...

Join Geometry		
Tab	Panel	Tool Button
Modify	**Geometry**	**Join**	**Join Geometry**

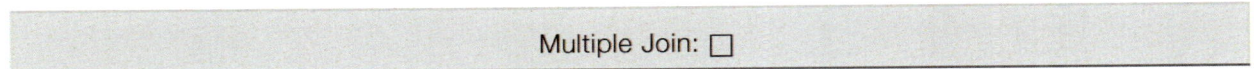

Multiple Join: ☑

10. First pick the ceiling, then pick each wall individually.

11. Reset the Join Geometry tool options...

Multiple Join: ☐

12. **Exit** the Join Geometry tool. Your ceiling view should appear as illustrated below.

Coffered Ceiling After Geometry Joined

 When using any of the modify tools that have a "multiple" option, such as *Align*, or *Join Geometry*, it is best to uncheck this box when finished with the operation, and just prior to exiting the tool. Revit remembers this setting, and automatically uses it the next time you use the tool. If you forget to look at the options bar, you may get unexpected results, as well as experience some frustration until realizing this checkbox is selected!

13. Open the section view **Living-Kitchen-Garage (Cross)** to view the results of the coffered ceiling. Your view should look similar to the illustration below.

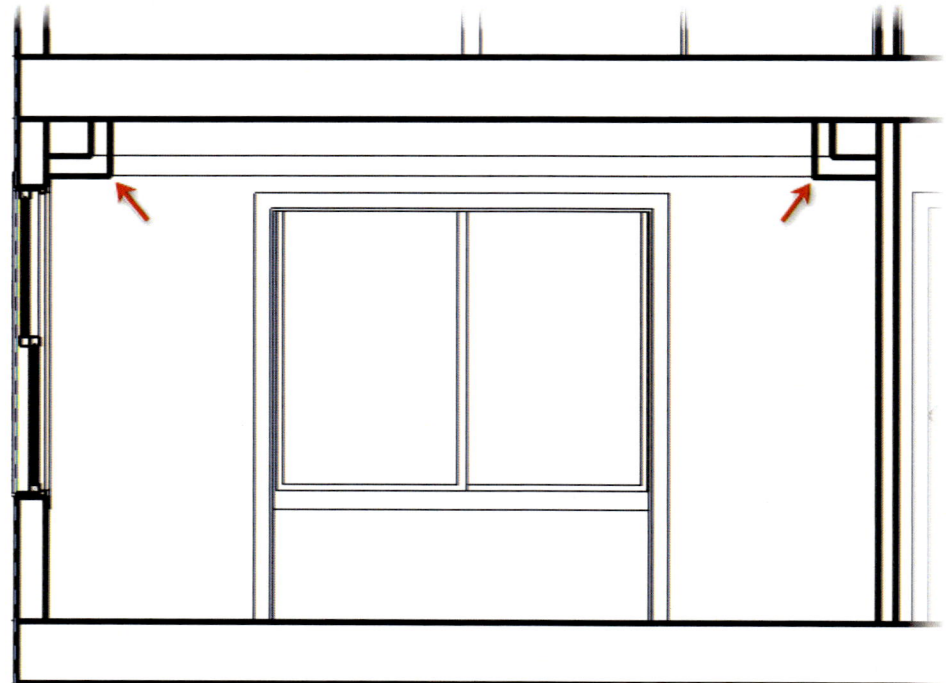

Section View of Coffered Ceiling

Create a Single-Layer 1/2" GWB Ceiling Type

In a future chapter you will create compound floors to place in your model. These floors will consist of multiple layers that represent joists and floor sheathing. You could also include a ceiling layer at the underside of the 2nd floor assembly to simplify the initial modeling process. However, this would create a few challenges and and potentially create extra work as follows:

- First, the ceiling material would extended out to the exterior where the floor cantilevers at the south side of the house. There's no way of adjusting layer extents on ceiling elements.

- If you later decide to place light fixtures in the ceiling, these family types are mostly ceiling-based (requires a *ceiling* as a host), and as a result couldn't be placed because the ceiling finish layer is actually part of a *floor* family.

- If you later replace the floor's core mass with discrete framing elements, you would need to model a separate ceiling anyway.

Therefore, the remainder of the ceilings on the first floor will consist of a single layer of gypsum wall board (GWB), and be associated with *T.O.W. - 1st FLR*. Additionally, you will use the Automatic Ceiling tool to model the remainder of the ceilings.

1. **Duplicate** one of the ceiling types containing *GWB* in the name, and name the new ceiling **GWB - 1/2"**.

Remember that you can select a family and duplicate it from within the Project Browser.

2. Edit the ceiling structure to represent the properties shown in the table below (*move the finish layer up and delete the structure layer*).

Ceiling Structure: Gwb - 1/2"

Layer	Function	Material	Thickness
1	Core Boundary	Layers Above Wrap	0' 0"
2	Finish 2 [5]	Gypsum Wall Board	0' 0 1/2"
3	Core Boundary	Layers Below Wrap	0' 0"

The structure of a compound element such as a wall, ceiling, floor, or roof, must have a core layer. Therefore, a single layer type will require the layer to be located between the core boundaries, even if the layer's function is other than *Structure*.

Set Up an Additional RCP View

When placing elements in Revit architecture, the default behavior is for the elements to be associated with the same level as is the view in which you are working. In the case of our existing RCP views, they are both associated with their respective finish floor levels. Therefore any ceilings placed from within either of these views will be associated with the respective view's level. This can be overridden; however, the override will reset back to the default level after each ceiling instance is placed, requiring this property to be overridden for each ceiling placement.

To eliminate the need for overriding the level property, we'll create an additional RCP view associated with the correct level for the the ceilings. Per design intent, the correct level for these ceilings is *T.O.W. - 1st FLR*.

The design intent for any ceiling finish layer in this project, other than the furred down portion of the coffer, is for the gypsum wall board to be attached to the underside of structural framing members such as trusses or joists. These framing members rest on the top plate of the corresponding walls, and are therefore associated with the corresponding T.O.W. level. Therefore, it makes sense that the ceiling finish layer be referenced to the same level, since all these elements share a common relationship to elevation. Then, should a plate height change be required in the future, a single change to level elevation will move all related elements without the need for additional editing.

Chapter 6: Ceilings

View Templates Refinement

Rather than create another view template for the new ceiling plan view, we'll reuse one created earlier in this chapter. However, there will be distinct differences in view range between the existing ceiling plans and the new one. Therefore, in their current state, the ceiling plan view templates are incompatible with the new view, since they include view range properties in their settings. In the following steps you will exclude the view range settings from the ceiling plan view templates.

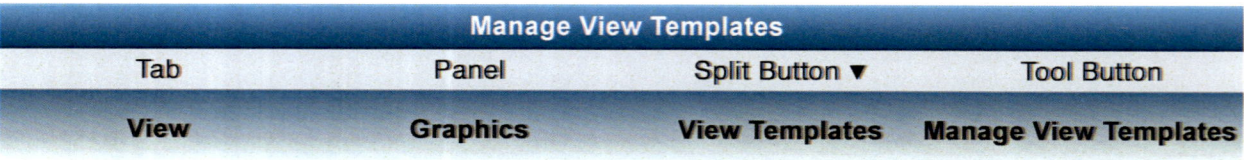

Manage View Templates			
Tab	Panel	Split Button ▼	Tool Button
View	Graphics	View Templates	Manage View Templates

 You can filter view templates by type using the *View type filter* drop-down list.

1. Select the view template named *Plan-RCP*, then **uncheck** the **Include checkbox** associated with *View Range*.

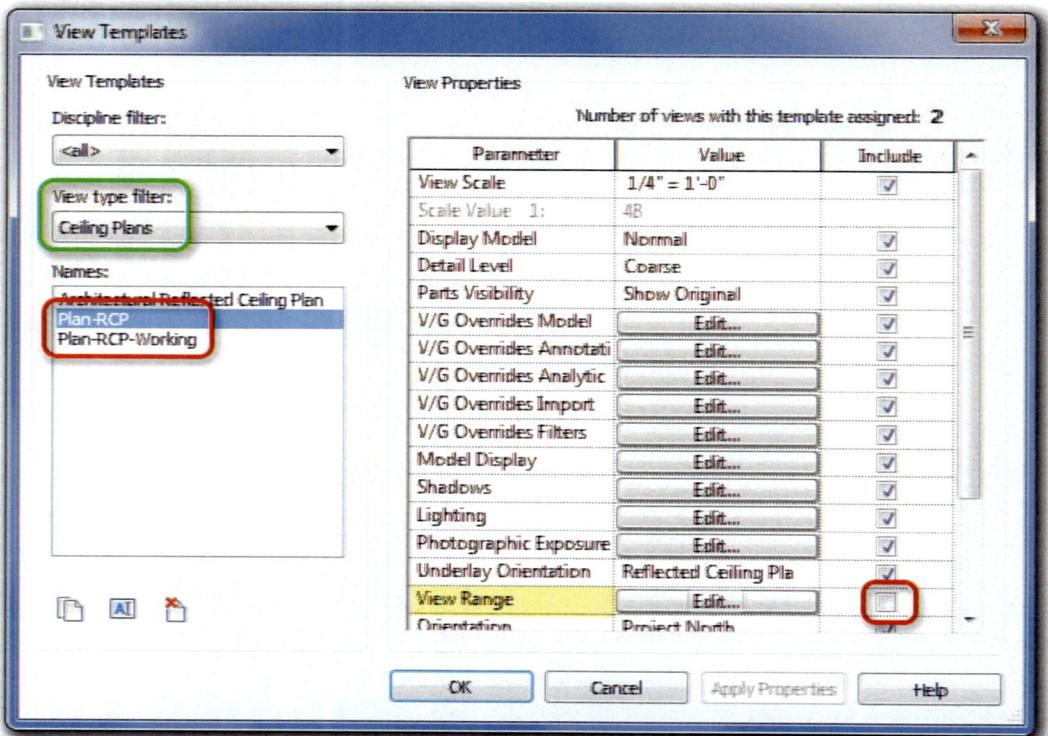

2. Select the view template named *Plan-RCP-Working*, and repeat the process.
3. Click **OK** to apply the changes.

190

Create the New View

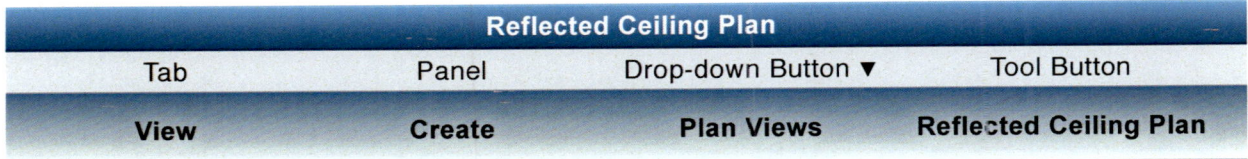

4. In the New RCP dialog box, select *T.O.W. 1st Floor*, then click **Edit Type...**

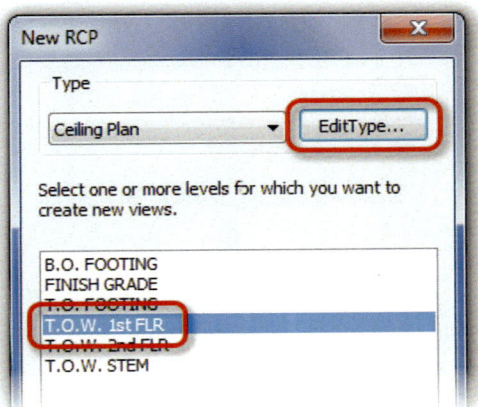

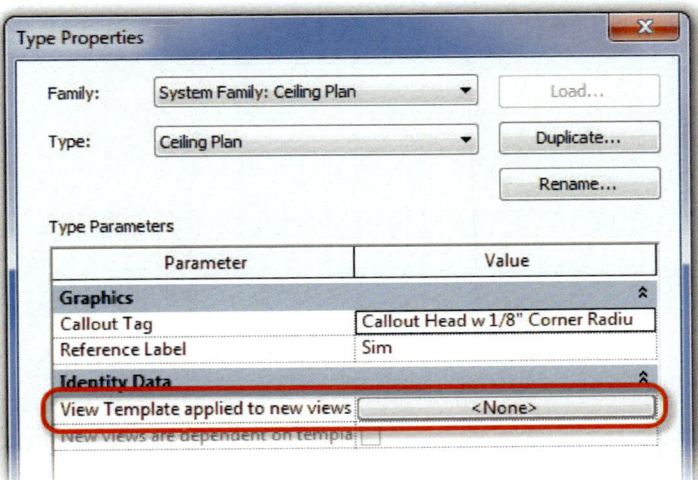

5. In the Type Properties dialog box, click the button **<None>** next to *View Template applied to new views*.

6. In the Apply View Template dialog box, select **Plan-RCP-Working**, then click **OK**.

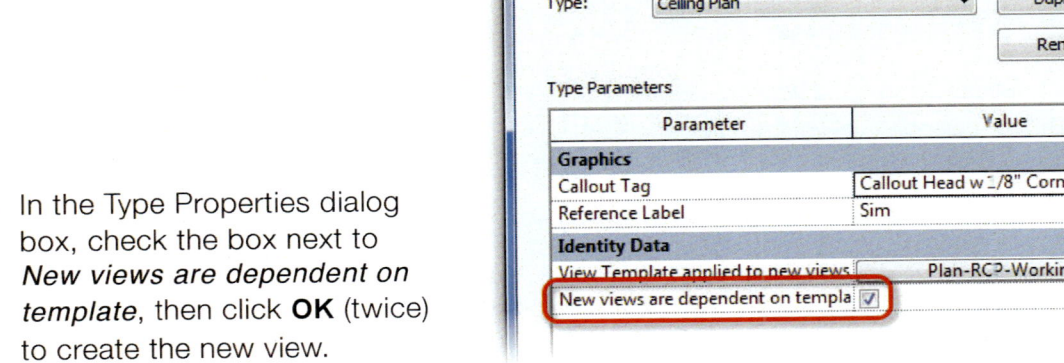

7. In the Type Properties dialog box, check the box next to *New views are dependent on template*, then click **OK** (twice) to create the new view.

Chapter 6: Ceilings

8. Rename the new view to **RCP - 1st Floor - T.O.W**. Answer **No** to the rename prompt.

 Answer **No** to the "...*rename corresponding level and views*" prompt.

9. Set the *View Range* properties for *RCP - 1st Floor - T.O.W* as illustrated below.

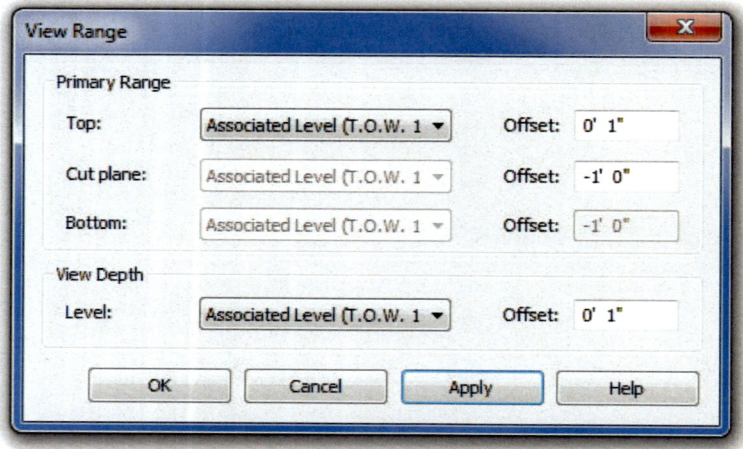

View Range Settings: RCP - 1st Floor - T.O.W.

10. The new ceiling plan should now appear identical to *RCP - 1st Floor* when the Temporary View Properties are set to view template *Plan-RCP-Working*.

Add the Remaining Ceilings

1. Open the ceiling plan view *RCP - 1st Floor - T.O.W*.

Ceiling		
Tab	Panel	Tool Button
Architecture	**Build**	**Ceiling**

Modify	Place Ceiling
Ceiling
Automatic Ceiling

Properties	
Type: **GWB - 1/2"**	
Level:	**T.O.W. 1st FLR**
Height Offset From Level:	**-0 0 1/2"**

Make sure you are working in the correct view. If not, the *Level* value in the Properties palette will reset back to the default level for that view after each ceiling placement.

2. Place ceilings in the spaces that don't already have a ceiling, including closets, pantry, and recessed portion of the coffered ceiling. These areas should be easily identifiable due to the existence of a surface pattern on existing ceilings. If you don't see any ceilings at this point, then you either haven't created them, or your Visibility/Graphics Overrides are incorrect.

3. **Exit** the Ceiling tool when done.

 Notice that the large ceiling that spans several rooms also overlaps a portion of the ceiling at the hall between the laundry room and garage. Next you will correct this by editing the ceiling boundary.

4. Select the ceiling highlighted in yellow in the illustration below.

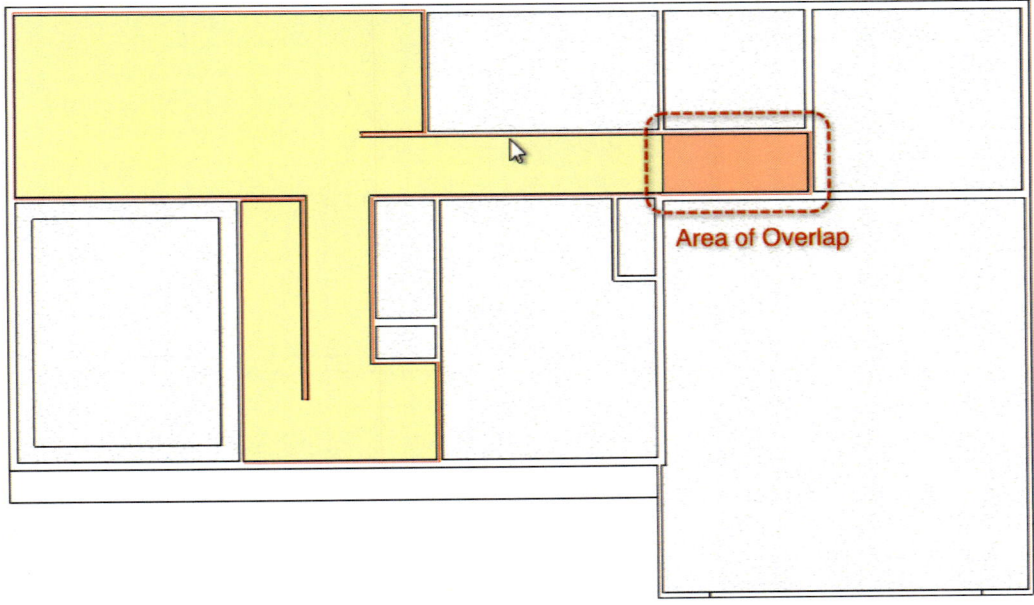

Select Ceiling To Edit (Illustration Colored for Clarity)

5. Click **Edit Boundary** in the contextual ribbon tab.

6. Edit the ceiling boundary as follows. Refer to the illustration below for clarity.

   a) **Delete** the ceiling boundary line at the end of the hall, as well as the short section at the south side of the hall.

   b) Add a new boundary line at the reference plane indicated in the illustration.

   c) **Align/Lock** the new boundary line to the reference plane.

   d) Trim the boundary lines as necessary, then click the **Finish Edit Mode** button ✓

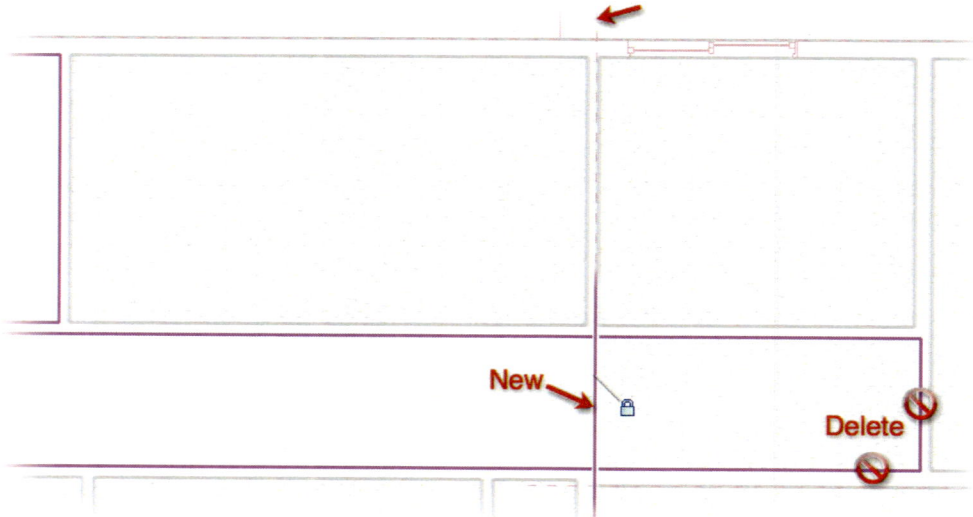

Edit The Ceiling Boundary

7. Use **Join Geometry** to join the two ceilings where they come together.

 To select the two ceilings for joining, move the cursor over the line where they come together, then click twice. The join line should disappear.

EXERCISE 6.2: CEILING FINISH LAYERS

8. When complete, your ceiling plan should look like the illustration below. Make sure the edge between the ceilings that were joined in the previous step is no longer visible. If it is, check your geometry conditions and ceiling properties closely to find the problem.

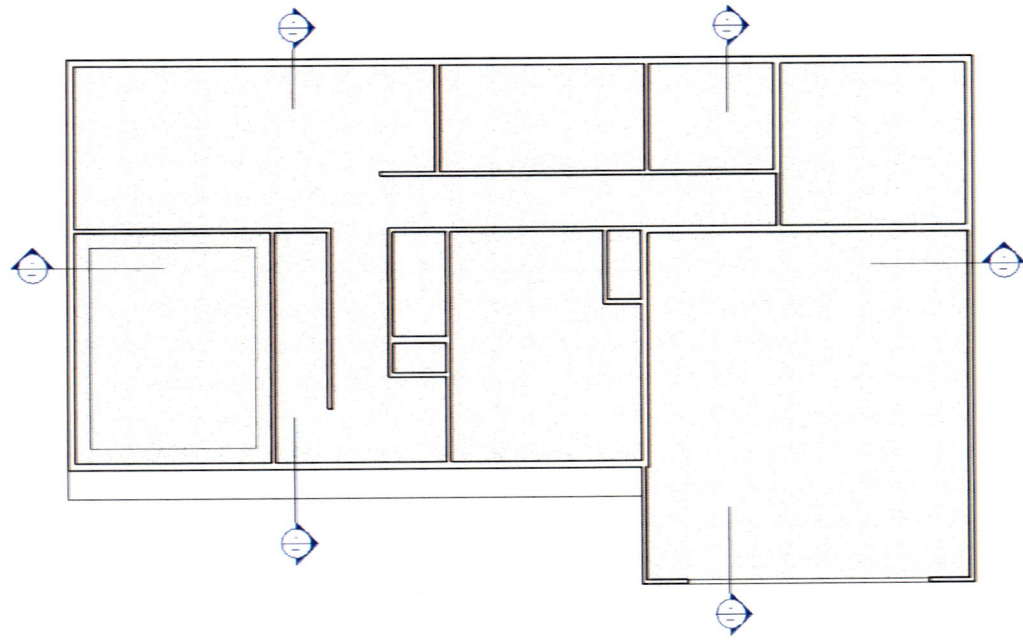

9. Open the various building section views to verify ceilings are at the correct elevation.

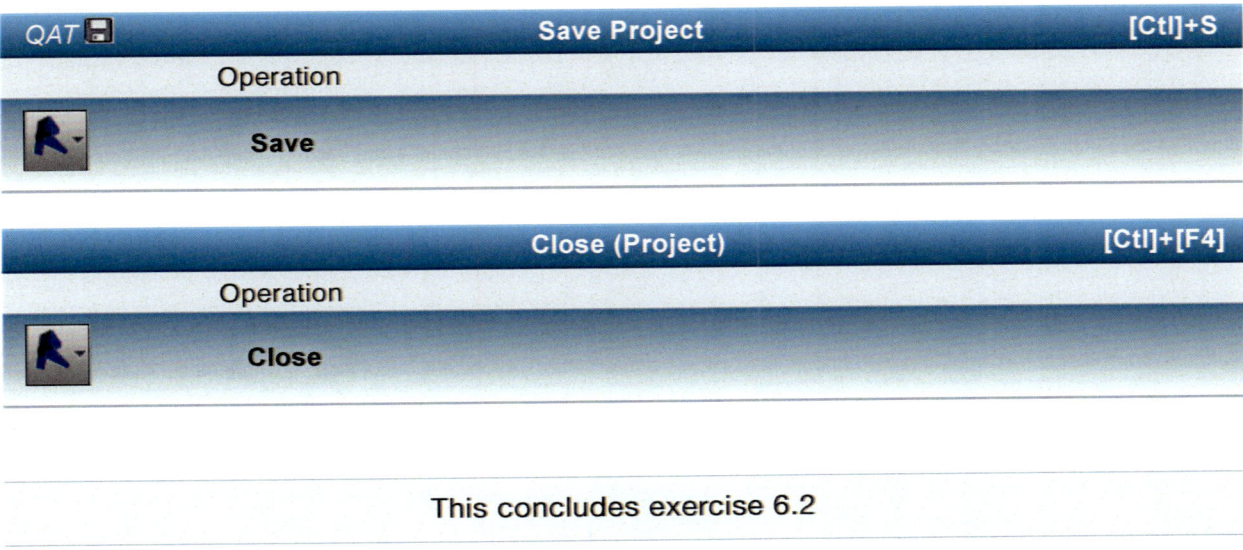

This concludes exercise 6.2

Chapter Summary

In this exercise you learned about the different tools and approaches to creating ceilings, as well as working in ceiling plan views. Additionally, you reinforced your skills in applying Visibility/Graphics Overrides and creating view templates.

Chapter 7

Foundation and Topography

Overview

This chapter will introduce you to foundation and topography elements, as well as reinforce view management and constraining techniques you learned in previous chapters.

Learning Objectives

After completing this chapter you should have a basic understanding of the following tools and concepts.

- View Discipline
- Modeling structural foundation elements
- Creating sloped surfaces using a slope arrow
- Basic topography modeling tools
- Building pads

Project Objectives

- Refined structural foundation plan view
- Model all spread footings and stem walls
- Add a sloped garage slab
- Add site topography and a foundation crawlspace
- Create additional 3D section views
- Additional views refinement
- Create additional view templates
- General model refinement

CHAPTER 7: FOUNDATION AND TOPOGRAPHY

Chapter Contents

Exercise 7.1: Modeling the Basic Foundation 199
    Set up the Foundation Plan View 199
    Create New Materials 200
    Create a New Foundation Wall Type 200
    Model the Stem Walls 201
    Refine Garage Walls, Doors, and Window 206
    Model the Spread Footings 207
    Model the Garage Slab 209
    Add a slope to the Garage Floor 213
    Refine foundation Plan View Graphics 216

Exercise 7.2: Modeling Topography 218
    Model the topography 218
    Add Crawlspace Using a Building Pad 222
    Create a 3D Foundation Section View 225

Exercise 7.1: Modeling the Basic Foundation

QAT 📂	Open Project		[Ctl]+O
	Operation	Option	File Name
🅡	Open ▶	Project	BIMHOUSE-EX06-2.rvt

	Save As (Project)		
	Operation	Option	File Name
🅡	Save As ▶	Project	BIMHOUSE-EX07-1.rvt

Set up the Foundation Plan View

Foundation plan views have some unique graphic requirements. Most obviously, it needs to clearly display foundation elements, both visible and hidden. In order to achieve this, there are a few view properties that need to be set differently than in a typical floor plan.

1. Open the floor plan view *Foundation Plan*, and make the following changes to the view properties.

 This is a good time to verify the associated level for the *Foundation Plan* view is set to **T.O.W. STEM**. If not, delete the view and recreate it before proceeding.

View Properties: Foundation Plan

Parameter	Value	Alternate Access
Underlay	None	
Discipline	Structural	
Crop View	✓	View Control Bar (VCB)
View Range...		
Top – Offset:	0' 0"	
Cut Plane – Offset:	0' 0"	
Bottom	Unlimited	
View Depth: Level	Unlimited	

 After setting the view properties, you should see only reference planes.

Create New Materials

 For a refresher on creating new materials, refer back to Chapter 6.

Materials		
Tab	**Panel**	**Tool Button**
Manage	Settings	Materials

1. Select the material *Concrete, Cast-in-Place gray* in the list of materials.
2. Make 3 duplicates of the selected material.
3. Rename the new materials using the following names.
   a) **Concrete, Cast-in-Place Footings**
   b) **Concrete, Cast-in-Place Floors**
   c) **Concrete, Cast-in-Place Stem Walls**
4. Open the *Identity* tab in the Material Browser.
5. For each of the new materials, edit the *Description* and *Comments* fields as shown in the table below.

Materials Properties: Identity Data

Material Name	Description	Comments
Concrete, Cast-in-Place Floors	CONCRETE SLAB	(SEE STRUCTURAL)
Concrete, Cast-in-Place Footings	CONCRETE FOOTING	(SEE STRUCTURAL)
Concrete, Cast-in-Place Stem Walls	CONCRETE STEM WALL	(SEE STRUCTURAL)

6. Click **OK** to close the Material Browser and complete the new materials.

Create a New Foundation Wall Type

As a final step before we begin to model the foundation, we'll create a new wall type to use for the stem wall. This wall type will be set up as a foundation wall, which will have an effect on modeling behavior. When modeling foundation walls in Revit, you specify the *depth* of the wall instead of the *height*.

1. Expand the Project Browser tree *Families* → *Walls* → *Basic Wall*.
2. Find the wall type *Generic - 6"*, and open its Type Properties dialog box.
3. Click **Duplicate...**, and enter **Stem - 6" Concrete** for the name.
4. Change the following properties...

Wall Type Properties: Stem - 6" Concrete

Parameter	Value
Function	Foundation

5. Edit the structure as follows...

Wall Structure: Stem - 6" Concrete *(Edit Assembly Dialog Box)*

Layer	Function	Material	Thickness
1	Core Boundary	Layers Above	
2	Structure [1]	Concrete - Cast-in-Place Stem Walls	0' 6"
3	Core Boundary	Layers Below	

Model the Stem Walls

1. Verify the floor plan view *Foundation Plan* is open. If not, open it now.

 Be sure to set up the wall tool and its options in the exact order shown...

Wall			
Tab	Panel	Split Button ▼	Tool Button
Architecture	**Build**	**Wall**	**Wall: Structural**

Properties
Type: **Stem - 6" Concrete**

Modify	Place Wall		
	Draw		
	Pick Lines		
Depth: **T.O. FOOTING**	Location Line: **Core Face: Exterior**		Offset: **0' 0"**

 When modeling walls that have their *Function* parameter set to **Foundation**, the *Height/Depth* selector on the options bar is grayed out and forced to the *Depth* setting.

2. Model the stem walls by picking each of the reference planes that define the footprint of the building. Make sure the walls are created to the interior side of the reference planes.

 Model only one wall per reference plane. You should end up with a total of eight walls.

3. When placing the second stem wall at the west side of the garage, you'll receive the overlapping walls warning illustrated below. Just close it; you'll correct this shortly.

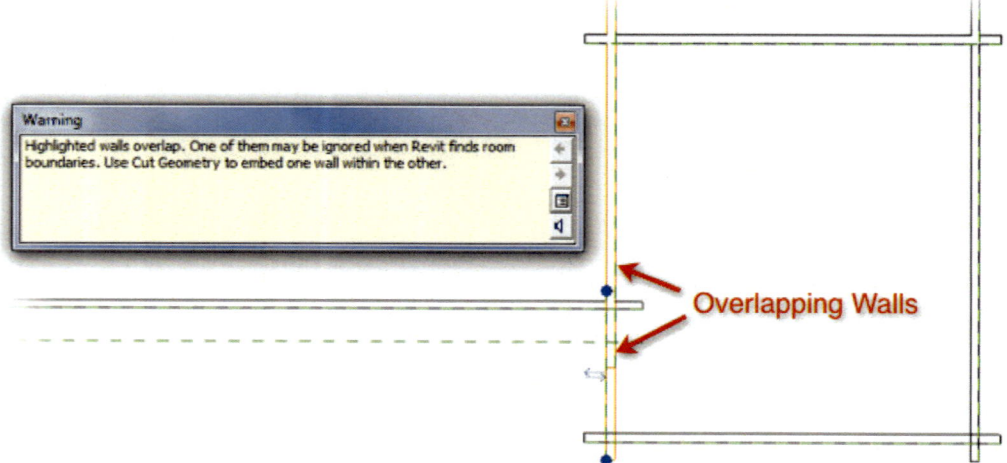

4. When done placing stem walls, use the best-suited trim tools to clean up the wall joins. Make sure that the previously overlapping walls remain as two separate walls that meet at the intersecting wall. When done, your plan view should appear as illustrated below.

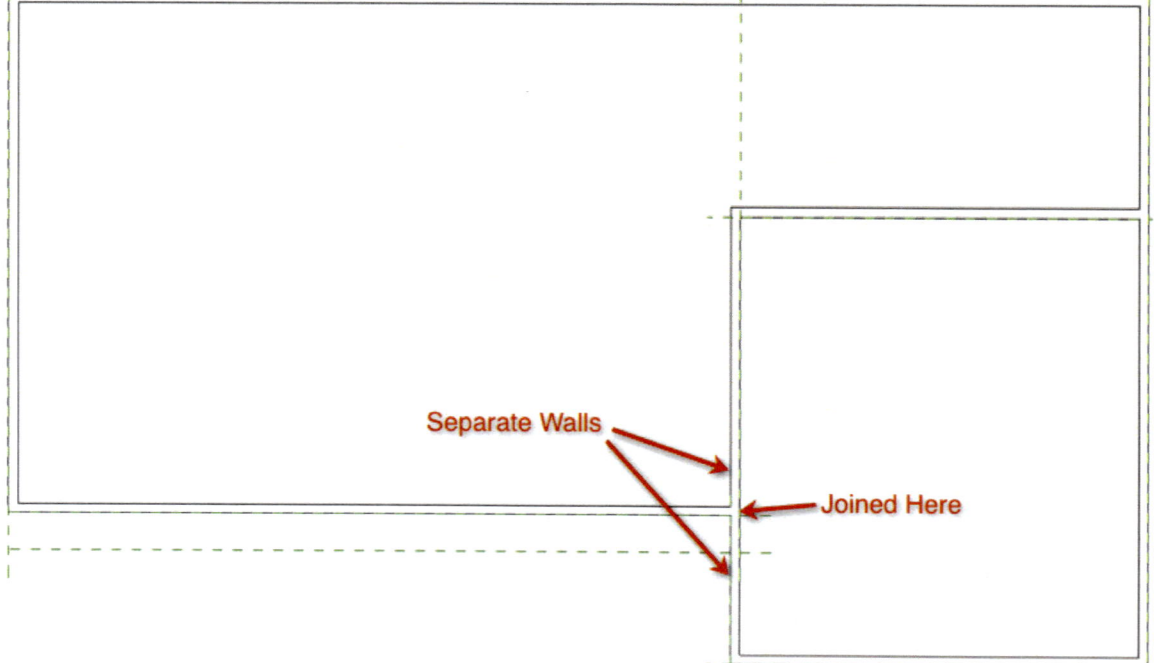

Stem Walls After Trimming

EXERCISE 7.1: CREATE A BASIC FOUNDATION

Adjust Wall Join Condition

As with earlier exercises, where the three walls come together on the west side of the garage, there is the potential for the automatic wall joins to generate constraints errors. Therefore, in the next steps you'll modify this wall join as you did in previous chapters.

 Depending on how the walls were trimmed, you might need to use the **Wall Joins** tool in the following operation. Unfortunately, when using this tool you can only see the join configuration if the adjoining walls intersect the view cut plane. If you recall, we set the cut plane to 0' 0". Therefore, the stem walls don't intersect it, and the join configuration won't be visible.
There are a number of ways to get around this. Since it's only a single join condition, you can just select the wall to determine if it's correct. If correct, leave it alone; if not, use **Wall Joins** to change the configuration. Since there are only two possible join configurations, clicking **Next** once will correct it. Note that if there were several join locations that needed editing, or the join was more complex with many possible join conditions, it would be more efficient to use *Temporary View Settings* and temporarily override the cut plane so it intersects the walls.

5. While referring to the illustration below, perform the following steps to modify the wall join condition.

    a) Drag the short wall end into the clear, then set the end to **Disallow Join**.

    b) Verify the corner join condition is as illustrated. If not, use the **Wall Joins** tool to correct it.

    c) **Align** and **Lock** the end of the wall to reference plane *Ext-South-1*.

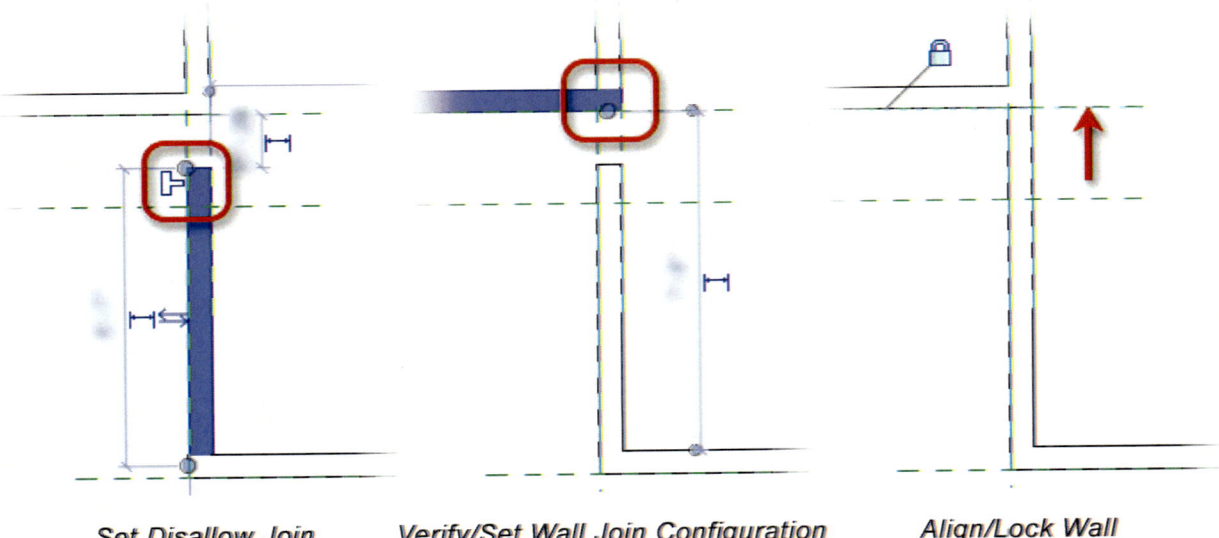

Set Disallow Join   Verify/Set Wall Join Configuration   Align/Lock Wall

6. Use **Join Geometry** to clean up the manual join.

CHAPTER 7: FOUNDATION AND TOPOGRAPHY

Align		AL
Tab	Panel	Tool Button
Modify	**Modify**	**Align**
Multiple Alignment: ☐	Prefer: **Faces of core**	

7. **Align** and **Lock** the *core face* of each stem wall to its respective reference plane.
8. **Exit** the Align tool when done.
9. Verify all stem walls are locked: select all of the walls, then click **Activate Dimensions** in the Options Bar. You should see a closed padlock on each wall as illustrated below.

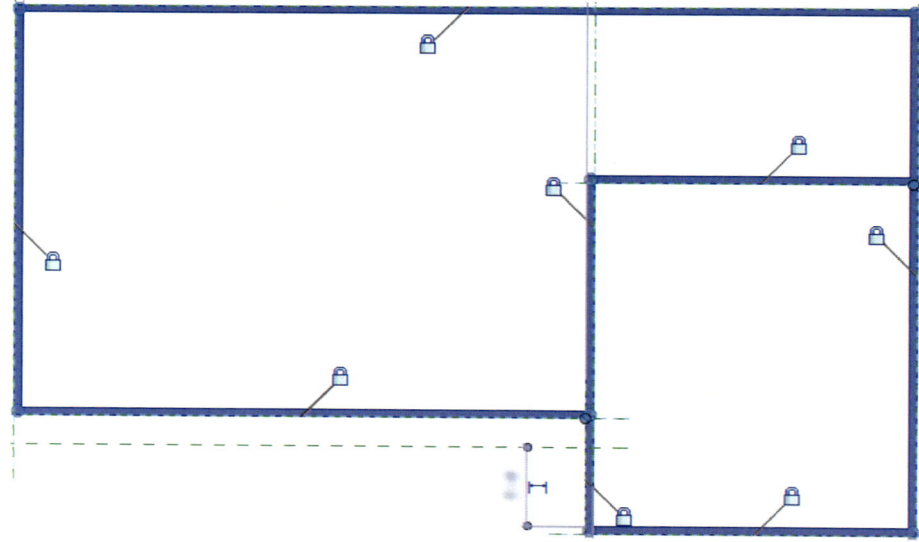

Split Stem Walls at Garage Door

Next you will create an opening at the garage door, allowing the garage slab to extend to the exterior face of the stem wall.

Split Element		SL
Tab	Panel	Tool Button
Modify	**Modify**	**Split Element**
Delete Inner Segment: ☑		

10. Split the stem wall and remove the inner wall segment as illustrated on the following page. Split locations are approximate; we'll adjust the wall ends steps that follow.

204

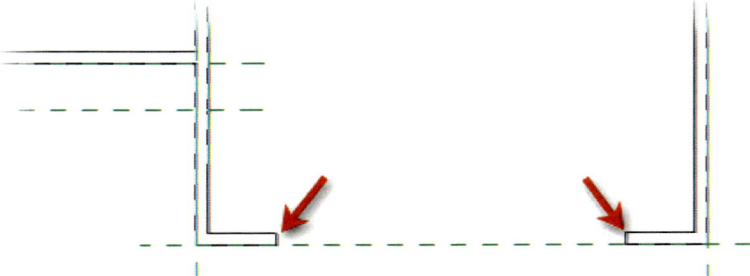

11. **Align/Lock** the two resulting stem walls to the associated reference plane (*Ext-Garage-South*)

 When splitting a constrained element, such as the stem wall in the previous steps, one of the resulting segments will lose its constraint. It's not obvious which one without selecting each of the resulting elements. Make sure to add constraints back in where necessary!

12. Open the *South* building elevation view.

13. **Align** and **Lock** the stem wall ends to the garage *wall opening* as shown in the illustration on the following page. Be sure to pick the <u>wall</u> as the alignment reference, <u>NOT</u> the overhead garage door.

 Use **[Tab]** to cycle through the possible selections in order to select the wall.

 Picking the garage door as the alignment reference will cause constraint errors if the garage door is later moved.

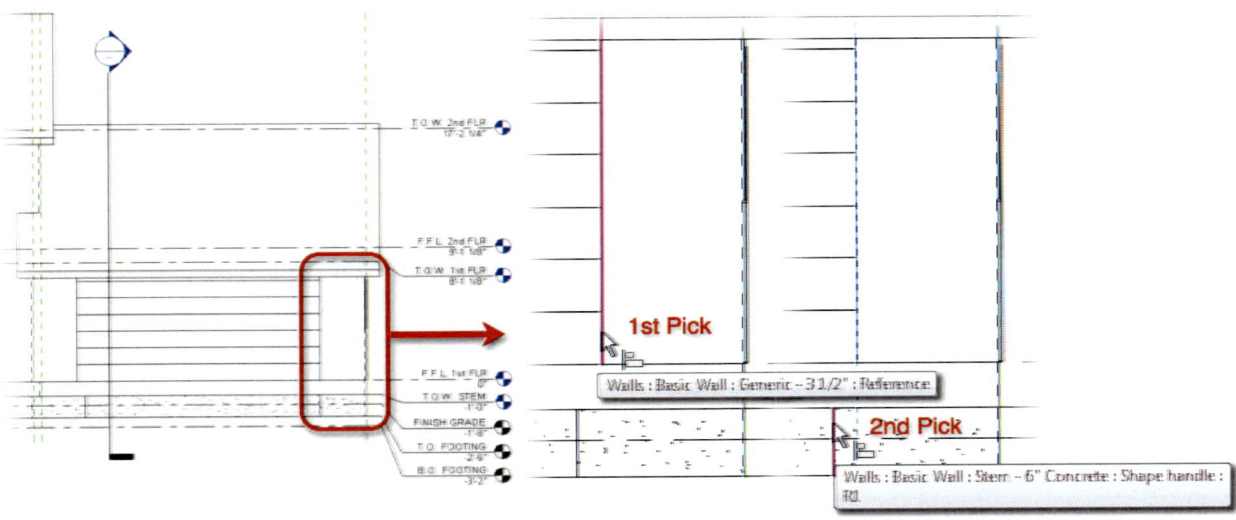

Aligning Stem Wall to Garage Opening

Refine Garage Walls, Doors, and Window

By now you have likely noticed that the garage walls and doors are floating above the stem wall. In the following steps you will correct this.

1. Open the floor plan view *F.F.L. 1st FLR*, then close hidden windows...

QAT	Close Hidden Windows	
Tab	**Panel**	**Tool Button**
View	Windows	Close Hidden

2. Open the default *{3D}* view, and orient it so you can see the southeast corner of the garage.

> Clicking on the *TOP-FRONT-RIGHT* corner of the view cube will orient the model to the southeast isometric view.

3. **Tile** the two windows, **Zoom All to Fit**, and make *F.F.L. 1st FLR* the active window.
4. Select the three *Generic - 3 1/2"* garage walls as illustrated below.

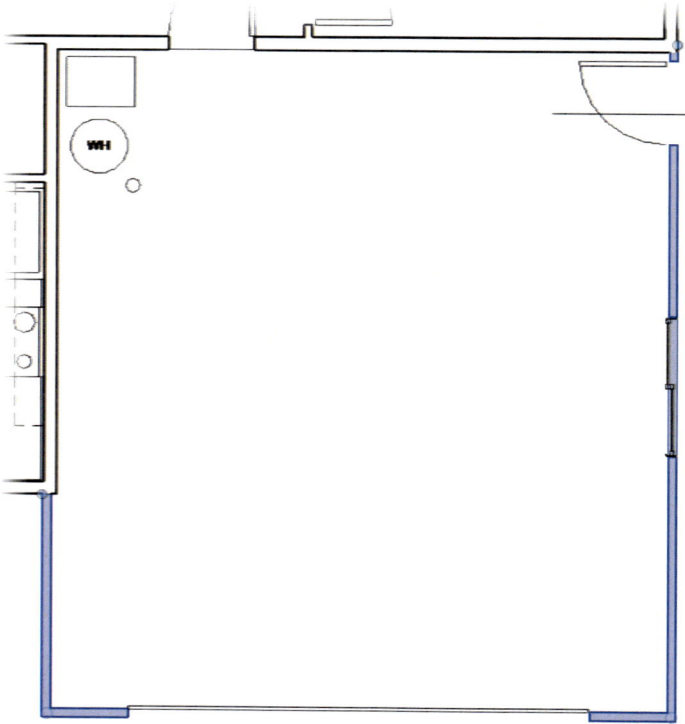

5. In the Properties palette, set *Base Constraint* to **T.O.W. STEM**.

   Notice the change in the *{3D}* view. The base of the garage walls should now rest on top of the stem wall.

6. Next select the following garage elements. You can do this from within either of the two open views.

    a) Overhead door

    b) Side-access door

    c) Window

7. In the Properties palette, set the *Level* parameter to **T.O.W. STEM**.

    Note the change in the *{3D}* view. Both garage doors should now go down to the top of the stem wall, and the window should follow to maintain the header height in relation to the doors as illustrated below.

 In future a future chapter, as the model is further developed, the door and window elevations will be further refined and adapted to correspond with design changes.

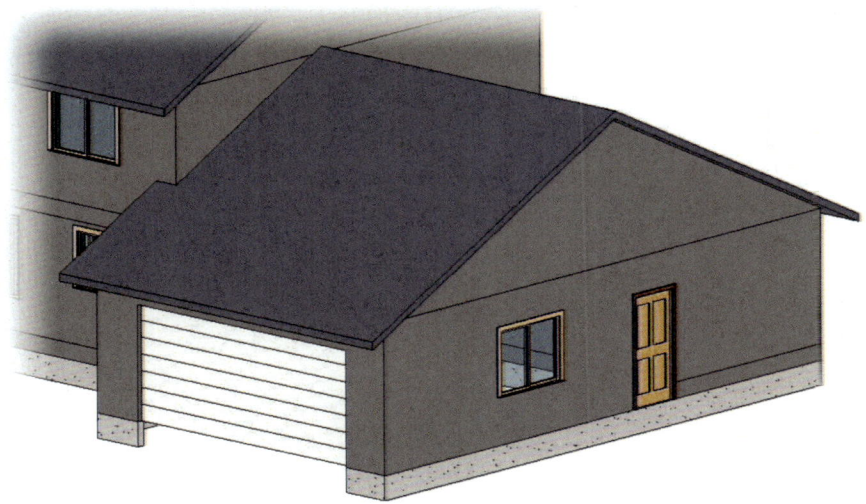

3D View of Garage After Re-associating Walls, Doors, and Window

Model the Spread Footings

In the following steps you will attach spread footings to the base of the stem walls. But first, you'll need to create a new footing type. This is a system family, therefore, we'll start with a footing already in the project.

1. Expand the Project Browser tree: *Families → Structural Foundations → Wall Foundation*

2. **Double-click** on *Bearing Footing - 36" x 12"* to open the Type Properties dialog box.

3. Click **Duplicate...** and enter **Bearing Footing - 15" x 8"** for the name.

4. In the Type Properties dialog box, change the parameters in the table on the following page.

Wall Foundation Properties: Bearing Footing - 15" x 8"

Parameter	Value
Material	Concrete, Cast-in-Place Footings
Width	1' 3"
Foundation Thickness	0' 8"
Default End Extension Length	0' 4 1/2"

5. Click **OK** to exit the dialog box.

6. Open the floor plan view *Foundation Plan* or the *{3D}* view and place the footings...

Wall Foundation		
Tab	Panel	Tool Button
Structure	Foundation	Wall

Properties
Type: **Bearing Footing - 15" x 8"**

Eccentricity:	0' 0"

7. Pick each of the stem walls (once each) to place the footings.

 You can place several footings at once by pre-highlighting a chain of walls using **[Tab]**, and then clicking once on the highlighted set.

8. **Exit** the Wall Foundation tool when done. Your *Foundation Plan* view should appear as illustrated below.

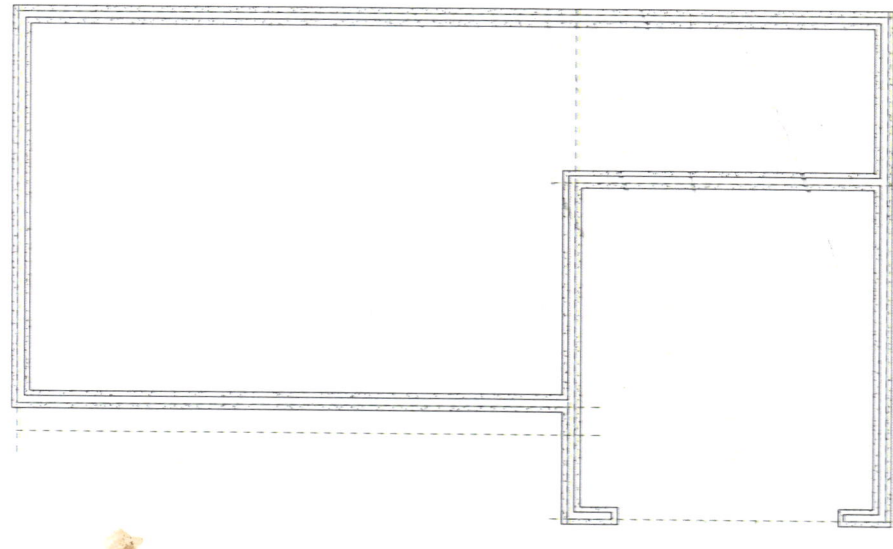

The footing end extension – where the stem walls end at the garage door opening – was automatic because we specified this in the *Default End Extension Length* property. Had we not specified this parameter, the end of the footing would have been flush with the end of the stem wall. This can however be manually adjusted after footings have been placed.

9. Open the default *{3D}* view and orbit the view to make the underside of the building visible. Your footings should appear as illustrated below.

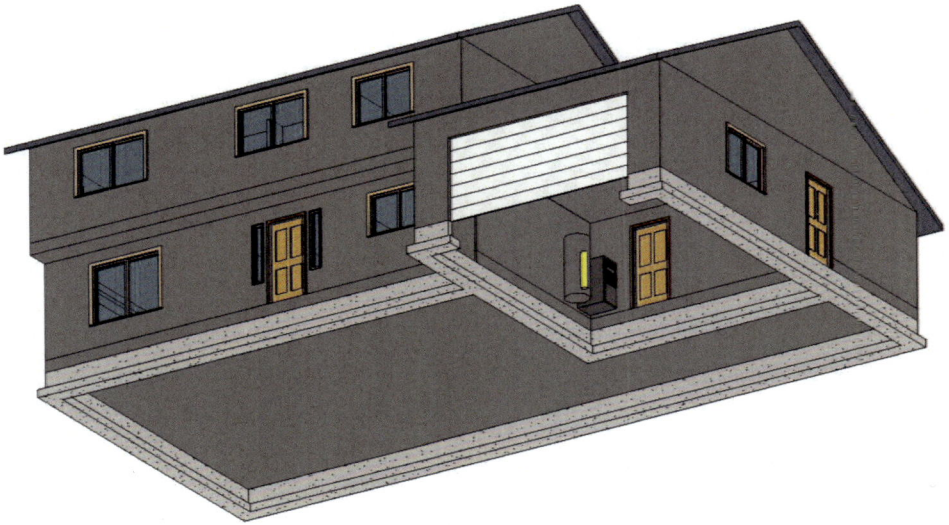

10. Open a section view to see the added stem walls and footings.

11. Adjust the *T.O. FOOTING* level up or down to see the stem wall flex, and the footing track it. Make sure to use undo to return the level to the correct elevation!

 At this time, there is no association between the B.O. FOOTING level and any of the foundation elements.

Model the Garage Slab

1. Open the floor plan view *Foundation Plan*.

Floor			
Tab	Panel	Split Button ▼	Tool Button
Architecture	Build	Floor	Floor: Architectural

2. Click **Edit Type** in the Properties palette.
3. Select *Generic - 12"*, and click **Duplicate...**
4. Enter **Slab on Grade - 4" Concrete** for the name.
5. Click on **Edit...** to open the Edit Assembly dialog box and set the following properties...

CHAPTER 7: FOUNDATION AND TOPOGRAPHY

Floor Structure: Slab On Grade - 4" Concrete

Layer	Function	Material	Thickness
	Core Boundary	Layers Above	
	Structure [1]	Concrete - Cast-in-Place Floors	0' 4"
	Core Boundary	Layers Below	

6. Click **OK** to exit all dialog boxes when done.

Properties	
Type: **Slab on Grade - 4" Concrete**	
Level:	**FINISH GRADE**
Height Offset From Level: **0' 2"**	

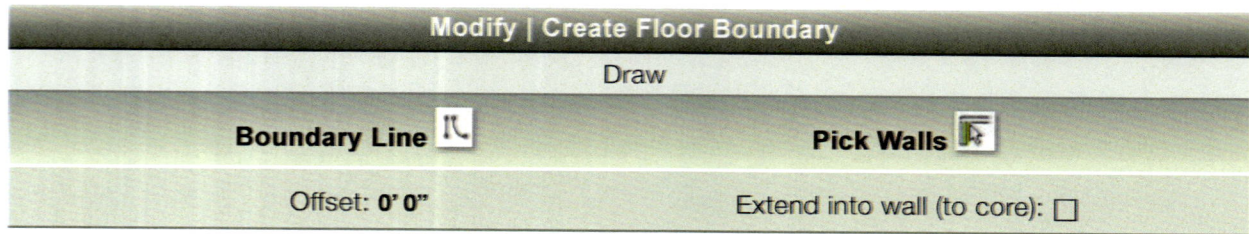

7. **Pick** the <u>five</u> walls indicated in the illustration below.

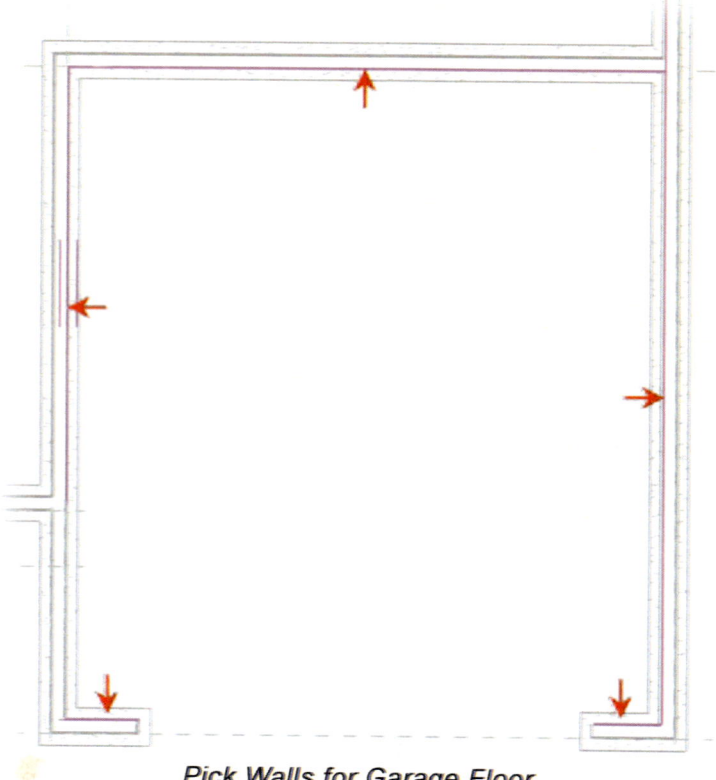

Pick Walls for Garage Floor

210

8. Next, add the boundary lines that define the footprint of the garage floor apron...

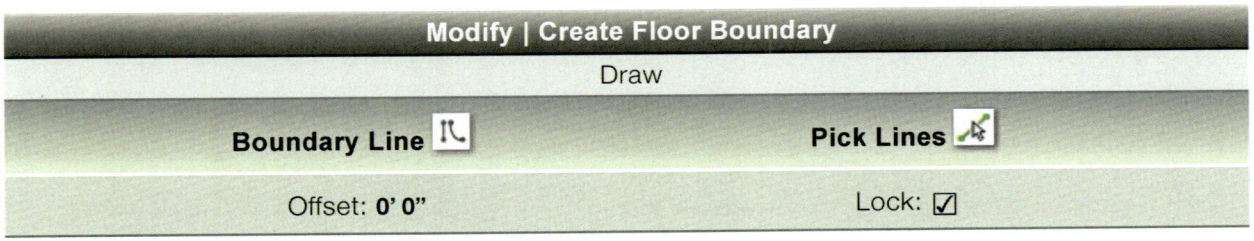

9. Click <u>once</u> on the reference plane associated with the south edge of the garage (*Ext-Garage-South*), then pick the end of each stem wall at the garage door opening as illustrated below:

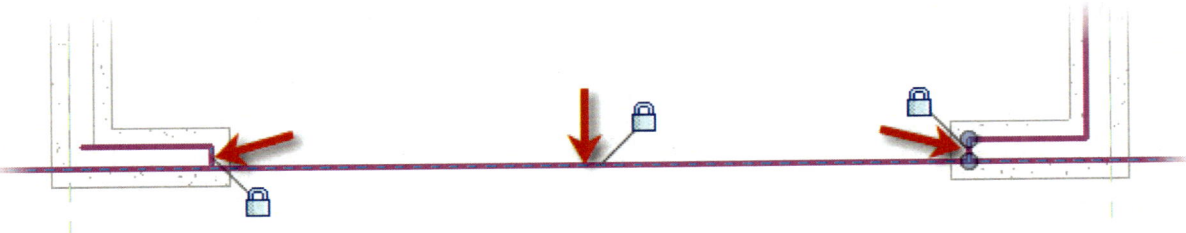

10. Use the **Trim/Extend to Corner** tool to create a closed-loop boundary, which should appear as illustrated below when done.

Completed Garage Floor Boundary Sketch

11. When done, click the **Finish Edit Mode** button

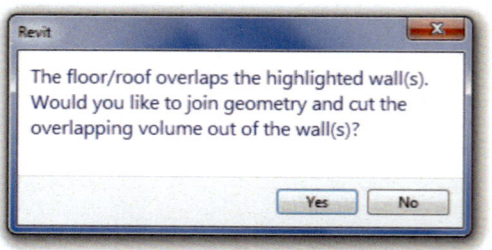

If you receive this dialog box, then the *Extend into wall* checkbox in the Options Bar was not cleared before picking walls. Answer **No**, then use undo to go back into the sketch mode. Select all boundary lines that were placed using the Pick Walls tool, and clear the *Extend into wall* checkbox in the Options Bar.

12. The garage portion of your foundation plan should now look like the following illustration. Note the hidden lines where the slab obscures the footing below.

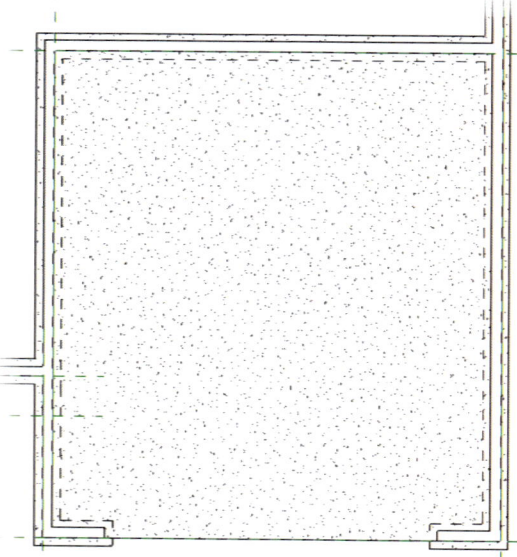

13. Open the section view *W-Laundry-Garage (Long)*. The new floor should appear as illustrated below.

Add a slope to the Garage Floor

When you open the building section view *W-Laundry-Garage (Long)*, you likely noticed that the garage floor is flat. In the next steps you'll use the slope arrow tool to add slope the floor for drainage.

1. Open the floor plan view *Foundation Plan*.
2. Select the garage floor and click the **Edit Boundary** button in the Contextual Ribbon tab.

3. Pick the mid-point of the north slab boundary line as the starting point, and then sketch downward to connect to the south boundary line.

 Make sure slope arrow stays perpendicular to the north boundary line while sketching.

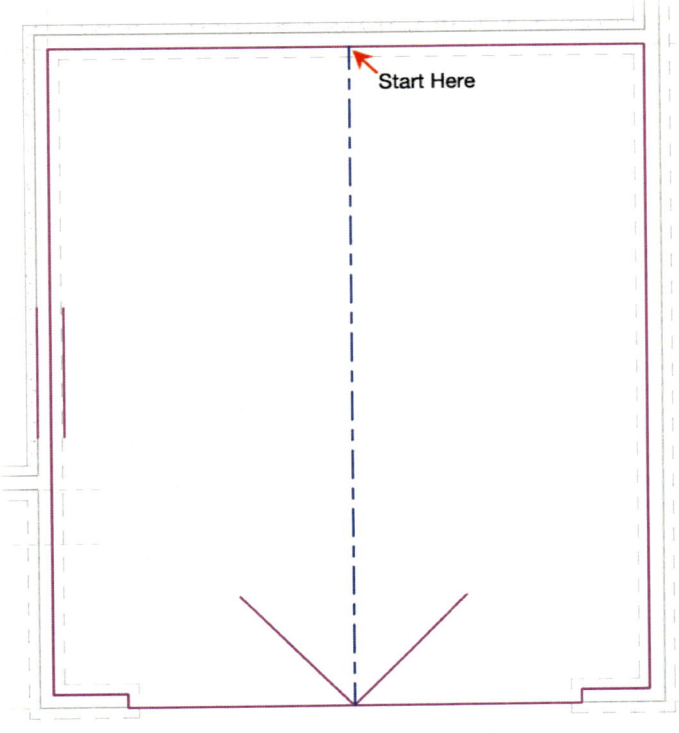

Sketch Slope Arrow

4. In the Properties palette, with the slope arrow still selected, set the properties as shown in the table below.

Slope Arrow Properties

Parameter	Value
Specify	**Height at Tail**
Level at Tail	**Default**
Height Offset at Tail	**0' 2"**
Level at Head	**Default**
Height Offset at Head	**0' 0"**

 As with any other element in Revit, the slope arrow needs to be selected in order to modify its properties. If somehow you accidentally deselected it after creating it, just select it again to access and modify its properties.

5. When done, click the **Finish Edit Mode** button ✓

6. Open the section view *W-Laundry-Garage (Long)*. The garage floor should be sloped as illustrated below.

Section View of Sloped Garage Floor

EXERCISE 7.1: CREATE A BASIC FOUNDATION

Refine the Overhead Garage Door Elevation

7. Select the <u>overhead</u> garage door. In the Properties palette set the following properties...

Door Properties: Overhead-Sectional: 16' x 8'

Parameter	Value
Level	**FINISH GRADE**
Sill Height	0' 2"

8. The overhead garage door should now be resting on the garage floor slab as illustrated below.

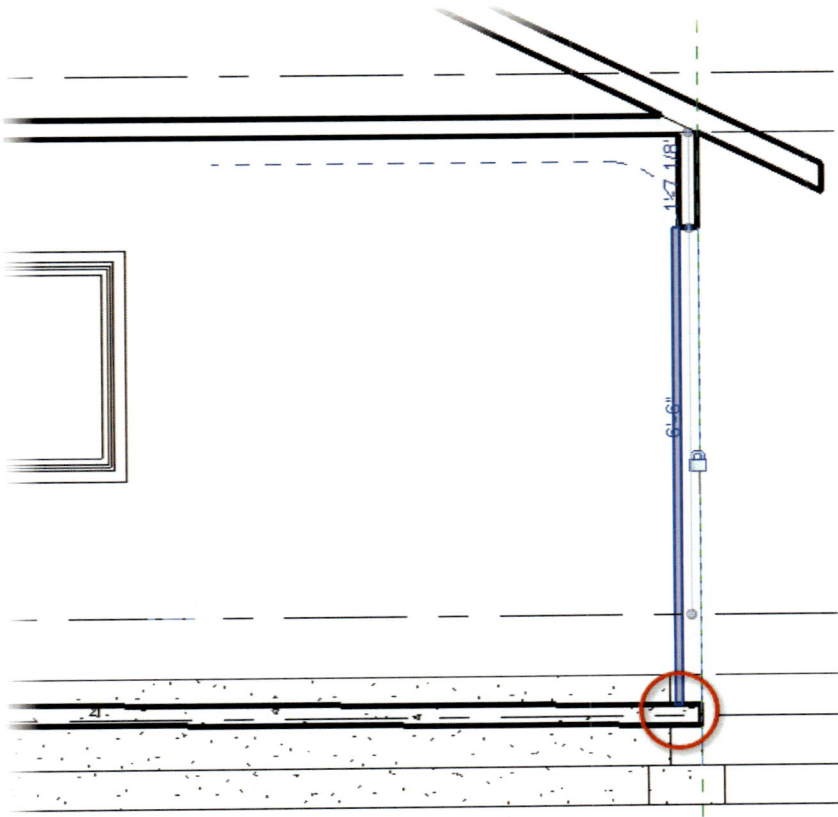

 This is a good time to flex the model to test the constraints created so far. You should flex all reference planes associated with a stem wall (8 total). Be aware of flexing distance limitations. As more constrained elements are added to the model, the more restrictive the limits can become. It's always a good idea to have a 3D view open and tiled, since a constraint error could be caused by an element not visible from the active view.

Refine foundation Plan View Graphics

1. Open the floor plan view *Foundation Plan*.

2. Edit the Visibility/Graphics Overrides as shown in the table below. Note that these overrides are only a starting point and will be modified as the model progresses.

 Periodically, you will be instructed to hide surface patterns. This instruction will be presented as "*Surface Patterns:* **Hidden**." This translates into unchecking the *Visible* checkbox. The procedure for overriding projection line weights is similar to patterns. Instead, click the corresponding **Override...** button in the *Lines* column under the Projection/Surface grouping.

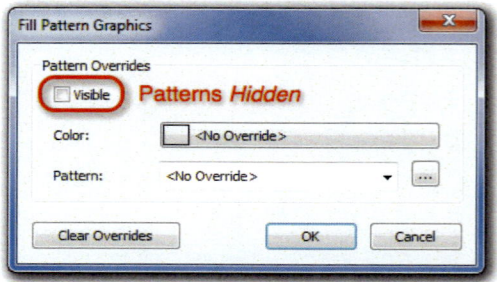

V/G Overrides: Foundation Plan

Category Tab / Category / Subcategory	Visibility	Other
Model / Doors	OFF	
Model / Floors	ON	Surface Patterns: **Hidden**
Model / Walls	ON	Projection Line Weight: **4**

3. When done, the view should appear as illustrated below.

EXERCISE 7.1: CREATE A BASIC FOUNDATION

4. Create a view template from the *Foundation Plan* view, and name it **Plan-Floor-Foundation**. (*Accept the default settings*)
5. Set the *View Template* property for *Foundation Plan* to **Plan-Floor-Foundation**.

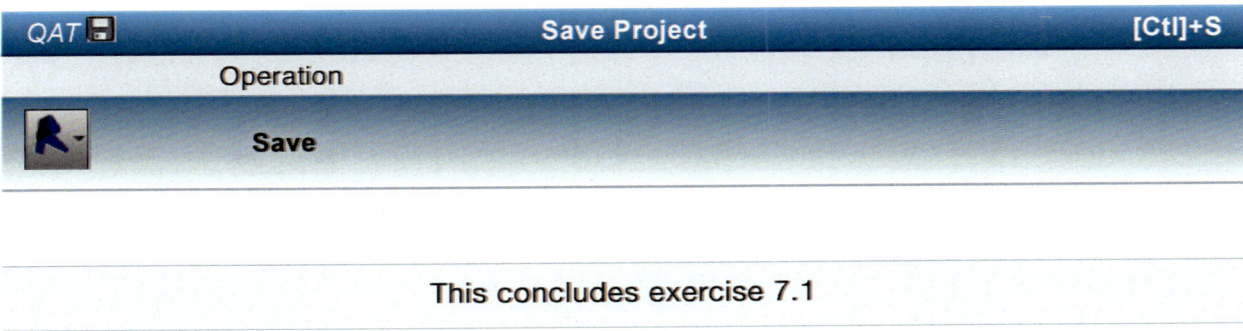

This concludes exercise 7.1

Exercise 7.2: Modeling Topography

QAT 📂	Open Project		[Ctl]+O
	Operation	Option	File Name
![R]	Open ▶	Project	BIMHOUSE-EX07-1.rvt

	Save As (Project)		
	Operation	Option	File Name
![R]	Save As ▶	Project	BIMHOUSE-EX07-2.rvt

Model the topography

Before placing a toposurface, you'll need to adjust the view properties and Visibility/Graphics Overrides for the *Site* plan view. Additionally, we'll sketch some temporary lines to use as a reference when creating the boundary of the toposurface.

Set Up the View

1. Open the floor plan view *Site*, and make the following changes to the view properties and Visibility/Graphics Overrides

View Properties: Site

Parameter	Value
View Range...	
Bottom	**Unlimited**
View Depth: Level	**Unlimited**

Visibility/Graphics Overrides: Site

Category Tab / Category / Subcategory	Visibility
Annotation / Elevations	**OFF**
Annotation / Reference Planes	**OFF**

Sketch Detail Lines as a Boundary Reference

 When creating a toposurface, there are no tools available for creating orthogonal lines and boundaries. However, the points that are placed to define a toposurface can be snapped to existing geometry or lines. The following steps are not normally required when creating a toposurface; however, they will allow us to create an orthogonal boundary with a predictable surface area.

Exercise 7.2: Modeling Topography

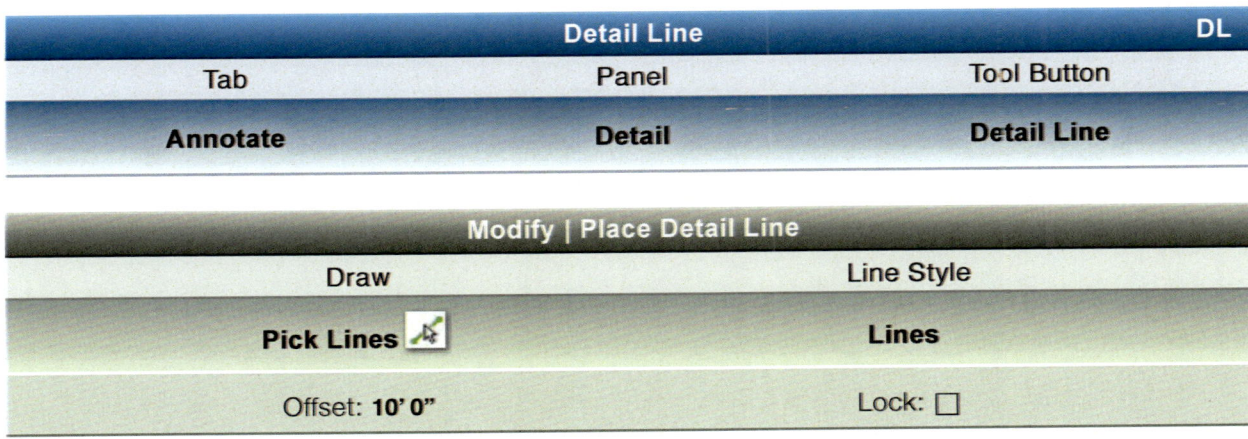

Tab	Panel	Detail Line	DL
Annotate	Detail	Tool Button	
		Detail Line	

Modify | Place Detail Line		
Draw		Line Style
Pick Lines		Lines
Offset: **10' 0"**		Lock: ☐

2. Pick four edges of the roof elements to place the detail lines. For the south line, pick the garage roof as illustrated below.

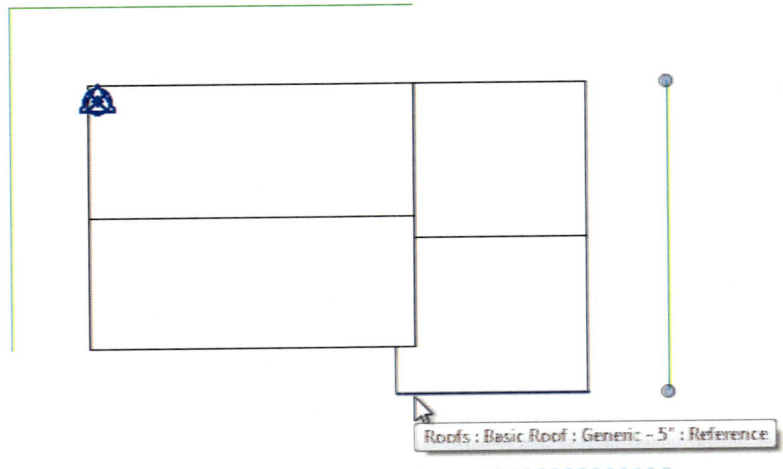

3. **Trim** the four lines to create a closed rectangle.

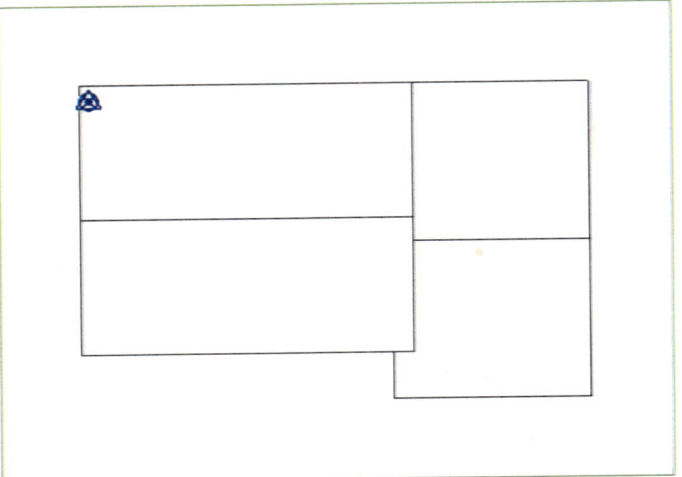

CHAPTER 7: FOUNDATION AND TOPOGRAPHY

Create the Topography

Toposurface		
Tab	Panel	Tool Button
Massing & Site	Model Site	Toposurface

Modify	Contextual Tab	
Panel	
Place Point	
Elevation: -1' 8"	Absolute Elevation

 The elevation of a toposurface is determined by the elevation of the points that define it. These points are always relative to the project base point, not a level. Even though we've created a FINISH GRADE level, the toposurface cannot be associated with this level.

4. Place four points at the corners of the reference rectangle as illustrated below.

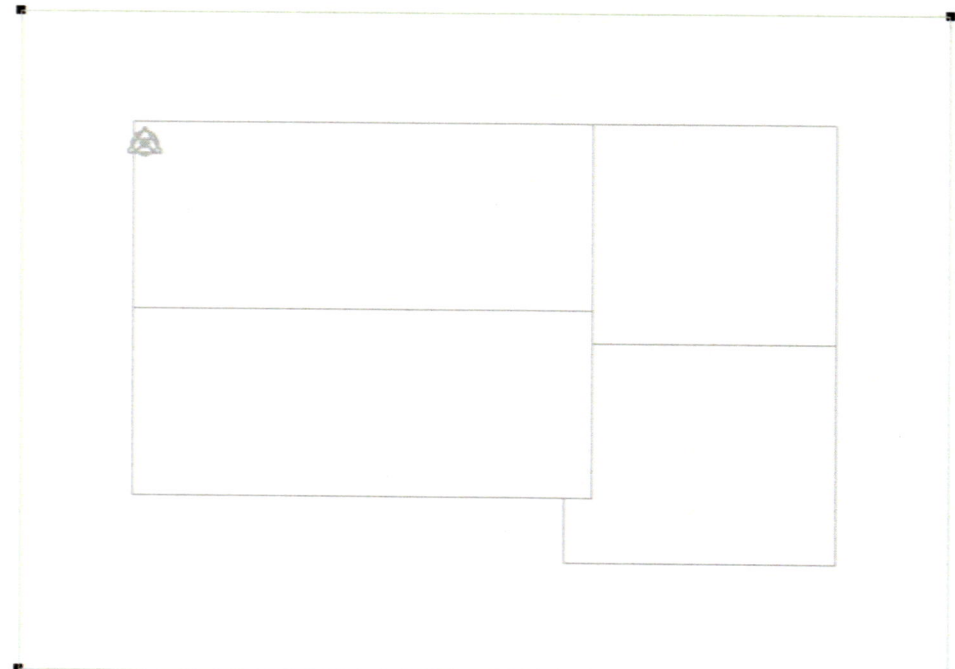

Add Points to Define Toposurface

5. When done, click the **Finish Edit Mode** button ✓
6. Select the four detail lines you previously created for reference and delete them.

7. Open a section view, and verify that the top of the toposurface is at *FINISH GRADE* level.

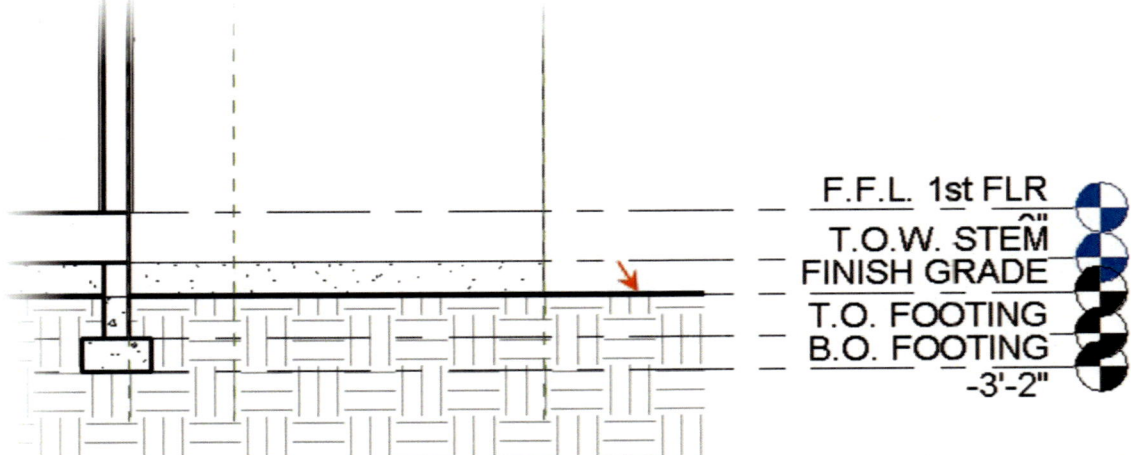

Section View of Toposurface

8. Select the toposurface, and in the Properties palette, enter **TOPOSURFACE** in the *Comments* field, then click **Apply** to accept the changes.

9. Open the default *{3D}* view to examine the toposurface.

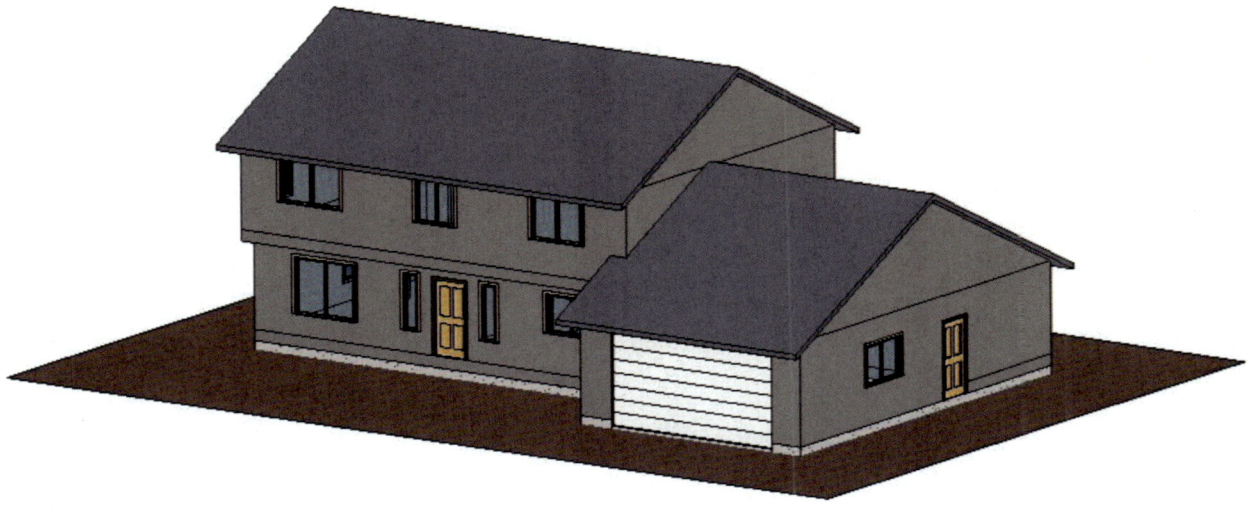

 Notice how in a section view the toposurface appears to be a cut solid element, as it's displayed with a cut line as well as a cut pattern representing earth. However, in the default *{3D}* view, it's displayed as a surface. That's because it *is* a surface. Whenever a toposurface is cut in a view, Revit applies additional graphics to help represent it as a cut solid. This includes 3D views with a section box cutting through the surface.

CHAPTER 7: FOUNDATION AND TOPOGRAPHY

Add Crawlspace Using a Building Pad

Edit the Building Pad Type and Place a Building Pad

System site families such as toposurface and building pads are not accessible via the project browser, and must therefore be created on-the-fly while the related tool is active. Since we'll be using only one type of building pad in this project, we'll go ahead and edit the existing type rather than duplicating it to create a new one.

1. Open the floor plan view *Foundation Plan*.
2. If any of the toposurface boundaries are visible in this view, adjust the crop region to hide them. <u>Do not</u> hide the toposurface element or category.

Create Building Pad		
Tab	Panel	Tool Button
Massing & Site	**Model Site**	**Building Pad**

3. In the Properties palette, click **Edit Type** to open the Type Properties dialog box.
4. **Rename** *Pad 1* to **Pad - Crawl Space**.
5. Click **Edit...** to open the Edit Assembly dialog box.
6. Change the *Thickness* value to **0' 0 1/16"**.
7. Click **OK** to exit all dialog boxes.

Modify	Create Pad Boundary	
Draw	
Boundary Line	**Pick Walls**
Offset: **0' 0"**	Extend into wall (to core): ☐

Properties	
Type: **Pad - Crawl Space** *(already set in Type Properties)*	
Level:	**B.O. FOOTING**
Offset From Level:	**0' 0 1/16"**

222

8. Pick the **exterior** side of the 6 stem walls defining the perimeter of the livable space as illustrated below. (*You will need to trim one of the corners*)

Building Pad Boundary Lines

9. When done, click the **Finish Edit Mode** button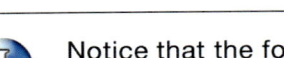

> Notice that the footing lines inside of the crawl space are no longer represented as hidden. This is because the building pad has depressed the topography down to the bottom of the footings, and therefore the topography no longer obscures the inner footing edges.

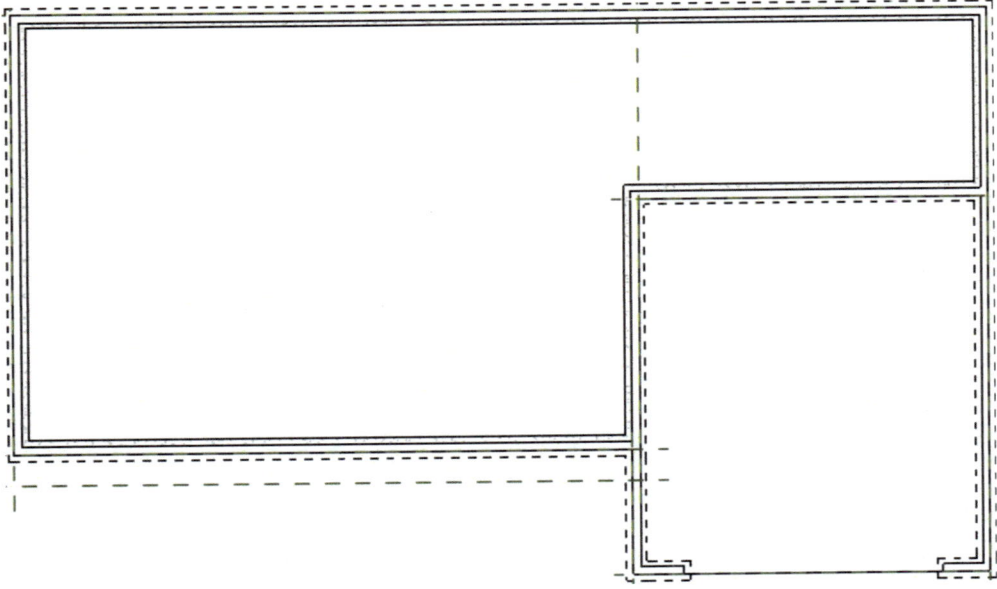

Foundation Plan View After Building Pad

10. Open building section view *Family-Stairs-Porch (Long)* and zoom in around a footing.

    Note the dissimilar cut line weight between the topography and cut foundation elements, and the undesirable graphic effect at the footing resulting from placing the building pad. The following steps will correct this.

Modify Object styles

Object Styles		
Tab	Panel	Tool Button
Manage	**Settings**	**Object Styles**

11. For the *Topography* category, set the *Cut Line Weight* to **5**.

12. Click **OK** to exit. The topography cut line in your section view should now blend with the rest of the cut foundation elements as illustrated below.

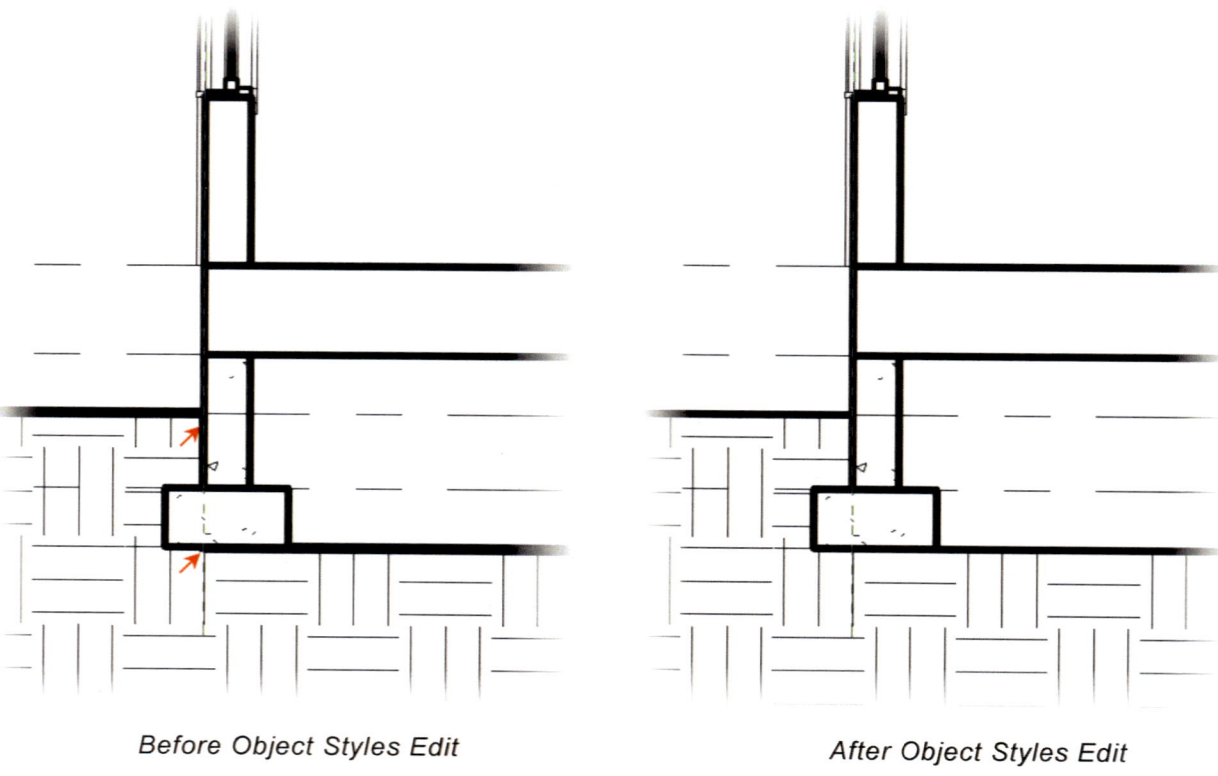

Before Object Styles Edit   After Object Styles Edit

 By adding the building pad, the toposurface was actually split into two separate elements. The area that exists within the boundary of the building pad is now separate from the remaining topography.

13. Select the toposurface directly beneath the building pad. To be sure that the toposurface is selected, and not the building pad, verify that it is highlighted as illustrated on the following page.

The tendency will be for the building pad to be pre-highlighted for selection. Remember to use **[Tab]** if necessary to cycle between the building pad and the toposurface. Alternately, you can enable **Select Elements by Face** in the Status Bar, which will allow you to select the toposurface by clicking anywhere on it.

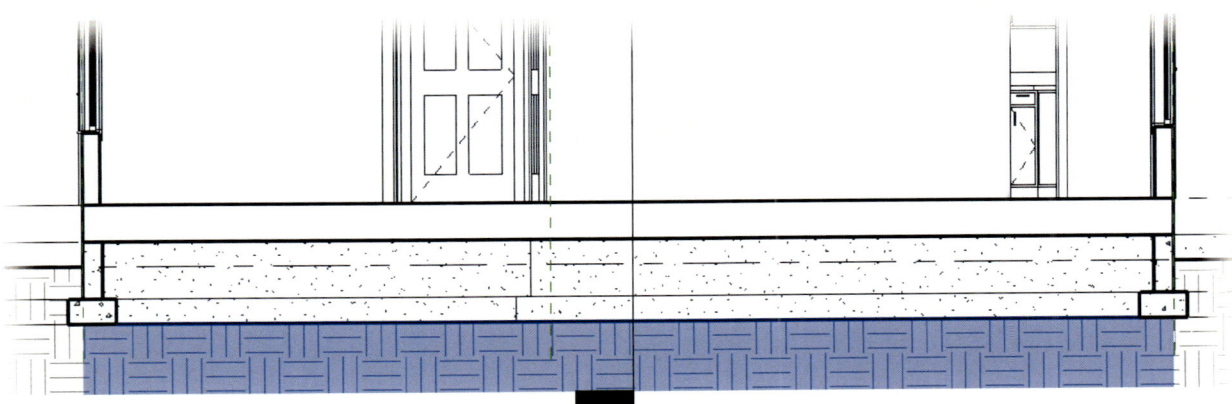

Toposurface Beneath Building Pad Selected

14. In the Properties palette, enter **CRAWLSPACE** in the *Comments* field, then click **Apply** to accept the changes.

Create a 3D Foundation Section View

1. **Duplicate** the default *{3D}* view.
2. **Rename** the new view **3D Section - Foundation**.

 To access the View Cube context menu, move the cursor in the vicinity of the view cube to reveal additional controls. Look for the small down-pointing arrow and click on it.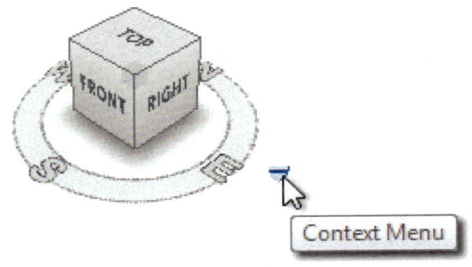

3. Open the View Cube context menu, and select:

   Orient to View → *Floor Plans* → *Floor Plan: Foundation Plan*

4. Click on the View Cube **Home** icon.

CHAPTER 7: FOUNDATION AND TOPOGRAPHY

Adjust View Properties and Visibility Graphics

5. In the *3D Section - Foundation* view properties, set *Discipline* to **Structural**.

6. Hide the floor element over the crawl space using the contextual menu **Hide in View ▶ Elements** as illustrated below.

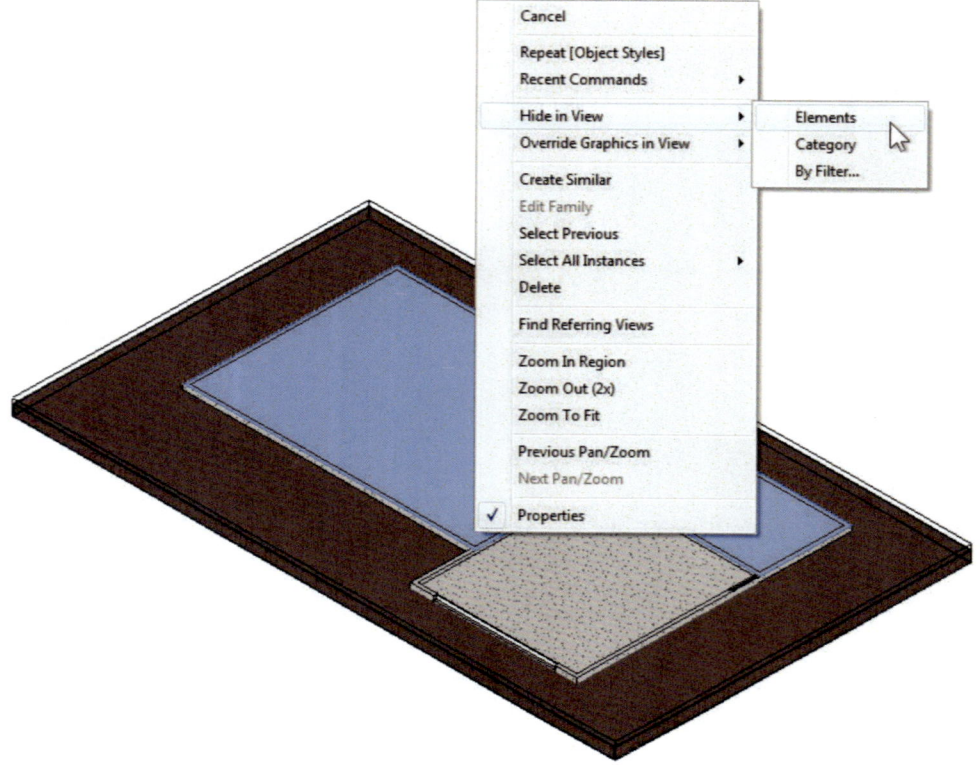

7. Hide the *Doors* category.

8. After changing the view properties and applying overrides, your 3D section view should appear as illustrated below.

226

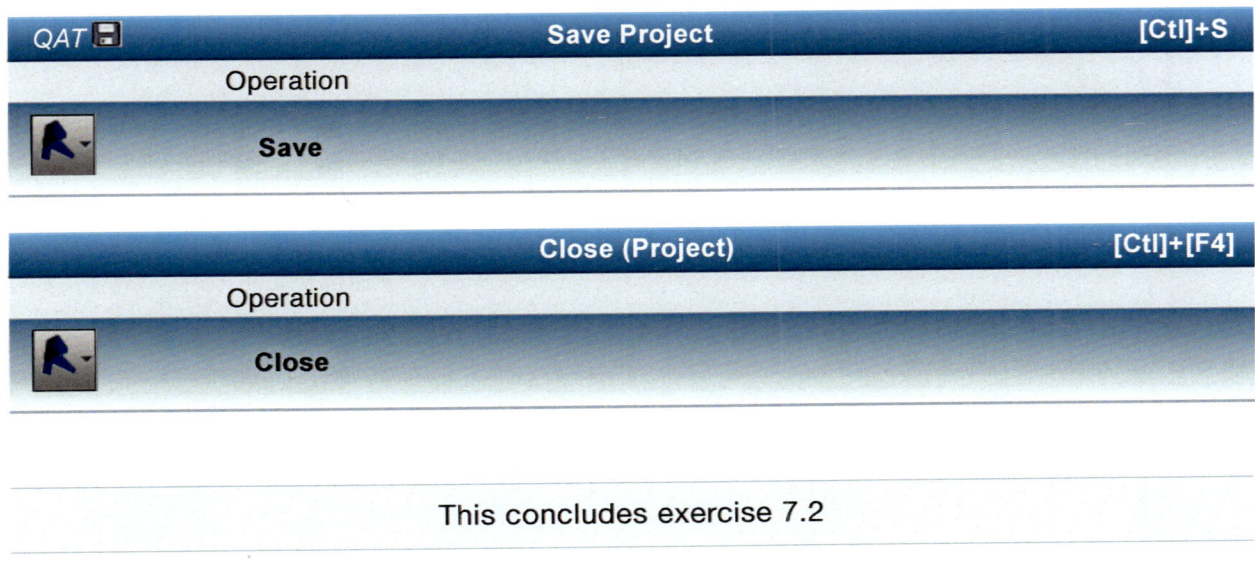

This concludes exercise 7.2

Chapter Summary

In this exercise you were introduced to foundation elements, structural views, and slope arrows, as well as site elements, such as the toposurface and building pad.

You are very likely beginning to recognize that there are a lot of similarities between various elements and tools in Revit. But despite the similarities, every category of element has its own idiosyncrasies, which require careful attention in order to yield the correct result.

Chapter 8
Compound Elements & Model Refinement

Overview

This chapter is intended to demonstrate creation of compound elements, such as roofs, floors, and walls, and how they fit into the process of progressive refinement of a building model. This is where the building model begins to take on more meaningful information as to how it's constructed, what materials are used, etc.

Learning Objectives

After completing this chapter you should have a basic understanding of the following new tools and concepts.

- Creating and working with compound walls
- Creating and working with compound floors
- Creating and working with compound roofs
- Replacing generic geometry with compound geometry
- Creating and working with stacked walls

Project Objectives

- Replace generic roofs with a compound roof type
- Replace generic floors with compound floor types
- Replace existing stem walls with stacked walls to include a mud sill
- Replace exterior generic walls with compound walls
- Replace interior generic walls with compound walls
- Adjust and constrain level elevations according to new floor assembly thicknesses

Chapter Contents

Exercise 8.1: Compound Roofs 231
- Transfer Project Standards 231
- Create New Roofing Materials 232
- Create a New Roof Type 235
- Replace Generic Roof Elements 236

Exercise 8.2: Compound Floors 237
- 1st Floor 237
- 2nd Floor 238
- Adjust Level Elevations 239

Exercise 8.3: Stacked Foundation Walls 242
- Create a Stacked Wall Assembly 242
- Replace Existing Stem Walls With Stacked Wall 244
- Correcting Effects of the Stem Wall Change 246

Exercise 8.4: Compound Walls 250
- Create New Wall Materials 250
- Create Exterior Compound Wall Types 251
- Create Interior Compound Wall Types 253
- Replace Generic Exterior Walls 255
- Replace Generic Interior Walls 259

Exercise 8.1: Compound Roofs

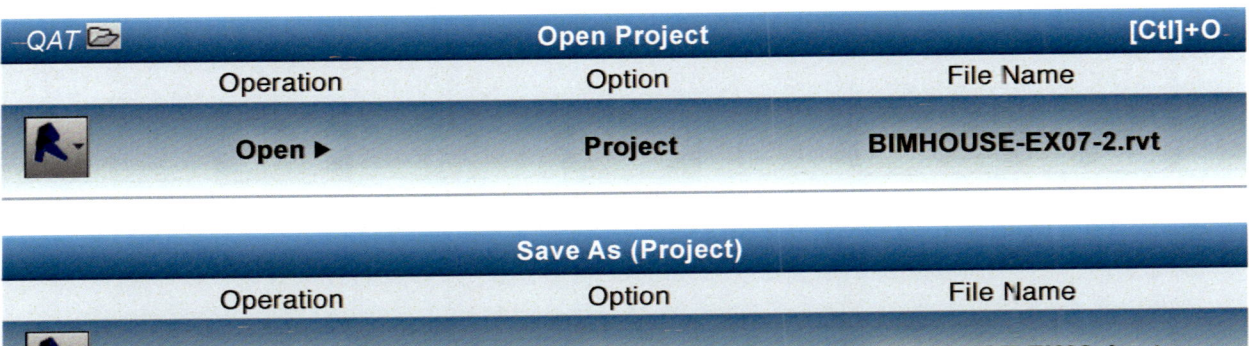

Transfer Project Standards

In this section you will be creating new materials that are suited to the roof structure for this project. For the shingle layer material, we want to use a custom surface pattern that doesn't exist in the project. Therefore, we need to transfer this pattern from another project file. This file is included with the content provided for this project.

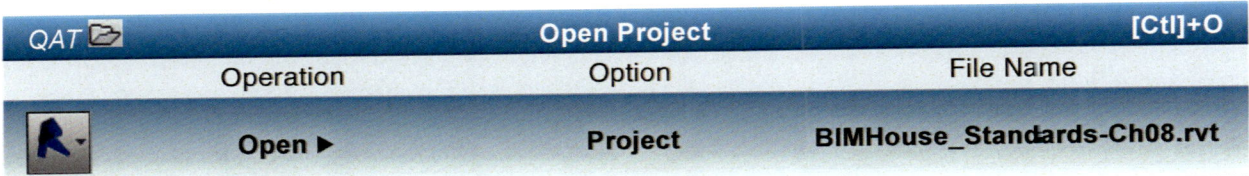

1. Switch back to an open window in your *BIMHOUSE-EX08-1* project file. **[Ctrl]+[Tab]**

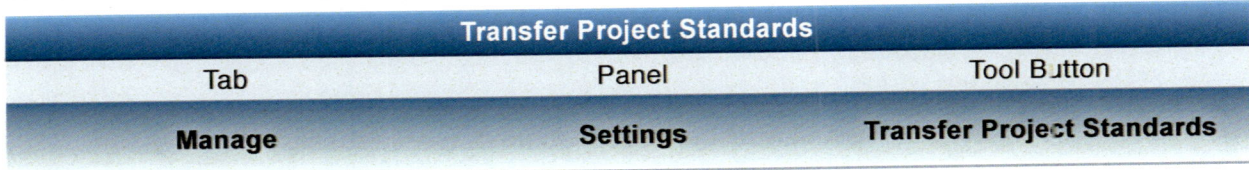

2. In the Select Items To Copy dialog box, do the following.

    a) Verify that *Copy from* is set to **BIMHouse_Standards-Ch08**. If not, select it from the drop-down list.
    b) Click **Check None**.
    c) Check the **Fill Patterns** checkbox in the list of selectable items.
    d) Click **OK** to start the transfer.

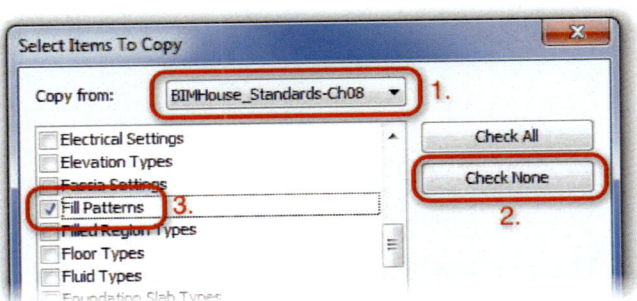

3. When the Duplicate Types dialog box appears, click **New Only** to complete the transfer.
4. You may now **Close** the project file *BIMHouse_Standards-Ch08*.

Chapter 8: Compound Elements & Model Refinement

Create New Roofing Materials

Materials Editing Overview

Many materials contain appearance assets, which is the information Revit uses when rendering or displaying materials using the Realistic visual style.

 The following steps are intended as a basic guide for editing material appearances. Refer back to these steps as necessary when creating the composite shingle material outlined on the following pages.

1. Replace the appearance:
   a) Open the Material Browser and select the material you wish to edit.
   b) Open the Appearance tab.
   c) At the bottom of the Material Browser, click the Open/Close asset browser button.
   d) Expand the Appearance Library on the left and select the desired category.
   e) Select the desired appearance on the right, then click the Replace button.

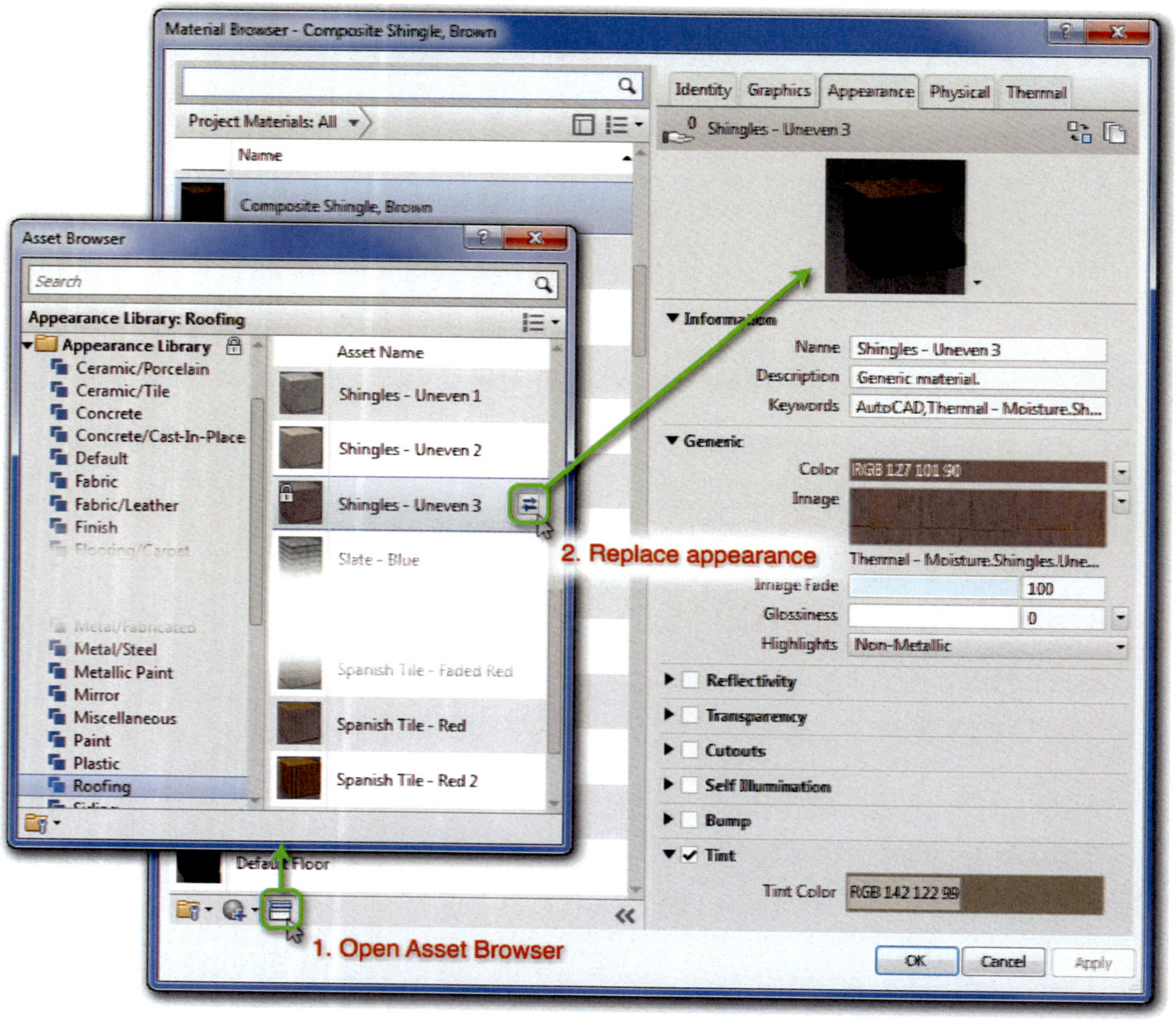

232

2. Edit the material texture properties:
   a) Click on the image to open the Texture Editor.
   b) Make the desired changes, and then click **Done**.
3. Edit the *Tint Color*:
   a) Click on the color swatch.
   b) Edit the *RGB* values, then click **OK**.

By default scale values in the texture editor are linked . This means that the Height value will change proportionately to Width, and vise-versa. To edit the values independently, click on the link icon to unlink the properties .

New Materials

 As you work through the remainder of this project, you will periodically be instructed to create new materials by duplicating existing materials. Most often these will be materials you have already created. Whenever you are instructed to do this, you will only be given new parameter values; I.E., those that need to be edited. Therefore, it is important that you create new materials carefully to ensure all parameters are correct, as any errors might propagate to new materials in the future.

Materials		
Tab	Panel	Tool Button
Manage	**Settings**	**Materials**

1. Create the materials shown in the following new materials tables. All materials are created by duplicating an existing material. Refer back to the *Materials Editing Overview* as necessary for specifics on adding appearance assets and editing textures.

New Roof Material 1: Roof Finish Layer

Property	Value
Existing Material to Duplicate	**Asphalt Shingle**
New Material Name	**Composite Shingle, Brown**
Graphics Tab	
Shading Color	**RGB 142-122-99**
Surface Pattern	**Composite Shingles** (Model Pattern)
Appearance Tab	
Appearance (Asset)	Appearance Library > Roofing > **Shingles - Uneven 3**
Texture Editor: Scale	Height = 2'-0" – Width = 3'-4" (linked)
Shading Color	**RGB 142-122-99**
Identity Tab	
Material Class	**Composites**
Description	**COMPOSITE ROOF SHINGLES**

New Roof Material 2: Roof Underlayment

Property	Value
Graphics Tab	
Existing Material to Duplicate	**Default Roof**
New Material Name	**Roofing Felt, #30**
Identity Tab	
Description	**#30 FELT UNDERLAYMENT**

Edit Existing Material: Structure, Wood Truss BC

Property	Value
Identity Tab	
Material Name	**Structure, Wood Truss BC**
Description	**PREFAB TRUSS**
Comments	**(SEE STRUCTURAL)**

New Roof Material 3: Truss Top Chord

Property	Value
Graphics Tab	
Existing Material to Duplicate	**Structure, Wood Truss BC**
New Material Name	**Structure, Wood Truss TC**

New Roof Material 4: OSB Sheathing

Property	Value
Graphics Tab	
Existing Material to Duplicate	**Plywood, Sheathing**
New Material Name	**OSB, Sheathing**
Identity Tab	
Description	**OSB SHEATHING**
Comments	**(SEE STRUCTURAL)**

Create a New Roof Type

2. In the Project Browser, navigate to the Families section and expand the following tree:

    Families → Roofs → Basic Roof

3. **Double-click** on *Wood Rafter 8" - Asphalt Shingle - Insulated* to open the Type Properties dialog box.

4. Click **Duplicate...**, enter **Wood Truss T.C. 4" - Composite Shingle+1/2"OSB** for the name *(T.C. stands for "top chord")*, and click **OK**.

5. Click **Edit...** next to the *Structure* parameter to open the Edit Assembly dialog box, then add/edit the roof layers as shown in the table on the following page.

CHAPTER 8: COMPOUND ELEMENTS & MODEL REFINEMENT

Roof Structure: Wood Truss T.C. 4" - Composite Shingle+1/2"OSB

Layer	Function	Material	Thickness
1	Finish 1 [4]	Composite Shingle, Brown	0' 0 1/4"
2	Membrane Layer	Roofing Felt, #30	0' 0"
3	**Core Boundary**	**Layers Above Wrap**	**0' 0"**
4	Substrate [2]	OSB, Sheathing	0' 0 1/2"
5	Structure [1]	Structure, Wood Truss TC	0' 3 1/2"
6	**Core Boundary**	**Layers Below Wrap**	**0' 0"**

6. Click **OK** to exit all dialog boxes and complete the new roof.

Replace Generic Roof Elements

1. Open the default *{3D}* view
2. Using **[Ctrl]**, select both roofs simultaneously.
3. In the Properties Palette, select **Wood Truss T.C. 4" - Composite Shingle+1/2"OSB** using the Type Selector. Your model should appear as illustrated below.

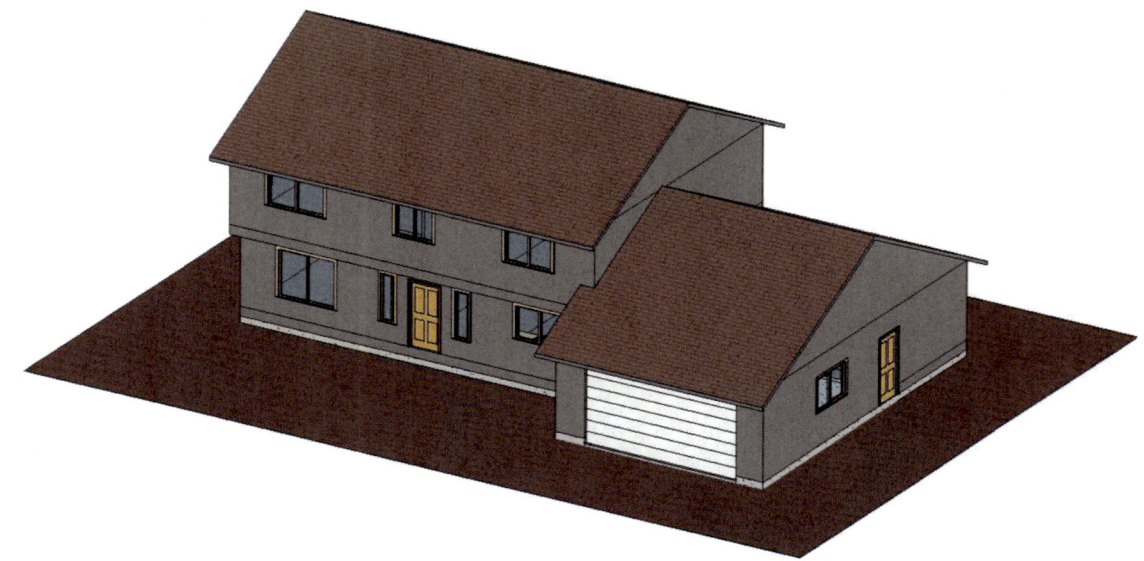

QAT	Save Project	[Ctl]+S
	Operation	
	Save	

This concludes exercise 8.1

Exercise 8.2: Compound Floors

The floor systems for the first and second floors are similar, the only difference being the joist height. Therefore, when creating the the second of the two, it's only a matter of duplicating the first and changing the name and layer thickness. Using this approach to creating new family types whenever possible is always more efficient than starting from scratch.

QAT	Open Project		[Ctl]+O
	Operation	Option	File Name
R	Open ▶	Project	BIMHOUSE-EX08-1.rvt

	Save As (Project)		
	Operation	Option	File Name
R	Save As ▶	Project	BIMHOUSE-EX08-2.rvt

1st Floor

1. Open the building section view *Family-Stairs-Porch (Long)*.
2. Select the *Generic 12"* floor at the 1st floor.
3. In the Properties palette, click **Edit Type** to open the Type Properties dialog box.
4. Click **Duplicate...**, and enter *TJI 9 1/2" - 3/4"T&G* for the name.
5. Open the Edit Assembly dialog box, and set the following layer properties:

Floor Structure: TJI 9 1/2" - 3/4"T&G

Layer	Function	Material	Thickness
1	Core Boundary	Layers Above Wrap	0' 0"
2	Structure [1]	Plywood, Sheathing	0' 0 3/4"
3	Structure [1]	Structure, Wood Joist/Rafter Layer	0' 9 1/2"
4	Core Boundary	Layers Below Wrap	0' 0"

6. Click **OK** twice to exit, which will exit all dialog boxes, complete the new floor, and apply the change to the selected floor element. Your section view should appear as illustrated on the following page.

CHAPTER 8: COMPOUND ELEMENTS & MODEL REFINEMENT

 Note the mismatch between the bottom of the new floor and the T.O.W. STEM. This is due to the overall thickness change in the new floor assembly. Don't worry about this right now, as we'll correct it shortly.

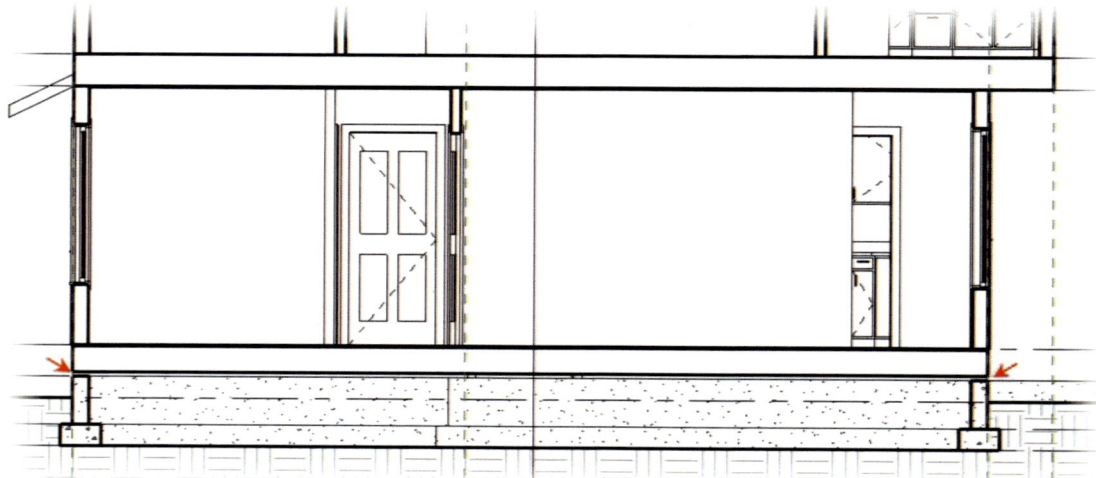

2nd Floor

1. If not already open, open the building section view *Family-Stairs-Porch (Long)*.
2. Select the *Generic 12"* floor at the 2nd floor.
3. Click **Edit Type** to open the Type Properties dialog box.
4. Select **TJI 9 1/2" - 3/4"T&G** for the *Type*.
5. Click **Duplicate...** and change the name to **TJI 11 7/8" - 3/4"T&G**.
6. Open the Edit Assembly dialog box, and set the following layer properties (*you should only have to change the thickness of Layer 3*).

Floor Structure: TJI 11 7/8" - 3/4"T&G

Layer	Function	Material	Thickness
1	Core Boundary	Layers Above Wrap	0' 0"
2	Structure [1]	Plywood, Sheathing	0' 0 3/4"
3	Structure [1]	Structure - Wood Truss Joist/Rafter Layer	0' 11 7/8"
4	Core Boundary	Layers Below Wrap	0' 0"

7. Click **OK** twice to exit all dialog boxes, complete the new floor, and apply the change to the selected floor element.

 Similar to the previous floor, you should see a mismatch between the bottom of the new floor assembly and the T.O.W. 1st FLR level, except that this time there is an interference condition instead of a gap.

Adjust Level Elevations

In the previous steps you replaced the generic 12" floors with floor assemblies of different thicknesses. This created an elevation mismatch between the bottom of the floors and their respective bearing levels. In the following steps you will correct this by adjusting level-to-level distances to match floor assembly thicknesses.

1. Open the building elevation view *W-South - Constraints*.
2. Place a *single* dimension string as illustrated below.

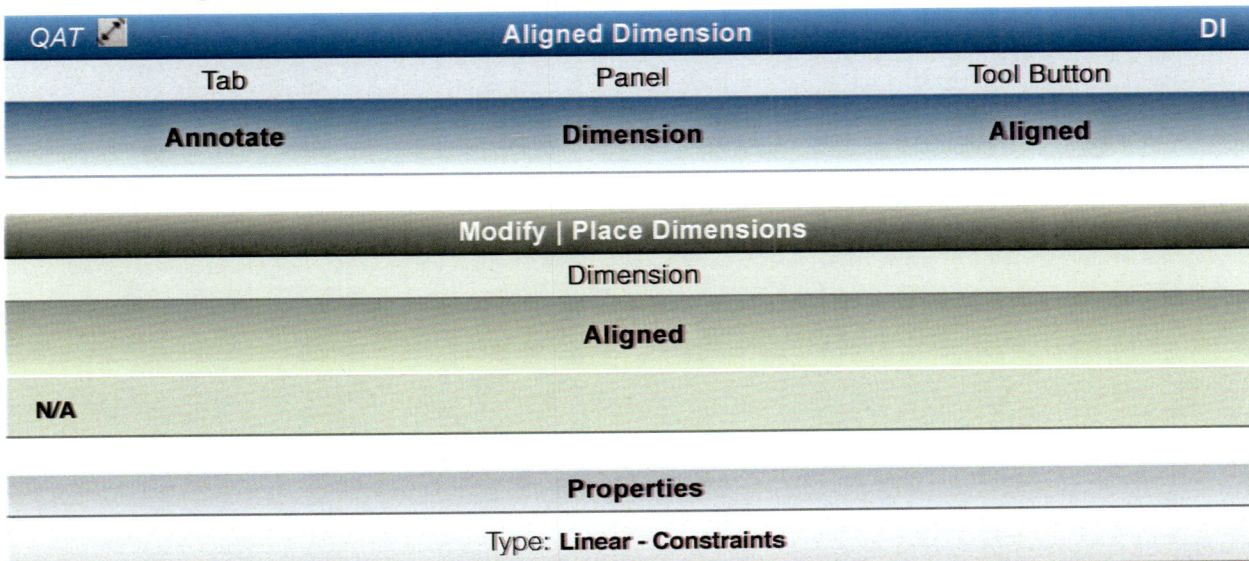

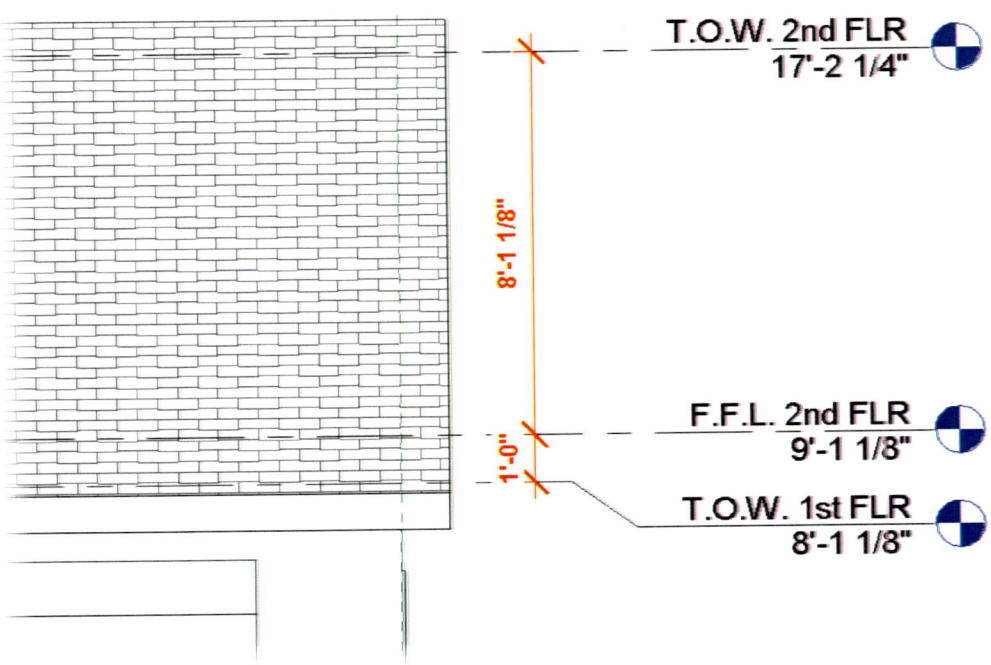

3. **Lock** the *8'-1 1/8"* dimension segment only. *Do not* lock to 1'-0" segment.

4. Select the level *F.F.L. 2nd FLR*.
5. Click on the 1'-0" dimension value between *F.F.L. 2nd FLR* and *T.O.W. 1st FLR* to activate the field, then change it to **1'-0 5/8"**.

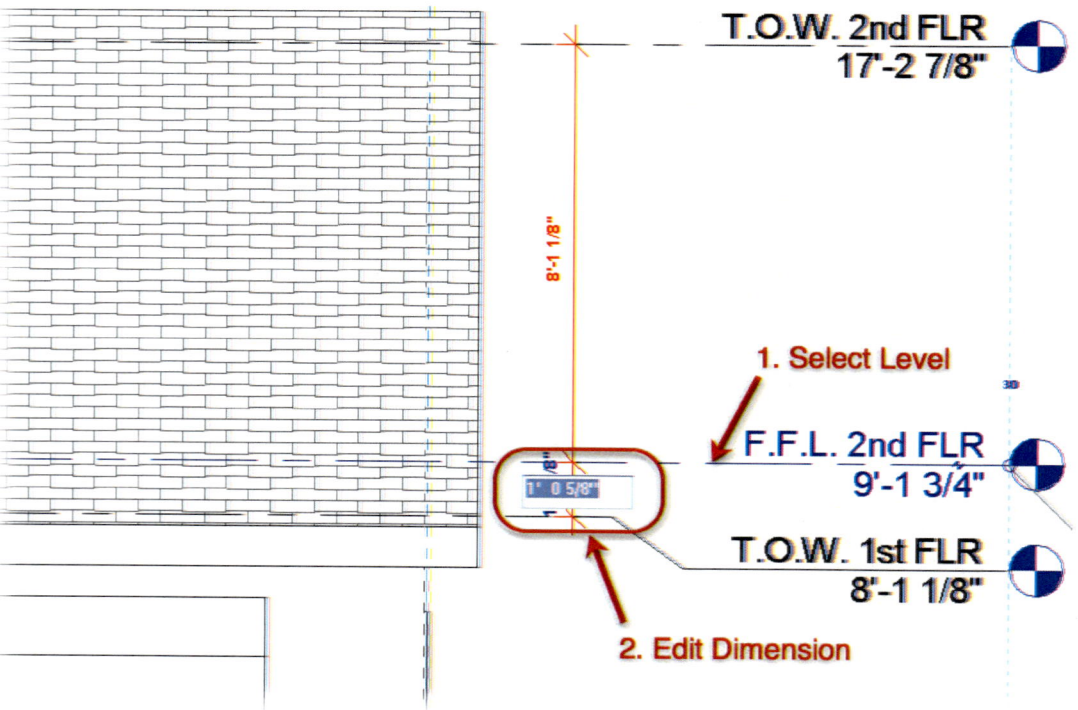

 Under certain conditions Revit it will not display temporary dimensions, nor will it allow you to edit an existing dimension value after selecting an element. This is often the case when multiple elements have been selected, or there is a large number of possibilities. When this happens, Revit will provide you with an **Activate Dimensions** button in the Options Bar. Clicking this button will reveal temporary dimensions, as well as allow editing of existing dimension values.

 When the *F.F.L. 2nd FLR* elevation was changed, the *T.O.W. 2nd FLR* level should have tracked to maintain the 8'-1 1/8" spacing between levels.

6. Select the dimension string between levels and **lock** the *1'-0 5/8"* dimension. This constrains the distance between the *T.O.W. 1st FLR* and *F.F.L. 2nd FLR* levels.
7. Select the level *T.O.W. STEM* and change its elevation to **-0'-11 3/4"**.
8. Open building section view *W-Laundry-Garage (Long)*. Your model should exhibit 1 1/2" gaps between the tops of the stem walls and bottom of the floor assembly as illustrated on the following page.

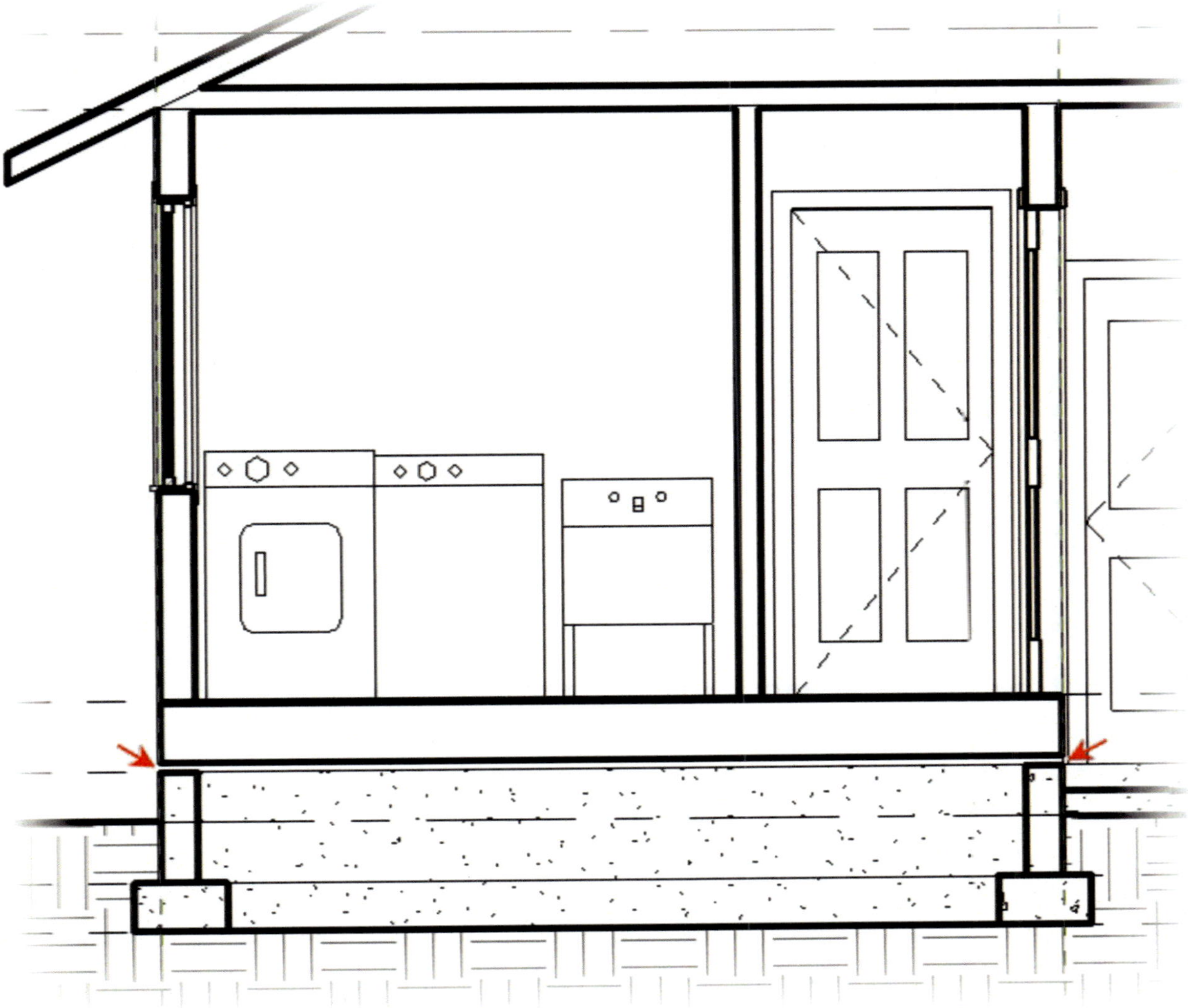

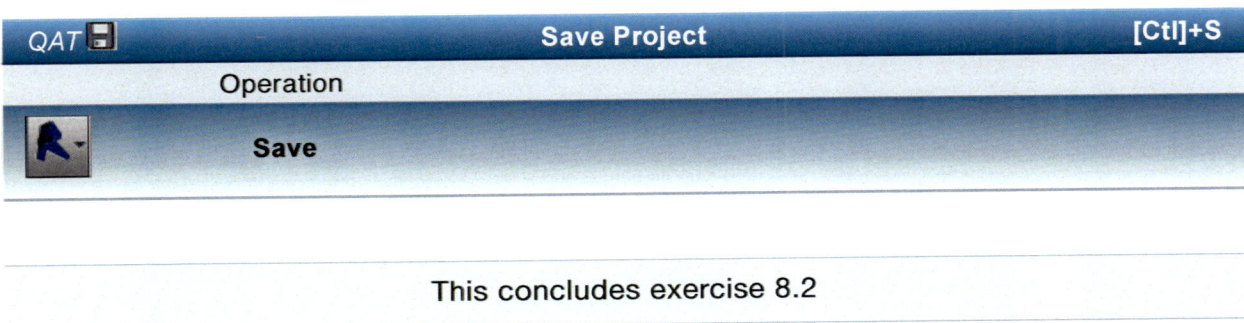

 The reason that the distance between *T.O.W. STEM* and *F.F.L. 1st FLR* is 1 1/2" greater than the thickness of the 1st floor assembly is to provide space to insert a pressure treated plate (mud sill) between the bottom of the floor and top of the stem wall.

QAT	Save Project	[Ctl]+S
	Operation	
	Save	

This concludes exercise 8.2

Exercise 8.3: Stacked Foundation Walls

As briefly mentioned in the last chapter, there needs to be a pressure treated plate between the bottom of the 1st floor assembly and the top of the stem wall. There are a number of ways we could accomplish this. However, for the sake of exploring the creation and application of stacked walls, this is the approach that will be used.

In the following steps you will first create a new stacked wall type consisting of a 6" concrete stem wall, and a 1 ½" x 5 ½" wall to represent the sill. You will then replace the instances of stem wall that support the 1st floor assembly with the new stacked wall.

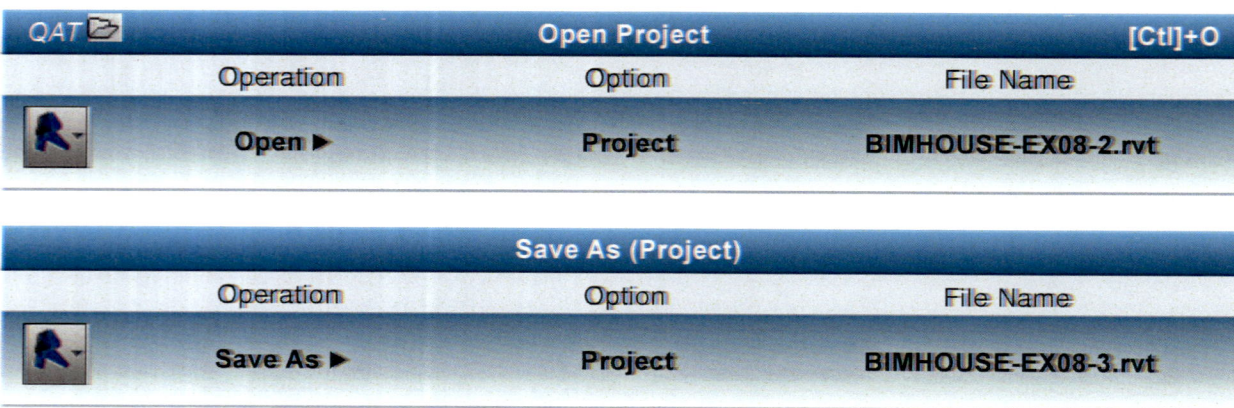

Create a Stacked Wall Assembly

You will need to create a basic wall type to use for the pressure treated plate prior to creating the stacked wall type.

New Basic Wall Type

1. Duplicate the *Generic - 5 1/2"* wall type, and name it **Exterior - Wood 5 1/2" P.T.**
2. Edit the structure as shown in the table below.
3. To create the material shown for Layer 2:
    a) **Duplicate** the material *Structure, Wood Joist/Rafter Layer*
    b) Name the new material **Structure, Wood, Pressure Treated**.
    c) Set the *Shading* value to a dark green color, such as **RGB 000-128-064**.

Wall Structure: Exterior - Wood 5 1/2" P.T.

Layer	Function	Material	Thickness
1	Core Boundary	Layers Above Wrap	0' 0"
2	Structure [1]	Structure, Wood, Pressure Treated	0' 5 1/2"
3	Core Boundary	Layers Below Wrap	0' 0"

4. Click **OK** to exit all dialog boxes and complete the wall type.

Build the Stacked Wall

5. In the Project Browser, navigate to the Families section and expand the following tree:

    Families → Walls → Stacked Wall

6. **Double-click** on *Exterior - Brick Over CMU w Metal Stud* to open the Type Properties dialog box
7. Click **Duplicate...**, and enter **Stem Wall - 2x6 Sill on 6" Concrete** for the name.
8. Click **Edit...** next to the *Structure* parameter to open the Edit Assembly dialog box.
9. Set the following properties:
    a) *Offset:* **Core Face: Exterior**
    b) *Sample Height:* **3' 0"**
10. In the Types pane, configure the stacked wall as shown in the table below.

 There can be only on variable layer in a stacked wall. To change the variable layer assignment, first select the layer, then click the **Variable** button at the bottom of the Types pane.

Stacked Wall Configuration: Stem Wall - 2x6 Sill on 6" Concrete

	Name	Height	Offset	Top	Base	Flip
1	Exterior - Wood 5 1/2" P.T.	0' 1 1/2"	0' 0"	0' 0"	0' 0"	
2	Stem - 6" Concrete	Variable	0' 0"	0' 0"	0' 0"	

11. Click **<< Preview** to expand the wall section preview and verify the wall section looks as illustrated below. You may need to zoom in to get a good look.

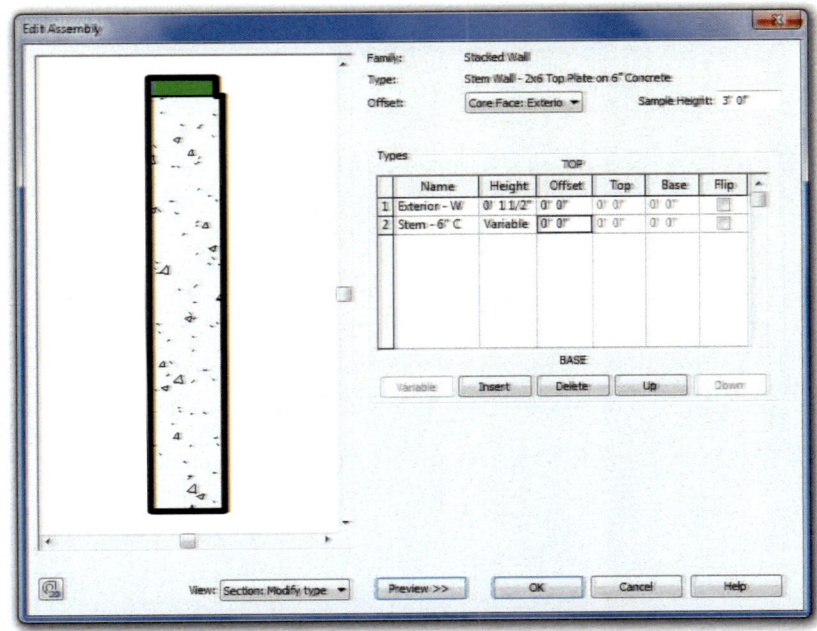

12. Click **OK** to exit all dialog boxes and complete the wall type.

Replace Existing Stem Walls With Stacked Wall

We'll assume that the garage walls will be constructed with a pressure treated sill. Therefore, there's no need to change the exterior garage stem walls to include a plate. However, the stem walls that define the livable area of the house will support the TJI floor system, and therefore require that the mud sill be included.

Along the east side of the house, you originally created a single stem wall that spans full length of the structure. You'll need to split this into two walls, allowing application of the stacked stem wall to the livable portion only.

1. Open the floor plan view *Foundation Plan*.
2. Zoom into the east side of the foundation where the three walls come together, and **split** the east stem wall where indicated in the illustration below.

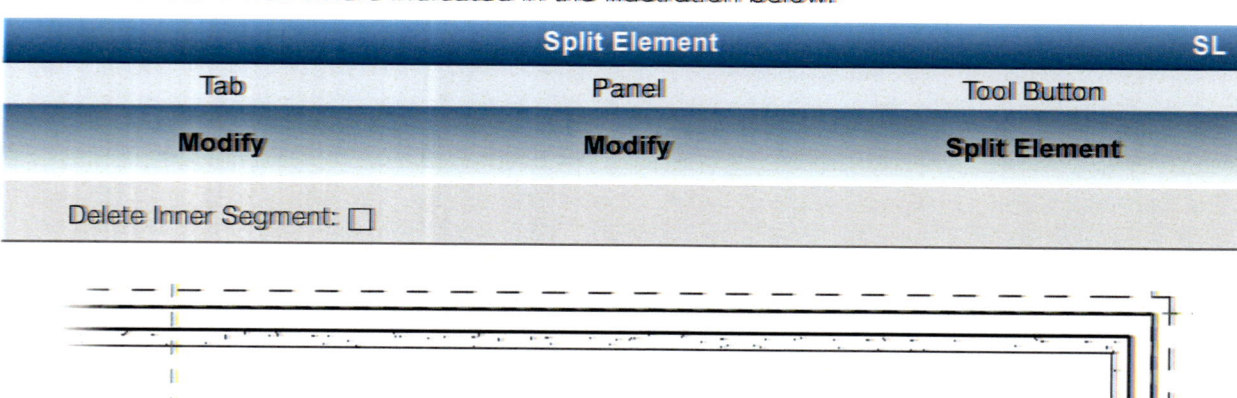

Stem Wall Split Location

3. Select the chain of walls as illustrated below.
   a) Click **Activate Dimensions** in the Options Bar.
   b) **Unlock** all 7 padlock icons.
   c) Set the *Top Offset* property to **0' 1 1/2"**.

 Do not proceed with the next step until the *Top Offset* property has been correctly set as instructed in the previous step. Due to the behavior of stacked walls, setting the *Top Offset* property after converting the wall type to a stacked wall will cause the top layer of the stacked wall (sill) to change in height, even though it is fixed.

   d) With the chain of walls still selected, change the wall type to **Stem Wall - 2x6 Sill on 6" Concrete**.

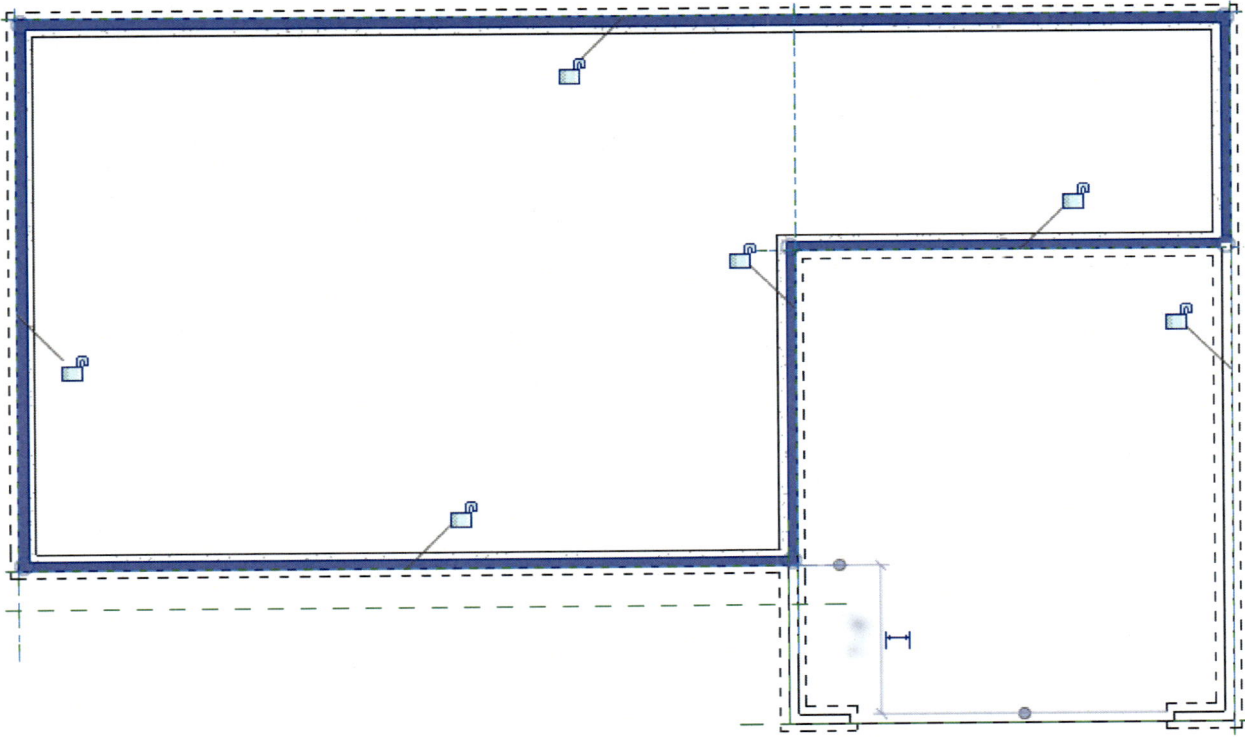

Select and Unconstrain Chain of Stem Walls

4. Open the view **3D Section - Foundation**
5. Adjust the top plane of the section box upward slightly to reveal the mud sill as illustrated below.

Correcting Effects of the Stem Wall Change

By changing the stem wall from a Basic family to a Stacked family, several artifacts were generated that need to be addressed. The following is a list of these items, which we'll address in the remainder of this section.

- Exterior 1st floor wall join at northeast corner of garage interfering with plate.
- Relocated association between garage slab and stem walls.
- Relocated association between building pad and stem walls.
- Additionally, you will want to re-constrain stem walls to reference planes.

Modify 1st Floor Exterior Wall Join at NE Corner of Garage

1. Open the view **3D Section - Foundation**, and zoom into the NE corner of the garage where the stem walls come together to form a "T". Notice the notch taken out of the sill. This has to do with the join condition created by the hidden garage wall.

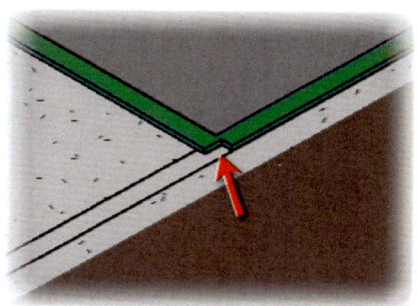

The reason for not seeing the offending garage wall is that the view *Discipline* property is set to **Structural**, which automatically hides non-structural walls. To see this wall, set the view *Discipline* property to **Coordination**. Experiment with dragging the end of the garage wall away from the stem wall join to see the effects on the sill.

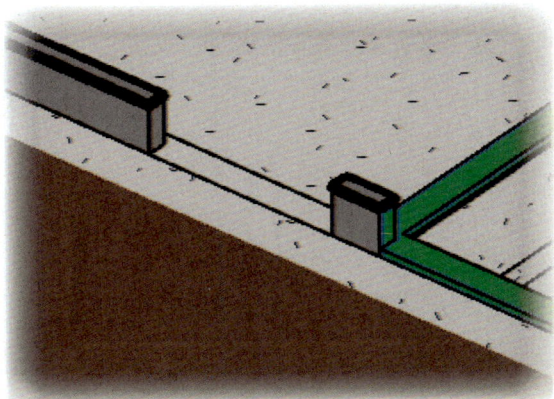
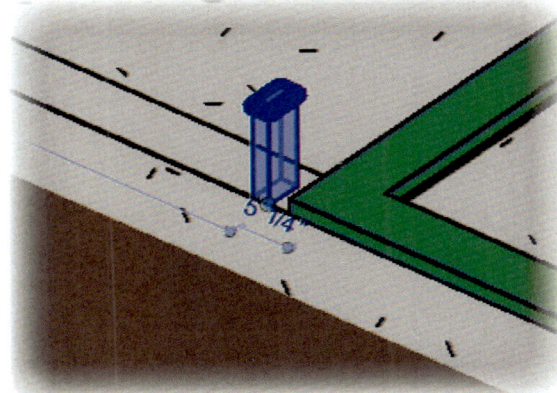

Remember to set the view *Discipline* property back to **Structural** when done.

2. Open floor plan view *W-1st Floor - Constraints*.
3. Drag the *Generic - 3 1/2"* wall end away from the join and set the end to **Disallow Join** as illustrated.
4. **Align** and **Lock** the end of the wall to reference plane *Int-Garage-North* as indicated in the illustration above.

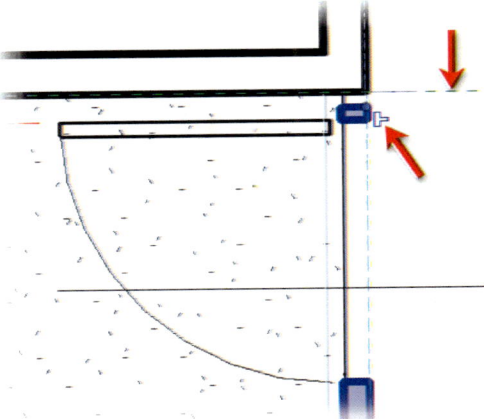

5. Use **Join Geometry** to clean up the join.
6. Open the view *3D Section - Foundation*. The sill should now form a clean corner as illustrated.

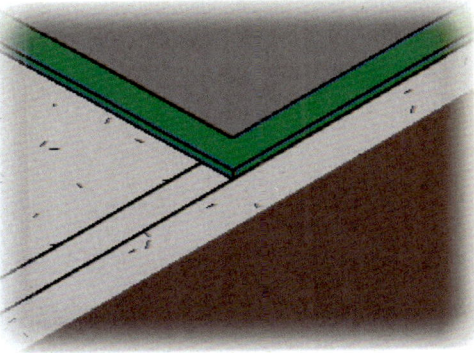

Re-lock Stacked Stem Walls to Reference Planes

7. Open plan view *Foundation Plan*.

8. **Align** and **Lock** the six stacked stem walls, as well as the east garage stem wall to their respective reference planes. Be careful to select **Faces of core** for the *Prefer* setting in the Options Bar, and make sure the *Detail Level* for the view is set to **Coarse**.

9. Test the constraints by flexing the 6 reference planes associated with the stacked stem walls. Remember to re-pin the reference planes when done.

Relocate Garage Slab Boundary Lines

When you split the garage stem wall, and changed the six stem walls from basic to stacked, the garage floor's association with these walls shifted from face to centerline. Therefore, you will need to edit the floor boundary to correct this.

 In the following steps you will realign the boundary lines to the core face of the stem walls; however, you will not lock them. When in the edit mode, if you select one of the boundary lines you will notice that there is still a flip arrow. This indicates that the boundary line is still associated with the wall. If you later select one of the boundary lines after it has been realigned, you will notice that it now has an offset value associated with it (Options bar).

10. Select the garage floor, then click **Edit Boundary** in the contextual ribbon tab.

11. Find the three boundary lines that shifted to the center of a stem wall and **Align** them back to the appropriate core face. If a boundary line is already at the face of a wall, there is no need to do anything with it.

12. When your boundary lines have all been repaired, your sketch should appear as illustrated below.

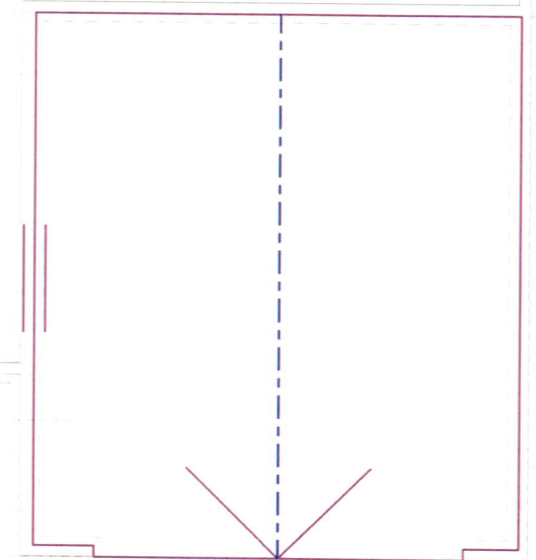

13. When done, click the **Finish Edit Mode** button ✓

Relocate Building Pad Boundary Lines

14. Open plan view *Foundation Plan*.
15. **Select** the building pad, then click **Edit Boundary** in the contextual ribbon tab.

 To select the building pad, you can create a crossing selection over a stacked stem wall, then use the filter tool to narrow down the selection set to Pads only. Alternately, enable **Select Elements by Face**; you can then click anywhere within the crawlspace to select the pad.

16. As you did with the garage slab, **Align** all boundary lines back to the exterior core face of the stem walls (do not lock).
17. When done, click the **Finish Edit Mode** button ✓

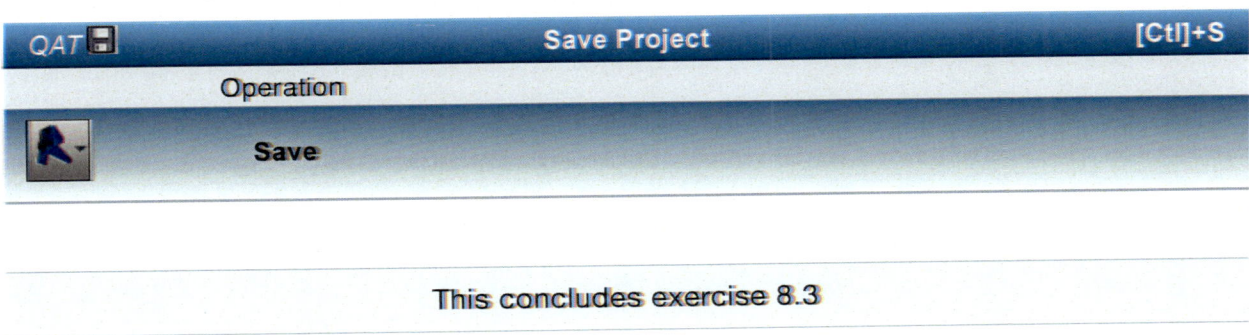

This concludes exercise 8.3

Exercise 8.4: Compound Walls

QAT 📂	Open Project	[Ctl]+O
Operation	Option	File Name
Open ▶	Project	BIMHOUSE-EX08-3.rvt

	Save As (Project)	
Operation	Option	File Name
Save As ▶	Project	BIMHOUSE-EX08-4.rvt

Create New Wall Materials

Prior to creating new wall types for the project, you'll need to create some new materials.

	Materials	
Tab	Panel	Tool Button
Manage	Settings	Materials

1. Create the following materials by duplicating and/or renaming as indicated in the tables below. Additionally, set any properties indicated for the new materials.

 Refer back to the beginning of this chapter for a refresher on creating materials if necessary.

New Wall Material 1: Gable Wall Finish Layer – Shake Siding

Property	Value
Existing Material to Duplicate	**Composite Shingle, Brown**
New Material Name	**Siding, Wood, Shake**
Graphics Tab	
Surface Pattern	**Shake 6"** (Model Pattern)
Appearance Tab	
Appearance (Asset)	Appearance Library > Roofing > **Shake - Handsplit**
Identity Tab	
Material Class	**Wood**
Description	**WOOD SHAKE SIDING**

New Wall Material 2: Exterior Wall Finish Layer – Horizontal Siding

Property	Value
Existing Material to Duplicate	**Siding, Wood, Shake**
New Material Name	**Siding, Wood, Horizontal, 6" Beige**
Graphics Tab	
Shading Color	**RGB 242-231-197**
Surface Pattern	**6" Parallel** (Model Pattern)
Cut Pattern	**Diagonal down** (Drafting Pattern)
Appearance Tab	
Appearance (Asset)	Appearance Library > Siding > **Horizontal 6in - Beige**
Identity Tab	
Description	**6" HORIZONTAL SIDING**

2. **New Wall Material 3: Exterior Wall Core Framing Layer**

Property	Value
Existing Material to Duplicate	**Structure, Wood Joist/Rafter Layer**
New Material Name	**Structure, Wood Stud Layer**
Identity Tab	
Description	**WOOD STUD FRAMING**

3. Click **OK** to exit the Material Browser when done.

Create Exterior Compound Wall Types

Exterior 2x6 Wall Type

1. In the Project Browser, navigate to the Families section and expand the following tree:
   Families → Walls → Basic Wall

2. **Double-click** on *Generic - 5 1/2"* to open the Type Properties dialog box.

3. Click **Duplicate...** and enter **Exterior - Wood 2x6 - 5/8"Siding+7/16"OSB+_+1/2"GWB** for the name.

4. Verify that the *Function* property is set to **Exterior**.

5. Click **Edit...** to open the Edit Assembly dialog box.

6. Build the wall structure as shown in the table on the following page.

Chapter 8: Compound Elements & Model Refinement

Compound Wall Structure: Exterior – Wood 2x6 - 5/8"Siding+7/16"OSB+_+1/2"GWB

Layer	Function	Material	Thickness
1	Finish 1 [4]	Siding, Wood, Horizontal, 6" Beige	0' 0 5/8"
2	Membrane Layer	Damp proofing	0' 0"
3	Substrate [2]	OSB, Sheathing	0' 0 7/16"
4	**Core Boundary**	**Layers Above Wrap**	**0' 0"**
5	Structure [1]	Structure, Wood Stud Layer	0' 5 1/2"
6	**Core Boundary**	**Layers Below Wrap**	**0' 0"**
7	Finish 2 [5]	Gypsum Wall Board	0' 0 1/2"

7. Open the preview pane, and set the *View* drop-down to **Section: Modify Type**.
8. Click **Modify** in the Modify Vertical Structure pane.
9. Zoom into the base of the wall in the preview pane, then select and **unlock** the base of layers 1 & 2 (one at a time) as illustrated below.

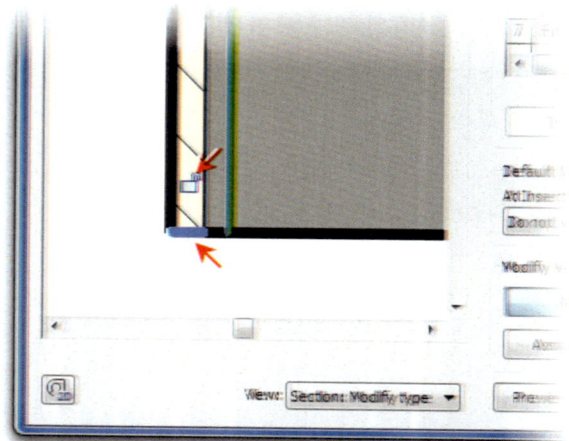 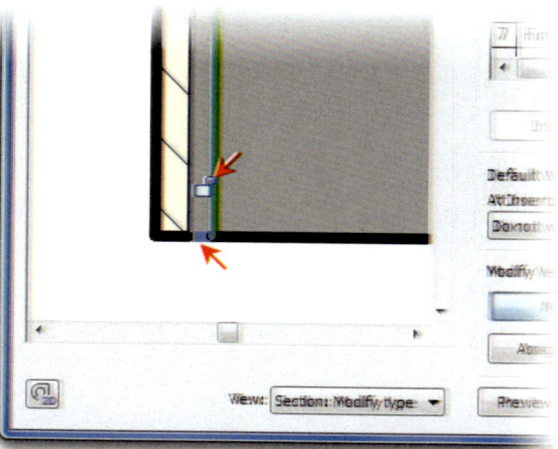

Unlock Base of Siding Layer (1)   Unlock Base of Sheathing Layer (2)

10. Click **OK** once to return to the Type Properties dialog box.

Exterior 2x4 Wall Type

11. Click **Duplicate...** and enter **Exterior - Wood 2x4 - 5/8"Siding+7/16"OSB+_+1/2"GWB** for the name. *(Hint: the only difference is 2x4 in lieu of 2x6, and you must remove the "2" that Revit adds to the end when duplicating an element.)*
12. Click **Edit...** to open the Edit Assembly dialog box.
13. Change the thickness of the core layer (*Structure [1]*) to **0' 3 1/2"**.
14. Click **OK** once to return to the Type Properties dialog box.

Exterior Gable Wall Type

15. Click **Duplicate...** and enter **Exterior - Wood 2x - 5/8"Shake+7/16"OSB** for the name.
16. Click **Edit...** to open the Edit Assembly dialog box.

17. Edit the wall structure as shown in the table below.

Compound Wall Structure: Exterior - Wood 2x - 5/8"Shake+7/16"OSB

Layer	Function	Material	Thickness
1	Finish 1 [4]	Siding, Wood, Shake	0" 0 5/8"
2	Membrane Layer	Damp proofing	0" 0"
3	Substrate [2]	OSB, Sheathing	0" 0 7/16"
4	**Core Boundary**	**Layers Above Wrap**	**0" 0"**
5	Structure [1]	Structure, Wood Stud Layer	0" 1 1/2"
6	**Core Boundary**	**Layers Below Wrap**	**0" 0"**

18. Click **Modify** in the Modify Vertical Structure pane.
19. Zoom into the base of the wall in the preview pane, then select and **lock** the base of layers 1 & 2 (one at a time) as illustrated on the following page.

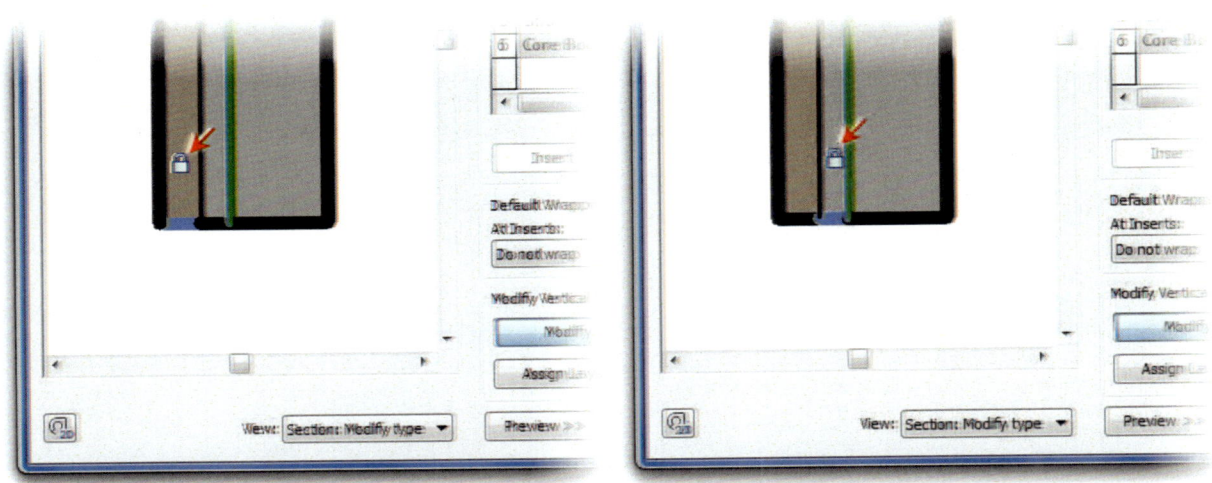

Lock Base of Siding Layer (1)   *Lock Base of Sheathing Layer (2)*

20. Click **OK** twice to exit all dialog boxes and complete the walls.

Create Interior Compound Wall Types

Interior 2x6 Wall Type

1. In the project browser, **double-click** on the wall type *Interior - 4 7/8" Partition (1-hr)* to open the Type Properties dialog box.
2. Click **Duplicate...** and enter **Interior - Wood 2x6 - 1/2"GWB+_+1/2"GWB** for the name.
3. Verify the *Function* property is set to **Interior**.
4. Edit the wall structure as shown in the table on the following page.

Compound Wall Structure: Interior - Wood 2x6 - 1/2"GWB+_+1/2"GWB

Layer	Function	Material	Thickness
1	Finish 2 [5]	Gypsum Wall Board	0' 0 1/2"
2	**Core Boundary**	**Layers Above Wrap**	**0' 0"**
3	Structure [1]	Structure, Wood Stud Layer	0' 5 1/2"
4	**Core Boundary**	**Layers Below Wrap**	**0' 0"**
5	Finish 2 [5]	Gypsum Wall Board	0' 0 1/2"

5. Click **OK** once to return to the Type Properties dialog box.

Interior 2x4 Wall Type

6. Click **Duplicate...** and enter **Interior - Wood 2x4 - 1/2"GWB+_+1/2"GWB** for the name.
7. Click **Edit...** to open the Edit Assembly dialog box.
8. Change the thickness of the core layer (*Structure [1]*) to **0' 3 1/2"**.
9. Click **OK** once to return to the Type Properties dialog box.

Interior 2x4 Soffit Wall Type

10. Click **Duplicate...** and enter **Soffit - Wood 2x4 - 1/2"GWB+_+0** for the name.
11. Change the *Function* property to **Soffit**.
12. Edit the wall structure as shown in the table below.

Compound Wall Structure: Soffit - Wood 2x4 - 1/2"GWB+_+0

Layer	Function	Material	Thickness
1	Finish 2 [5]	Gypsum Wall Board	0' 0 1/2"
2	**Core Boundary**	**Layers Above Wrap**	**0' 0"**
3	Structure [1]	Structure, Wood Stud Layer	0' 3 1/2"
4	**Core Boundary**	**Layers Below Wrap**	**0' 0"**

13. Click **OK** to exit all dialog boxes.

Exercise 8.4: Compound Walls

Replace Generic Exterior Walls

 You may want to have the {3D} view open and tiled while making the following changes so you can see the changes happening in more detail.

1. Open the floor plan view *F.F.L. 1st FLR*.
2. Set the view *Detail Level* to **Medium**. To do this, you will need to edit the view template associated with this view.
3. Select the four *Generic - 5 1/2"* walls as illustrated below (selection highlighted in blue).

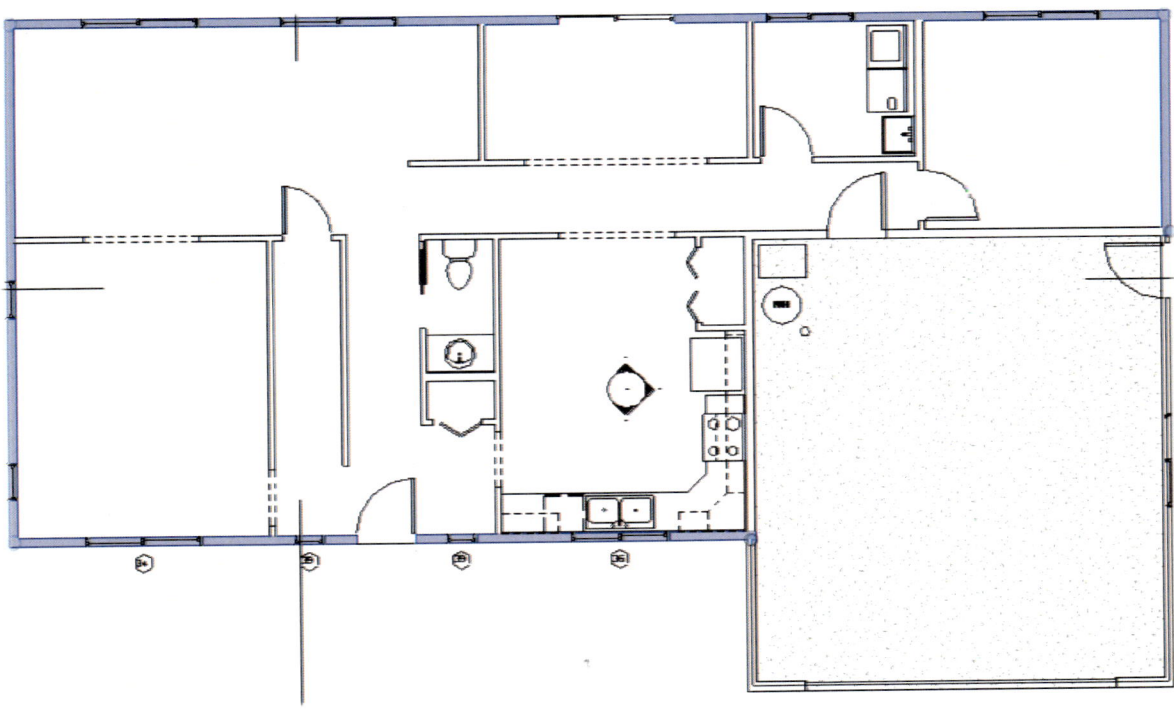

1st Floor Exterior Wall Selection

4. Change the properties of these four walls...

Properties
Type: **Exterior - Wood 2x6 - 5/8"Siding+7/16"OSB+_+1/2"GWB**
Base Extension Distance: **-1' 0 3/4"**

 Since the siding and sheathing need to extend down passed the floor level to the stem wall, the Base Extension Distance was entered as a negative number. The siding and sheathing layers were unlocked when the wall type was created, which is what enabled the Base Extension Distance parameter.

CHAPTER 8: COMPOUND ELEMENTS & MODEL REFINEMENT

5. Select the three *Generic - 3 1/2"* garage walls as illustrated below (selection highlighted in blue).

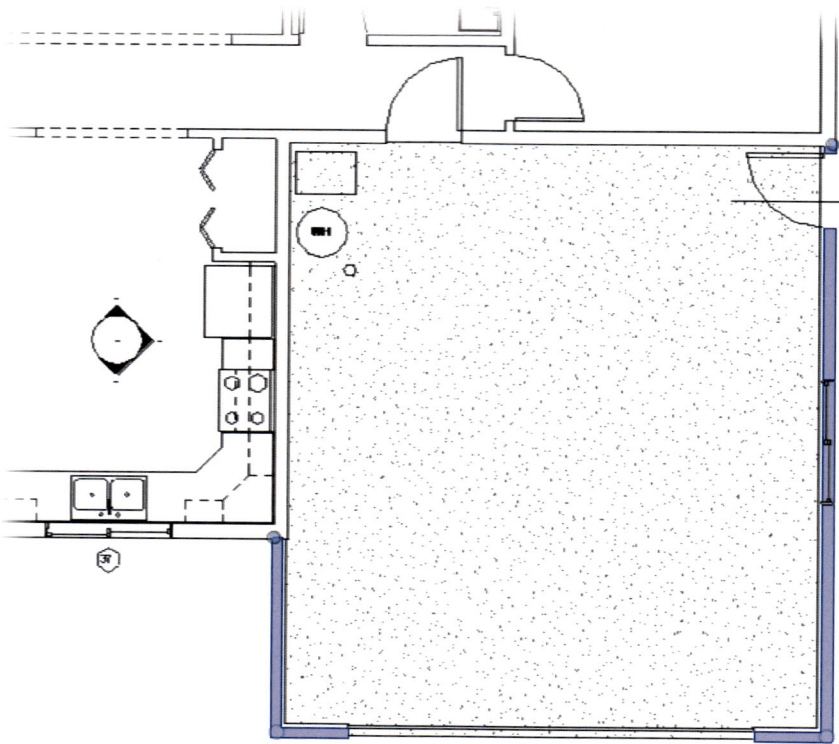

6. Change the properties of these three walls...

Properties
Type: **Exterior - Wood 2x4 - 5/8"Siding+7/16"OSB+_+1/2"GWB**
Base Extension Distance: **-0' 1"**

1. Open the floor plan view *F.F.L. 2nd FLR*.
2. Select the four *Generic - 5 1/2"* walls that define the exterior walls for the 2nd floor.
3. Change the properties of these four walls...

Properties
Type: **Exterior - Wood 2x6 - 5/8"Siding+7/16"OSB+_+1/2"GWB**
Base Extension Distance: **-1' 0 5/8"**

4. Open section view *Family-Stairs-Porch (Long)* to view the changes.
5. Toggle **Thin Lines** to get a better view of the wall layer extensions at the floor assemblies.

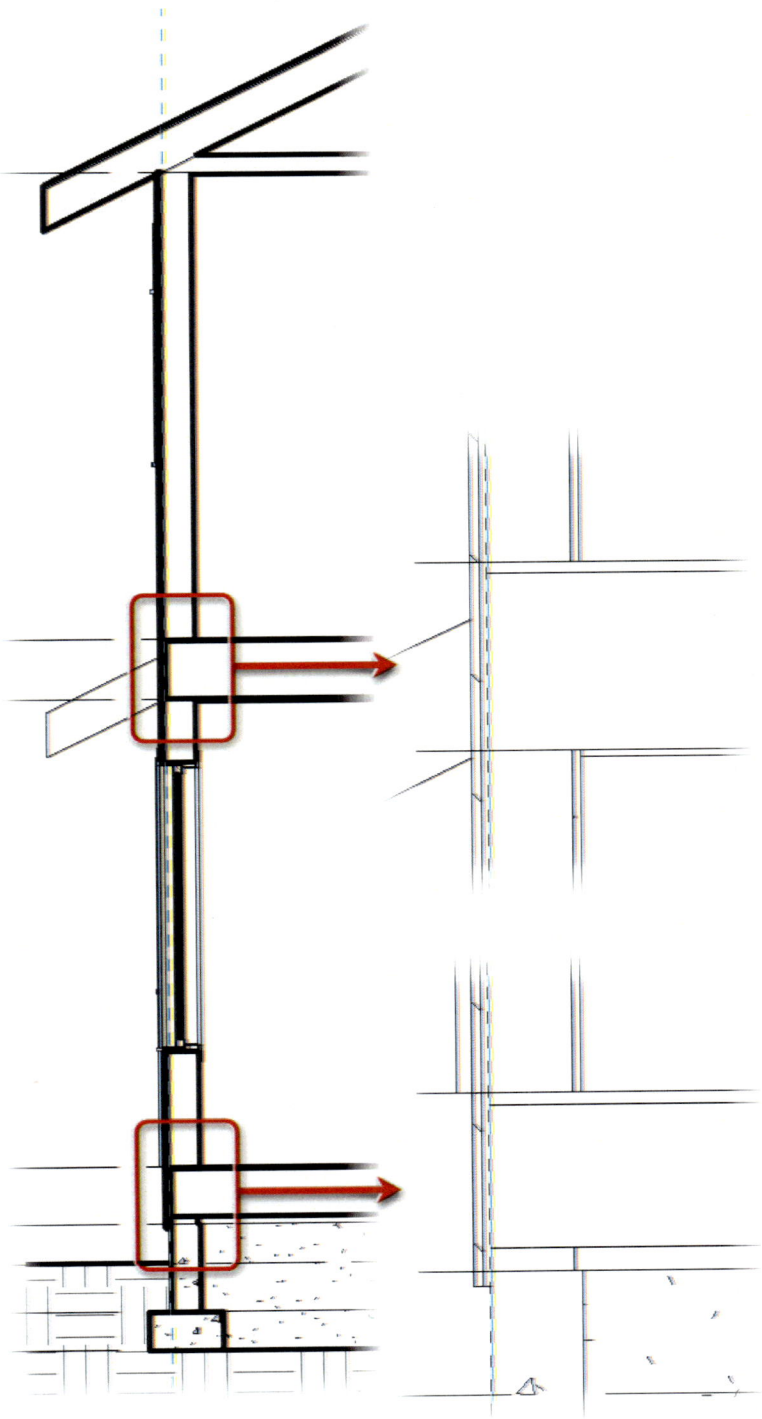

6. Reset Thin Lines mode.
7. Open the default *{3D}* view and orbit to view the changes.

CHAPTER 8: COMPOUND ELEMENTS & MODEL REFINEMENT

8. Select all four gable walls, and change their properties as follows.

Properties
Type: **Exterior - Wood 2x - 5/8"Shake+7/16"OSB**

9. When done, your model should look like the illustrations below.

3D Model Views After Exterior Walls Refinement

10. Use **Join Geometry** where the 1st floor roof intersects 2nd floor exterior walls.

 If you don't see the shake pattern on the gable walls, try zooming in. If it still doesn't appear, one or more of the gable walls may be oriented inside-out.

Replace Generic Interior Walls

1st Floor Partition Walls

1. Open the floor plan view *F.F.L. 1st FLR*.
2. Select the *Generic - 3 1/2"* interior walls as illustrated below (selection highlighted in blue).

 To select all the walls of a specific type within the current view, select one of the walls, right-click, and from the contextual menu pick *Select All Instances → Visible In View*.

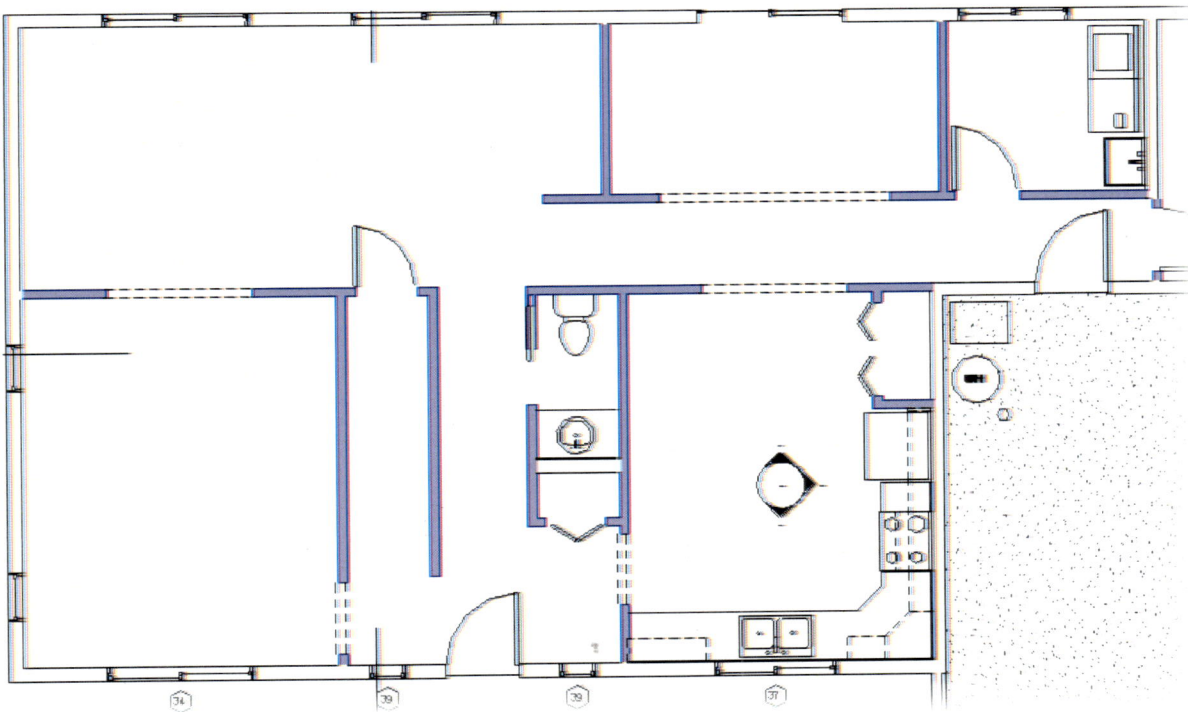

3. Change the wall type....

Properties
Type: **Interior - Wood 2x4 - 1/2"GWB+_+1/2"GWB**

 If you receive *Constraints Not Satisfied* errors when changing the walls, you can choose to remove the constraints if you're comfortable that you know what your doing based the visual feedback. Otherwise, cancel the operation and repeat the previous steps with a smaller selection set, or by converting one wall at a time.

CHAPTER 8: COMPOUND ELEMENTS & MODEL REFINEMENT

4. Select the *Generic - 5 1/2"* interior walls as illustrated below.

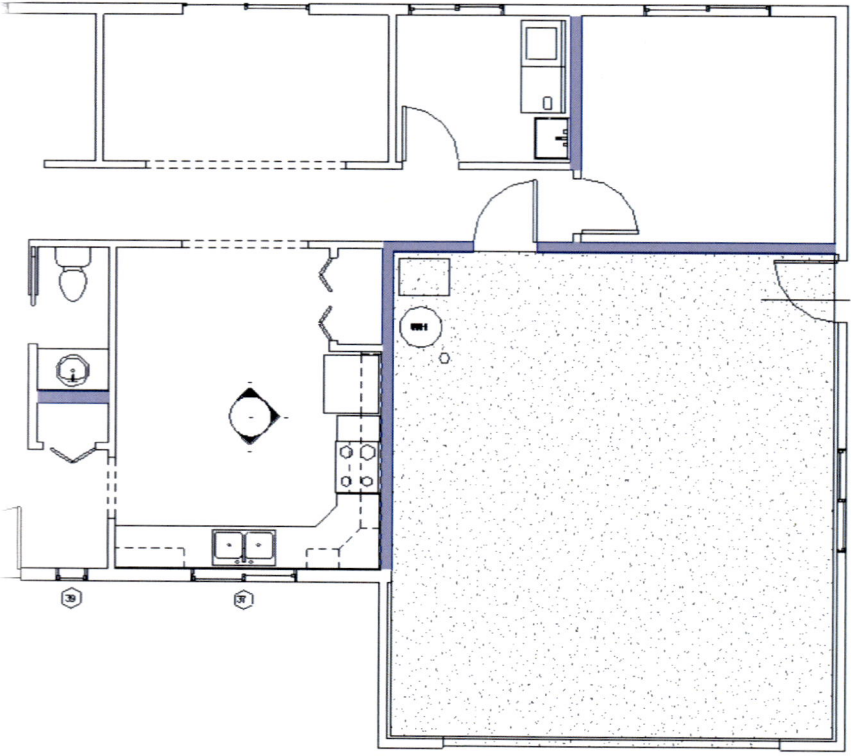

5. Change the wall type...

Properties
Type: **Interior - Wood 2x6 - 1/2"GWB+_+1/2"GWB**

2nd Floor Partition Walls

6. Open the floor plan view *F.F.L. 2nd FLR*.
7. Repeat the previous steps to convert all generic interior walls to compound interior walls.

1st Floor Soffit Walls

8. Open the ceiling plan view *RCP - 1st FLR*.
9. Select the 4 soffit walls at the coffered ceiling in the living room, then change the wall type to **Soffit - Wood 2x4 - 1/2"GWB+_+0**.

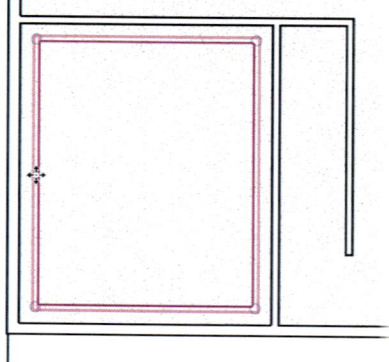

 The soffit walls won't be visible in this view, however, hovering over the edge of the coffered ceiling and pressing **[tab]** should pre-highlight one of the soffit walls. You can then press **[tab]** again to chain highlight all 4 walls, then **click** to select them all at once.

260

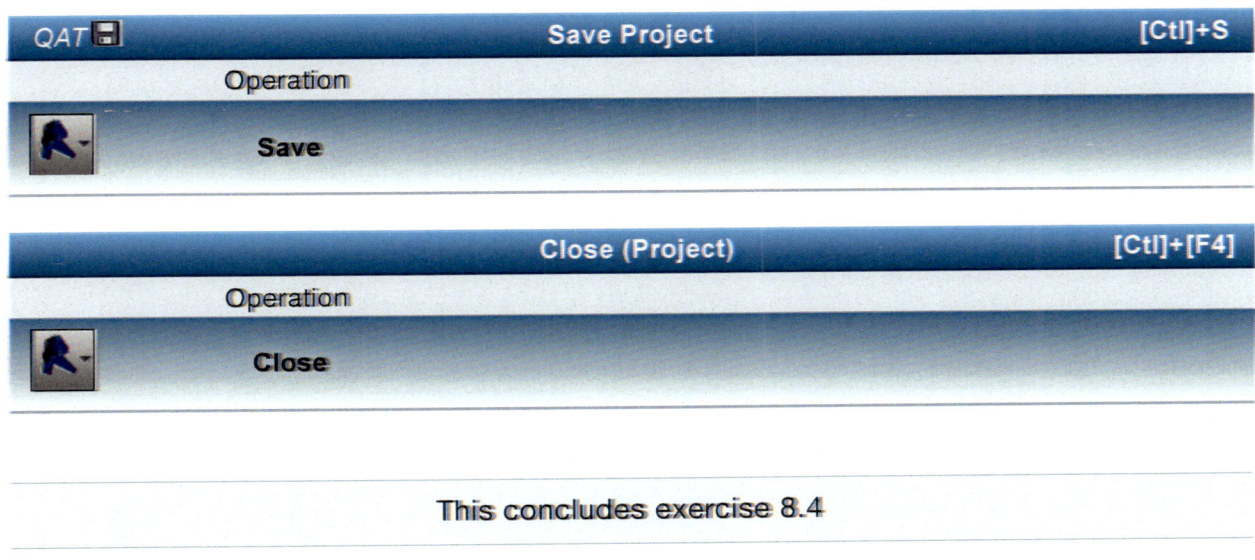

This concludes exercise 8.4

Chapter Summary

In this chapter you practiced creating compound elements, an experienced the process of refining your building model by replacing generic "placeholder" elements with the new compound elements you created. These compound elements contain useful information – the "I" in BIM – which can later be extracted for construction and cost analysis.

In converting generic elements to compound elements, you likely experienced some unexpected behavior of model elements, constraints errors, etc., reinforcing the need to understand and properly set element properties, as well as the importance of selective and proper application of constraints.

Chapter 9
Structural Elements

Overview

This chapter is intended to provide exposure to basic modeling with structural elements. The extent to which these elements are covered are to provide accurate geometric and graphic information in the building model. However, specifics related to modeling for structural analysis is beyond the scope of this course and will not be covered.

Learning Objectives

After completing this chapter you should have a basic understanding of the following new tools and concepts.

- Working with grids
- Modeling structural columns, beams, and isolated foundations
- Column and beam properties
- Column/footing attachments
- Column/beam attachments
- Using the Array tool

Project Objectives

- Create a structural grid for locating structural columns and footings
- Model foundation and framing elements in the crawl space
- Add isolated pad footings at the garage portal
- Model the porch foundation and framing elements
- Create additional working views
- Refinement of various existing views

CHAPTER 9: STRUCTURAL ELEMENTS

Chapter Contents

Exercise 9.1: Grid Layout for Footings & Columns 265
- Create a Working Foundation Plan View 266
- Sketch Grids 266
- Using Array to Add Grids 268
- Dimension, Refine, and Constrain the Grids 269

Exercise 9.2: Columns, Isolated Footings, and Beams 273
- Add Structural Columns 273
- Add Isolated Footings at Crawl Space and Porch 277
- Refine Footing Materials & Elevations 280
- Add Structural Beams 283
- Adjust Structural Element Joins 287
- Add Isolated Footings at the Garage Portal 289
- Adjust Foundation Plan View Graphics 292
- Check Your Work 293

Exercise 9.1: Grid Layout for Footings & Columns

 Be sure to use the exact steps outlined below to open your project file.

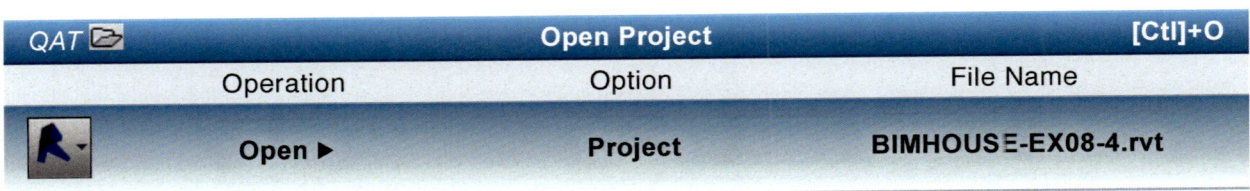

QAT	Open Project		[Ctl]+O
	Operation	Option	File Name
	Open ▶	Project	BIMHOUSE-EX08-4.rvt

1. In the Open dialog box, check the **Audit** checkbox and answer **Yes** to the Audit Warning as illustrated below, then select your *BIMHOUSE-EX08-4.rvt* file and click **Open**.

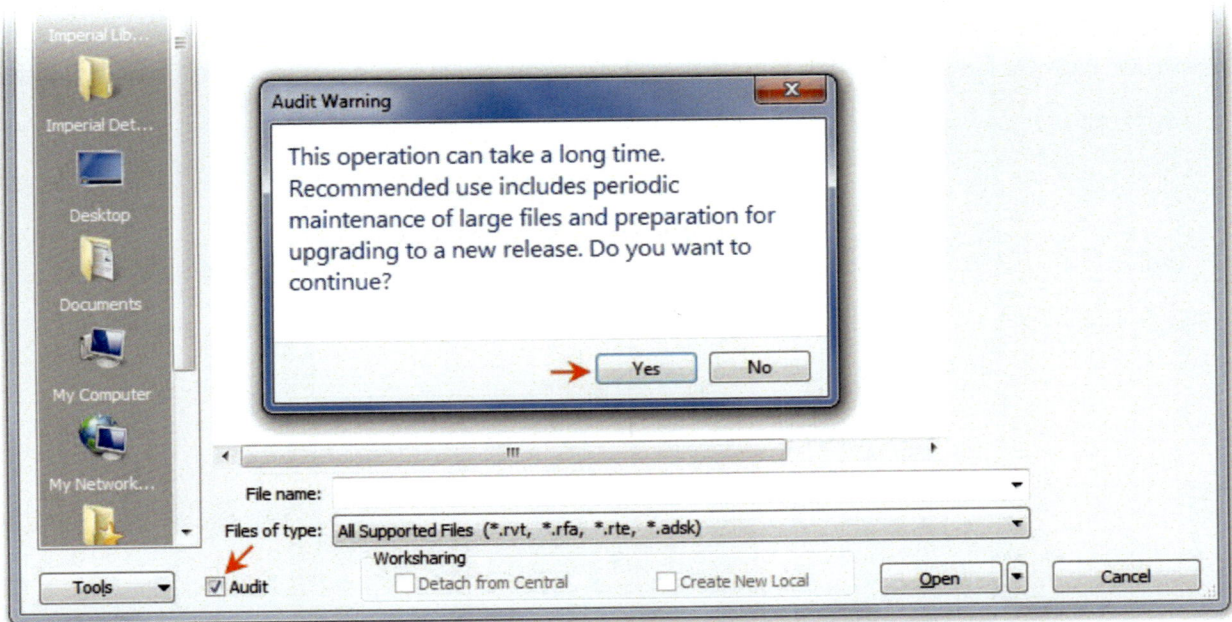

	Save As (Project)		
	Operation	Option	File Name
	Save As ▶	Project	BIMHOUSE-EX09-1.rvt

 To avoid file corruption, it is advised to periodically run Audit on opening of a file. This is particularly true after adding or doing extensive work with walls.

Create a Working Foundation Plan View

In a typical residential plan set, it is uncommon to use column grids – or grids in general – to identify building layout. This is not to say that grids shouldn't be used to control the layout of the model, they're just not normally a visible part of residential construction documents. Therefore, we'll create a working foundation plan view where we can leave the grids fully visible.

1. **Duplicate** the floor plan view *Foundation Plan*.
2. Name the new view **W-Foundation - Constraints**.
3. Set the *View Template* property to **<None>**.

Sketch Grids

1. Verify the *W-Foundation - Constraints* view is open, and sketch grids as follows...

Grid			GR
Tab	Panel	Tool Button	
Architecture	Datum	Grid	

Modify | Place Grid
Draw
Line
Offset: 0' 0"
Properties
Type: 1/4" Bubble

> Default sketch behavior of the specified grid type is as follows: First pick = no bubble, second pick = grid bubble.

2. Sketch the grids labeled *1* and *2* in the illustration on the following page, starting with the grid *#1*. If the first grid you sketch does not start with number 1, edit the value immediately after sketching it, and prior to sketching the next grid. Don't worry about exact location at this time, but do make sure that the extents line up between the grids using the remote snapping feature.

3. Sketch the grids labeled *AA* through *CC* in the illustration on the following page, starting with *Grid AA* at the left and working toward the right with each consecutive grid. Be sure to relabel the first grid with **AA** immediately after sketching it, and prior to sketching the next grid. This will allow grids *BB* and *CC* to be labeled automatically when sketched.

EXERCISE 9.1: GRID LAYOUT FOR FOOTINGS & COLUMNS

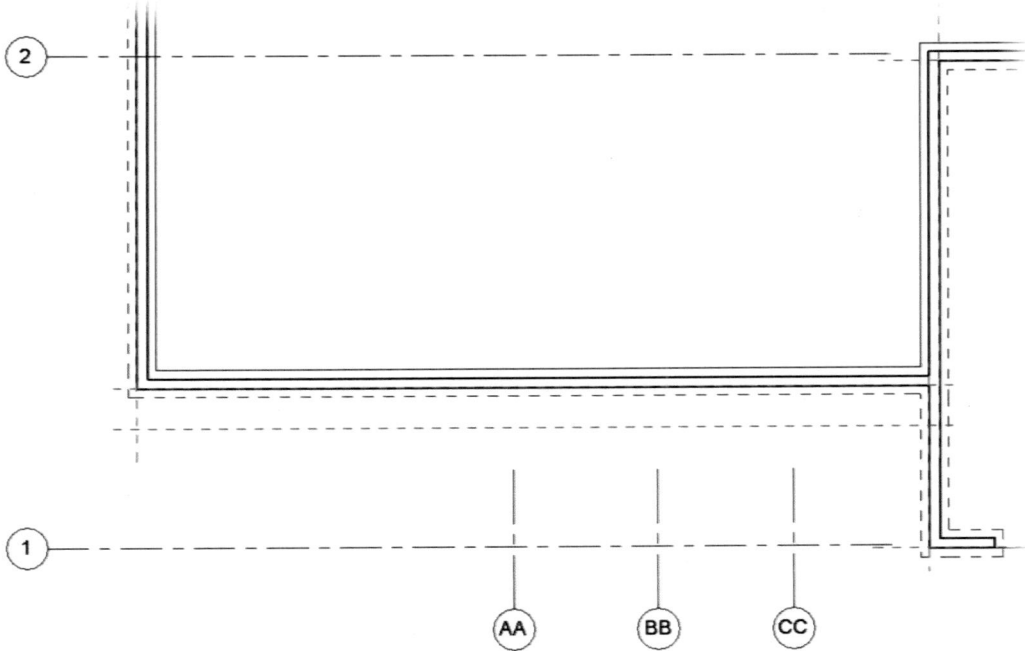

Sketch Grids Part 1

4. Sketch the grid labeled **A** in the illustration below. Be sure to relabel the grid value with **A** immediately after sketching it (click the value to activate the field).

5. Edit the temporary dimension so that the grid is **3'-0"** from the centerline of the west stem wall as shown.

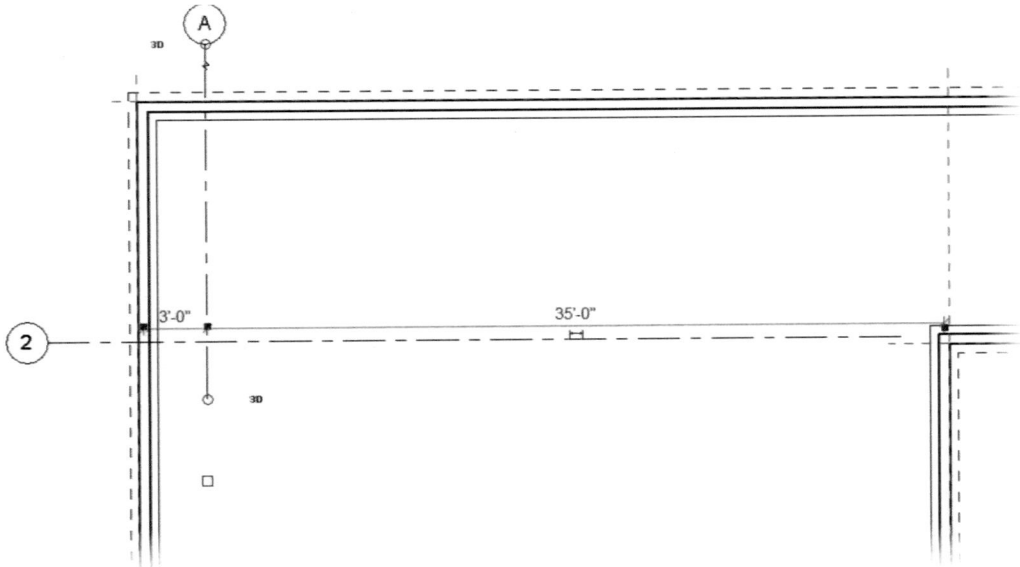

Sketch Grids Part 2

6. **Exit** the Grid tool when done.

Using Array to Add Grids

1. Select grid *A* and then perform the following array operation...

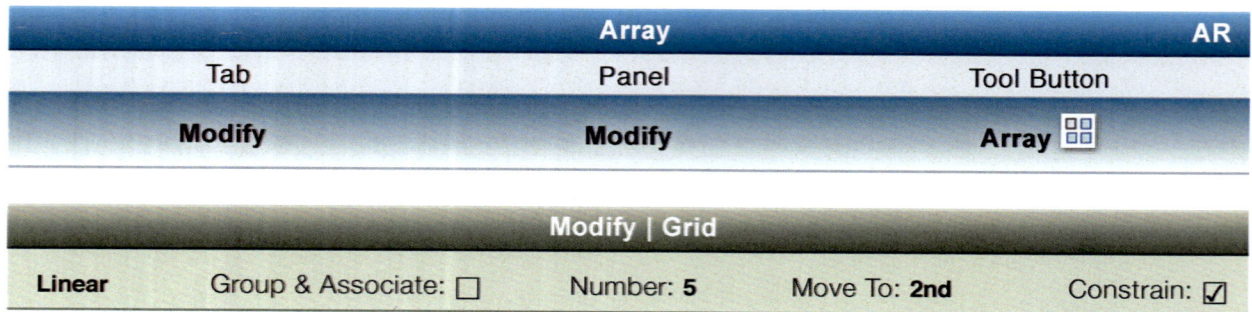

Array		AR
Tab	Panel	Tool Button
Modify	Modify	Array

Modify | Grid				
Linear	Group & Associate: ☐	Number: **5**	Move To: **2nd**	Constrain: ☑

2. **Click** anywhere on-screen, move the cursor to the right 8'-0" as illustrated below, then **click** to complete the array.

 While moving the cursor to the right, you can also take advantage of the listening dimension: type **8 [enter]**, and this will complete the array.

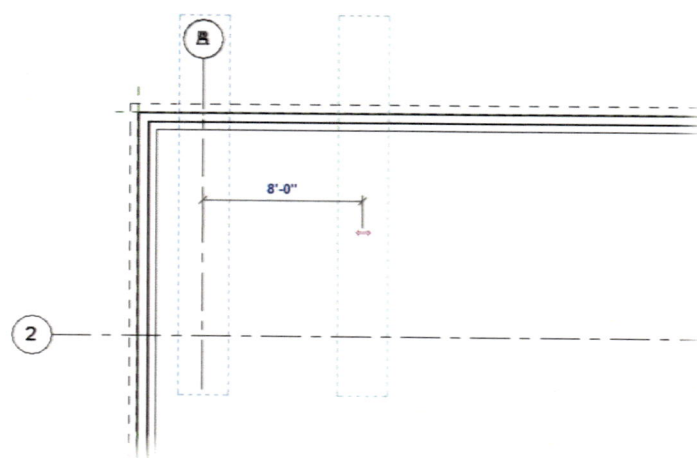

3. When complete, the new arrayed grids should appear as illustrated below.

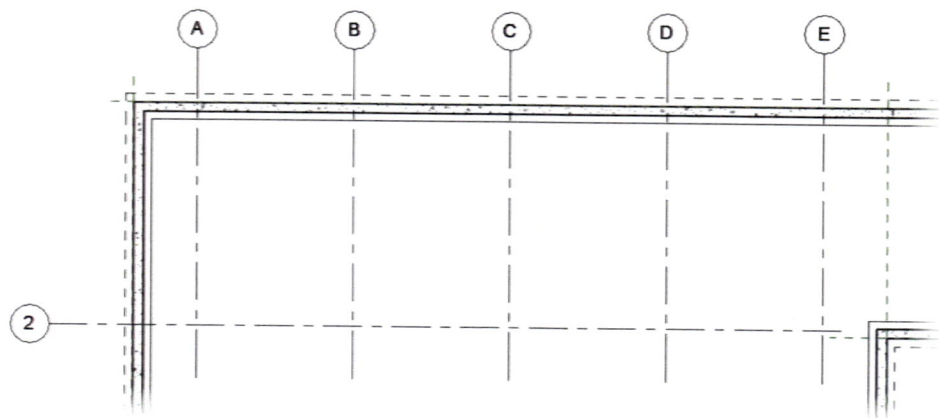

The default setting for *Group & Associate* when using the grid tool is *enabled*. This causes to tool to create a grid element, which has properties that can be edited as needed. *Unchecking* Group & Associate results in equally spaced copies of the starting element, but array properties are not preserved after completing the array operation.

Dimension, Refine, and Constrain the Grids

Dimension, Locate, and Pin

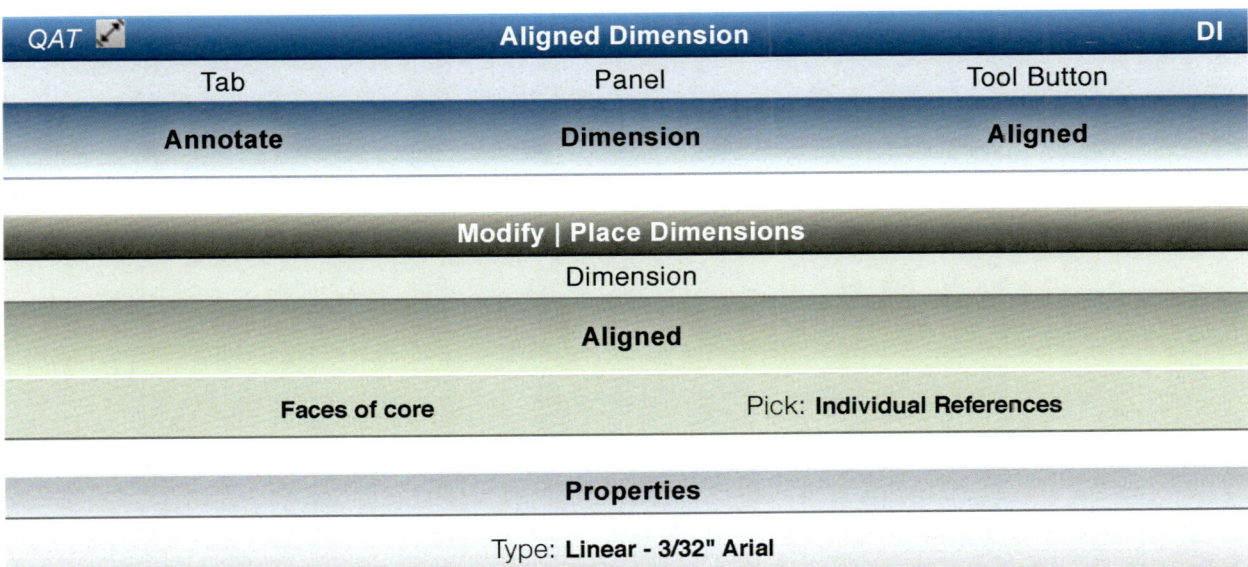

1. Place dimension strings illustrated on the following page, then locate each grid to the correct position as indicated by the dimension values shown – *don't* lock the dimensions! Note that you shouldn't have to relocate the *arrayed* grids. If they aren't positioned correctly, undo the array then go back and repeat the previous array steps.

 Witness lines at walls can be referenced to either the wall face, or the associated reference plane. If using a wall face, just be sure to pick the correct face as illustrated.

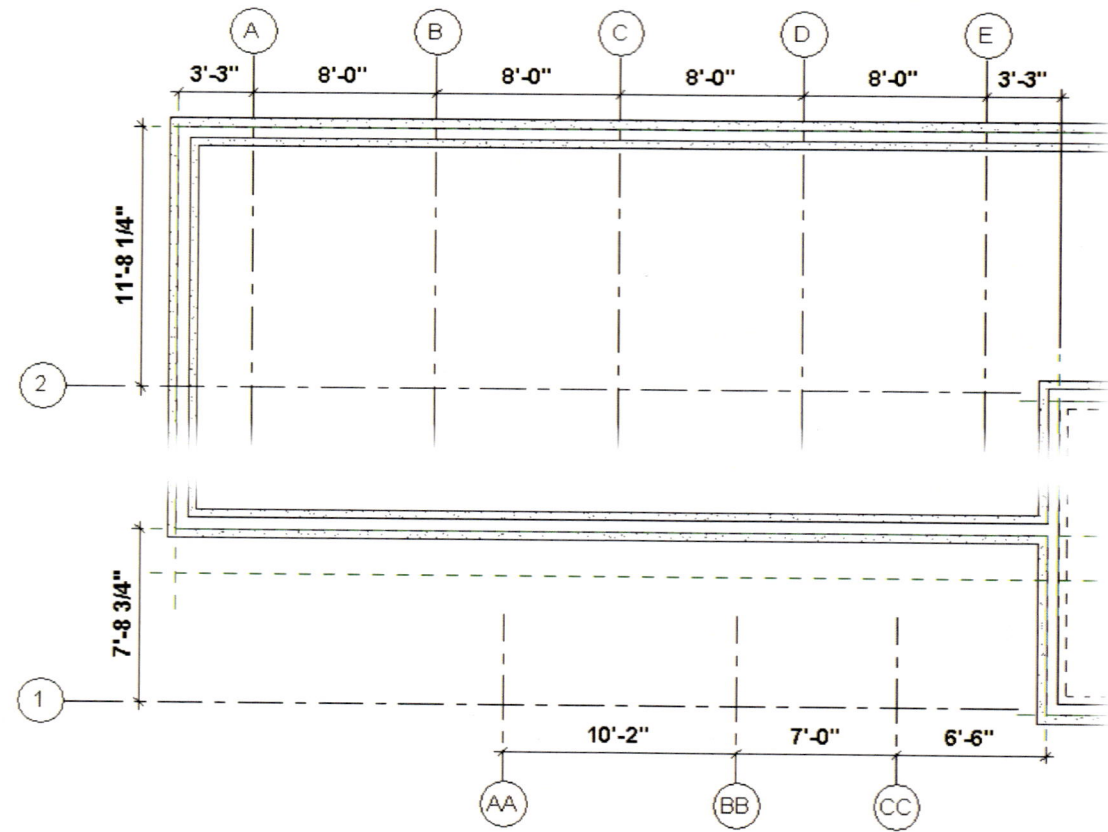

Dimension & Locate Grids
(Dimensions shown are over-sized for readability)

2. **Pin** all grids after they have been properly located.

Refine the Grid Appearance in the Foundation Plan View

As mentioned in the beginning of this exercise, the foundation plan to that will appear on the construction documents need not have visible grids. However, some portion of the line can be useful when dimensioning. Therefore, we won't completely hide the grids, but we'll remove the identifier bubbles and adjust the 2D extents.

3. Open the floor plan view *Foundation Plan*.

4. Select each grid one at a time and convert its extents to **2D** by clicking on the *3D* icon, then **hide** the grid bubble by unchecking the associated checkbox as illustrated on the following page.

 You can convert multiple 3D extents to 2D at once. To do so, enable the *Crop View* and *Crop Region Visible* properties, then drag the crop boundary across the group of 3D extents. When the ends of the grids begin to move and track the crop boundary, they have been converted to 2D. If you plan to move the crop boundary back, make sure to adjust the 2D extents first; otherwise they will return to 3D. Note that this works for reference planes and levels as well.

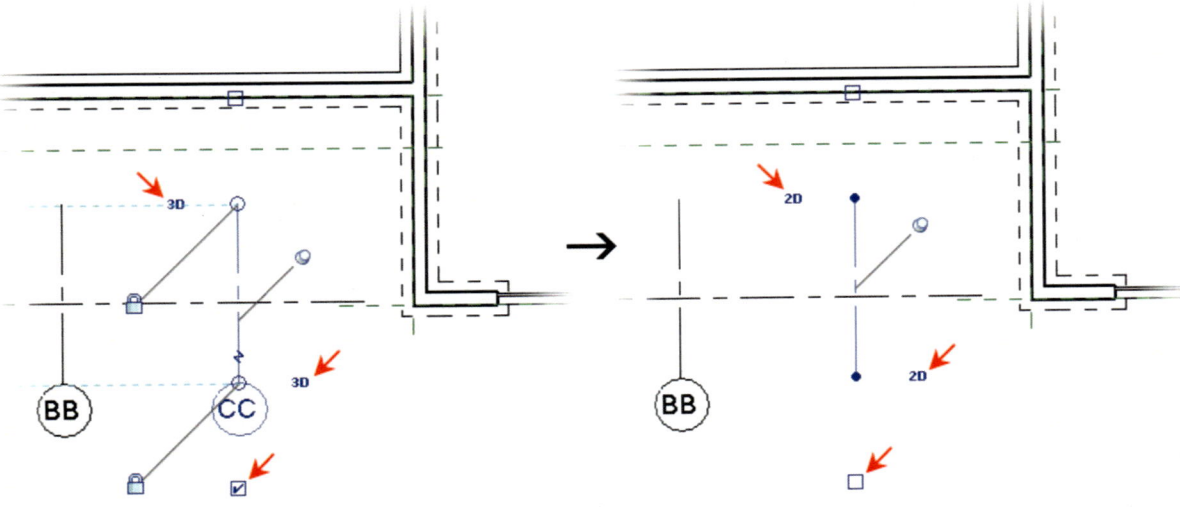

Set Grid Extents to 2D & Hide Grid Bubbles

5. After all 3D extents have been converted to 2D, and the grid bubbles hidden, adjust the grid lengths by selecting a 2D extent control, then dragging it into the desired location.

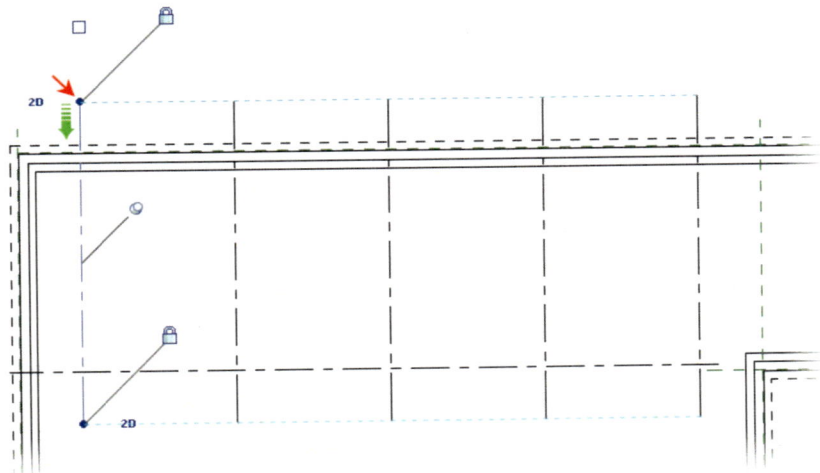

Select and Drag 2D Grid Extents

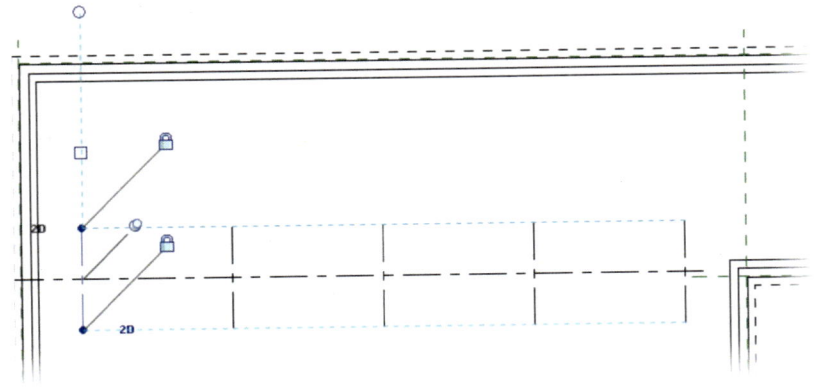

Grid Extents After Dragging Into Position

CHAPTER 9: STRUCTURAL ELEMENTS

 While dragging a 2D extent, the grid's 3D extent appears and is indicated by a light-blue dashed line. By moving the 2D extent, you adjusted the graphic representation of these grids for the current view only. You can open any other plan view where grids are visible and verify that those grid lines remain unchanged.

6. Continue the process for the remaining grids until your view appears as illustrated below.

 When adjusting the horizontal grid lines, they'll default to moving together since they are locked. To allow independent movement of an extent, select a grid and open the padlock at the end you wish to drag *prior* to dragging the extent control.

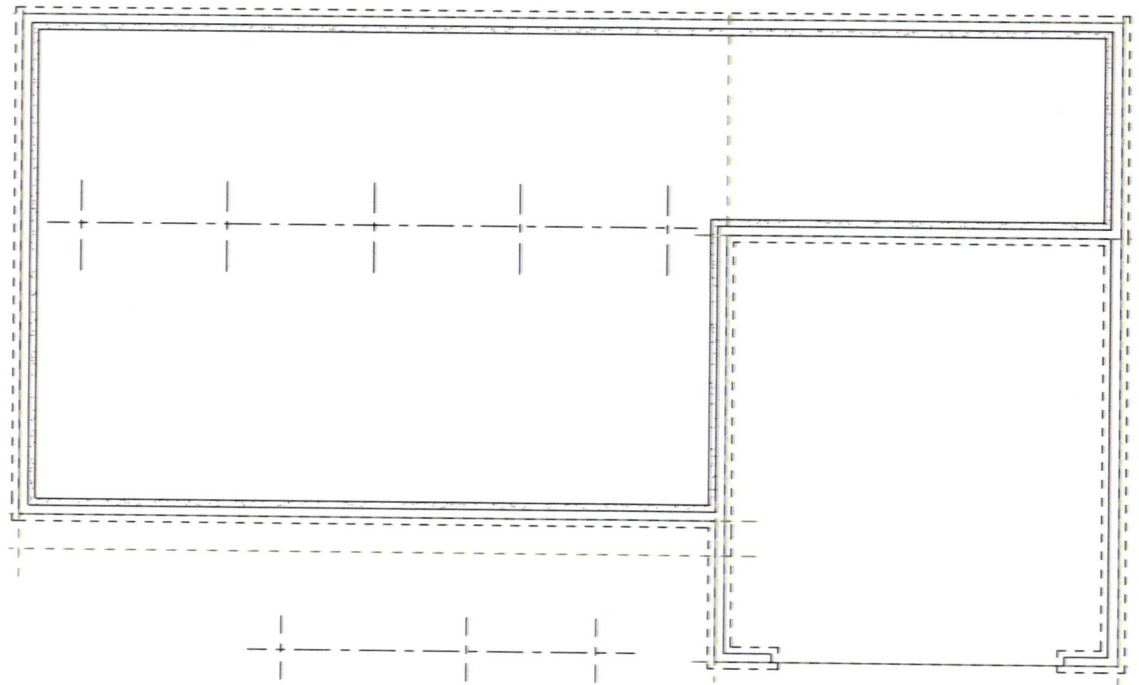

2D Grid Extents Adjusted in the Foundation Plan View

7. Open the floor plan view W-*Foundation - Constraints* and verify the 3D grid extents have not moved. If so, undo the work in the *Foundation Plan* and repeat the previous steps.

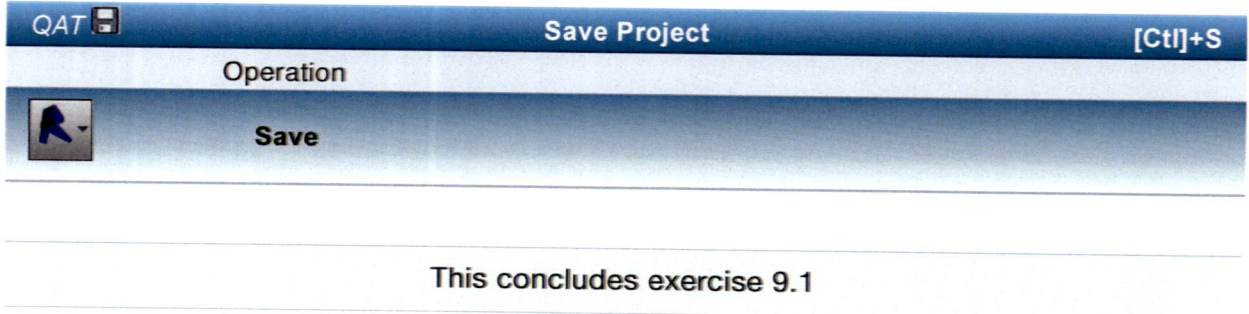

This concludes exercise 9.1

Exercise 9.2: Columns, Isolated Footings, and Beams

QAT	Open Project		[Ctl]+O
	Operation	Option	File Name
	Open ▶	Project	BIMHOUSE-EX09-1.rvt

	Save As (Project)		
	Operation	Option	File Name
	Save As ▶	Project	BIMHOUSE-EX09-2.rvt

Add Structural Columns

From a construction sequencing standpoint, concrete footings would be poured prior to adding columns. However, due to the way Revit attaches isolated footings to a host, it is best to place the columns followed by the footings.

Load Structural Columns

> **Type Catalogs**: Families that contain a large number of types will typically have an associated type catalog. This is a text file containing the parameter data for all defined types within the family. In this situation, the family file itself does not contain the individual types. When loading this type of family, the type catalog (*Select Types dialog box*) is automatically opened, allowing the user to select and load only those types required.

Load Family		
Tab	Panel	Tool Button
Insert	Load from Library	Load Family

Load Families

Family	File Location	Type
Dimension Lumber-Column.rfa	...Imperial Library\Structural Columns\Wood\	**4x4**

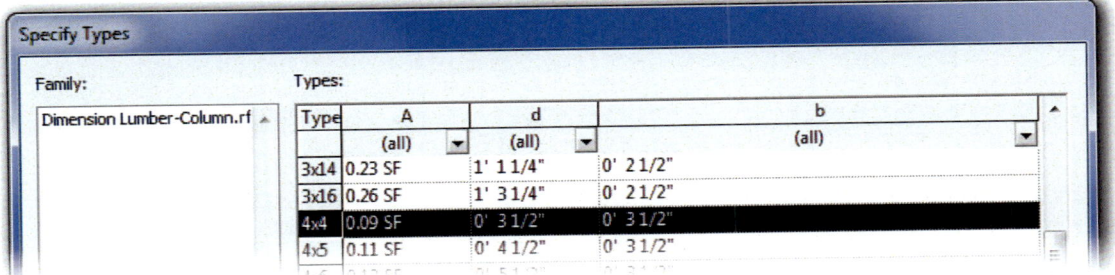

CHAPTER 9: STRUCTURAL ELEMENTS

Load Family		
Tab	Panel	Tool Button
Insert	Load from Library	Load Family

Load Families

Family	File Location	Type
Glulam-Western Species-Column.rfa	...Imperial Library\Structural Columns\Wood\	5.125x6

Adjust Visibility/Graphics in View

8. Open the floor plan view *W-Foundation - Constraints*.
9. Set/verify the Visibility/Graphics Overrides shown in the following table (*make sure the View Template property for this view is set to* **<None>**).

V/G Overrides: W-Foundation - Constraints

Category Tab / Category / Subcategory	Visibility
Model / Structural Columns	ON
Model / Structural Framing	ON

Place Bearing Posts in the Crawl Space

Structural Column		
Tab	Panel	Tool Button
Structure	Structure	Column

Properties
Type: **Glulam-Western Species-Column: 5.125x6**

Moves With Grids: ☑

 Be sure to select **At Grids** in the Multiple panel only *after* setting the properties in the Options Bar and the Properties palette. Once the *Place Structural Column > At Grid Intersection mode* has been entered, most properties are no longer available for editing.

Modify	Place Structural Column			
Mode	Placement	Multiple	Tag
N/A	Vertical Column	At Grids	Tag on Placement
	Rotate after placement: ☐	Depth: T.O. FOOTING	

10. While in the *Place Structural Column > At Grid Intersection* mode, draw a selection box around the 6 column grids located within the foundation crawl space.

11. After you see the 5 columns appear, press the **[space]** bar once to orient the columns as illustrated below.

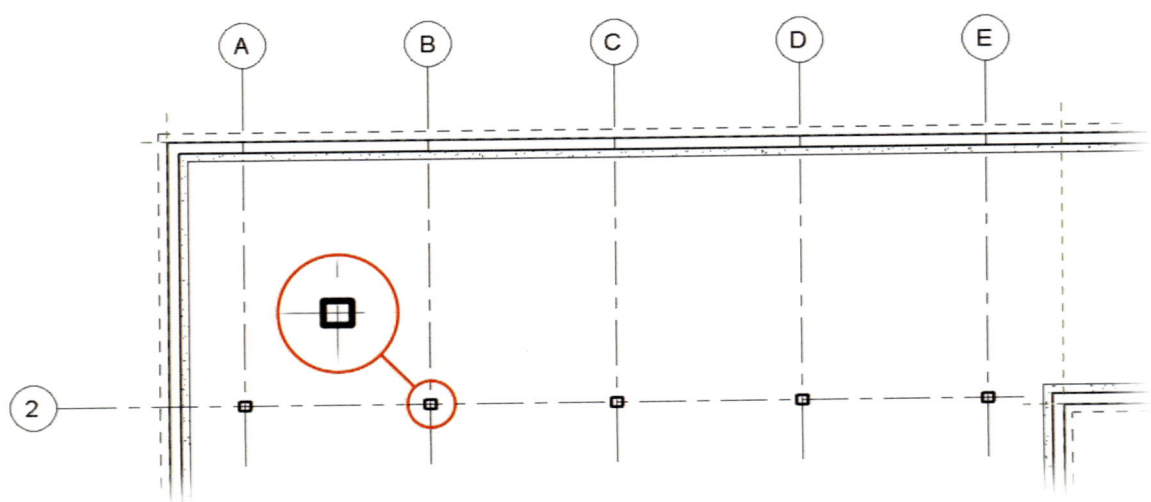

Foundation Columns in Crawl Space

12. Click the **Finish** button ✓

13. **Exit** the Place Structural Column tool.

14. Open the building section view *3D Section - Foundation* to view the columns. Your view should resemble the illustration below.

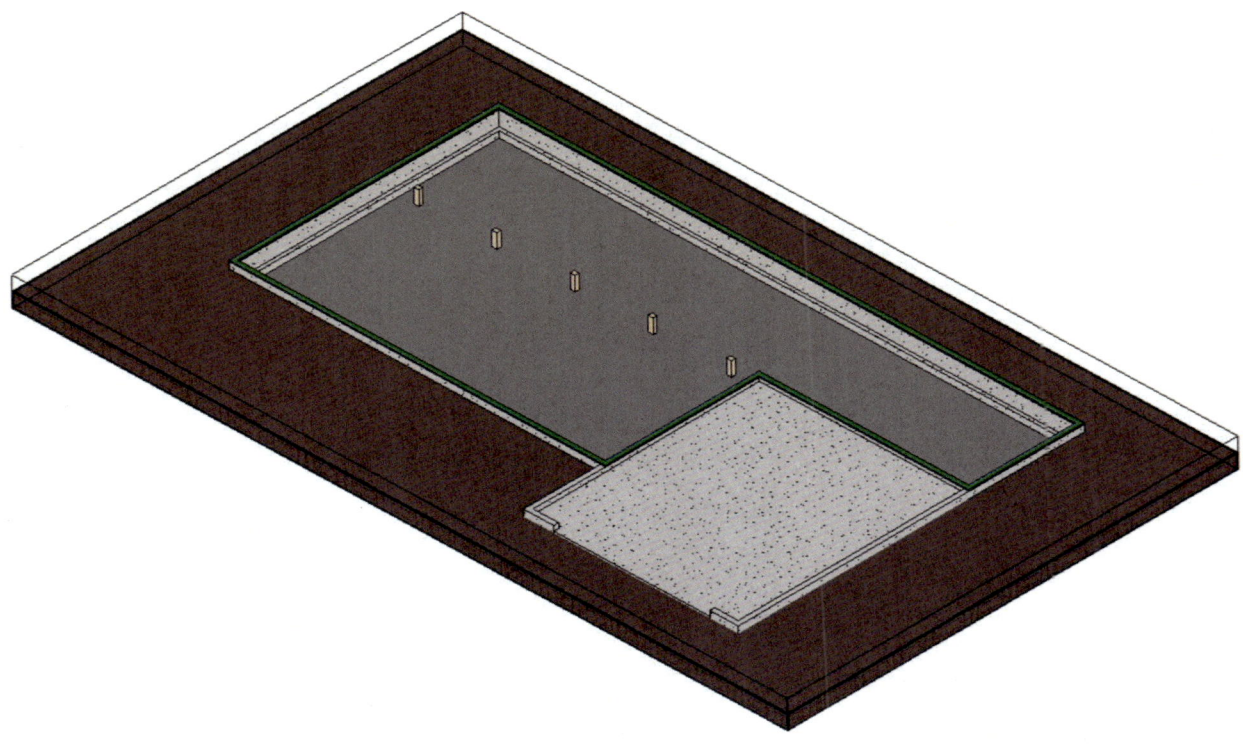

Place the Porch Columns

15. Open the floor plan view *T.O.W. 1st FLR*.

Structural Column		
Tab	Panel	Tool Button
Structure	**Structure**	**Column**

Properties
Type: **Dimension Lumber-Column: 4x4**
Moves With Grids: ☑

Modify | Place Structural Column			
Mode	Placement	Multiple	Tag
N/A	**Vertical Column**	**At Grids**	**Tag on Placement**
Tag Style:	Rotate after placement: ☐		Depth: **FINISH GRADE**

16. While in the mode *Place Structural Column > At Grid Intersection*, draw a selection box around the 4 column grids located at the porch area.

17. After you see the 3 columns appear, click the **Finish** button ✓

18. **Exit** the Place Structural Column tool.

19. Open the *South* elevation view to verify the column's base and top levels appear at the correct levels as illustrated below.

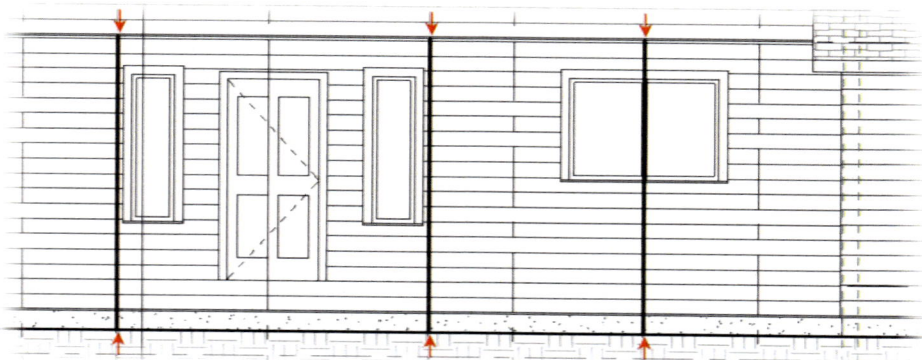

 Note that in the elevation view the columns are represented as stick symbols. This is the default behavior of structural elements in views with the *Detail Level* set to **Coarse**.

20. In the Project Browser, simultaneously select all exterior elevation views.

21. In the Properties Palette, set *Detail Level* to **Medium** and **Apply** the change. The columns should display with model geometry as illustrated below (*South* elevation view).

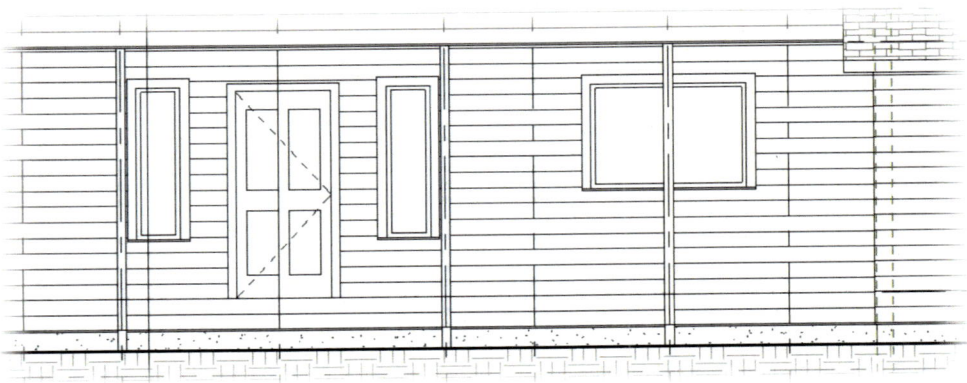

 Remember that when changing properties for a multi-view selection made in the Project Browser, you must make the change in the Properties Palette, *not* the VCB. Changes made with the VCB affect only the active view.

Add Isolated Footings at Crawl Space and Porch

Since no isolated footings are loaded into the project, you will first need to load them as well as create a new type.

Load Family		
Tab	Panel	Tool Button
Insert	Load from Library	Load Family

Load Families

Family	File Location
Footing-Rectangular.rfa	...Imperial Library\Structural Foundations\
Footing-Round.rfa	*Provided Chapter 9 custom content*

Create a New Footing Type

1. In the Project Browser, navigate to the *Families* section and expand the following tree:

    Families → *Structural Foundations* → *Footing Rectangular*

2. Duplicate either of the two existing footing types and name the new type **30" x 30" x 12"**.

3. Edit the following type properties:

CHAPTER 9: STRUCTURAL ELEMENTS

Footing Type Properties: 30" x 30" x 12"

Parameter	Value
Width	2' 6"
Length	2' 6"
Thickness	1' 0"

4. Click **OK** to close the Type Properties dialog box and create the new footing type.

Place Footings in the Crawl Space

5. Open floor plan view *W-Foundation - Constraints*.

Isolated Foundation		
Tab	Panel	Tool Button
Structure	**Foundation**	**Isolated**

Modify	Place Isolated Foundation	
Mode	Multiple
(Not Applicable)	At Grids
Rotate after placement: ☐	

Properties
Type: **Footing-Rectangular: 30" x 30" x 12"**

6. While in the mode *Place Isolated Foundation > At Grid Intersection*, draw a selection box around the 6 column grids located within the foundation crawl space.

7. After you see the 5 footings appear, click the **Finish** button ✓

8. Close the following warning dialog *(do not exit the Place Isolated Foundation tool)*.

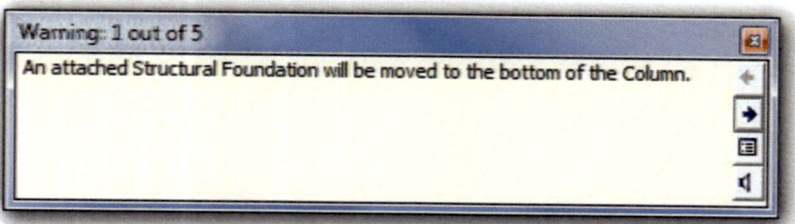

 Regarding the warning: in this case we *do* want the foundation to be moved to the bottom of the column. This additionally creates a relationship between the column and the footing where the base height of the column controls the footing elevation.

9. The footings should appear as illustrated below.

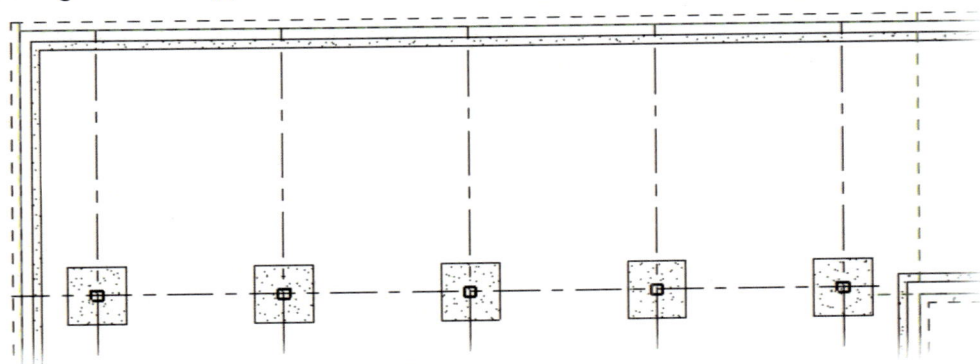

Isolated Footings In Crawl Space

10. Continue placing footings *(do not exit the Place Isolated Foundation tool)*...

Place Footings at the Porch

Modify	Place Isolated Foundation	
Mode	Multiple
(Not Applicable)	At Grids
Rotate after placement: ☐	
Properties	
Type: **Footing-Round: 12" x 20"**	

11. While in the mode *Place Isolated Foundation > At Grid Intersection*, draw a selection box around the 4 column grids located located at the porch area.

12. After you see the 3 footings appear, click the **Finish** button ✓

13. Close the warning dialog.

14. **Exit** the Place Isolated Foundation tool. The footings should appear as illustrated below.

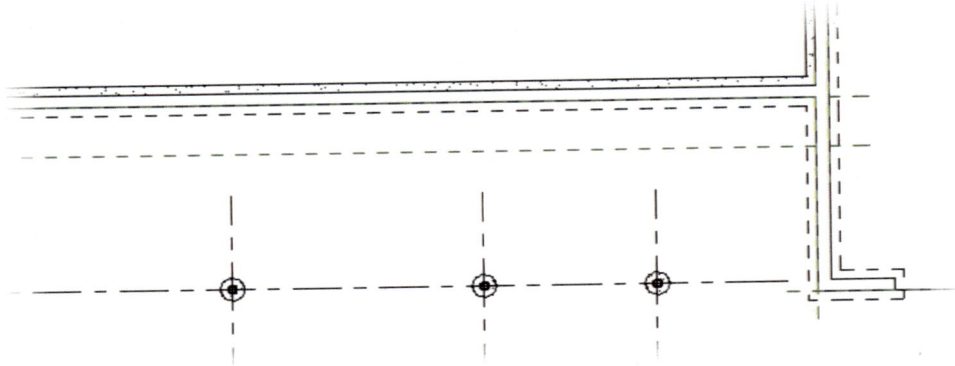

Isolated Footings At Porch

Refine Footing Materials & Elevations

Change Footing Material

1. Simultaneously select the five *30" x 30" x 12"* rectangular footings in the crawl space.
2. In the Properties palette, click on the dialog launcher button for the *Footing Material* to open the Materials dialog box.
3. Select **Concrete, Cast-in-Place Footings** for the material and click **OK** to apply the new material.
4. Select the three *12" x 20"* round footings.
5. Enter **12" DIA. SONOTUBE CONCRETE FORM** in the *Comments* field of the Properties Palette.

Create a Working Section

To help facilitate the steps that follow, we'll create a section view at the porch.

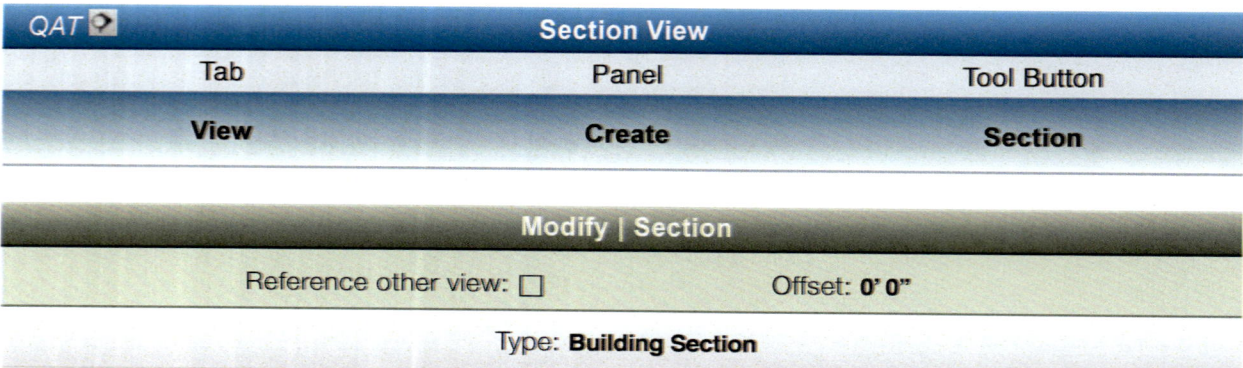

QAT	Section View		
Tab	Panel		Tool Button
View	Create		Section

Modify | Section		
Reference other view: ☐		Offset: **0' 0"**
Type: **Building Section**		

6. Create the section as illustrated below. Be sure to adjust the view direction and far clipping plane as shown.

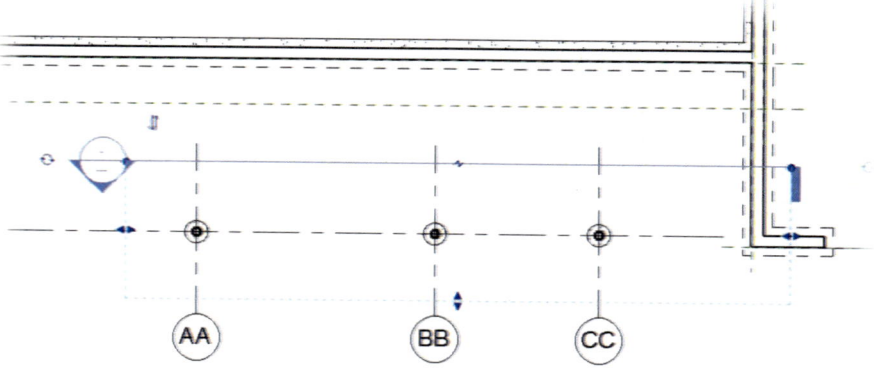

Add Section Marker

7. Rename the new section view **W-Porch (Cross)**.

Adjust Footing Elevations at the Porch

8. Open the new section view *W-Porch (Cross)*, and set the *Detail Level* to **Medium**.
9. Select the three 4x4 columns.
10. In the Properties Palette, set the *Base Offset* property to **0' 2"**. Click **OK** when you receive the warning regarding attached structural foundations.

 In general, it's advisable to address warnings in Revit so they don't accumulate and bloat the model. However, certain warnings are only tied to the immediate action and don't remain in the model database; the previous warning is such an example. To illustrate, after performing the action you can go back and select any of the elements that were associated with the warning message and verify there are no lingering warnings attached.

11. The bases of all three columns should rise 2" above the *FINISH GRADE* level, and the footings should follow as illustrated below.

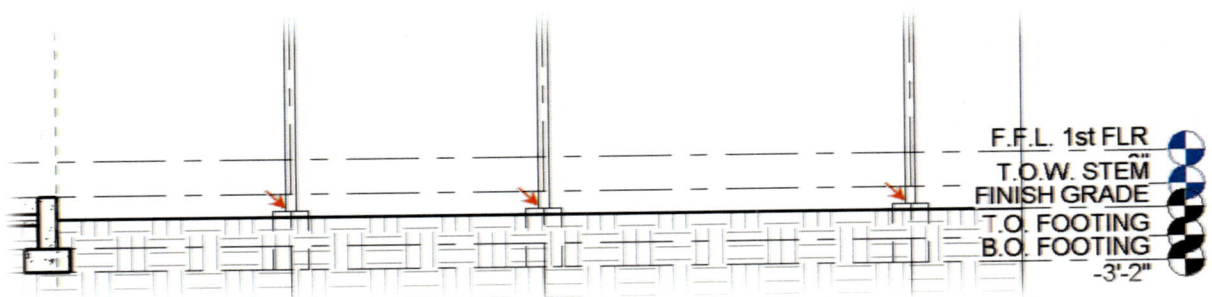

Column Bases and Footings Raised Above Finish Grade

Re-Host Footings at the Porch

Although the tops of the isolated footings are attached to the bases of their respective columns, the host level of the footings was automatically set to the level associated with the view in which the footings were placed; in this case the associated level is *T.O.W. STEM*. Although the following steps to re-host the footings are not necessary for a properly functioning model, doing so will help in maintaining clarity of design intent; that is, the tops of these footings should be located at 2" above *FINISH GRADE*.

 Since this section view was created from within a structural plan view, its discipline is also set to Structural. Therefore, the footings will be represented by hidden lines.

12. Simultaneously select the three porch footings, then edit the instance properties shown in the table below.

 When changing *Level* and *Offset* values on the following page (3 places), make sure to change both properties before applying the change.

Select Porch Footings

Footing Instance Properties: Footing-Round 12" x 20"

Parameter	Value
Level	FINISH GRADE
Offset	0' 2"

Adjust Footing Elevations in Crawl Space

13. Open the section view *Living-Kitchen-Garage (Cross)*.

14. Simultaneously select the five *5.125" x 6"* posts in the crawl space, then edit the instance properties shown in the table below. Click **OK** when you receive the warning regarding attached structural foundations.

Column Instance Properties: Glulam-Western Species-Column 5.125x6

Parameter	Value
Base Level	B.O. FOOTING
Base Offset	1' 0"

15. The bases of all five columns should rise a total of 4", placing them 12" above the crawl space floor. Additionally, the bottoms of the attached footings should now be resting on the crawl space floor as well.

Re-Host Footings in Crawl Space

As with the round footings, we want to keep design intent clearly reflected in the rectangular footing properties.

16. Simultaneously select the five *30" x 30" x 12"* footings in the crawl space, then edit the instance properties shown in the table below. Click **OK** when you receive the warning regarding attached structural foundations.

Footing Instance Properties: Footing-Rectangular 30" x 30" x 12"

Parameter	Value
Level	B.O. FOOTING
Offset	1' 0"

17. Open the *3D Section - Foundation* view, and verify the isolated footing elevations with respect to finish grade and the crawl space surface per the illustration below.

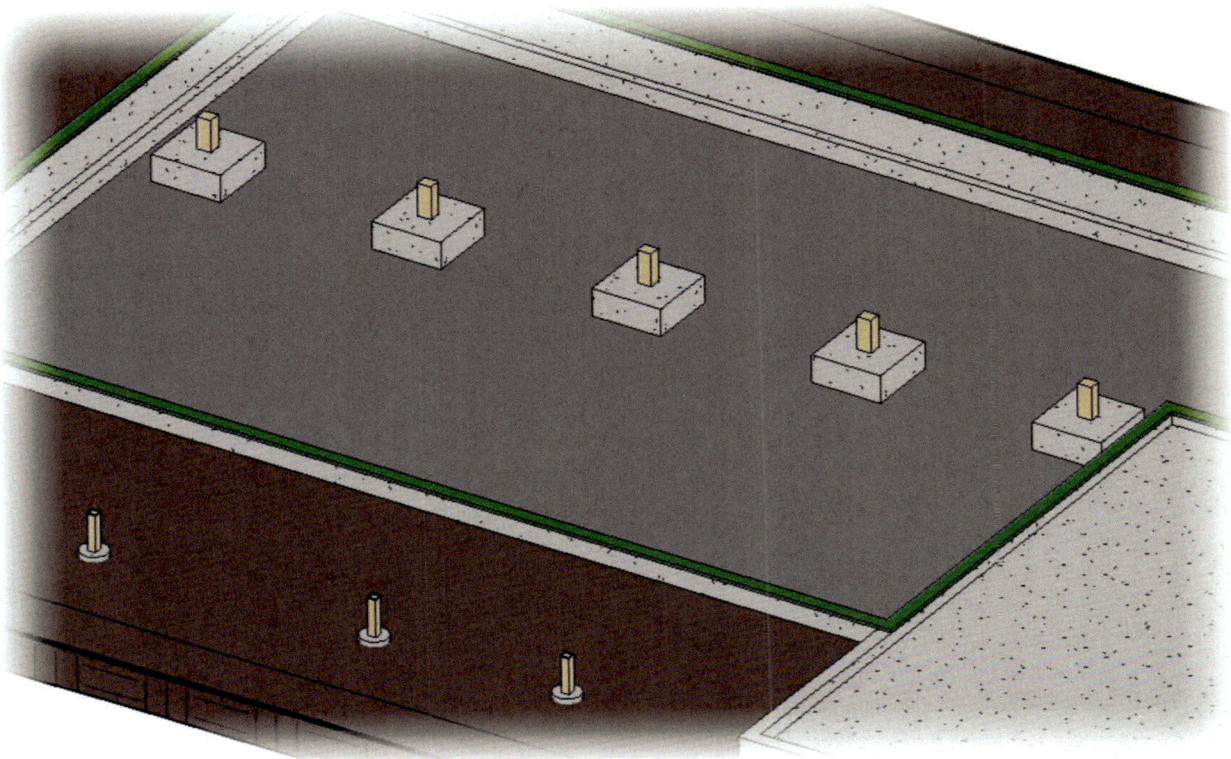

Add Structural Beams

1. Open the floor plan view *W-Foundation - Constraints*.

Beam		
Tab	Panel	Tool Button
Structure	Structure	Beam

2. Click **Load Family** in the Contextual Ribbon Tab.

Load Families

Family	File Location	Type
Glulam-Western Species.rfa	...Imperial Library\Structural Framing\Wood\	5.125x9

Properties	
Type: **Glulam-Western Species: 5.125x9**	
z Offset Value:	0' 1 1/2"

CHAPTER 9: STRUCTURAL ELEMENTS

	Modify	Place Beam		
Mode	Draw	Multiple	Tag
Load Family	Pick Lines	N/A	Tag on Placement

Placement Plane: **T.O.W. STEM**   Structural Usage: **<Automatic>**   3D Snapping: ☐   Lock: ☑

3. **Pick** *Grid 2* <u>once</u> to place the beam.
4. **Exit** the Place Beam tool.
5. Set the *Detail Level* for the view to **Medium**. The beam geometry should appear.
6. Select the beam, and adjust the ends to be 1" from the inside face of each stem wall as illustrated on the following page.

 The final beam length should be 37'-4". You can start by positioning the entire beam at one end to be 1" away from the face of the stem wall by using temporary dimensions. Next, grab the grip at the other end of the beam and hold down the mouse button. The temporary beam length dimension is now a listening dimension. Type the length value **37' 4"**, press **[enter]**, and the beam length will update and be properly located. (You can release the mouse button after typing the first character)

 For this example, when selecting a grip to resize the beam, be sure the status bar and/or tool tip reads "Drag Structural Framing Component End." This grip is indicated on the beam end by the filled dot, NOT the double arrow.

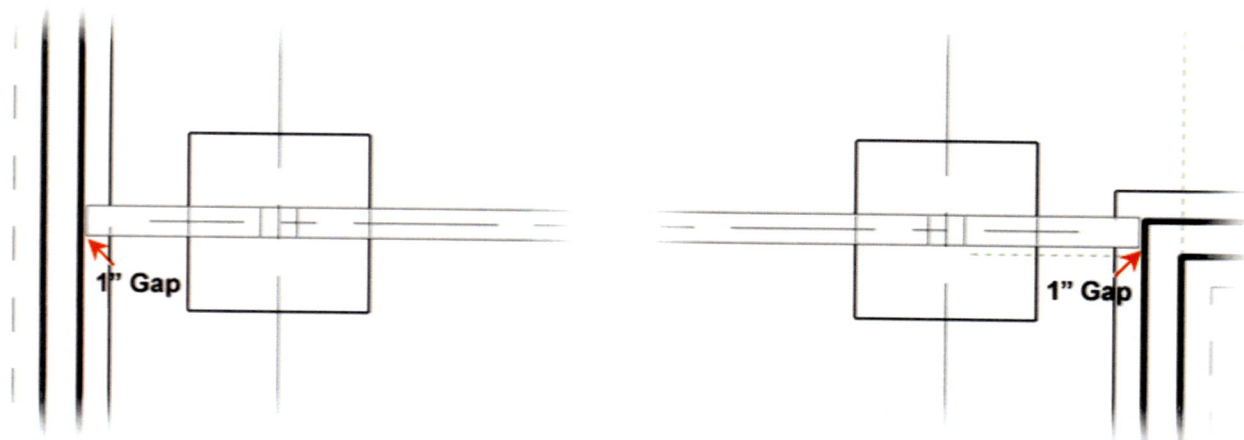

Adjusted Beam Length

Place the Header Beam at the Porch

7. Open floor plan view *T.O.W. 1st FLR*.

Beam		
Tab	Panel	Tool Button
Structure	Structure	Beam

Load Families

Family	File Location	Type
Dimension Lumber.rfa	...Imperial Library\Structural Framing\Wood\	4x8

Properties	
Type: **Dimension Lumber: 4x8**	
z Offset Value:	0' 0"

Modify	Place Beam			
Mode	Draw	Multiple	Tag
Load Family	Line	N/A	~~Tag on Placement~~
Placement Plane: **T.O.W. 1st FLR**	Structural Usage: **<Automatic>**	3D Snapping: ☐	Chain: ☐

8. Begin sketching the beam on *Grid 1* starting slightly to the left of *Grid AA* as illustrated below. Don't worry about exact dimensions right now, we'll refine the length of the beam later.

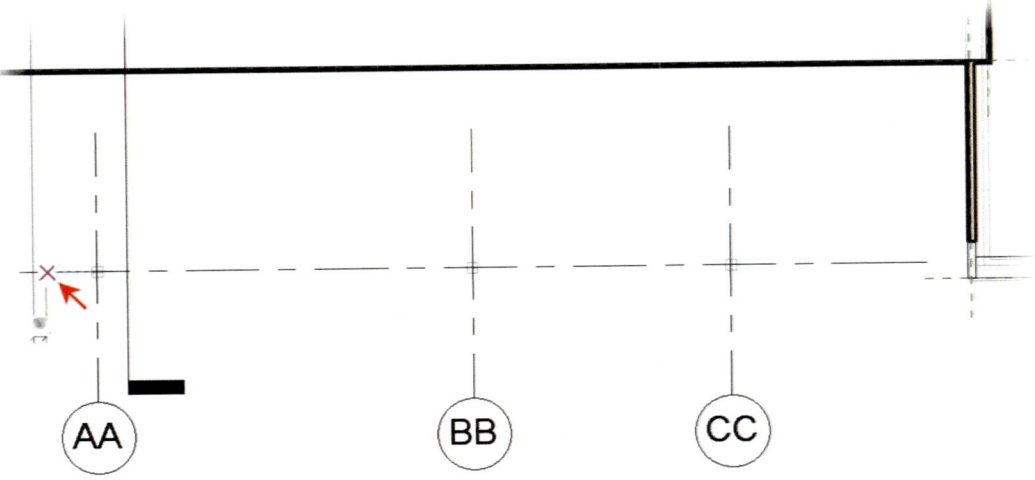

Sketch Beam – Approximate First Pick Location

9. Sketch to the right and place the endpoint of the beam roughly at the inside face of the west garage wall as illustrated below.

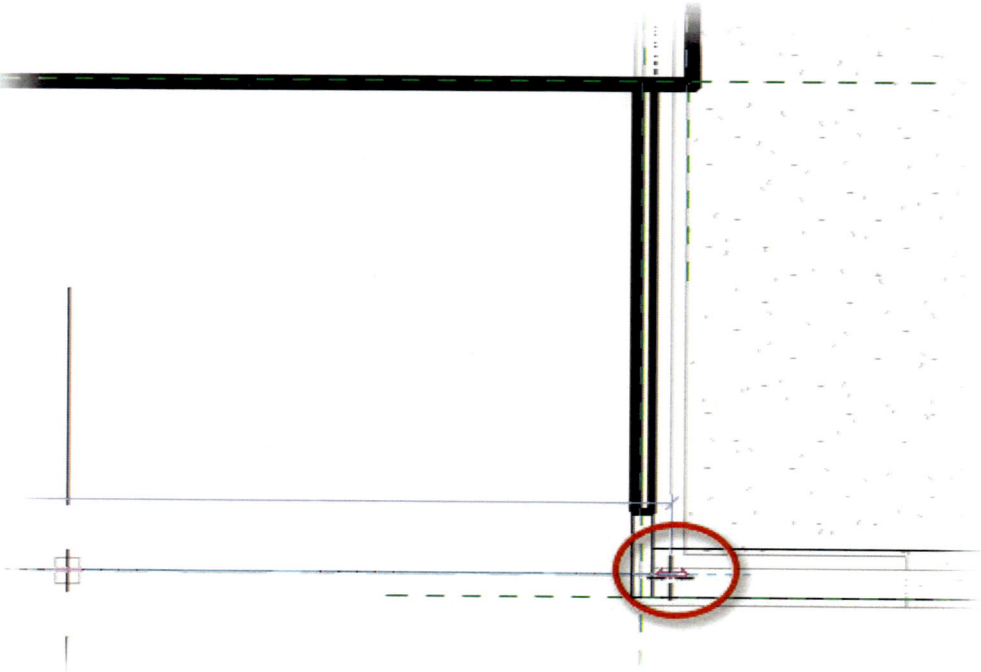

Sketch Beam – Second Pick Location

10. **Exit** the Place Beam tool.

11. **Align** and **Lock** the centerline of the beam to *Grid 1*.

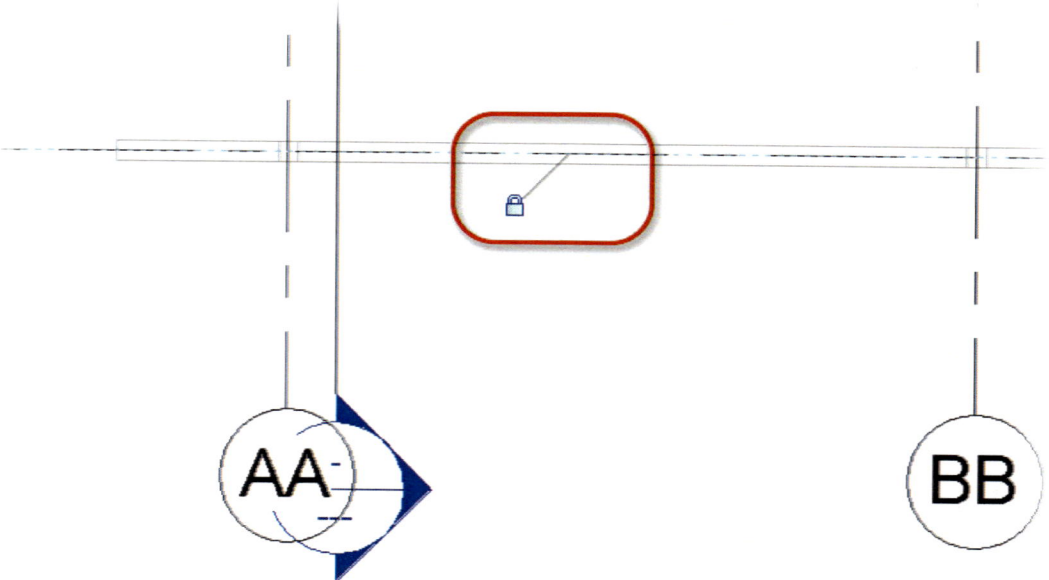

Adjust Structural Element Joins

Create a 3D Structure View

1. Duplicate the default *{3D}* view.
2. Set the following properties and Visibility/Graphics Overrides for the new view:

View Properties

Parameter	Value	Alternate Access
Discipline	Structural	
View Name	3D Structure	Contextual menu

3. Open the Visibility/Graphics Overrides dialog, and in the Model tab do the following:

    a) Click **All**.
    b) Turn all categories off by clicking on a checkbox.
    c) Click **None**.
    d) Make the changes indicated in the following table.

V/G Overrides: 3D Structure

Category Tab / Category / Subcategory	Visibility
Model / Floors	ON
Model / Structural Columns	ON
Model / Structural Foundations	ON
Model / Structural Framing	ON
Model / Walls	ON

4. Hide the two TJI floors by selecting them, then **right-click** and from the contextual menu select **Hide in View → Elements**, or use the keyboard shortcut **[EH]**.
5. Your view should now appear as illustrated Below.

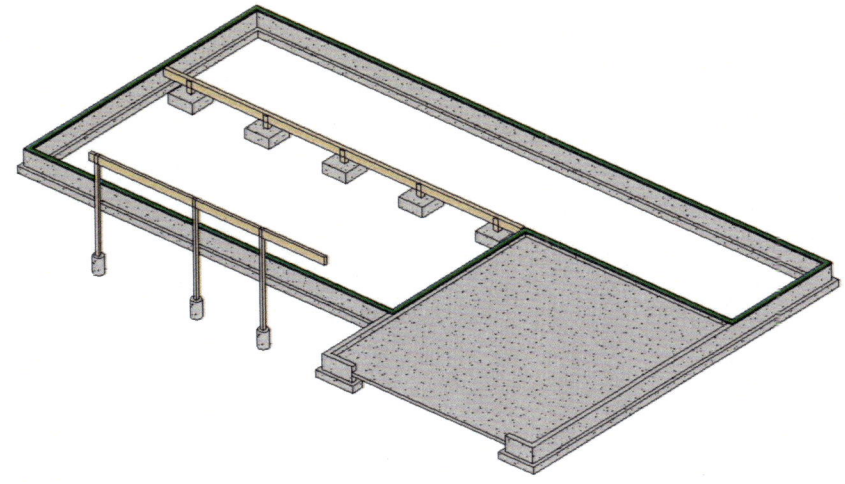

CHAPTER 9: STRUCTURAL ELEMENTS

Attach Columns to Beams

6. Simultaneously select the three columns at the porch.

 Right-click on one column, then from the contextual menu pick **Select All Instances → Visible in View** (or **In Entire Project**).

Modify	Structural Column
Modify Column	
Attach Top/Base	
Attach Column: **Top** Attachment Justification: **Minimum Intersection**	Attachment Style: **Cut Column** Offset From Attachment: **0' 0"**

7. **Pick** the 4x8 beam over the selected columns to complete the attachment.

8. Repeat the previous process to attach the 5 Glulam columns in the crawl space to the Glulam beam.

9. Verify the column/beam attachments appear as illustrated below.

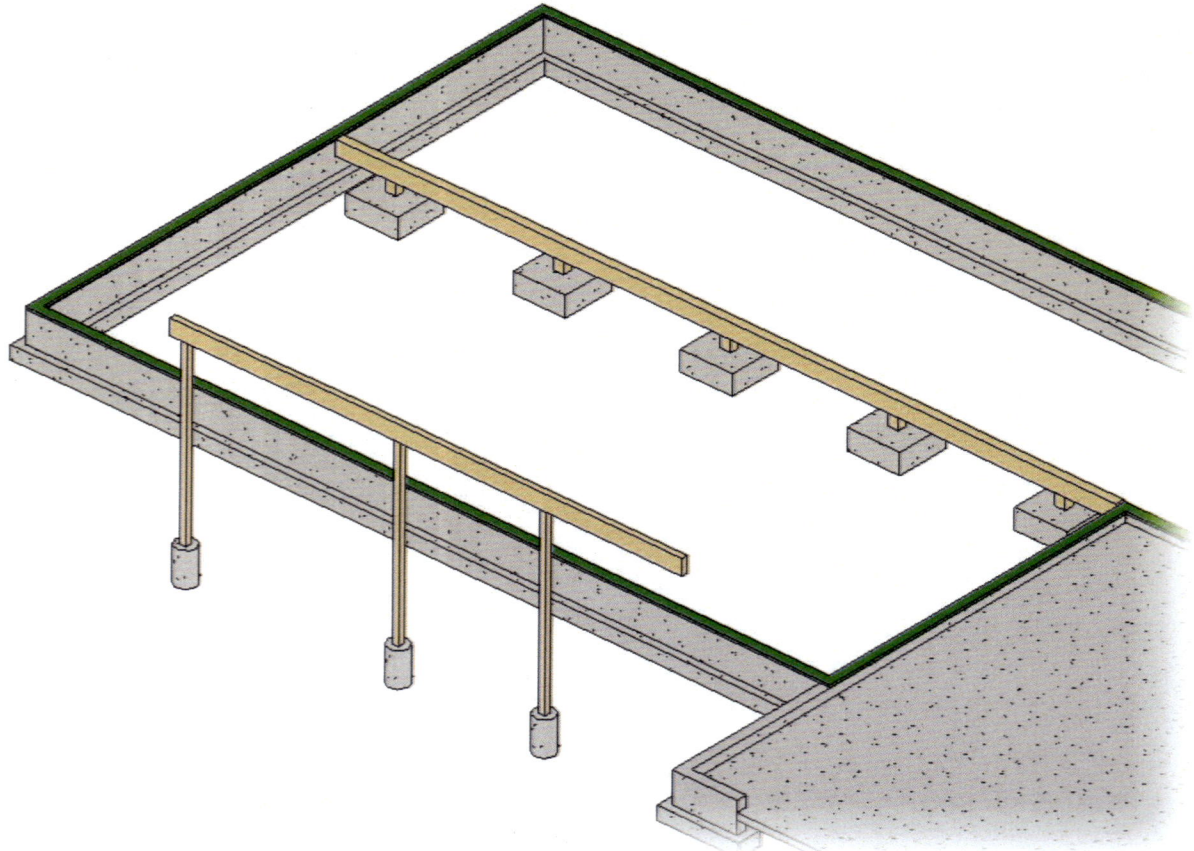

Add Isolated Footings at the Garage Portal

In this project we'll assume a break in the footing at the garage door, and provide a pad footing at each end of the garage portal to handle the concentrated point loads.

1. Open the floor plan view *W-Foundation - Constraints*.
2. Open the Visibility/Graphics Override dialog box, and make the following changes:

V/G Overrides: W-Foundation - Constraints

Category Tab / Category / Subcategory	Visibility
Model / Site	OFF
Model / Topography	OFF

 The footings you are about to place are not located at a column. Therefore, the footings will attach and host themselves to a toposurface or building pad if these elements are visible in the view. Failure to hide these categories will result in incorrectly hosted footings.

Create a New Isolated Footing Type.

3. In the Project Browser, navigate to the Families section and expand the following tree:

    Families → Structural Foundations → Footing-Rectangular

4. **Double-click** on one of the types to open the Type Properties dialog box.
5. Click **Duplicate…**, then enter **24" x 24" x 8"** for the name and click **OK**.
6. Edit the following properties:

Footing Properties: Footing-Rectangular: 24" x 24" x 8"

Parameter	Value
Width	2' 0"
Length	2' 0"
Thickness	0' 8"

7. Click **OK** when done.

Place the Isolated Footings

Isolated Foundation		
Tab	Panel	Tool Button
Structure	**Foundation**	**Isolated**

CHAPTER 9: STRUCTURAL ELEMENTS

Properties	
Type:	**Footing-Rectangular: 24" x 24" x 8"**
Level:	**T.O. FOOTING**
Offset:	**0' 0"**
Moves With Grids:	☐
Structural Material:	**Concrete, Cast-in-Place Footings**

Modify	Place Isolated Foundation	
Mode	Multiple
N/A	N/A
Rotate after placement: ☐	

8. Place two footings, one at each end of the garage portal as illustrated below. Try to place them so the center of the footing is beneath the stem wall, preferably a few inches back from the end of the wall.

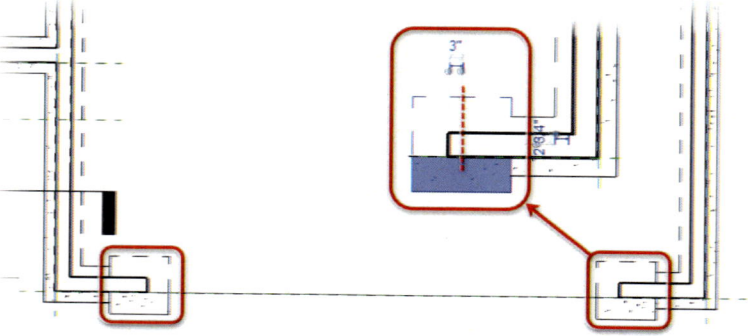

9. **Exit** the Place Isolated Foundation tool.

Constrain the Footings

In the following steps you will constrain the isolated pad footings to the stem walls, both along the wall's center axis, as well as the wall ends. To do this we'll need to use both length and alignment constraints.

 Make sure you have placed the footings as explained in step 8 above, and that the footing center is set back from the end of the stem wall. If not, move them now.

10. Place the dimensions to be used for length constraints...

EXERCISE 9.2: COLUMNS, ISOLATED FOOTINGS, AND BEAMS

QAT	Aligned Dimension	DI
Tab	Panel	Tool Button
Annotate	Dimension	Aligned

Modify | Place Dimensions
Dimension
Aligned
Faces of Core — Pick: **Individual References**

Properties
Type: **Linear - Constraints**

11. Place a dimension from the vertical center reference of each footing to the end of its respective stem wall as illustrated below.

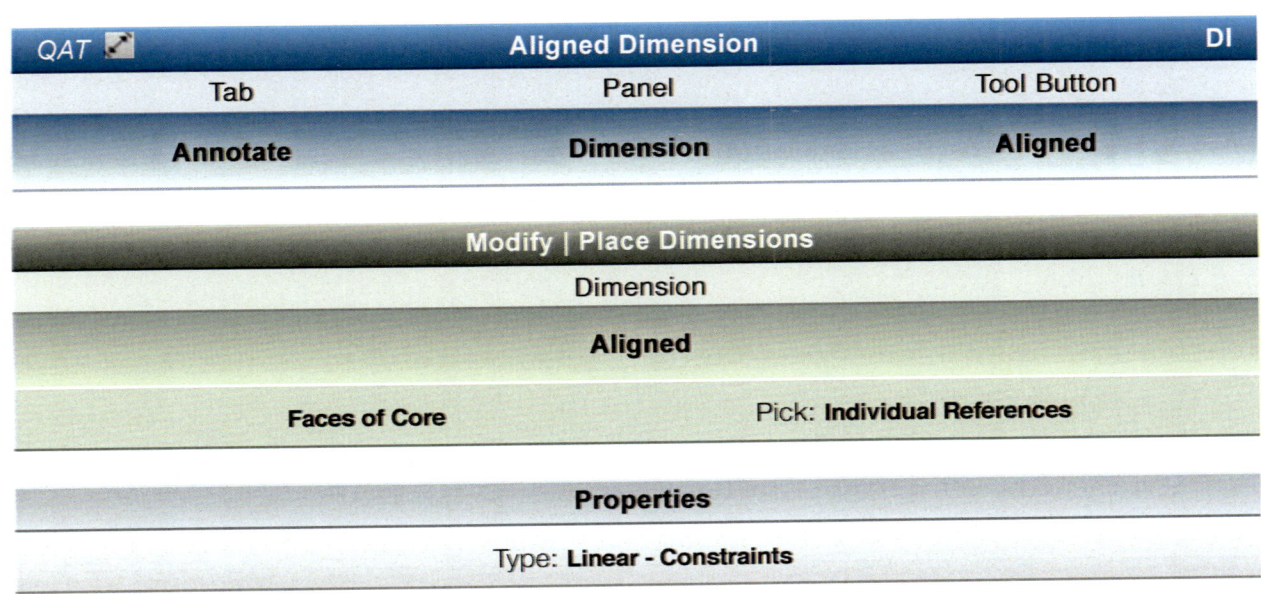

12. If either of the dimensions do not read **2"**, select the related footing to activate the dimension, then adjust the dimension to **0' 2"** as illustrated.

13. After both dimensions read correctly, select each dimension and **lock** it.

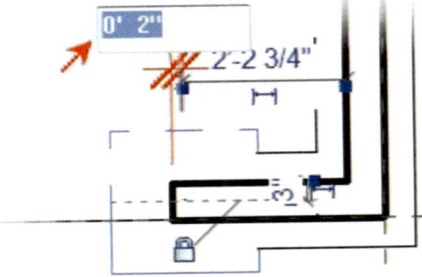

14. **Align** and **Lock** the horizontal center reference of each footing to the *core centerline* of its respective stem wall as illustrated below.

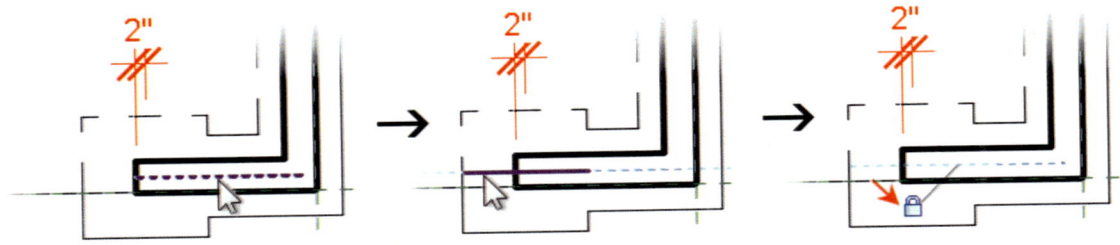

Adjust Foundation Plan View Graphics

Since the Foundation Plan view is linked to a view template, any permanent changes to the Visibility/Graphics Overrides must be made directly within the view template.

1. Open the floor plan view *Foundation Plan*.

2. In the Properties Palette, click *View Template* button (it should be labeled **Plan-Floor-Foundation**). This will open the Apply View Template dialog box with the assigned view template selected.

3. Click on the **Edit...** button associated with any of the *V/G Overrides* to open the Visibility/Graphics Overrides dialog box.

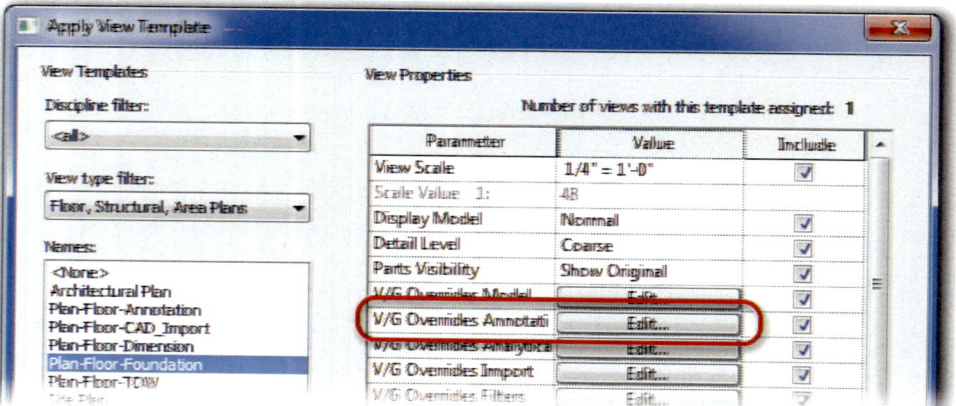

4. Select the appropriate tab and then set the overrides as shown in the table below. Verify your view appears as illustrated below when done.

V/G Overrides - Filter Settings: Foundation Plan

Category Tab / Category / Subcategory	Filter	Overrides
Annotation / Reference Planes		Visibility = OFF
Filters	View Markers - Working	Visibility = OFF

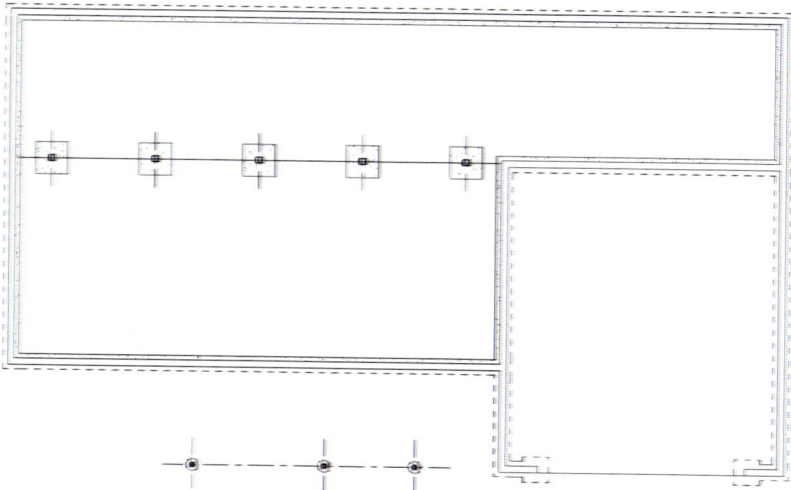

Check Your Work

1. Open the plan view *W-Foundation Constraints*.

2. **Close Hidden Windows**.

3. Open the default *{3D}* view

4. Open the *3D Structure* view

5. **Tile Windows**, and **Zoom All to Fit**.

6. In the *W-Foundation Constraints view*, **unpin** and **move** reference planes and grids to verify the structural elements are correctly associated and flex as expected. At the same time, verify that the integrity of the remainder of your model is still intact. Remember to return the reference planes and grids to their original location and **pin** them when done.

 When moving grids, use arrow keys to nudge in small increments, otherwise you may receive warnings indicating that columns can't maintain attachments to their target.

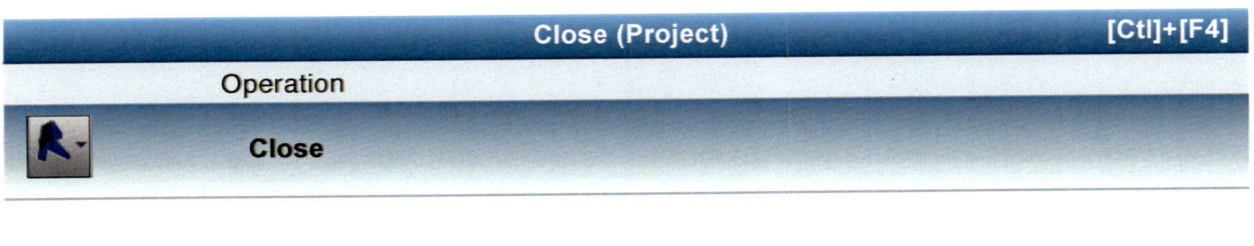

This concludes exercise 9.2

Chapter Summary

In this exercise you were exposed to structural elements. As you have probably noticed, structural elements add a whole new level of complexity to modeling, and have their own unique set of parameters and behaviors. While it is beneficial to have a basic understanding of these elements as an architectural modeler, in-depth structural modeling is often better left to structural engineers, or advanced users that have a solid understanding of Revit's structural features.

Chapter 10
Porch Construction

Overview

This chapter is intended primarily to reinforce concepts you've previously learned and used in earlier lessons and exercises.

Learning Objectives

After completing this chapter you should have a basic understanding of the following new tools and concepts.

- Creating a fill pattern
- Adding dimension text

Additionally, you will practice many concepts learned in previous chapters.

Project Objectives

- Complete the roof/ceiling portion of the porch
- Add a deck to the porch
- Create additional 3D section views
- Revise the building layout by extending the garage

Chapter Preface

By now you should be getting familiar with certain tools and processes. Therefore, as you may have already noticed in previous chapters, various steps might not use the familiar tool banners to guide you to the tool's location. Furthermore, certain detailed step-by-step instructions may be abbreviated.

 In the case where your instructed to place aligned dimensions and then lock them, be sure to use the dimension type **Linear - Constraints** for easy identification of constraints.

Chapter Contents

Exercise 10.1: Porch Deck 297
    Porch Deck Layout 297
    Model The Porch Deck 298

Exercise 10.2: Porch Roof & Ceiling 302
    Model The Porch Roof 302
    Adjust the Beam Length & Position 307
    Create New Ceiling Types 308
    Model the Ceiling Structure Layer 310
    Update RCP View Template Settings 313
    Model the Ceiling Finish Layer 313
    Add a Porch Gable Wall 317
    3D Porch Section View 323

Exercise 10.3 Floor Plan Design Revision 325
    Extend the Garage 325
    Revise the CAD Import View 326

Exercise 10.1: Porch Deck

QAT 📂	Open Project		[Ctl]+O
	Operation	Option	File Name
R▼	Open ▶	Project	BIMHOUSE-EX09-2.rvt

	Save As (Project)		
	Operation	Option	File Name
R▼	Save As ▶	Project	BIMHOUSE-EX10-1.rvt

Porch Deck Layout

1. Open floor plan view *W-1st Floor - Constraints*.
2. Place two **Reference Planes** to outline the porch as illustrated below. Exact location isn't critical at this point.

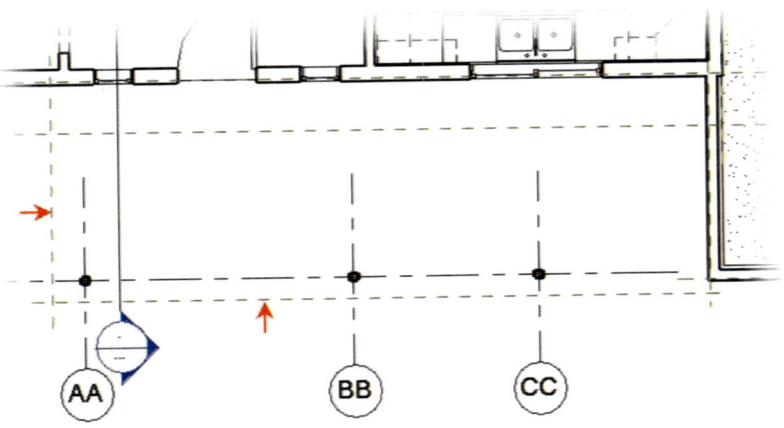

3. Name the reference planes as follows:
   a) **Porch - West**
   b) **Porch - South**
4. Add a length constraint between the new reference planes and the porch grids...

QAT 🗡	Aligned Dimension		DI
	Tab	Panel	Tool Button
	Annotate	Dimension	Aligned

Properties
Type: **Linear - Constraints**

CHAPTER 10: PORCH CONSTRUCTION

Modify	Place Dimensions	
Dimension		
Aligned		
N/A		Pick: **Individual References**

5. After placing the dimensions, adjust the location of each reference plane so they are **3 1/4"** from the grids as illustrated below.

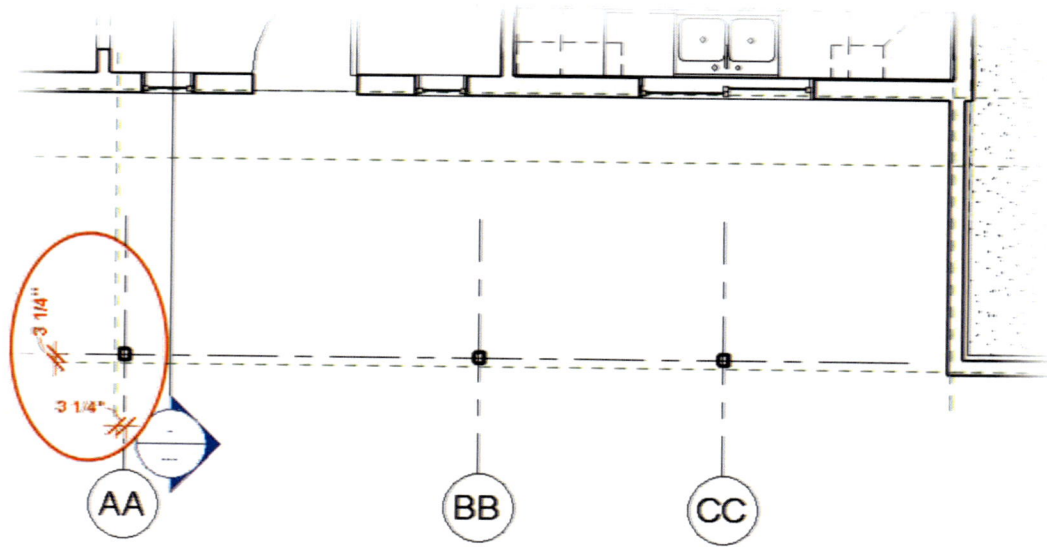

6. **Lock** both dimensions *after* the reference planes are correctly located.

Model The Porch Deck

When creating the porch deck, you will use a compound floor element that uses a mass layer to represent the framing layer, just as you did with the interior floor systems.

Create a New Floor Type

1. In the Project Browser, navigate to the Families section and expand the following tree:

    Families → Floors → Floor

2. Double-click on *Wood Joist 10" - Wood Finish* to open the Type Properties dialog box.
3. Click **Duplicate...**, and enter **Wood Joist 2x8 - 15/16" Composite Deck** for the name.
4. **Edit** the structure to match the following table. For the finish layer you'll need to create a new material as specified in the second table below.

 Refer back to Chapter 8 for a refresher on creating and editing materials.

Compound Floor Structure: Wood Joist 2X8 - 15/16" Composite Deck

Layer	Function	Material	Thickness
1	Finish 1 [4]	Flooring, Composite Decking *(new)*	0' 0 15/16"
2	**Core Boundary**	**Layers Above Wrap**	**0' 0"**
3	Structure [1]	Structure, Wood Joist/Rafter Layer	0' 7 1/4"
4	**Core Boundary**	**Layers Below Wrap**	**0' 0"**

New Material

Property	Value
Existing Material to Duplicate	**Oak Flooring**
New Material Name	**Flooring, Composite Decking**
Graphics Tab	
Shading Color	**RGB 142-122-99**
Surface Pattern	**6" Parallel** (Model Pattern)
Appearance Tab	
Appearance (Asset)	Appearance Library > Flooring/Wood > **Beechwood - Mystic Brown**
Identity Tab	
Material Class	**Composites**
Description	**COMPOSITE DECKING**

5. Click **OK** to exit all dialog boxes and complete the new floor type.

Add the Deck

Floor			
Tab	Panel	Split Button ▼	Tool Button
Architecture	**Build**	**Floor**	**Floor: Architectural**

Properties	
Type Selector:	**Wood Joist 2x8 - 15/16" Composite Deck**
Level:	**F.F.L. 1st FLR**
Height Offset From Level:	**-0' 1"**

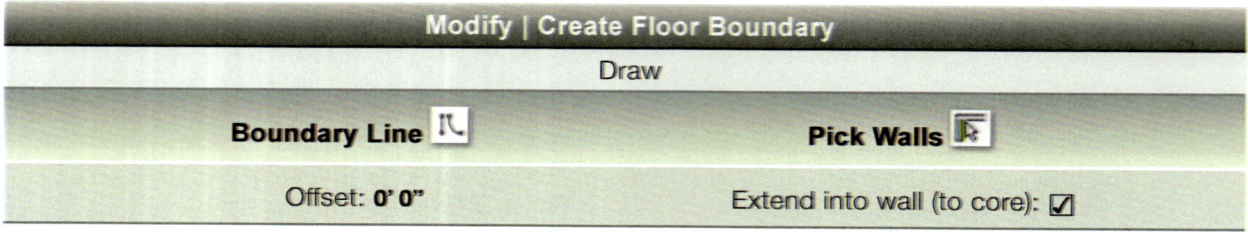

6. Pick the two walls of the house where the deck will attach as shown in the illustration below.

7. Next pick the two reference planes that define the outer perimeter of the porch deck as shown in the illustration below.

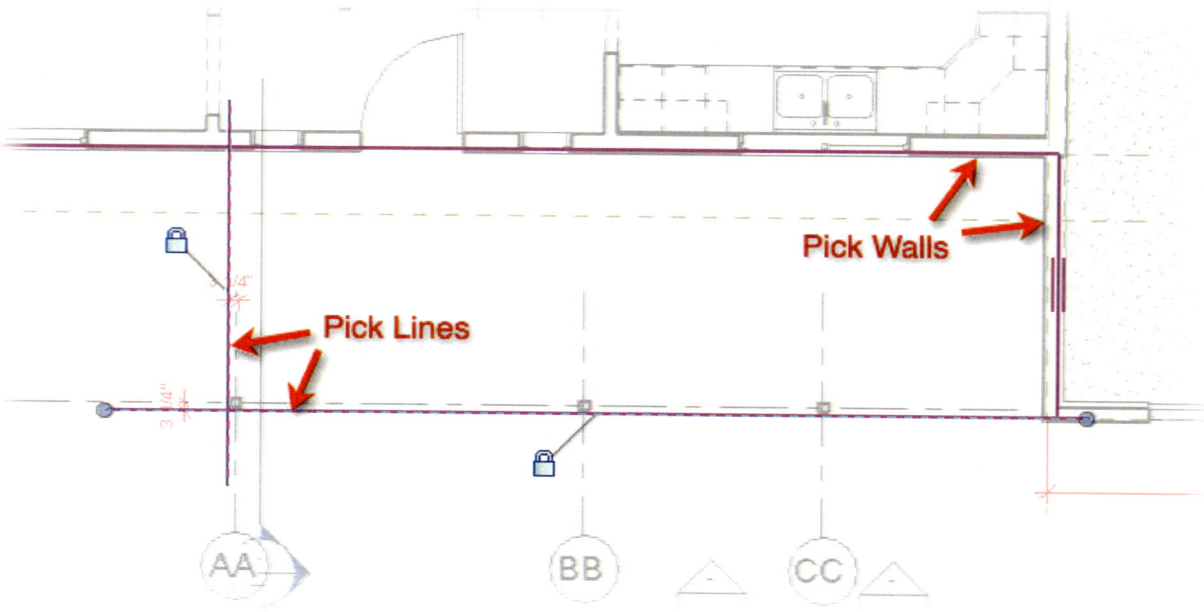

8. Use **Trim/Extend to Corner** to trim the corners.

9. When done, click the **Finish Edit Mode** button ✓

10. Answer **YES** when prompted to cut the overlapping geometry from the walls. The deck should appear as illustrated on the following page.

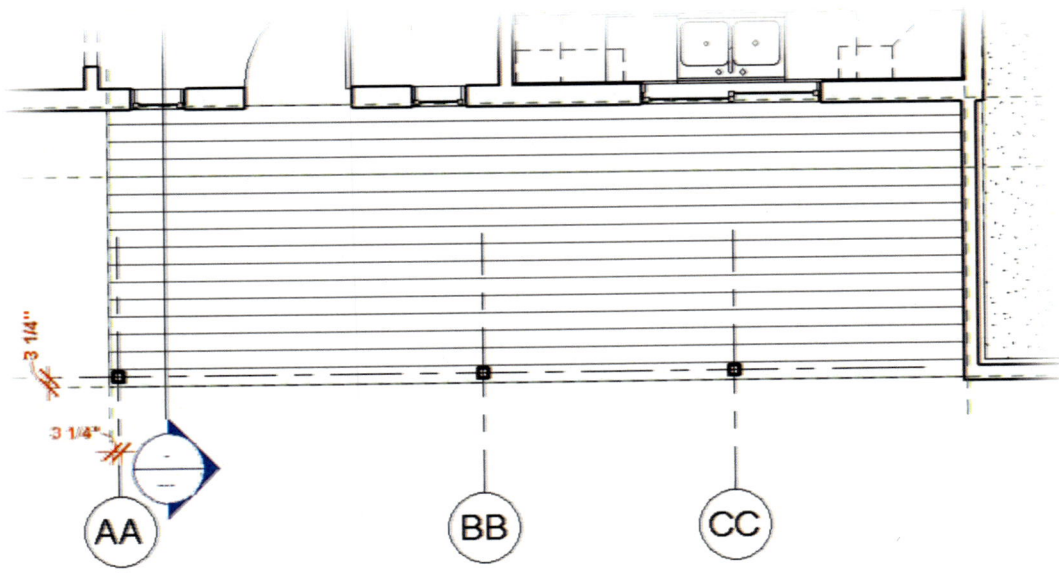

Completed Porch Deck

11. Open the default *{3D}* view. The deck should appear as illustrated below.

QAT 💾	Save Project	[Ctl]+S
	Operation	
🔧	Save	

This concludes exercise 10.1

Exercise 10.2: Porch Roof & Ceiling

QAT	Open Project	[Ctl]+O
Operation	Option	File Name
Open ▶	Project	BIMHOUSE-EX10-1.rvt

	Save As (Project)	
Operation	Option	File Name
Save As ▶	Project	BIMHOUSE-EX10-2.rvt

Model The Porch Roof

To model the porch roof, we'll use the *Roof Plan* view. This isn't the only view where we could create this roof. However, we'll use this opportunity to set up the Visibility/Graphics Overrides for the *Roof Plan* so that it's closer to being complete, and ready for use in the CD sheet set.

Set Up the Roof Plan View

1. Open the floor plan view *Roof Plan*.
2. Set up the view properties as indicated in the following tables.

View Properties: Roof Plan

Parameter	Value	Alternate Access
Detail Level	Medium	View Control Bar (VCB)
Visual Style	Hidden Line	View Control Bar (VCB)
Underlay	None	
View Range		
Top:	Unlimited	
Cut Plane – Offset:	20' 0"	
Bottom:	F.F.L. 1st FLR	
Bottom – Offset:	0' 0"	
View Depth Level:	F.F.L. 1st FLR	
View Depth Level – Offset:	0' 0"	

 Remember that you can quickly hide several categories at once by first creating a selection set with one or more elements from each category, then right-clicking to open the contextual menu and selecting **Hide in View → Category**.

V/G Overrides: Roof Plan

Category Tab / Category / Subcategory	Visibility	Other
Model / Ceilings	OFF	
Model / Mechanical Equipment	OFF	
Model / Plumbing Fixtures	OFF	
Model / Roofs	ON	Surface Patterns Visibility = OFF
Model / Specialty Equipment	OFF	
Annotation / Elevations	OFF	
Annotation / Grids	OFF	
Annotation / Sections	OFF	

3. When done, your *Roof Plan* view should appear as illustrated below.

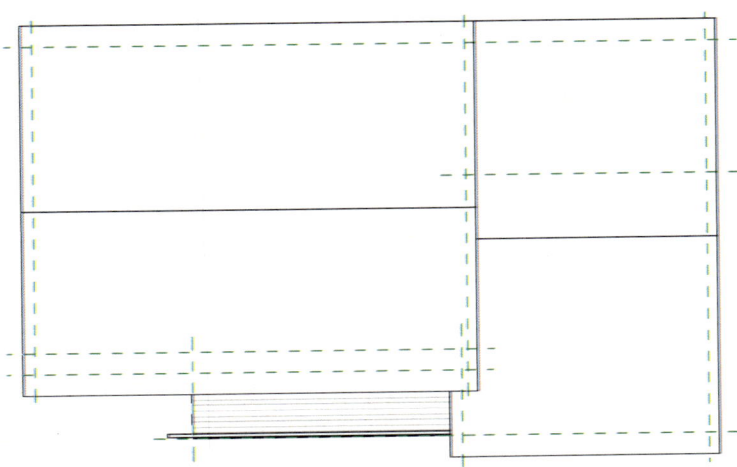

Create Template from Current View

Tab	Panel	Split Button ▼	Tool Button
View	Graphics	View Templates	Create Template from Current View

In the following steps you will create two view templates. The first template will capture the existing view settings. You will then make a change to V/G Overrides and then create the second template with the updated view settings.

4. Name the new view template **Plan-Roof-Working**. Click **OK** to accept all of the default settings and create the template.
5. Edit the V/G Overrides again: set visibility for the *Reference Planes* category to **OFF**.
6. Create another view template named **Plan-Roof**. Click **OK** to accept all of the default settings and create the template.
7. Set the *View Template* property for *Roof Plan* to **Plan-Roof**.

CHAPTER 10: PORCH CONSTRUCTION

Model the Porch Roof

8. We'll need reference planes accessible while modeling this roof. Use *Temporary View Properties* → *Temporarily Apply Template Properties...* **Plan-Roof-Working**.

9. Using **Temporary Hide/Isolate**, hide the following *elements*.

 Selecting the roofs first will render them transparent, allowing selection of the gable wall below.

 a) Both roofs

 b) The gable wall on the west side of the garage next to the porch

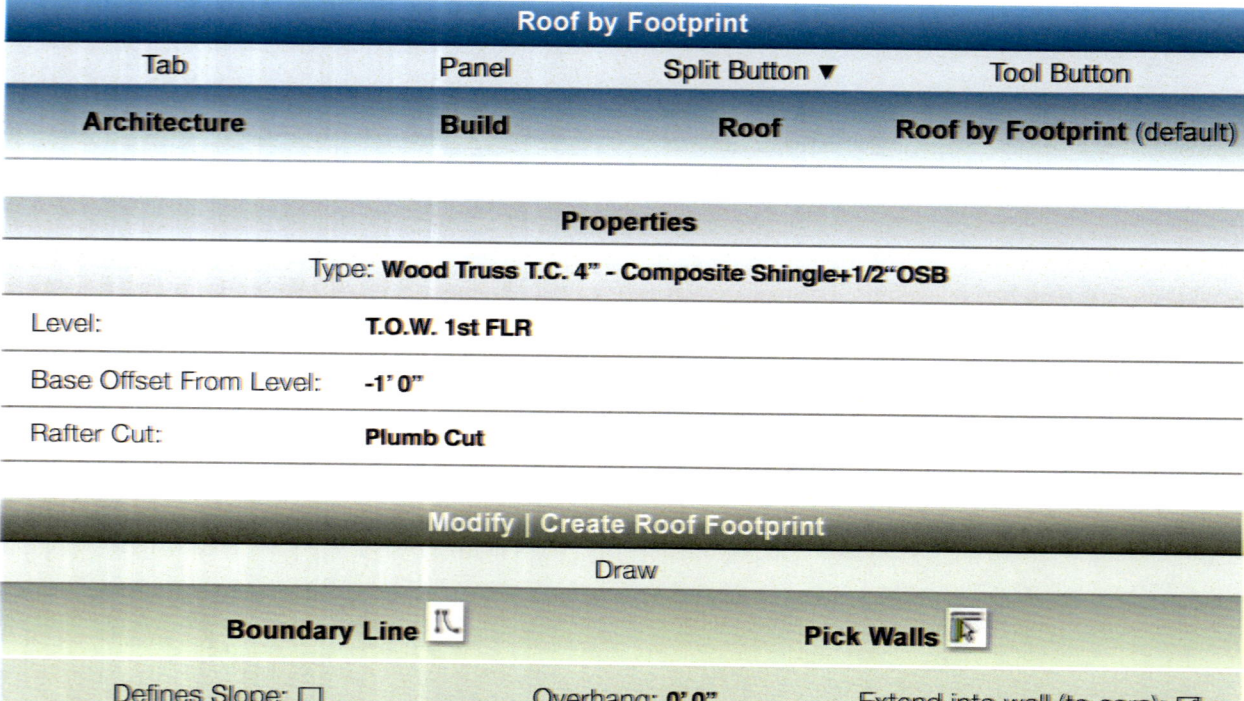

Roof by Footprint			
Tab	Panel	Split Button ▼	Tool Button
Architecture	**Build**	**Roof**	**Roof by Footprint** (default)

Properties	
Type: **Wood Truss T.C. 4" - Composite Shingle+1/2"OSB**	
Level:	**T.O.W. 1st FLR**
Base Offset From Level:	**-1' 0"**
Rafter Cut:	**Plumb Cut**

Modify | Create Roof Footprint	
Draw	
Boundary Line	**Pick Walls**
Defines Slope: ☐ Overhang: **0' 0"** Extend into wall (to core): ☑	

10. Pick the west garage wall and the south wall of the 2nd floor as illustrated below.

11. Update the Draw tools and Options Bar settings...

EXERCISE 10.2: PORCH ROOF & CEILING

Modify | Create Roof Footprint		
Draw		
Boundary Line		Pick Lines
Defines Slope: ☐	Offset: 1' 0"	Lock: ☐

12. Pick the reference plane that defines the west side of the porch as illustrated below, making sure the offset direction is to the west.

13. Update the Options Bar settings...

Defines Slope: ☑	Offset: 2' 0""	Lock: ☐

14. Pick the the south edge of the 4x8 beam as illustrated below. Make sure the offset direction is to the south.

15. Verify the slope value for the last boundary line is **6"/12"**. If not, change it now.

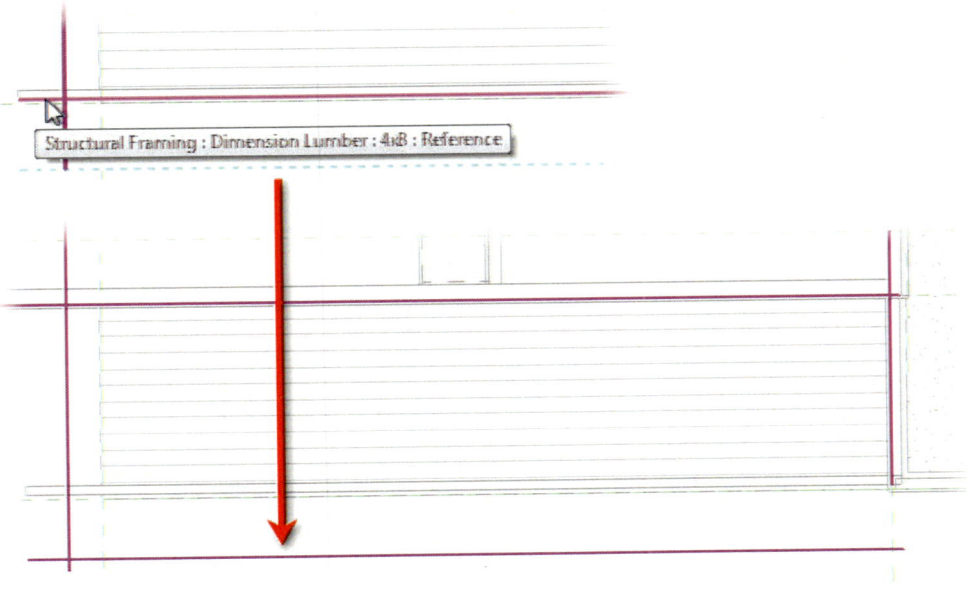

16. Click **Modify** to exit the *Pick Lines* tool.

17. Use **Trim/Extend to Corner** to clean up the boundary lines.

 Since there aren't any walls to pick and associate with the south and west roof boundary lines, no parametric relationships have been created between these two edges of the roof and the porch structure. To create the desired parametric relationships, length constraints must be added between the floating boundary lines and corresponding reference planes.

18. Place two aligned dimensions as illustrated below, and **lock** each one.

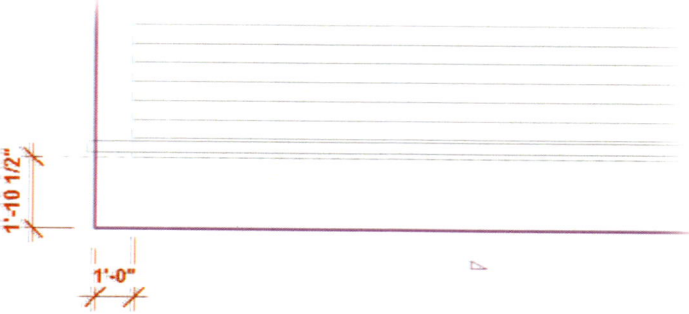

> ⚠ As with any other model element created by sketching boundaries, constraints *must* be created while in the boundary sketch mode for the element to remain flexible outside of sketch mode. Make sure you dimension to the reference planes and *not* the porch deck.

19. When done, click the **Finish Edit Mode** button

20. Answer **YES** when prompted to cut the overlapping geometry from the walls.

21. Open the *Default {3D}* view. Your porch roof should appear as illustrated below. Notice the overlap and slight mismatch to the garage roof. We'll correct this later.

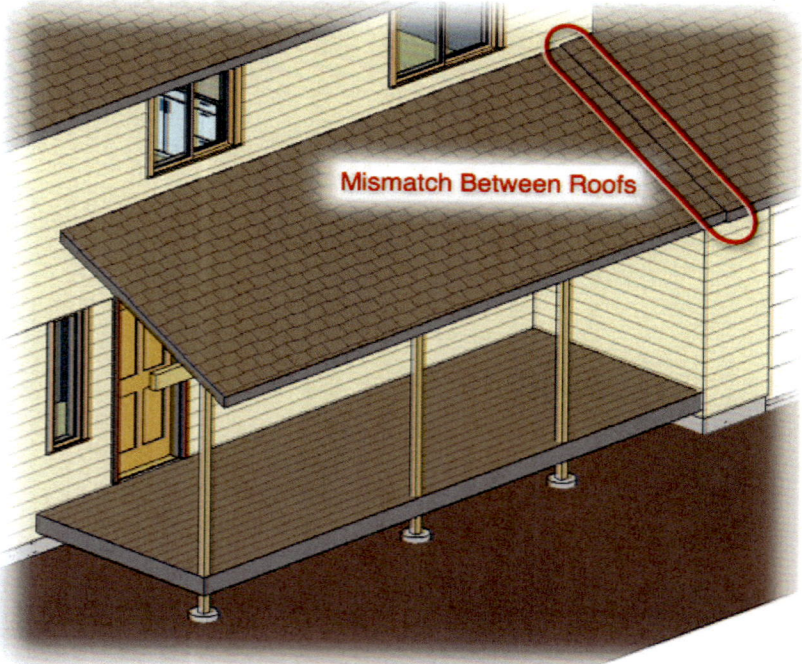

22. Open the floor plan view *Roof Plan*.

23. *Temporary Hide/Isolate* → **Reset Temporary Hide/Isolate**.

24. *Temporary View Properties* → **Restore View Properties**.

EXERCISE 10.2: PORCH ROOF & CEILING

 Depending on where you started to sketch the beam in the previous chapter, it may or may not be protruding from the west side of the porch roof at this time.

Adjust the Beam Length & Position

In the following steps we'll adjust the beam length based on the bearing points, as well as the required physical beam length

1. Open the floor plan view *T.O.W. 1st FLR*.

2. Select the 4x8 beam at the porch, then drag the west end so that it snaps to the intersection of *Grid 1* & *Grid AA* as illustrated below.

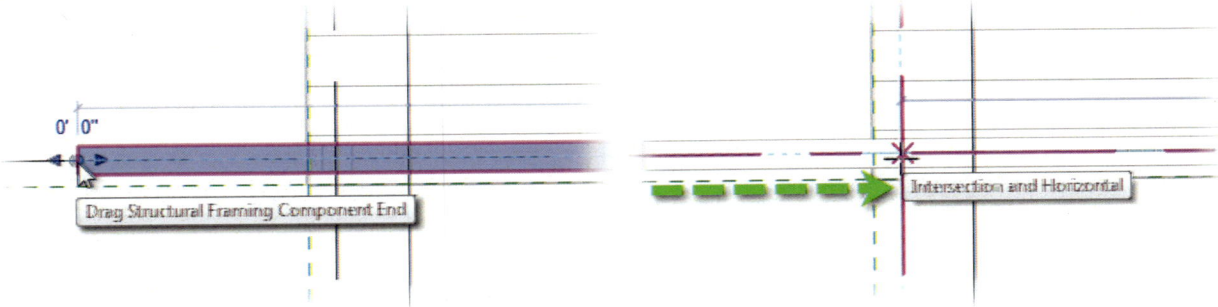

3. Adjust the opposite end of the beam using the drag handle, and then keying the length value of **23' - 9 3/4"** into the listening dimension. This will place the endpoint of the beam at the center of the wall core.

4. With the beam still selected, adjust the following properties.

Properties	
Type: **Dimension Lumber: 4x8**	
Start Extension:	**0' 3 1/4"**
End Extension:	**0' 1 3/4"**

5. The beam should appear as illustrated below. Notice the offset between the *drag handles* and the physical ends of the beam.

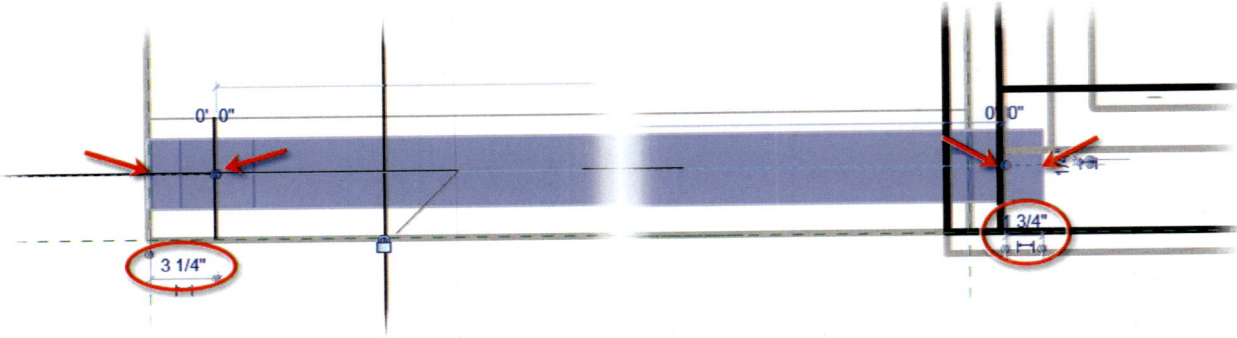

307

Create New Ceiling Types

Before we add the ceiling elements to the porch, we'll need to create a couple new ceiling types. One to represent the bottom chord of the jack truss, the other for the *Hardie Soffit* finish layer, which will also extend underneath the 2nd floor cantilever along the south face of the house. The *Hardie Soffit* finish layer will require a new material, as well as a new fill pattern to be used for the surface pattern of the new material.

New Fill Pattern

Tab	Panel	Drop-down Button ▼	Tool Button
Manage	Settings	Additional Settings	Fill Patterns

1. In the Fill Patterns dialog box, select the **Model** radio button, then click **New**.

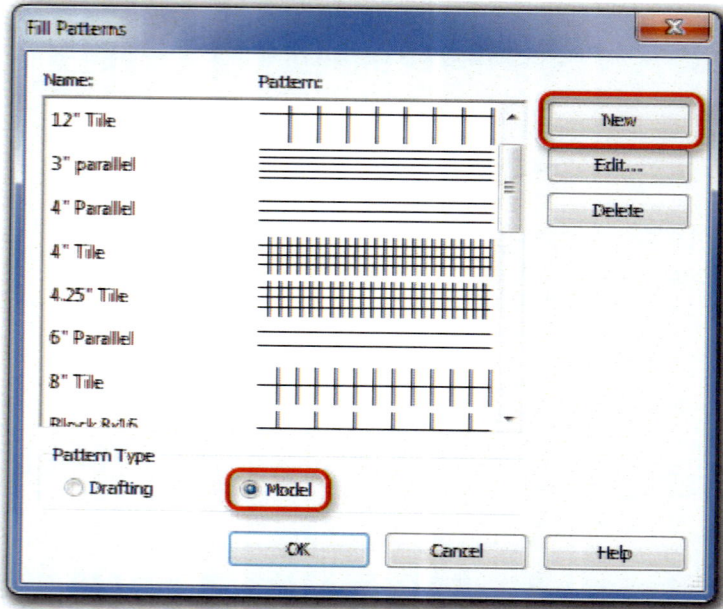
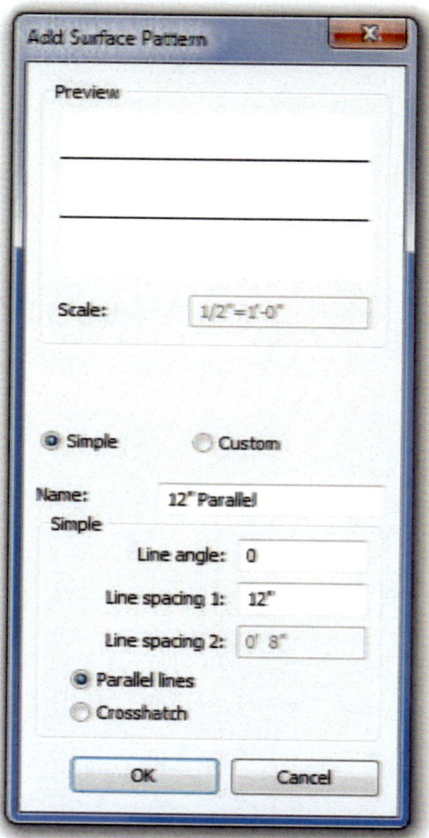

2. In the Add Surface Pattern dialog box, edit the properties as illustrated in the image to the right.
3. Click **OK** twice to complete the fill pattern.

New Material

4. Create the material described in the table below.

New Ceiling Material

Property	Value
Existing Material to Duplicate	Siding, Wood, Horizontal, 6" Beige
New Material Name	Fiber Cement, HardieSoffit, Beige
Graphics Tab	
Surface Pattern	12" Parallel
Cut Pattern	Sand - Dense
Identity Tab	
Material Class	Fiber Cement
Description	12" WIDE SOFFIT PANELS
Manufacturer	JAMES HARDIE
Model	12" X 12' NON-VENTED CEDARMILL

New Ceiling Types

5. **Duplicate** the ceiling *GWB on 4" Truss B.C.* and rename the duplicate to **HardieSoffit on 3/8" OSB**.

6. **Edit** the structure of the new ceiling to match the table below.

Ceiling Structure: HardieSoffit on 3/8" OSB

Layer	Function	Material	Thickness
1	Core Boundary	Layers Above Wrap	0' 0"
2	Structure [1]	OSB, Sheathing	0' 0 3/8"
3	Core Boundary	Layers Below Wrap	0' 0"
4	Finish 1 [4]	Fiber Cement, HardieSoffit, Beige	0' 0 1/4"

7. Click **OK** *once*, then click **Duplicate...**

8. Enter **4" Truss B.C** for the name, and **Edit** the structure to match the table below.

Ceiling Structure: 4" Truss B.C.

Layer	Function	Material	Thickness
1	Core Boundary	Layers Above Wrap	0' 0"
2	Structure [1]	Structure, Wood Truss BC	0' 3 1/2"
3	Core Boundary	Layers Below Wrap	0' 0"

9. Click **OK** to exit all dialog boxes.

CHAPTER 10: PORCH CONSTRUCTION

Model the Ceiling Structure Layer

1. Open the plan view *T.O.W. 1st FLR*.

2. Using *Temporary Hide/Isolate*, hide the gable wall at the west side of the garage next to the porch.

Ceiling		
Tab	Panel	Tool Button
Architecture	Build	Ceiling

3. Select **Sketch Ceiling**.

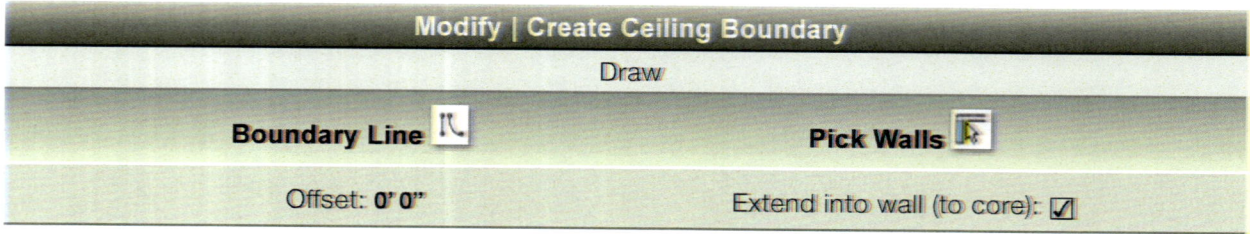

4. Pick the west garage wall and the south exterior wall of the 2nd floor as shown in the illustration.

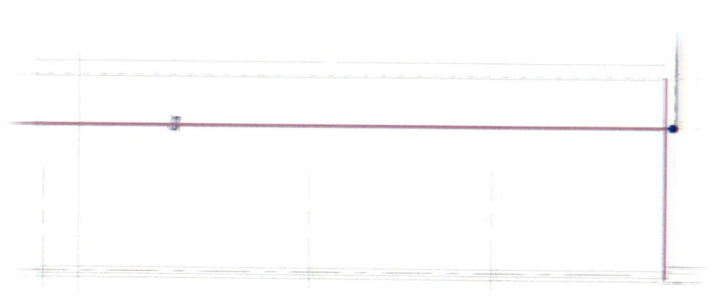

 Only the base extension (siding and sheathing) portion of the 2nd floor exterior wall should be visible in this view. If you are unable to pick the 2nd floor wall, chances are that its *Base Extension Distance* property is set incorrectly.

5. Update the Draw tools and Options Bar settings...

310

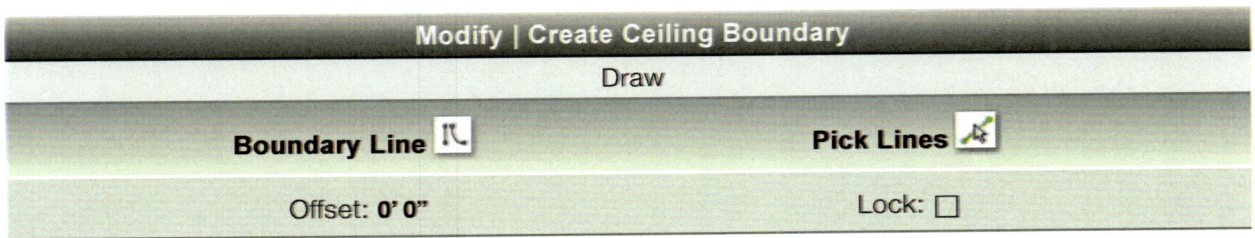

6. Pick the *Porch - West* reference plane as illustrated below and **Lock** the boundary line.
7. Pick the south edge of the *beam* as illustrated below. *Do not* lock.

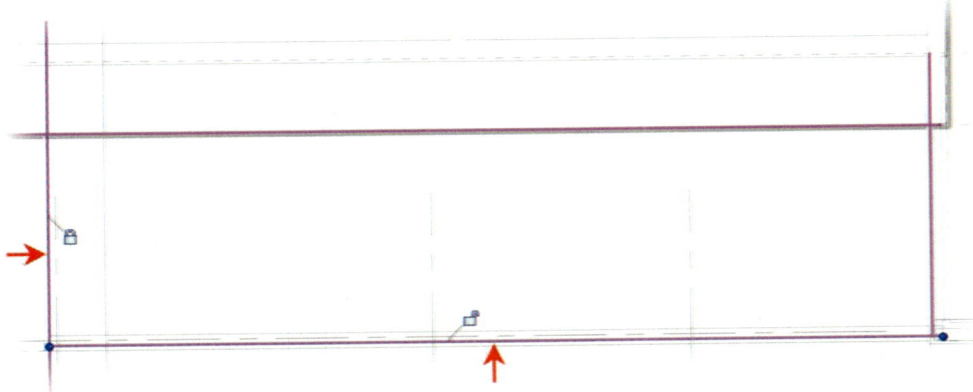

8. Click **Modify** to exit the *Pick Lines* tool.
9. Use **Trim/Extend to Corner** to clean up the boundary lines.
10. Place an aligned dimension between the *Porch - South* reference plane and the south boundary line as illustrated below, then **Lock** it to create a length constraint.

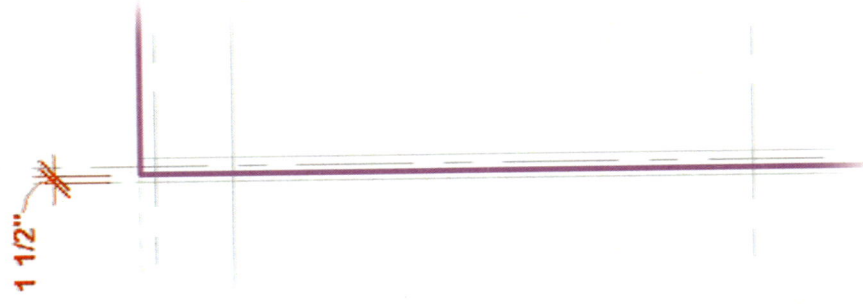

11. When done, click the **Finish Edit Mode** button ✓
12. **Reset Temporary Hide/Isolate**.

13. Open the section view *Family-Stairs-Porch (Long)* and zoom in around the porch. Your section should appear as illustrated below.

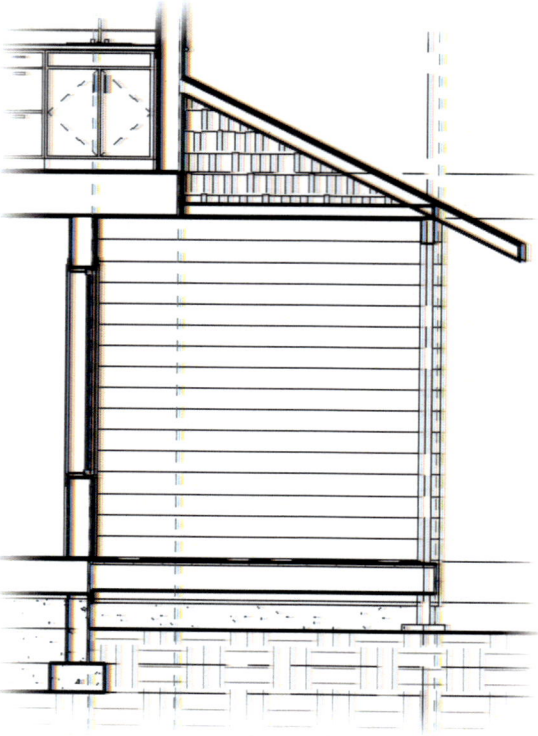

Longitudinal Building Section View of Porch

14. Use **Join Geometry** to clean up the view as illustrated below.

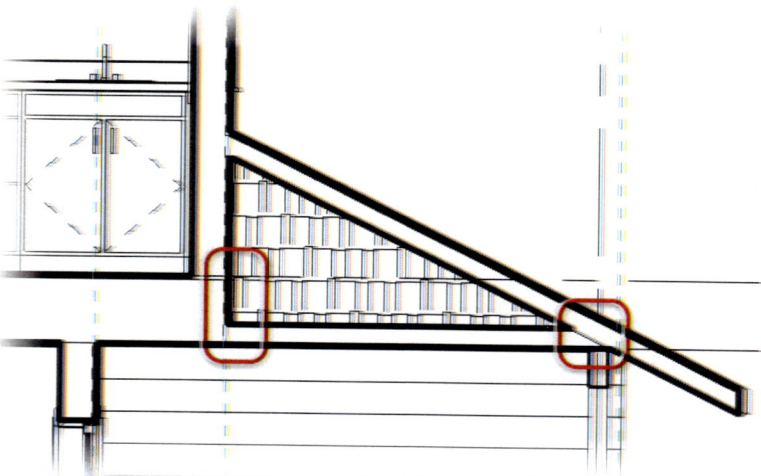

> The element picked first with Join Geometry will remove volume from the element picked second; however, if you pick in the incorrect oder, you can reverse the join this by using **Switch Join Order** in the Join tool drop-down.

Update RCP View Template Settings

Prior to adding the ceiling finish layer, we need to update the visibility graphics for the 1st floor reflected ceiling plans to show structural framing. We'll do this by editing the view templates.

View Template Settings			
Tab	Panel	Split Button ▼	Tool Button
View	Graphics	View Templates	Manage View Templates

1. Make the changes for each of the view templates indicated in the tables below.

View Template Setting Updates: *Plan-RCP*

Property	Value	Include
Detail Level	Medium	✓
V/G Overrides Model		✓
Structural Framing	Visibility = ON	
V/G Overrides Annotation		✓
Grids	Visibility = OFF	

View Template Setting Updates: *Plan-RCP-Working*

Property	Value	Include
Detail Level	Medium	✓
V/G Overrides Model		✓
Structural Framing	Visibility = ON	

Model the Ceiling Finish Layer

1. Open the ceiling plan view *RCP - 1st Floor - T.O.W.*

Ceiling		
Tab	Panel	Tool Button
Architecture	Build	Ceiling

2. Select **Sketch Ceiling**.

Properties	
Type: **HardieSoffit on 3/8" OSB**	
Level:	**T.O.W. 1st FLR**
Height Offset From Level:	**-0' 0 5/8"**

CHAPTER 10: PORCH CONSTRUCTION

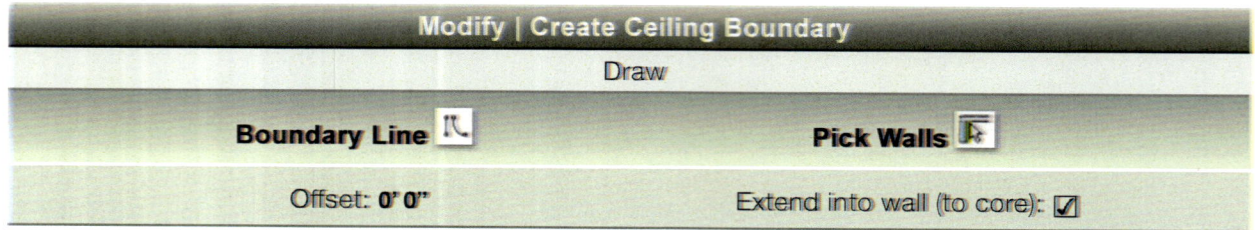

3. Pick the four walls illustrated below.

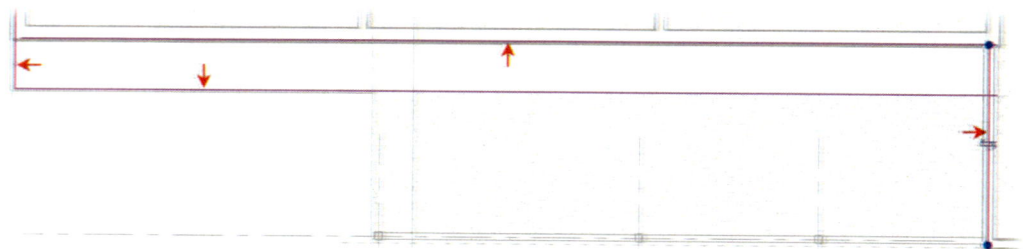

4. Update the Draw tools and Options Bar settings...

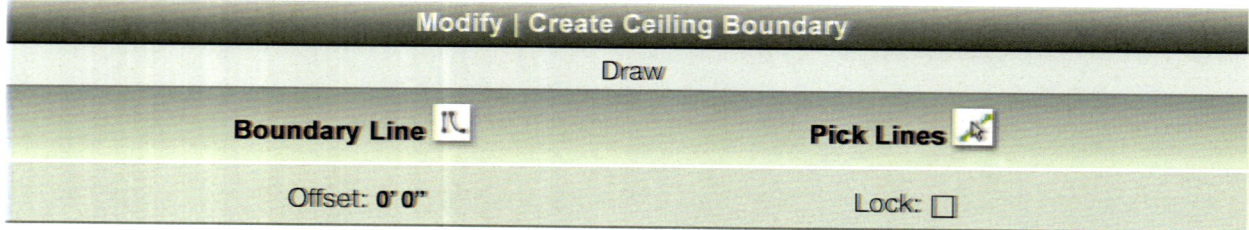

5. Pick the *Porch - West* reference plane and **Lock** it as illustrated below.
6. Pick the north edge of the beam as illustrated below. *Do not* lock.

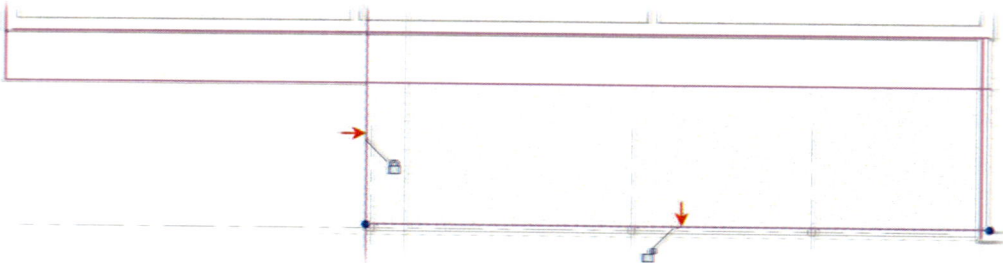

7. Click **Modify** to exit the *Pick Lines* tool.
8. Use **Trim/Extend to Corner** to clean up the boundary lines as illustrated below.

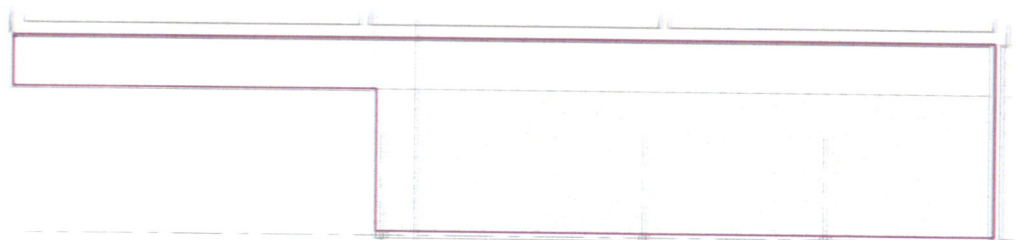

9. Place an aligned dimension between the *Porch - South* reference plane and the south boundary line as illustrated below, then **Lock** it to create a length constraint.

 Be sure to pick the boundary line for the ceiling and *not* the beam! If the dimension is visible after exiting the ceiling edit mode, the dimension is incorrectly referenced.

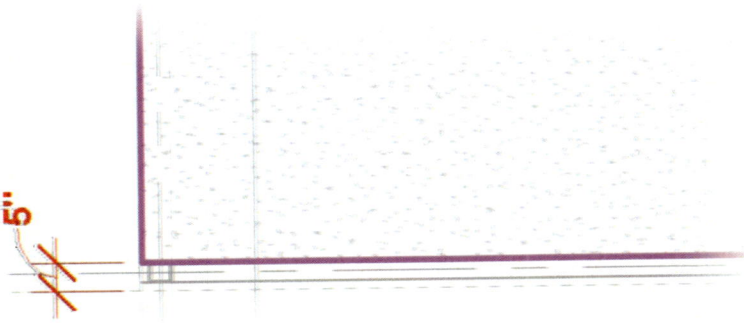

10. When done, click the **Finish Edit Mode** button ✓

11. Open the section view *Family-Stairs-Porch (Long)*.

12. Zoom in around the porch ceiling, then use **Join Geometry** to join the ceiling finish layer to all intersecting geometry to achieve the results illustrated below.

13. Open the default *{3D}* view, then orbit and zoom to the underside of the southwest corner of the building where the 2nd floor cantilevers as illustrated below.

14. Select the two exterior 2nd floor walls as illustrated, then set their **Base Extension Distance** to **-1 1 1/4"** so the siding extends down to the bottom face of the ceiling finish layer (HardieSoffit).

Orient 3D View *Select Walls*

15. Use **Join Geometry** to join the 1st & 2nd floor exterior walls on the west side where the siding overlaps. When done, the adjusted conditions should appear as illustrated below.

Add a Porch Gable Wall

1. Open the plan view *T.O.W. 1st FLR*.

2. **Right-click** on the gable wall over the west garage wall, and from the contextual menu click **Create Similar**, then set/verify the properties shown below.

Modify	Place Wall
Draw	
Line	

| Height: **Unconnected 6' 0"** | Location Line: **Core Face: Exterior** | Chain: ☐ | Offset: **0' 0"** | Radius: ☐ |

Properties
Type Selector: **Exterior - Wood 2x - 5/8"Shake+7/16"OSB**
Base Constraint:	**T.O.W. 1st FLR**
Base Offset:	**0' 0"**

 Make sure to set the unconnected height to at least 6' 0", otherwise it will be represented as a low wall, and the core layers will not be visible for alignment in the next steps.

3. Sketch the wall on the *Porch - West* reference plane. Start sketching the wall where the *Porch - West* reference plane and the south face of the beam intersect as shown in the first illustration below. Sketch the wall toward the 2nd floor south exterior wall as shown in the second illustration below, but <u>do not intersect the wall</u>.

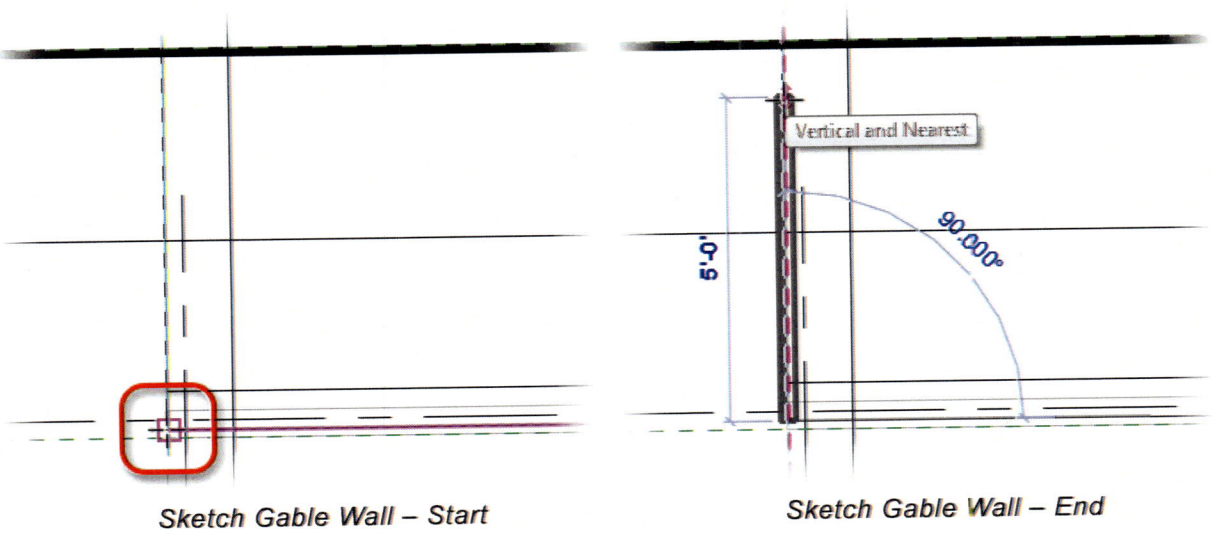

Sketch Gable Wall – Start   Sketch Gable Wall – End

CHAPTER 10: PORCH CONSTRUCTION

4. Exit the wall tool and set the free end of the gable wall to **Disallow Join** as illustrated below.

5. **Align** and **Lock** the free end of the gable wall to the reference plane *Ext-South-2*.
6. Use **Join Geometry** to clean up the join condition.
7. **Duplicate** the view *T.O.W. 1st FLR*.
8. **Rename** the new view to **W-T.O.W. 1st Floor - Constraints**, and leave it open.

Constrain the Gable Wall to the Porch

9. **Align** and **Lock** the exterior core face of the gable wall to the *Porch - West* reference plane. Be sure to use **Faces of core** for the *Prefer* setting.
10. Place an aligned dimension from the *Porch - South* reference plane to the nearest end of the gable wall as illustrated below, then **lock** the dimension to create a constraint.

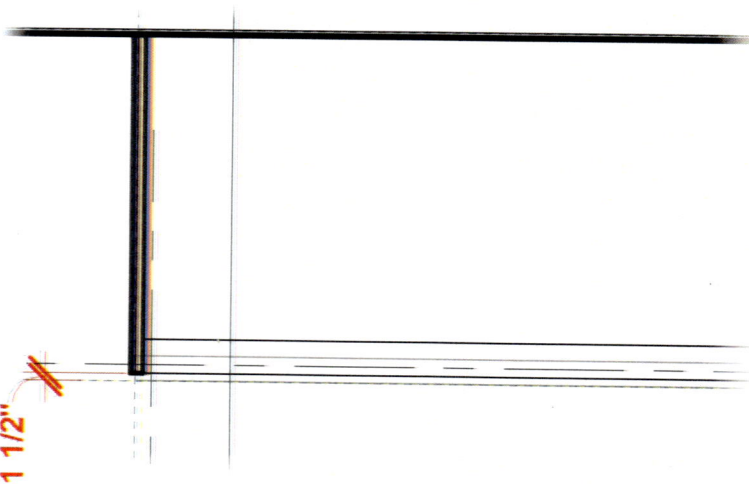

Exercise 10.2: Porch Roof & Ceiling

Attach the Gable Wall to the Roof

11. Open the *Default {3D}* view.

12. Select the new gable-end wall and use **Attach Top/Base** to attach the wall's *top* to the porch roof. When done, your porch should appear as illustrated below.

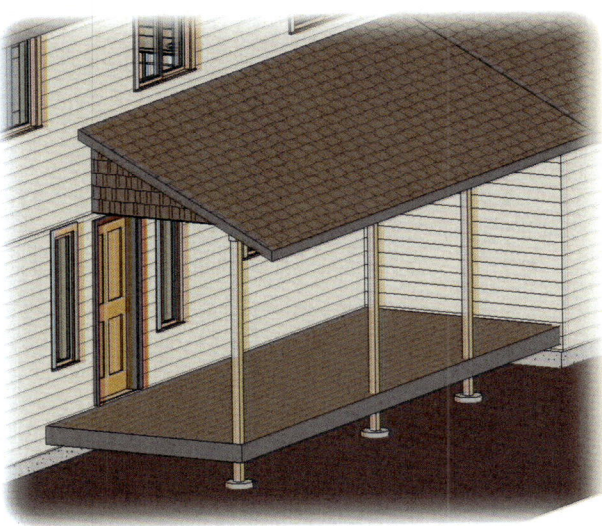

Completed Porch

Join the Gable Wall to the Ceiling

13. Open the section view *W-Porch (Cross)*.

14. Set the *Discipline* property to **Coordination**. The gable wall at the west end of the porch should appear.

15. Set *View Scale* to **1/2" = 1'-0"**.

16. Zoom in around the porch gable end, then use **Join Geometry** to join the gable wall to both ceiling elements. The join condition should appear as illustrated.

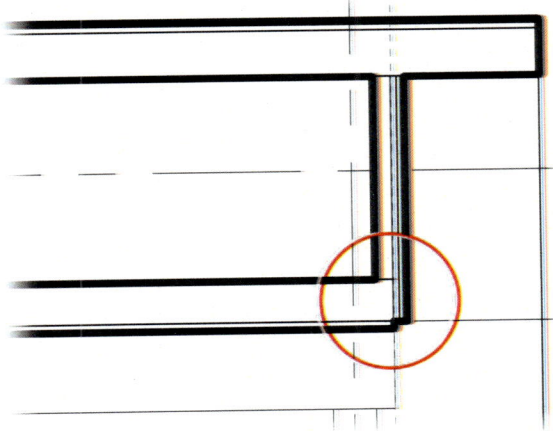

 Notice that in the join condition between the gable wall and ceiling elements the siding finish layer of the gable wall does not extend down flush with the bottom of the ceiling. Furthermore, if it did there would be a small gap due to the OSB sheathing between the truss and siding.

Modify Ceiling / Gable Connections

17. Select the gable wall at the west end of the porch, and click **Edit Type** in the Properties Palette.
18. Rename the wall to **Exterior - Wood 2x - 5/8"Shake(BU)+7/16"OSB**. *(Add (BU))*
19. Click **Edit...** to open the Edit Assembly dialog box.
20. Open the Preview pane and set *View* to **Section: Modify type attributes**.
21. Click **Modify**, and unlock layer 1 *(Finish 1 [4])* at the bottom of the wall as illustrated on the following page.

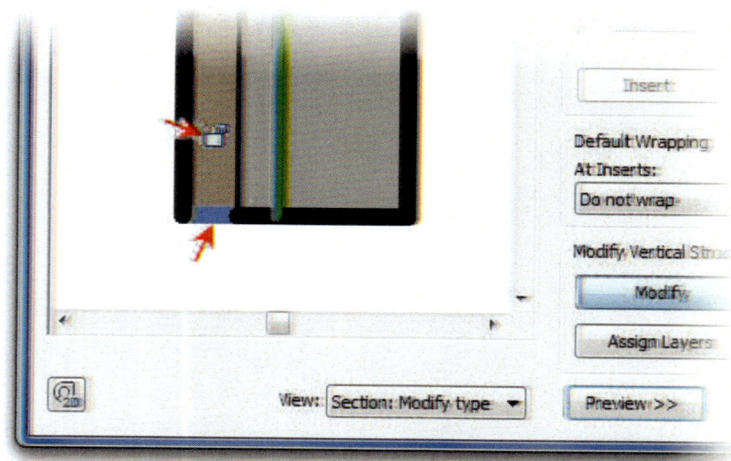

22. Click **OK** twice to exit all dialog boxes and complete the changes.
23. With the wall still selected, set the *Base Extension Distance* to **-0" 0 5/8"** so the bottom of the siding moves flush with the bottom of the ceiling finish layer. The join condition should appear as illustrated below. Notice there are a couple of conditions that are still incorrect.

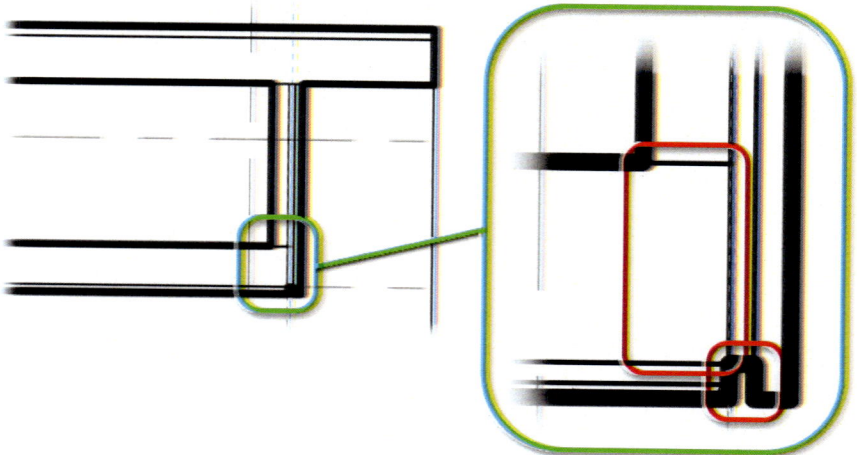

24. Open the floor plan view *W-T.O.W. 1st Floor - Constraints*.

25. Select the *4" Truss B.C.* ceiling element, then click **Edit Boundary**.

26. **Delete** the boundary line associated with the *Porch - West* reference plane.

 If you are unable to associate the boundary line in the following steps to the interior face of the gable wall, it is likely due to an automatic join condition between the gable wall and the 2nd floor exterior wall. Revit uses automatic wall join information to synchronize boundary lines when using the flip arrow. The only way to gain individual flip arrow control of boundary lines is to set corresponding wall joins to **Disallow Join**.

27. Using the **Pick Walls** draw tool, replace the boundary line by associating it to the <u>interior</u> face of the gable wall as illustrated.

28. **Trim/Extend** the corners as necessary, then click **Finish Edit Mode** ✓ to complete the ceiling.

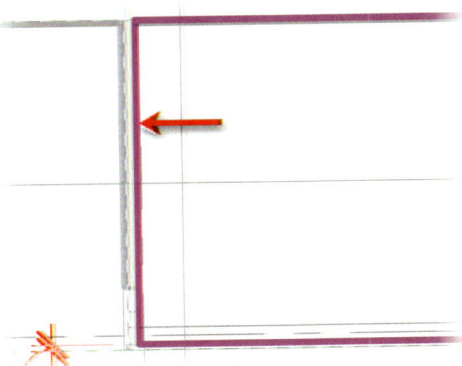

29. Open the section view *W-Porch (Cross)* and notice the change.

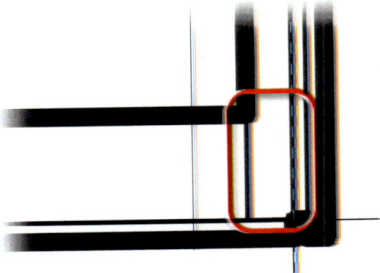

30. Open the ceiling plan view *RCP - 1st Floor - T.O.W.*

31. Select the ceiling element *HardieSoffit on 3/8" OSB*, then click **Edit Boundary**.

32. Select the boundary line associated with the *Porch - West* reference plane and **unlock** it.

33. **Align** and **Lock** the boundary line to the edge of the gable wall between the siding layer and OSB layer as illustrated below.

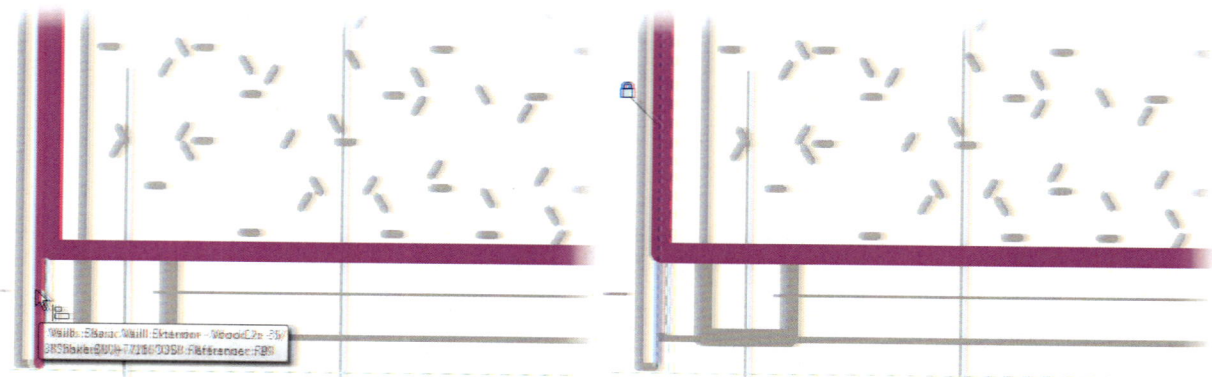

34. **Trim/Extend** the corners as necessary, then click **Finish Edit Mode** ✓ to complete the ceiling.

35. Open the section view *W-Porch (Cross)* and notice the change.

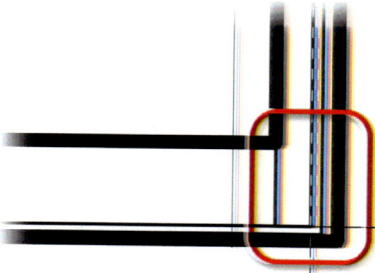

3D Porch Section View

To help better view the porch from various angles, you will create a 3D section view and override some of the visibility and graphics.

1. Duplicate the *Default {3D}* view.
2. Rename the new view **3D Section - Porch**.
3. Using either of the methods you previously learned, create a 3D section box around the porch and adjust it so it resembles the illustration below.
   a) Method 1: Use the *Orient to View* option in the View Cube context menu.
   b) Method 2: Enable the *Section Box* parameter in the view properties.
4. Use visibility/graphics overrides to get your views to reflect the illustrations below. Use the *Transparency* override where context is desired, but shouldn't obscure the view. The idea is to be able to view the porch from the interior side of the south wall, but retain the walls, windows, and door as part of the context.

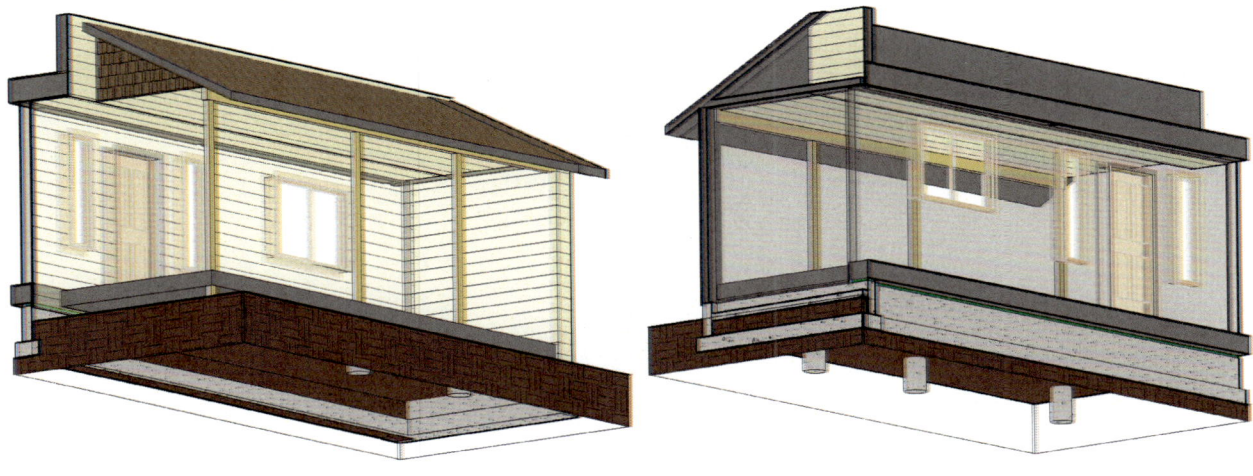

 To get your view to resemble the illustration above, you'll need to perform a number of visibility/graphics overrides, both *by element* and *by view*.

5. Zoom in around the underside of the porch ceiling as illustrated below. Notice that the siding of the 2nd floor wall protrudes through to the face of the porch ceiling.

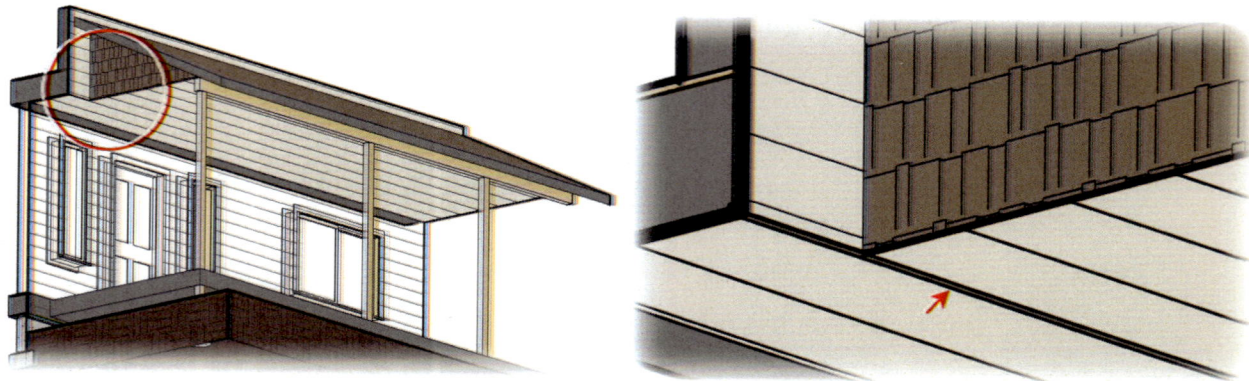

6. Use **Join Geometry** to clean up this condition. Pick the porch ceiling first, then the 2nd floor exterior wall. The resulting join is illustrated below.

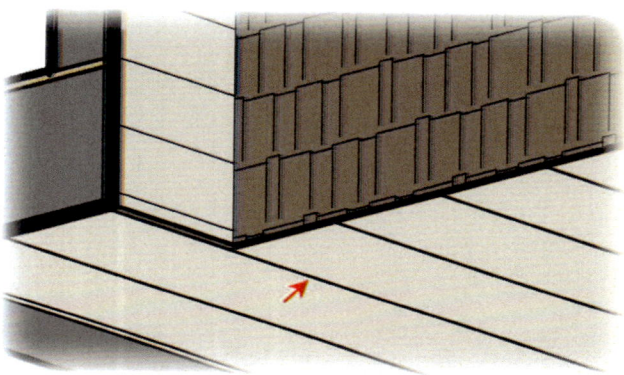

This concludes exercise 10.2

Exercise 10.3 Floor Plan Design Revision

In the previous section we modeled the porch roof, and this resulted in a mismatch between the porch and garage roofs. There are a number of ways we could address this mismatch. However, in this case we'll assume a design change to the original floor plan that involves lengthening the garage.

Extend the Garage

1. Open the floor plan view *W-1st Floor - CAD Import*.
2. **Close Hidden Windows**.
3. Open the default *{3D}* view, then **Tile Windows**.
4. Select the reference plane *Ext-Garage-South* and **unpin** it.
5. **Move** the reference plane to the south **2'-4"**. The condition at the porch/garage intersection should appear as illustrated.
6. Orbit the 3D view and verify that all related model elements adjust as expected. Be sure to look under the building for dissociated foundation elements.

CHAPTER 10: PORCH CONSTRUCTION

7. Use **Join Geometry** to join the porch roof to the intersecting gable and exterior garage walls. Your results should reflect the illustration below.

Porch / Garage Roof Condition After Join Geometry

Revise the CAD Import View

1. Open the floor plan view *W-1st Floor - CAD Import*.

2. Open the view template settings for this view (*Plan-Floor-CAD_Import*) and set the *Dimensions* category in the view to **Visible**.

3. Using the dimension style *Linear - Constraints*, add an aligned dimension between the reference plane and CAD import geometry as illustrated below.

 DO NOT LOCK THIS DIMENSION!

4. Select the dimension added in the previous step, then click on the dimension value to open the Dimension Text dialog box.

5. Enter **CORRECT LENGTH = 2'-4"** in the *Below* field as illustrated.

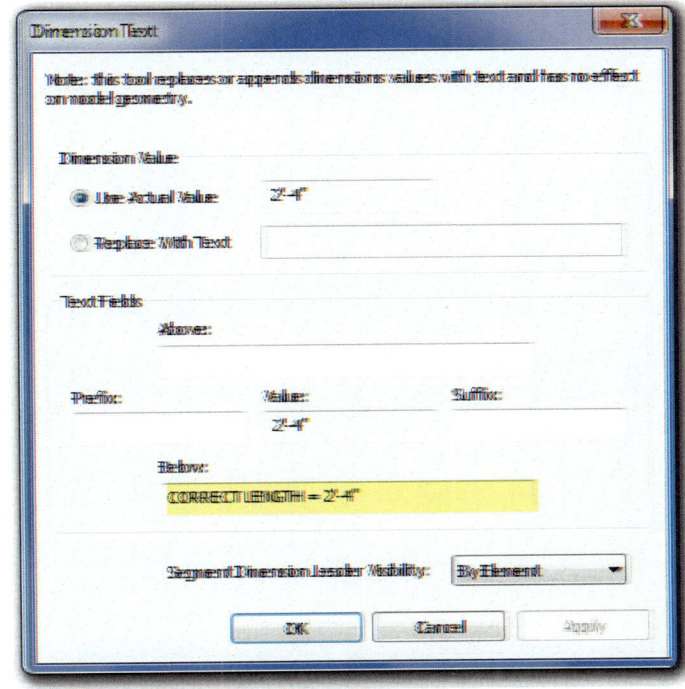

6. Click **OK** to apply the change. The dimension should update as illustrated below.

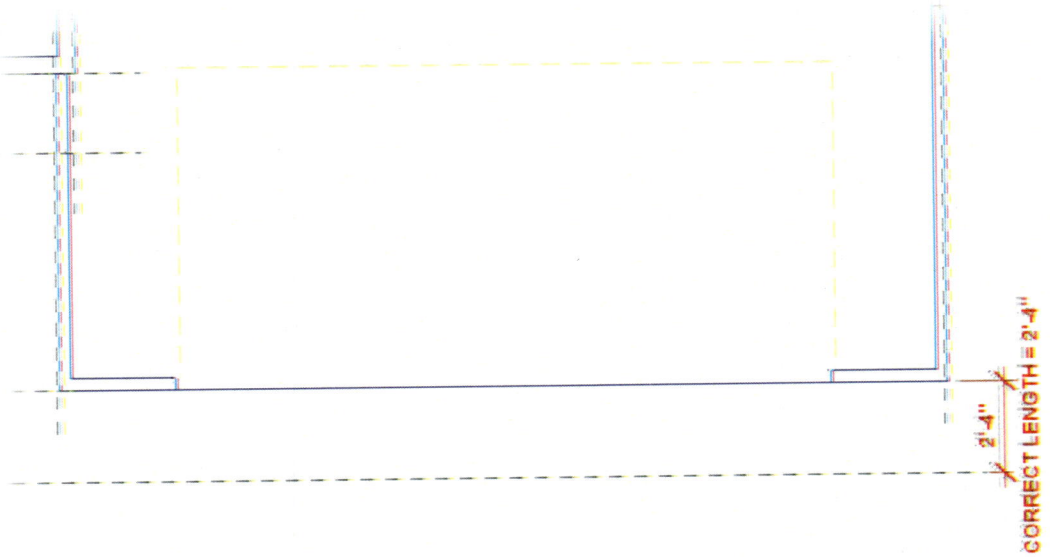

 The CAD Import views are used as a reference to verify correct locations of reference planes, ensuring correctness of the building layout. However, since the 1st floor layout has changed and we don't have an update CAD file to import, we needed something in this view to inform us of the correct *revised* location of the south garage reference plane.

7. Re-pin the *(Ext-Garage-South)* reference plane.

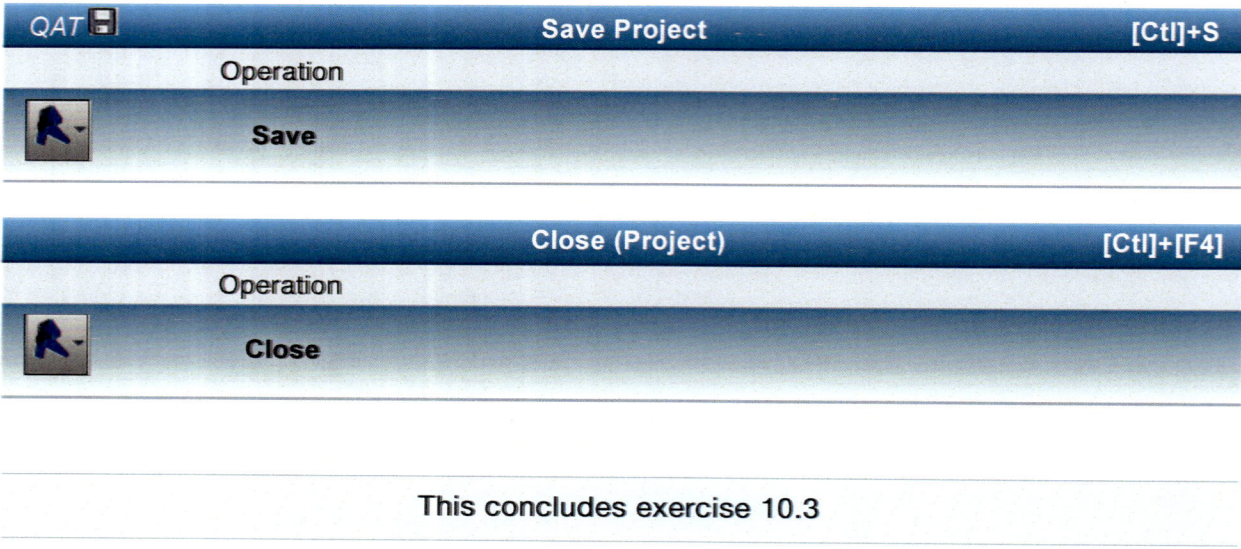

This concludes exercise 10.3

Chapter Summary

In this exercise you learned some new tips and tricks, as well as exercised concepts learned in earlier lessons in order to bring the porch closer to completion. In the next chapter you will add steps and railings to complete the porch.

Chapter 11
Stairs & Railings

Overview

This chapter is intended to introduce you to working with stair and railing elements. Given the complexity of these elements, the concepts and techniques used in this exercise will only cover the basics.

Learning Objectives

After completing this chapter you should have a basic understanding of the following new tools and concepts.

- Working with stairs
- Working with railings
- Split section markers
- Editing wall profiles

Project Objectives

- Add porch steps and railings
- Add monolithic steps at the rear patio entrance
- Add steps at the interior garage entrance
- Add Interior stairway
- Modify stairway walls with wall caps
- Add wall-mounted hand rail at the interior stairway
- Create additional 3D section views

CHAPTER 11: STAIRS & RAILINGS

Chapter Contents

Exercise 11.1: Entry Stairs 334
    Concrete Pad 334
    Porch Stairs 339
    Garage Stairs 344
    Patio Stairs 348

Exercise 11.2: Interior Stairs 354
    Floor Opening 354
    Stair by Component 362
    Guard Walls 367
    3D Interior Stair Section - East 374

Exercise 11.3: Porch Railings 376
    Porch Stair Railings 376
    Porch Deck Railings 381

Exercise 11.4: Interior Railings 386
    Wall Caps 386
    Handrail 393
    Plan View Graphics Refinement 396
    3D Interior Stair Section - West 397

Exercise 11.1: Entry Stairs

Open Project		[Ctl]+O
Operation	Option	File Name
Open ▶	Project	BIMHOUSE-EX10-3.rvt

Save As (Project)		
Operation	Option	File Name
Save As ▶	Project	BIMHOUSE-EX11-1.rvt

Concrete Pad

Before adding stairs leading up to the porch, we need to add a portion of the walkway. This will consist of a concrete slab to support the stairs, and will become part of the complete walkway in a future chapter.

We'll use reference planes to lay out the slab. These reference planes will then be used to constrain both the slab and the stair elements.

Lay Out the Slab

1. Open the floor plan view *W-1st Floor - Constraints*.
2. Referring to the illustration on the following page, sketch a reference plane from north to south starting at the centerline of the main entry door at the porch.
   a) Name the reference plane **Entry CL**.
   b) Place the reference dimension shown between the *Entry CL* and *Ext-West* reference planes. It should read *19'-5"*. If not, go back to the plans provided for this project to help identify the problem.
   c) **Pin** the reference plane.
3. Referring to the same illustration, sketch three more reference planes to define the outline of the entry path, and name them as follows.
   a) **Walk - West**
   b) **Walk - South**
   c) **Walk - East**
4. Referring to the same illustration, add the dimensions and equality constraints as shown. Note that some dimensions are shown in blue for clarity. You do not need to create a new dimension type for these unless you wish to do so.

EXERCISE 11.1: ENTRY STAIRS

 Do not constrain the dimensions shown in blue. You can use any dimension type for these dimensions that you prefer. However, since you won't be locking them, don't use the type *Linear - Constraints*. This will help to avoid confusion.

5. Adjust the three walkway reference plane locations per the dimensions shown in the illustration below.

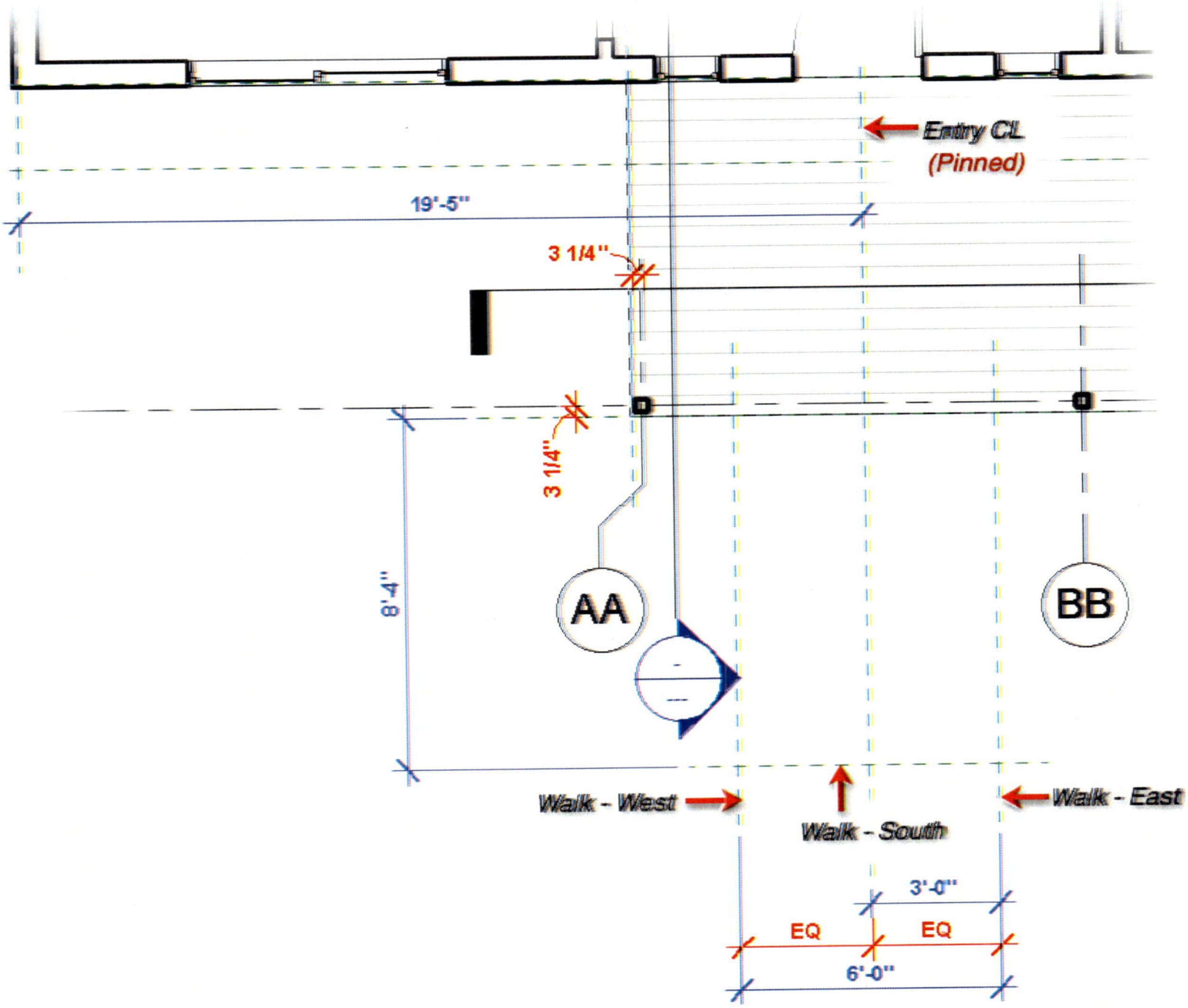

(Reference dimensions shown in blue for clarity)

CHAPTER 11: STAIRS & RAILINGS

Model the Slab

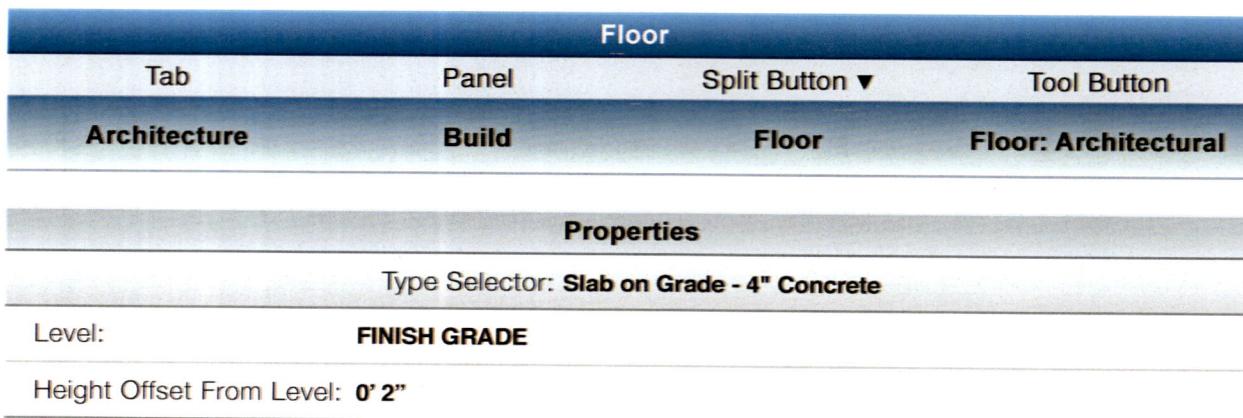

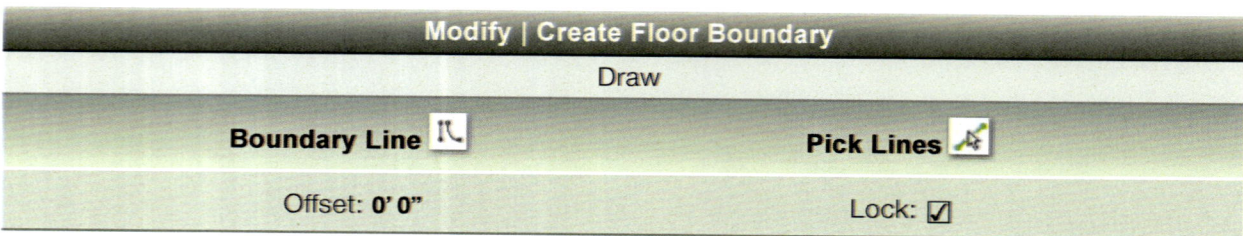

6. Pick the reference planes *Walk - West*, *Walk - South*, *Walk - East*, and *Porch - South* to create four boundary lines. Make sure they're locked to their respective reference planes.

7. Use **Trim/Extend to Corner** to clean up the boundary lines. Your boundary should appear as illustrated below.

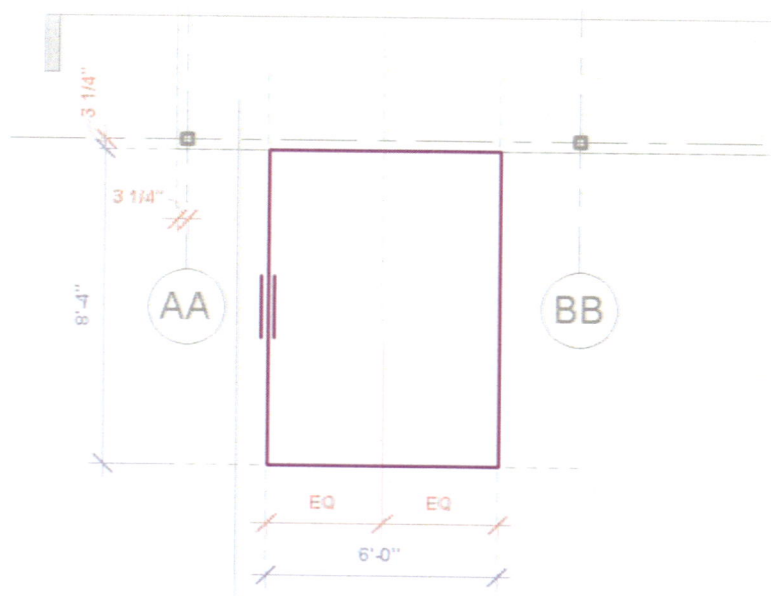

8. When done, click the **Finish Edit Mode** button ✓

Split Section Marker

In the following steps you will split the section marker *Family-Stairs-Porch (Long)* to create an offset – or "jog" – that will include the porch steps and walkway as part of the section.

9. Select the section marker for *Family-Stairs-Porch (Long)*.

Tab	Panel	Tool Button
	Modify	Views	
Modify	Section	Split Segment

10. **Split** the section marker, and adjust the lower segment as illustrated below.

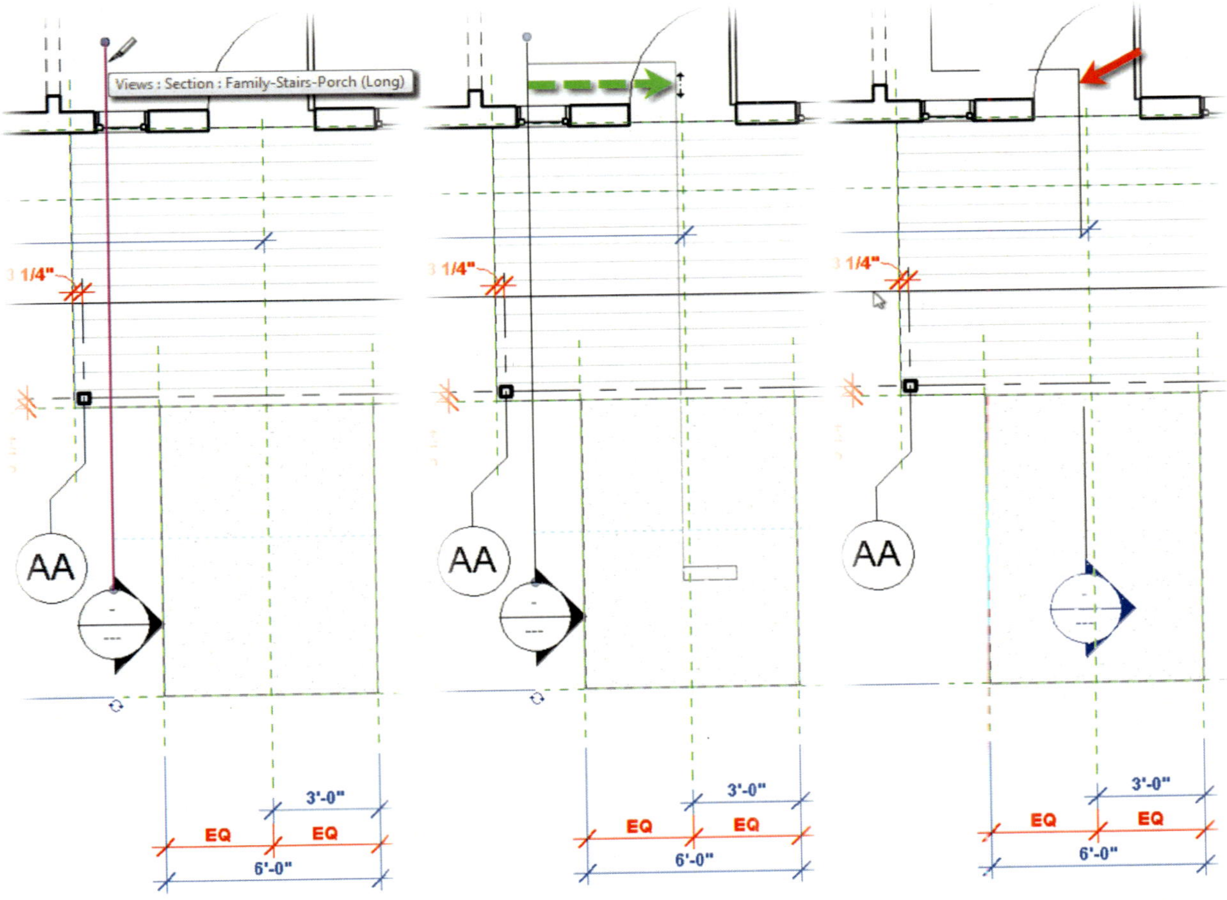

1. Segment Split Location   2. Move Lower Segment   3. Completed

 Consider adjusting the section head down and away from the concrete slab.

11. Open the section view *Family-Stairs-Porch (Long)* to examine the changes.

12. Adjust the right edge of the crop region and level 2D extents as necessary to expose the entire slab previously created. The porch area of your edited section view should appear as illustrated below.

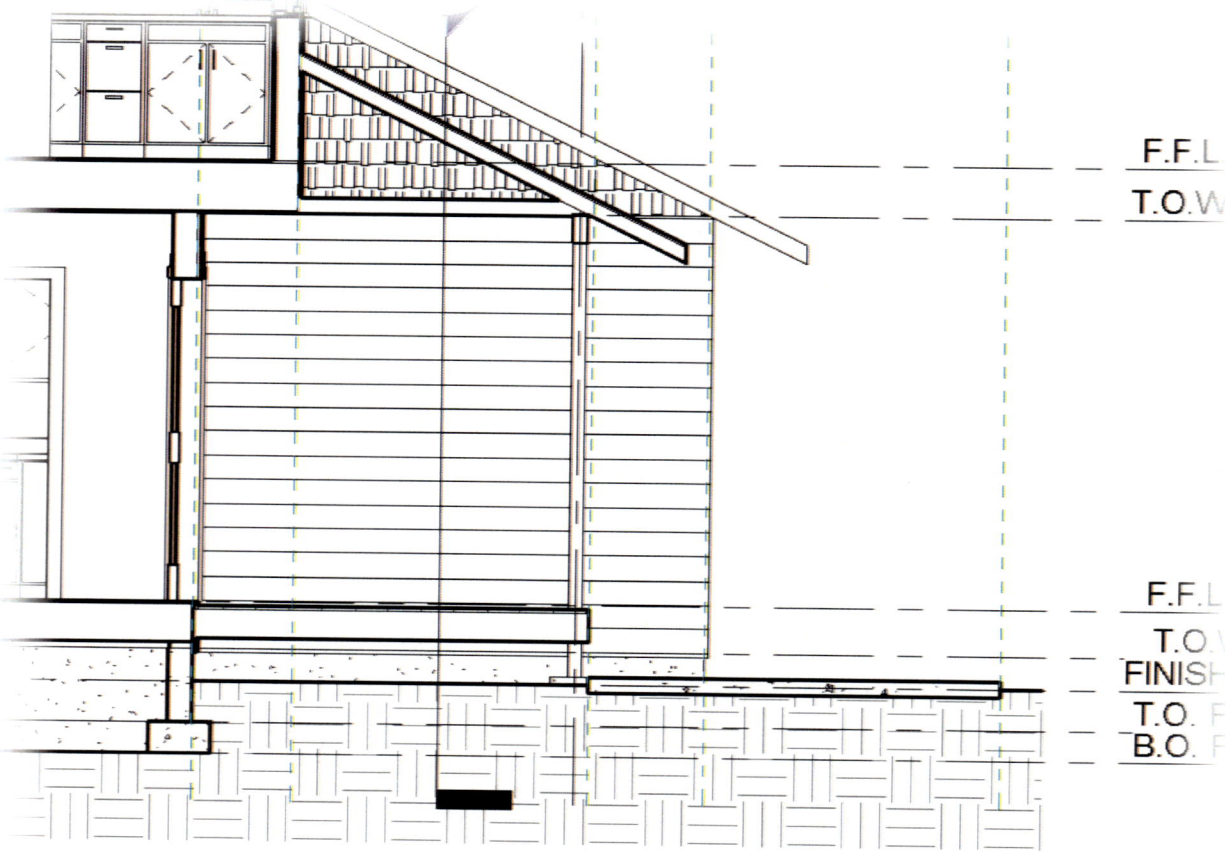

Family-Stairs-Porch (Long) - Crop & Level Extents Adjusted

13. Use the **Measure Between Two References** tool to measure from the top of the porch deck to the top of the walkway slab. The result should be *1' 5"*. If not, correct this before moving on to the next steps.

   Hint: the walkway slab should be 2" above the **FINISH GRADE** level, and the porch deck should be 1" below the *F.F.L. 1st FLR* level.

 When using the measure tool **Measure Between Two References**, the tool snaps to *points*, not *planes* as does the **Aligned Dimension** tool. Therefore by default, the tool will measure a straight, non-orthogonal line between two points. However, you can override this by pressing **[shift]** before picking the second point of the measurement.

EXERCISE 11.1: ENTRY STAIRS

Porch Stairs

Create a New Stair Type

 Make sure you duplicated the correct stair type, and modify *only* those properties shown.

1. In the Project Browser, navigate to the *Families* section and expand the following tree:

    Families → Stairs → Stair

2. **Double-click** on the family *7" max riser 11" tread* to open the Type Properties dialog box.
3. Click **Duplicate...**, and enter **Porch Steps** for the name.
4. Edit the properties listed in the table below. *Properties not listed should not be changed!*

Stair Type Properties: Porch Steps

Parameter	Value	Comment
Calculation Rules		
Minimum Tread Depth	1' 3 1/2"	
Construction		
Function	**Exterior**	
Materials & Finishes		
Tread Material	**Flooring, Composite Decking**	
Riser Material	**Siding, Wood, Horizontal, 6" - Beige**	
Stringer Material	**Trim**	
Treads		
Tread Thickness	0' 0 15/16"	Thickness of composite decking
Nosing Length	0' 0 1/2"	
Nosing Profile	**Default**	
Risers		
End with Riser	**Clear checkbox**	Ends with tread
Riser Thickness	0' 0 5/16"	
Stringers		
Trim Stringers at Top	**Match Level**	Cut off at porch deck level
Middle Stringers	2	
Stringer Thickness	0' 2"	
Stringer Height	0' 9 1/2"	

339

CHAPTER 11: STAIRS & RAILINGS

Model the Porch Stairs

5. Open the floor plan view *W-1st Floor - Constraints*.

Stair by Sketch			
Tab	Panel	Split Button ▼	Tool Button
Architecture	Circulation	Stair	Stair by Sketch

Properties	
Type: **Porch Steps**	
Base Level:	**FINISH GRADE**
Base Offset:	**0' 2"**
Top Level:	**F.F.L. 1st FLR**
Top Offset:	**-0' 1"**
Multistory Top Level:	**None**
Up Text:	**UP**
Up Label:	☑
Up Arrow:	☑
Show Up arrow in all views:	☑
Width:	**5' 5"**
Desired Number of Risers:	**3**
Actual Tread Depth:	**1' 3 1/2"**

Modify	Create Stairs Sketch			
Mode	Draw	Work Plane	Tools
Run	Line ╱	N/A	N/A

 Be sure to select the correct stair type before sketching.

6. Referring to the illustrations on the following page, start sketching on the *Entry CL* reference plane in an upward direction over the concrete walkway. Continue to sketch until the on-screen feedback reads *3 RISERS CREATED, 1 REMAINING*. If the temporary dimension for the run length reads **2' 7"** then click to complete the run; otherwise, enter **2' 7"** into the listening dimension.

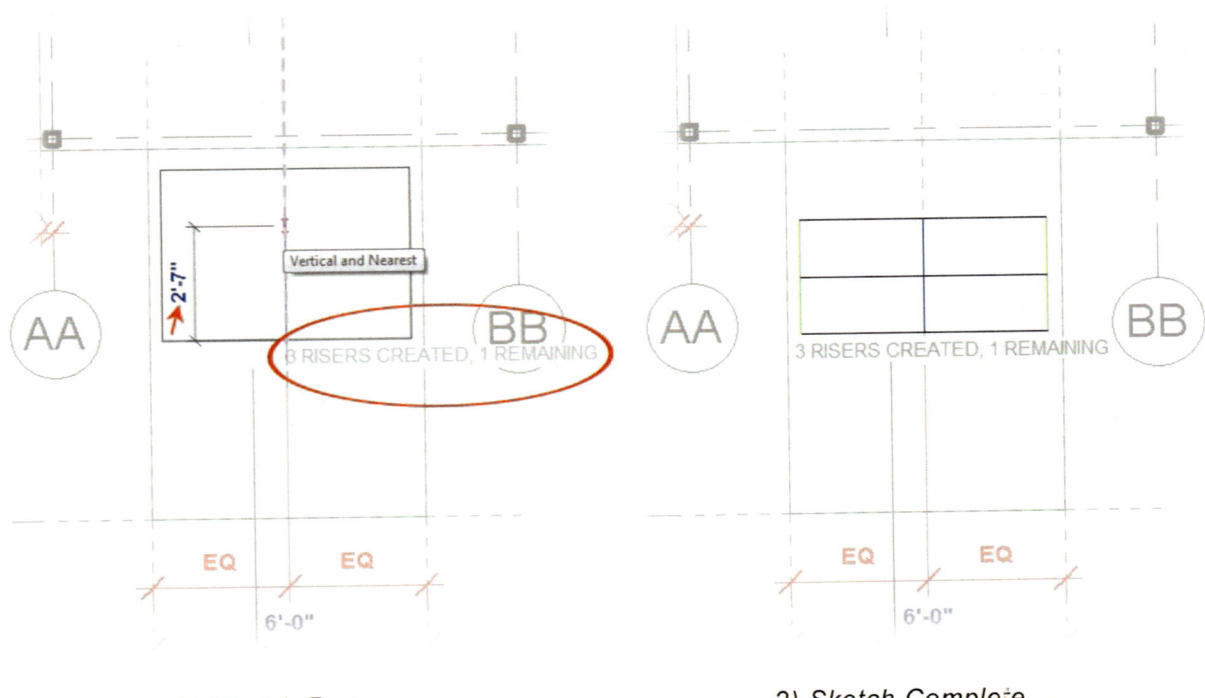

1) Sketch Run 　　　　　　*2) Sketch Complete*

7. When done, click the **Finish Edit Mode** button ✓.

8. Close the warning regarding the desired vs. actual number of risers.

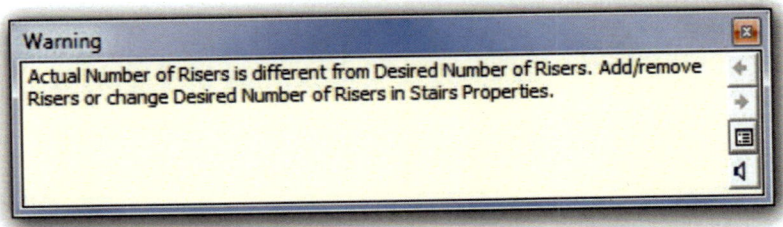

 Due to the way Revit uses rules to construct stairs when using the *Stair by Sketch* tool, the desired configuration of the porch steps combined with the stair type properties will generate this warning. A detailed explanation of the cause is beyond the scope of this exercise. Alternately, using the *Stair by Component* tool could help prevent this warning.

CHAPTER 11: STAIRS & RAILINGS

Position & Constrain the Stairs

9. **Align** and **Lock** the north edge of the stair to the reference plane *Porch - South* as illustrated below.

 Be sure to align the stair to the *reference plane*, and <u>not</u> the porch-deck floor element.

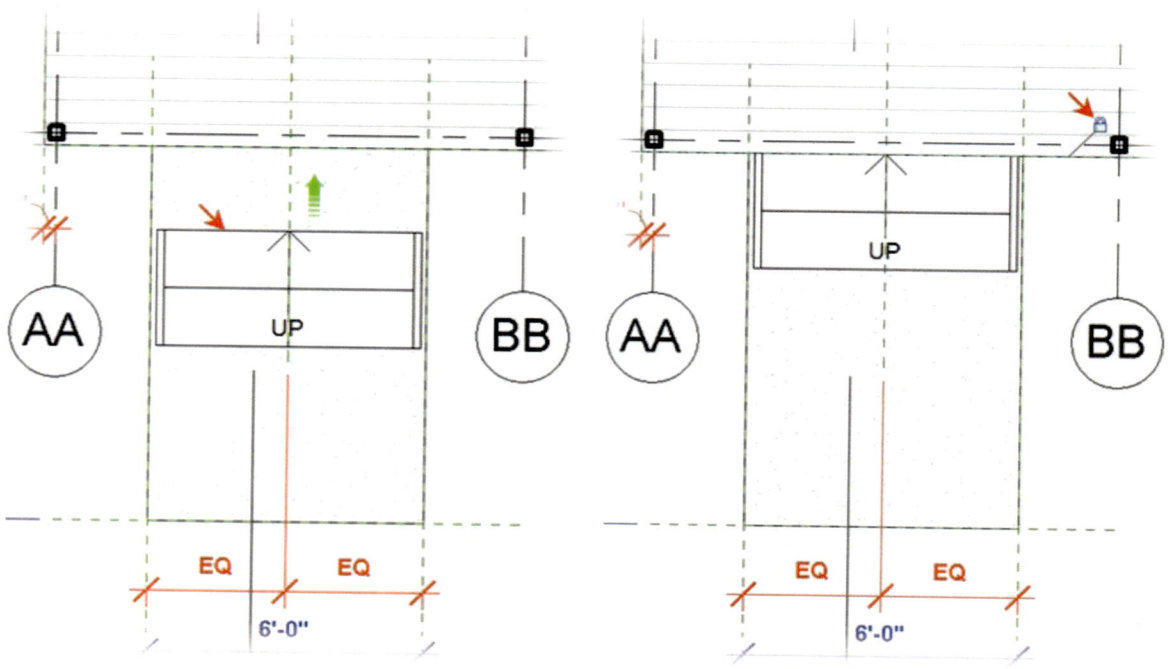

1. Align Stair Edge to Reference Plane   2. Constrain Alignment

10. Open the default {3D} view. The porch steps should appear as illustrated below.

11. Open the floor plan view *W-1st Floor - Constraints*.

12. Select the porch stair, and click **Edit Sketch** in the Contextual Ribbon tab.

13. Dimension the outer boundaries of the stair sketch to the *Walk - West* and *Walk - East* reference planes as illustrated on the following page. **Lock** these dimensions.

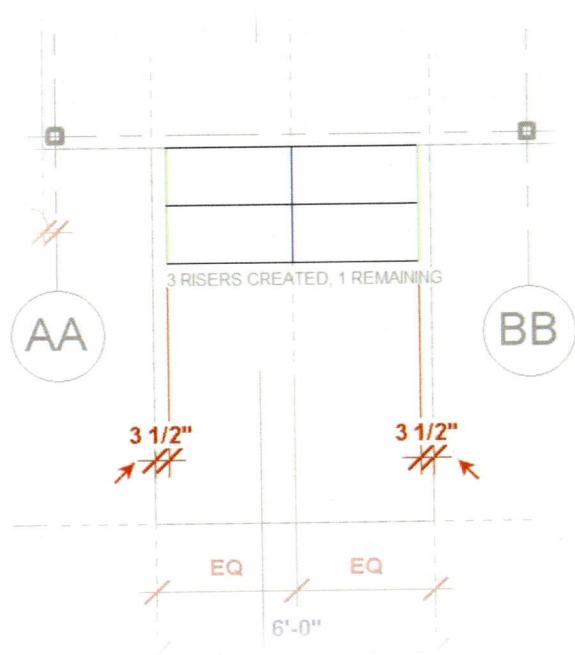

14. When done, click **Finish Edit Mode** ✓

 When the intent is to constrain the *location* of a stair element, then constrain the references of the *completed stair element*. When the intent is to *flex* the stair geometry through relationships, then constrain the *sketch lines*.

15. Test the constraints:

   a) Move the *Walk - East* and *Walk - West* reference planes left/right. The stair and concrete walk should flex in width and remain centered on the *Entry CL* reference plane.

   b) Unpin and move *Grid 1* up/down; the stair should *move* north/south, and the concrete walk should *flex* with the south edge of the porch deck.

   c) Remember to return the reference planes and grid back to their original positions and re-pin the grid.

Garage Stairs

New Stair Type

 Make sure you duplicate the correct stair type, and modify *only* those properties shown.

1. In the Project Browser, navigate to the *Families* section and expand the following tree:

    Families → Stairs → Stair

2. Open the Type Properties for *Porch Steps*.
3. Click **Duplicate...**, enter **Garage Steps** for the name, then edit the following properties.

Stair Type Properties: Garage Steps

Parameter	Value	Comment
Calculation Rules		
Minimum Tread Depth	0' 11"	
Materials and Finishes		
Tread Material	**Softwood, Lumber**	
Stringer Material	**Softwood, Lumber**	
Treads		
Tread Thickness	0' 1 1/2"	
Nosing Length	0' 0"	
Risers		
Riser Type	**None**	Open riser
Stringers		
Right Stringer	**Open**	
Left Stringer	**Open**	
Middle Stringer	1	
Stringer Thickness	0' 1 1/2"	
Stringer Height	1' 6"	
Open Stringer Offset	0' 1"	
Stringer Carriage Height	1' 0"	

Model the Garage Stairs

4. Open the floor plan view *W-1st Floor - Constraints*.

Stair by Sketch			
Tab	Panel	Split Button ▼	Tool Button
Architecture	Circulation	Stair	Stair by Sketch

Properties	
Type:	**Garage Steps**
Base Level:	**FINISH GRADE**
Base Offset:	**0' 4"**
Top Level:	**F.F.L. 1st FLR**
Top Offset:	**-0' 5 3/8"**
Multistory Top Level:	**None**
Up Text:	**UP**
Up Label:	☑
Up Arrow:	☑
Show Up arrow in all views:	☑
Width:	**3' 6"**
Actual Tread Depth:	**0' 11"**

Modify	Create Stairs Sketch			
Mode	Draw	Work Plane	Tools
Run	Line 	N/A	Railing Type

5. After clicking the **Railing Type** button, select **None** from the Railing dialog box.

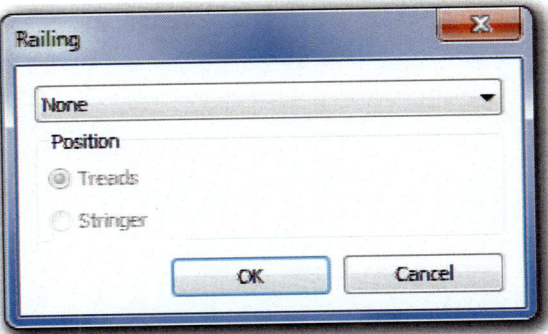

6. Sketching in an upward direction over the garage slab, sketch until the on-screen feedback reads *3 RISERS CREATED, 0 REMAINING* as illustrated on the following page. Don't worry about exact location at this time.

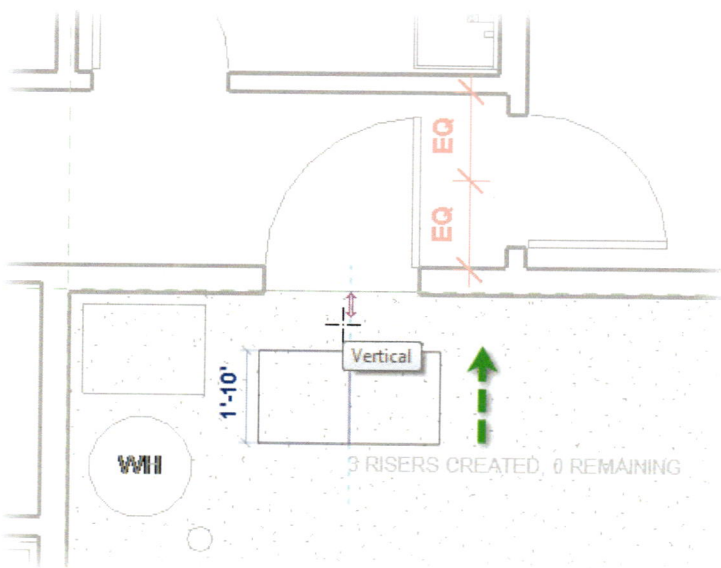

7. When done, click **Finish Edit Mode** ✓

Constrain the Garage Stairs

8. **Align** and **lock** the stair element as follows (refer to illustration below):

   a) Centerline of stair *to* centerline of interior garage door.

   b) End reference of stair (top edge in plan view) to reference plane *Int-Garage-North*

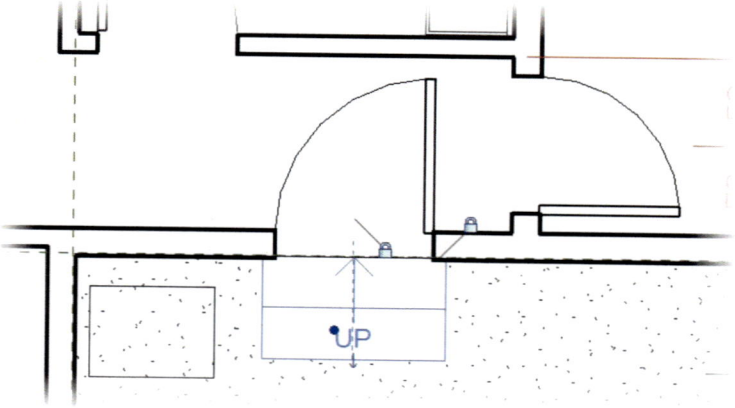

 When creating alignment constraints between a door and a stair element, there is a priority that determines which element can be moved. In this case, moving the stair will drive the location of the door. However, the door cannot drive the location of the stair. Therefore, to move the pair, you must move the stair element.

9. Make sure the section marker for *W-Laundry-Garage (Long)* cuts through the garage steps. If not, move it now, then open the section view *W-Laundry-Garage (Long)*. Zoom in around the steps. Your view should appear as illustrated below.

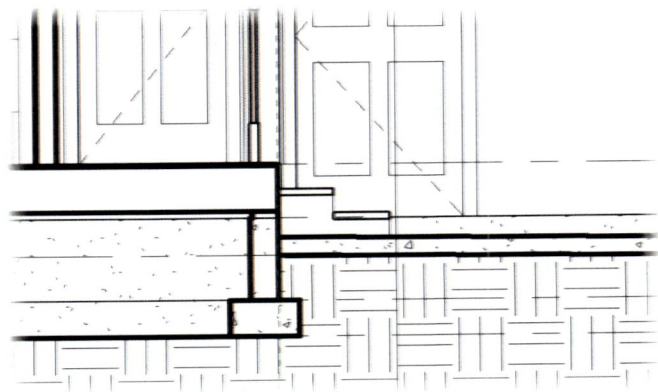

10. Duplicate the default *{3D}* view, and rename it **3D Section - Garage**.

11. Using either of the methods you previously learned, create a 3D section view of the garage and adjust it so you can see the garage steps similar to that illustrated below.

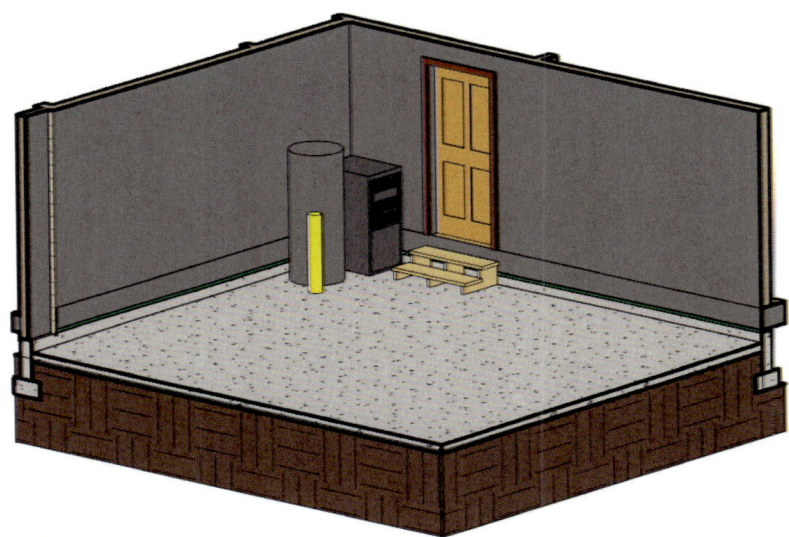

12. Select the bollard post, water heater, and furnace, then set the following properties:

    a) *Level:* **FINISH GRADE**

    b) *Offset:* **0' 4"**

 There are many design, as well as code considerations that affect the installation of water heaters and furnaces. The previous steps of placing these elements on the garage slab is intended for simplification, not as a final configuration. Furthermore, the bollard post would extend below the slab and be embedded in concrete.

CHAPTER 11: STAIRS & RAILINGS

Patio Stairs

The purpose of the following exercise steps is to demonstrate working with a monolithic stair type. Actual construction methods for the patio stairs would likely vary somewhat. The ideal method for modeling these steps involves the topic of in-place families, and is beyond the scope of this exercise.

Patio Slab

Prior to creating the steps at the rear entrance, we'll add a small patio slab in the backyard.

1. Open the floor plan view *W-1st Floor - Constraints*.

2. Add reference planes as as illustrated below, and lay out a 24' x 10' patio slab footprint, centered on the sliding glass door. *Note that the dimensions shown in blue are for reference only. You may add them if you wish.*

3. Name the reference planes **Patio - West**, **Patio - North**, and **Patio - East**.

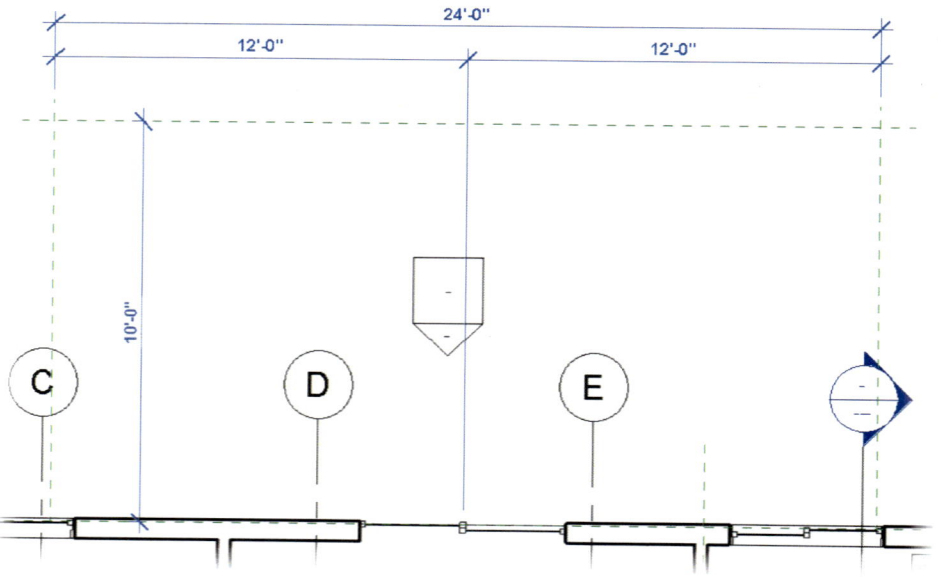

(Dimensions shown in blue are for reference only)

		Floor	
Tab	Panel	Split Button ▼	Tool Button
Architecture	Build	Floor	Floor: Architectural

Properties
Type: **Slab on Grade - 4" Concrete**

Level: **FINISH GRADE**

Height Offset From Level: **0' 2"**

EXERCISE 11.1: ENTRY STAIRS

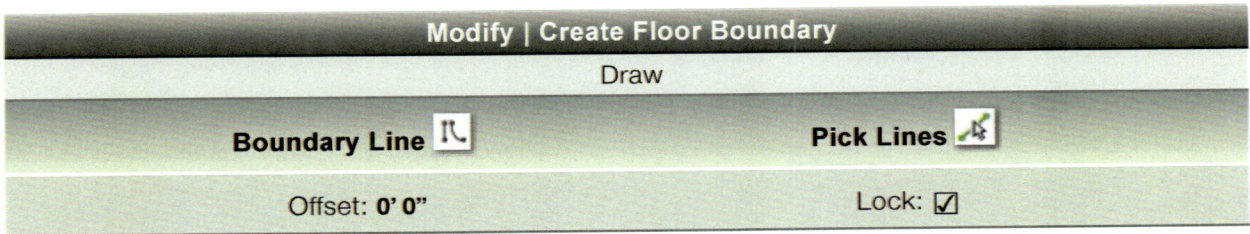

4. Pick the three reference planes that define the patio layout, and the *Ext-North* reference plane that defines the north side of the house footprint.

5. Use **Trim/Extend to Corner** to clean up the boundary lines.

6. When done, click the **Finish Edit Mode** button ✓

7. Select the *North* exterior elevation marker *arrowhead*, then move the view's clipping plane (click-drag) up until it is clear of the patio slab as illustrated below.

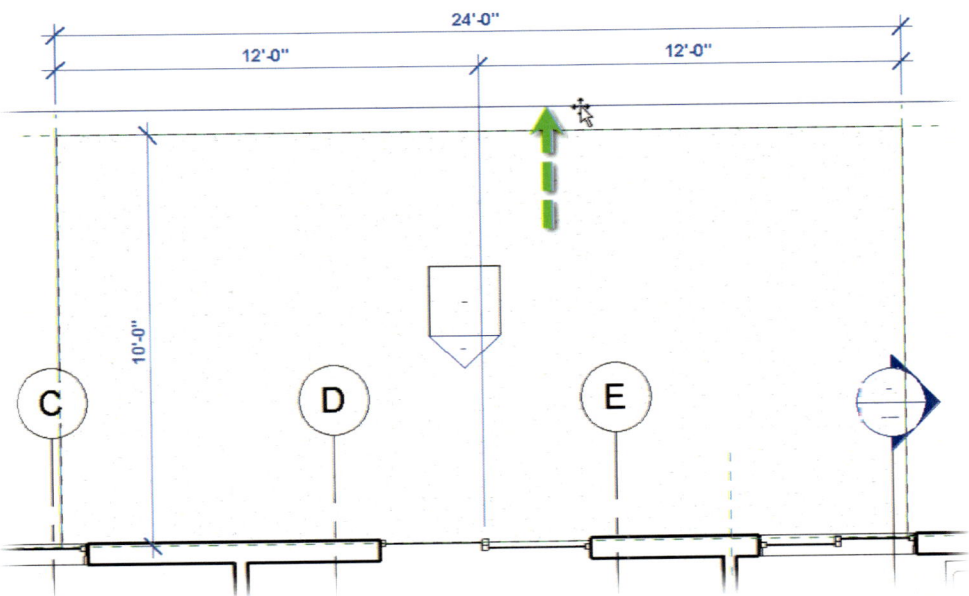

New Stair Type

8. In the Project Browser, navigate to the *Families* section and expand the following tree:

    Families → Stairs → Stair

9. Open the Type Properties for *Monolithic Stair*.

10. Click **Duplicate...**, enter **Patio Steps** for the name, then edit the following properties.

 Make sure you duplicate the correct stair type, and modify *only* those properties shown.

CHAPTER 11: STAIRS & RAILINGS

Stair Type Properties: Patio Steps

Parameter	Value	Comment
Construction		
Function	**Exterior**	
Materials and Finishes		
Monolithic Material	**Concrete, Cast-in-Place Steps**	Create new material (see below)
Treads		
Tread Thickness	**0' 0"**	
Nosing Length	**0' 0"**	
Nosing Profile	**Default**	
Risers		
Riser Type	**Straight**	
Stringers		
Trim Stringers at Top	**Match Landing Stringer**	
Landing Carriage Height	**1' 5"**	Results in a full thickness at landing

New Stair Material: Concrete - Cast-in-Place Steps

Property	Value
Existing Material to Duplicate	**Concrete, Cast-in-Place gray**
New Material Name	**Concrete, Cast-in-Place Steps**
Identity Tab	
Description	**MONOLITHIC CONCRETE STEPS**

Model the Patio Stairs

11. Open the floor plan view *W-1st Floor - Constraints*.

Stair by Sketch			
Tab	Panel	Split Button ▼	Tool Button
Architecture	**Circulation**	**Stair**	**Stair by Sketch**

Properties	
Type: **Patio Steps**	
Base Level:	**FINISH GRADE**
Base Offset:	**0' 2"**
Top Level:	**F.F.L. 1st FLR**
Top Offset:	**-0' 1"**
Multistory Top Level:	**None**
Up Text:	**UP**
Up Label:	☑
Up Arrow:	☑
Show Up arrow in all views:	☑
Width:	**7' 0"**
Actual Tread Depth:	**1' 0"**

Modify	Create Stairs Sketch			
Mode	Draw	Work Plane	Tools
Run	**Line** /	**N/A**	**Railing Type**

12. Select **None** from the Railing Type dialog box.

13. Sketching in a downward direction over the patio slab, sketch until the on-screen feedback reads *4 RISERS CREATED, 0 REMAINING* as illustrated below. Don't worry about exact location at this time, just start in the vicinity of the north edge of the slab.

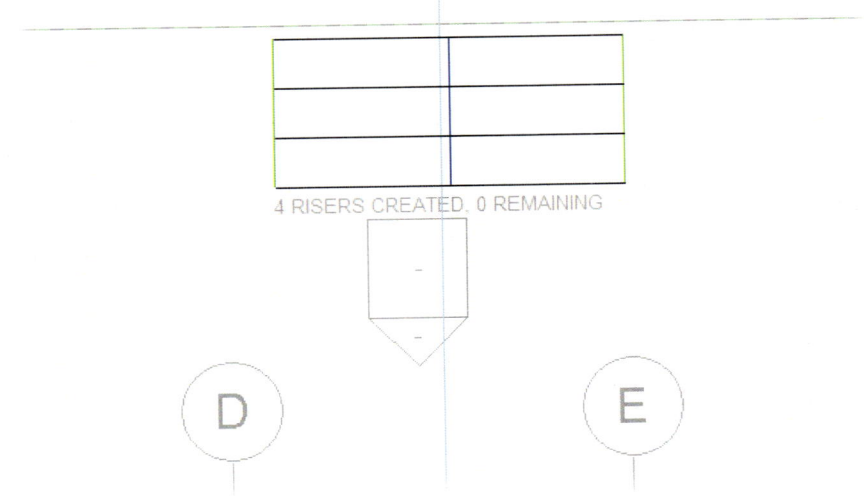

14. Select the end riser sketch line, and adjust its position using temporary dimensions as illustrated below. This will create a small landing at the top of the steps.

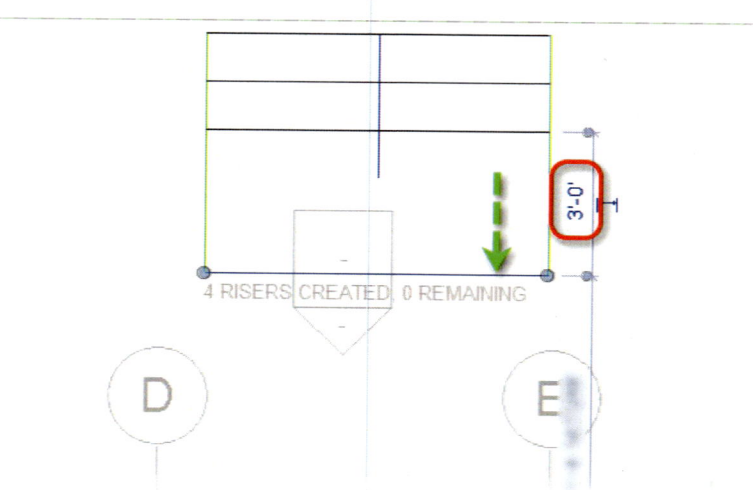

15. When done, click **Finish Edit Mode**

> Actual construction methods would likely dictate that the monolithic stair be placed on or below grade, and then the patio slab be poured around it. However, due to the limitations of the stair tool, the patio stair has been placed on top of the slab. To model a stair that represents the construction method mentioned above would require an in-place family, which is beyond the scope of this exercise.

16. **Align/Lock** the stair element as follows. Additionally refer to the illustration below.

   a) Centerline of stair *to* centerline of sliding glass door.

   b) South reference of stair *to* the *Ext-North* reference plane that defines the north side of the house footprint.

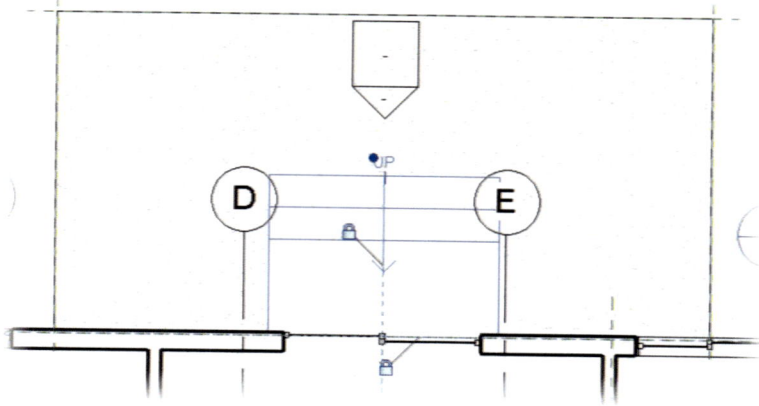

Patio Steps Aligned

17. Open the default *{3D}* view to examine your work. Your patio steps should appear as illustrated below.

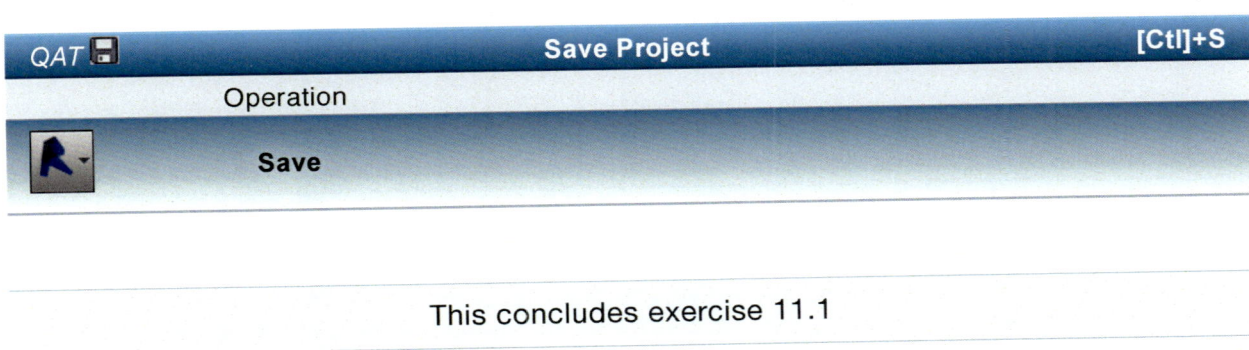

This concludes exercise 11.1

Exercise 11.2: Interior Stairs

QAT	Open Project		[Ctl]+O
Operation	Option		File Name
Open ▶	Project		BIMHOUSE-EX11-1.rvt

	Save As (Project)	
Operation	Option	File Name
Save As ▶	Project	BIMHOUSE-EX11-2.rvt

Floor Opening

In the following steps we'll cut an opening for the stairway in the floor/ceiling assembly. This will leave the floor layers exposed within the opening. To correct this, we'll replace the 2nd floor stairwell walls with a new wall type that has the interior GWB finish layer unlocked at its base. We'll then apply a negative *Base Extension Distance* to the 2nd floor walls in the stairwell, which will extend the GWB down over the face of the floor opening and create a continuous GWB surface from the base of the 1st floor up to the top of the 2nd floor.

Split the Walls Around the Stairway

Prior to applying the base extension described above, we need to split the walls around the stairway opening. This will confine the extension of the GWB finish layer within the stair opening.

After going through all of the steps consisting of splitting walls, cutting the floor / ceiling openings, and then applying base extension distance to the 2nd floor walls, you may question the order in which the steps are performed. It may seem reasonable that the walls could be split after creating the opening. However, to create the opening you will associate boundary lines with the walls that define the stairwell. If you associate the boundary with a wall, and then later split the wall, there is no way to control which one of the new wall segments will be associated with the boundary line. Therefore, knowing that a wall needs to be split and splitting it ahead of time allows us to be deliberate when associating a boundary line to a wall.

1. Open the floor plan view **W-2nd Floor - Constraints**, and set the *Underlay* property to **None**.

Failure to set *Underlay* to **None** may result in split walls on the 1st floor!

2. **Split** the walls shown in the illustration below at the locations specified by red arrows. Note that split location 1 is approximate. Anywhere on, or slightly north of the grid line is acceptable.

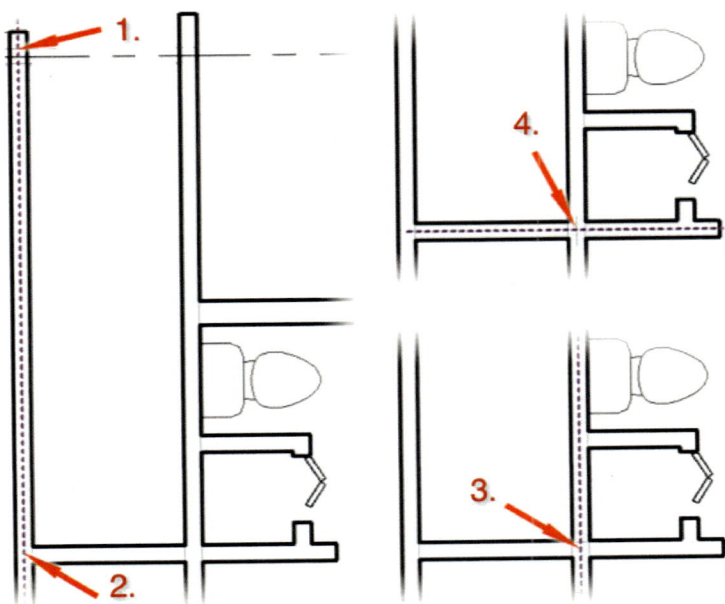

3. Set *Underlay* to **F.F.L. 1st FLR**.

4. **Align** and **Lock** the north end of the wall at the east side of the stairway *to* the *core face* of the 1st floor wall below as shown in the following illustration.

 Make sure to double-check the status bar when picking the wall!

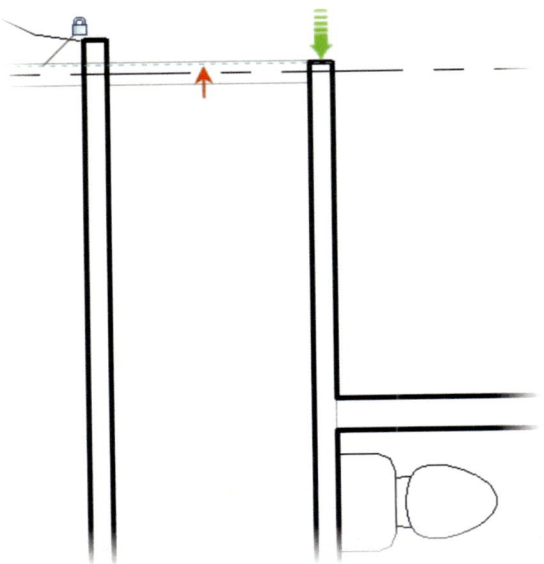

5. Use **Wall Joins** to configure the wall join conditions as illustrated below.

 Although there's only one join configuration for the end-to-end wall join near the bedroom door, it may still require that you select it and click **Next** to get the join to clean up.

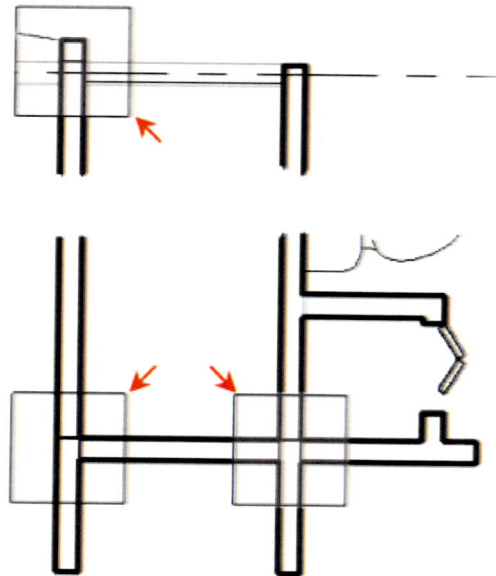

6. Select the short wall at the south side of the stairway and verify it's oriented such that the exterior side is facing away from the stairway. If not, click on the flip arrow to reorient it.

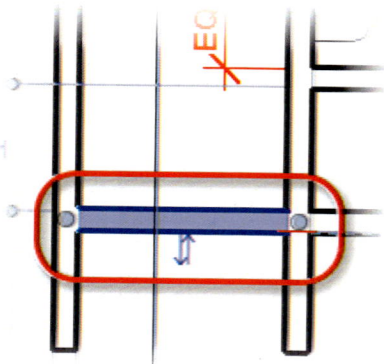

Cut the Opening

 Be sure that your walls have been properly split before proceeding. The openings you are about to create will be associated to these walls. Splitting the walls after creating the opening creates the potential for dissociating the opening boundaries from these walls.

7. Select the floor element at the 2nd floor *(TJI 11 7/8" - 3/4"T&G)*, and click **Edit Boundary** in the Contextual Ribbon tab.

Remember that the default behavior for selecting an element requires clicking on an *edge*. This can be challenging when the element's edges are all masked by other elements, as is the case with this floor. Enabling **Select Elements by Face** will make it easier to select the floor.

Modify | Floors > Edit Boundary	
Draw	
Boundary Line	**Pick Walls**
Offset: 0' 0"	Extend into wall (to core): ☑

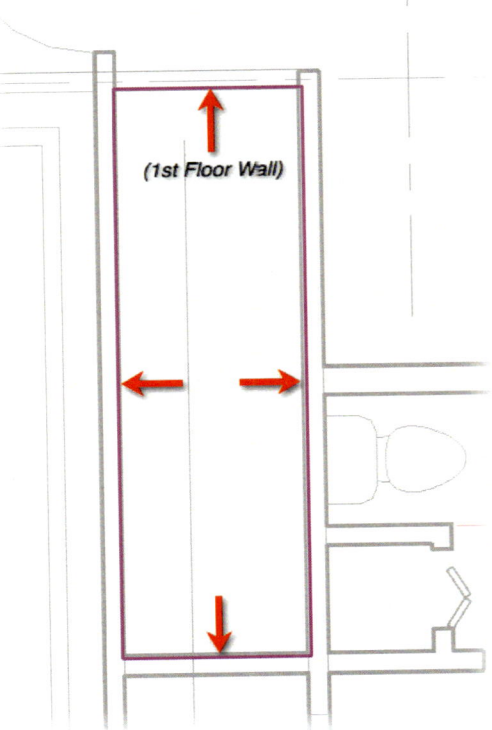

8. Pick the four walls as illustrated to the right.
9. Use **Trim/Extend to Corner** as needed to clean up the boundary lines.
10. When done, click **Finish Edit Mode**
11. Answer **YES** when prompted to cut the overlapping geometry from the walls.
12. Open any one of the section views that cuts through the stairway. Notice that the floor has been cut, but the ceiling element still covers the opening.

13. With the section view still open, select the ceiling *(GWB - 1/2")*, and click **Edit Boundary** in the Contextual Ribbon tab.
14. When the Go To View dialog box appears, select *Floor Plan: W-2nd Floor - Constraints*, then click **Open View**.

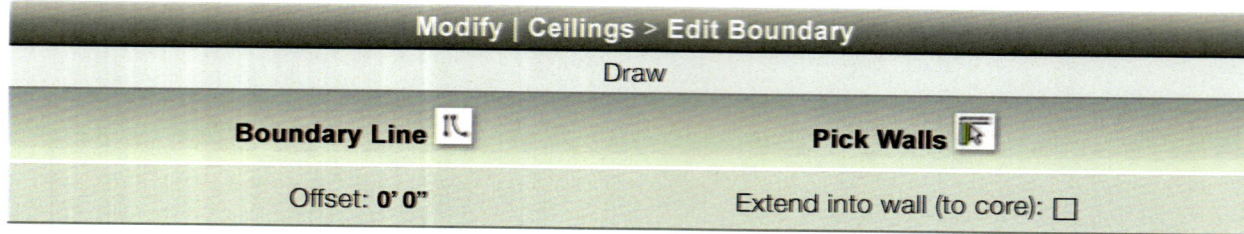

15. Referring to the illustration below,

    a) Add the new boundary line indicated.
    b) Exit the *Pick Walls* tool.
    c) **Delete** the boundary line indicated.
    d) Use **Trim/Extend to Corner** to clean up the boundary lines indicated.

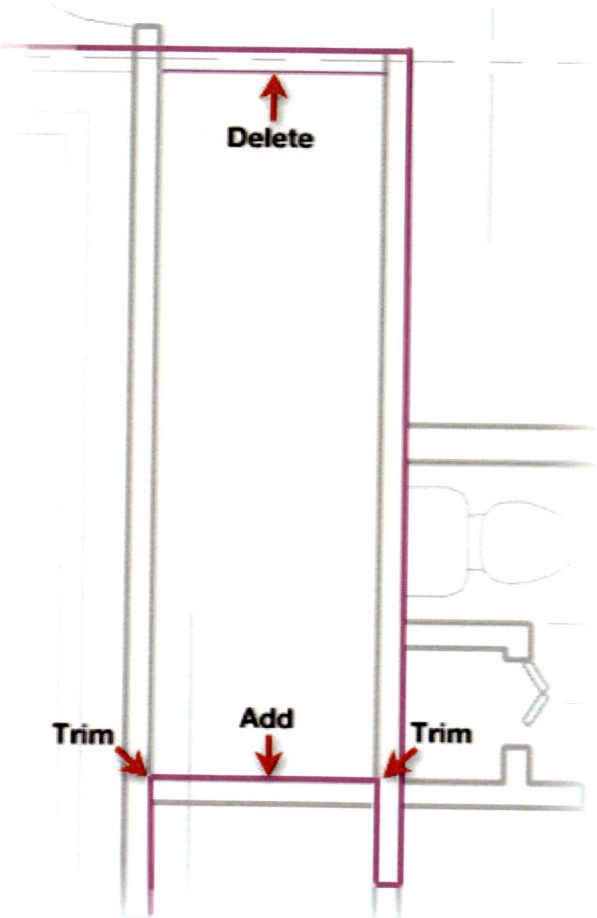

16. When done, click **Finish Edit Mode** ✓
17. Open the section view *Family-Stairs-Porch (Long)* and verify the ceiling protrudes into the opening by 1/2" as illustrated on the following page.

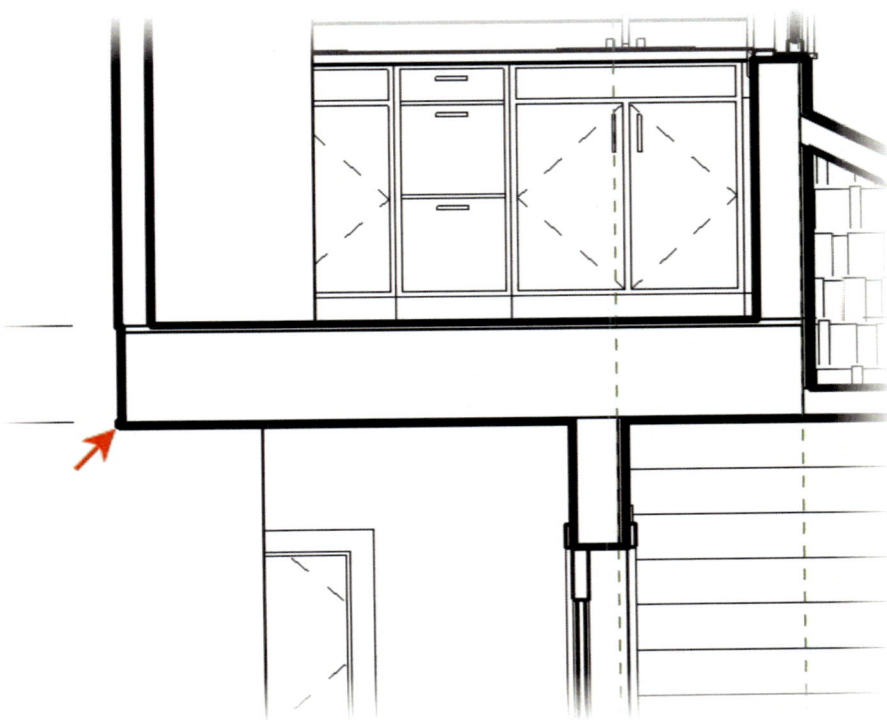

Longitudinal Section View - Stairway Opening

18. Open the section view *Living-Kitchen-Garage (Cross)* and verify the edge of the floor is recessed from the finish face of walls by 1/2" on each side as illustrated below.

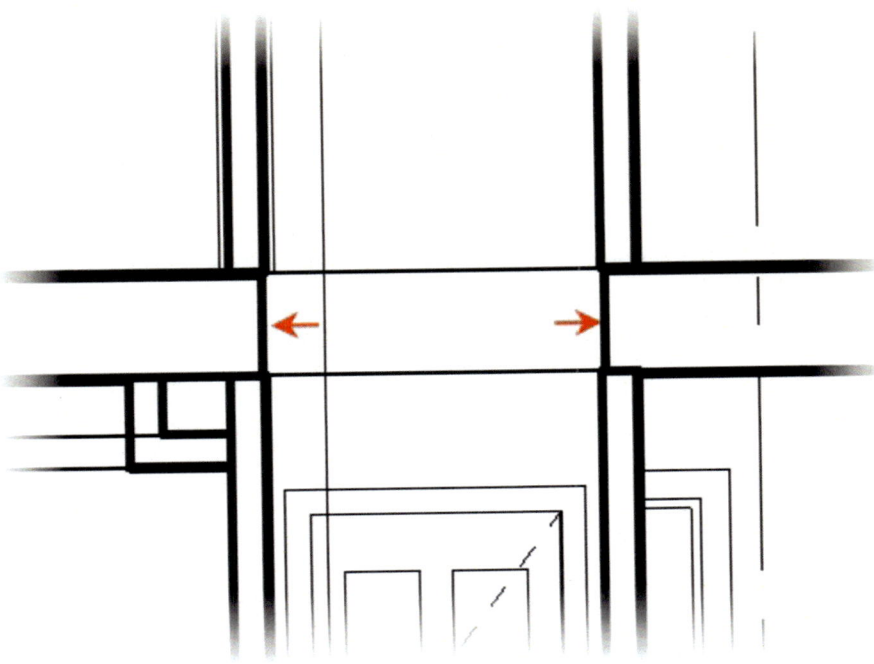

Cross Section View - Stairway Opening

1. Open the floor plan view *W-2nd Floor - Constraints*.

2. *Simultaneously* select the three walls that surround the stairway as illustrated, and verify the the *Location Line* is set to **Core Face: Interior**. If not, set it now.

3. With the three walls still selected, click **Edit Type**.

4. Click **Duplicate...** and enter **Interior - Wood 2x4 - 1/2"GWB+_+1/2"GWB(BU)** for the name.

5. Open the Edit Assembly dialog box and do the following:

    a) Open the Preview pane, and set *View:* **Section: Modify Type Attributes**.

    b) Click **Modify** in the Modify Vertical Structure pane.

    c) Zoom in on the base of the wall

    d) Pick the base of the interior finish layer, and **unlock** it as illustrated below.

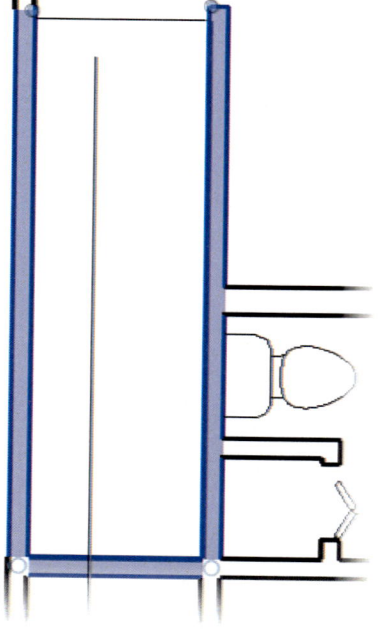

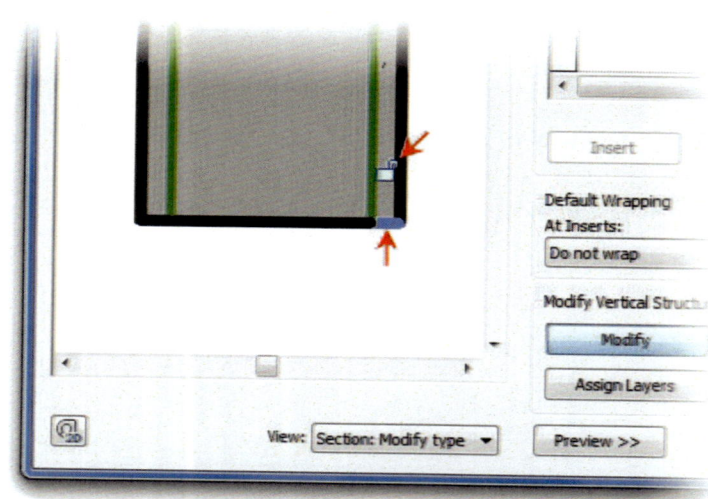

6. Click **OK** twice to close all dialog boxes and complete the wall type.

7. While all three walls are still selected, in the Properties palette set the *Base Extension Distance* to **-1' 0 5/8"** and apply the change.

8. Set *Underlay* for *W-2nd Floor - Constraints* to **None**.

9. Open the section view *Family-Stairs-Porch (Long)* verify the drywall extends down to the ceiling layer as illustrated below.

10. Use **Join Geometry** to achieve the results illustrated below.

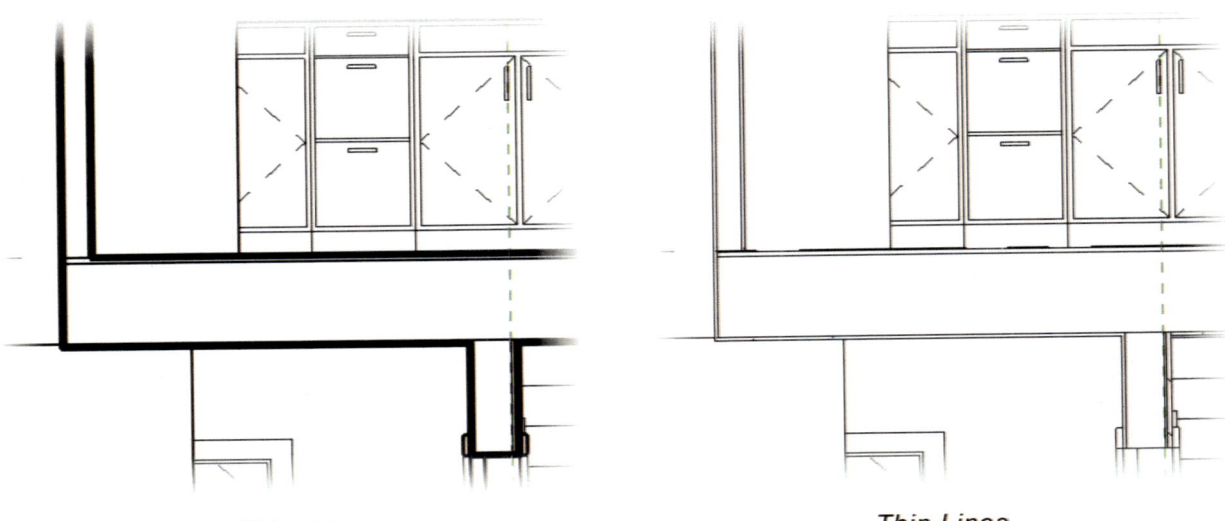

Thick Lines   Thin Lines

Longitudinal Section View - Wall Base Extension - Geometry Joined

11. Open the section view *Living-Kitchen-Garage (Cross)* and verify the drywall extends down to the top of the 1st floor walls as illustrated below.

12. Use **Join Geometry** to achieve the results illustrated below.

Thick Lines   Thin Lines

Cross Section View - Wall Base Extension - Geometry Joined

 When joining geometry in section views, join all intersecting interior walls, ceilings, and floors.

CHAPTER 11: STAIRS & RAILINGS

Stair by Component

For the interior stairs we will explore the *Stair by Component* tool. Modeling stairs with this tool provides for better control, particularly with post-editing of a stair. However, a component stair does not respond well to constraints intended to control its width.

New Carriage Type

1. In the Project Browser, navigate *Families* → *Stairs* → *Carriage*
2. Open the Type Properties for *Carriage - 2" Width*.
3. **Duplicate** *Carriage - 2" Width* and enter **Carriage - 1 1/2" Width - Wood** for the name.
4. Edit the following properties:

Carriage Type Properties: Carriage - 1 1/2" Width - Wood

Parameter	Value	Comment
Materials and Finishes		
Material	Softwood, Lumber	
Dimensions		
Structural Depth On Run	0' 5"	
Width	0' 1 1/2"	

New Run (Tread / Riser) Type

1. In the Project Browser, navigate *Families* → *Stairs* → *Non-Monolithic Run*
2. Open the Type Properties for *2" Tread 1" Nosing 1/4" Riser*.
3. **Duplicate** *2" Tread 1" Nosing 1/4" Riser* and enter **3/4" Tread 1/2" Straight Riser** for the name.
4. Edit the following properties:

Run Type Properties: 3/4" Tread 1/2" Straight Riser

Parameter	Value	Comment
Materials and Finishes		
Tread Material	Plywood, Sheathing	
Riser Material	Plywood, Sheathing	
Treads		
Tread Thickness	0' 0 3/4"	
Nosing Length	0' 0"	
Nosing Profile	Default	
Risers		
Riser Thickness	0' 0 1/2"	
Riser To Tread Connection	Join All Risers And Treads	

New Stair Type

1. In the Project Browser, navigate *Families* → *Stairs* → *Assembled Stair*
2. Open the Type Properties for *7" max riser 11" tread*.
3. **Duplicate** *7" max riser 11" tread* and enter **Interior Stairs** for the name.
4. Edit the following properties:

Stair Type Properties: Interior Stairs

Parameter	Value	Comment
Calculation Rules		
Maximum Riser Height	0' 7 3/4"	
Minimum Tread Depth	0' 10"	
Construction		
Run type	3/4" Tread 1/2" Straight Riser	
Landing Type	Non-monolithic landing	
Supports		
Right Support	Carriage (Open)	
Right Support Type	Carriage - 1 1/2" Width - Wood	
Right Lateral Offset	0' 0"	
Left Support	Carriage (Open)	
Left Support Type	Carriage - 1 1/2" Width - Wood	
Left Lateral Offset	0' 0"	
Middle Support	☑	
Middle Support Type	Carriage - 1 1/2" Width - Wood	
Middle Support Number	1	

Model the Interior Stairs

5. Open the floor plan view *F.F.L.1st FLR*.

Stair by Component			
Tab	Panel	Split Button ▼	Tool Button
Architecture	Circulation	Stair	Stair by Component

CHAPTER 11: STAIRS & RAILINGS

Properties	
Type: **Assembled Stair / Interior Stairs**	
Base Level:	**F.F.L. 1st FLR**
Base Offset:	**0' 0"**
Top Level:	**F.F.L. 2nd FLR**
Top Offset:	**0' 0"**

Modify | Create Stair			
Mode	Components	Work Plane	Tools
Run	**Straight**	**N/A**	**Railing Type**
Location Line: **Exterior Support Right**	Offset: **0' 0"**	Actual Run Width: **3' 6"**	Automatic Landing: ☐

6. Select **None** from the Railing Type dialog box.

7. Sketching in an upward direction within the stairway area, sketch until the on-screen feedback reads *15 RISERS CREATED, 0 REMAINING* as illustrated below. Don't worry about exact location at this time, just place it in the general vicinity.

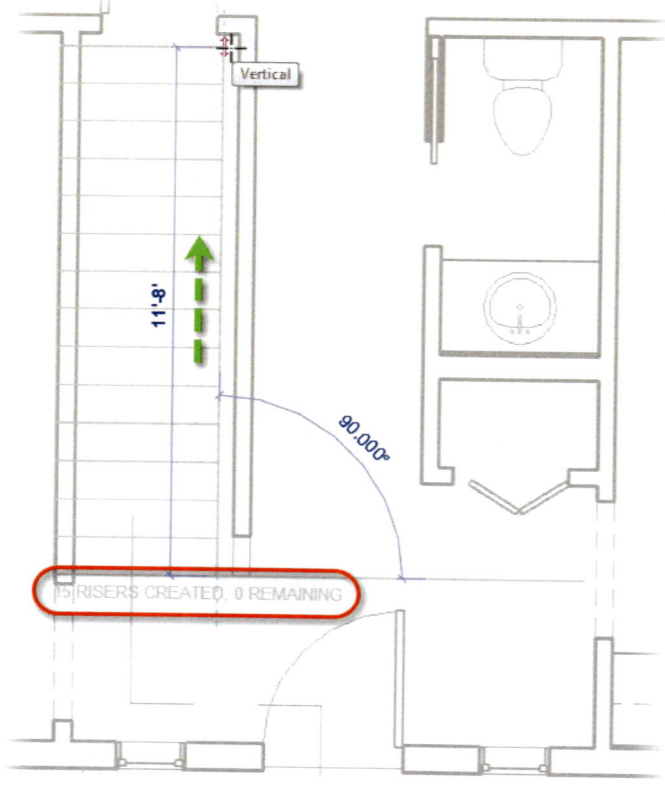

8. Click **Modify** or press **[esc]** to exit the Run tool.

9. Select the stair element.

10. In the Properties Palette, **uncheck** End with Riser. Notice the change in *Relative Top Height* when you do this. Additionally, notice the *Actual Riser Height*. This is the amount by which the *Relative Top Height* changed.

11. When done, click **Finish Edit Mode** ✓ and read the warning.

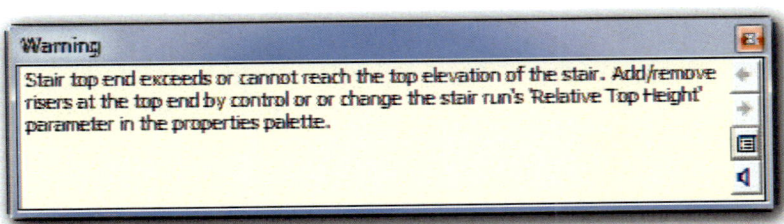

12. Close the warning and clear all selections.

13. Select the newly created stair. Notice the warning icon in the Contextual Ribbon Tab.

14. In the Properties Palette, look for the *Actual Riser Height* and enter this value as a <u>negative</u> number for the *Top Offset* property. The warning icon should disappear from the Contextual Ribbon Tab.

15. Referring to the illustrations below,

    a) **Align** and **Lock** the east edge of the stair to the <u>core face</u> of the east wall in the stairway.

    b) **Align** and **Lock** the north edge of the stair to the <u>core face</u> of the north wall in the stairway.

    c) Select the stair element, then use the drag handle on the UP text to move it down and away from the first tread.

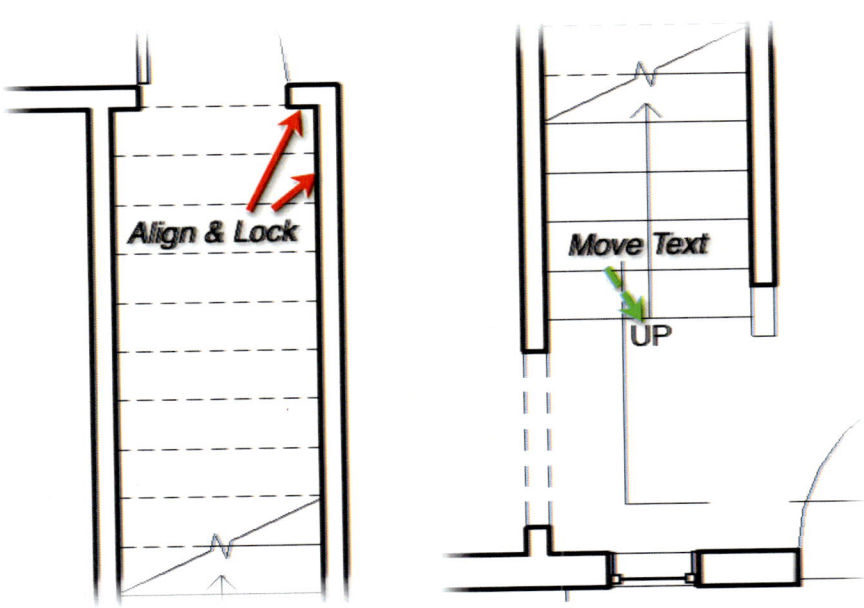

16. Open the section view *Family-Stairs-Porch (Long)*. Your stairway should appear as illustrated below.

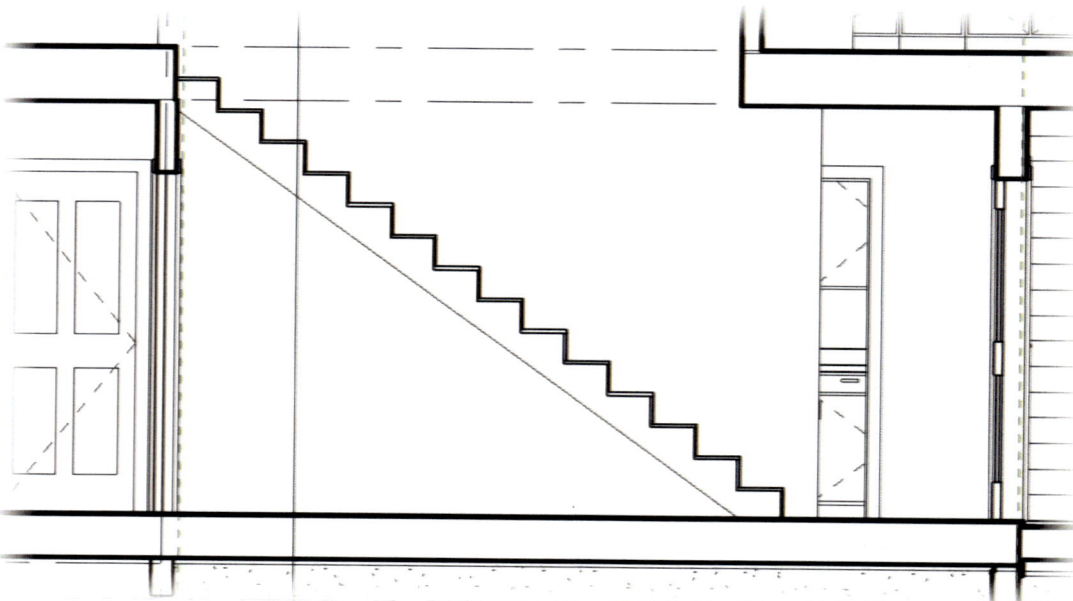

17. Open the section view *Living-Kitchen-Garage (Cross)*. Your stairway should appear as illustrated below. Note that the stair treads, risers, and outer stringers should cut through the drywall to the face of the core where indicated in the illustration.

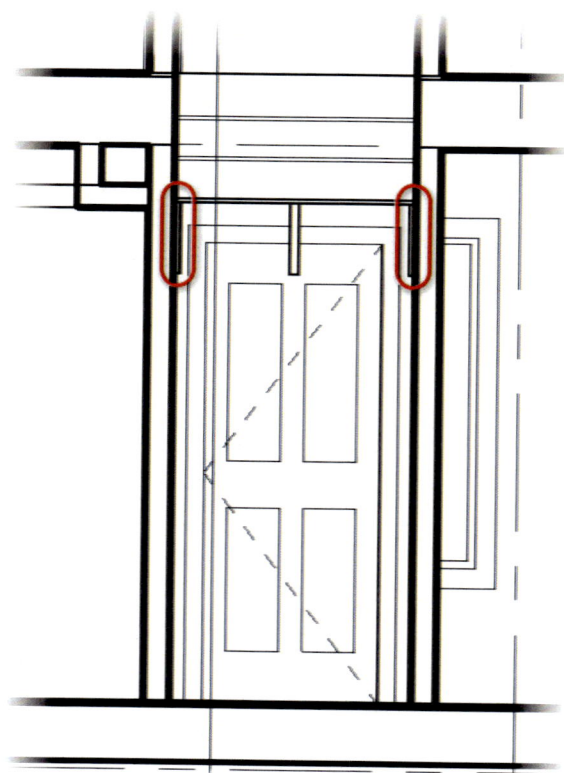

Guard Walls

Next we'll open up the wall between the stairway and the hall, and in doing so create a sloped guard wall that follows the stairs. Additionally, we'll create a low guard wall at the 2nd floor loft area. To accomplish this, we'll use the *Edit Profile* tool to modify the profile of the walls associated with the change.

Sloped Guard Wall at Stairs

1. Open the section view *Family-Stairs-Porch (Long)*.
2. Sketch a reference plane as illustrated below. Be sure to snap to the top corners of the tread nose while sketching to ensure the correct angle and elevation.
3. Name the reference plane **Stair Wall - Angled**.

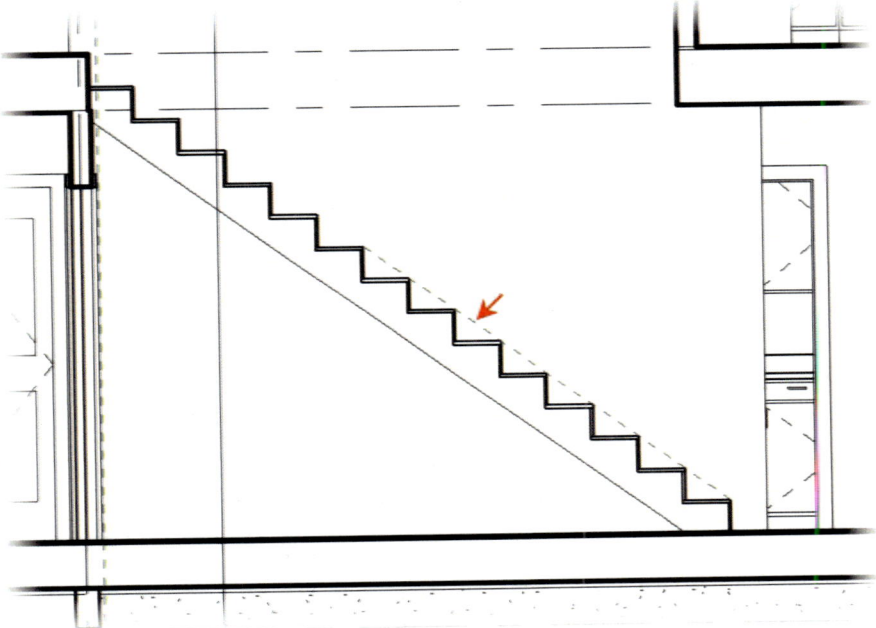

4. Select the reference plane, and **move** it *vertically* **3' 0"** as illustrated on the following page.

 Use the **Move** tool to move the reference plane vertically, *not* perpendicular to the stair slope.

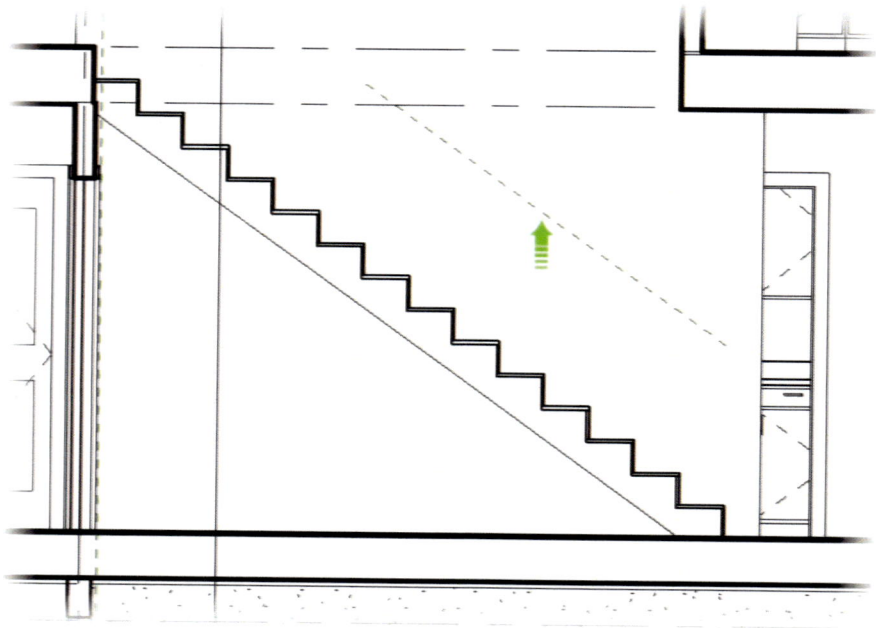

Move Reference Plane Straight Up

5. Sketch a second reference plane and position it as illustrated below. Name the reference plane **Stair Wall - Vert**.
   Note: the 6'-3" temporary dimension in the illustration is referenced to the core face of the wall.

 Make sure the lower 3D extent of the vertical reference plane extends down far enough to pass through the cut plane of 1st floor plan views (4' 0"), or it won't be visible in these views.

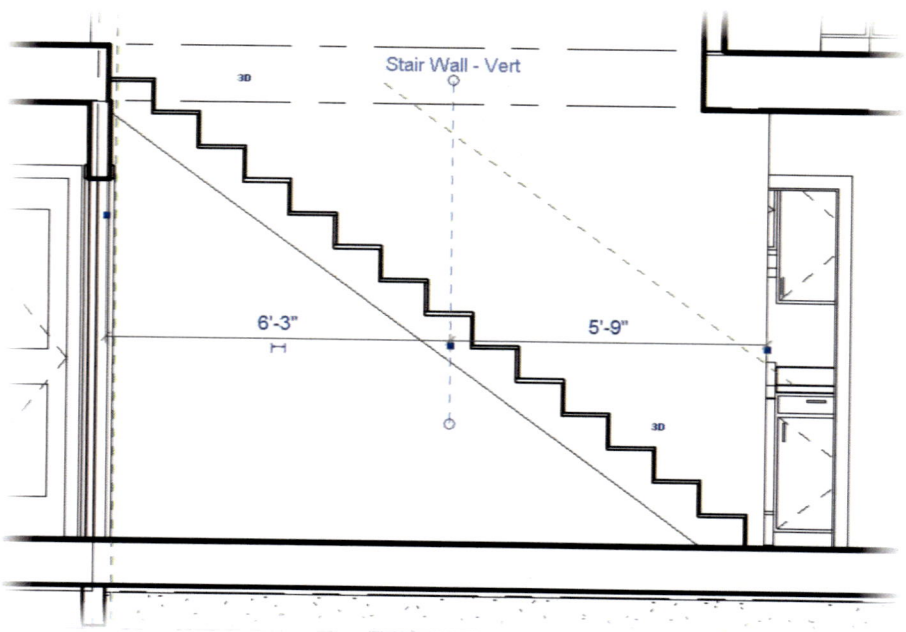

6. Select the wall behind the stairway on the 1st floor, and click **Edit Profile** in the Mode panel of the Contextual Ribbon tab.

7. Sketch, locate, and trim the boundary lines as illustrated below.

8. **Align** and **Lock** the sloped sketch line to the *Stair Wall - Angled* reference plane.

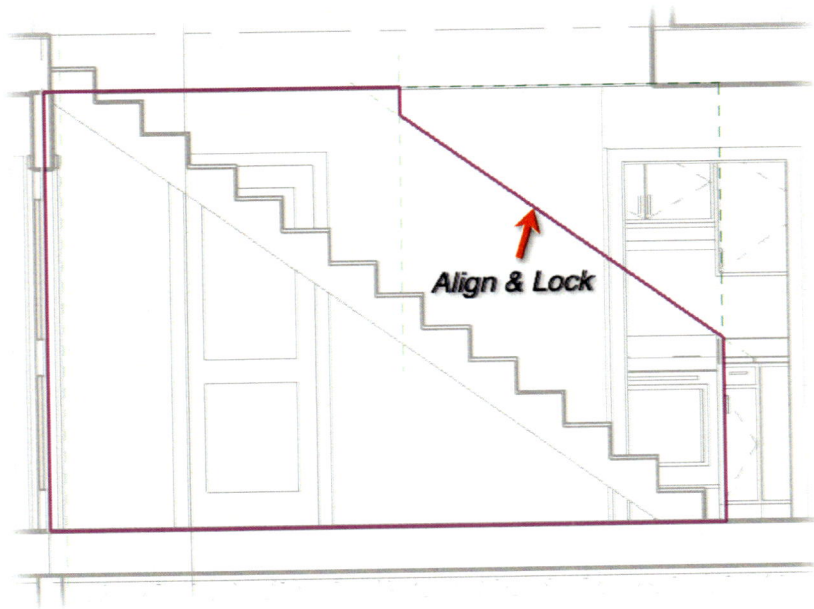

9. When done, click **Finish Edit Mode** ✓. Your wall should appear as illustrated below.

10. **Align** and **Lock** the vertical profile line to the *Stair Wall - Vert* reference plane as indicated in the illustration below.

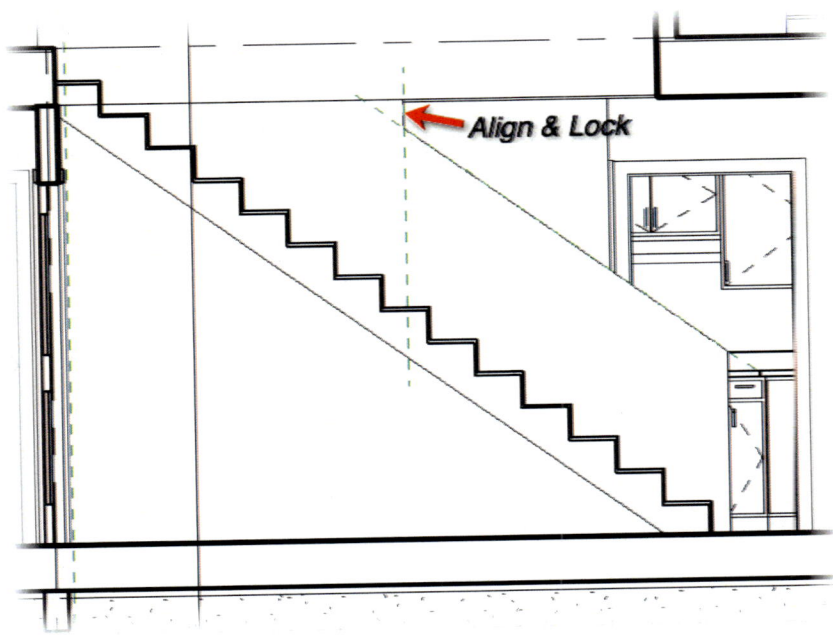

CHAPTER 11: STAIRS & RAILINGS

Guard Wall at Loft

11. Select the wall behind the stairway on the 2nd floor, and click **Edit Profile** in the Mode panel of the Contextual Ribbon tab.

12. Sketch, locate, and trim the boundary lines as illustrated below.

 You should not have to create any of the constraints shown in the illustration.

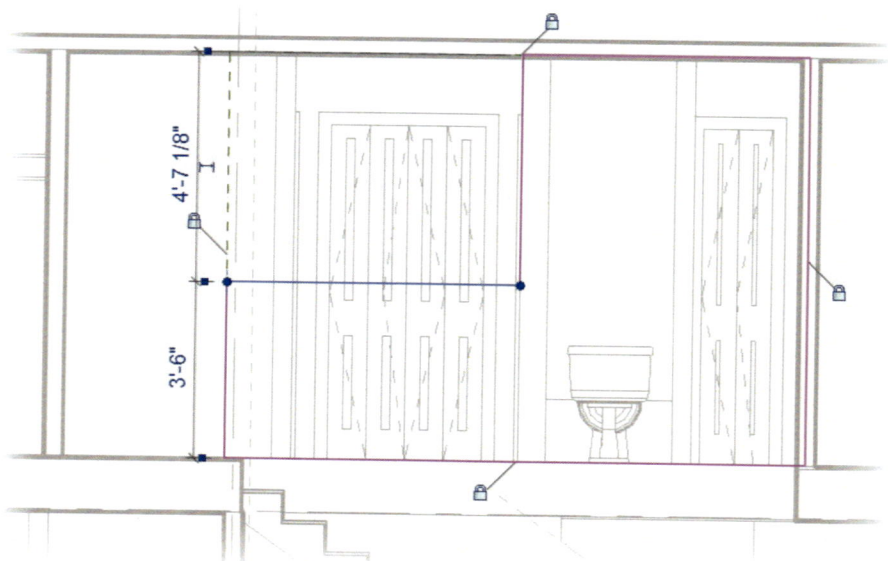

13. When done, click **Finish Edit Mode** ✓. Your wall should appear as illustrated below.

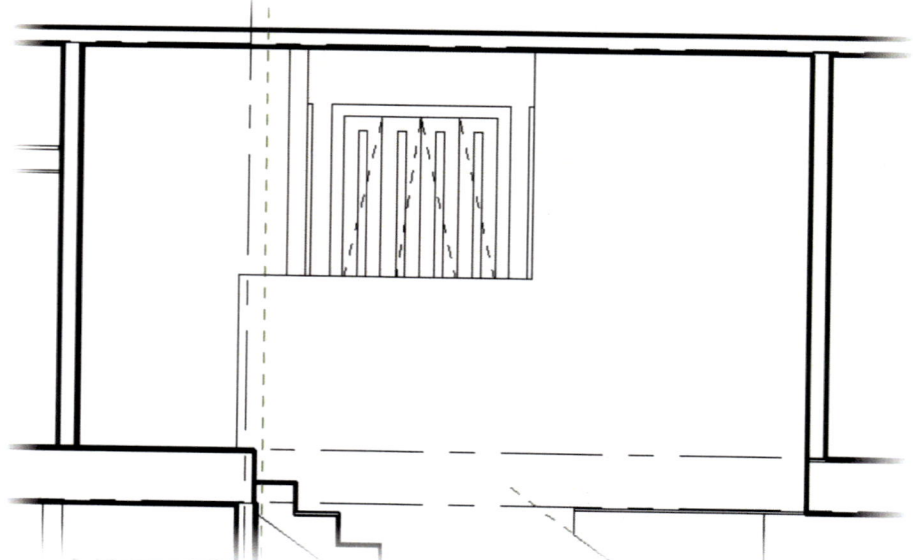

14. Open the floor plan view *F.F.L. 2nd FLR*. Notice the section of wall you converted to a low wall is now represented with a *projected* line style instead of *cut*.

15. **Move** the *DN* text as illustrated.

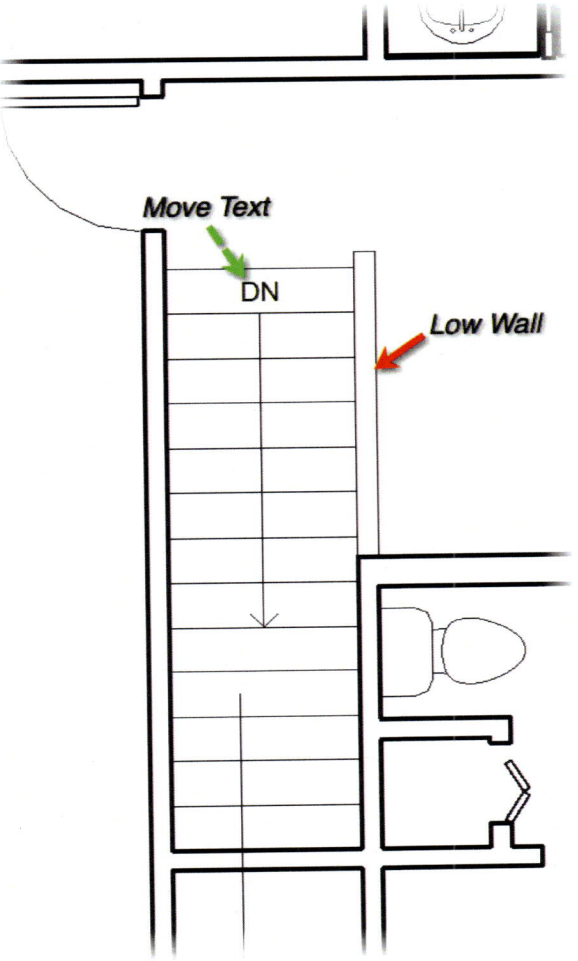

 Walls in Revit Architecture that have an *Unconnected Height* property of less than 6' 0" are considered low walls, and are represented with projection lines even if they pass through the cut plane for the view. However, in the In the case of the low wall in the illustration above, it's represented with projected lines strictly because the top of the wall is below the cut plane. Even though we edited the profile to shorten a portion of this wall, it's still part of a wall that has an Unconnected Height property of 8' 1 1/8". Therefore, if the lower portion of this wall was to pass through the cut plane, it would be displayed with cut lines.

1st Floor Ceiling Refinement

A byproduct of creating the sloped guard wall is that a portion of that wall no longer extends to the floor/ceiling assembly, where it previously defined the boundary for the 1st floor ceiling. Therefore, the ceiling in this area needs to be edited to fill in the area previously occupied by the wall.

1. Open the ceiling plan view *RCP - 1st Floor - T.O.W*.
2. Select the reference plane *Stair Wall - Vert* and adjust its 3D extents as illustrated below.

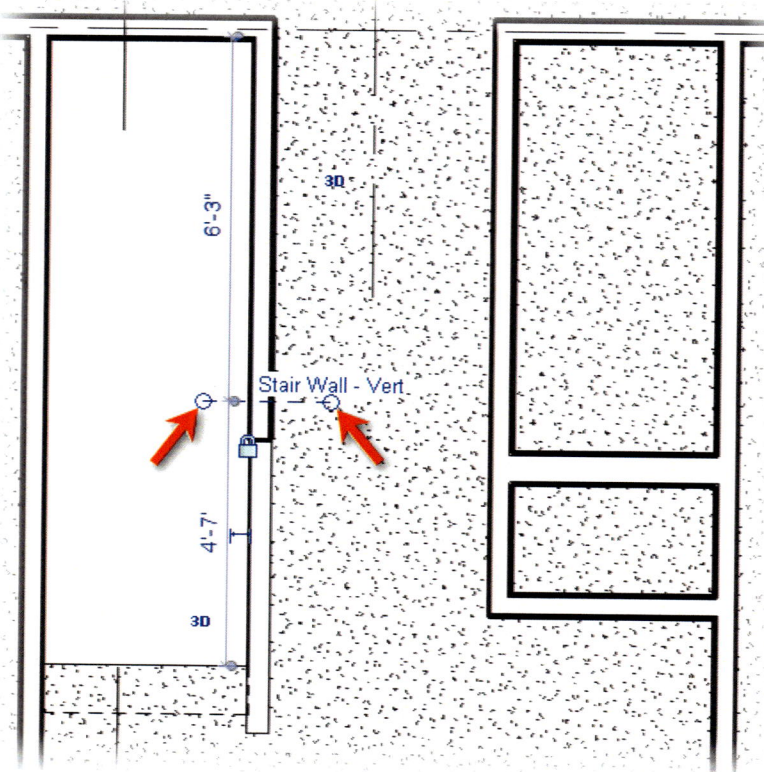

3. Select the ceiling, and click **Edit Boundary** in the Contextual Ribbon tab.

4. **Align** and **Lock** the boundary line indicated *to* the reference plane *Stair Wall - Vert* as illustrated below.

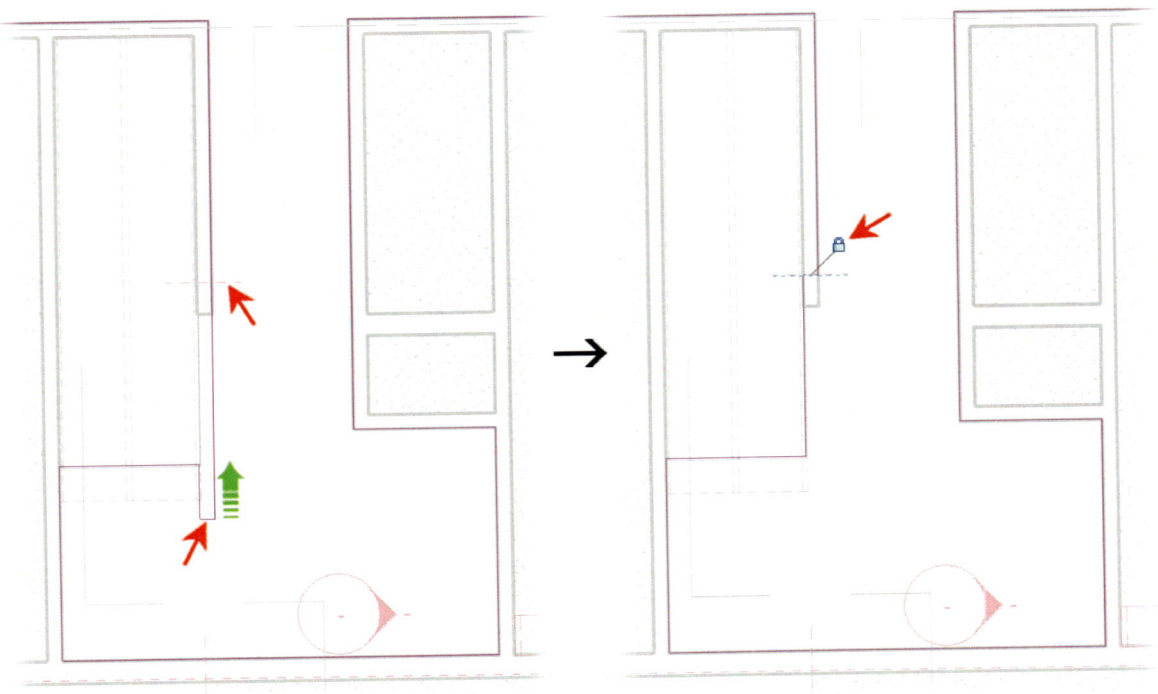

Edit Ceiling Boundary

5. When done, click **Finish Edit Mode** ✓
6. Close the ceiling plan view.
7. Open the section view *Family-Stairs-Porch (Long)*. Your ceiling/wall join should appear as illustrated below. If not, you may need to use **Join Geometry** to clean up the join between the ceiling and the wall above to remove the join line.

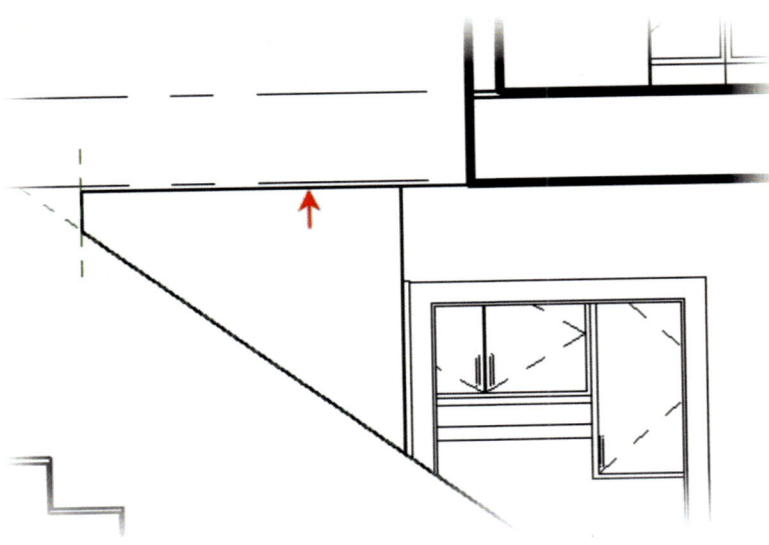

CHAPTER 11: STAIRS & RAILINGS

3D Interior Stair Section - East

1. Duplicate the default *{3D}* view, and rename the new view **3D Section - Stairs East**.

2. Using either of the methods you previously learned, create a 3D section box around the stairway and adjust it to appear similar to the illustration below.

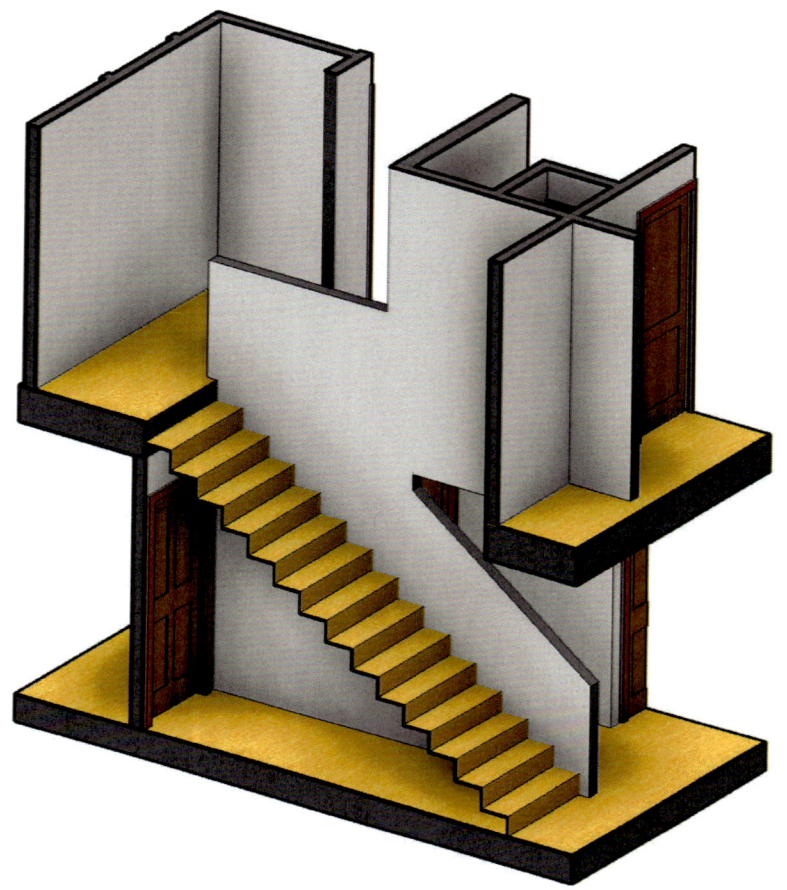

 If you wish to achieve the graphic results illustrated above, you need to set the *Visual Style* to **Realistic**, and set the *Show Ambient Shadows* checkbox in the Graphic Display Options dialog box. This will only work if *Use Hardware Acceleration* is enabled in the Options dialog box. Additionally, the section box has been hidden using V/G Overrides.

QAT	Save Project	[Ctl]+S
Operation		
	Save	

This concludes exercise 11.2

Exercise 11.3: Porch Railings

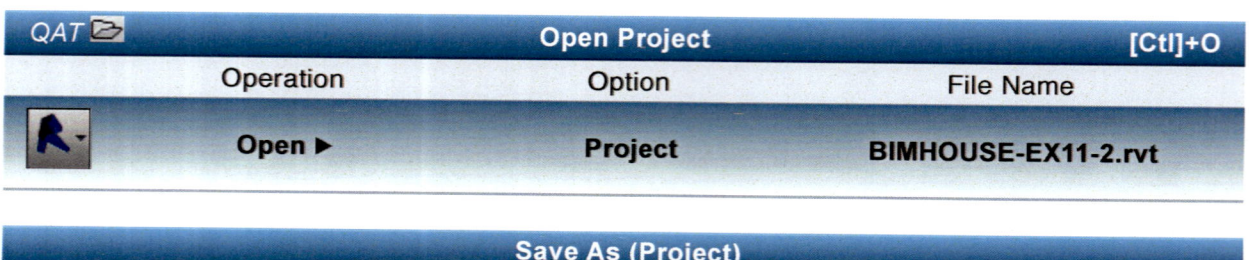

QAT	Open Project		[Ctl]+O
Operation	Option		File Name
Open ▶	Project		BIMHOUSE-EX11-2.rvt

	Save As (Project)	
Operation	Option	File Name
Save As ▶	Project	BIMHOUSE-EX11-3.rvt

 By default, Revit adds railings to stairs when they are created. The added railings might not be the desired final configuration, but they do serve as a starting point from which to work. The default railing settings can be edited while creating a stair instance if desired.

Porch Stair Railings

Load Railings

Railings are system families, and therefore cannot be loaded into a project in the same manner as loadable families. Rather, they need to be copied or transferred from one project to another. In the following steps you will transfer railing types from a provided project file into your BIM house project using *Transfer Project Standards*. This will transfer all railing types required for the remainder of this chapter.

1. Open the provided project file *BIMHouse_Railings-Ch11.rvt*.
2. Return to the BIM House project file (**[ctrl]+[tab]**).

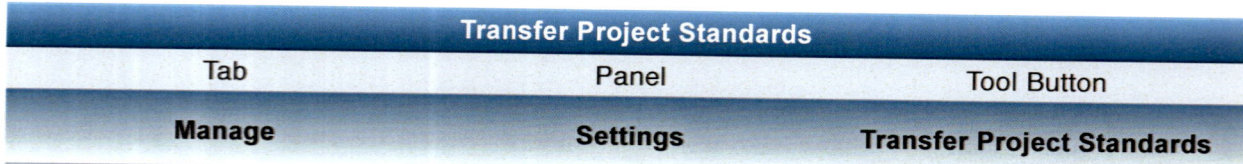

Transfer Project Standards		
Tab	Panel	Tool Button
Manage	Settings	Transfer Project Standards

3. In the Select Items to Copy dialog box, do the following:

   a) Select **BIMHouse_Railings-Ch11** in the *Copy from* drop-down list.

   b) Click **Check None**.

   c) Select the **Railing Types** category.

   d) Click **OK**.

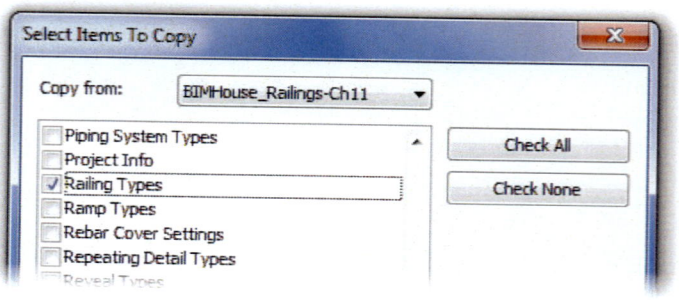

4. In the Duplicate Types dialog box, click **New Only**.
5. In the Project Browser, navigate to the *Families* section and expand the following tree:

    Families → Railings → Railing

6. Verify the railing types indicated in the following illustration are present in your project.

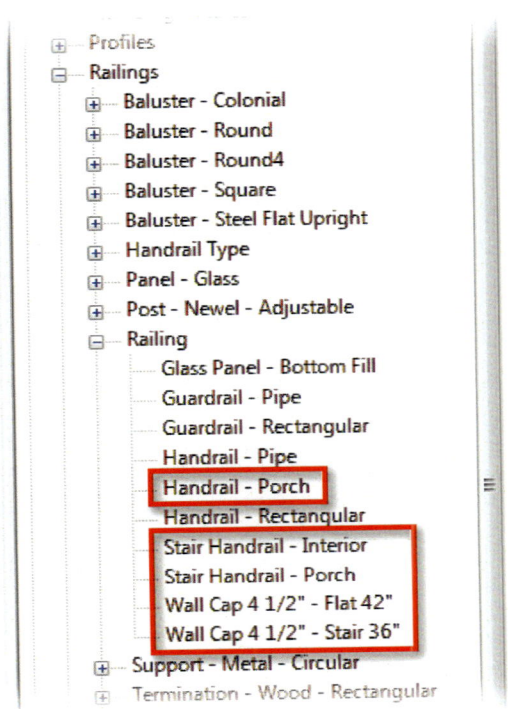

7. Close the file *BIMHouse_Railings-Ch11.rvt*

Replace the Default Stair Railings

8. Open the floor plan view *W-1st Floor - Constraints*.
9. Select both of the handrails simultaneously at the the porch steps as illustrated below.
10. Using the Type Selector, change the selected railings to **Stair Handrail - Porch**.

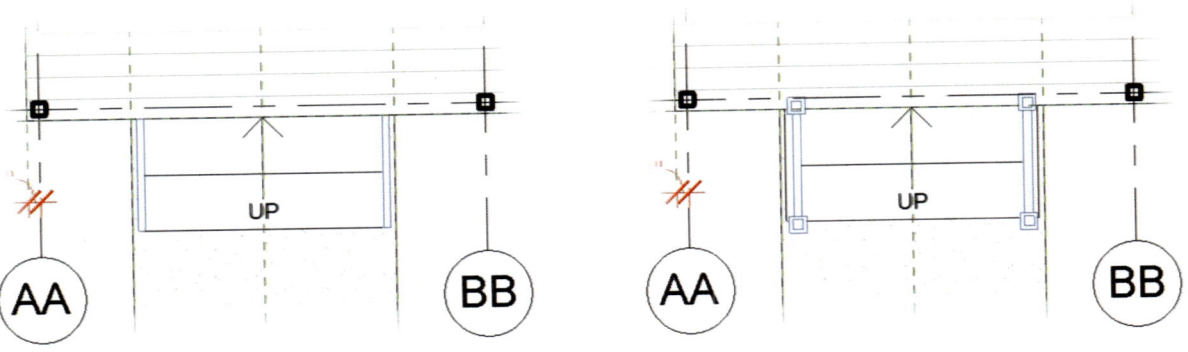

Selected Handrails   Selected Handrails - New Type

CHAPTER 11: STAIRS & RAILINGS

11. Notice that handrails are offset from the stringers and are resting on the treads. To correct this, select each railing one at a time and do the following:

    a) Click on the **Flip Arrow.**

    b) Set the *Tread/Stringer Offset* property to **0' 0"**.

12. Open the *Default {3D}* view, as well as the section view *Family-Stairs-Porch (Long)* to view the changes. Your railings should appear as illustrated below. Notice that the newel posts at the railing ends are not positioned correctly.

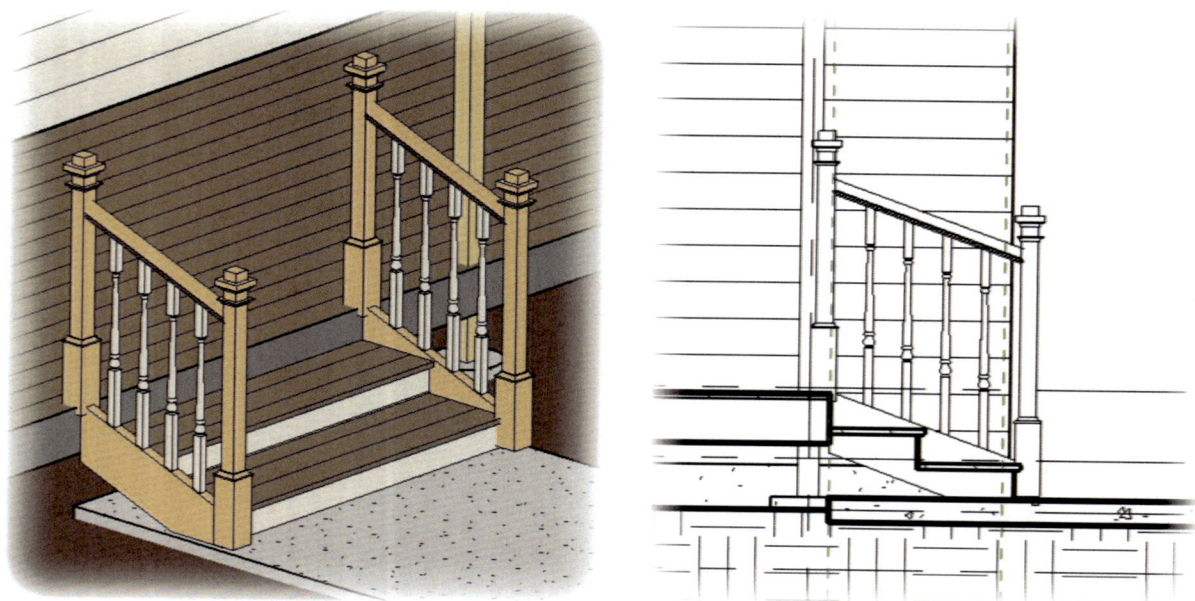

Porch Stair Railings - Initial Placement

Adjust and Constrain Stair Railings

As observed in the previous illustrations, the newel posts are not positioned correctly with respect to both the stair run-length, as well as in elevation. This is a result of the railing type properties, as well as the default railing path length that was automatically created with the stair element. In the following steps you will correct this.

13. Open the floor plan view *W-1st Floor - Constraints*.

14. Select the left railing and click the **Edit Path** button in the Contextual Ribbon tab.

15. Using temporary dimensions, adjust the sketch line length and position as illustrated on the following page. Make sure to adjust the temporary dimension references so the north end of the path is referenced to *Grid 1* prior to making any adjustments.

    a) *Path length* = **2'–9 5/8"**

    b) *End distance from Grid 1* = **1 3/8"**

When using temporary dimensions to adjust the length *and* position of an unanchored linear element (both ends unjoined) such as a wall or line, adjusting the dimension that defines the element's length will adjust the length as expected. However, adjusting a dimension between an endpoint and other geometry will *move* the selected element; it *will not* stretch the element's length. Therefore, when needing to adjust both, it's best to adjust the element length first (assuming you know it), then its position.

16. **Align** and **Lock** the sketch line to the stair boundary as illustrated below.

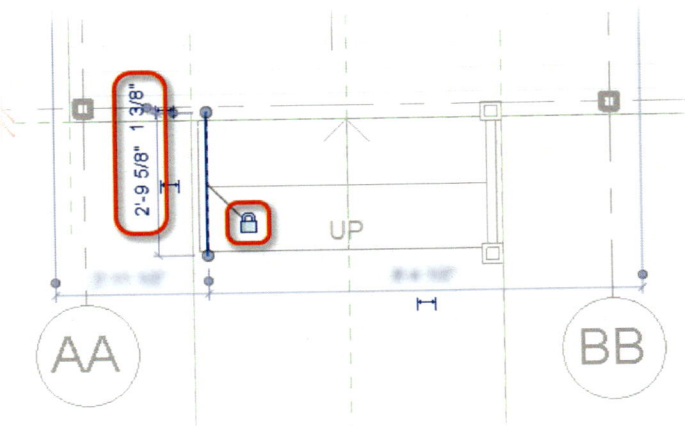

Railing Path Adjustments & Alignment Constraint

 Initially, when railings are automatically created through the use of the stair tool, their path lines are automatically associated to the stair boundary. Editing the railing path breaks this relationship, requiring a manual alignment constraint to be applied.

17. Add a dimension string as illustrated below, then **lock** both dimension values.

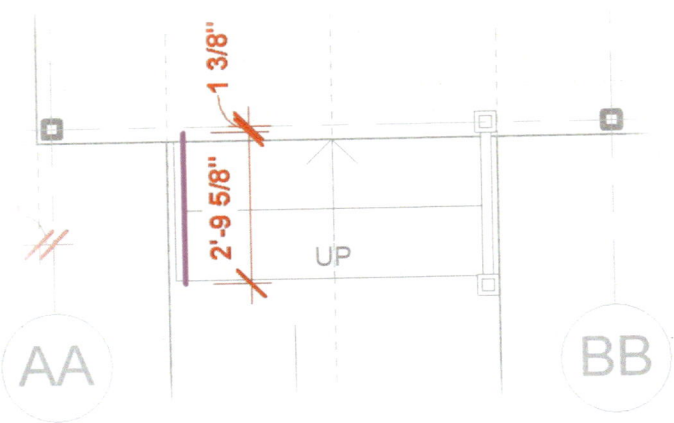

Railing Path Length Constraints

CHAPTER 11: STAIRS & RAILINGS

18. When done, click **Finish Edit Mode** ✓
19. Repeat the previous process for the opposite railing.
20. Open the default *{3D}* view, as well as the section view *Family-Stairs-Porch (Long)* to view the changes. Your railings should appear as illustrated below.

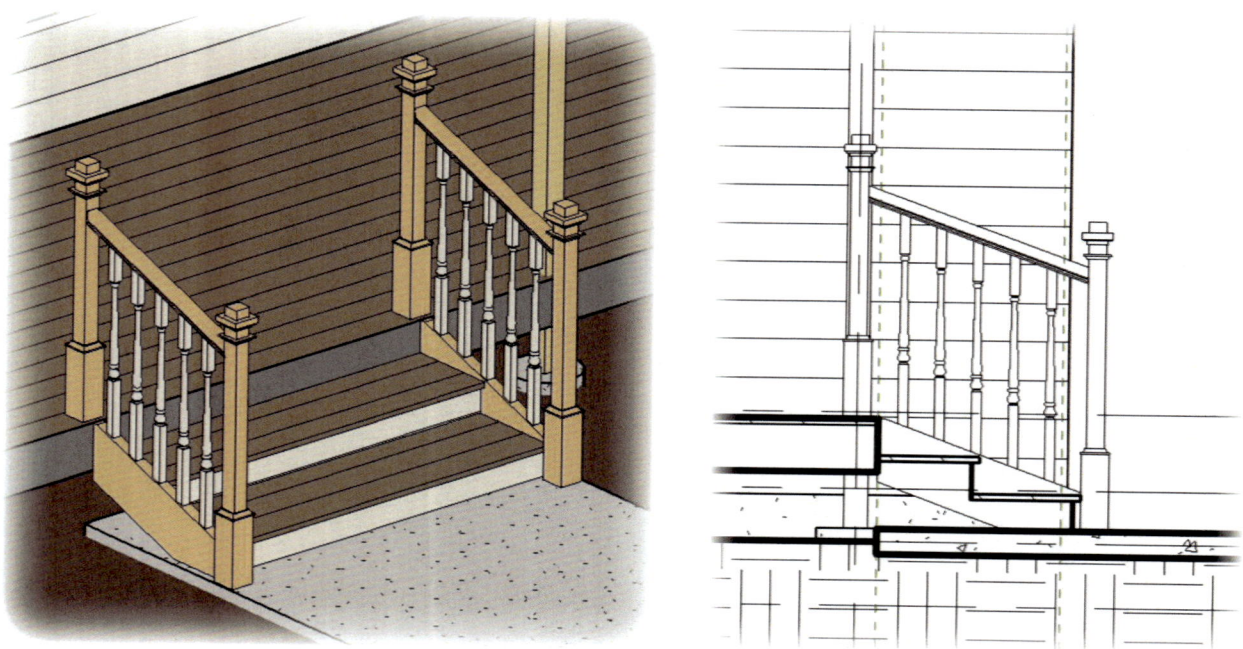

Porch Stair Railings - Length Adjusted

Porch Deck Railings

1. Open the floor plan view *W-1st Floor - Constraints*.

2. Immediately after clicking the *Pick New Host* tool, **pick the porch deck** (floor element).

3. Sketch the path for the first railing as illustrated below. It doesn't matter at which end you start the sketch, since this railing family has no offset.

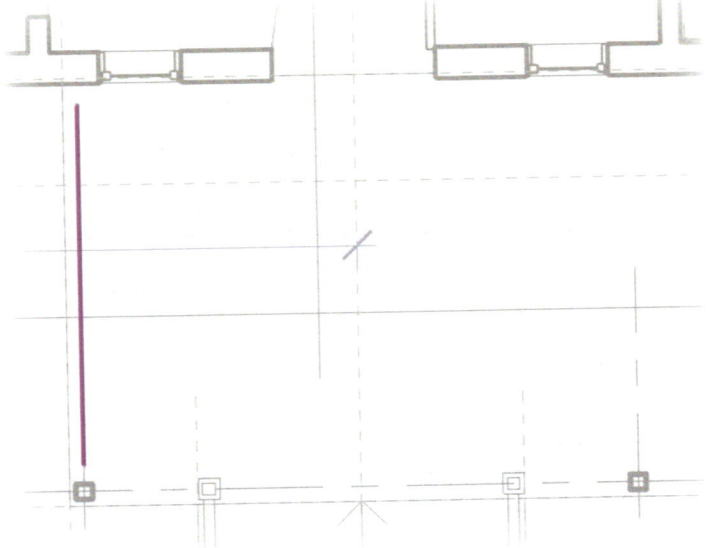

Initial Railing Path Sketch

4. **Align** and **Lock** the path line as follows. Refer to the following three illustrations for details. Be sure to lock each alignment operation.

   a) The lower endpoint of the path to the face of the structural column.

   b) The upper endpoint of the path to the *Wall Face* of the 1st floor south wall.

   c) The path line to *Grid AA*.

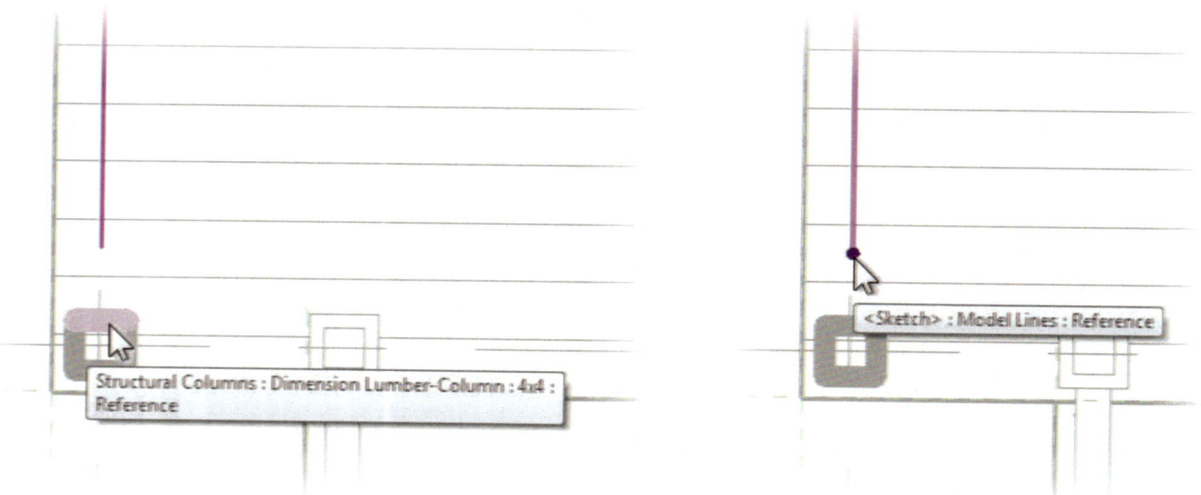

1) Align the Path-end: Pick 1   *2) Align the Path-end: Pick 2*

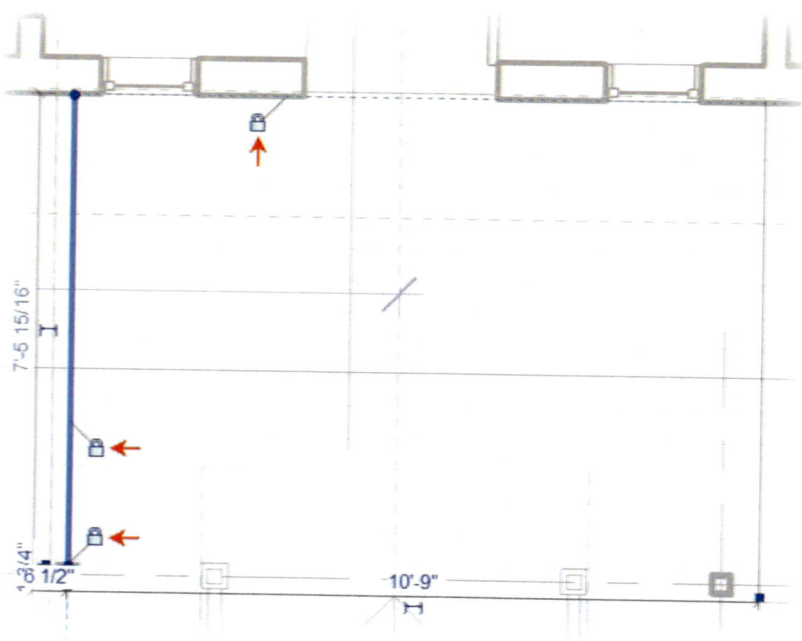

3) Completely Aligned & Locked Railing Path

5. When done, click **Finish Edit Mode** . The railing should appear as illustrated below.

6. Open the view *3D Section - Porch*. Verify the balusters are resting on the surface of the deck. If they are floating, the railing wasn't properly hosted.

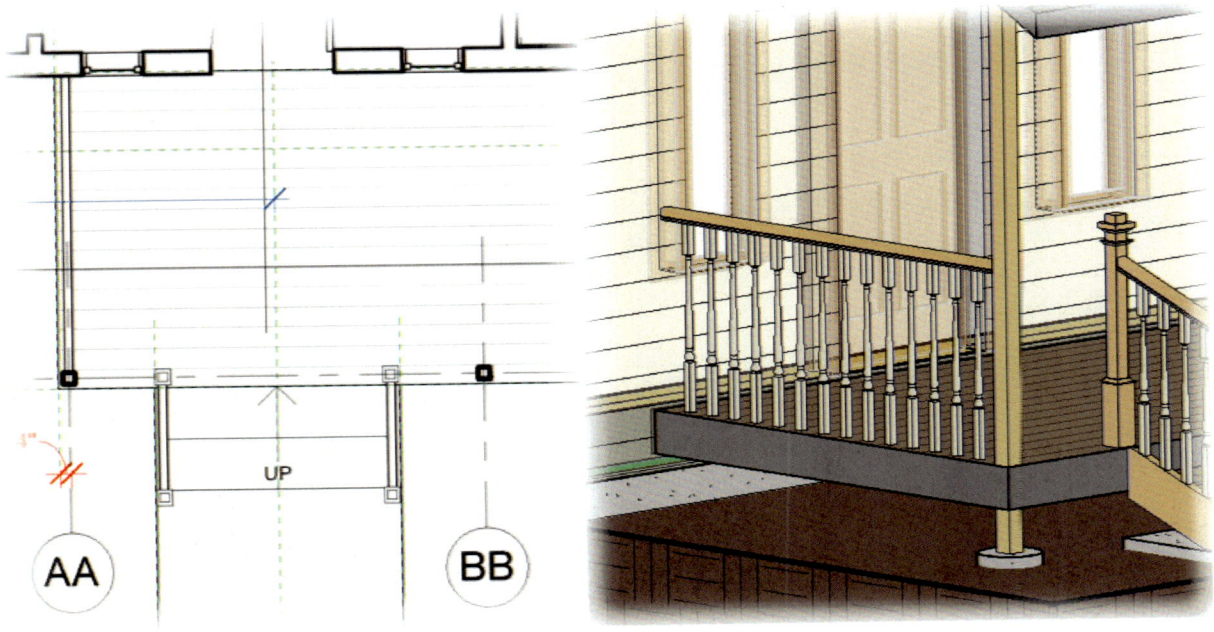

7. Repeat the previous steps to create the two additional railing segments indicated in the illustration below. Use alignment targets that are appropriate for the railing segment.

> ⚠ You must remember to host each railing segment to the deck.

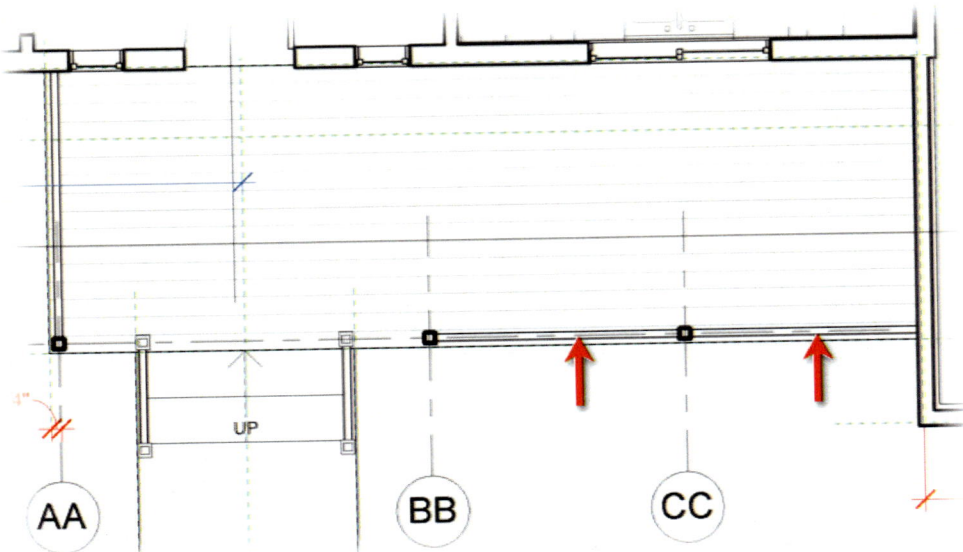

CHAPTER 11: STAIRS & RAILINGS

The final two railing segments require a slightly different approach to constraining the ends where they intersect the newel posts at the steps.

	Railing: Sketch Path		
Tab	Panel	Split Button ▼	Tool Button
Architecture	Circulation	Railing	Sketch Path

 You must remember to host each railing segment to the deck.

8. Referring to the illustrations below,

   a) Sketch a path between the column at *Grid AA* and the nearest newel post as shown in the first illustration below. Make sure the path crosses over reference plane *Walk - West*.

   b) Add an **Aligned Dimension** from the reference plane *Walk - West* to the endpoint of the path closest to the newel post.

   c) Adjust the path so the added dimension = **1 1/8"** (*select line and then edit the temporary dimension value*).

   d) **Lock** the dimension.

   e) **Align** and **Lock** the opposite end of the path to the column.

   f) When done, click **Finish Edit Mode** ✓.

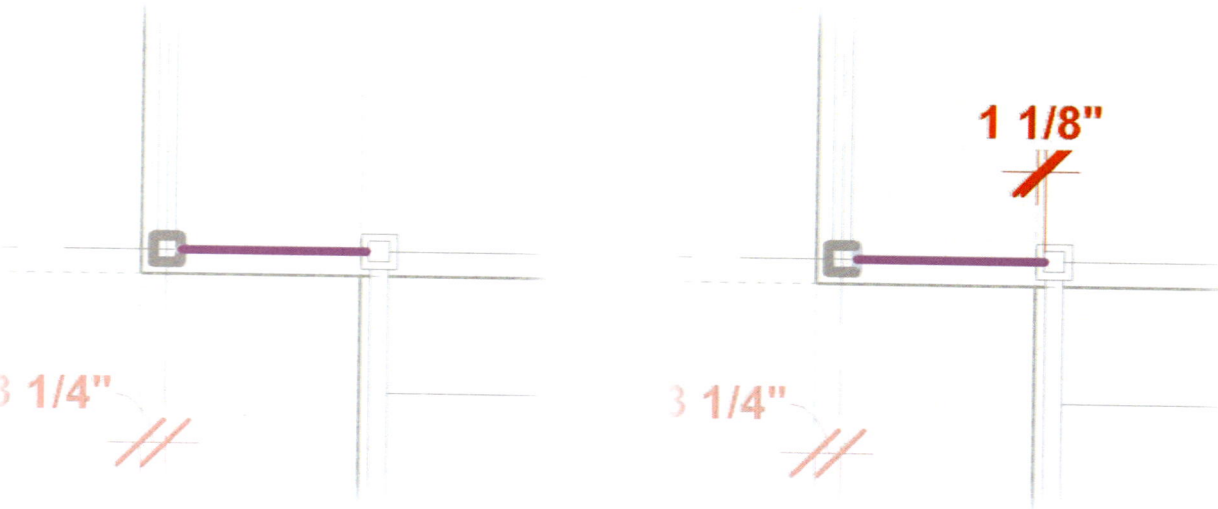

Sketch Path at Newel Post   Constrain Path-end to Reference Plane

9. Repeat the previous process for the rail at the east side of the steps.

10. After completing all of railing segments, open the view *3D Section - Porch* to see the additions. Verify all balusters are seated on the deck.

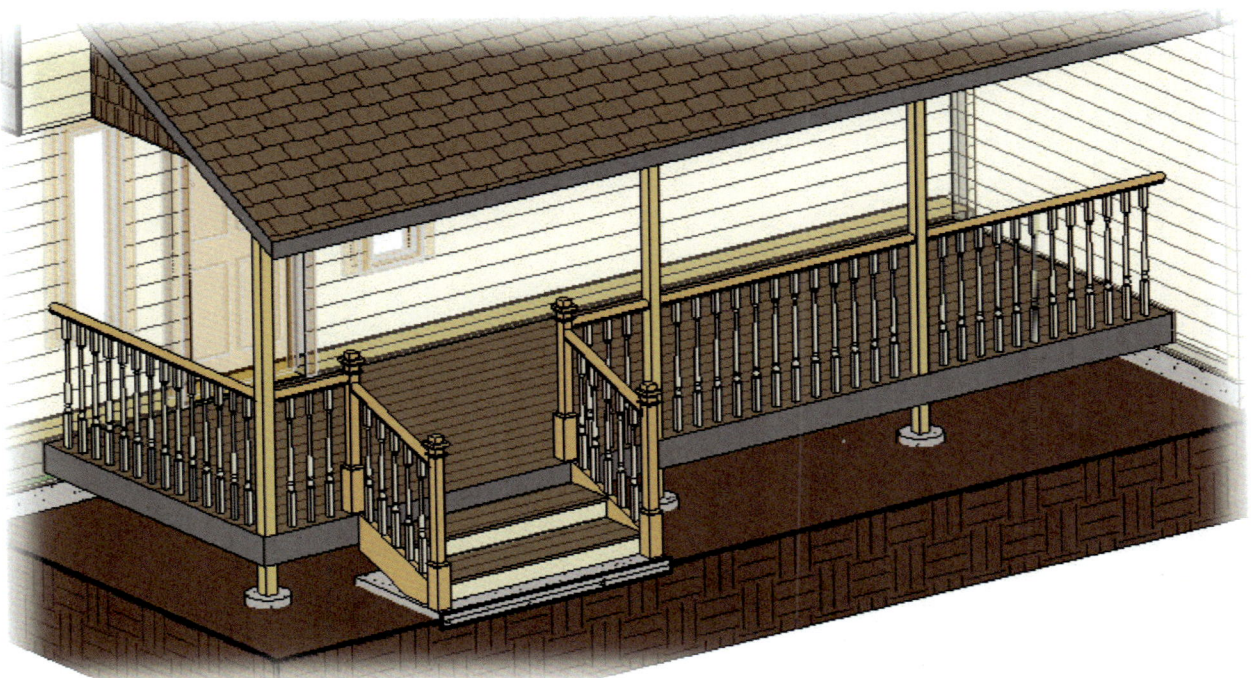

11. Close all open views except for *3D Section - Porch* and *W-1st Floor - Constraints*, then **Tile** these two windows.

12. Test your porch constraints by adjusting the grids associated with the porch *(Grids 1, AA, BB, CC)*, as well as the *Walk - East/West/South* reference planes.

 Remember to return all grids and reference planes back to their original locations and re-pin anything unpinned during the testing process.

 To pick a new host for a railing, you must first select the railing, then click the **Pick New Host** button. You can do this from any view where both the railing and the target host are visible.

QAT	Save Project	[Ctl]+S
	Operation	
R	Save	

This concludes exercise 11.3

Exercise 11.4: Interior Railings

QAT 📂	Open Project		[Ctl]+O
	Operation	Option	File Name
R.	Open ▶	Project	BIMHOUSE-EX11-3.rvt

	Save As (Project)		
	Operation	Option	File Name
R.	Save As ▶	Project	BIMHOUSE-EX11-4.rvt

Wall Caps

To finish off the top of the low walls at the stairs and landing, we'll add wall caps. The wall cap railing families were previously loaded into the project during the Transfer Project Standards operation.

Plan Region at Sloped Guard Wall

If we open any of our first floor plan views, will see that our cut plane intersects the sloped guard wall at the stairway. This gives us an inaccurate representation of the full length of the sloped portion. We'll remedy this by adding the plan region around this portion of wall.

1. Open the floor plan view *W-1st Floor - Constraints*.

Plan Region			
Tab	Panel	Drop-down Button ▼	Tool Button
View	**Create**	**Plan Views**	**Plan Region**

2. Sketch the Plan Region as shown in the first illustration on the following page.
3. Edit the View Range properties as follows:

View Range Adjustments

Parameter	Value
Top – Offset:	8' 0"
Cut Plane – Offset:	7' 10"

4. When done, click **Finish Edit Mode** ✓. Your view should appear as shown in the second illustration on the following page.

EXERCISE 11.4: INTERIOR RAILINGS

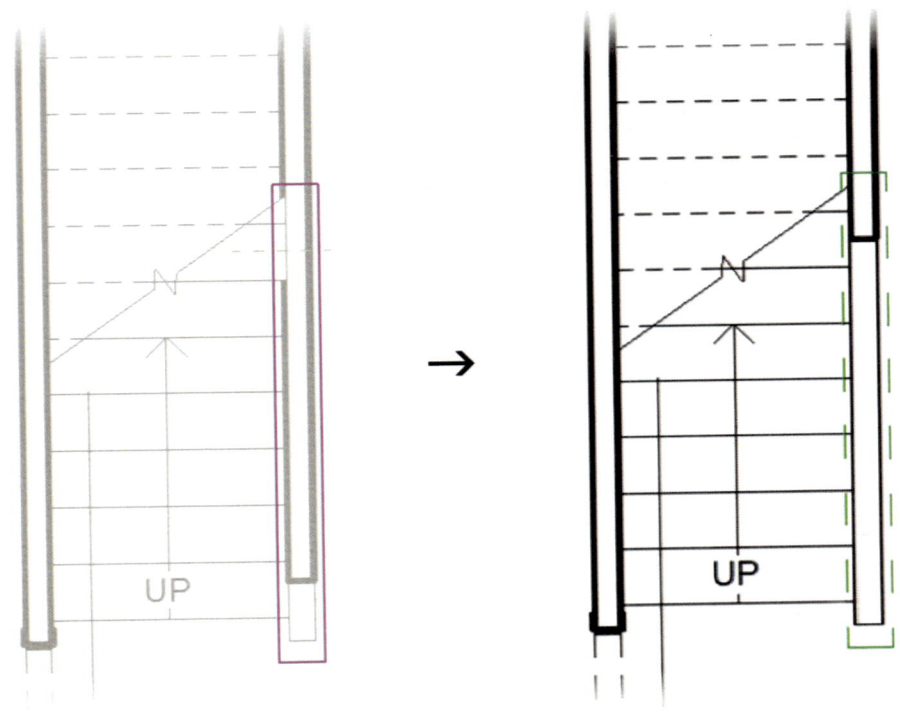

1. Sketch Plan Region   2. Completed Plan Region

Copy the Plan Region

5. Select the plan region, and in the Clipboard panel of the Modify tab click **Copy to Clipboard**, or press **[Ctrl]+C**.

\multicolumn{4}{c}{Paste: Aligned to Selected Views}
Tab	Panel	Split Button ▼	Tool Button
Modify	**Clipboard**	**Paste**	**Aligned to Selected Views**

6. From the Select Views dialog box, use **[Ctrl]+Click** to select the the following views.

   a) *Floor Plan: 1st Floor - Dimension*

   b) *Floor Plan: F.F.L. 1st FLR*

   c) *Floor Plan: W-1st Floor - Working Notes*

7. Click **OK**.

8. Verify all copies of plan region were created by opening the views listed above.

CHAPTER 11: STAIRS & RAILINGS

Model the Sloped Stair Wall Cap

9. Open the floor plan view *W-1st Floor - Constraints*, and zoom into the area around the base of the interior stairway.

10. To properly locate the wall cap, we'll need access to the edge of the stair family, which is currently hidden because it extends through the drywall to the wall core. However we'll need to maintain visibility of the wall. Therefore, set the *Visual Style* view property to **Wireframe** (VCB).

Railing: Sketch Path			
Tab	Panel	Split Button ▼	Tool Button
Architecture	Circulation	Railing	Sketch Path

Properties	
Type:	**Wall Cap 4 1/2" - Stair 36"**
Base Level:	**F.F.L. 1st FLR**
Base Offset:	**0' 0"**

Modify	Create Railing Path		
Draw	Work Plane	Tools
Pick Lines	N/A	Pick New Host
Offset: **0' 0"**		Lock: ☑

11. **Pick** the *Interior Stairs* element to select it as the host.

 In the next step you will be picking a hidden edge of the stair to place the railing path. If you have a difficult time locating this edge with the cursor, set the *Visual Style* to **Wireframe**.

12. To place the railing path, **Pick** the right edge of the *Interior Stairs* as illustrated below. Verify that padlock icon indicates locked. If not, **lock** it now.

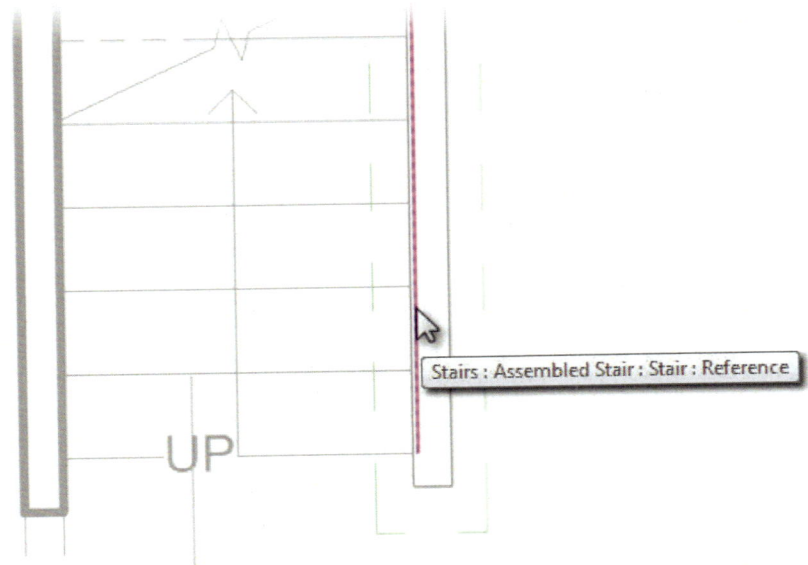

13. **Align** and **Lock** the endpoints of the path line as follows (refer to the illustration below).

   a) Lower endpoint of the railing path to the end of the sloped stair wall.

   b) Upper endpoint of the railing path to the reference plane *Stair Wall - Vert*.

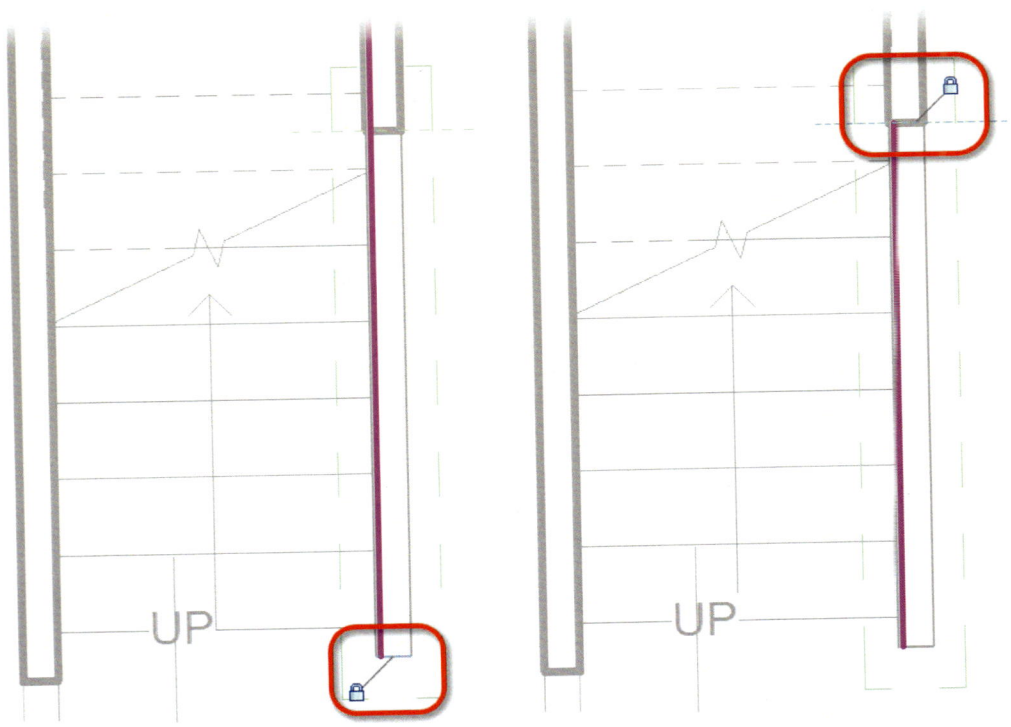

14. When done, click the **Finish Edit Mode** button ✓

CHAPTER 11: STAIRS & RAILINGS

15. Your view should appear as illustrated below. If your wall cap is not centered on the stair wall, select the cap and click the **Flip Arrow**.

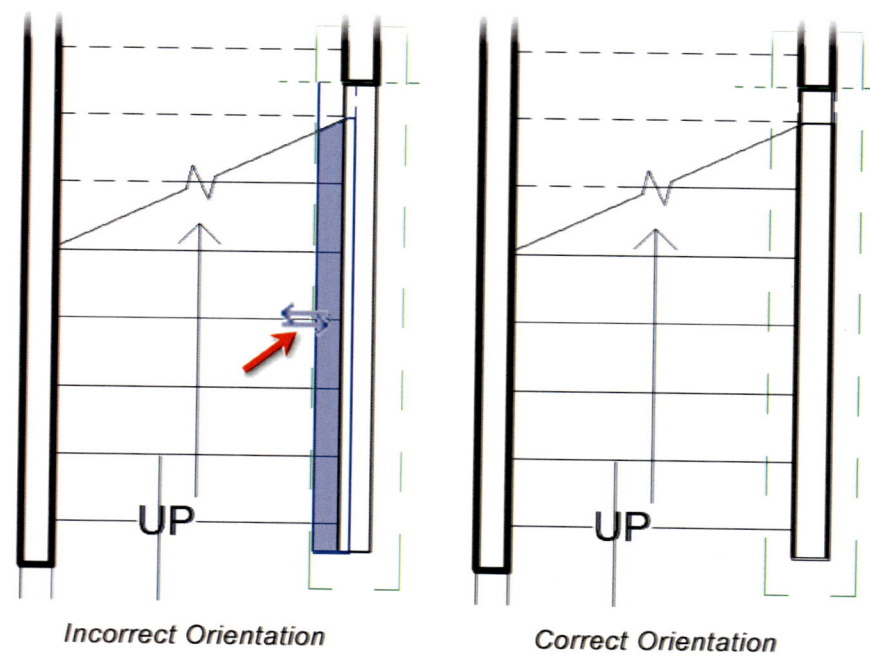

Incorrect Orientation   Correct Orientation

Model the Wall Cap at Loft

16. Open the floor plan view **W-2nd Floor - Constraints**, and zoom into the area around the top of the interior stairway.

Tab	Panel	Split Button ▼	Tool Button
		Railing: Sketch Path	
Architecture	Circulation	Railing	Sketch Path

Properties
Type: **Wall Cap 4 1/2" - Flat 42"**

Base Level:	F.F.L. 2nd FLR
Base Offset:	0' 0"

Draw	Work Plane	Tools
	Modify	Create Railing Path	
Pick Lines	N/A	N/A
Offset: **0' 0"**		Lock: ☑

390

17. Pick the centerline of the wall as illustrated below to place the railing path.

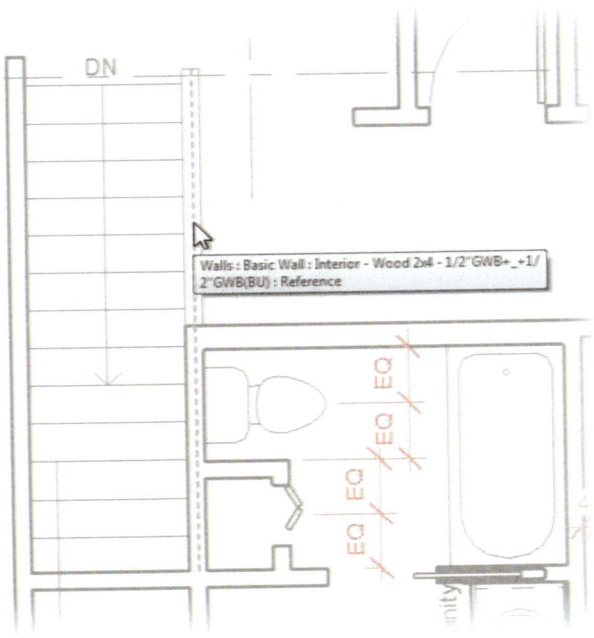

Railing Path - Pick Wall

18. **Align/Lock** the ends of the path line as follows. Refer to the illustrations below for details.

   a) Lower endpoint of the railing path *to* the *finish face* of the intersecting wall.

   b) Upper endpoint of the railing path *to* the end of the low wall.

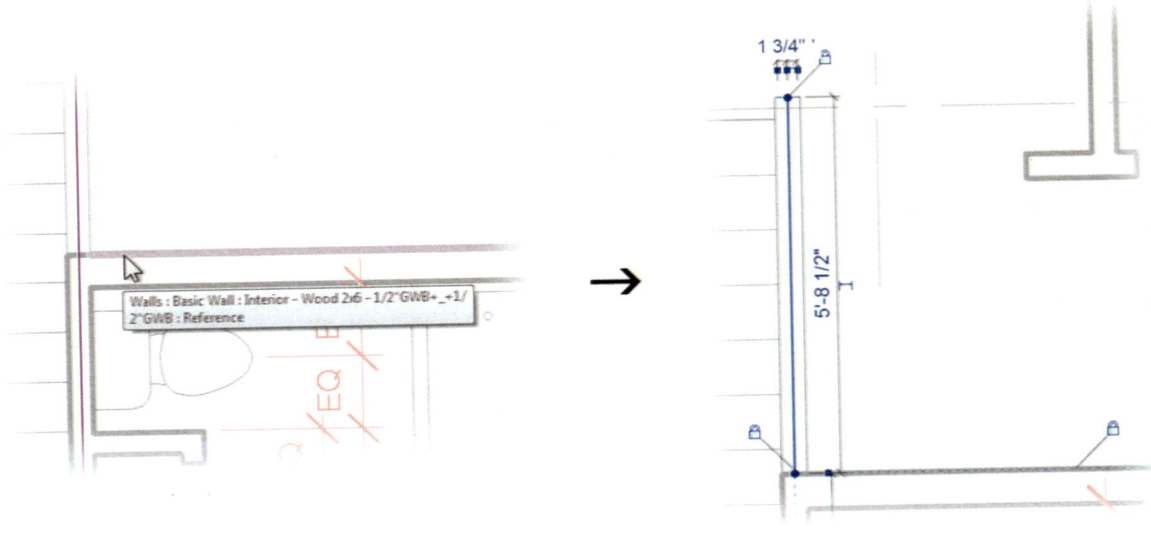

Pick Wall Face for Path-end Alignment   Completed Alignments & Constraints

19. When done, click **Finish Edit Mode** ✓

20. Open the *3D Section - Stairs East* view. The wall caps should appear as illustrated below.

 If either of the end caps is at the wrong end of the wall cap, you will need to edit the sketch, and reverse the sketch direction. I.E., unlock the ends of the sketch, drag them to the opposite ends, and then realign and lock.

Handrail

To meet code, the interior stairs need a handrail. This handrail will be placed on west wall of the stairway.

1. Open the floor plan view *W-1st Floor - Constraints*.

Railing: Sketch Path			
Tab	Panel	Split Button ▼	Tool Button
Architecture	Circulation	Railing	Sketch Path

Properties	
Type:	**Stair Handrail - Interior**
Base Level:	**F.F.L. 1st FLR**
Base Offset:	**0' 0"**

Modify	Create Railing Path		
Draw	Work Plane	Tools
Pick Lines	N/A	Pick New Host
Offset: **0' 0"**		Lock: ☑

2. Pick the *Interior Stairs* element to select it as the host.

3. Pick the <u>Finish Face</u> of the west stairway wall as illustrated to place the path.

4. Click **Modify** to exit the Pick Lines tool.

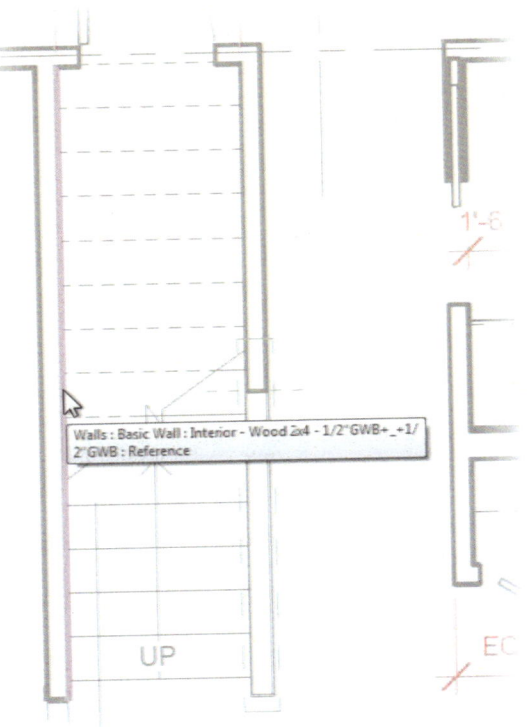

5. Refer to the illustrations below, select the railing path and adjust the endpoints as follows.

   a) Drag the lower end so it snaps to the first stair tread.

   b) Drag the upper end so it snaps to the face of the wall shown.

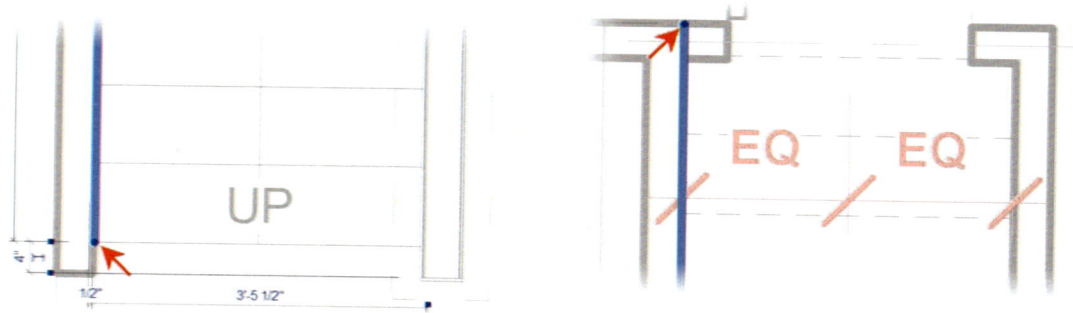

   Adjust South End of Railing Path   Adjust North End of Railing Path

6. When done, click **Finish Edit Mode** ✓. The stair railing will likely be buried in the wall.

7. Click the **Flip Arrow** – if required – to move the handrail to the outside face of the wall as illustrated below.

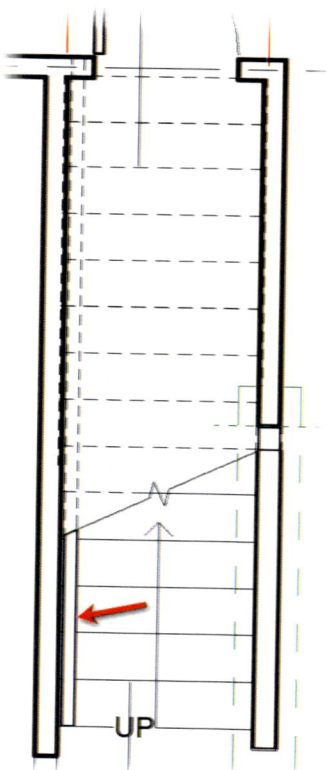

8. Create a section as illustrated below, and rename it **W-Stairs (Long)**. Be sure that the section is viewing to the west (use the flip arrow if necessary after creating it).

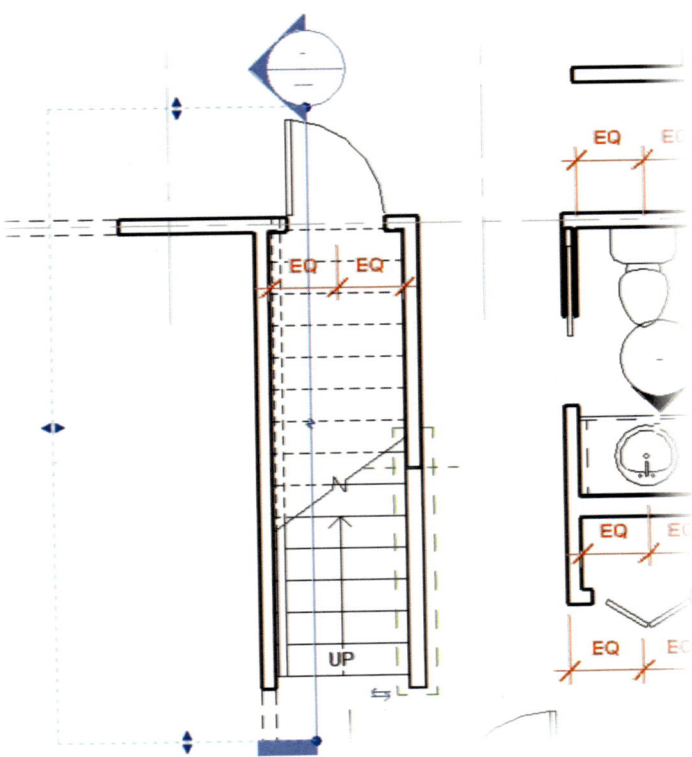

9. Open the section view *W-Stairs (Long)* and set the *Detail Level* to **Medium**. The railing should appear as illustrated below.

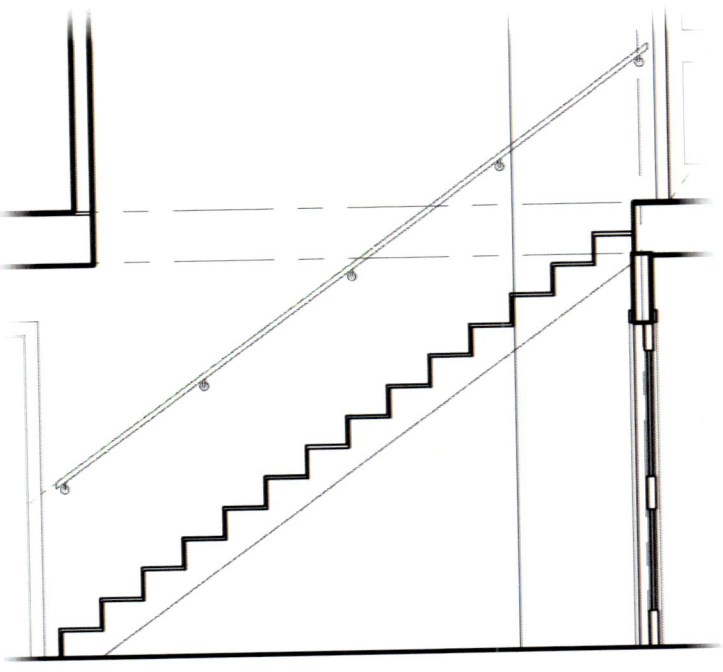

Plan View Graphics Refinement

You may have noticed some strange graphics around to top of the sloped wall cap. This is a result of both Object Styles and stair properties. We'll refine this in the steps that follow.

1. Open floor plan view *F.F.L. 1st FLR*.
2. Zoom in to inspect the area near the top of the sloped wall cap.

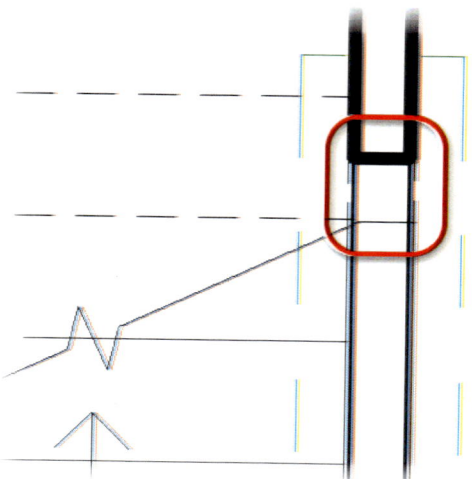

3. Select the interior stair element and click **Edit Type**.
4. Under the *Graphics* heading, locate *Cut Mark Type* and click the dialog launcher button to open **Single Zigzag** type properties.
5. Change the *Cut Line Angle* to **35°**.
6. Click **OK** twice to apply and view the changes.

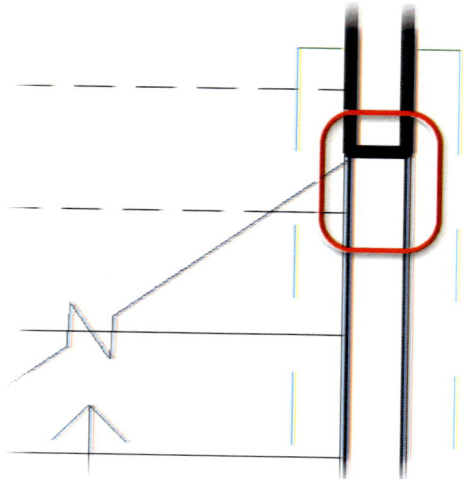

3D Interior Stair Section - West

1. Duplicate the *3D Section - Stairs East* view, and rename the new view **3D Section - Stairs West**.

2. Open the view *3D Section - Stairs West*, and adjust the section box to yield a view similar to that illustrated below.

QAT 💾	Save Project	[Ctl]+S
	Operation	
R	Save	

	Close (Project)	[Ctl]+[F4]
	Operation	
R	Close	

This concludes exercise 11.4

Chapter Summary

In this exercise you were exposed to stairs and railings. The intentions were only to expose you to basic modeling methods related to these elements. The details of how these elements are constructed and edited run deep, and are well beyond the scope of what you have learned so far.

Congratulations!

Congratulations on completing volume one of the BIM House. You may have encountered some challenges along the way; that's okay! Parametric modeling, whether buildings or mechanical objects, is challenging and has a much steeper learning curve than traditional CAD drafting – that's because parametric modeling isn't drafting!

So far you have only scratched the surface of Revit's capabilities. In Volume II of the BIM House, the focus will be more on leveraging the information in the model – the "I" in BIM – to create meaningful and accurate construction documents.

In closing, if you are serious about mastering this software it is important to exercise what you've learned on a regular basis, and continue to expand your skill-set beyond what is taught in this curriculum. Even seasoned pros are always learning new tools and techniques, and they do get rusty when not exercising their skills for a while! To be good at it, and stay that way requires a long-term commitment.